Excavations at Tel Michal, Israel

Tel Aviv University
Sonia and Marco Nadler Institute of Archaeology

Publications of the Institute of Archaeology
Number 8

EXCAVATIONS AT
TEL MICHAL, ISRAEL

Edited by
Ze'ev Herzog
George Rapp, Jr.
and
Ora Negbi

Published by
The University of Minnesota Press, Minneapolis

and

The Sonia and Marco Nadler Institute of Archaeology,
Tel Aviv University

Published by the University of Minnesota Press,
2037 University Avenue Southeast, Minneapolis, MN 55414
and The Sonia and Marco Nadler Institute of Archaeology,
Tel Aviv University, Tel Aviv.
Published simultaneously in Canada
by Fitzhenry & Whiteside Limited, Markham.
Printed in the United States of America.

Library of Congress Cataloging-in-Publication Data

Excavations at Tel Michal, Israel / Ze'ev Herzog, George Rapp, Jr.,
and Ora Negbi.
    p.   cm. — (Publications of the Institute of Archaeology; no. 8)
A cooperative project of the University of Minnesota Press and the
Institute of Archaeology at Tel Aviv University.
Includes index.
ISBN 0-8166-1622-1
    1. Michal Site (Israel)   2. Israel—Antiquities.   3. Excavations
(Archaeology)—Israel.   I. Herzog, Ze'ev.   II. Rapp, George Robert,
1930–   .   III. Negbi, Ora.   IV. University of Minnesota.   Press.
V. Universitat Tel-Aviv.   Makhon le-arkhe′ologyah.   VI. Series.
DS110.M53E83 1988   88-2962
933—dc19   CIP

This volume is dedicated
to the memory of

Shmuel (Shmulik) Moshkovitz,

partner, friend, and a moving spirit
of the Tel Michal expedition.

Contents

Preface

The decision to publish this volume as a cooperative project of the University of Minnesota Press and the Institute of Archaeology at Tel Aviv University reflects the real significance of the Expedition to the Coastal Plain of Israel. Working simultaneously in two editorial teams at Duluth and Tel Aviv involved the challenge of overcoming gaps of thousands of miles and differences in approach, style, and even spelling.

The multidisciplinary character of this project is clearly demonstrated by the wide variety of analyses, subjects, studies, and methods presented by the more than 40 contributors to the volume. By dividing the material and responsibility among so many authors, we have managed to publish all the available material from the excavation as well as a number of in-depth studies within a reasonably short period of time after the end of the excavations. Most chapters were submitted for publication between 1982 and 1984.

All three editors reviewed the articles in this volume; however, out of personal interest and specialization, the chapters on stratigraphy and architecture were closely supervised by Ze'ev Herzog, the archaeometric and environmental studies by George Rapp, and the chapters on pottery and other small artifacts by Ora Negbi.

The difficult task of editing these articles, also conducted on two sides of the Atlantic, was undertaken by Irene Aranne at Tel Aviv University and Judy Holz at the University of Minnesota in Duluth. Production of plates and figures was the responsibility of Lily Singer-Avitz at Tel Aviv. Ora Paran and Judith Dekel drew the plans and sections, and Mira Ben-Zvi, Rodica Penchas, and Josef Kepelyan illustrated the pottery and other small finds. Josef Kepelyan also arranged the plates. At Duluth these jobs were performed by Sharon Hongell and James Allert, who drafted several figures. Avis Hedin was responsible for word processing the many drafts of each chapter.

The Tel Michal project could not have reached fruition without the generous support of the participating institutions and the following major contributors, to whom we express sincere gratitude: The Cleveland-Cliffs Foundation, Dorothy Moore Congdon, Control Data Corporation, the Jacob E. Goldenberg Foundation, the Mary Livingston Griggs and Mary Griggs Burke Foundation, the Alice Tweed Tuohy Foundation, and the Twin Ports Jewish Federation and Community Council.

The volume is dedicated to the memory of our beloved Shmuel Moshkovitz, who was not only the expedition surveyor and stratigrapher but also a moving spirit of the project and a personal friend to the volunteers and staff who dug at Tel Michal (Pl. 56). His contribution to the results may be detected in many of the individual chapters even though they do not bear his name.

We deeply regret that two more of our contributors have passed away since this project was first initiated: Prof. Raphael Giveon, the senior Egyptologist at Tel Aviv University, and Prof. Alexandru Lupu, who divided his time between the Institute of Technology (Technion) at Haifa and metallurgical analyses for the Tel Aviv Insitute of Archaeology. The loss of these two distinguished colleagues will be sorely felt in our future research.

Z. H.
G. R.
O. N.

Figures

Plates

Tables

Expedition Staff*

Project Director: James D. Muhly (Penn)
Archaeological Director: Ze'ev Herzog (TAU)
Archaeometric Director: George Rapp, Jr. (UMD)
Educational Director and
  Area Supervisor: Anson F. Rainey (TAU)
Find Processing Coordinator and
  Area Supervisor: Ora Negbi (TAU)
Project Coordinator and
  Area Supervisor: Fredric R. Brandfon (CMU)
Surveyor and Stratigraphy
  Consultant: Shmuel Moshkovitz (TAU)
Registrar of Finds: Lily Singer-Avitz (TAU)
Photographer: Avraham Hay (TAU)
Regional Survey: Ram Gophna (TAU)
  Bruce Warren (BYU)
Geologist: John A. Gifford (UMD)
Area Supervisors: Diethelm Conrad (Philipps U)
  William Coulson (UM)
  LeGrande Davies (BYU)
  Steven Derfler (Hamline U)
  John C. Lawrenz (WLS)
  John Nelson (BYU)
  Ronald T. Marchese (UMD)
  Ray Matheny (BYU)
  Sariel Shalev (TAU)
  Mark Dorenfeld (U Wisc)
  Amy Eisenstadt (UM)
  Rebecca Friedman (Penn)
  Richard Hanson (BYU)
  Ekhard Heuer (Philipps U)
  Anat Honigman (TAU)
  Judith Johnson (UM)
  Ronald Jyring (UMD)
  Erik Klucas (UM)
  Katherine Kostamo (UMD)
  Wade Kotter (BYU)
  Kathryn Murray (BYU)

Glena Nielson (BYU)
Avi Ofer (TAU)
Mitchell Pratt (California)
Janette Ridley (UM)
Robyn Rogin (UM)
Volkmar Rumpf (Philipps U)
Jonathan Ship (Penn)
Robert Schuman (WLS)
Michael Stacy (BYU)
Delany Stinson (UM)
Christina Sumner (Macquarie)
Jane Sutter (OSU)
Carla Van Aalderen (Groningen U)
Zvi Zuk (TAU)
Physical Anthropologists: Sara C. Bisel (UMD)
  Michele Hogan (UMD)
Pottery Restoration: Mira Barak (TAU)
  Amalia Katzenelson (TAU)
Field Conservator: Virginia Green (Penn)
  Rosa Lowinger-Brandfon (NYU)
Drawing of Finds: Michal Ben-Gal (IDA)
  Hannah Kek (TAU)
  Yarden Piri (IDA)
Photography Assistants: Ben Agar (UM)
  Christopher Sheriff (BYU)
  James Walker (BYU)
Site Surveyors: Deanne Gurr (BYU)
  Brent Harmon (BYU)
  Howard Kempton (BYU)
Regional Survey Assistants: Etan Ayalon (TAU)
  Shlomo Bonimovitz (TAU)
  Israel Drori (TAU)
Secretaries: Karen Benson (Tel Aviv)
  Jane Brandfon (Penn)
  Sara Eliazar (Tel Aviv)
Camp Administrators: Maurice Ben-Ami (Tel Aviv)
  Zvi Kaplan (Tel Aviv)
  Yoram Moshkovitz (Tel Aviv)

Registration Assistants: Sari Arad (TAU)
Mira Barak (TAU)
Semadar Harpazi (TAU)
Hadas Kirsh (TAU)
Site Reconstruction: Sariel Shalev (TAU)

*Key to abbreviations:
BYU: Brigham Young University, Provo, Utah
CMU: Central Michigan University, Mt. Pleasant
Groningen U: Groningen University, Groningen, Holland
Hamline U: Hamline University, St. Paul, Minnesota

IDA: Israel Department of Antiquities and Museums
Macquarie U: Macquarie University, New South Wales, Australia
NYU: New York University
OSU: Ohio State University, Columbus
Penn: University of Pennsylvania, Philadelphia
Philipps U: Philipps Universität, Marburg, Germany
TAU: Tel Aviv University, Israel
UM: University of Minnesota, Minneapolis
UMD: University of Minnesota, Duluth
U Wisc: University of Wisconsin, Madison
Wash U: Washington University, St. Louis, Missouri
WLS: Wisconsin Lutheran Seminary, Mequon

Authors

Shua Amorai-Stark, Hebrew University, Jerusalem

Arthur C. Aufderheide, University of Minnesota, Duluth

Etan Ayalon, Haaretz Museum, Tel Aviv

Natan Bakler, Geological Survey of Israel, Jerusalem

Mira Barak, Tel Aviv University

Sara C. Bisel, University of Minnesota, Duluth

Fredric R. Brandfon, Central Michigan University, Mt. Pleasant

Christa Clamer, Department of Antiquities and Museums, Jerusalem

Diethelm Conrad, Philipps Universität, Marburg, Germany

LeGrande Davies, Brigham Young University, Provo, Utah

Steven Derfler, Hamline University, St. Paul, Minnesota

Nurit Feig, Department of Antiquities and Museums, Jerusalem

Moshe Fischer, Tel Aviv University

John A. Gifford, University of Minnesota, Duluth

Raphael Giveon (deceased), Tel Aviv University

Jonathan Glass, Ministry of Interior, Jerusalem

Paul Goldberg, Hebrew University, Jerusalem

Ram Gophna, Tel Aviv University

Salo Hellwing, Tel Aviv University

Ze'ev Herzog, Tel Aviv University

Christopher L. Hill, University of Minnesota, Duluth

Michele Hogan, University of Minnesota, Duluth

Aharon Horowitz, Tel Aviv University

Ronald Jyring, University of Minnesota, Duluth

Debra F. Katz, University of Minnesota, Minneapolis

Trude Kertesz, Tel Aviv University

Arie Kindler, Haaretz Museum, Tel Aviv

Katherine Kostamo, University of Minnesota, Duluth

Mordechai Lamdan, Prehistoric Museum, Haifa

Nili Liphschitz, Tel Aviv University

Alexandru Lupu (deceased), Tel Aviv University

Ronald T. Marchese, University of Minnesota, Duluth

Shmuel Moshkovitz (deceased), Tel Aviv University

James D. Muhly, University of Pennsylvania, Philadelphia

Polymnia Muhly, University of Pennsylvania, Philadelphia

Ora Negbi, Tel Aviv University

Anson F. Rainey, Tel Aviv University

George Rapp, Jr., University of Minnesota, Duluth

Lily Singer-Avitz, Tel Aviv University

Margaret Thomson, University of Minnesota, Duluth

Vanda Vitali, University of Toronto

Yoav Waisel, Tel Aviv University

Jo Ann E. Wallgren, University of Minnesota, Duluth

Participating Institutions

Tel Aviv University (Institute of Archaeology)
University of Minnesota, Duluth (Archaeometry
  Laboratory)
Brigham Young University, Provo, Utah
University of Pennsylvania, Philadelphia
Macquarie University, New South Wales, Australia

Wisconsin Lutheran Seminary, Mequon, Wisconsin
Hamline University, St. Paul, Minnesota
Central Michigan University, Mt. Pleasant
Philipps Universität, Marburg, Germany
Municipality of Herzliya, Israel

Abbreviations

AAA	*Annals of Archaeology and Anthropology.* Liverpool.
AASOR	*Annual of the American Schools of Oriental Research.*
ADAJ	*Annual of the Department of Antiquities of Jordan.*
AfO	*Archiv fur Orientforschung;* continuation of AfK.
AG I–IV	Petrie, W. M. F. 1931–34. *Ancient Gaza I–IV.* London.
Agora IV	Howland, R. 1958. *The Athenian Agora IV: Greek Lamps and Their Survivals.* Princeton.
Agora V	Robinson, H. S. 1959. *The Athenian Agora V: Pottery of the Roman Period: Chronology.* Princeton.
Agora XII	Sparkes, B. A., and Talcott, L. 1970. *The Athenian Agora XII: Black and Plain Pottery of the 6th, 5th and 4th Centuries B.C.* Princeton.
Agora XXII	Rotroff, S. I. 1982. *The Athenian Agora XXII: Athenian and Imported Mold-made Bowls.* Princeton.
Ain Shems III	Grant, E. 1934. *Rumeilah, Being Ain Shems Excavations III.* Haverford, Pa.
Ain Shems IV–V	Grant, E., and Wright, G. E. 1938–39. *Ain Shems Excavations IV, V.* Haverford, Pa.
AJA	*American Journal of Archaeology.*
Am. Antiquit.	*American Antiquity*
ANET	Pritchard, B., ed. 1969. *Ancient Near Eastern Texts.* 3d ed. with supplement. Princeton.
Anthedon	Petrie, W. M. F. 1937. *Anthedon, Sinai.* London.
Aphek-Antipatris I	Beck, P., and Kochavi, M. *Aphek-Antipatris I.* Tel Aviv. In press.
Ashdod I	Dothan, M., and Freedman, D. N. 1967. Ashdod I. *'Atiqot* 7 (English series).
Ashdod II–III	Dothan, M. 1971. Ashdod II–III. *'Atiqot 9–10* (English series).
Ashdod IV	Dothan, M., and Porath, Y. 1982. Ashdod IV: Excavation of Area M. *'Atiqot 15* (English series).
'Atiqot	Journal of the Israel Department of Antiquities (Hebrew and English series).
Ayios Iakovos	Åström, P., et al. 1962. Supplementary Material from Ayios Iakovos Tomb 8. *Opuscula Atheniensia* 4:207–279.
BA	*Biblical Archaeologist.*
BAR	*Biblical Archaeology Review.*
BASLS	*Bulletin Académie et Société Lorraines des Sciences.*
BASOR	*Bulletin of the American Schools of Oriental Research.*
Beer-sheba I	Aharoni, Y., ed. 1973. *Beer-sheba I: Excavations at Tel Beer-sheba, 1969–1971 Seasons.* Tel Aviv.
Beer-sheba II	Herzog, Z. 1984. *Beer-sheba II: The Early Iron Age Settlements.* Tel Aviv.
Berytus	The American University of Beirut.
Beth-Pelet	Petrie, W. M. F. 1930. *Beth-Pelet (Tell Fara),* vol. 1. London.
Beth-shan 1966	James, F. W. *The Iron Age at Beth-shan.* Philadelphia.
Beth-zur 1933	Sellers, O. *The Citadel of Beth-zur.* Philadelphia.
Beth-zur 1968	Sellers, O. R., et al. The 1957 Excavations at Beth-zur. *AASOR* 38.
BIES	*Bulletin of the Israel Exploration Society* (continuation of *BJPES;* Hebrew).
BMC Alexandria	Poole, R. S. 1892. *Catalogue of the Greek Coins in the British Museum, Alexandria and the Nomes.* London.

BMC Arabia	Hill, G. F. 1922. *Catalogue of the Greek Coins in the British Museum, Arabia, Mesopotamia and Persia.* London.
BMC Lycia, Pamphylia	Hill, G. F. 1897. *Catalogue of the Greek Coins in the British Museum, Lycia, Pamphylia and Pisidia.* London.
BMC Palestine	Hill, G. F. 1914. *Catalogue of the Greek Coins in the British Museum, Palestine.* London.
BMC Phoenicia	Hill, G. F. 1910. *Catalogue of the Greek Coins in the British Museum, Phoenicia.* London.
BMP 1932	*Photographs of Casts of the Persian Sculptures of the Achaemenid Period, Mostly from Persepolis.* British Museum, Department of Egyptian and Assyrian Antiquities. London.
Corinth XII	Davidson, G. R. 1952. *Corinth XII: The Minor Objects.* Princeton.
CPP	Duncan, J. G. 1930. *Corpus of Dated Palestinian Pottery.* London.
Dura Europos IV.2	Cox, D. H. 1949. *The Greek and Roman Pottery: The Excavations at Dura Europos, Final Report IV, 1, fasc. 2.* New Haven, Conn.
Early Arad	Amiran, R., et al. 1978. *Early Arad: The Chalcolithic Settlement and Early Bronze City I: First-Fifth Seasons of Excavations, 1962–1966.* Jerusalem.
EI	*Eretz-Israel.* (Hebrew and English) Archaeological, Historical and Geographical Studies.
Enc. Arch. Exc. I–IV	Avi-Yonah, M., ed. 1975–78. *Encyclopedia of Archaeological Excavations in the Holy Land, I–IV.* Jerusalem.
Enc. Miqr. II	*Encyclopaedia Miqra'it (Encyclopaedia Biblica;* Hebrew). 1954. Jerusalem.
En-gedi 1966	Mazar, B., Dothan, T., and Dunayevsky, I. En-gedi Excavations in 1961–1962. *'Atiqot 5* (English series).
Enkomi I–III	Dikaios, P. 1969. *Enkomi I–III.* Mainz am Rhein.
Gerar	Petrie, W. M. F. 1928. *Gerar.* London.
Gezer I–III	Macalister, R. A. S. 1911–12. *The Excavation of Gezer I–III.* London.
Gezer 1974	Dever, W. F., et al. *Gezer II: Report of the 1967–1970 Seasons in Fields I and II.* Annual of the Hebrew Union College/Nelson Glueck School of Biblical Archaeology 2.
Had. Arch.	*Hadashot Archeologiot (Archaeological News;* Hebrew).
Hama II,3	Riis, P. J. 1948. *Hama II.3: Les cimetières à crémation.* Copenhagen.
Hazor I–IV	Yadin, Y., et. al. 1958, 1960–61. *Hazor I–IV.* Jerusalem.
Hazor 1972	Yadin, Y. *Hazor* (Schweich Lectures 1970). London.
HTR	*Harvard Theological Review.*
IEJ	*Israel Exploration Journal.*
IG I	*Inscriptiones Graecae,* Vol. 1. A. Kirchhoff, ed. 1873.
Iraq	British School of Archaeology in Iraq.
Isr. J. Earth	*Israel Journal of Earth Sciences.*
Isr. J. Zool.	*Israel Journal of Zoology.*
JAOS	*Journal of the American Oriental Society.*
JAS	*Journal of Archaeological Science.*
JEA	*Journal of Egyptian Archaeology.*
Jericho I–II	Kenyon, K. M. 1960, 1965. *Excavations at Jericho I–II.* London.
Jericho IV	Kenyon, K. M., and Holland, T. A. 1982. *Excavations at Jericho IV.* London.
JFA	*Journal of Field Archaeology.*
JHS	*Journal of Hellenic Studies.*
JNES	*Journal of Near Eastern Studies.*
JPOS	*Journal of the Palestine Oriental Society.*
KAI	Donner, H., and Röllig, W. 1962. *Kanaanäische und aramäische Inschriften I–III.* Wiesbaden.
Kalopsidha	Åström, P., et al. 1966. *Excavations at Kalopsidha and Ayios Iakovos in Cyprus (SIMA 2).* Lund.
Kamid el-Lōz 2	Poppa, R. 1978. *Kamid el-Lōz 2. Der eisenzeitliche Friedhof. Befunde und Funde.* Bonn.
Kush V	Reisner, G. A. 1963. *The Royal Cemeteries of Kush V: El Kurru.* Cambridge, Mass.
Lachish II	Tufnell, O., et al. 1940. *Lachish II: The Fosse Temple.* London.
Lachish III	Tufnell, O. 1953. *Lachish III: The Iron Age.* London.
Lachish IV	Tufnell, O., et al. *Lachish IV: The Bronze Age.* London.
Lachish V	Aharoni, Y. 1975. *Investigations at Lachish: The Sanctuary and the Residency (Lachish V).* Tel Aviv.
Levant	Journal of the British School of Archaeology in Jerusalem and the British Institute at Amman for Archaeology and History.
Liber Annuus	Studii Biblici Franciscani.
MASCA Journal	Museum of Applied Science and Center for Archaeology.
MDIK	*Mitteilungen des Deutschen Archäologischen Instituts, Abteilung Kairo.*
Megiddo I	Lamon, R. S., and Shipton, G. M. 1939. *Megiddo I.* Chicago.
Megiddo II	Loud, G. 1948. *Megiddo II.* Chicago.

Megiddo Tombs	Guy, P. L. O. 1938. *Megiddo Tombs*. Chicago.
Memphis I	Petrie, W. M. F. 1909. *Memphis I*. London.
Meydum and Memphis III	Petrie, W. M. F. 1910. *Meydum and Memphis III*. London.
Mitekufat Haeven	(*From the Stone Age*; Hebrew). Israel Prehistoric Society.
MUSE	Annual of the Museum of Art and Architecture, University of Missouri, Columbia.
MVAG	*Mitteilungen der Vorderasiatisch-Agyptischen Gesellschaft.*
Nessana I	Colt, H. D., ed. *Excavations at Nessana I*. London.
Nichoria I	Rapp, G., Jr., and Aschenbrenner, S. E., eds. 1978. *Excavations at Nichoria in Southwest Greece I: Site, Environs and Techniques*. Minneapolis.
Nush-i Jan III	Curtis, J. 1984. *Nush-i Jan III: The Small Finds*. London.
Olynthus X	Robinson, D. M. 1941. *Excavations at Olynthus. Part X: Metal and Minor Miscellaneous Finds, An Original Contribution to Greek Life*. Baltimore.
Paphos I	Erdmann, E. 1977. *Ausgrabungen in Alt-Paphos auf Cypern, I. Nordosttor und persische Belagerungsrampe in Alt-Paphos*. Konstanz.
PEFQSt	*Palestine Exploration Fund, Quarterly Statement.*
PEQ	*Palestine Exploration Quarterly* (continuation of *PEFQSt*).
Persepolis II	Schmidt, E. F. 1957. *Persepolis II: Contents of the Treasury and Other Discoveries*. Chicago.
Praktika	*Tes en Atenais Archaiologikes Etaireias.*
Qadmoniot	*Quarterly for the Antiquities of Eretz-Israel and Bible Lands.* (Hebrew).
QDAP	Quarterly of the Department of Antiquities in Palestine.
Qedem	Monographs of the Institute of Archaeology. Hebrew University of Jerusalem.
Quartär	*Jahrbuch für Enforschung des Eiszeitalters und der Steinzeit.*
Quatern. Res.	Quaternary Research.
Ramat Raḥel II	Aharoni, Y. 1964. *Excavations at Ramat Raḥel, Seasons 1961 and 1962.*
RB	*Revue Biblique.*
RDAC	*Report of the Department of Antiquities, Cyprus.*
Salamis II.4	Karageorghis, B. 1970. *Excavations in the Necropolis of Salamis II*. Nicosia.
Samaria 1924	Reisner, G. A., Fischer, C. S., and Lyon, D. G. *Harvard Excavations at Samaria 1908–1910*. Cambridge, Mass.
Samaria-Sebaste III	Crowfoot, J. W., Crowfoot, G. M., and Kenyon, K. M. 1957. *The Objects from Samaria*. London.
SCE IV, 1B	Åström, P. 1972. *The Swedish Cyprus Expedition IV, 1B: The Middle Cypriote Bronze Age*. Stockholm.
SCE IV, 2	Gjerstad, E. 1948. *The Swedish Cyprus Expedition IV, 2: The Cypro-Geometric, Cypro-Archaic and Cypro-Classical Periods*. Stockholm.
SCE IV, 3	Vessberg, O., and Westholm, A. 1956. *The Swedish Cyprus Expedition IV, 3: The Hellenistic and Roman Periods in Cyprus*. Stockholm.
Shechem	Wright, G. E. 1956. *Shechem*. London.
Shiqmona I	Elgavish, J. 1968. *Archaeological Excavations at Shikmona. Field Report No. 1: The Levels of the Persian Period, Seasons 1963–1965*. (Hebrew). Haifa.
Shiqmona II	Elgavish, J. 1974. *Archaeological Excavations at Shikmona. Field Report No. 2: The Level of the Hellenistic Period—Stratum H. Seasons 1964–1970*. (Hebrew). Haifa.
Shiqmona III	Elgavish, J. 1977. *Archaeological Excavations at Shikmona: The Pottery of the Roman Period*. (Hebrew). Haifa.
SIG	Dittenberger, W., ed., 1915–24. *Sylloge Inscriptionum Graecorum*. Leipzig.
SIMA	*Studies in Mediterranean Archaeology.*
SNG Copenhagen, Macedonia II	1943. *Sylloge Nummorum Graecorum, Macedonia, Part II*. Copenhagen.
SNG Copenhagen Macedonia III	1943. *Sylloge Nummorum Graecorum Macedonia, Part III*. Copenhagen.
SNG Copenhagen, Seleucid Kings	Morkholm, O. 1959. *Sylloge Nummorum Graecorum, Syria, Seleucid Kings*. Copenhagen.
SNG Oxford, Macedonia III	1976. *Sylloge Nummorum Gracecorum, Ashmolean Museum, Oxford, Vol. V, Part III, Macedonia*. London.
Stephania	Hennessy, J. B. 1963. *Stephania, A Middle and Late Bronze Age Cemetery in Cyprus*. London.
Sukas II	Ploug, G. 1973. *Sukas II: The Aegean, Corinthian and Eastern Greek Pottery and Terracottas*. Copenhagen.

Sukas VII   Buhl, M. L. 1983. *Sukas VII. The Near Eastern Pottery and Objects of Other Materials from the Upper Strata*. Copenhagen.

SWP I–III   Conder, C. R. and Kitchener, H. H. 1881–88. *The Survey of Western Palestine, Memoirs I–III*. London.

Taanach I   Rast, W. 1978. *Taanach I: Studies in the Iron Age Pottery*. Cambridge, Mass.

TAH   Hamilton, R. M. 1935. Excavations at Tell Abu Hawam. *QDAP* 4:1–69.

Tarsus III   Goldman, H. 1963. *Excavations at Gozlu Kule: Tarsus III: The Iron Age*. Princeton.

TBM I   Albright, W. F. 1932. The Excavation of Tell Beit Mirsim in Palestine I: The Pottery of the First Three Campaigns. *AASOR* 12.

TBM III   Albright, W. F. 1943. The Excavations of Tell Beit Mirsim III: The Iron Age. *AASOR* 21–22.

Tel Aviv   *Journal of the Tel Aviv University Institute of Archaeology*.

Tell el Mazar I   Yassine, K. 1984. *Tell el Mazar I. Cemetery A*. Amman.

Tell Halaf IV   von Oppenheim, M. F. 1962. *Tell Halaf IV*. Berlin.

Tell Keisan   Briend, J., and Humbert, J. B. 1980. *Tell Keisan (1971–1976): Une cité phénicienne en Galilée*. Paris.

Tell Qasile   Mazar, A. 1980. *Excavations at Tell Qasile. Part One: The Philistine Sanctuary: Architecture and Cult Objects*. Qedem 12. Jerusalem.

Tel Mevorakh I   Stern, E. 1978. *Excavations at Tel Mevorakh (1973–1976). Part One: From the Iron Age to the Roman Period*. Qedem 9. Jerusalem.

Tel Mevorakh II   Stern, E. 1984. *Excavations at Tel Mevorakh (1973–1976). Part Two: The Bronze Age*. Qedem 18. Jerusalem.

TN I   McCown, C. C. 1947. *Tell en Nasbeh I: Archaeological and Historical Results*. Berkeley.

TN II   Wampler, J. C. 1947. *Tell en Nasbeh II: The Pottery*. Berkeley.

Tyre   Bikai, P. M. 1978. *The Pottery of Tyre*. Warminster.

Ugaritica II   Schaeffer, C. F. A. 1949. *Ugaritica II*. Paris.

Ugaritica VI, VII   Schaeffer, C. F. A., et al. 1969, 1978. *Ugaritica VI, VII*. Paris.

VT Sup.   *Vetus Testamentum Supplements*.

ZA   *Zeitschrift für Assyriologie und verwandte Gebiete*.

ZDPV   *Zeitschrift des Deutschen Palästina-Vereins*.

Excavations at Tel Michal, Israel

1

Introduction

by Ze'ev Herzog, George Rapp, Jr., and James D. Muhly

Tel Michal is located in the coastal plain of Israel, within the municipal boundaries of Herzliya (map ref. 131/174; Fig. 1.1). The site lies on a *kurkar* ridge overlooking the beach (Pls. 1; 2) 12.5 km north of Jaffa (Joppa) and 6.5 km north of the Yarkon estuary. From 1977 to 1980, large-scale excavations initiated by the Institute of Archaeology at Tel Aviv University were conducted at the site by the Archaeological Expedition to the Central Coastal Plain of Israel. Before this, a small-scale salvage dig was carried out on the northeastern hillock (Makmish) by N. Avigad on behalf of Museum Haaretz of Tel Aviv and the Hebrew University at Jerusalem.

1.1. PROJECT ORGANIZATION

The concept of regional archaeology has deep roots at the Institute of Archaeology ever since its introduction by Yohanan Aharoni in 1969. For Aharoni, the regional approach was not merely a theoretical concept but emanated from his intuitive feeling for the discipline, in which the geography of a region is studied along with an intensive archaeological survey, excavations in selected sites, and a careful analysis of historical sources that are then integrated into an overall view of cultural change. Such were Aharoni's researches in the early 1950s in the Upper Galilee (Aharoni 1957) and from the early 1960s in the biblical Negev (*Beersheba I*; Aharoni 1976) until his untimely death in 1976. It was therefore natural that the new project started by Aharoni's colleagues and students follow a similar cultural-regional methodology. Since the University of Minnesota has also developed a regional approach, as applied to the environmental study of Messenia in Greece and the excavations at Nichoria (McDonald and Rapp 1972; *Nichoria I*), our mutual background and interests have led to sound cooperation.

Accordingly, the decision to dig at Tel Michal was made not on the basis of its size or importance as a site but as a first step in a much broader regional project whose objective was to explore the central coastal plain of Israel. Moshe Kochavi, then director of the Institute of Archaeology at Tel Aviv University, had already undertaken a regional study of the eastern Yarkon basin as an adjunct of the Aphek-Antipatris excavations. It therefore seemed appropriate that a second team based at the same institute would complete the study by exploring the western part of this geographic unit. Following Kochavi's advice, two tells were chosen: Tel Michal, a relatively small site on the coastal cliffs north of Tel Aviv, and Tel Gerisa, a large mound on the southern bank of the Yarkon. Tel Michal, which became our pilot project, was excavated during four seasons in the summers of 1977–80, followed by four seasons (1981–83, 1986) at Tel Gerisa (Herzog 1983; 1984), with a renewal of digging scheduled for 1988. Concurrently the regional survey is being conducted (Chap. 3).

The project soon attracted several institutions and scholars who were considering archaeological work in Israel. Upon joining the Tel Michal expedition, Brigham Young University of Provo, Utah, represented by LeGrande Davies of the Department of Religious Instruction, increased the extent of its financial contribution and participation in the excavations of the Institute of Archaeology, with which it had been associated since 1976 at Tel Beer-sheba. Davies' main interest was the Persian period cemetery (Chap. 11).

The University of Pennsylvania, represented by Prof. James D. Muhly of the Department of Oriental Studies, was a major partner from the first season. It included the project in its summer program, and Professor Muhly agreed to serve as the project director; he also undertook the responsibility for publishing the metal finds (Chap. 25).

Through Professor Muhly's good offices, Prof. George Rapp, Jr., Dean of the College of Science and Engineering at the University of Minnesota in Duluth, and director of its Archaeometry Laboratory, joined the expedition together with his archaeometric staff and a large complement of students. As archaeometric director of the expedition, he stimulated the application of the latest research methods from the natural sciences (Rapp and Gifford 1985) in a number of specialized studies—for example, analysis of

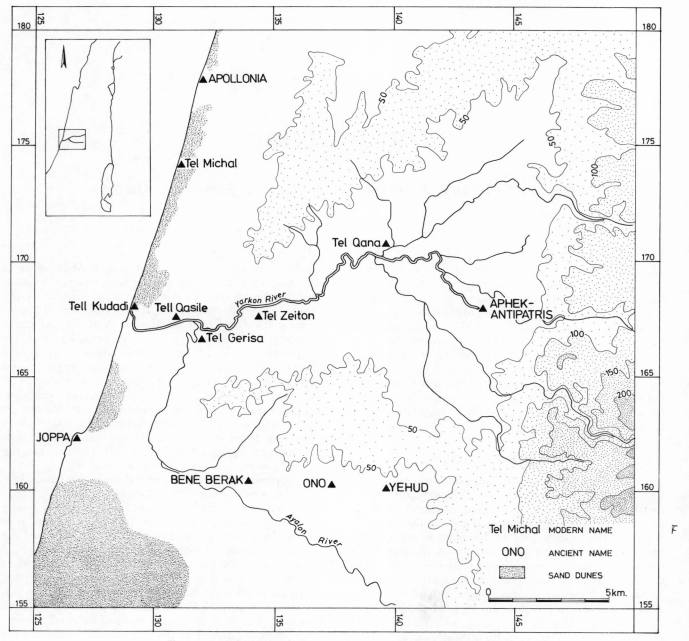

Figure 1.1. Tel Michal and other ancient sites in central coastal plain of Israel.

paleobotanical phytoliths (Chap. 20) and the nutritional chemistry of human bones (Chap. 21b), as well as the by-now familiar reports on paleobotany (Chap. 19), zooarchaeology (Chap. 22), nuclear activation analysis (Chap. 24a), and petrography (Chaps. 24b, 24c).

A team from Macquarie University, New South Wales, Australia, was organized by Dr. Geoffrey Cowling of the School of History, Philosophy, and Politics, supported by a donation from the Sir Asher Joel Foundation. The Aus-

tralian team was with us all four seasons and continues at Tel Gerisa. In 1978 and 1980 (second and fourth seasons), the Wisconsin Lutheran Seminary of Mequon included the project in its Summer Quarter in Israel program codirected by Profs. John C. Jeske and John C. Lawrenz. A large group of students participated in the dig. Other groups joining the expedition included contingents organized by Prof. Diethelm Conrad of Philipps Universität, Marburg, Germany; Steven Derfler of Hamline University, St. Paul, Minnesota; Dr. Gerald Shin of the University of North Carolina in Wilmington; and Fredric R. Brandfon of Central Michigan University, Mount Pleasant. A complete list of the expedition staff is presented on pages xvi–xvii, and the list of participants appears in Appendix II.

A major backer of our project was the Municipality of Herzliya, which set up the expedition camp at Nof Yam (Pl. 54), a few kilometers north of the excavation site, provided the infrastructure (electricity, sanitary facilities, concrete tent platforms, kitchen and dining facilities, fencing and guard services), and erected two buildings for the expedition's offices; the municipality also piped water and prepared a road to the site itself. We are deeply grateful to Shmuel Degani, head of the Culture, Youth and Sport Department, who represented the municipality and coordinated its activities, and to Mayor Yoseph Nevo, his deputy, Haim Blas, and the workers of the Education Department and the Department of Municipal Engineering, all of whom were most helpful to the expedition. The municipality also provided a special budget for the preservation of the more interesting architectural features of the site, mainly the Roman fortress and the Ptolemaic winepress (Pl. 45), which have now been restored for the benefit of scholars, students, and the general public.

The contributions and support of all the above assured the financial basis of the project and attracted a large number of students who participated in our academic summer courses (Pl. 55). The multidisciplinary methods and the multinational joint effort and groups of participants are a good illustration, in our opinion, of the new trends advocated and praised by Dever (1980:46) for expanding archaeological horizons today.

1.2. SITE AND EXCAVATIONS

1.2.1. Site

Tel Michal is an unusual phenomenon in the archaeological landscape of Israel. It is not simply an ancient tell or mound (although it includes one), but a group of separate components spread over five hills of varying heights, sizes, and shapes (Fig. 1.2; Pls. 1; 2).

The high tell (Area A) overlooks the beach and covers about 1,600 m². It rises about 10 m above the terrain to its east, with an original elevation (before removal of the overlying sand dunes) of 30 m above sea level (Pls. 3; 4). This part of the site witnessed the most continuous occupation and had the deepest deposits, probably because it was a compact unit demarcated by the ravines running into the sea at its northern and southern ends. The top of the hill commands a fine view of the open sea to the west, to the south as far as Jaffa, and to the north as far as Arsuf-Apollonia. To the east may be seen the second *kurkar* ridge and the *hamra* hills beyond it. (See Chaps. 16 and 17 for geographic details.)

Before our excavations, the top and eastern side of the high tell were covered by a thick layer (more than 2 m deep) of windblown sand that buried and protected the ancient

remains (Pl. 3). The other three sides, especially the western, seaward side, suffered from continuous erosion and tectonic upheavals. Chapter 18 details the long-term physiographic changes in the tell. A platform erected during the Middle Bronze Age in the center of the mound (Chap. 4) created an upper terrace, whereas the northern end was considerably lower. Consequently, entry into the settlement was effected from the east, first with a moderate ascent to the northern, lower terrace and then another climb to the upper terrace. In Strata XIV–XII, III, and II, drainage channels were found leading downward in the reverse direction.

The northern hill (Areas D, E, and F) is a much larger unit but was occupied over a shorter time than the high tell, mainly during the Persian and Hellenistic periods, with a correspondingly shallower accumulation of debris. The hill covers an area of 4 hectares (40,000 m²), but it was inhabited only on its southern side (Chaps. 8, 12). The northern slope of this hill was used as a cemetery in the Persian period (Chap. 11). The slope terminates with a twisting ravine, now called Nahal Gelilot (Arabic: Wadi el-Gharbi or Wadi Makmish; Pl. 1).

The northeastern hillock (Makmish), located 400 m northeast of the high tell, covers an area of some 1,000 m². Avigad excavated it in 1958–60 and discovered cultic installations of the Iron Age, Persian, and Hellenistic periods.

The eastern hillock (Area C), located about 150 m southeast of the high tell, is small and sandy, covering only about 625 m². Its history and function appear to be similar to those of the northeastern hillock (see Chaps. 6a, 8, 12).

The southeastern hillock (Area B), which covers about 1,000 m², was apparently occupied by farmsteads in the Iron Age and the late Persian period (see Chaps. 6a, 8).

In addition to these areas of occupation, isolated *winepresses* were uncovered in three locations around the site. The earliest complex, which dates from the Iron Age (Chap. 6b), is located approximately 180 m east of the high tell. A second winepress, previously cleaned by Avigad, who dated it to the Persian period, lies between Areas B and C. Finally, S. Lev-Yadon discovered a small winepress in the sand dunes about 200 m south of Area B, which we subsequently excavated and dated to the Hasmonean period (Chap. 12).

1.2.2. Research History

The site was first mentioned in official records in 1922 by J. Ory, who surveyed the area and noted its considerable extent. He reported that what we refer to as the high tell was called Tell el-Qantur by the local Arabs, and the surrounding area was called Dhahrat Makmish. Ory speculated that *Makmish* was derived from *Mekal* of the Phoenician god Reshef-Mekal, which corresponds to the Greek Apollo-Amyklos (for further discussion of the name, see Herzog, Negbi, and Moshkovitz 1978:100). The name Tel Michal was given to the site by the Israel Government Names Committee (the Survey of Israel uses the spelling Mikhal). The available data do not establish the ancient name of the site.

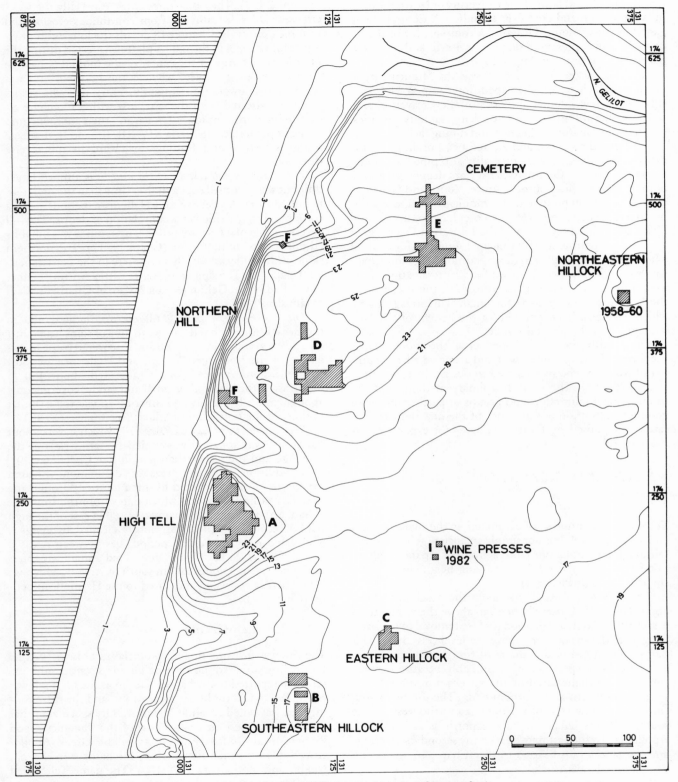

Figure 1.2. Topography of Tel Michal and location of excavated areas.

In 1958 and 1960, small-scale excavations were carried out on the northeastern hillock by N. Avigad (1960; 1961; 1977). The excavation, published under the name Makmish, yielded figurines, altars, and other cult objects, indicating that this was a sacred area during the Iron Age and the Persian and Hellenistic periods. Tel Michal was surveyed again in 1966 and was viewed as a port settlement founded during Middle Bronze Age II (Gophna and Kochavi 1966). The large-scale excavations undertaken by our expedition were conducted from 1977 to 1980. Two years later, bulldozers working in the area uncovered some plastered remains that were excavated by Z. Herzog and turned out to be a complex of Iron Age winepresses (Chap. 6b).

Some of the objects discussed in this publication, such as flint tools, scarab impressions, coins, and metal objects, were collected from the surface before our excavations and presented to us for study by a number of archaeological enthusiasts. We would especially like to note the contributions of Y. Davidor (see Schulman 1978), D. Weiss (see Mozel 1978), and Y. Friedman.

1.2.3. Progress of the Excavations

Since most of the prospective digging areas were covered by thick layers of sand, it was next to impossible at the outset to determine the nature, extent, and duration of the settlements in different parts of the site. The first season was therefore planned as a 4-week trial excavation to probe all the areas. Expansion or discontinuation would be decided upon according to the results. From the very beginning, however, it was obvious that the high tell was the focus of interest, and three large excavation areas were opened there.

On the northern hill, two probes at the northern and southern ends of the western side revealed Persian period kilns and a dumping area (Area F). In a third spot, on the southeastern side, a sloping stone surface was uncovered, resulting from leveling of Persian period houses by the builders of a Hellenistic winepress (Chaps. 8, 12). The fourth area, on the northern end of the hill, was opened in a place where hewn stones of graves were visible on the surface (Area E). This was the cemetery of the Persian period (Chaps. 11, 21). Additional areas were opened on the eastern hillock (Area C) and the southeastern hillock (Area B).

In the second season, the poor state of preservation caused us to discontinue excavation of Area F and to limit the size of Areas B and C. In the third season, our major efforts were devoted to excavating the high tell and the Hellenistic winepress on the northern hill, where some deep probes were made to determine the stratigraphy of the Persian occupation there (Chap. 8). The high tell became the focus of our fourth and last season, when we aimed to reach the lowest Bronze Age levels (Chap. 4).

Site preservation was an important factor in planning the progress of the excavations. Since the Roman fortress was designated for restoration from the very beginning, we had to dig between its walls (mainly in the courtyard) to reach the underlying strata. This further limited our ability to retrieve full data on the earlier levels in this area.

1.2.4. Notes on Plans

All field plans were drawn on a scale of 1:50 and later reproduced at 1:100. As far as possible, the detailed plans are printed in this volume on a scale of 1:200, but for some of the larger areas we had to further diminish the scale. The reference point for measuring elevations, designated as zero level, was set at the top of the high tell, 30 m above sea level. All elevations were measured from this point (i.e., subtracted from zero) and hence are negative values.

The excavation boundaries vary from stratum to stratum. In some cases, the lower excavated area was decreased because of the danger of collapse of the side balks. In other cases, the excavated area in a lower stratum may be larger than that above because there was less erosional damage at these points than higher up. The dotted outline of the Roman fortress was imposed over the plans of the earlier strata partly to help orient the reader and partly because its walls served as the limits of the excavated area in many parts of the high tell.

Sections were drawn on enlarged photographs during the entire excavation and used for our analysis of the stratigraphy (see, e.g., A. F. Rainey in Herzog 1980:121, Pl. 30:1). However, drawings based on such sections are reproduced in this volume only when we feel that they explain the stratigraphy more clearly than do the plans, as with the processes of construction and destruction of the Bronze Age earthworks (Chap. 4).

1.3. STRATIGRAPHY

The results of the excavations are arranged in seventeen strata from the earliest Middle Bronze Age IIB (Stratum XVII) up to the latest Early Arab occupation (Stratum I). Table 1.1 summarizes the stratigraphic sequence and emphasizes the gaps in occupation and the expansion of settlement to different areas of the site in various periods. In addition to temporal and spatial dimensions, Figure 1.3 demonstrates the ratio between the estimated original size of the site, its preserved part, and its excavated area.

In retrospect, the results of the four excavation seasons may be viewed ambivalently. The poor state of preservation limited the clear-cut architectural plans and the number of rich object assemblages in secure stratigraphic contexts. The material came mainly from fills and from the cemetery; only a few of the floors yielded any. Nevertheless, our method of extensive exposure and intensive excavation allowed us to retrieve a large quantity of artifacts and other archaeological remains. This rich material, presented throughout the volume, shows how much can be learned about a site and its environment, even a poorly preserved one.

Table 1.1. Stratigraphic and Chronological Chart

Stratum	Former Abbreviation	Period	Approximate Date	Areas Occupied
I	Ar.	Early Arab	8th-9th centuries C.E.	A,C
		G A P		
II	R	Roman	10-50 C.E.	A
IIIa	L.Has.	Late Hasmonean ⎫	100-50 B.C.E.	A
IIIb	Has.	Early Hasmonean ⎭		
IV	H1	Hellenistic (Seleucid)	200-100 B.C.E.	A, D
V	H2	Hellenistic (Ptolemaic)	300-200 B.C.E.	A, C, D
VI	P1	Persian/Hellenistic	350-300 B.C.E.	A, B, C, D, F
VII	P2	Persian period	400-350 B.C.E.	A, B, C, D, F
VIII	P3	Persian period	430-400 B.C.E.	A, D, E, F
IX	P4	Persian period	450-430 B.C.E.	A, E
X	P5	Persian period	490-450 B.C.E.	A, E
XI	P6	Persian period	525-490 B.C.E.	A, E
		G A P		
XII	Iron 1	Iron Age IIC	8th century B.C.E.	A, C
		G A P		
XIII	Iron 2	Iron Age IIA	10th century B.C.E.	A, B, C, I
XIV	Iron 3	Iron Age IIA	10th century B.C.E.	A, B, C, I
		G A P		
XV	LB II	Late Bronze Age II	14th-13th centuries B.C.E.	A
XVI	LB I	Late Bronze Age I	16th-15th centuries B.C.E.	A
XVII	MB IIB	Middle Bronze Age IIB	17th century B.C.E.	A, D

1.4. NATURE OF THE TEL MICHAL SETTLEMENTS

The environmental conditions around Tel Michal did not encourage the establishment of permanent settlement (there was none in the area from premodern times either). The *kurkar* ridges present an obstacle to transportation and also prevent proper drainage from the hinterland into the sea. Hence the interridge troughs to the east of the site are covered by marshes during long periods in winter. The soils in the near vicinity are sandy and salty. The *ḥamra* (red sandy soil) is not arable; furthermore, a great deal of the region is covered by wind-borne sand dunes.

Under such conditions, the existence of a settlement at Tel Michal cannot be explained by favorable subsistence conditions like those that prevailed at Tel Aphek and Tel Gerisa in the fertile Yarkon basin. The construction of a settlement on this barren cliff facing the Mediterranean can only be ascribed to external factors. We assumed a priori that this external factor was its seacoast location. Throughout most of its periods of occupation, Tel Michal was very likely a maritime station—military, commercial, or both—engaging in international trade and providing services to ships and seafarers.

The archaeological data unearthed in our excavations show a clear correlation between the periods of developed trade contacts along the coasts of the eastern Mediterranean and the periods of most intensive occupation at Tel Michal. Absence of a natural bay near the site leads to the assump-

tion that a suitable anchorage may have existed in a natural channel located at the foot of the original hill, possibly once protected by a *kurkar* ridge whose abraded remains are still visible under the water (Pl. 2).

The results of our excavations clearly indicate the nature of the first two settlements: small (about one-half acre) trading posts in both the Middle and Late Bronze ages. Evidence from Iron Age IIA indicates that, in addition to engaging in trade, the population looked for opportunities to widen its economic base. Grapevines are one of the few types of cultivated plants that grow in the red sandy soils, and the complexes of twin winepresses (Chap. 6b) nicely confirm the use of the land for viticulture. In the Iron Age we also find small religious installations on the northeastern and eastern hillocks, which may reflect the expanding cultic role of the site.

After a long hiatus (with only brief and poor occupation in the later part of the Iron Age), the site was resettled and flourished in the Persian period. The high tell could no longer accommodate the population, and a large "lower city" developed on the northern hill. The eastern hillocks were used once again for ceremonial and religious functions, and in the open areas winepresses and pottery kilns were erected. Some of their products may have been exported. The abundance of retrieved metal objects may point to a forge, although no such workshop was found. The large population is also reflected by the extensive cemetery on the northern outskirts of the town. A central political or military authority erected a sequence of forts on the northern

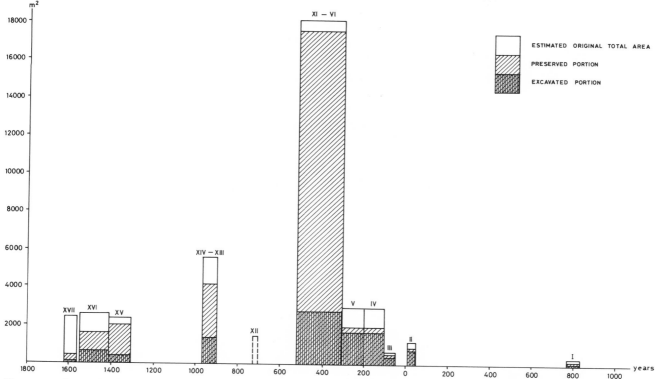

Figure 1.3. Occupational periods, gaps, and relative sizes of settlements at Tel Michal. Each column represents (estimated) total size of settlement, its relative preserved portion, and excavated portion.

end of the high tell that dominated the approach from the sea, as well as the hills and hillocks north and east of the tell.

In the Hellenistic period the military function of Tel Michal became dominant: a large fortress covers most of the high tell, with only a few houses at its northern end. The northern hill was occupied by a large winepress that suggests centralization of production. In Hasmonean times, the high tell was occupied only by a small fort with a small winepress 200 m to its south. The Roman fort marks the last extensive usage of Tel Michal by a centralized authority. Following a gap of about 700 years, a small watchtower or lighthouse was constructed on the high tell in the Early Arab period. After its abandonment, Tel Michal remained unknown and forgotten until modern times.

REFERENCES

Aharoni, Y. 1957. *The Settlement of the Israelite Tribes in the Upper Galilee.* Jerusalem. (Hebrew).

Aharoni, Y. 1976. Nothing Early and Nothing Late: Re-Writing Israel's Conquest. *BA* 39:55–78.

Avigad, N. 1960. Excavations at Makmish, 1958. *IEJ* 10:90–96.

Avigad, N. 1961. Excavations at Makmish, 1960. *IEJ* 11:97–100.

Avigad, N. 1977. Makmish. *Enc. Arch. Exc. III*: 768–770.

Dever, W. G. 1980. Archeological Method in Israel: A Continuing Revolution. *BA* 43:41–48.

Gophna, R., and Kochavi, M. 1966. Notes and News: An Archaeological Survey of the Plain of Sharon. *IEJ* 16:143–144.

Herzog, Z., ed. 1980. Excavations at Tel Michal 1978–1979. *Tel Aviv* 7:111–150.

Herzog, Z. 1983. Notes and News: Tel Gerisa 1982. *IEJ* 33: 121–123.

Herzog, Z. 1984. Notes and News: Tel Gerisa 1983. *IEJ* 34:55–56.

Herzog, Z., Negbi, O., and Moshkovitz, S. 1978. Excavations at Tel Michal, 1977. *Tel Aviv* 5:99–130.

McDonald, W. A., and Rapp, G., Jr. 1972. *The Minnesota Messenia Expedition.* Minneapolis.

Mozel, I. 1978. A Note on the Flint Implements from Tel Michal and Nahal Poleg. *Tel Aviv* 5:152–158.

Rapp, G., Jr., and Gifford, J. 1985. *Archaeological Geology.* New Haven.

Schulman, A. R. 1978. Two Scarab Impressions from Tel Michal. *Tel Aviv* 5:148–151.

2

The Sharon Coastal Plain: Historical Geography

by Anson F. Rainey

The ensuing survey will give the background for our research in this area. There are many gaps in both the historical and the archaeological records, but this does not release us from the obligation to make some attempt at connecting the evidence from both sources. Our approach is regional, applying Alt's method of *territorial geschichte* to the Sharon plain while seeking fresh evidence by archaeological survey and excavation.

2.1. DISTRICT

2.1.1. Name

The meaning of the term *Sharon* (Hebrew *šārôn*) is somewhat obscure. Contrary to some opinions, it cannot be derived from the Semitic root *yšr*, meaning "straight," etc. That root contains the voiceless palatoalveolar sibilant *š* (sh), but the place name Sharon (1 Chron. 5:16) appears in Egyptian transcription as *ša-ru-na* (Thutmose III, No.21) and in el-ʿAmarna Akkadian as ^{uru} *ša-ru-na*^{ki} (*EA* 241:4). These spellings (Egyptian *š* and Akkadian *š*) suggest an original root with voiceless interdental *t* (th)—e.g., *try* / *trw*, *trr*, or *wtr*. Although the LXX usually accepts the name as a proper noun, once it renders τουπεδίου as "the plain" (SS 2:1) and once τῷ δρυμῷ as "the oak coppice" (Isa. 65:10). This latter association is taken up by Josephus (*War* I, xiii, 2 [250] = *Antiq.* XIV, xiii, 3 [334]) and also by Strabo (XVI, ii, 27, 28). Interestingly enough, an ancient Greek term for "old hollow oak" was σαρωνίς, as known also to Pliny (*N.H.* IV, 18). Whether or not there is some generic connection between the word *Sharon* and the oak tree, the presence of an oak forest along the western ridges of the central Sharon doubtless led to its application and may even account for the word's having been carried abroad to other parts of the Mediterranean.

2.1.2. Geography

Biblical references would be inadequate to define the Sharon as a geographic entity. Where MT has a king of Aphek followed by one "of the Sharon" (*melek laššārôn*; Josh. 12:18), LXX has a conflation of the two, βασιλέα Αφεκ της Σαρων, "king of Aphek of the Sharon." If the latter text represents the original, then Hebrew *laššārôn* would simply be an epithet to distinguish that Aphek from others in the country. The sarcophagus inscription of Eshmunezer, king of Sidon (mid-5th century B.C.E.), refers to "Dor and Joppa, the mighty grain lands which are in the territory of Sharon" (*KAI* 14:19; *ANET* 662), thus encompassing the entire coastal plain from the shadow of Carmel to the headland of Joppa. Eusebius seems to limit the Sharon on the north when he refers to "Sarōnas, the country from Caesarea to Joppa" (*Onom.* 162:5–6). But he probably assumes here that the metropolitan district of Caesarea extends to the Carmel.

As mentioned above, Josephus and Strabo both allude to the "forest" along the coastal plain south of Carmel. The presence of this forest is attested to in the 19th century by the Jacotin and *PEF* maps (Har-el 1977:79–82). The coastal topography consisted of a series of elements arrayed along a north-south axis parallel to the shoreline: the coastal cliff and an adjacent narrow plain behind which was a "trough" or longitudinal, channellike depression. To the east of this trough was the first sandstone (*kurkar*) ridge, one of three (counting the coastal cliffs), and behind it was a deep trough (the modern railway line between Tel Aviv and Haifa) followed by another sandstone belt. In this larger depression, the accumulated drainage of the various streams (see below) formed swamps, especially in the north, because their flow to the sea was hindered by the sandstone ridges. The easternmost sandstone belt developed a covering of red Mousterian sand (*ḥamra*); here the oak forest was prevalent (Bakler 1978; Karmon 1971:214–216).

It would appear from written sources that the Sharon included the region of Dor (Naphoth-dor; Josh. 11:2; 12:13; 1 Kings 4:11), the southern border of which was at the Chróseos River (*Wâdī ed-Diflā* = Naḥal Daliyya) during Roman times. On the east, the Sharon was bounded by the Hill Country of Ephraim (Samaria) and the Carmel. The hinterland of Joppa formed the southern district of the Sharon (cf. Eshmunezer above), probably identical to the Plain of Ono (Neh. 6:2) though it is separated from the central Sharon by the modern Yarkon River (Nahr el-Aujā'). This river rises at Aphek (Râs el-'Ain = Rosh Ha 'Ayin) and winds a tortuous path to its outlet 3.5 miles (6 km) north of Joppa, thus forming a natural barrier to commerce from the south.

The identification of the Yarkon (Hebrew *mê hayyār-qôn*; Josh. 19:46) with Nahr el-Aujā' is taken for granted by most scholars today (Kallai 1958); others have raised serious doubts, however, suggesting that the Naḥal Ayalon is the better candidate (Noth 1953:121–122). The latter suggestion has much to commend it, modern usage notwithstanding. The Yarkon is joined from the south by the Naḥal Ayalon (*Wâdī esh-Shellâl*), which begins at the Valley of Ayalon and works its way northwest until, failing to break through the *kurkar* ridges behind Joppa, it meets the modern Yarkon near Tel Gerisa (Tell Jerîsheh; Avnimelech 1950–51). The sandstone ridges of the Sharon north of the modern Yarkon do not continue uniformly to the south. The main ridge east of the coastal cliffs is prominent, however, and it is the cause for the deflection of Naḥal Ayalon northward. To the east of Naḥal Ayalon, one finds clusters of sandstone hills and ridges, which pass eastward into hills of the red Mousterian sand. They form a barrier between the modern Yarkon basin and that around Lod, the Plain of Ono (Neh. 6:2), probably identical with the Valley of the Craftsmen (Neh. 11:35; Har-el 1977; Karmon 1971:228–231, esp. map [Fig. III.16] on p. 228).

The Brook Kanah (*Wâdī Qânah*), coming down from the hills of Samaria and forming the traditional border between Ephraim and Manasseh (Josh. 16:8; 17:9), joins the modern Yarkon on the north near Tel Qana (Tell Qânah). These three streams comprise the principal drainage basin across the southern third of the Sharon and form a natural corridor leading inland from the coast.

Several other streams work their way from the foothills of Samaria westward through the *kurkar* ridges. Among the most important are the Crocodile River (Naḥal Tanninim = Nahr ez-Zerqā), Naḥal Ḥadera (Nahr el-Mefjir / Wâdī Khudeirah), and Naḥal Alexander (Nahr Iskanderûneh), the last of which runs north/northeast across the plain, collecting several minor streams along the way. Of lesser importance was Naḥal Poleg (Nahr el-Fâliq). The northward detour of Naḥal Alexander was necessitated by the zone of higher ground in the middle of the plain, viz., the "island" of Mousterian red soil. The long line of *kurkar* ridges blocked effective drainage for some of the wadis, thus creat-

ing marshes and swamps that, along with the oak forest, made human occupation quite difficult on the western side of the plain (Karmon 1971:214–220). The areas of documented settlement will be treated below.

2.2. OCCUPATIONAL HISTORY

2.2.1. Early Settlement Patterns

The presence of Early Bronze Age I campsites along the coastal strip, west of the swamp zone, is reported by Gophna (1978). Patterns of settlement, especially EB II and III sites along the main wadis, were discovered by Gophna and Kochavi (1966); more recently, the rise of fortified urban settlements in the Middle Bronze Age IIA has been discussed by Kochavi et al. (1979). Historically, the 3d and early 2d millennia B.C.E. of the Sharon plain are a blank except for the appearance of Aphek among the towns and rulers of the later Execration texts (Posener 1940:69, No. E9), contra Helck (1971:52), who thinks that the Aphik on the plain of Acco is meant. The ruler of Aphek bore a typical Amorite name, Yanki-'ilu, or "God has smitten."

2.2.2. Late Bronze Age

The focus of attention in the latter half of the 2d millennium is the area south of the modern Yarkon and along the eastern edge of the Sharon, beside the foothills of Samaria. The literary tale about the conquest of Joppa (*ANET* 22–23) during the reign of Thutmose III must be understood against the background of that pharaoh's topographical inscriptions (Aharoni 1979:152–158). During his first campaign, he progressed along the great trunk route from northern Sinai to the pass leading toward Megiddo from the northern Sharon (Nos. 57–71; these and subsequent numbers in the paragraph refer to cities listed in the topographical inscription of Thutmose III). Of special interest for the Sharon plain is the sequence from Joppa (No. 62) to Gath (No. 63; Gath-rimmon, Josh. 19:45; 21:34; 1 Chron. 6:69), to Lod (No. 64), to Ono (No. 65), to Aphek (No. 66). The continuation reflects the fact that it was necessary to go past Aphek in order to progress northward to Socoh (No. 67), Yaḥm (No. 68), Gath (No. 70; Gath-padalla of the el-'Amarna texts; Rainey 1968), and Migdal (No. 71).

The same line of march is reflected in the second campaign of Amenhotep II (cf. Aharoni 1979:166–168). The pharaoh and his troops came to Aphek and then marched on to Socoh and Yaḥm. The army conducted raids westward against two settlements in the plain from which they brought back human captives and "much cattle." A crucial battle was evidently fought against the Canaanite rebels somewhere in the northern Sharon (Mazar 1974:90) before the pharaoh continued on to the Jezreel Valley.

These texts reflect the fact that the major urban settlements from the Early Bronze Age II through the Middle Bronze Age II and the Late Bronze Age were along the western edge of the Samarian foothills. The modern Yarkon and the forest swamps to the north of it discouraged traffic, whereas the rich alluvial soil and plentiful water sources in the eastern Sharon (plus the higher altitude and healthier atmosphere) led to the establishment of a line of important towns there. All major caravans went around Aphek toward Socoh. The eastern edge of the Sharon plain was thus a major link in the international trunk route connecting Egypt with North Syria and Mesopotamia, erroneously called Via Maris.

2.2.3. Iron Age

The Sea Peoples occupied coastal sites such as Dor (the Sekels, according to Wenamon; Aharoni 1979:269) and Tel Qasila. Aphek was also a chief rallying point for them (1 Sam. 4:1; 29:1). However, archaeological survey has revealed that there was also another Early Iron Age development in the central and northern Sharon plain. In addition to the many new settlements that sprang up on the hills east of the Sharon (e.g., 'Izbet Ṣartah), others appeared along the courses of the streambeds. These were to be found along the course of Naḥal Ḥadera, in the lower basin of Naḥal Alexander, and near Naḥal Tanninim. Some excavations have been conducted at a few of these sites, such as Tel Zeror (Tell edh-Dhurûr) and Tel Burgata (Khirbet el-Burj).

This northern area of the Sharon plain was assigned to Manasseh (Josh. 17:9–10), i.e., north of Naḥal Qana. Although Manasseh is credited with failure to occupy the towns given to it from neighboring tribes (Josh. 17:11–12; Judg. 1:27–28), including Dor, nothing is said about the major eastern and central zones of the Sharon plain. South of the modern Yarkon, the Danites had failed to possess their territory (Judg. 1:34–36; Josh. 19:40–47), and the Ephraimites failed to drive out the Canaanites of Gezer (Josh. 16:10; cf. Judg. 1:35). But there is no intimation that the Manassehites did not occupy the main portion of the Sharon plain. Well-known Canaanite towns such as Socoh, Yaḥm, and Gath-padalla may well have succumbed to the Israelites. At least, they were surrounded by newly established settlements in the Early Iron Age.

Therefore, it is not unreasonable to argue, as we will below, that the eastern and central Sharon was settled by one of the leading Manassehite clans, namely Hepher (Josh. 17:2; 1 Kings 4:10). A negative argument may also be deduced, viz., the absence of any Levitical cities in this area. The newly incorporated territories, such as the Jezreel Valley and the Danite area south of the present Yarkon, were dotted with Levitical centers, apparently established there to strengthen monarchial authority among the formerly Canaanite populations. So all indications are that Israelite clans, evidently from the tribe of Manasseh, gained a foothold on the Sharon plain during the Early Iron Age.

It was probably between the Yarkon and the Alexander streams that David had his royal herds, under the charge of Shitrai the Sharonite (1 Chron. 27:29). It is also interesting that cattle herding on the Sharon was administered separately from that in "the Plains," presumably the Jezreel and Beth-shan valleys.

Against the background of the former Canaanite urban centers, the Sea Peoples' occupation of Dor and the area south of the modern Yarkon, and the Manassehite settlement in the central Sharon, one must understand the division of the area among Solomon's commissioners. Ben-deker had the territory south of the present Yarkon (1 Kings 4:9); his district is incompletely described in Kings and evidently has to be filled in by utilizing the list of Danite towns (Josh. 19:40–46; Aharoni 1976; 1979:311–313). Ben-abinadab had Naphoth-dor (1 Kings 4:11). Ben-hesed had the territory between them, including the unidentified Arubboth (1 Kings 4:10). The inclusion of Socoh assures that his district was on the Sharon and not in the hill country of Manasseh (contrary to popular opinion). The "land of Hepher" is most logically to be equated with the Manassehite territory that experienced a new settlement density during the Early Iron Age (cf. above). There is no valid reason to locate Hepher in the same area as his "descendants," the daughters of Zelophahad, who appear in the hill country according to the Samaria Ostraca (Aharoni 1979:368), as should be obvious from perusal of other genealogical lists (e.g., 1 Chron. 2 and 4 [Aharoni 1979:245–248]).

Pharaoh Shishak also attacked the cities on the eastern Sharon plain (Aharoni 1979:327). His inscription bears witness to the existence of Borim, Gath-padalla, and Yaḥm, besides Socoh, in 926 B.C.E. The mysterious Arubboth of 1 Kings 4:10 is strangely unattested in the Shishak list; perhaps it is a scribal corruption.

The accepted theory, first proposed by Forrer (1922:60–61), that Tiglath-pileser III formed a province with Dor as its capital and most of the Sharon as its territory is without foundation, especially with regard to Forrer's equation of his alleged province with "the way of the sea" in Isaiah 8:3. The biblical expression "way of the sea" had nothing to do with the great trunk route passing along the eastern Sharon plain. I have recently proposed that it be identified with the route connecting Dan with Tyre (Rainey 1981:146–149). Although Dor does appear on Assyrian lists of towns (Forrer 1922:52, 54), there is no evidence that it ever had status as a province with an eponym as governor. In the 7th century B.C.E., Dor was awarded to Tyre as a port of trade (*ANET* 534a). As a recognized commercial port, it would have been listed along with other such centers of trade in Assyrian rosters. But the assumed province of Dor is evidently a figment of Forrer's imagination. As for the Sharon plain, there is testimony, albeit from a corrupt spelling, in Esarhaddon's annals that Aphek still belonged to Samaria in the early 7th century (Borger 1956:112, 16–17; *ANET* 292b).

2.2.4. Persian Period

The fate of the coastal plain during the late 7th and most of the 6th centuries is unknown. The Assyrian administrative arrangements were probably inherited by the Egyptians after 609 B.C.E. and by the Babylonians after 605. In the very early stages of Persian rule, the Achaemenid kings had taken over the Levant, known as "Beyond the River" (Rainey 1969:51–52; *ANET* 316), and must have administered it pretty much as the Babylonians had. A crucial factor in the history of the coastal regions is the role of the Phoenician navies as the sea arm of the Persian empire. The Tyrians had obtained rights to the seaport of Dor under Esarhaddon (see above), and there is every reason to assume that the Persians granted similar rights to the Phoenicians. The Phoenician fleet would have been vital to the support of Persian campaigns along the coast in the direction of Egypt. Active naval operations of this nature would have led to the establishment of garrisons and lookout points such as Tel Michal.

It is now possible to attempt a correlation between the historical events of the Levant in this period and the stratigraphy of Tel Michal. Thus, Stratum XI may have been founded in connection with the campaign by Cambyses against Egypt in 525 B.C.E. (Herodotus III, 1ff.) or else that by Darius in 519/518 B.C.E. (Herodotus IV, 166–167, 200–203; Parker 1941; Cameron 1943). During the late 6th and early 5th centuries, the island of Cyprus and the cities of "eastern Greece"—i.e., Asia Minor, the eastern coasts of the Aegean—were part of the Persian empire and doubtless conducted extensive trade with the Phoenicians (cf. Ezek. 27:12–15). The revolt of Egypt from Persian rule in 486 B.C.E. (Herodotus VII, 1, 4, 7) led to other disturbances in the Levant (cf. Ezra 4:6) that may have curtailed coastal activities and perhaps led to the abandonment or destruction of Stratum XI.

The construction of a substantial fort at a place like Tel Michal (Stratum X) may be associated with the reconquest of Egypt (483 B.C.E.) or the Persian preparations for their war against the Greeks. It was essential that Xerxes have a strong fleet, the backbone of which was Phoenician (Herodotus VII, 89). He must have made favorable inducements to the Phoenician cities to ensure their loyalty. The broader historical background is thus Xerxes' campaign against Greece in 479 B.C.E.

The end of Stratum X can perhaps be associated with events following 460 B.C.E. when Egypt again revolted from Persian rule. An Athenian fleet was sent to Egypt in 459 (Diodorus XI, 71, 74–75; Herodotus III, 12, 15, VII, 7; Thucydides I, 104, 110), and it seems to have attacked the Phoenician coast (Olmstead 1948:304, basing his argument on an inscription, *IG* I, 433).

The reconstruction of Tel Michal in Stratum IX suggests the return of a strong administration to the Phoenician coast. A royal brother-in-law, Megabyzus, was sent out to quell the revolt in Egypt; he concurrently became governor of the Province Beyond the River. He was supported in his Egyptian campaign by the Phoenician fleet (Herodotus III, 160; Diodorus XI, 74, 77). During this time, the Persian authorities evidently made a concerted effort to secure the loyalty of the peoples in their Levantine province. In the seventh year of Artaxerxes' reign (458 B.C.E.), Ezra was sent to Jerusalem to see to the legal and social organization of the Jewish millet (ethnic group) (Ezra 7:7, 11–26). But the provincial administrators were extremely sensitive to

any signs of independence on the part of local ethnic groups in view of the dangerous situation in Egypt. Therefore, when the Jews began to rebuild their walls, they urgently requested, and received, a restraining order from the king (Ezra 4:7–23). On the other hand, the Phoenician involvement in the Egyptian campaign, doubtless motivated by the desire to get revenge on the Greek fleet, would have necessitated rebuilding the coastal stations, such as that at Tel Michal.

This is most likely the background of the Eshmunezer inscription (*ANET* 662). That king of Sidon claims that the "Lord of Kings," an illusion to the Persian monarch (Galling 1963), gave him the towns of Dor and Joppa. He stresses that these were grain-producing areas in the "field [territory] of Sharon," and their importance was not only as seaports but also as a source of wheat for feeding the Sidonians. Most Phoenician manpower was engaged in maritime activities: building, maintaining, and sailing the ships of the great fleet (cf. Ezek. 27:8–9). The date of the Eshmunezer inscription has been much disputed but seems most likely to come from the second quarter of the 5th century B.C.E. (Peckham 1968:78–87).

Megabyzus himself rebelled against the Persian monarch because of his displeasure at the way the Egyptian rebel leadership was subsequently treated. A loyal army, under an Egyptian, was sent to the Levantine coast to force Megabyzus back into line; though the attempt was not successful, the invading troops must have wreaked havoc with many Phoenician sites. This could account for the destruction of Stratum IX, ca. 448–447 B.C.E. (Ctesias, *Persica* 37).

The establishment of the settlement in Stratum VIII must have followed the restoration of tranquility after the retirement of Megabyzus from the scene. The coastal areas, such as the Plain of Ono, were firmly under Persian control (cf. Neh. 6:2). Phoenicia maintained its loyalty to the Persian authority, and its fleet continued to operate in the Persian cause (e.g., Diodorus XII, 27:4, concerning events after 445 B.C.E.), even through the reign of Darius II (Diodorus XIII, 36:5, 38:4, for events in 413–412 B.C.E.). The revolt of Egypt in 404 B.C.E. (Demotic Chronicle III, 18–19; cf. Diodorus XIV, 35:3–5) under Amyrtaeus (Kienitz 1953:72) at the death of Darius II did not shake the allegiance of Phoenicia. On the contrary, Abrokomas, now satrap of Beyond the River, had massed a large army (Xenophon, *Anabasis* I, 4:5), doubtless with the intent of invading Egypt. He was diverted, of course, by the revolt of Cyrus the Younger. A scaraboid of the next Egyptian king, Nepherites (398 B.C.E.), found at Gezer (Rowe 1936:320–321), is hardly sufficient to prove that he conducted a military campaign in the southern Levant. The Phoenician fleet was quite active in support of the Persians in their war against Sparta (Diodorus XIV, 79:8) in 396 B.C.E.

But not long thereafter, Achoris came to the Egyptian throne and, by 386 B.C.E., had entered into an alliance with Evagoras, king of Salamis (Diodorus XV, 2:3). The latter made himself master of Cyprus and then, while

Abrokomas and other Persian satraps were attacking Egypt, he occupied Tyre and some other Phoenician towns (Isocrates, *Evagoras*, 62, *Panegyric*, 161; Diodorus XV, 2:4). This conquest of the coast probably brought about the end of Stratum VIII at Tel Michal. The Persian forces were beaten and forced to retreat from Egypt (Isocrates, *Panegyric*, 140). But Evagoras was ousted from the Levant and compelled to accept peace terms with the Persians (381–379 B.C.E.; Diodorus XV, 8–9).

Sidon's role in the conflict with Evagoras is not known. Tyre had given him support, but Sidon may have kept itself out of the war or even sided with the Persians. At any rate, a strong Sidonian dynast soon appeared on the scene, known in the Greek sources as Straton I. His Phoenician name was evidently 'Abd-'ashtart, only partly preserved on an inscription from Delos (*CIS* I, 114; cf. the Tyrian king from the 10th century B.C.E. called Αβδαστρατος, [Josephus, *Apion*, 1, 122]). The fact that he took a Greek name is indicative of the strong Hellenic influence at his court. During his reign, ca. 378–358, firm diplomatic and commercial ties were established with Athens. As a reward for assisting an Athenian embassy on its way to treat with Artaxerxes II (either in 378 or 368; Tod 1948:119), he was awarded the title of "guest-friend" at Athens, and Sidonian merchants were granted special exemptions from certain local Athenian taxes (*SIG* I, No. 185; Tod 1948:116–119). Coins credited to him bear the typical Sidonian ship and, on the reverse, a deity in a chariot followed by the king in ceremonial attire (Seyrig 1959:52ff.), above them the letters '-b.

Just such a coin of Straton/ 'Abd-'ashtart was found on the floor of a room from Stratum VII at Tel Michal (Reg. No. 5743/60; Locus 347; Chap. 27: No. 4). Therefore, it would appear that Stratum VII, with its especially substantial fort on the northern end of the high mound, was constructed by 375 B.C.E. or thereabouts. Such a date would correspond well to the need for coastal installations in support of the mighty naval force gathered at Acco in 373 B.C.E. for a renewed attack on Egypt (Diodorus XV, 41:3; Polyaenus III, 9:56; Isaeus, Nicostratus, 7). The commander, Pharnabazus, satrap of Cilicia, had 300 ships and a great land force including 12,000 Greek mercenaries. The invasion was repelled by Pharaoh Nectanebes (Nekhtnebef; Diodorus XV, 42–44).

Even though the Periplus of Pseudo-Scylax may have been composed some decades later (Avi-Yonah 1977:28, n. 127), its assignment of Dor to Sidon conforms to what is known from the Eshmunezer inscription (cf. above). On the other hand, the following town (possibly Crocodilonpolis: Strabo XVI, 2:27; Galling 1964:198) and a river mouth of the Tyrians indicate that Sidonian control had not necessarily been uniform during the late 5th and 4th centuries. The Tower of Straton, documented for the mid-3d century (Pap. Zenon, Cairo 59004), is also skipped over by Pseudo-Scylax, whose text moves on to Joppa. This has suggested to some that the Tower of Straton was founded not by Straton I but by Straton II (Avi-Yonah 1977:30–31).

From about 368 to 360 B.C.E., the Satraps' Revolt nearly destroyed the Persian Empire. Syrians and Phoenicians also took part in the rebellion (Diodorus XV, 90:3). Tachos (Teos), now pharaoh of Egypt (362 B.C.E.), mobilized a great army and, in collaboration with the rebel satraps, executed an invasion of the Levantine coast (Diodorus XV, 92). He was supposed to join a satrap, Aroandas, in Syria and march eastward in support of Datames, who was crossing the Euphrates. Ochus, younger son of Artaxerxes, was trying to hold off this maneuver in Phoenicia, and Tachos's nephew, Nectanebos (Nekhtharehbe), was attacking cities in Syria. The conspiracy against Tachos, in which Nectanebos became pharaoh, left the hapless Tachos at the mercy of Artaxerxes. The notation that Tachos found refuge first with Straton at Sidon (Xenophon, *Agesilaus* II, 30) indicates that the Phoenician towns had not necessarily been damaged by the Egyptian invasion. So one need not assume that coastal sites like Tel Michal were destroyed at this time.

As the aftermath of his victory in the Levant, Ochus, who had succeeded to the throne as Artaxerxes III (358), managed to regain control over the entire empire except for Egypt. In 351 B.C.E. he made another attempt to conquer the land of the Nile, but without achieving his goal (Demosthenes XV, 11, 12; Isocrates, *Philip*, 101; Diodorus XVI, 44:1, 48:1, contra Diodorus XVI, 40:3). This failure evidently led to a further revolt by the Phoenician cities, with Sidon at their head. The Sidonian ruler now was Tennes, who also received support from Nectanebos of Egypt. Although the Phoenicians managed to repulse an attack by the satraps of Cilicia and the province Beyond the River, they eventually succumbed to the massive forces of Artaxerxes himself. Tennes treacherously surrendered Sidon to the Persian monarch, who intended to make an example of it to the other rebels (Diodorus XVI, 43–45; Isocrates, *Philip*, 102). It is quite likely, therefore, that settlements belonging to Sidon also suffered at this time (cf. Barag 1966), so one may propose a date between 346 and 345 B.C.E. for the destruction of Stratum VII at Tel Michal.

Nevertheless, Sidon seems to have revived soon in spite of the severity of its punishment. Artaxerxes launched a massive campaign against Egypt (343 B.C.E.), and this time he brought it to its knees (Diodorus XVI, 46:4–52:3). The need to move forces down the Levantine coast and to support them logistically could have led to the rapid reconstruction of both Sidon and the outposts. Thus, the rebuilding of the fort at Tel Michal, Stratum VI, may have been carried out in the process.

Subsequent events during the reigns of Arses and Darius III (338–334), including another Egyptian revolt and reconquest, seem not to have affected the coastal cities of the Levant. When Alexander marched down the coast after his victory at Issus (333), he was welcomed by Sidon, whose ruler was Straton II (Arrian II, 15:6; Curtius IV, 1:15ff.). A coin bearing Alexander's likeness was found on the floor of the entryway to Fort 324 (Reg. No. 5584/60; Locus 322; Chap. 27: No. 28) from Stratum VI, suggesting that the fort did not suffer at this time. It represents another parallel between Tel Michal and Sidon, in contrast to Tyre, which was reduced after the famous seven-month siege. During the seesaw affairs between Alexander's generals, the Levantine coast was part of the province, now called Syria, established by Alexander. The Battle of Gaza between Ptolemy and Demetrius (312 B.C.E.; Diodorus XIX, 80–86) was not followed by an advance up the coast. On the other hand, after the battle of Ipsus, Ptolemy took advantage of the situation and occupied the Syrian (including the Phoenician) coast up to the Eleutheros (Nahr el-Kebir). So this event, in 301 (Diodorus XX, 113), probably brought an end to the settlement of Stratum VI at Tel Michal.

2.2.5. Hellenistic Period

The Sidonian hegemony over the Sharon coast may have been terminated when Artaxerxes razed Sidon in 345 (cf. above), but the seaport towns continued to exist. They probably were not grouped into a larger administrative district by the Ptolemies, who preferred to leave their subject territories in smaller units (Avi-Yonah 1977:34–35). Under the Seleucids, who favored larger administrative divisions, the coastal zone was called Paralia (1 Macc. 15:38), which extended from "the Ladder of Tyre" (1 Macc. 11:59; apparently Josephus, *Antiq.* XIII, v, 4 [146] should be emended accordingly: Marcus 1943:297, n. *f*), i.e., the territory of Ptolemais (2 Macc. 13:24), to the "border of Egypt" (1 Macc. 11:59; Josephus, *Antiq.* XIII, v, 4 [146]). The province was, in fact, split into two separate units by the assignment of coastal towns such as Azotus and Jamnia to Idumaea and Joppa to Samaria (Avi-Yonah 1977:48–49). Zenon, a subordinate to the Ptolemaic minister of finance under Ptolemy II, visited the Tower of Straton and Pegae during his visit to the country. He also had agents at such coastal towns as Joppa (Aharoni and Avi-Yonah 1977:113, Map 177).

Only after 103 B.C.E. was the Sharon coastal plain added to Judea by Alexander Jannaeus. A local tyrant named Zoilus had established himself at the Tower of Straton and Dora (Dor); he was removed at Jannaeus's behest by Ptolemy Latherus during the Machiavellian negotiations in a three-cornered conflict that included Cleopatra III of Egypt (*Antiq.* XIII, xii, 2–4 [324–337]). Probably, it was then that a large community of Jews began to settle in the Sharon. They joined in the conflict for the Hasmonean succession when the Parthian prince Pacorus invaded the country by way of Ptolemais (*Antiq.* XIV, xiii, 3 [334]; *War* I, xiii, 2 [250]).

The establishment of Caesarea by Herod the Great completely changed the urban pattern in the Sharon. A new metropolis was founded, using Greco-Roman technology to provide a water supply, make the terrain suitable, and build a harbor.

REFERENCES

Aharoni, Y. 1976. The Solomonic Districts. *Tel Aviv* 3:5–15.

Aharoni, Y. 1979. *The Land of the Bible.* 2d ed. Translated and edited by A. F. Rainey. London and Philadelphia.

Aharoni, Y., and Avi-Yonah, M. 1977. *The Macmillan Bible Atlas.* 2d rev. ed. New York.

Avi-Yonah, M. 1977. *The Holy Land.* Grand Rapids, Mich.

Avnimelech, M. 1950–51. The Geological History of the Yarkon Valley and Its Influence on Ancient Settlements. *IEJ* 1:77–83.

Bakler, N. 1978. Geology of Tel Michal and the Herzliya Coast. *Tel Aviv* 5:131–135.

Barag, D. 1966. The Effects of the Tennes Rebellion on Palestine. *BASOR* 183:6–12.

Borger, R. 1956. *Die Inschriften Asarhaddons Königs von Assyrien.* Archiv für Orientforschung Beiheft 9. Osnabrück.

Cameron, C. G. 1943. Darius, Egypt and "The Lands Beyond the Sea." *JNES* 2:307–313.

Forrer, E. 1922. *Die Provinzeinteilung des assyrische Reiches.* Leipzig.

Galling, K. 1963. Eschmunazer und der Herr der Könige. *ZDPV* 73:140–151.

Galling, K. 1964. *Studien zur Geschichte Israels im persischen Zeitalter.* Tübingen.

Gophna, R. 1978. Archaeological Survey of the Central Coastal Plain, 1977. *Tel Aviv* 5:136–147.

Gophna, R., and Kochavi, M. 1966. Notes and News: An Archaeological Survey of the Plain of Sharon. *IEJ* 16:143–144.

Har-el, M. 1977. The Valley of the Craftsmen (Geʾ Haḥarašîm). *PEQ* 109:75–86.

Helck, W. 1971. *Die Beziehungen Ägyptens zu Vorderasien im 3. und 2. Jahrtausend v. Chr.* 2., verbesserte Auflage. Wiesbaden.

Kallai, Z. 1958. Yarqon, mei Hayarqon. *Enc. Miqr.* II: 886–889 (Hebrew).

Karmon, Y. 1971. *Israel: A Regional Geography.* London.

Kienitz, F. K. 1953. *Die politische Geschichte Ägyptens vom 7. bis zum 4. Jahrhundert vor der Zeitwende.* Berlin.

Kochavi, M., Beck, P., and Gophna, R. 1979. Aphek-Antipatris, Tel Poleg, Tel Zeror and Tel Burga: Four Fortified Sites of the Middle Bronze Age IIA in the Sharon Plain. *ZDPV* 95:121–165.

Marcus, R., ed. 1943. *Josephus with an English Translation.* Vol. VII. Loeb Classical Library. Cambridge, Mass.

Mazar, B. 1974. *Canaan and Israel.* (Hebrew) Jerusalem.

Noth, M. 1953. *Das Buch Josua.* 2d ed. Handbuch zum Alten Testament I: 7. Tübingen.

Olmstead, A. T. E. 1948. *History of the Persian Empire.* Chicago.

Parker, R. A. 1941. Darius and His Egyptian Campaign. *American Journal of Semitic Languages and Literature* 58:373–377.

Peckham, J. B. 1968. *The Development of the Late Phoenician Scripts.* Harvard Semitic Series 20. Cambridge, Mass.

Posener, G. 1940. *Princes et pays d'Asie et de Nubie.* Brussels.

Rainey, A. F. 1968. Gath-padalla. *IEJ* 18:1–14.

Rainey, A. F. 1969. The Province "Beyond the River." *Australian Journal of Biblical Archaeology* 1:51–78.

Rainey, A. F. 1981. Toponymic Problems (cont.). *Tel Aviv* 8:146–151.

Rowe, A. 1936. *A Catalogue of Egyptian Scarabs, Scaraboids, Seals and Amulets in the Palestine Archaeological Museum.* Cairo.

Seyrig, H. 1959. Antiquités syriennes. *Syria* 36:37–89.

Tod, M. N. 1948. *A Selection of Greek Historical Inscriptions.* Oxford.

3

History of Settlement in the
Tel Michal Region

by Ram Gophna and Etan Ayalon

The purpose of this review is to throw light on the history of settlement in the vicinity of Tel Michal and particularly to clarify the relationship between the site and its hinterland during various periods. An attempt is made to elucidate the nature of the settlement at Tel Michal and the factors that played a role in its development throughout different periods. This includes an evaluation of its relative importance in the history of the whole Sharon coastal plain (from Dor to Jaffa) in comparison with other sites such as Mikhmoret and Tel Poleg. Finally, an attempt will be made to understand the reasons for the transfer of settlement from Tel Michal to Apollonia and the differences in nature and importance of the two settlements.

The area to be discussed in detail is the geographic niche adjacent to Tel Michal that is part of the coastal strip between the Poleg basin in the north and the Yarkon basin in the south. This review may be divided chronologically into three main parts: the background before the establishment of the first settlement at Tel Michal (Section 3.2); the period of settlement on the tell itself, during which two phases of development were distinguished (Sections 3.3 and 3.4); and the period after the site's abandonment (Section 3.5). The history of the region after abandonment of the site, which is connected with processes that took place in the southern Sharon in general and the harbor town of Apollonia in particular, is dealt with in detail elsewhere (Roll and Ayalon 1982; in press). Therefore, it will only be discussed briefly here.

Our review is based on the excavations that were conducted at different sites on the southern Sharon coast, particularly at Tel Michal and Apollonia, and the complementary archaeological survey carried out in the region by the authors (Gophna 1978a; Gophna and Ayalon 1980).[1,2]

3.1. THE TEL MICHAL REGION AS A SUBSISTENCE AREA IN THE SOUTHWESTERN SHARON

Between the Yarkon River in the south and Naḥal Tanninim in the north, the Sharon is divided into a number of parallel longitudinal strips (Karmon 1961; 1971; Bakler 1978). In the west along the coast there are three parallel *kurkar* (sandstone) ridges and between them two low-lying valleys covered with alluvial deposits, called *marzeva* zones or troughs. Until recently, swamps and marshy pools abounded in these valleys. Today the coastal road lies in the western trough between the first (western) and the second *kurkar* ridges. The railway line runs along the middle trough between the second and third (eastern) *kurkar* ridges. The third ridge is covered extensively by hills of sandy red soil (*hamra*). On the coast itself, and particularly adjacent to the river outlets, sand dunes have accumulated, especially in more recent periods. The central Sharon consists of *hamra* hills, once covered by an oak forest. Along the foothills of the Sharon in the east stretches a broad valley, rich in alluvial deposits, that is known as "the *marzeva*" (trough). Since this term is also applied to the two parallel valleys next to the coast (which are called the "western trough" and the "central trough," respectively), this valley will be called the "eastern trough" in the discussion below.

This geomorphologic pattern is uniform and continuous in the southern Sharon between the Yarkon River and Naḥal Poleg. On the other hand, farther north the Sharon is cut by the beds of the Alexander, Hadera, and Tanninin streams that cross it from east to west. These streams flow in alluvial valleys similar in nature to the eastern trough and, like the latter, well suited for settlement. Fertility of soil, communication facilities, and availability of water sources and building materials vary considerably in the different parts of the Sharon and had a strong influence on

Table 3.1. Sites in the Vicinity of Tel Michal

No.	Name	Other Names	Map Reference	Character of Site	Periods[a]
1	Apollonia	Arshaf, Arsuf, Arsur	131/177	Prehistoric site, town, port	PPNB, EB I, Ir II, P-Cr
2	Bir el-'Ababsheh		1349/1783	Settlement	H, R, B
3	Balaqiya, Khirbet el	Ga'ash	1333/1818	Settlement	EB I, B
4	'Einan el-Qibli	"Country Club"	1309/1723	Prehistoric site	EP, PN, EB I, MB IIA
5	Ga'ash		1343/1823	Prehistoric site	PPNB
6	Herzliya		1354/1746	Prehistoric site, settlement	PPNB, B
7	Herzliya cemetery		1342/1752	Settlement	B, A
8	Herzliya B		1328/1749	Prehistoric site, settlement, cemetery	EP, R, B
9	Jaiyus, Khirbet		1367/1810	Settlement	R, B, A
10	Jelil	Gelilot	1325/1743	Settlement, cemetery	P, B, A
11	Kefar Shemaryahu		1333/1771	Temple, cemetery	MB IIA, R-B
12	Michal, Tel	Makmish	1310/1742	Settlement, port	MB IIB-R I, A
13	Ra'anana	el-Habas	1348/1769	Prehistoric site	EP
14	Ra'anana		1357/1782	Prehistoric site	PPNB
15	Rishpon		1336/1783	Prehistoric site, cemetery	EP, R-B
16	Shefayim		1329/1804	Prehistoric site, cemetery	PPNB, EB I, MB IIA
17	Shefayim (east)		1353/1811	Settlement, cemetery	MB IIA, H, R
18	Sidna 'Ali	el Haram	1318/1773	Mosque, port, cemetery	A, Med
19	12/1, 12/2		1318/1726	Settlement, cemetery	MB IIA
20	13/4		1311/1735	Campsite	MB IIA
21	13/7		1317/1737	Campsite	MB IIB, P
22	13/8		1315/1736	Prehistoric site	PN

[a] EP = Epipaleolithic, PPNB = Prepottery Neolithic B, PN = Pottery Neolithic, EB = Early Bronze Age, MB = Middle Bronze Age, Ir = Iron Age, P = Persian, H = Hellenistic, R = Roman, B = Byzantine, A = Early Arab, Cr = Crusader, and Med = Medieval.

the intensity and distribution of settlements and sources of livelihood (Karmon 1961; 1971).

The maximum dimensions of the Tel Michal region as a subsistence area are about 7 km × 12 km (Fig. 3.1). This includes the *kurkar* coastal cliff in the west, the second *kurkar* ridge in the center (exposed only in the southern part), and the western margins of the low *hamra* hills in the east. Between these units lie the two longitudinal troughs: the western trough, partially covered by sand dunes, where until recently there were small seasonal swamps, and the central trough, east of Tel Michal, where an extensive swamp (Bahret Katurieh; *SWP II*: Sheet XIII) dominated the landscape in the past. The economic and agricultural value of the area was thus rather limited, but there was sufficient potential in different periods to support at least one large settlement as well as a number of smaller agricultural sites.

The area between the coast and the second *kurkar* ridge consists of *hamra* suitable for agriculture, especially for viticulture. Numerous winepresses found in archaeological surveys and excavations testify to the extent of grape cultivation in the past (Roll and Ayalon 1981; in press). The sand dunes that cover this area today apparently accumulated only after the Byzantine period. The region was also exploited for hunting and pasturing (Gophna 1978a) and for fishing along the coast (Herzog et al. 1978:128). In the central trough, east of the second *kurkar* ridge, were once swamps rich in game. The importance of animal husbandry

in the economy finds expression in the quantity of sheep and cattle bones at Tel Michal – about 90 percent of the total (see Chap. 22). Hunted animals represent 7.2 percent of the finds, a quantity that accords in general with finds from these periods at other sites. The majority of wild animals belong to the Cervidae family (red deer, fallow deer). The finds from Apollonia (I. Drori, unpublished) show that even in relatively late periods (Byzantine, Early Arab, and Crusader) the inhabitants hunted and fished (activities that supplied about 4.3 percent of the total bones retrieved, with a similar component of species).

The heavy soil at the margins of the swamps became fertile agricultural land only after drainage and channeling operations were undertaken. Once the swamps were drained, probably in the Byzantine period, the whole valley became an excellent agricultural area. The *hamra* hillocks that extend over the southern Sharon were covered by an oak forest that, until the Roman period, served only for hunting and grazing. In the Roman and Byzantine periods, the forest was partially cleared and the hilly areas were exploited for agriculture.

3.2. PREHISTORIC PERIOD TO MIDDLE BRONZE AGE II (Fig. 3.1)

There are no sites from the Lower Paleolithic (until 80,000 B.C.E.) in this area, their western extent being the third

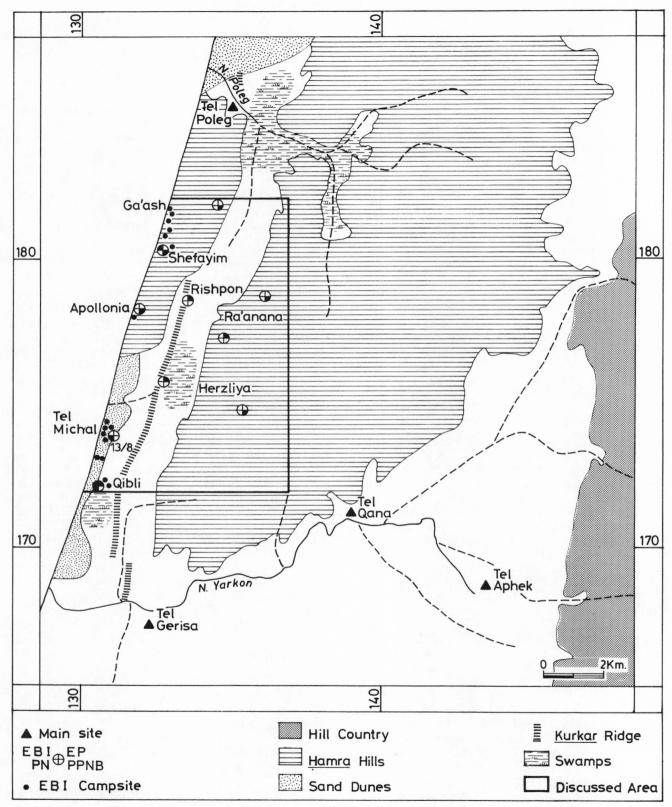

Figure 3.1. Epipaleolithic to Early Bronze I sites in southern Sharon.

kurkar ridge (Gilead 1970:2). Nor are there any from the Middle (80,000-35,000 B.C.E.) and Upper Paleolithic (35,000–15,000 B.C.E.), since sites of these periods were concentrated on Mount Carmel and its margins (Ronen 1975:240–242).

3.2.1. Epipaleolithic Period (15,000–8000 B.C.E.)

The end of the Würm glaciation is characterized, especially in its second half, by a relative increase in precipitation that led to the spread of vegetation and the increase of fauna. The coastline was 8–10 km west of the present line (Gilead 1970:33). Sites from the Epipaleolithic (Table 3.1) were found at Rishpon (Gilead 1974:Fig. 1), Herzliya B, 'Einan el-Qibli, and Ra'anana. The relatively small number of sites and their limited size illustrate the marginal nature of the region as a subsistence area in this period for a population of hunter-gatherers who lived in the Sharon, particularly in the low *hamra* hills (Gilead 1974). Because of the paucity of flint implements, it is not possible to determine exactly the place of the assemblages within the sequence of the microlithic industry of the period (Bar-Yosef 1970; 1975). There is no doubt, however, that the tools under discussion belong to Kebaran assemblages. The sites were adjacent to swamps and seasonal water pools that existed in the western trough ('Einan el-Qibli), in the central trough (at the edge of the *kurkar* ridge at Rishpon and Herzliya B), and at the edge of the *hamra* hillocks (Ra'anana). The inhabitants of these sites exploited the forest of the hills and the swamps of the *marzeva* zones for hunting and foraging.[3]

As in other parts of the Sharon, no Natufian (10th-9th millennia B.C.E.) or Pre-Pottery Neolithic A (8th millennium) sites were found.

3.2.2. Pre-Pottery Neolithic B (7000–6000 B.C.E.)

In the *hamra* hills, important Epipalaeolithic sites and those of the Pre-Pottery Neolithic B (situated on top of the hills) overlap. Farther west, the record of human presence is sporadic and concentrated at incidental locations: Shefayim and Apollonia on the coastal cliff, Ga'ash in the western trough, Ra'anana and Herzliya at the edges of the hills, close to the Katurieh swamp. The finds from the southern Sharon show a distinction between sites rich in arrowheads and those with many small axes, suggesting differing activities of the inhabitants (Noy 1977:32), even though it is quite probable that these settlements were occupied by the same population. The absence of sickle blades and adzes connected with agricultural activity suggests a population of transient hunters. In the Jordan Valley and the hill country, on the other hand, there already existed sites whose inhabitants were engaged to some extent in agriculture (Noy 1975; 1981).

3.2.3. Pottery Neolithic (6000–4000 B.C.E.)

Sites known from this period—'Einan el-Qibli (Prausnitz 1970; Prausnitz et al. 1970; Noy 1977) and Site 13/8, east of Tel Michal (*Had. Arch.* 72:25–26)—are adjacent to small winter swamps in the western trough. These were seasonal settlements of hunters who were occupied in sporadic agriculture (Noy 1977:32–33; 1981), as evidenced by grain pits, pottery storage vessels, and flint sickle blades. The incidental uncovering of Site 13/8, after the removal of layers of sand and *hamra* during developmental works, suggests that the number of settlements in this period was greater than previously suspected. The extent and nature of the remains show, however, that they were small, temporary sites.

3.2.4. Chalcolithic Period (4000–3150 B.C.E.)

During the Chalcolithic period, occupation of the coastal plain is represented by isolated finds, mainly flint tools (Gophna 1978a:138), with the exception of one small site discovered at Kibbutz Shefayim in 1981. It seems that the area served mainly as pastureland for the settlements that existed at the same time in the Yarkon basin to the south (Perrot 1961:21–27, 36–37); in the lower Alexander basin in the central Sharon (Paley and Porath 1979); in the Hadera basin (Sukenik 1937) in the northern Sharon; and along the eastern *marzeva* and the edge of the hills in the eastern Sharon (Gophna 1974; *Had. Arch.* 67–68:27 –28).

3.2.5. Early Bronze Age I (3150–3000 B.C.E.)

In the first phase of the Early Bronze Age, the area continued to be used for hunting and grazing. Intensity of exploitation increased significantly along the coast and the western trough, however; many small sites were found with remains of this period, particularly hearths and pottery, apparently from huts and temporary encampments. The three largest campsites were found at Shefayim, 'Einan el-Qibli, and Ramat Aviv (Gophna 1978a). An additional site of this group was discovered at Apollonia. These remains of shepherds and hunters throw light on a particular aspect of settlement in the southern Sharon at the beginning of the Early Bronze Age: the land in the west was still used solely for grazing and hunting at a time when village and town life was already developing in the eastern Sharon at the foot of the hills and in the eastern *marzeva*. Such sites include Tel Aphek and Tel Qana (Gophna 1974; Kochavi 1975:21–23, 38; *Had. Arch.* 69–71:52). Perhaps it was the settlers of the eastern Sharon themselves who were exploiting these lands for such purposes.

From the subsequent stages of the Early Bronze Age (EB II-III), no sites at all have been discovered in the region.

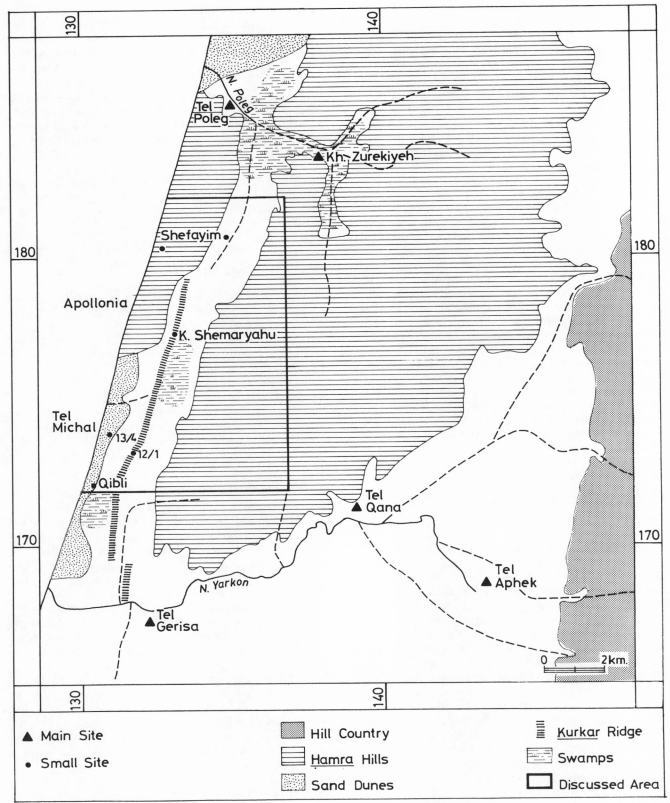

Figure 3.2. Middle Bronze Age IIA sites in southern Sharon.

3.2.6. Middle Bronze Age I
(2200–2000 B.C.E.)

Isolated finds reflect the temporary presence of people in the region (Gophna 1978a), which also served in this period as a hunting ground and pastureland between the settlements in the Poleg basin in the north (Gophna 1973:111, n. 3; *Had. Arch.* 78–79:38) and those in the Yarkon area in the south (Mazar 1978:963).

3.2.7. Middle Bronze Age IIA (2000–1750 B.C.E.) (Fig. 3.2)

For the first time in the southwestern Sharon, real settlements began to appear, and the subsistence area was exploited mainly for agricultural purposes. This settlement pattern existed for some time before the establishment of the first settlement at Tel Michal. It included villages (Shefayim east, Site 12/1 on the coastal road), a sanctuary (Kefar Shemaryahu), cemeteries (Shefayim east, Site 12/1), and campsites of herders and hunters not far from the coast (Shefayim, Site 13/4, 'Einan el-Qibli) (Gophna and Beck 1981:71). All these new sites were part of the general wave of settlement that took place in the southern Sharon. Perhaps this increase in population is connected with the city-state that existed at Aphek (Gophna and Ayalon 1980), like the large settlements that existed along the coast at that time (Tel Burga, Tel Zeror, Tel Poleg, Tel Gerisa, Yavneh Yam) (Kaplan 1978; Kochavi et al. 1979). The distribution of these settlements in a line paralleling the coast (especially along the second *kurkar* ridge), as well as the special character and location of the sanctuary exposed on a hilltop at Kefar Shemaryahu, suggest that during this period the coastal road was exploited for the first time as an important highway. (The density of agricultural settlements in this region was repeated only much later in the Roman period; see Section 3.4 below.)

3.3. MIDDLE BRONZE AGE IIB TO IRON AGE (Fig. 3.3)

3.3.1. Middle Bronze Age IIB to Late Bronze Age (1750–1200 B.C.E.)

After the desertion of the large MB IIA settlements, a new settlement development began in the Middle Bronze Age IIB. It is possible to see the founding of Tel Michal as part of a general phenomenon at this time: the establishment or revival of port cities and forts along the coast of Israel. Examples are Tel Mevorakh (*Tel Mevorakh II*: 46–98), Tel Gerisa (Avigad 1976; Geva 1982; Herzog 1984), Jaffa (Kaplan and Kaplan 1976), Tel Mor (Dothan 1977), Ashdod (Dothan 1975), and others. The first settlement at Tel Michal was limited in size, but in the light of the many imported vessels found and the lack of agricultural settlements around the tell, it may be surmised that the site was a harbor fort or trading station, part of a larger political unit

that developed marine trading activity. The results of the survey show that the founding of the first settlement at Tel Michal did not lead to the emergence of agricultural settlements around it like those that existed in the region during the Middle Bronze Age IIA, and its agricultural potential was not exploited.

During the 16th-14th centuries B.C.E., the situation around Tel Michal remained similar to that of the previous period, with no agricultural development of its hinterland.

3.3.2. Iron Age (1200–586 B.C.E.)

In the first phase of the Iron Age, there was no settlement at Tel Michal. This is noteworthy in light of the flourishing contemporaneous Philistine city at nearby Tell Qasile (Mazar 1978; *Tell Qasile*: 3–12, 74–77). In Iron Age II, Tel Michal was settled for two short periods with a gap in occupation following each. For the first time it is possible to point to an increase in the size of the settlement, when buildings of a cultic nature were set up on hillocks to the east of the high tell (Avigad 1977b). As a settlement that depended on outside initiative, Tel Michal can be compared to the Iron Age agricultural settlement at Tel Poleg (Kochavi et al. 1979:133). Like Tel Michal, Tel Poleg was settled intermittently with periods of abandonment in between. In the Iron Age, however, a large agricultural settlement existed there. The material culture exposed at Tel Poleg indicates that it was connected with the Israelite network of settlements in the eastern Sharon. Tel Michal, on the other hand, was apparently linked to the sites of the lower Yarkon basin: Tell Qasile, Tel Gerisa, Tell Kudadi (Avigad 1977a). The occupation of Tel Michal in the Iron Age, like that of the Middle and Late Bronze ages, did not lead to agricultural development of the region nor to the foundation of new settlements.[4]

3.4. PERSIAN TO ROMAN PERIODS (Fig. 3.4)

3.4.1. Persian Period (586–332 B.C.E.)

After an occupational gap at the end of the Iron Age, settlement was renewed at Tel Michal at the beginning of the Persian period. This included a fort, workshops, and a sanctuary.[5] For the first time the development of Tel Michal resulted in peripheral settlements, although it was important mainly as a harbor for the army and ships of the Persians, Phoenicians, and Egyptians (Herzog 1981). Thus, new settlements were founded in the area, apparently as part of the Phoenician interests along the entire Levantine coast that are hinted at in the inscription of Eshmunezer (see Chap. 2). The most important of these settlements, which in time superseded Tel Michal as the central site of the region, was founded at Apollonia, apparently called Arshaf by its Phoenician founders (S. Izre'el, personal communication). The architectural remains, the rich grave finds, the pottery assemblages, and many Phoenician coins, most of them from Sidon, testify to the importance of the settlement (Roll and Ayalon 1982:17; in press).

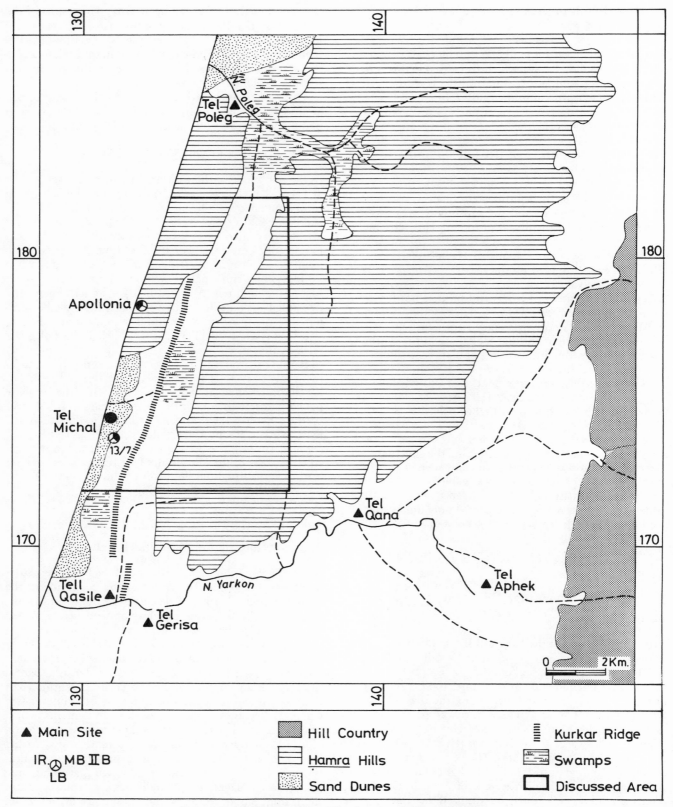

Figure 3.3. Middle Bronze Age IIB to Iron Age sites in southern Sharon.

The coexistence of Tel Michal and Apollonia, two nearby ports about 3 km apart, suggests that the two were controlled by different factors—Tyre or Sidon, as may be understood from the list of Pseudo-Scylax (Avi-Yonah 1979:27–31). The founding of two satellite settlements to the east of Tel Michal—Site 13/7 at the edge of the *marzeva* and Jelil on the second *kurkar* ridge—attests to the intensive agricultural exploitation of the area, both in the *marzeva* zones and at the edge of the forest and swamps. Apollonia and Jelil reflect the beginning of agricultural settlement in the region, a process that continued to develop, reaching its peak in the Byzantine period. These sites existed for a long time and are known from archaeological records as well as from historical sources (Roll and Ayalon, in press).

When one adds to this picture other sites that existed contemporaneously on the southern Sharon coast, such as the extensive agricultural settlement at Tel Poleg and its surrounding villages or that at Tell Qasile and its environs, it is possible to observe the formation of a new settlement pattern with a broad economic basis, which included ports, workshops, and agricultural villages, as well as sanctuaries. Such a varied pattern had existed in the area only in the Middle Bronze Age IIA, but at that time it was isolated chronologically and of short duration, whereas the pattern renewed in the Persian period marked the beginning of a settlement expansion process that continued—albeit intermittently—in the following periods.

3.4.2. Hellenistic Period (332–37 B.C.E.)

During the Hellenistic period, the settlement at Tel Michal gradually decreased in size until its total desertion in the 1st century C.E. At the same time, Apollonia increased in importance and dimension and was already mentioned in historical sources by its Greek name. Quite possibly, Hellenistic authorities intentionally transferred the administrative, military, and economic center from Tel Michal to Apollonia, a small and relatively new settlement that may have had more advantageous harbor capabilities and land routes leading to it. A fort and a few other buildings still stood on the high tell at Tel Michal, a large winepress to the north and a cultic site to the east. The fort was also in use at the time of Hasmonean control of the coast. At Apollonia, a workshop for the extraction of purple dyes was found, as well as graves and rich pottery assemblages (Roll and Ayalon 1982:17). Small villages were discovered at Shefayim north of Apollonia (one on the coast and the other at the edge of the western *marzeva*) and at Bir el-'Ababsheh, east of Apollonia at the edge of the central *marzeva*. These settlements were now concentrated in the vicinity of Apollonia rather than around Tel Michal, as they had been during earlier periods. Perhaps because of the decline of Phoenician presence and influence (Avi-Yonah 1979:38–39) or as a result of the Hasmonean wars, the population of the coast decreased during this period, as indicated by the absence of significant remains at Tel Poleg (Gophna 1973:111, n.3) and Tell Kudadi (Avigad 1977a) and the paucity of finds at Tell Qasile, the central settlement of the lower Yarkon basin (*Tell Qasile*: 12).

3.4.3. Early Roman Period (37 B.C.E.–70 C.E.)

The Early Roman period concludes the history of settlement at Tel Michal, the occupation having been reduced to a large fort established at the summit of the high tell. This citadel existed in the first half of the 1st century C.E. After its destruction (before the Great Jewish Revolt?), the site was completely deserted for about 700 years (apart from a short, limited presence at the beginning of the Early Arab period). The settlement at Tel Poleg, which existed from the Persian period onward, was also deserted at this time, indicating an overall change in the pattern of settlement on the southern Sharon coast. At Apollonia, no remains of this period were uncovered except isolated finds in the area of the city and burial caves in Kefar Shemaryahu to the east; however, historical sources attest to the importance of the settlement there, which continued to increase with time (Roll and Ayalon 1982:18; in press).

To date, no agricultural settlements of this period have been identified with any certainty. Although this lack may be the result of the chance of discovery, it is also possible that a crisis in the settlement of the region found expression in the desertion of Tel Michal and Tel Poleg and the dwindling size of Apollonia and its transfer in location.[6] One possible explanation is the declining importance of the small port cities in the Sharon after the founding of the large port city at Caesarea. On the other hand, around Tell Qasile a settlement pattern developed that included an urban center and agricultural villages. Tell Qasile may be connected with the flourishing of Antipatris and Jaffa, two important Roman centers in the Yarkon basin (Roll and Ayalon, in press).

3.5. MIDDLE ROMAN PERIOD (2D CENTURY C.E.) ONWARD (Fig. 3.5)

Apollonia flourished as a port city in the Late Roman, Byzantine, and Early Arab periods when Antipatris and Tell Qasile, the earlier urban centers in the southern Sharon, lost their importance and became secondary settlement points (Kochavi 1975:40; Mazar 1978:968). The settlement process gained impetus in the Middle Roman period (2d century C.E.) when the first agricultural settlements were founded on and along the *hamra* hills, and it reached its peak in the 6th-8th centuries C.E. Most important was the establishment of villages and farmsteads along the southern Sharon coast, mainly on the *kurkar* ridges, where many burial caves from the Roman and Byzantine periods were uncovered (Gophna 1978b). The earliest site, Herzliya B, was founded in the 2d century. Others were founded on the coast and in the swampy areas that were drained by digging a canal at Tel Poleg and a tunnel at Her-

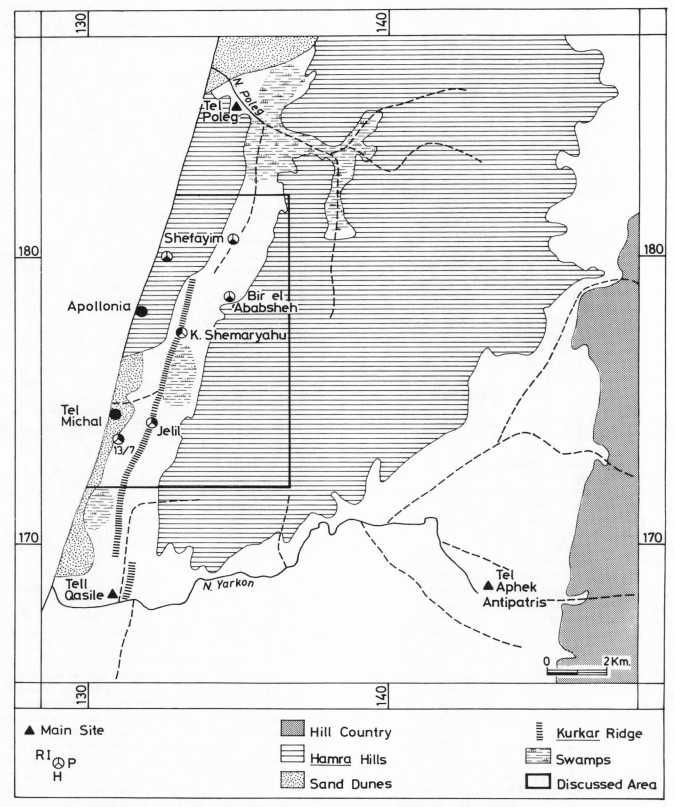

Figure 3.4. Sites of Persian to Roman I periods in southern Sharon.

zliya B. These drainage works probably date to the Byzantine period, when settlements were founded in the former swamplands (Herzliya cemetery). Settlements and farms were also set up in the low *hamra* hills of the central Sharon, where the oak forest had been cleared. The Sharon forest, called Drymus in Greek sources, is mentioned up to the Early Roman period, again from the Crusader period onward (Conder 1897:276), and in the descriptions of travelers in the last century (see *SWP II*: 136). On the other hand, there is no mention of the forest in historical or geographic records from the Late Roman, Byzantine, or Early Arab periods.

Oak represents about 50 percent of the total Tel Michal wood samples (see Chap. 19) from the Late Bronze Age to the Hellenistic period, but only 20 percent in the Roman period. In similar examinations from Apollonia (Liphschitz and Waisel 1978a; 1978b), oak represents 66 percent of the samples from the Persian period but only 5 percent from the Byzantine period and 9 percent from the Early Arab period; however, in the Middle Ages (the Crusader and Mameluke periods), it returns to a high level: 75 percent. In wood samples collected at Kefar Saba on the eastern fringes of the southern Sharon, no oak was found dating to the Byzantine and Early Arab periods, whereas all the samples from the Ottoman period were oak (Liphschitz and Waisel 1979). Although this evidence is indirect, it indicates that wood samples taken from a site tend to reflect the natural vegetation in the region during different periods. It is therefore probable that the oak forest was much reduced in the Late Roman, Byzantine, and beginning Early Arab periods. The forest was cleared to make land available for settlements, fields, and roads. Oak wood, which burns well, was used as fuel for the development of the glass industry that flourished in the region during these periods and that required large quantities of wood for its furnaces. Glass manufacturing was practicable here because the necessary raw materials, sea sand and limestone, were abundantly available in the vicinity.

Figure 3.5 illustrates the intensity of this pattern of settlements in the southern Sharon, which reached a peak in the 6th-8th centuries C.E. In the Tel Michal region, it included one large city (Apollonia), four villages (including Khirbet el-Balaqiya on the coast and Jelil), and 11 farmsteads (including Khirbet Jaiyus on the margins of the *hamra* hills, where the main building is preserved, with dimensions of 30 m × 40 m). Six burial sites on the second *kurkar* ridge, including Herzliya (Gophna 1978b), Kefar Shemaryahu (Sukenik 1944), and Jelil, are also preserved.[7]

The economy was based mainly on agriculture and the processing of agricultural products (as shown by the remains of numerous wine and olive presses) and on industry, particularly glass production. Remains of glass workshops were found at most of the large sites in the southern Sharon, including Khirbet Jaiyus, Bir el-'Ababsheh, Herzliya, and Herzliya B. They were extensive at Apollonia, where glass furnaces were excavated in 1950 at the north of the city (Yeivin 1951:86–87). Installations and other evidence for the extraction of purple dye were found at Apollonia and

Khirbet Jaiyus. At least seven winepresses were uncovered at Apollonia (Roll and Ayalon, in press) and others at Khirbet Jaiyus, Tel Michal, Herzliya B, and Jelil. The Sharon wine was renowned for its quality in the Roman and Byzantine periods (Mishnah, Nida V7; Jer., Nida II). Olive presses were uncovered at Apollonia, Khirbet el-Balaqiya, and the Herzliya cemetery. Wine and oil presses, numerous throughout the area, attest to the nature of some of the crops suited to the *hamra* soil of the central Sharon (Roll and Ayalon 1981). Although not mentioned in written sources, glass manufacturing may have developed in the region because of the need to consolidate the economic basis of the population, which had increased beyond the limited agricultural capacity of this soil (Karmon 1961).

In the Roman period, a network of roads developed through the southern Sharon to the harbor at Apollonia (Roll and Ayalon 1984). The most important route, which served until modern times, turned off from the Roman road Shechem-Jaffa and led via Kefar Saba to Apollonia. Then as now, it was an important transport axis between Jaffa, Sidna 'Ali, Apollonia, the southern Sharon, and Shechem. Other roads led from Sebaste and Antipatris to Apollonia. The most important route in the coastal region was the road established on a north-south axis in the Middle Bronze Age IIA, running west of the second *kurkar* range. It was paved for the first time in the Roman period (Avi-Yonah 1951:55), and its importance increased or decreased in the various periods according to the rising or falling fortunes of the coastal cities in the Sharon and the relationships among them.

Under these circumstances, Apollonia's sphere of influence as an urban center increased to encompass a broader region than that under the control of Tel Michal at any time during its history: the entire southern Sharon, up to the western fringes of the Samarian hills (Roll and Ayalon, in press). In this context, an interesting relationship may be discerned between the development of the rural hinterland and the physical expansion of Apollonia itself, whose size increased rapidly to about 60 hectares in the middle of the Byzantine period. Apollonia also included a large manufacturing center at its northern edge, a church on the eastern side, and an extensive anchorage into the sea (Roll and Ayalon 1982). This settlement pattern continued without significant change through the beginning of the Early Arab period and up to about the 8th century C.E., when a severe crisis occurred (Sharon 1976). As a result, most of the settlements in the southern Sharon were abandoned, particularly those on the coast and in the central hills. At this time the oak forest began to renew itself. In the eastern *marzeva*, by contrast, some settlements continued to exist because of their proximity to the international highway. Forest and swamp again dominated the landscape, as mentioned in Crusader sources. From the 9th century C.E. onward, settlement in the region reverted to the limited pattern prevailing in the MB IIB-Iron Ages. Only one settlement— Apollonia / Arsuf—dominated the coast, probably from the need for a point of control over the southwestern Sharon coast. It remained an important city throughout the Early

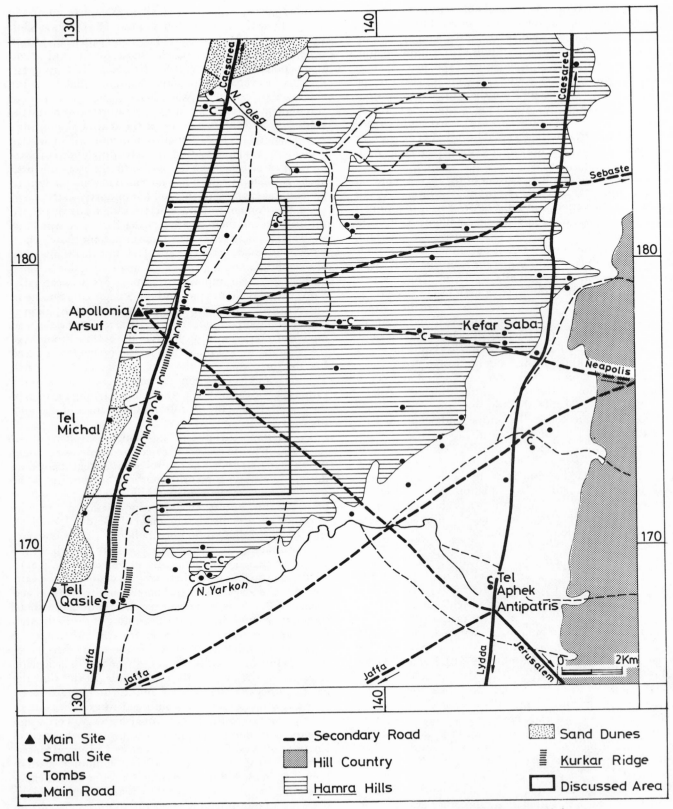

Figure 3.5. Roads and sites of southern Sharon in Late Roman, Byzantine, and Early Arab I periods.

Arab and Crusader periods, until its destruction by the Mamelukes in the 13th century. It is interesting to note the lack of agricultural settlements around Apollonia/Arsuf in the Crusader period, in contrast to the situation around Akko at the time (Benvenisti 1970:214–215; Barag 1979). Perhaps its importance is to be understood (like that of Tel Michal from the Middle Bronze Age IIB to the Iron Age) as a military and maritime post, rather than as a regional center.

During the Mameluke and Ottoman periods, Sidna 'Ali became a military-religious center and a harbor market for agricultural produce (Avitsur 1977:244). As in the Hellenistic period, when the main settlement was removed from Tel Michal to Apollonia, the transfer of the regional center from Apollonia to adjacent Sidna 'Ali was the result of the external initiative of the new rulers.

3.6. SUMMARY

The existence of a central settlement surrounded by satellite villages in the coastal area of the southwestern Sharon between Naḥal Poleg and the Yarkon River has been demonstrated by archaeological and historical research. Such a center existed almost continuously from the middle of the 2d millennium B.C.E., first at Tel Michal, then at Apollonia, and finally at Sidna 'Ali. In all three sites there were military installations, harbors, civilian trading stations, and shrines or places of worship. There seems to have been a direct relationship between the character and the size of the central settlement and its hinterland. Three situations express this connection in the different periods covered by this review:

1. During the periods before any permanent settlement, the region served mainly for hunting and grazing (Prehistoric period to Middle Bronze Age II).

2. Periods of intermittent settlement followed, during which Tel Michal's existence was based on military, trading, and marine activity along the coast but was separated from the agricultural settlements in the eastern Sharon by a hilly, forested strip about 10 km wide (MB IIB to Iron Age). The excavations at Tel Michal and the survey carried out in the vicinity point to the sporadic nature of settlement on the site in the Bronze and Iron Ages and force us to try to place local events within the historical geographic context of the Sharon as a whole. In the Middle Bronze Age IIA, the regional settlements may have been part of the city-state centered in the Yarkon basin to the south (Aphek?), whose northern border was the Naḥal Poleg basin. The foundation of the first settlement at Tel Michal at the end of the Middle Bronze Age II and its existence in the Late Bronze Age raise the question about the extent to which it may have been associated with the political framework that existed in these periods in the lower Yarkon basin and in Jaffa. In any case, it seems that Tel Michal marked the northern border of the settled area of this dispersal pattern. Examining the Iron Age archaeological material from Tel Michal, we find it difficult to determine the ethnic identity

of its occupants and the degree of their affinity with those of the Yarkon basin. Whatever the case, the absence of sites around Tel Michal in the Middle Bronze, Late Bronze, and Iron Ages and the lack of apparent contact with the eastern *marzeva* and Samarian hills point toward the possible association of Tel Michal with its neighbors to the south.

3. From the Persian period onward, settlement in the region gained momentum, apparently beginning with the entrenchment of the Phoenicians along the coast. In the Late Roman, Byzantine, and beginning Early Arab periods, settlements and farms sprang up all over the southern Sharon, and various branches of agriculture and manufacturing were developed. In this phase, the entire southern Sharon became the direct hinterland connected with the major coastal city. The settlement at Tel Michal went into a decline and then ceased to exist. The center was transferred to Apollonia, which became a large and important city. Thus, the dependence of Tel Michal on external factors and the absence of an agricultural hinterland during most of its history led to chronological gaps and lack of continuous settlement on the site. The town of Apollonia followed a different path, enjoying continuous development on the basis of a strong connection with a very broad hinterland.

NOTES

1. It was not possible in this review to show the development of the pattern of settlement in the region graphically or statistically. First, the nature and different sizes of the sites (city, village, campsite, farmstead, burial) prevent any grouping under a common denominator. Second, several sites (e.g., Site 13/8) have been covered over the years by sand or alluvium and are exposed only by chance as a result of development works. Other sites were damaged and have disappeared because of building and agricultural activity. A statistical study of the pattern of settlement would therefore be misleading from the outset.

2. The survey was carried out by the Archaeological Survey of Israel and the Institute of Archaeology of Tel Aviv University in the framework of the Tel Michal excavations sponsored by the Archaeological Expedition to the Central Coastal Region of Israel. S. Bunimovitz, I. Drori, and members of the Tel Michal excavation project participated.

3. At the Ḥefzibah site (Hadera), which is similar in its location to the sites discussed, bones were found of wild ox (*Bos taurus*), goat or sheep (*Ovis/Capra*), gazelle (*Gazella gazella*), deer (*Capreolus capreolus*), and fallow deer (*Dama mesopotamica*); all are forest, swamp, or open parkland animals. Mortars and pestles found there are evidence of grain gathering and pounding (Haker 1974; Ronen 1975:243; Ronen et al. 1975:57–58).

4. Iron Age II sherds, including "Samaritan bowls," have recently been found at Apollonia, suggesting that a small settlement existed there in the 9th-8th centuries B.C.E. We are grateful to Prof. I. Roll for his permission to mention these finds.

5. The phenomenon of sanctuaries on routes close to the coast, known at the end of the Iron Age and particularly in the Persian period, may be connected with Phoenician settlement in this region (Stern 1982:237–240). Such sanctuaries or hints of their existence have been found at Akko (Dothan 1981), Dor (Stern 1980:212), and Elyakhin (Stern 1982:16) in the northern Sharon, at Tel Yaoz near Palmaḥim (*Had. Arch.* 67:30–31), Mispeh Yonah at Ashdod (Cross 1964), Ashkelon (Stern 1982:159), and others.

6. At this time, the settlement at Apollonia moved from its former lo-

cation during the Persian and Hellenistic periods (in the center of the city, according to its later dimensions) to the southern edge, closer to the convenient descent to the sea and harbor. The new settlement was apparently set up in the second half of the 1st century C.E. (*Had. Arch.* 74–75:16–17; Roll and Ayalon 1982).

7. Burial in caves hewn in the *kurkar* ceased at the end of the Byzantine period. In the Early Arab period, the settlers of Apollonia/Arsuf and the environs were buried in graves dug in the *hamra* hills to the north and south of the city.

REFERENCES

Avi-Yonah, M. 1951. The Development of the Roman Road System in Palestine. *IEJ* 1:54–60.

Avi-Yonah, M. 1979. *The Holy Land from the Persian to the Arab Conquests (536 B.C. to A.D. 640): A Historical Geography.* Grand Rapids, Mich.

Avigad, N. 1976. Tell Jerishe. *Enc. Arch. Exc.* II: 575–578.

Avigad, N. 1977a. Tell Kudadi. *Enc. Arch. Exc.* III: 720.

Avigad, N. 1977b. Makmish. *Enc. Arch. Exc.* III: 768–770.

Avitsur, S. 1977. *Changes in the Agriculture of Eretz-Israel.* (Hebrew) Tel Aviv.

Bakler, N. 1978. Geology of Tel Michal and the Herzliya Coast. *Tel Aviv* 5:131–135.

Bar-Yosef, O. 1970. *The Epi-Palaeolithic Cultures of Palestine.* Ph.D. dissertation. Hebrew University, Jerusalem.

Bar-Yosef, O. 1975. The Epi-Palaeolithic in Palestine and Sinai. Pages 363–378 in: *Problems in Prehistory: North Africa and the Levant.* F. Wendorf and A. E. Marks, eds. Dallas.

Barag, D. 1979. A New Source Concerning the Ultimate Borders of the Latin Kingdom of Jerusalem. *IEJ* 29:197–217.

Benvenisti, M. 1970. *The Crusaders in the Holy Land.* Jerusalem.

Conder, C. R. 1897. *The Latin Kingdom of Jerusalem.* London.

Cross, F. M. 1964. An Ostracon from Nebī Yūnis. *IEJ* 14:185–186.

Dothan, M. 1975. Ashdod. *Enc. Arch. Exc.* I: 103–118.

Dothan, M. 1977. Tel Mor. *Enc. Arch. Exc.* III: 889–890.

Dothan, M. 1981. New Aspects of the Phoenician Culture during the Persian Period. *Eighth Archaeological Conference in Israel: Abstracts of Lectures,* 3. Jerusalem.

Geva, S. 1982. *Tell Jerishe: The Sukenik Excavations of the Middle Bronze Age Fortifications.* Qedem 15. Jerusalem.

Gilead, D. 1970. Handaxe Industries in Israel and the Near East. *World Archaeology* 2:1–11.

Gilead, D. 1974. Epi-Palaeolithic Find-Spots in the Eastern Sharon. *Mitekufat Haeven* 12:32–35.

Gophna, R. 1973. The Middle Bronze Age II Fortifications at Tel Poleg. *EI* 11:111–119 (Hebrew); 26 (English summary).

Gophna, R. 1974. *The Settlement of the Coastal Plain of Eretz Israel during the Early Bronze Age.* (Hebrew) Ph.D. dissertation. Tel Aviv University.

Gophna, R. 1978a. Archaeological Survey of the Central Coastal Plain, 1977. Preliminary Report. *Tel Aviv* 5:136–147.

Gophna, R. 1978b. Sharon Plain. *Enc. Arch. Exc.* IV: 1071–1074.

Gophna, R., and Ayalon, E. 1980. Survey of the Central Coastal Plain, 1978–1979: Settlement Pattern of the Middle Bronze Age IIA. *Tel Aviv* 7:147–151.

Gophna, R., and Beck, P. 1981. The Rural Aspect of the Settlement Pattern of the Coastal Plain in the Middle Bronze Age II. *Tel Aviv* 8:45–80.

Haker, D. 1974. The Fauna of Ḥefsibah. *Mitekufat Haeven* 12:2–6 (Hebrew); 77 (English summary).

Herzog, Z. 1981. Six Settlement Phases of the Persian Period of Tel Michal. *Eighth Archaeological Conference in Israel: Abstracts of Lectures,* 2. Jerusalem.

Herzog, Z. 1984. Notes and News: Tel Gerisa 1983. *IEJ* 34:55–56.

Herzog, Z., Negbi, O., and Moshkovitz, S. 1978. Excavations at Tel Michal, 1977. *Tel Aviv* 5:99–130.

Kaplan, J. 1978. Yavneh-Yam. *Enc. Arch. Exc.* IV: 1216–1218.

Kaplan, H., and Kaplan, J. 1976. Jaffa. *Enc. Arch Exc.* II: 532–541.

Karmon, Y. 1961. Geographical Influences on the Historical Routes in the Sharon Plain. *PEQ* 93:43–60.

Karmon, Y. 1971. *Israel: A Regional Geography.* London.

Kochavi, M. 1975. The First Two Seasons of Excavations at Aphek-Antipatris: Preliminary Report. *Tel Aviv* 2:17–44.

Kochavi, M., Beck, P., and Gophna, R. 1979. Aphek-Antipatris, Tel Poleg, Tel Zeror and Tel Burga: Four Fortified Sites of the Middle Bronze Age IIA in the Sharon Plain. *ZDPV* 95:121–165.

Liphschitz, N., and Waisel, Y. 1978a. *Analysis of the Botanical Material of Tel Apollonia Collected during the 1977 Season.* (Hebrew) Unpublished report, Tel Aviv University.

Liphschitz, N., and Waisel, Y. 1978b. *Dendroarchaeological Investigations No. 80: Apollonia 1979.* (Hebrew) Unpublished report, Tel Aviv University.

Liphschitz, N., and Waisel, Y. 1979. *Dendroarchaeological Investigations No. 66: Kefar Saba 1978.* (Hebrew) Unpublished report, Tel Aviv University.

Mazar, A. 1978. Tell Qasile. *Enc. Arch. Exc.* IV: 963–975.

Noy, T. 1975. *Six Neolithic Sites: A Sample from Different Geographical Zones of Israel.* Ph.D. dissertation. Hebrew University, Jerusalem.

Noy, T. 1977. Neolithic Sites in the Western Coastal Plain. *EI* 13:18–33 (Hebrew); 290–291 (English summary).

Noy, T. 1981. The Early Neolithic Periods in the Levant. *EI* 15:7–14 (Hebrew); 78 (English summary).

Paley, S. M., and Porath, Y. 1979. Burial Caves in Kibbutz Ma'abarot. *IEJ* 29:238–239.

Perrot, J. 1961. Une tombe à ossuaires du IVᵉ millénaire à Azor, près de Tel-Aviv. *'Atiqot* 3:1–83 (English series).

Prausnitz, M. W. 1970. A Neolithic Hole-Mouth Jar. *'Atiqot* 6:76–77. (Hebrew series); 9*, English summary).

Prausnitz, M., et al. 1970. Excavations at the Neolithic Site of Herzliya, 1969. *Mitekufat Haeven* 10:11–16 (Hebrew; English summary).

Roll, I., and Ayalon, E. 1981. Two Large Wine Presses in the Red Soil Regions of Israel. *PEQ* 113:111–125.

Roll, I., and Ayalon, E. 1982. Apollonia/Arsuf—A Coastal Town in the Southern Sharon Plain. (Hebrew) *Qadmoniot* 15:16–22.

Roll, I., and Ayalon, E. 1984. Roman Roads in Western Samaria and Northern Judea. Pages 131–146 in: *Israel: People and Land* (Hebrew; 13*–14*, English summary). Haaretz Museum Yearbook I, 19.

Roll, I., and Ayalon, E. In press. Apollonia and the Southern Sharon: A Model of a Port and Its "Hinterland." (Hebrew) In *The Sharon.* A. Shmueli, ed. Tel Aviv.

Ronen, A. 1975. The Paleolithic Archaeology and Chronology of Israel. Pages 229–248 in: *Problems in Prehistory: North Africa and the Levant.* F. Wendorf and A. E. Marks, eds. Dallas.

Ronen, A., et al. 1975. The Epi-Palaeolithic Site Ḥefziba, Central Coastal Plain of Israel. *Quartär* 26:53–72.

Sharon, M. 1976. Processes of Destruction and Nomadisation in Palestine under Islamic Rule (633–1517). Pages 9–32 in: *Notes and Studies on the History of the Holy Land under Islamic Rule.* M. Sharon, ed. (Hebrew) Jerusalem.

Stern, E. 1980. Tel Dor, 1980. *IEJ* 30:209–213.

Stern, E. 1982. *Material Culture of the Land of the Bible in the Persian Period, 538–332 B.C.E..* Warminster.

Sukenik, E. L. 1937. A Chalcolithic Necropolis at Haderah. *JPOS* 17:15–30.

Sukenik, E. L. 1944. Kefar Shemaryahu. *QDAP* 10:195–196.

Yeivin, S. 1951. Archaeological News: Arsuf (Apollonia). *AJA* 55:86–87.

4

Middle and Late Bronze Age Settlements (Strata XVII-XV)

by Ze'ev Herzog

The sequence of Bronze Age strata at Tel Michal was clarified only during the fourth (and last) season of excavation, when the lowest levels on the high tell were reached (Figs. 4.1–4.9). In a number of deep probes at the center of the tell, we encountered layers of sloping fills of sand and *hamra* soil, which suggested that we were actually digging the artificial fills beyond the original eastern slope of the hill (Fig. 4.1). This led to the obvious conclusion that most of the Middle Bronze Age settlement must have been located on a sizable part of the natural *kurkar* hill that had subsequently split off and collapsed onto the beach below (Fig. 4.2).

The same phenomenon seems to have occurred once again at the end of the Late Bronze Age I—although perhaps not on such a drastic scale. This conclusion forms the basis for our interpretation of the different locations of the three Bronze Age settlements on the high tell, each somewhat more inland than its predecessor, and for our reconstruction of the continuing process of erection, destruction, and rebuilding of these settlements.

4.1. MIDDLE BRONZE AGE IIB (STRATUM XVII)

4.1.1. Constructional Remains

Western Slope

The earliest occupational remains at Tel Michal were uncovered on the western slope of the high tell where we excavated a stepped trench into the side of the steep slope facing the sea (Fig. 4.3). The top of the natural hill, reached at level 11.50 m, consisted of a layer of sand partly consolidated into soft *kurkar* (Locus 929), overlying consolidated *kurkar*.[1] The deepest level at which potsherds still appeared was 11.63 m. Above this were several types of horizontally

deposited soil layers that contained sherds solely of the Middle Bronze Age IIB, their total depth about 4 m. Since no floor or occupational level could be distinguished within these deposits, we assume that they were fills dumped against the slope by the inhabitants in order to level the top of the natural hill and create a broad, flat surface on which to build their settlement (see Herzog 1980:141–142). We shall refer to these fills as Platform 782, after the locus number for its uppermost layer in our stepped trench. The term is also applied to other remnants of this earthen platform encountered elsewhere on the tell, although they will generally be referred to by their original locus numbers.

In our stepped trench, Platform 782 was built up as follows (Fig. 4.3; Pl. 5). On top of the natural *kurkar* rock, several alternating layers of gray, ashy soil and yellow sand (Loci 927 and 922) were laid at elevations 11.63–9.50 m. Above these was a thin layer of clean yellow sand (Locus 916) that contained a few MB IIB sherds. The next deposit (Locus 911) consisted of a mixture of *hamra* soil with lenses of ash and stones. At one spot in this deposit was a concentration of medium-size stones, apparently the remains of a collapsed retaining wall that had supported the fills. Locus 911 also contained several MB IIB sherds (Figs. 5.2:9; 5.3:10, 13) and a broken grinding stone. Since there was no evidence of any occupational surface here, we assume these objects were discarded by the workers during construction of the earthen platform.

The uppermost level of the platform (Locus 782) consisted of a massive layer of hard-packed *hamra* more than 1 m thick. In our trench this layer reached elevation 7.50 m, but this was not yet the top of the original platform, since it was preserved at a higher level (up to 6.85 m) on the northern side of the tell (Locus 1664; see below). But on our western side of the tell, the original top was missing completely, because of the destructive forces that severed a large portion of the hill. Whatever remained of the upper part of Plat-

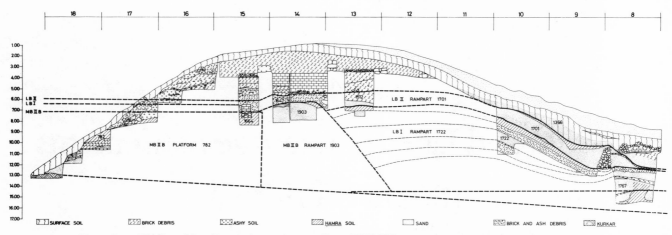

Figure 4.1. Middle and Late Bronze Age settlements (Strata XVII–XV) as seen in reconstructed west-east cross section.

form 782 in our stepped trench was also pockmarked by robbers' trenches and pits of the Late Bronze Age (Robbers' Trench 776) and Iron Age (Pit 378 of Stratum XIV).

Northern End of the High Tell

The second location in which MB IIB remains were reached was at the northern end of the mound. Here brick Wall S156 marked the junction between the northeastern end of Platform 782 and the sloping fills of the rampart that were laid against it from the outside. This part of Platform 782 (Locus 723) abutted onto the southwest face of Wall S156. Its top was preserved at elevation 7.00 m. A probe cutting through the hard-packed, dark red soil of the platform was discontinued at level 7.75 m.

Wall S156, 64 cm wide, was built of *ḥamra* bricks without stone foundations. Its base was at level 9.95 m and its highest point of preservation at 6.68 m, a total height of 3.27 m. It was evidently entirely underground, serving as a retaining wall for the earthen platform. We unearthed a stretch of about 8 m of its length, but its northwestern continuation was severed together with the overall collapse of this part of the mound. A thick layer of sand (Locus 719) extends downward beyond the base of the wall, lying against its outer side on the northeast (Pl. 7). We retrieved a few MB IIB sherds from this fill. Overlying it, a layer of red *ḥamra* soil (Locus 716), about 20–30 cm thick, inclined northward at elevations ranging from 6.70 m at the top to 8.70 m at the bottom. Where the two fills met, a saw-toothed color pattern occurs, probably resulting from the simultaneous dumping and partial overlapping of the last layer of yellow sand and the red *ḥamra*. The sloping layer of compact red *ḥamra* soil forms a glacis whose main purpose was to retain the underlying sand layers and to prevent them from sliding down or being washed down the slope.

Center of Mound

Here we reached additional MB IIB constructional remains in deep test pits (Figs. 4.6; 4.9).

Wall N156 is the only stone wall from this period found at Tel Michal. About 80 cm wide, it was constructed of two rows of *kurkar* fieldstone with a superstructure of *ḥamra* brick, badly disturbed at the top. A *ḥamra* fill (Locus 1664) appears on both sides of the wall. No floor could be discerned, since whatever floors might have existed were totally eroded. The base of Wall N156 is at about the same level as the top of Platform 782, located about 10 m to the southwest. This may indicate that the floors of the MB IIB settlement were laid on a higher elevation, possibly around level 6.70 m.

East of Locus 1664, sand and *ḥamra* fills once again occur, from which we may conclude that Wall N156 marked the eastern limit of the earthen platform on which the settlement was built.

In three separate probes on a north-south axis at the center of the high tell (Fig. 4.9), we reached a thick layer of sand forming a strip about 10 m long and 4 m wide (Loci 1657, 1663, and 1903). Because of the imminent danger of collapse of the excavation balks, we had to stop digging before we reached the bottom of this fill. Its excavated depth is about 2 m (between elevations 5.80 and 7.80 m). This continuous sandbank is undoubtedly part of the same artificial earthen rampart that encircled the settlement.

The total width of the sandbank (from west to east) is about 7 m; at its eastern edge, it rises slightly and then starts to slope downward at a gradient of 40 degrees. Covering the sand, a layer of hard-packed, red *ḥamra* soil (Loci 1665 and 1901) about 80 cm thick served as the glacis of the rampart. Although in many spots this mantle was eroded, in some it still retained its original steep incline (e.g., Fill 1901 in Fig. 4.9; Pl. 11).

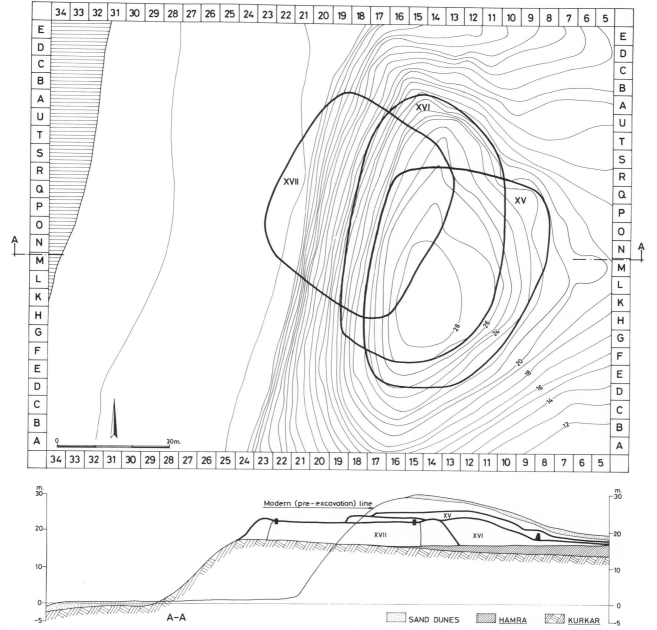

Figure 4.2. Schematic reconstruction of relative positions of Middle and Late Bronze Age settlements in relation to present topography of high tell.

Northern Hill

We found several MB IIB sherds, a flint sickle blade, some metal objects, and a worked bone in a deep trial pit (Locus 174) excavated on the southern slope of the northern hill. The limited size of the excavated area made it difficult to decide whether these remains came from an additional built-up area at Tel Michal or whether the objects were dumped there at a later date. Nowhere else at the site did

any MB IIB remains come to light.

4.1.2. Reconstruction of the Middle Bronze Age IIB Settlement

The main elements of the MB IIB settlement at Tel Michal are the *ḥamra* platform with retaining Walls S156 and

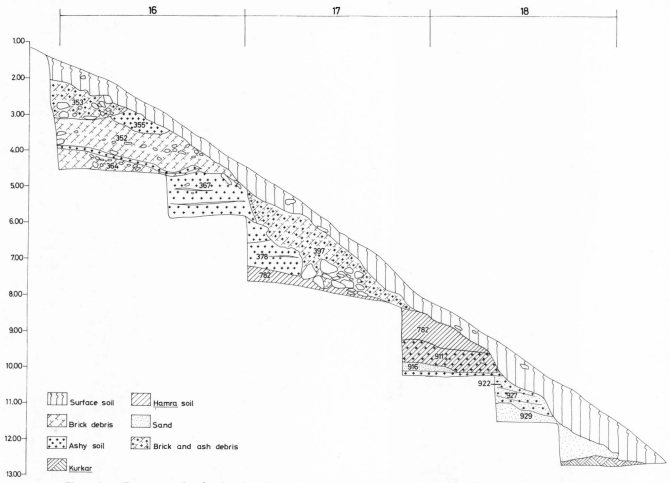

Figure 4.3. East-west section drawing through southern balk to ramparts on western slope of high tell (Squares M16–M18).

N156 and the earthen rampart encircling the entire construction. By extending the lines of the retaining walls, we get a wedge-shaped area that demarcates the inner core of the settlement, terminated on the west by the completely eroded slope. The surviving part of the platform covers an area of about 500 m². If we assume that the preserved eastern side of the wedge is almost its complete original length (about 50 m) and that the platform was roughly rectangular (Fig. 4.2), the size of the settlement may be estimated at 2,500 m² and the preserved part would be about 20 percent of its original area. By adding the earthen rampart and glacis (a strip 15 m wide all around), we arrive at a total area of about 6,400 m². From these figures we can calculate the volume of the different materials used in construction. The *ḥamra* platform would have required approximately 12,500 m³ and the earthen rampart some 15,000 m³ of sand plus 4,000 m³ of *ḥamra* for the glacis. Since there is a convenient source for both of these materials immediately east of the high tell and since both of them are sandy, easily quarried soils, we may estimate a rate of 1 m³ of *ḥamra* construction

or 2 m³ of sand-filling per workday. At this rate, the workers would have required 16,500 days to lay the *ḥamra* and 7,500 days to dump the sand—a total of 24,000 workdays. This means that it would have taken 200 workers about 4 months to complete this project.[2]

Evidence for the possible source of some of the *ḥamra* soil came from the extreme end (Square M8) of the section on the eastern slope of the tell (Fig. 4.4), where several sand-filled pits cut into the natural *ḥamra* soil were observed (e.g., Locus 1767). These pits were probably dug by the workers to obtain material for the *ḥamra* glacis. The sand that refilled the pits could have been blown into them by the wind or dumped into them on purpose when the area was leveled for the next occupational phase.

The absence of a defensive city wall around the MB IIB settlement at Tel Michal indicates that the purpose of the earthworks described above was not primarily military. The considerable time and effort expended in constructing them can best be explained as an attempt to create a broad level area, clearly defined and high above the surrounding

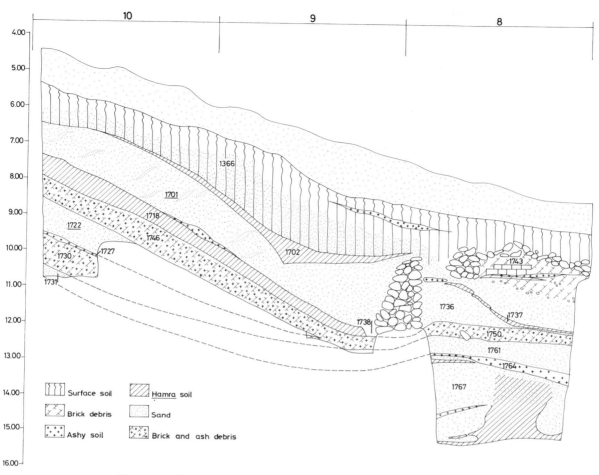

Figure 4.4. West-east section through ramparts in Squares M10–M8 (eastern slope).

terrain. The purpose of the circumferential *ḥamra*-covered sand rampart was to protect the core of the platform against erosion; any damage to the rampart caused by wind or rain could be easily and quickly repaired before the platform itself (and the settlement built upon it) was endangered.

Middle Bronze Age IIB settlements of various sizes surrounded by earthen ramparts that are not defended by city walls are well known throughout Syria and Israel (Kaplan 1975). In the coastal plain of Israel, such ramparts (without city walls) were discovered at Achzib (Prausnitz 1975:207–208), Akko (Dothan and Raban 1980), Tel Mevorakh (*Enc. Arch. Exc. III*: 861–871), Tel Burga (Kochavi et al. 1979), Yavneh Yam (Kaplan 1975), Tel Mor and Tel Ashdod (Dothan 1973), and Tel Poran (Gophna 1977).

Lacking city walls, these settlements were unable to protect themselves effectively against powerful enemies, since even if the slopes of the ramparts were steep and slippery, their effectiveness as a military deterrent is debatable—the enemy could still climb up or over them without undue difficulty. It therefore seems that the term "fortified cities" often applied to such settlements is incorrect.[3] But if the

military function is ruled out (or at least plays only a minor role), how should we interpret this phenomenon? The answer seems to lie in technical and economic considerations, for despite the enormous size and volume of these earthworks, they were easier and quicker to construct than a city wall. Whereas earthen ramparts may be erected simply by dumping the local soils in alternate layers, erection of a wall necessitates thousands of hours by skilled workers to quarry and transport the building stones and hundreds of stonemasons to lay the foundations. The mudbrick superstructure requires clay, straw, and an abundant water supply; moreover, the molding and drying of millions of bricks is a time-consuming and laborious process.

We may thus assume that, in times of rapid population increase and peaceful political conditions, construction of an earthen rampart was preferred, at least by settlements that did not feel threatened by military attack. These earthworks provided the settlers with a relatively quick and cheap method of creating a framework for their city. On level terrain like that at Yavneh Yam, the settlers threw up a circumferential rampart with a craterlike cross section and

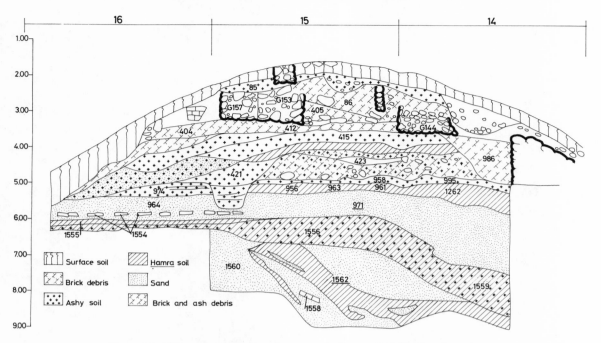

Figure 4.5. West-east section through ramparts in Squares G16–G14 (southern slope).

built their houses and other structures inside. On existing hills like Tel Michal, settlers enlarged the horizontal building area at the summit by dumping earth against the slopes and then built their settlement on top.

4.1.3. Founding of Tel Michal in the Light of Settlement Patterns in the Coastal Plain

The intensive occupation of the coastal plain of Israel from Haifa southward during the Middle Bronze Age II has been well documented in studies of settlement patterns (Gophna 1974; Gophna and Beck 1981). When we take this information and rearrange it into a separate scheme for each subperiod (MB IIA and MB IIB), an interesting picture emerges.

Table 4.1 classifies the recorded sites into four categories: (A) large settlements, mostly cities of 30,000 m² or more; (B) villages, hamlets, farmsteads, trading stations, and forts (less than 10,000 m²); (C) isolated structures, mainly temples; and (D) cemeteries or single graves. Sites with both graves and habitations are classified according to group A or B depending on the size of the settlement.

The total number of recorded sites in the surveyed area shows 52 from the Middle Bronze Age IIA and 67 from IIB, an increase of 29 percent in the second phase. When the coastal plain is subdivided into two regions, however, one north and one south of the Yarkon River, two different patterns emerge: north of the Yarkon there were 25 sites in Phase A and only 19 in Phase B, representing a decrease of 24 percent,[4] whereas south of the Yarkon there were 27

Table 4.1. Comparison of Middle Bronze Age IIA and IIB Settlement Patterns in the Coastal Plain

Region	Middle Bronze Age IIA					Middle Bronze Age IIB				
	A	B	C	D	Total	A	B	C	D	Total
Northern coastal plain	6	15	1	3	25	6	13	···	···	19
Southern coastal plain	2	21	2	2	27	13	24	···	11	48
Total	8	36	3	5	52	19	37		11	67

sites in Phase A and 48 in Phase B—an increase of 78 percent.

The difference in regional settlement patterns between the two phases of Middle Bronze Age II is also striking: whereas the total number of MB IIA sites is divided almost equally (25:27), the MB IIB north-south ratio is 19:48—an increase of more than 152 percent. Moreover, several of the southern sites are more than twice as large as the northern ones. The ratio of large settlements (category A) in the south during each subperiod is most significant: 13 during the Middle Bronze Age IIB, compared with only 2 in the previous phase. This undoubtedly reflects a population explosion in the southern coastal plain in the later phase. The settlement at Tel Michal is the northernmost site erected in the Middle Bronze Age IIB to be discovered to date along the coast of Israel; all others were located along the road at

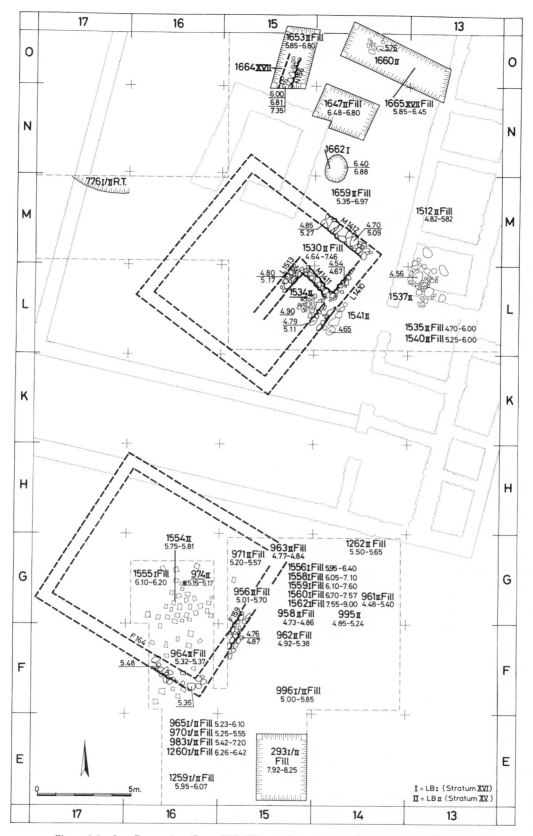

Figure 4.6. Late Bronze Age (Strata XVI–XV) remains at center and southern end of high tell.

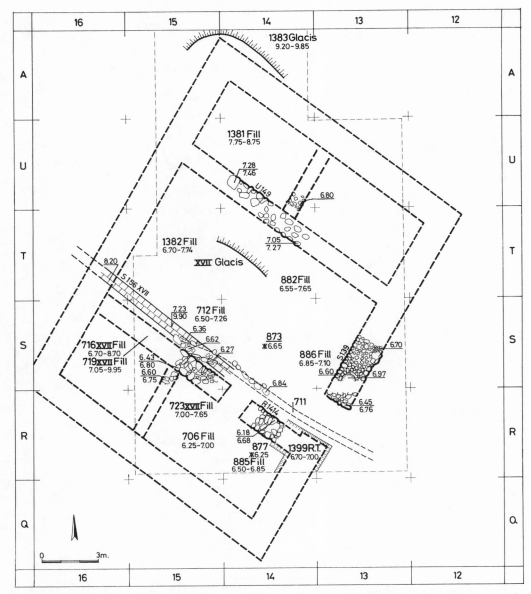

Figure 4.7. Late Bronze Age I remains (Stratum XVI) at northern end of high tell (Fort 873), with elements of Stratum XVII.

the foot of the hill country. The founding of Tel Michal at that time is undoubtedly connected with a wave of settlement in the southern coastal plain.

The impetus for settlement in the north during the Middle Bronze Age IIA is generally considered to have originated on the Syro-Lebanese coast, but what is the historical background for developments in the southern coastal plain? The answer to this question involves setting the precise date for the earliest pottery assemblage (see Chap. 5), which belongs to the latter stages of the Middle Bronze Age IIB (or Middle Bronze Age IIC, as it is often called).[5] This

date is contemporary with the 15th (Hyksos) Dynasty that ruled over Lower Egypt and the southern coastal plain of Canaan in the late 17th and early 16th centuries B.C.E. (Kempinski 1974:126–132). To refine the date even further, I would suggest a correlation with Apophis I, as proposed by Dothan (1973) for the founding of Tel Mor and Tel Ashdod, which resemble Tel Michal in many respects. Tel Michal would then have been the northernmost station among the newly established sites during this flourishing phase of the 15th dynasty and may mark the northern limit of direct Hyksos suzerainty in the coastal plain in the Mid-

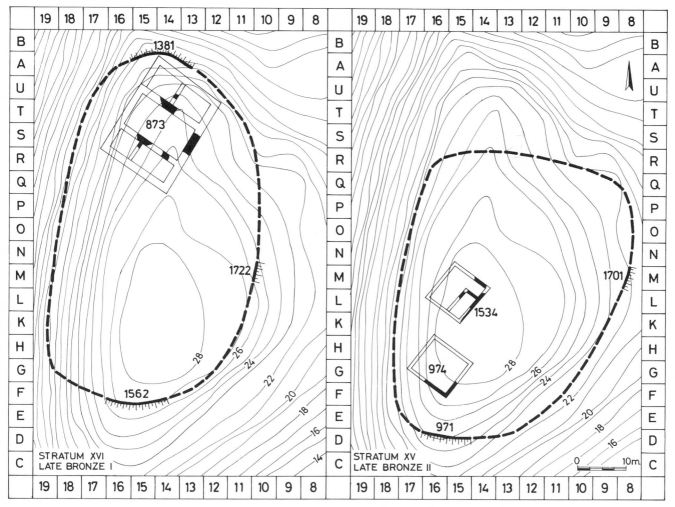

Figure 4.8. Comparison of size and location of architectural remains of Late Bronze I–II settlements.

dle Bronze Age IIB.

The absence of fortifications at our site supports the assumption of peaceful and prosperous conditions in the region at this time, undoubtedly related to intensified trade in the eastern Mediterranean. Archaeologically, this commerce is represented by the abundance of Cypriote imports found in various sites along the coast. Historical attestation comes from the second stele of Kamose, which mentions hundreds of cedar ships owned by the Hyksos ruler Apophis I that carried merchandise from R*t*nw (Habachi 1972:37; Kempinski 1974:127–129).

Evidence of maritime trade, together with the nonmilitary nature of the newly founded settlements, indicate that the stimulus for the wave of settlement on the southern coast of Canaan did not come from any threat of Egyptian attack as suggested by Dothan (1973:16–17), but quite the opposite; the prevailing peace and prosperity created by

flourishing international trade were both the cause and result of this population expansion.[6]

The location of Tel Michal on the coastal cliff overlooking the sea corroborates its raison d'être as a maritime trading station. Although international shipping probably operated through the harbor cities located at the outlets of main rivers, small vessels serving the coastal trade needed intermediate stations such as Tel Michal.

Our attempts to locate a likely place at the foot of the tell for these boats to anchor have been only partially successful. In aerial photographs taken in 1949 and 1977, remnants of an abraded *kurkar* ridge lying in the shallow waters of the surf zone parallel to the coastal cliff are clearly visible (Fig. 18.1; Pl. 2). Immediately below the tell there is one patch of *kurkar* much wider than the narrow strips to its north and south, somewhat crescent shaped with a small cove facing the beach. No signs of human activity such as

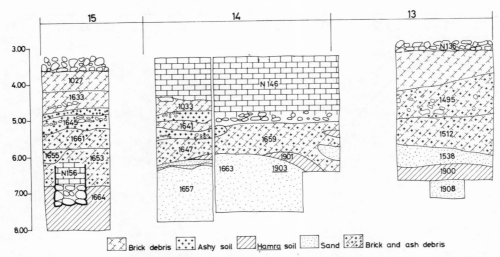

Figure 4.9. West-east section drawing combined from probes in center of high tell in Squares N13–N15.

quarrying or construction were found in the underwater survey conducted here by the Center for Maritime Studies of Haifa University.[7] However, the survey team recorded a channel about 30–40 m wide and up to 2 m deep between this abraded *kurkar* ridge and the beach. This channel may have afforded a safe anchorage, the *kurkar* ridge on the seaward side serving as a breakwater. The logical place for the entrance into the channel would have been from the north near the estuary of Naḥal Gelilot where there is a gap in the underwater *kurkar* ridge (see Chap. 17). Although it is possible that light vessels were pulled up onto the beach (like the fishing boats of today) or moored to a wooden pier or the like, it is difficult to understand why the first settlers chose this particular cliff top on which to found Tel Michal if there was not some topographical feature of the coastline at this spot that made it suitable for anchoring small coastal craft at least.

4.1.4. Destruction of the Middle Bronze Age Settlement

The destruction of the MB IIB settlement at Tel Michal was so drastic that no traces of any architectural remains or occupational levels were preserved, even on the surviving part of the *ḥamra* platform. This points toward a tectonic cause for the disaster, which is the only way to explain why so much of the settlement is completely missing.

Additional evidence for tectonic faulting and the concurrent disappearance of most of the western side of the high tell is the considerable filling activity on the opposite side of the mound in the succeeding Late Bronze Age I, undoubtedly intended to compensate for the lost area of the former settlement (Figs. 4.1; 4.2; Pl. 9). It should be stressed that the topographical change between Stratum XVII and Stratum XVI was greater than all those occurring

during the ensuing 3,500 years. Whereas at the end of the Middle Bronze Age IIB the high tell suddenly lost what we estimate to be about 80 percent of its volume (including part of its natural *kurkar* base), only about 30 percent of the Roman fortress is missing, mainly as a result of slow but continuous surface erosion.

The archaeological evidence therefore seems to support the theory of a number of geologists who argue that the coastal line of Israel has been strongly influenced by a series of neotectonic movements (Neev et al. 1973; see also Chap. 16). The destruction of the MB IIB maritime station at Tel Michal around 1570 B.C.E. was most likely a result of such tectonic activity.[8]

4.2. LATE BRONZE AGE (STRATA XVI-XV)

The transition from the Middle to the Late Bronze Age at Tel Michal was accompanied by an eastward shift of the settlement and a radical change in its shape. The horizontal area remaining at the top of the mound was expanded by massive earthworks on three sides — north, east, and south. On the eastern, inland side, a strip varying from 15 to 20 m in width and composed of alternating soil layers was added to the remains of the Stratum XVII ramparts. Similar earthworks were thrown up at the southern end of the mound and, on a lesser scale, at the northern end. Undoubtedly, this inland expansion of the mound in the Late Bronze Age I was required to compensate for the loss of terrain on the seaward side. At the beginning of Stratum XV the mound was once again expanded eastward, although not as extensively (Figs. 4.1; 4.2; 4.8).

Both Late Bronze Age strata suffered severely from natural forces. At the end of the Late Bronze Age I, another tectonic movement apparently caused additional destruction on the western side. No Stratum XVI occupational remains survived on the southern spur of the mound, and on the northern terrace there are only a few badly preserved architectural remnants (Fig. 4.7). In Stratum XV the northern end of the mound was not occupied at all, and only in the central and southern parts of the mound did any remains survive (Fig. 4.6). This stratum, however, suffered considerably from surface erosion that wrought havoc with the ruins during the occupational gap of several hundred years following the abandonment of the site at the end of the Late Bronze Age. As a result, only scanty patches of Stratum XV floors are preserved.

Earthen ramparts and other fills provided the main evidence of LB I and II settlements. It was relatively easy to distinguish between the two construction phases, since builders in all three Bronze Age strata consolidated earth or sand fills with a layer of hard-packed, red *hamra* soil. In addition, the presence of large quantities of MB IIB pottery in the lower fills points toward an LB I filling operation, whereas those soil layers containing both MB IIB and LB I sherds were presumably dumped during the Late Bronze Age II.

After we began to understand the peculiar phenomenon of the successive eastward shifts of the artificial mound, we decided to cut sections into it to learn how the earthen ramparts were constructed. Naturally, this evidence is best seen on the vertical section drawings (Figs. 4.4; 4.5). The description is therefore presented primarily according to the subareas in which these trenches and probes were made and only secondarily in chronological order.

4.2.1. Eastern Slope (Fig. 4.4; Pl. 9)

A trench 5 m wide cut perpendicular to the eastern slope of the tell (Squares M8-M10) by a bulldozer (with final straightening of balks by hand) provided the clearest picture. However, since a great deal of the rampart consists of sand, the balks of the trench collapsed almost as soon as the sand was exposed to air (Pl. 9) and prevented us from excavating deeper than about 5 m. Only in a probe at the eastern end of the trench (Square M8) were we able to penetrate deeper, and there we reached the natural *hamra* soil, which started at level 14 m. Several sand-filled pits (e.g., Pit 1767) cut into this soil, which may have been "quarried" for this material during the Middle Bronze Age II (see Section 4.1.2).

Rampart 1722 (Stratum XVI)

The layers of this rampart deposited against the slope increase in thickness as they approach the top of the mound. As a result, their angle becomes wider (and the slope becomes steeper) until the uppermost *hamra* layer (Locus 1718) reaches an angle of 30 degrees.

The lowest rampart layer here is a thin strip of ashy soil (Locus 1764) lying directly above the sand fill of Pit 1767. Above it is another sand layer about 70 cm thick (Locus 1761), which is probably a continuation of the sloping sand layer whose traces were found at the western end of the

rampart in Square M10 (Locus 1731). The next layer (Locus 1750) is a mixture of broken bricks and ashy soil full of potsherds and animal bones, obviously taken from the ruins of the MB II settlement at the top of the mound. The western part of the rampart included a layer of brick-and-ash debris (Locus 1730), a thin ash layer (Locus 1727), a thick sand layer (Locus 1722), and another thick layer of brick-and-ash debris (Locus 1746) that continued on a horizontal plane at the bottom of the mound in Square M8 (Locus 1750). The face of the rampart was consolidated with a layer of compacted *hamra* (Locus 1718). We observed traces of this capping on top of the horizontal layer of brick-and-ash debris (Locus 1750) at the east. Although the junction between the sloping and horizontal parts of the rampart was interrupted by retaining Wall M91, it was not difficult to recognize the original continuity of the layers on either side.

Rampart 1701 (Stratum XV)

The LB II addition to the ramparts on this side of the mound is more limited in extent and constructed somewhat differently. Most of it consists of huge quantities of sand, up to 2 m in depth. To retain such a mass of sand, the builders were obliged to erect retaining Wall M91 as the first stage of the operation. This wedge-shaped wall is 2.15 m high and 1.3 m wide at its base. Its foundation trench (Locus 1738) cuts into *hamra* layer 1718. The western face of the wall has an angle of 110 degrees, whereas the outer face is almost vertical. The V-shaped space between this retaining wall and the Stratum XVI rampart was then filled in with sand to the height of the wall. After that, the builders dumped a very thick layer of sand on the upper stretches of the slope (Locus 1701) and against the outer side of the retaining wall (Locus 1736). Both of these fills were capped with a layer of hard-packed *hamra*: Locus 1702 on the slope above the retaining wall and Locus 1737 below it. On the left-hand side of the section drawing (Fig. 4.4), the *hamra* layer (1702) appears as a very thin strip, the rest probably having been washed away by surface erosion.

Above the Stratum XV *hamra* capping are mixed deposits of *hamra*, sand, and streaks of ash (Locus 1366), probably destruction debris that was washed down the slope. In the Persian period a structure was erected at the bottom of the rampart (Building 1743), demonstrating that there was no major change in the topography of the high tell following the end of the Late Bronze Age.

4.2.2. Southern Slope (Fig. 4.5)

We obtained additional data regarding the ramparts surrounding the LB settlements in our excavations at the southern end of the high tell. Because sand fills in the balks of our section collapsed, we had to stop work here at level 9 m. The earthworks of Stratum XVI (Rampart 1562) and Stratum XV (Rampart 971) are shown in the west-east cross section through Squares G16-G14 (Fig. 4.5).

Rampart 1562 (Stratum XVI)

Like Rampart 1722 on the eastern slope, the LB I rampart

here is also composed of brick-and-ash debris taken from the ruins of the previous settlement, alternating with layers of the *ḥamra* soil and yellow sand (Pl. 10).

The lowest unit (Locus 1562) consists of a deep deposit of sand interspersed at the east with strips of *ḥamra*, which help to prevent sand sliding down the slope. A diagonal line of bricks (Locus 1558) incorporated into this locus no doubt was intended to serve the same purpose; presumably the bricks came from the debris of the Stratum XVII settlement, like the deposits of brick and ash in Loci 1556 and 1559 that covered the sand of Locus 1562. The gray-brown soil of these deposits contained large quantities of MB IIB sherds as well as animal bones. The face of Rampart 1562 presumably was completely covered with a layer of compacted *ḥamra*, but only a thin strip of it has been preserved (Locus 1555) in the western part of the section.

From the considerable depth of these deposits—down to level 9.00 m—we may assume that these fills were added to the hill during the Late Bronze Age I and that the original MB IIB settlement did not extend this far south. The LB I addition lies between 6 m and 9 m, about the same elevation as the earthworks of this period excavated on the northern and eastern sides of the high tell.

Rampart 971 (Stratum XV)

The earthworks added in the Late Bronze Age II are characterized by a sandy fill (Locus 971), piled up in some places as high as 2 m and totally covering the previous rampart. In the western part of the area, a layer of *ḥamra* bricks (Locus 1554), scattered about at different angles and including many broken pieces, is incorporated into the sand layer (Locus 964). Although some of the bricks are stacked on top of others, they clearly were not part of a structure but were intended instead to consolidate the sand layer (Pl. 8).

The upper part of Rampart 971 suffered considerably both from surface erosion during the long occupational gap that followed the end of the Late Bronze Age II and also from intrusive pits and foundation trenches of the Iron Age and Persian period. Nevertheless, several patches of the *ḥamra* mantle of the rampart were still preserved (Loci 956, 963, 961, and 1262). Ash layers 974, 958, and 995 (the latter two lying above the *ḥamra* strip) were probably occupational surfaces, although no real floors were preserved from this stratum.

Two poorly preserved, rather thin wall segments (F159 and F164) are evidently foundations of an LB II building, presumably a private dwelling (Fig. 4.6).

Mixed Deposits from Late Bronze Age I and II

South of the above-mentioned wall segments starts the steep southern slope from which some of the richest LB pottery assemblages were collected. The broken vessels were found in mixed deposits (Loci 293, 965, 983, 996, 1259, and 1260) that probably originated from debris thrown down the slope in the occupied part of the tell when it was dug out or leveled off by the 10th-century B.C.E. builders

of the Iron Age settlement (Stratum XIV). This would explain why the pottery is a mixture of LB I and II sherds, with no later ones.

4.2.3. Center of the High Tell

We unearthed Late Bronze Age remains in the center of the tell mainly under the courtyard of the Roman fortress and in small probes at its east and north. Here again, our data come mostly from the earthen fills making up the various layers of the rampart. In addition, we found parts of a building and several paved areas. The best way to explain the correlation of the various fill layers is by reference to the sectional drawings of the three probes, arranged in Figure 4.9 according to their relative positions (Pls. 11; 12).

Stratum XVI

The LB I earthen rampart was badly eroded and there was no evidence of it on top of the MB IIB sand layers (Fills 1657, 1663, and 1903 in Square N14), which were covered directly by LB II fills. Only in Square N13 did we encounter LB I remains: a sand fill in Locus 1908 and a hard-packed *ḥamra* layer (Locus 1900) that covered it and probably joined *ḥamra* layer 1718 on the eastern slope. In the Late Bronze Age I, an ash pit (Locus 1662) was dug into one of the MB II sand fills (Locus 1657).

Stratum XV

The LB II rampart is represented by a sand fill (Locus 1538) in Square N13 and above it a thick layer of brick-and-ash debris (Locus 1512), with extensions 1647 and 1653 to the north, 1659 in the center, and 1530, 1535, and 1540 in the west. This debris apparently came from the ruins of the LB I settlement, which were leveled off and incorporated into the new rampart. Its *ḥamra* capping is missing, probably having washed away.

Remains of LB II Structure 1534 include Walls L1410, M1411, L1513, and M1412, all built of two rows of *kurkar* fieldstones (Fig. 4.6). These walls apparently formed the eastern corner of a rectangular building. In Room 1534, a stone pavement was partially preserved at level 4.90 m (Pl. 13). There were several other pavements nearby; Pavement 1541 next to the building was laid over a heavy *ḥamra* fill. One of its paving stones was an anchor (a large block with a perforation smoothed by contact with the anchor rope) in secondary use, the earliest anchor found in a stratigraphic context at Tel Michal (see Chap. 31). Pavement 1537 was a few meters to the east. Here we found a storage jar, probably of Egyptian origin, sunk into the earth of Fill 1540. Pavement 1660 in Square O14 was lower by 1 m than the others; hence we assume that the central and northern parts of the LB II settlement were built on a lower terrace than the southern end—a topographical feature of the high tell that remained unchanged throughout succeeding periods.

The Late Bronze Age is not represented in the stepped trench on the western slope (Fig. 4.3), where Iron Age deposits lie directly over the remains of the MB IIB platform.

4.2.4. Northern Slope

Stratum XVI

The LB I remains at the northern end of the high tell consist of Structure 873 and Rampart 1381, with continuation in Locus 882 (Figs. 4.6; 4.7). These fills lie directly on top of the MB IIB earthworks, creating a new rampart with sloping *ḥamra* glacis (Locus 1383) in Squares T/U14–15 and extending the mound northward.

The remains of Structure 873 are badly damaged, and any reconstruction is purely hypothetical. However, Wall S139, 1.60 m wide and located on the northern spur of the mound, may have served as a military fort guarding approaches from the north.

The beaten earth floor (Locus 873) at level 6.65 m may have been part of the central courtyard of Structure 873. Southwest of this floor are two segments of a wall (R1414) about 1.20 m wide that could have separated the courtyard from a roofed room or rooms. Only a patch of flooring is preserved here (Floor 877), with pottery in a burnt layer at 6.25 m. If our reconstruction is correct, then the floor of the room (or rooms) would have been about 40 cm higher than the courtyard level.

The remains farther north are even less well preserved. Wall U149 may have been the northeastern closure of the courtyard. Two rooms that might have existed at the far northern end of the high tell were almost totally destroyed at the end of the Late Bronze Age. Since the western part of the building is completely missing, it is also impossible to know whether there were any rooms on that side. Our hypothetical estimate is that the structure originally measured about 16 m × 22 m (Fig. 4.7).

Along the face of Wall R1414, a stone-lined channel (Drain 711) slopes from west to east. Assuming that this drainage channel passed under the gate or entrance to the building through Wall S139, we may locate this opening at the southeast side of the structure. The junction of Walls S139 and R1414, however, is missing because of Robbers' Trench 1399 of a later period. In any case, the existence of this drain supports our assumption that Structure 873 had an open, central courtyard.

Stratum XV

In view of the complete absence of any LB II ceramic material in this area, we assume that the northern end of the high tell was unoccupied during this period.

4.2.5. Summary of Late Bronze Age Remains

Tel Michal is one of the few coastal sites that does not show signs of a decline during the transitional period between the Middle and Late Bronze Ages. Despite the catastrophe that razed the settlement at the end of Stratum XVII and severed from it a large mass of its area, not only was the settlement rebuilt in Stratum XVI but considerable effort was invested to restore it to its original size by expanding the

habitable area eastward. Perhaps it was even larger than the MB IIB settlement.

The labor required to construct the LB I earthern ramparts may be estimated as follows: assuming that the cross section of the eastern rampart was 20 m long and 7 m high and that the sloping eastern part was 12 m long with a gradient of 30 degrees, the area of this section would be $8 \times 7 + (12 \times 7)/2 = 98m^2$. Since the length of the eastern rampart was about 70 m, its volume would therefore be about 6,860 m³. If each worker transported and dumped about 1 m³ of earth per day, the rampart could have been erected by 200 workers in about 34 workdays.

NOTES

1. This unit is defined as the upper part of the Dor *kurkar* bed, which consists of a very friable, calcareous sandstone (Bakler 1978: 132–133; see also Chap. 16, where it is called Wingate *kurkar*).

2. In our preliminary calculation, based on a smaller estimated area, the figures came out much lower (Herzog 1980:141–142).

3. The occasional presence of a city gate built into such ramparts does not contradict the thesis that these rampart-surrounded cities were not really fortified. The gates were required to provide daily access into the city on the original surface level. They also gave lateral support to the earthworks on both sides of the gate passage, whereas the gatehouse chambers could be used as guardrooms manned by a limited number of armed men who functioned to keep out undesirable visitors or to protect the palace of the settlement's ruler or chief (Herzog 1976:66–80).

4. This figure supports Na'aman's theory regarding a population decrease in the Sharon between the Middle Bronze Age IIA and IIB (Na'aman 1982:168).

5. Although we believe that the settlement at Tel Michal was established during a late phase of the Middle Bronze Age IIB, we have avoided using the term Middle Bronze Age IIC, mainly because the distinction between phases B and C is not manifest in the ceramic material published so far from any of the coastal sites. A detailed study of this question led Kempinski (1974:140) to conclude that there is no justification for dividing this period into two separate phases.

6. Dothan's assumption is refuted by his own chronology, which attributes the founding of Ashdod to the beginning of Aphosis I's reign, whereas the struggle with the 17th dynasty started only at the *end* of Aphosis's 41-year reign (Dothan 1973:16–17).

7. The research was conducted by Avner Raban and Yoseph Tur-Caspa in December 1979.

8. On tectonic and eustatic changes in the Mediterranean coast of Israel, see Flemming et al. 1978.

REFERENCES

Bakler, N. 1978. Geology of Tel Michal and the Herzliya Coast. *Tel Aviv* 5:131–135.

Dothan, M. 1973. The Foundation of Tel Mor and of Ashdod. *IEJ* 23:1–17.

Dothan, M., and Raban, A. 1980. The Sea Gate of Ancient Akko. *BA* 43:35–39.

Flemming, N. C., Raban, A., and Goetschel, C. 1978. Tectonic and Eustatic Changes on the Mediterranean Coast of Israel in the Last 9000 Years. Pages 33–94 in: *Progress in Underwater Science*, vol. 3. J. C. Gamble and R. A. Yorke, eds. London.

Gophna, R. 1974. *The Settlement of the Coastal Plain of Eretz Israel during the Early Bronze Age.* (Hebrew) Ph.D. dissertation. Tel Aviv University.

Gophna, R. 1977. A Fortified Settlement from the Early Bronze and Middle Bronze II at Tel Poran. (Hebrew) *EI* 13:87–90.

Gophna, R., and Beck, P. 1981. The Rural Aspect of the Settlement Pattern of the Coastal Plain in the Middle Bronze Age II. *Tel Aviv* 8:45–80.

Habachi, L. 1972. *The Second Stela of Ramose and His Struggle against the Hyksos Ruler and His Capital.* Gluckstadt.

Herzog, Z. 1976. *The City Gate in Eretz Israel and Its Neighboring Countries.* (Hebrew) Ph.D. dissertation. Tel Aviv University.

Herzog, Z., ed. 1980. Excavations at Tel Michal 1978–1979: Summary and Conclusions. *Tel Aviv* 7:141–146.

Kaplan, J. 1975. Further Aspects of the Middle Bronze Age II Fortifications in Palestine. *ZDPV* 91:1–17.

Kempinski, A. 1974. *Canaan (Syria-Palestine) during the Last Stage of the MB IIB (1650–1550 B.C.).* (Hebrew with English summary) Ph.D. dissertation. Hebrew University, Jerusalem.

Kochavi, M., Beck, P., and Gophna, R. 1979. Aphek-Antipatris, Tel Poleg, Tel Zeror and Tel Burga: Four Fortified Sites of the Middle Bronze Age IIA in the Sharon Plain. *ZDPV* 95:121–165.

Na'aman, N. 1982. Eretz Israel in the Second Intermediate Period. Pages 161–175 in: *The History of Eretz Israel I.* (Hebrew) Y. Eph'al, ed. Jerusalem.

Neev, D., Bakler, N., Moshkovitz, S., Kaufman, A., Magaritz, M., and Gophna, R. 1973. Recent Faulting along the Mediterranean Coast of Israel. *Nature* 245:254–256.

Prausnitz, M. W. 1975. The Planning of the Middle Bronze Age Town at Achzib and Its Defences. *IEJ* 25:202–210.

5

Bronze Age Pottery (Strata XVII-XV)

by Ora Negbi

The earliest pottery assemblages found at Tel Michal belong to three successive phases of occupation on the high tell during the Middle Bronze Age II (MB IIB), the Late Bronze Age I (LB I), and the Late Bronze Age II (LB II) (see Chap. 4).

5.1. MIDDLE BRONZE AGE II REPERTORY

The only substantial constructions from the first occupational phase are a retaining wall and a glacis in the northwestern sector of the high tell and a brick platform in the western sector. A few MB II sherds were found in a sand fill (Locus 719) laid against the retaining wall (S156) in the northern sector. The brick layers of the platform in the center of the high tell (Loci 782, 911) and the *hamra* layer that served as a glacis in northern Area A (Locus 716) have yielded several fragmentary vessels of the same period. Unfortunately, dwellings of the first occupational phase that stood on the platform were either eroded westward or razed by the people of the second occupational phase (LB I) in order to expand their available living space. These people covered the top of the MB II platform and glacis in the northwest sector with gray fill (Loci 712, 1382), which contained sherds of the first occupational phase. At the same time they removed a large amount of MB II debris to the eastern and southern sectors of the high tell. As a result, the bulk of MB II pottery was not found in proper stratigraphic context but in LB I fills. Of special importance are deposits containing a large quantity of MB II vessels found in alternating layers of fill in the southern (Loci 1556, 1558, 1559, 1560, 1562) and eastern sectors (Loci 1702, 1718). These deposits, sealed by huge accumulations of sand (Loci 971, 1701) piled above them during the filling operation, have not yielded a single sherd of the succeeding occupational phase (LB I). The same situation prevails in the eastern sector of the high tell (Loci 1900, 1903, 1535, 1664, 1665), where fills contain pottery that is diagnostic only to the earliest phase (MB II).

Middle Bronze Age II pottery appears sporadically in the sand accumulation and in occupational debris above it. The few specimens found in these mixed deposits, mainly fills and pits, were for the most part excluded from our study.

5.1.1. Local Wares

Local wares include the following types of vessels:

1. Plain Bowls. Plain bowls with inverted rims are the most common (Fig. 5.1:1–9). The only complete specimen (Fig. 5.1:4) has a convex disk base typical of the MB IIB-C repertory (Amiran 1969:91). The rims of these bowls, however, have their closest counterparts in MB IIC contexts of Shechem (Seger 1974:123, Fig. 4:1, 5–6, Fig. 6:37–42) and Ashdod (Dothan 1973:11, Fig. 6:2–4). Other shallow and deep bowls with either inverted or plain rims (Fig. 5.1:10–12) are less common (Amiran 1969:91, Pl. 26:5). Of special interest is a bowl of coarse and gritty ware decorated on the exterior with horizontal lines in monochrome red (Fig. 5.1:1). The painted decoration is applied on a white slip in a fashion typical of the closing phase of Middle Bronze Age II (Amiran 1969:103; Dothan 1973:13; and see below, 5.2.1.B5b).

2. Carinated Bowls. Bowls of this type appear in several variants, ranging from specimens with everted rims and rounded or moderated carination (Fig. 5.2:1–12) to those having flaring rims with sharp carination (Fig. 5.2:13–24). The majority of bowls (Fig. 5.2:1–15) are common to the MB IIB-C repertory (Amiran 1969:94; *Lachish IV*: 174–180, Bowls Classes B-C). The complete lack of slip and burnishing (Kempinski 1974:74, 109; Dever 1974:45) indicates that they belong to the latest phase of the Middle Bronze Age. Among the bowls of the latter variant are many specimens of thin, well-levigated ware (Fig. 5.2:16–24; see *Lachish IV*: 178, Bowls Class A). In contrast to bowls of the former variants, they are also distinguished by high ring bases or trumpet bases (Fig. 5.2:19, 22–24) and are occasionally classified as chalices or goblets (Amiran 1969:94–95). Pedestal bowls of this distinctive type are diagnostic of the latest MB II assemblages at various sites (Kempinski 1974:54, 110, 113; Dever 1974:45, Fig. 14:3;

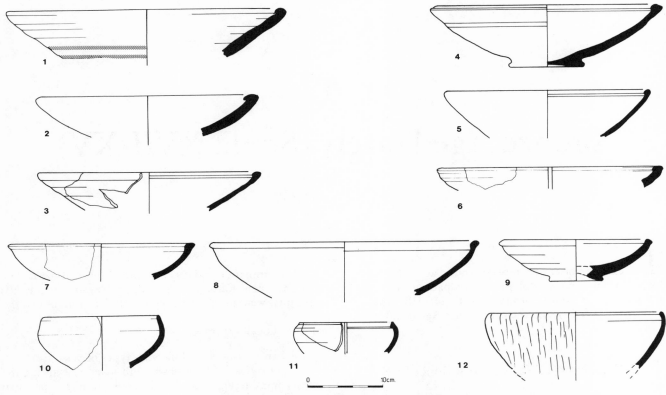

Figure 5.1. Middle Bronze Age II Pottery.

Legend for Fig. 5.1

No.	Type	Reg. No.	Locus	Description
1	Bowl	9739/2	1556	Gray-black (black), small white grits; exterior and interior white slip, red slip.
2	Bowl	9747/1	1558	Brown (brown), small white grits, large gray grits; vertical burnish.
3	Bowl	9797/5	1562	Brown (light brown), small white and gray grits.
4	Bowl	9767/6	1559	Brown (brown), small gray grits; exterior horizontal burnish.
5	Bowl	9782/3	1558	Brown (brown), small white grits.
6	Bowl	10869/1	1718	Brown (gray), small white grits.
7	Bowl	10790/7	1718	Brown (gray), small white grits.
8	Bowl	9782/2	1558	Brown (gray), small white and gray grits.
9	Bowl	9758/1	1559	Brown (gray), small white and gray grits, large white grits.
10	Bowl	10909/1	1718	Brown (brown), small gray grits.
11	Bowl	9758/3	1559	White (light brown), small white and gray grits.
12	Bowl	9764/9	1559	Brown (brown), small white and gray grits; exterior hand burnish.

Seger 1974, Fig. 3:12, 16–18, Fig. 4:21, Fig. 6:29, 31–32). It is noteworthy that the pedestal bowl (Fig. 5.2:23; Pl. 57:1) and one of the carinated bowls (Fig. 5.2:9) were found in the platform in the center of the high tell (Locus 911), and another carinated bowl of the same type is recorded from the *ḥamra* layer of the glacis at the northern end (Locus 716). These bowls are of special importance since they are among the few vessels of the first occupational phase found in proper stratigraphic context at the site. The closest analogy to the carinated bowls appears in well-dated MB IIC contexts from the lowest level of Area G at Ashdod (Dothan 1973:13, Fig. 6:6–7) and the Northwest Gate Area at Shechem (Dever 1974:45, Fig. 14:1–2, 4–5). Con-

sequently, the three bowls found in the platform and the glacis at Tel Michal should date the first occupational phase to Middle Bronze Age IIC.

3. Miniature Bowls. One of the miniature bowls (Fig. 5.2:27) was found in the MB IIC platform (Locus 911) in the center of the high tell, and the other two (Fig. 5.2:25–26) originated in the LB I fill above the platform at the northern end (Locus 712) and below the sand (Locus 1556) in the southern sector of Area A. The bowl in Figure 5.2:26 is a coarse vessel that does not give any chronological clues. The bowls in Figure 5.2:25 and 27, which correspond to larger versions of plain and carinated bowls recovered from the fill in the southern sector of Area A (Figs. 5.1:9;

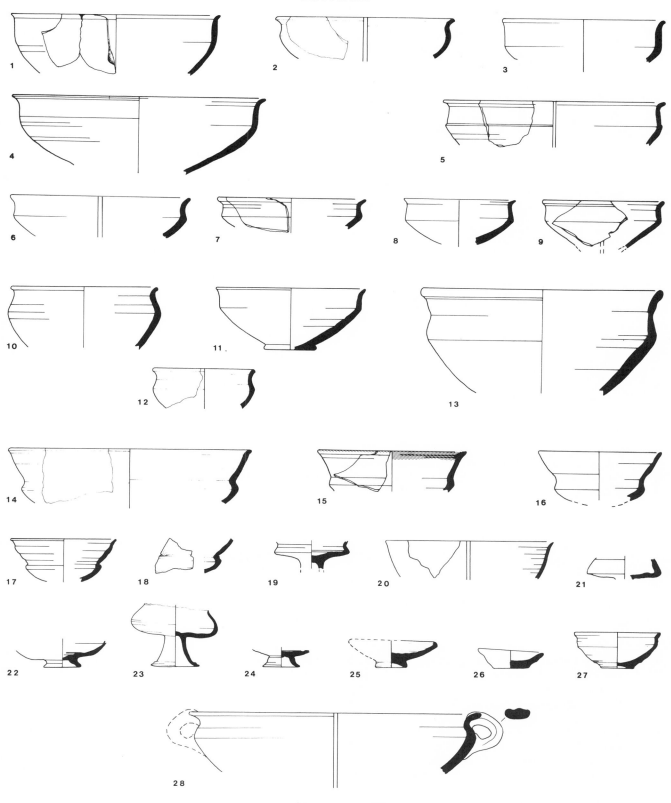

Figure 5.2. Middle Bronze Age II Pottery.

Legend for Fig. 5.2

No.	Type	Reg. No.	Locus	Description
1	Bowl	9758/9	1559	Brown (gray), small white and gray grits.
2	Bowl	10909/2	1718	Brown (gray), small and large white grits.
3	Bowl	9754/1	1558	Brown (gray), small and large white grits.
4	Bowl	9782/7	1558	Brown (black), small white and gray grits, large white grits; interior horizontal burnish.
5	Bowl	9767/1	1559	Brown (gray), small white grits.
6	Bowl	9747/6	1556	Brown (gray), small white and gray grits.
7	Bowl	9791/5	1562	Brown (light gray), small white grits.
8	Bowl	9742/1	1556	Brown (gray), small white and gray grits.
9	Bowl	6040/1	911	Brown (gray), small white grits.
10	Bowl	9764/10	1559	Brown (gray), small white and gray grits; horizontal burnish.
11	Bowl	9796/1	1558	Brown (black), small white and gray grits.
12	Bowl	10790/5	1718	Brown (gray), small gray grits.
13	Bowl	9754/3	1556	Brown (brown), small and large white and gray grits.
14	Bowl	10925/1	1718	Brown-gray (gray), small white grits.
15	Bowl	9781/2	1559	Brown (gray), small white grits; interior horizontal burnish; red line on rim.
16	Bowl	9797/7	1562	Brown-light gray (gray), small white grits.
17	Bowl	9787/9	1559	Brown (gray), small gray grits.
18	Bowl	10821/1	1718	Brown (gray), small white grits.
19	Bowl	9794/3	1562	Brown (brown), small white and gray grits, large white grits.
20	Bowl	9739/3	1556	White (light brown), small white grits.
21	Bowl	9775/2	1559	White (light gray), small white and gray grits.
22	Bowl	9758/2	1559	White (white), small white grits.
23	Bowl	6045/1	911	Yellow (red-brown); horizontal wheel burnish, yellow slip.
24	Bowl	9787/1	1559	Brown (gray), small gray grits.
25	Bowl	8826/1	712	Brown-gray (gray), small white grits.
26	Bowl	9739/1	1556	Brown (gray), small white grits.
27	Bowl	6045/2	911	Brown (gray), small white grits.
28	Krater	9751/1	1556	Brown (gray), small white grits.

5.2:10), appear in MB IIC context elsewhere (Dever 1974:45, Fig. 14:22–23). It is noteworthy that the miniature bowl in Figure 5.2:27 was found in the brickwork of the platform together with a carinated bowl and pedestal bowl (Fig. 5.2:9, 23) that can be safely assigned to Middle Bronze Age IIC.

4. Kraters. The two-handled krater found in the sealed fill in the southern sector of Area A (Fig. 5.2:28) belongs to a well-known type that appeared during the later phase of the Middle Bronze Age (Amiran 1969:99, Pl. 29:7; Kempinski 1974:55, 110, Pl. 3:S39, S41).

5. Cooking Pots. All come from sealed fills in the southern and eastern sectors of the high tell and are distinguished by three types of rims:

(a) *Folded rims* (Fig. 5.3:1–4) are very common at Tel Michal but are comparatively rare at other sites (Amiran 1969:102, Pl. 30:7). Elsewhere, they are recorded mainly from "northern contexts," dating to Middle Bronze Age IIB-C (Kempinski 1974:55, 110, Pls. 5–6:S67, T102; Dever 1974:44, Fig. 13:4; Seger 1974:123, Fig. 3:1).

(b) *Everted rims,* characterized by their inner gutter, are less common (Fig. 5.3:5–7). Rims of this type, which seem to be a throwback to prototypes of the Middle Bronze Age IIA (Amiran 1969:102, Pl. 30:2), became very popular during the Middle Bronze Age IIC, as indicated by parallels from Shechem (Seger 1974:123, Fig. 4:30–31, Fig. 6:3–7) and Ashdod (Dothan 1973:11, Fig. 6:15–16, lowest level in Area G).

(c) *Flaring rims* appear in two variants. Most of them (Fig. 5.3:8–9) belong to handleless pots that predominated during the latter phases of Middle Bronze Age II (Amiran 1969:102, Pl. 30:5; Kempinski 1974:55, Pl. 3:S48, S49) and are especially popular in MB IIC assemblages (Seger 1974:123, Fig. 4:32; Dothan 1973:5, Fig. 3:6–7). A single specimen with a loop handle (Fig. 5.3:10) is a later variant (Amiran 1969:102, Pl. 30:4) diagnostic of "northern contexts" of Middle Bronze Age IIC (Kempinski 1974:110, Pl. 6:T98). The latter pot and its counterparts of the first variant are regarded as ancestors of the more developed flared-rim pots of Late Bronze Age I.

6. Storage Jars. These are represented by simple flaring rims (Fig. 5.3:11–13) and thickened profiled rims (Fig. 5.3:14) characteristic of MB IIB-C assemblages at other sites (Amiran 1969:103; Seger 1974:123, Fig. 5:25, 27, Fig. 6:14). The repertory of Tel Michal also includes rims with an inner gutter (Fig. 5.3:15–16) that are diagnostic to MB IIC contexts elsewhere (Dothan 1973:13, Fig. 6:7; Dever 1974:41, Fig. 13:9, 12; Seger 1974:123, Figs. 5:28, 6:15). Several specimens that have a ridged band at the bottom of the neck (Fig. 5.3:13, 15) or a band with rope decoration on the shoulder (Fig. 5.3:18) recall MB IIB-C parallels from various sites (Amiran 1969:103, Pl. 32:1, 3–4, 9; Seger 1974:123, Fig. 5:14; *Hazor I*: Pl. CXVII:12–14). All the jar fragments illustrated in Figure 5.3:11–16 and 18 came from the sealed fills in the south and east of Area A. However, another body fragment with rope decoration is also

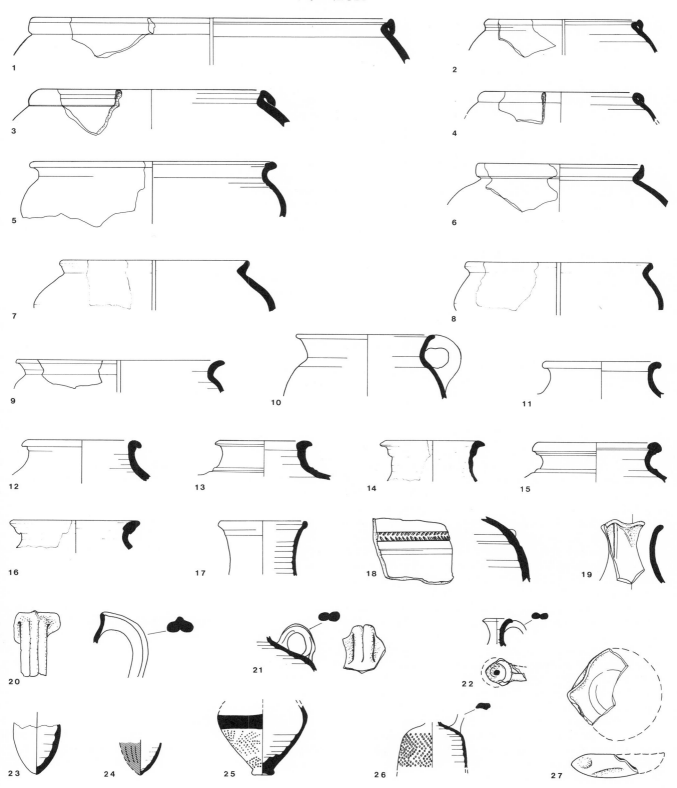

Figure 5.3. Middle Bronze Age II Pottery.

Legend for Fig. 5.3

No.	Type	Reg. No.	Locus	Description
1	Cooking pot	9758/5	1559	Dark brown (black), small white and gray grits, large white grits.
2	Cooking pot	9787/4	1559	Brown (gray), small white and gray grits.
3	Cooking pot	9797/8	1562	Brown (brown), small white and gray grits.
4	Cooking pot	9788/2	1560	Brown (gray), small white and gray grits.
5	Cooking pot	10790/8	1718	Brown (gray), small gray grits.
6	Cooking pot	9767/2	1559	Black (black), small and large white grits.
7	Cooking pot	10821/2	1718	Dark brown (black), small and large white grits.
8	Cooking pot	10809/5	1718	Brown (black), small white grits, large white and gray grits.
9	Cooking pot	9717/8	1556	Brown (black), small white grits.
10	Cooking pot	9797/9	1562	Dark brown (black), small white and gray grits, large white grits.
11	Storage jar	9782/10	1558	Brown (gray), small white grits, large gray grits.
12	Storage jar	9742/5	1556	Brown (gray), white and gray grits, large gray grits.
13	Storage jar	9758/6	1559	Brown (gray), small white and gray grits.
14	Storage jar	8825/3	1382	Orange-brown (orange-brown), small white grits.
15	Storage jar	9791/6	1562	Brown (dark gray), small white and gray grits.
16	Storage jar	8805/5	1382	Brown (gray), small white grits.
17	Jug	9796/3	1558	Light brown (light brown), small white and gray grits, few large white grits.
18	Storage jar	9781/6	1559	Brown (gray), small white grits.
19	Jug	9764/3	1559	Brown (brown), small white grits.
20	Jug	9781/7	1559	Light brown (black), small white and gray grits.
21	Jug	9764/1	1559	Brown (gray), small white and gray grits; hand burnish.
22	Juglet	9767/3	1559	Brown (brown-light gray), small white grits.
23	Juglet	9747/17	1556	Yellow (yellow), small white and gray grits, large gray grits; vertical burnish.
24	Juglet	10790/3	1718	Brown (brown), small white grits; vertical burnish; red-brown slip.
25	Juglet	9781/12	1559	Black (black), small white grits.
26	Juglet	9592/1	1512	Gray (gray), horizontal burnish on shoulder.
27	Lamp	9764/5	1559	Brown (brown), small white grits.

recorded from the sand fill laid against the retaining wall in the northern end of Area A (Locus 719). This fragment may indicate that the MB IIC pottery found in the LB I fill in the eastern and southern sectors corresponds to earliest MB II deposits of the first occupational phase in the western sector.

7. Jugs and Juglets. Although the rims of two jugs (Fig. 5.3:17, 19) provide no chronological clues, the triple handle of another jug (Fig. 5.3:20) recalls MB IIA prototypes (Amiran 1969: Pl. 33:6) and the double shoulder handle of the fourth (Fig. 5.3:21) covers the entire duration of Middle Bronze Age II (Amiran 1969: Pls. 33:7, 34:7; Dothan 1973:13, Fig. 6:14). The main reason for regarding the Tel Michal jugs as products of Middle Bronze Age IIC is the rarity of painting, slip, or burnishing. Among the few fragmentary juglets recorded from the sealed fills in the southern and eastern sectors are the rim of a perfume juglet (Fig. 5.3:22), bases of two dipper juglets (Fig. 5.3:23–24), and a biconical juglet of Tell el-Yahudiyeh ware (Fig. 5.3:25). A cylindrical juglet of the same ware, found out of context in later debris in the center of Area A (Locus 1512 above sand), is illustrated in Figure 5.3:26. The juglet repertory as a whole has certain features diagnostic of the latest phase of Middle Bronze Age II, when there was a tendency to prefer plain juglets over slipped and burnished ones and to replace round-based dipper juglets with pointed-based ones, as demonstrated by Kempinski (1974:

56, 60, 111; see Dothan 1973:13, Fig. 6:13). The two Tell el-Yahudiyeh juglets have their closest parallels in Tomb II at Enkomi, dating to Middle Cypriote III (Amiran 1969:112, 118–120, Pl. 36:19–20; Saltz 1977:59). However, a recent study of this ware indicates that biconical and cylindrical juglets comparable to those of Tel Michal are to be classified as Egyptian types, with a few Syro-Palestinian copies (Kaplan 1980:63, Biconical juglets Type 1 and Cylindrical juglets Type 1). Relying on the conclusive data from Tell ed-Da'ba, it can be assumed that juglets of both types range from Level E/2 to the end of Level D/2, from the late 13th Dynasty to the end of the second Intermediate Period (Bietak 1970:40–41; Kempinski 1974:88–89; Kaplan 1980:70, 72). Later examples of that ware continue into the early 18th Dynasty, as recorded from other sites in Egypt and elsewhere (Kaplan 1980:70; Negbi 1978:147, n. 32; Dothan 1973:13; Amiran 1969:120).

8. Lamps. The fragmentary lamp (Fig. 5.3:27), showing a rather developed pinched mouth, fits well into the chronological horizon of the closing years of the Middle Bronze Age and the opening of the Late Bronze Age (Amiran 1969:190; *Lachish IV*: 184–185, Lamps Classes B-C).

5.1.2. Imported Wares

Imported wares include many fragments of Cypriote vessels, all found in LB I fills, mainly in the southern sector of

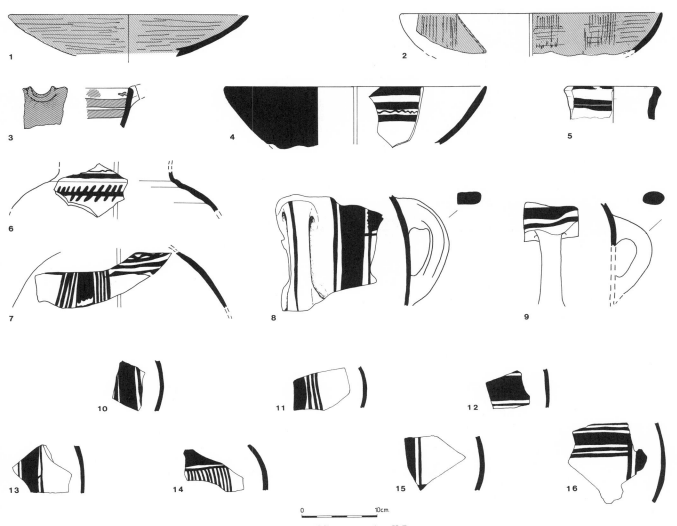

Figure 5.4. Middle Bronze Age II Pottery.

Legend for Fig. 5.4

No.	Type	Reg. No.	Locus	Description
1	Bowl	9764/8	1559	Brown (brown), small brown grits, large white grits; horizontal hand burnish; interior and exterior red slip.
2	Bowl	9742/11	1556	Brown-orange (gray); vertical and horizontal hand burnish; red slip.
3	Bowl	9675/1	1903	Light orange (light orange), small gray grits; exterior red slip; interior red decoration.
4	Bowl	9782/11	1558	White (white), small white grits; exterior black slip; interior black decoration.
5	Amphora	10488/13	1659	Green (green), small white grits; black decoration.
6	Amphora	9787/6	1559	Brown (gray), small gray grits; white slip; black decoration.
7	Amphora	9796/6	1558	White (white); exterior black decoration.
8	Amphora	9797/1	1562	Green (green), small white and gray grits; brown decoration.
9	Amphora	9797/2	1562	(White) white, small gray grits; white slip; black decoration.
10	Amphora	9782/13	1558	White (light), small white grits; black decoration.
11	Amphora	9767/4	1559	Yellow (brown-yellow), small gray grits; black decoration.
12	Amphora	9789/1	1562	White (white-light gray), small white grits; black decoration.
13	Amphora	9791/2	1562	Green (green), small gray grits; black decoration.
14	Amphora	9782/12	1558	Light (light), small white grits; black decoration.
15	Amphora	9791/1	1562	White (light brown), small white and gray grits; black decoration.
16	Amphora	8805/8	1382	Orange (light brown), small white grits; black decoration.

the high tell. They can be classified into three distinctive wares:

1. Red-on-Red. Two bowls with multiple bands painted in matte red inside and out belong to this ware (Fig. 5.4:1–2). Red-on-Red, usually classified as a variant of Red-on-Black ware, is comparatively rare in Cyprus and elsewhere (*SCE IV, 1B*: 118, 228). At Enkomi it appears in Level A, dating from the Middle Cypriote III (*Enkomi I*: 223). An intact bowl of this ware is recorded from Stratum 12 at Tel Mor and can be safely assigned to the closing phase of Middle Bronze Age II (Dothan 1973:8–9, Fig. 4:4).

2. Composite Ware. Included in this ware are a spouted bowl with red-slipped exterior and white-painted interior (Fig. 5.4:3) and a bowl with black-slipped exterior and white-painted interior (Fig. 5.4:4). Composite ware of these two variants (RS/BS + WP III-IV) is diagnostic to the Famagusta district and especially to Kalopsidha, where it appears in Middle Cypriote I-III contexts (*SCE IV, 1B*: 124–126; *Kalopsidha*: 68–69; Artzy et al. 1981:39). Early occurrences of this ware in Israel are recorded from MB IIA contexts at Akko and Megiddo XIIIA (Saltz 1977:57). A later specimen of this ware that originated in Area D at Hazor is assigned to Middle Bronze Age IIB through Late Bronze Age I (*Kalopsidha*: 68; *Hazor I*: Pl. CIV:16).

3. White Painted Ware. A rim, several handles, and many body fragments (Fig. 5.4:5–16) belong to amphorae of White Painted V ware. This ware appears in Cyprus in Middle Cypriote III (Saltz 1977:58) and is well represented in the context of Level A at Enkomi (*Enkomi I*: 223). The large amount of White Painted ware and other Middle Cypriote fabrics at Enkomi in contexts assigned to Level I (*Enkomi I*: 223–224) is probably the result of filling operations that took place in Late Cypriote I. That problem, however, is beyond the scope of the present study. The chronology of White Painted V in Israel is more decisive. A White Painted V krater is recorded from Stratum XI at Megiddo (*Megiddo II*: Pl. 36:3). A complete amphora has recently been found in the MB IIB stratum (Stratum XIII) at Tel Mevorakh (Stern and Saltz 1978:140, No. I), and at least three more fragments of the same type of vessel were uncovered in the MB IIB and MB IIC strata (Strata XIII-XII) at that site (Stern and Saltz 1978:142–143, Nos. II-IV).

5.2. LATE BRONZE AGE REPERTORY

There are comparatively few undisturbed loci containing LB I pottery that belongs to the second occupational phase on the high tell. Pottery of this period appears on fragmentary floors at the northern end (Loci 873, 877) and below LB II debris in the center of the high tell (Loci 1512, 1540, and 1660). Several intact and fragmentary vessels were also found in the accumulation of sand (Locus 971) that seals the layer of early fills in the southern sector (see 5.1 above), as well as on the *ḥamra* layer (Loci 956, 961) laid above the sand to stabilize it.

Late Bronze Age II pottery is recorded mainly from Iron Age fills in the center of the high tell (Loci 1530, 1535, 1653, 1659, and 1661). Since no LB II floors have been

found, it seems likely that they were washed away during the period of abandonment that followed the last phase of Late Bronze Age occupation on the site.

The bulk of LB I-II pottery from Tel Michal, including many intact vessels, was found on the southern slope (Loci 293, 965, 970, 983, 996, 1259, and 1260). It seems likely that at least some of these discarded vessels were piled against the slope in leveling operations carried out there during the Iron Age. No Iron Age pottery has been recorded from the slope, and the repertory as a whole is Late Bronze Age.

Stratigraphically, however, the distinction between LB I and LB II loci turns out to be unsatisfactory in most areas. We therefore have to rely mainly on typological considerations to separate the repertory of each phase. Late Bronze Age sherds from mixed deposits, especially Iron Age and Persian pits, were generally excluded from our study.

5.2.1. Local Wares

The local pottery has been classified into simple and decorated wares.

A. Simple Wares

The repertory of simple wares from Tel Michal includes the following types of vessels:

1. Plain Bowls. Three intact bowls with ring base were found on the southern slope of the tell (Fig. 5.5:4–6). These bowls and fragments of several others (Fig. 5.5:1–3) are characterized by several rim variants: inverted (Fig. 5.5:3–4), thickened (Fig. 5.5:1–2), and plain (Fig. 5.5:5–6). Bowls with inverted rims, predominant in the MB IIC repertory at Tel Michal (Fig. 5.1:1–6), are known to continue during LB I-IIA at other sites (Amiran 1969:125; *Ashdod II-III*: 78, 81, Fig. 31:5–6, Fig. 32:11, Area B, Strata 5–4). One of the thickened rim bowls (Fig. 5.5:1) that came from an LB I deposit in the center of the high tell (Locus 1660) corresponds to the bowls of Class G from Lachish, which prevail in the earliest phase of the Fosse Temple (*Lachish IV*: 181). Other bowls with thickened and plain rims (Fig. 5.5:2, 5–6) are common in the LB II repertory (Amiran 1969:125; cf. *Hazor I*: Pls. CX, CXXV:1–18, Area D, and CXLIII:6–17, Area E).

2. Carinated Bowls. The carinated bowls (Fig. 5.5:7–11) are mainly degenerated MB II types that span the entire duration of the Late Bronze Age (Amiran 1969:125, 129). Since most of them (Fig. 5.5:8–10; Pl. 57:2) came from the southern slope, their date cannot be pinpointed. However, one bowl from the same area (Fig. 5.5:7) was found on the *ḥamra* layer (Locus 956) above the sand and can therefore be safely assigned to Late Bronze Age I. Another bowl (Fig. 5.5:11) distinguished by its high base, which was discovered on an LB I floor at the northern end of the high tell (Locus 877), recalls MB IIC forerunners (cf. Fig. 5.2:22, 24). A fragmentary pedestal bowl, presumably a chalice or a goblet (Fig. 5.5:12), recorded from later debris in the center of the high tell, is of a type current in LB I-II assemblages elsewhere (Amiran 1969:129, 134).

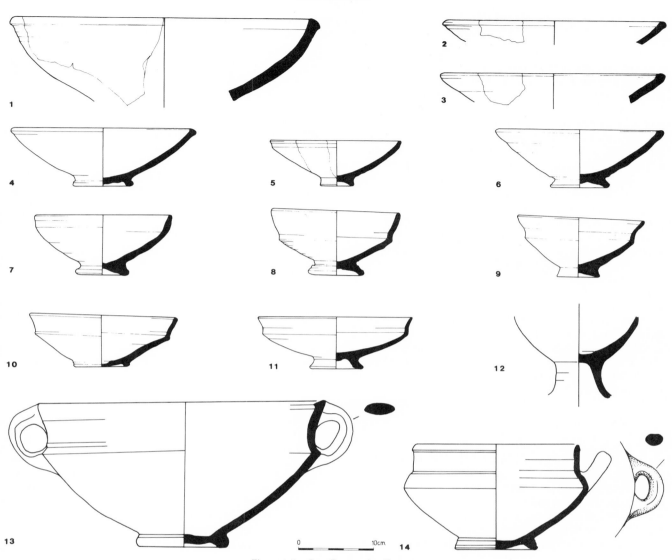

Figure 5.5. Late Bronze Age Pottery.

Legend for Fig. 5.5

No.	Type	Reg. No.	Locus	Description
1	Bowl	10375/1	1660	Brown (gray), small and large white grits.
2	Bowl	10445/1	1653	Orange (black), small white grits.
3	Bowl	9588/1	1512	Brown (black), small gray grits.
4	Bowl	6625/1	970	Brown (brown), small white grits.
5	Bowl	6547/1	965	Brown (light gray), small white and gray grits.
6	Bowl	8430/1	983	Brown (gray), small white and gray grits, large white grits; white slip.
7	Bowl	6526/1	956	Light brown (light brown), small and large white grits.
8	Bowl	6682/1	965	Brown (brown), small and large white grits; white slip.
9	Bowl	6675/1	965	Brown (brown), small and large white and gray grits.
10	Bowl	8431/1	1259	Brown (gray), small white and gray grits.
11	Bowl	5922/1	877	Light brown (light brown), small white and gray grits, large gray grits.
12	Chalice	10461/1	1653	Light brown (black), small white and gray grits.
13	Krater	8473/1	1262	Brown (gray-brown), small white and gray grits.
14	Krater	6471/2	965	Brown (gray), small white and gray grits, large white grits; white slip.

51

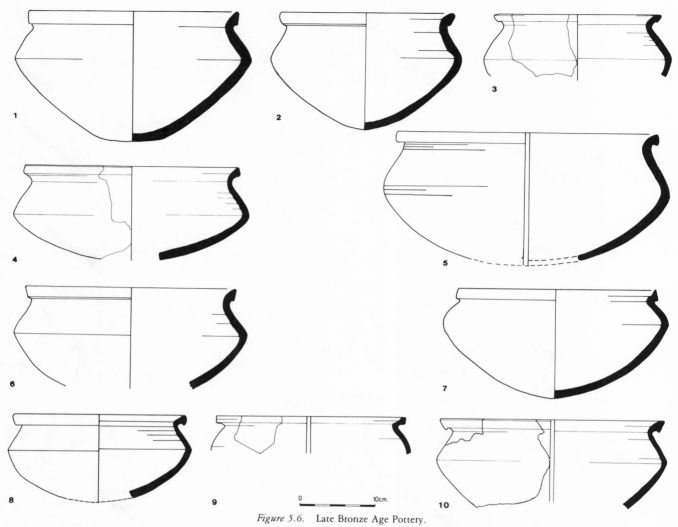

Figure 5.6. Late Bronze Age Pottery.

Legend for Fig. 5.6

No.	Type	Reg. No.	Locus	Description
1	Cooking pot	8431/3	1259	Brown (brown), small white and gray grits, many large white and gray grits.
2	Cooking pot	8431/5	1259	Brown (brown), small and large white grits.
3	Cooking pot	8862/1	873	Black-brown (black), small white and gray grits.
4	Cooking pot	6675/2	965	Brown (brown), small and large white and gray grits.
5	Cooking pot	8481/2	983	Brown (gray), small white and gray grits.
6	Cooking pot	9805/1	983	Brown (black), small and large white grits.
7	Cooking pot	8431/2	1259	Brown (brown), small white grits; large white and gray grits.
8	Cooking pot	5923/1	877	Dark brown (gray), small and large white grits.
9	Cooking pot	10411/1	1661	Brown (gray), small white and gray grits.
10	Cooking pot	8430/2	983	Dark brown (gray), small white and gray grits, large white grits.

3. *Kraters.* One of the two kraters (Fig. 5.5:13; Pl. 57:3) is a common type. The other krater with a single horizontal handle (Fig. 5.5:14; Pl. 57:4) is comparatively rare at other sites, but recalls LB II parallels elsewhere (*Hazor I:* Pl. CXXVII:10, Area D, Stratum 1; *Hazor II:* Pl. CXIX:1, Area C, Stratum 1B). It has already been noted that the horizontally placed handles of this type of krater seem to have been inspired by Cypriote pottery (Epstein 1966:3; Amiran 1969:134). The typological affinities of the krater from Tel Michal to decorated specimens of the same type (Fig. 5.8:11–14; Pl. 57:5) may support this assumption (see Section 5.2.1.B4 below).

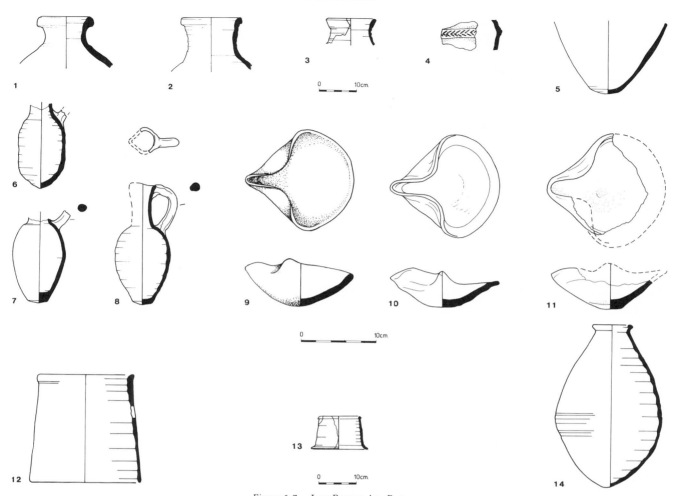

Figure 5.7. Late Bronze Age Pottery.

Legend for Fig. 5.7

No.	Type	Reg. No.	Locus	Description
1	Storage jar	8410/2	1259	Brown (black), small and large white grits.
2	Storage jar	8410/3	1259	Light brown (black), small white grits; few large white grits.
3	Storage jar	10444/2	1659	Light brown (gray), small white and gray grits.
4	Storage jar	9665/1	1540	Brown (black), small white and gray grits.
5	Storage jar	5924/1	877	Brown (gray), small white and gray grits; large white grits.
6	Juglet	6534/1	965	Brown (brown), small white and gray grits; few large white grits.
7	Juglet	5429/1	706	Buff (buff), small white grits.
8	Juglet	6506/1	965	Green (green), small gray grits.
9	Lamp	9709/1	971	Brown, small white grits.
10	Lamp	6458/1	961	Dark brown (brown-gray), small white and gray grits.
11	Lamp	6678/1	983	Light brown (light brown), small white grits.
12	Stand	6485/1	965	Brown (black), small white and gray grits; large white grits.
13	Stand	9596/2	1535	Brown (black), small white and gray grits.
14	Jar	9633/1	1540	Red (red), small white and gray grits.

4. Cooking Pots. The majority of the cooking pots have everted, triangular rims (Fig. 5.6:1–6; Pl. 57:8) that were most common during the entire Late Bronze Age (Amiran 1969:135–140). Several triangular rims with an inner gutter (Fig. 5.6:7–9; Pl. 57:6–7) that continue the tradition of their MB IIC forerunners (Fig. 5.3:6–7) are diagnostic of

Late Bronze Age I (*Hazor I*: Pl. CXXXIX:3, Area E; *Ashdod II–III*: 79, Fig. 31:12, Area B, Stratum 5). A rim of the latest pot in the series (Fig. 5.6:10) has the somewhat longer triangle typical of the last phase of Late Bronze Age II (Amiran 1969:140).

A selection of cooking pots from the southern slope,

which yielded many specimens (Fig. 5.6:1–2, 4–7), corresponds well with the cooking pots (Fig. 5.6:3, 8–9; Pl. 57:6) recorded from LB I floors at the northern end (Loci 873, 877) and the Iron Age fill in the center (Locus 1661) of the high tell.

5. Storage Jars. The rims of three storage jars—two from the southern slope (Fig. 5.7:1–2) and a third from the Iron Age fill in the center (Fig. 5.7:3)—lack any features that would help to date them precisely. A round base (Fig. 5.7:5) found on an LB I floor at the northern end (Locus 877) belongs to a "Canaanite commercial jar" of a type well known in the LB I repertory (Amiran 1969:140–141). A body sherd with a band of rope decoration (Fig. 5.7:4) found below LB II debris in the center of the high tell (Locus 1540) recalls MB II forerunners (Fig. 5.3:18) and can safely be assigned to Late Bronze Age I (cf. *Hazor I*: Pl. CXXIV:10–12).

6. Juglets. Two dipper juglets were found on the southern slope (Fig. 5.7:6, 8; Pl. 57:10). The shortened body and slightly pointed base of the first one recalls LB I–IIA parallels from other sites (Amiran 1969:146; *Hazor I*: Pl. CXXXI:22; *Hazor III-IV*: Pls. CCLXVI:3, CCLXXV:3). The second juglet, distinguished by an elongated neck and flattened base, recalls some juglets from the lower level of Stratum V at Tell Abu Hawam (*TAH*: 43, No. 260); Strata IX-VIII at Megiddo (*Megiddo II*: Pl. 50:15), and Stratum IB at Hazor (*Hazor II*: Pl. CXXXI:21). A third juglet was found in the fill of Locus 706 in the northern end of the high tell (Fig. 5.7:7).

7. Lamps. An intact lamp (Fig. 5.7:9) was found in the sand (Locus 971) that sealed the huge layers of fill in the southern sector. This lamp, with its pinched mouth and signs of flattened rim, is much more developed than its MB IIC forerunner recovered from the fill below it (Fig. 5.3:27). Lamps of this type are known from Structures I-II in the Fosse Temple at Lachish (*Lachish IV*: 184, Lamps Class D, Pl. 73) and LB I-IIA assemblages at Hazor (*Hazor I*: Pl. XLII:1–4; *Hazor II*: Pl. CXXXV:1–3; *Hazor III-IV*: Pl. CCLXVII:1–4). Another intact lamp and fragments of a third one found on the slope in the same area (Fig. 5.7:10–11) are the latest in the series. Lamps of this type prevail in Structures II-III of the Fosse Temple at Lachish (*Lachish IV*: 186, Lamps Class E, Pl. 73) and can safely be assigned to the Late Bronze Age IIA-B (Amiran 1969:190).

8. Stands. Two stands were found. The first (Fig. 5.7:12), which came from the southern slope (Locus 965), is fenestrated, and the second (Fig. 5.7:13), found in LB II debris (Locus 1535), is of the plain "squat" type. Stands of both variants did not change significantly over the ages and hence cannot be conclusively dated (cf. *Megiddo II*: Pl. 47:17, Stratum X, Pl. 55:17–18, Stratum IX).

9. Miscellaneous Vessels. A complete jar of Egyptian shape (Fig. 5.7:14; Pl. 57:12) discovered in the ash fill below LB II debris (Locus 1540) seems to belong to Late Bronze Age I. It is difficult to date it with precision on the basis of typological data, since tall and handleless jars of this type range from the 12th to the 18th dynasties in Egypt (Kelley 1976: Pls. 40:6, 42:5–6, 44:4, 45:5, 12th Dynasty;

Pls. 47:7, 48:5, Second Intermediate Period; Pls. 57:4, 58:1, early 18th Dynasty). A good parallel for the Tel Michal specimen is recorded from Tomb Z 330 at Zawyet el-Aryan, which dates from the reign of Thutmosis III (Merrillees 1968:14, Pl. XXVII). Amiran (1969:187) has pointed out that Egyptian imports are quite rare in Israel in the Late Bronze Age. The material and technique of the jar from Tel Michal, in comparison with counterparts from Megiddo (*Megiddo Tombs*, Pl. 57:9; *Megiddo II*, Pl. 65:1–2), do not exclude the possibility of local manufacture.

B. Decorated Wares

A large quantity of painted pottery was found at Tel Michal. In most cases the decoration is applied in two colors, generally red and black. However, only four fragments are bona fide Bichrome ware; all the other vessels are of coarser fabric.

Chemical and petrographic analyses have indicated that the coarse painted ware and the Bichrome ware are two distinctive groups. The first has been designated as "Local" and the second as "Foreign" (see Chaps. 24a and 24b). The latter ware is therefore treated together with the imported pottery (see 5.2.2.A1 below). The local ware includes the following types of vessels:

1. Plain Bowls. Two intact bowls found on the southern slope have string-cut bases (Fig. 5.8:1–2). The first (Fig. 5.8:1), which corresponds to an undecorated specimen from Tel Michal (Fig. 5.5:5), is painted inside with black and red lines. The second bowl (Fig. 5.8:2), distinguished by a red-painted rim, recalls undecorated specimens from LB I-IIA assemblages elsewhere (*Ashdod II-III*: 81, Pl. 32:6, Area B, Stratum 4; *Lachish II*: Pl. XXXVII:13–14, Fosse Temple II; *Hazor I*: Pl. CXLIII:3–4, Area E, LB II; *Hazor III-IV*: Pl. CCLXII:2–11, Area H, Stratum 2). Fragments of larger bowls (Fig. 5.8:4–6) decorated in the same fashion are also related to undecorated vessels from the site (Fig. 5.5:1–2). One of these fragments (Fig. 5.8:5), which came from sand sealing the early fills in the southern slope, might belong to the upper part of a chalice. Decorated bowls and chalices are recorded from LB I-IIA assemblages at other sites (Amiran 1969:125, Pl. 38:8; *Ashdod II-III*: 81, Fig. 31:7, Area B, Stratum 5; *Lachish II*, Pl. XLVI:207, Fosse Temple II; *Megiddo II*: Pl. 61:17, Stratum VIII). Of special interest is a fragment of a slipped and burnished bowl (Fig. 5.8:3) decorated on the inside with wavy and straight lines in monochrome black. It seems likely that this fragment represents a coarse version of Chocolate-on-White ware (Amiran 1969:158–159, Photo 150, Pl. 49:5).[1]

2. Carinated Bowls. Only two decorated bowls of this type have been found. One of them (Fig. 5.8:7) has red and black decoration inside and out. The other (Fig. 5.8:8) is decorated with a single line in monochrome red on the outside. The first bowl, which corresponds to undecorated forerunners found in MB IIC contexts at Tel Michal (cf. Fig. 5.2:14–15), was found on an LB floor at the northern end of the high tell (Locus 877). Parallels from LB I contexts elsewhere (*Hazor III-IV*: Pl. CCLXIII:36, Area H, Stratum

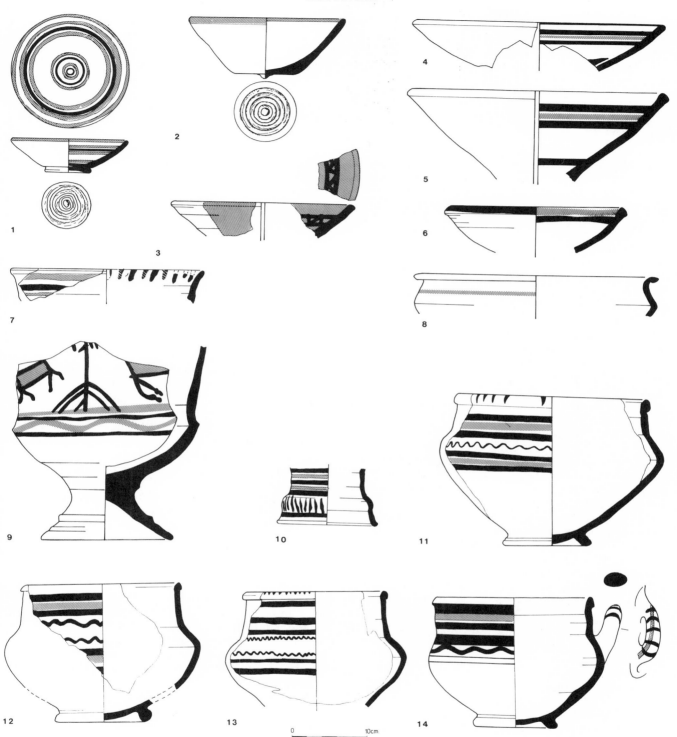

Figure 5.8. Late Bronze Age Pottery.

Legend for Fig. 5.8

No.	Type	Reg. No.	Locus	Description
1	Bowl	9800/1	983	White (white), small gray grits; red and black decoration.
2	Bowl	9800/2	983	Brown (gray), small white and gray grits, large white grits; red decoration.
3	Bowl	6493/3	965	Brown (light brown), small white and gray grits, large white grits; horizontal burnish; red slip; brown decoration.
4	Bowl	6684/1	996	Brown (brown), small white and gray grits, large white grits; red and black decoration.
5	Bowl	9712/1	971	Brown-red (brown), small and large white grits; red and black decoration.
6	Bowl	6625/2	970	Brown (gray), small white grits; black and red decoration.
7	Bowl	5903/1	885	Brown (brown-gray); brown and black decoration.
8	Bowl	6748/2	971	Brown (brown), small white and gray grits; white slip; red decoration.
9	Goblet	9800/5	983	Brown (brown-gray); black and red decoration.
10	Goblet	6677/1	965	Brown (brown), small white and gray grits; red and black decoration.
11	Krater	6662/1	956	Brown (brown-gray), small and large white and gray grits; white wash; red and black decoration.
12	Krater	6682/6	965	Brown (brown-gray), small white and gray grits, large white and black grits; white wash; black and red decoration.
13	Krater	6485/2	965	Light brown-cream (light brown), small gray grits; white slip; black and red decoration.
14	Krater	8431/4	1259	Brown (gray), small white and gray grits, large white grits; white slip; red and black decoration.

2) seem to confirm that date. The second bowl, characterized by white slip inside and out, looks like a coarse imitation of Chocolate-on-White ware (cf. Eisenberg 1976:108, Pl. A, Tel Kittan, LB I). Since this bowl originated in the sand deposit that seals the layers of fill in the southern sector of the high tell (Locus 971), it can safely be assigned to Late Bronze Age I.

3. Goblets. The southern slope has yielded one goblet whose uppermost part is missing as well as a trumpet base of another goblet. The tree and pair of quadrupeds painted in red and black on the body of the first goblet (Fig. 5.8:9) appear in the LB I repertory of Bichrome ware (Epstein 1966:40–53). The evolution of the tree (palm?) and quadruped motif (ibexes) is best exemplified in the successive structures of the Fosse Temple at Lachish (*Lachish II*: Pl. XLVII:229, 240; *Lachish IV*: 219). Relying on the evidence from Lachish and other sites, it is assumed that the antithetic arrangement is characteristic of Late Bronze Age II rather than I (Amiran 1969:161; *Ashdod II-III*: 83, Fig. 35:16; Stern 1976:111, Pl. B; Epstein 1966:140–142). The undecorated trumpet base of this goblet seems also to accord with the data gained from Lachish, where the fashion of decorating bases prevails in Structure I of the Fosse Temple and seems to disappear in the later structures (*Lachish II*: Pl. LXVII:222). The trumpet base of the second Tel Michal goblet (Fig. 5.8:10) has red and black lines painted on its unslipped surface and can therefore be assigned to Late Bronze Age I. Bases decorated in the same fashion are recorded among goblets of Bichrome ware (Epstein 1966:19), but they are more common in the repertory of the coarse, local ware (Amiran 1969:129, Pl. 40:2; *Lachish II*: Pl. XLVII:222–223).

4. Kraters. Kraters are the most distinctive vessels in the decorated repertory of Tel Michal. Their decoration consists of alternating wavy and straight lines in red and black (in several cases only reddish brown is discernible), either painted on a thin, whitish slip or on the plain, bare surface.

One krater (Fig. 5.8:14) that can certainly be reconstructed as having a single horizontal handle on the shoulder recalls an undecorated specimen of this type (Fig. 5.5:14). The fragmentary condition of the other three kraters does not allow for complete reconstruction (Fig. 5.8:11–13; Pl. 57:5). However, because of their similarity in shape and decoration to the first krater, it can be assumed that they had a single handle placed in the same fashion. Compared with the two-handled kraters, which predominate in the Bichrome ware repertory (Epstein 1966:3, 13–15, Pls. IV-V, Krater type A1 [a]), the one-handled type is relatively rare (Epstein 1966:3, 16, Pl. VI, Krater type A1 [b]). Decoration of the former type consists solely of geometric designs, mostly spoked wheels (Epstein 1966:58, Pl. VI:1–4) and, in a few cases, alternating triangles and straight bands on the shoulder (Epstein 1966:68, Pl. VI:5–6). Simple decorations of horizontal lines in red and black appear on a fragment of a single-handled krater from Sépulture I at Minet el-Beida dating to Ugarit Récent I (*Ugaritica II*: Fig. 54:15). Unlike its Bichrome ware counterparts, the decoration of the Minet el-Beida fragment is painted on unburnished white slip. In this respect it is close in style and execution to the kraters from Tel Michal.

Distribution of decorated kraters in the Fosse Temple at Lachish shows that the type with a single horizontal handle appears only in Structure I (*Lachish II*: 79). Two kraters of this variant (*Lachish II*: Pl. XLIX:253–254), regarded by Tufnell as "local versions and imitations of Bichrome forms" (*Lachish IV*: 219), are painted on the bare surface. Amiran notes that the first of these, decorated with lattice panels, "is related in shape and decoration to the Bichrome Style and should perhaps be considered as a crude imitation of this style" (Amiran 1969:134, Pl. 41:3). The second krater is decorated with an hourglass motif, undoubtedly borrowed from the Bichrome ware repertory (Epstein 1966:66–67). The simple pattern of straight and wavy lines is recorded from other kraters of local ware from the Fosse

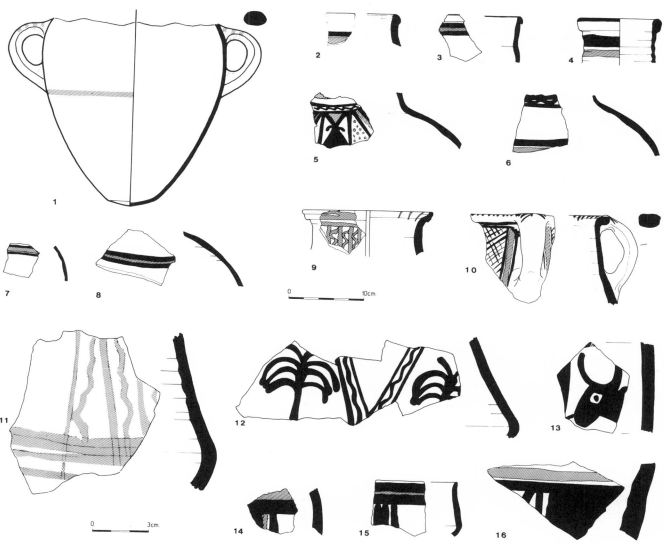

Figure 5.9. Late Bronze Age Pottery.

Legend for Fig. 5.9

No.	Type	Reg. No.	Locus	Description
1	Storage jar	508/4	293	Brown-red (brown-red), small white and gray grits; red and black decoration.
2	Storage jar	6471/5	965	Brown (light brown-gray), small white and gray grits; white wash; red and black decoration.
3	Storage jar	6542/2	956	Brown-orange (brown), many small white grits, large white grits; red and black decoration.
4	Storage jar	6542/1	956	Brown (brown), small white and gray grits; black and red decoration.
5	Storage jar	6520/1	965	Brown (black); red and black decoration.
6	Storage jar	6471/4	965	Light brown (light brown), small white grits; red and black decoration.
7	Storage jar	8431/8	1259	Orange (brown-orange), small white and gray grits; red and black decoration.
8	Storage jar	5905/2	877	Light brown (light brown), small white grits; red and black decoration.
9	Jug	6488/1	961	Brown (brown-gray), small white and gray grits; red decoration.
10	Jug	6547/4	956	Brown (gray), small white grits; red and black decoration.
11	Jug	9806/1	985	Brown (brown), small white and gray grits; red decoration.
12	Jug	6543/1	983	Brown (black-gray), small white and gray grits; black decoration.
13	Krater	9811/1	961	Brown (light brown); red and black decoration.
14	Jug	8414/1	1260	Light brown; black and red decoration.
15	Bowl	6631/1	956	White (white); horizontal burnish; black and red decoration.
16	Jug	8419/1	996	Yellow (yellow); black and red decoration.

Temple at Lachish. A fragment from Pit 210, attributed to Structure I or II (*Lachish II*: 90, Pl. LXII:8), and two handleless kraters from Structure II (*Lachish II*: Pl. XLIX: 261–262) are decorated in that fashion. Relying on the occurrence of the single horizontal handle at Lachish and Minet el-Beida, it seems likely that the Tel Michal kraters can be assigned to Late Bronze Age I rather than IIA. The fragments of three kraters from Tel Michal (Fig. 5.8:12–14) were found on the southern slope, and their date is inconclusive. The fragments of the fourth one (Fig. 5.8:11) came from the *ḥamra* layer (Locus 956) laid over the sand in Late Bronze Age I. Since the four kraters are closely related in both shape and decoration, it is tempting to regard them as products of the same workshop and to date them accordingly.

5. Storage Jars. Various fragments can be attributed to the type of decorated vessels designated by Amiran as "domestic jars" (Amiran 1969:142–143). The decoration, painted in red and black on white slip or smoothed surface, consists of three main elements: horizontal lines on rim, neck, and shoulder (Figs. 5.9:2–4, 6–8), sometimes also on the body below the handles (Fig. 5.9:1; Pl. 57:11); alternating straight and wavy lines, appearing horizontally at the bottom of the neck (Fig. 5.9:5–6) or vertically on the shoulder; and a series of metopes on the shoulder, with an hourglass and dot-filled triangle design (Fig. 5.9:5).

(a) *Straight-line decoration:* "Domestic jars" decorated with a series of horizontal lines are diagnostic to LB I contexts in Israel (Amiran 1969:142, Pl. 44:2; *Hazor II*: Pl. CXVI:28; *Hazor III-IV*: Pl. CCXL:6). Jars decorated in this fashion have been assigned by Epstein to the "Bichrome Style" (Epstein 1966:17, Pl. VIII:3–4, Jar Types B1 [b], C), in spite of the fact that they lack the distinctive burnished slip of that ware. Decorated rims, necks, and body sherds from jars of the same type have recently been published from Ugarit, where they are dated to Ugarit Récent 2/3 (Courtois 1978:236–237, Fig. 12:7–9, 16). Earlier specimens from the same site, dated to Ugarit Récent 1/2, include intact and fragmentary jars that have been designated as "*grandes céramiques bicolores locales*" (Courtois 1978: 238–239, Fig. 13:1–2, 5).

Most of the fragments from Tel Michal came from the southern slope (Fig. 5.9:1–2, 7), and their date is therefore inconclusive. However, two rims (Fig. 5.9:3–4) found on the *ḥamra* layer above the sand on the southern slope (Locus 956) and a body fragment (Fig. 5.9:8) recovered from a fragmentary floor at the northern end of the high tell (Locus 877) can safely be ascribed to Late Bronze Age I.

(b) *Straight- and wavy-line decoration:* This pattern does not occur on jars of Bichrome ware (Epstein 1966:77–81). A jar bearing the pattern is recorded from the repertory of Chocolate-on-White (Amiran 1969:159, Photo 156). The latter, however, is painted in monochrome reddish brown on the whitish, burnished slip diagnostic of that ware.

Jar fragments from Tel Michal (Fig. 5.9:5–6) have the closest parallels in the repertory of "*grandes céramiques bicolores locales*" from Ugarit (Courtois 1978:238–239, Fig.

13:5) and "domestic jars" from Hazor (*Hazor I*: Pls. LXXVI:10; XCVII:12) that prevails at both sites during the initial phase of the Late Bronze Age (*Ugaritica II*: Figs. 50:19, 75:19; Courtois 1978:216–217, Fig. 7:7; *Hazor I*: Pl. CXLI:12–13). There are indications that jars of this type were found in Israel during the closing phase of Middle Bronze Age II. Of special interest are intact jars from Megiddo (*Megiddo II*: Pl. 43:2, Tomb 3046, assigned to Stratum X) and Tell el-ʿAjjul (Amiran 1969:102–103, Photo 103), both of which belong to that period. The latter jars differ from their LB successors in the density of their patterns and the zones to which their white slip was applied. The decoration, a series of alternating straight and wavy lines in red and black, forms a wide band on the shoulder. The slip covers only the upper half of the vessel, leaving the lower, undecorated half unslipped.

White-slipped fragments of closed vessels (jars and jugs) decorated with straight and wavy lines are recorded also from MB IIC contexts at Shechem (Toombs and Wright 1963:51, 60, Fig. 26; Seger 1974:122, Fig. 3:25–26) and Ashdod (Dothan 1973:13, Fig. 7:4). Unlike Ashdod specimens, Shechem fragments are painted in monochrome brown. In that respect they bear certain stylistic affinities to jars and jugs of Chocolate-on-White ware (Amiran 1969:159, Photos 152, 156, Pl. 49:8). Seger (1974:130) has already demonstrated that previous assumptions claiming the Shechem fragments to be ancestors of Bichrome ware (*Shechem*: 76) are untenable. Since there is a consensus that Chocolate-on-White ware appears in Israel at the end of the Middle Bronze Age (Amiran 1969:159; Dothan 1973:13, Fig. 6:8; Seger 1974:123–130, Fig. 4:3, 11, 35, Fig. 6:8–9; Dever 1974:45, Fig. 14:9), it seems more likely that the Shechem fragments are coarser versions of the Chocolate-on-White ware fragments. The straight- and wavy-lined vessels from Tel Michal (Fig. 5.9:5–6) from the southern slope (Locus 965) lack a proper archaeological context. However, since no pottery diagnostic of the Middle Bronze Age is recorded from that area, they can safely be assigned to the Late Bronze Age. Based on analogies from Ugarit and Hazor (discussed above), it seems likely that they belong to Late Bronze Age I rather than II.

(c) *Metope-style decoration:* The metope decoration on the shoulder fragment from Tel Michal (Fig. 5.9:5) is unknown among jars of Bichrome ware and rarely appears on "domestic jars" (Amiran 1969:143). An amphoriskos of Chocolate-on-White ware from Tell el-Farʿah (N) has a metope consisting of an hourglass motif enclosed by dot-filled triglyphs on the shoulder (Amiran 1969:159, Photo 154, Pl. 49:10). Tell el-ʿAjjul has yielded a jar fragment of the same ware, bearing an hourglass and a dot-filled triangle similar to those depicted on the fragment from Tel Michal (*AG III*: Pl. XLIII:57, City II). In contrast to jars, however, these motifs are quite popular on other types of Bichrome vessels (Epstein 1966:66–67, 70–71; Amiran 1969:154; Stern 1976:111, Pl. B). There is no doubt that Cypriote Bichrome ware (see 5.2.2.A1) had a direct impact on certain decorative elements of Chocolate-on-White and other painted wares of local fabrics at the end of the Middle

Bronze Age and the beginning of the Late Bronze Age. On the other hand, it has been demonstrated elsewhere that certain types of Cypriote vessels bear distinctive Near Eastern shapes (Stern and Saltz 1978:142). This phenomenon is best exemplified by White Painted V amphorae (cf. Fig. 5.4:5–9 with Stern and Saltz 1978: Figs. 2–3), which seem to borrow their form from MB II forerunners of the "Canaanite commercial jars" (Amiran 1969:103, 140–141, Pls. 32:1–2).

6. Jugs. Three decorated fragments (Fig. 5.9:9–11) probably belong to biconical jugs, common in the local repertory during the Late Bronze Age. One fragment with a loop handle from rim to shoulder (Fig. 5.9:10) can be assigned to a distinctive type of biconical jug that appears in LB assemblages elsewhere (Amiran 1969:147). A metope of lattice pattern painted in red and black on its neck recalls an elaborate jug of the same type from Ugarit dating to the late 14th-early 13th centuries B.C.E. (Courtois 1978:232, Fig. 10:1). The fragments from Tel Michal, which came from the southern slope, are undated but seem to fit well into the chronological framework of Late Bronze Age II. Two other fragments (Fig. 5.9:9, 11) are decorated in monochrome red in a pattern of alternating straight and wavy lines placed vertically on both neck and shoulder. This pattern, occasionally applied to "domestic jars" and jugs of the previous type (Amiran 1969: Pl. 47:10; *Megiddo Tombs*: Pl. 55:1, Tomb 4; Courtois 1969: Fig. 4:C, Tomb 4253), prevails mainly on biconical jugs with shoulder handles (Amiran 1969:146, Pl. 47:1–2, 6–7; *Lachish II*: Pl. XLIX:260, Fosse Temple II). The best parallels for the Tel Michal fragments are the specimens with monochrome decoration from Hazor (*Hazor II*: Pl. CXX:15, Area C, Stratum IB; Pl. CXXXIV:8, 10–11, Area F, Stratum IB), Megiddo (*Megiddo Tombs*: Pl. 16:13, Tomb 989A1), and Ashdod (*Ashdod II-III*: 82, Fig. 34:5–7, Area D, Stratum 4; Fig. 36:7 is an unstratified specimen assigned to Stratum 2) dating to Late Bronze Age I-IIA. The two fragmentary jugs from Tel Michal should be dated accordingly. Since the body fragment (Fig. 5.9:11) originated on the southern slope, it is impossible to know whether it belongs to Late Bronze Age I or IIA, but the rim fragment (Fig. 5.9:9) found on the *ḥamra* layer above the sand from the same area (Locus 961) can be safely ascribed to Late Bronze Age I.

7. Miscellaneous Fragments. A shoulder fragment of a biconical krater or jug is decorated in monochrome black (Fig. 5.9:12) with elaborate palm trees enclosed between triglyphs of wavy and straight lines. The fragment seems to represent a late and somewhat degenerated version of the "palm-tree and ibex motif" (Amiran 1969:161–162). In contrast to the decorated goblet discussed above (Fig. 5.8:9), the trees of this fragment appear alone without quadrupeds. In spite of the fact that the fragment was found out of context on the southern slope (Loci 970, 983), it is undoubtedly of LB II horizon. Based on the evolution of the palm-tree motif in the Fosse Temple at Lachish, it seems to fit well into the 13th century B.C.E. (*Lachish II*: Pls. LXI:7, XLVIII:248–250, Structure III).

5.2.2. Imported Wares

The imported pottery of the Late Bronze Age has been classified into Cypriote and Aegean wares.

A. Cypriote Wares

A few intact vessels and many fragments belonging to the following wares were found at Tel Michal:

1. Bichrome Ware. Only four fragments from Tel Michal are of Bichrome ware; according to chemical and petrographic analyses, three of them may safely be designated as Cypriote imports (see 5.2.1.B above; Chap. 24a, Group 3). This finding accords with neutron activation analyses from other sites, indicating that the bulk of Bichrome ware originated in eastern Cyprus (Artzy et al. 1976:20).

All fragments of Bichrome ware from Tel Michal were found in the southern sector of the high tell. Three of them (Fig. 5.9:13–14, 16) came from the southern slope and cannot be dated with precision, but the fourth sherd (Fig. 5.9:15), uncovered on the *ḥamra* layer above the sand (Locus 956), can safely be assigned to Late Bronze Age I. This rim is decorated in a geometric pattern belonging to a well-known type of hemispheric bowl with a circular, horizontal handle (Epstein 1966:18, Pl. VII:10–13, Bowls Type B1(a); Amiran 1969:125, Pl. 48:2; *Enkomi I*: 227; *Enkomi III*: Pl. 58:1, Level 1A). The three sherds from the slope are tiny body fragments. Two of them (Fig. 5.9:14, 16) decorated with framed panels probably came from jugs or kraters (Epstein 1966:81–82). The bull's head portrayed on the third fragment (Fig. 5.9:13; Pl. 58:8) recalls the bull on a krater from Tel Nagila (Amiran and Eitan 1964:227, Fig. 5, Pl. 45), but it has its closest counterpart on a krater fragment from Tell el-'Ajjul (Epstein 1966:45–46, Fig. 3:7). Although the body of the Tel Michal bull is missing, it shares two features with the Tell el-'Ajjul bull: the eyes of both are portrayed by a black dot set in a small reserved circle and the horns of both are bow shaped. The krater from Tel Nagila is assigned to Late Bronze Age I (Amiran and Eitan 1964:223), and it seems likely that those of Tell el-'Ajjul and Tel Michal belong to the same period.[2]

2. White Slip Ware. The repertory of White Slip I-II from Tel Michal encompasses the main styles of this ware on Cyprus as classified by Popham (*Kalopsidha*: 95).[3] Several White Slip I bowls (Fig. 5.10:1–2, 4; Pl. 58:2–4) belong to the Bichrome variety of "framed wavy-line" style (*Kalopsidha*: 95, WS I: Type I). Others (Fig. 5.10:3, 6) are of the "framed row of lozenges" and "parallel line" styles (*Kalopsidha*: 95, WS I: Types II, V). One bowl (Fig. 5.10:5; Pl. 58:5) of the "ladder pattern with lozenges" style (*Kalopsidha*: 95, WS I: Type IV) is occasionally designated as transitional White Slip I/II or White Slip IIA (*Ayios Iakovos*: 22, 284). The thin and glossy fabric of our bowl, however, is diagnostic to White Slip I rather than to White Slip II (*Kalopsidha*: 96).

A fragment of a White Slip II bowl (Fig. 5.10:9) belongs to the "framed line-dot" style (*Kalopsidha*: 96, WS II: Type I) and two others (Fig. 5.10:7–8; Pl. 58:6) to the "framed hooked-line" style (*Kalopsidha*: 96, WS II: Type II). Most

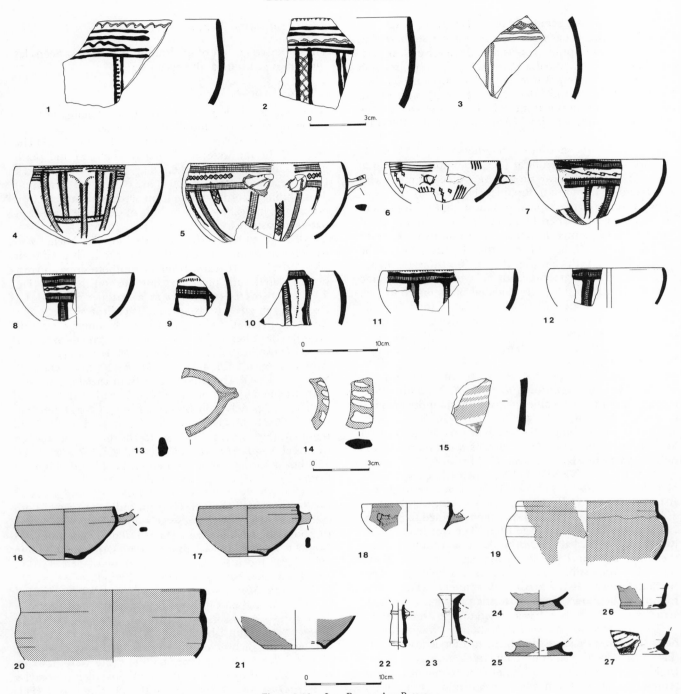

Figure 5.10. Late Bronze Age Pottery.

of the White Slip II bowls from Tel Michal are of the "ladder pattern" style (*Kalopsidha*: 96, WS II: Type III), including the "hanging dot" (Fig. 5.10:10) and the "plain ladder" (Fig. 5.10:11–12) varieties.

Based on typological data, it appears that the White Slip ware of Tel Michal covers the entire Late Bronze Age. Of special interest are Bichrome ware specimens of the "framed wavy-line" style (Fig. 5.10:1–2, 4), closely related to White Slip I bowls from Stephania dating to the initial phase of Late Cypriote I (*Stephania*: 56, Pl. XXXII:14–16, 23, Tomb 5). Bichrome bowls of this style, comparatively rare in Israel, are recorded from Tell el-'Ajjul, where they have been classified by Petrie as "Fine Anatolian Ware" (*AG I*§§45, 49; Pl. XXXIV:81–82). The earliest specimens

Legend for Fig. 5.10

No.	Type	Reg. No.	Locus	Description
1	Bowl	6506/7	965	Gray (gray); white slip; red and brown decoration; hand burnish.
2	Bowl	6695/2	983	Brown-gray (brown-gray); white slip; hand burnish; black and red decoration.
3	Bowl	6655/1	983	Light brown (light brown); hand burnish; white slip; red decoration.
4	Bowl	6471/1	965	Brown (gray); hand burnish; white slip; brown and red decoration.
5	Bowl	6676/1	965	Brown (brown); hand burnish; white slip; brown decoration.
6	Bowl	10453/2	1659	Gray (gray), small white grits; hand burnish; white slip; brown decoration.
7	Bowl	9668/4	1530	Brown-gray (gray), small white grits; hand burnish; white slip; brown decoration.
8	Bowl	6676/2	965	Brown (brown); hand burnish; white-gray slip; brown decoration.
9	Bowl	9505/4	1512	Brown (gray), small white grits; hand burnish; white-pink slip; brown decoration.
10	Bowl	10482/14	1659	Gray (gray), small white grits; hand burnish; white slip; brown decoration.
11	Bowl	6493/1	965	Brown (brown-gray); hand burnish; white-gray slip; brown decoration.
12	Bowl	9505/3	1512	Brown (gray), small white grits; white slip; brown decoration.
13	Bowl	6493/2	965	Light brown (light brown); gray slip.
14	Jug	6593/1	962	Gray (light gray); gray slip; white decoration.
15	Jug	10444/6	1659	Brown (gray), small white grits; gray slip; white decoration.
16	Bowl	6506/2	965	Brown-pink (brown-pink), small white grits; red wash.
17	Bowl	6429a/1	956	Brown-gray (gray), small white grits; hand burnish; brown slip.
18	Bowl	9505/2	1512	Gray (gray), small white grits; gray slip.
19	Krater	6655/3	983	Brown (brown), small white grits; gray slip.
20	Krater	8430/3	983	Brown (gray); gray slip.
21	Bowl	10421/5	1653	Brown-red (brown-red), small white grits; brown-red slip.
22	Jug	10453/7	1659	Gray (gray); hand burnish; black slip.
23	Jug	10482/11	1659	Brown-orange (brown-orange); brown slip.
24	Jug	8431/9	1259	Brown (gray); red slip.
25	Jug	10375/2	1660	Black (black), small white grits; brown-red slip.
26	Bowl	10443/4	1659	Gray (gray), small white grits; hand burnish; brown-red slip.
27	Jug	10437/1	1659	Black (black), small white grits; white decoration.

of "ladder pattern" style (Fig. 5.10:5) appear in Cyprus in Late Cypriote IB (*Ayios Iakovos*: 222; *Enkomi II*: Pl. 56:16, Level IB). Later varieties of this style (Fig. 5.10:7–12), found sporadically in LB I contexts, prevail in Israel during the Late Bronze Age II (Amiran 1969:172, Pl. 53:4–6, 8; *Ashdod II-III*: 82, Strata 4–3; Hankey 1981:108, Taanach).

Most of the White Slip I bowls from Tel Michal were found on the southern slope (Fig. 5.10:1–5), but they can safely be assigned to the Late Bronze Age I. The White Slip II Bowls came mainly from Iron Age fills in the center of the high tell (Fig. 5.10:6–7, 9–10, 12), so it is impossible to ascribe them to a specific phase of Late Bronze Age II (cf. Gittlen 1975:117).

3. Monochrome and Base Ring Wares. Two bowls of Monochrome ware were found in the southern sector, the first on the southern slope and the second on the *hamra* layer (Fig. 5.10:16–17; Pl. 58:1). A fragment of a third bowl (Fig. 5.10:18) came from the Iron Age fill in the center of the high tell (Locus 1512).

Base Ring I ware is represented by fragmentary kraters (Fig. 5.10:19–20), a wish-bone handle of a bowl (Fig. 5.10:13), and a jug base (Fig. 5.10:24), all found on the southern slope. Rim, neck, and base fragments of Base Ring I jugs (Fig. 5.10:22–23, 25) and a bowl (Fig. 5.10:21) are also recorded from LB II debris and Iron Age fills in the center of the high tell (Loci 1653, 1659, 1660).

Base Ring II ware is rare. A handle, body fragment, and bases of jugs (Fig. 5.10:14–15, 27) and bowls (Fig. 5.10:26)

are diagnostic of this ware. The body and base fragments (Fig. 5.10:15, 26–27) came from Iron Age fill in the central area (Locus 1659) and the handle (Fig. 5.10:14) from Bronze Age fill (Locus 962) in the southern area.

Monochrome and Base Ring I wares are diagnostic of Late Cypriote I. Both wares appear on Cyprus in Late Cypriote IA (*Ayios Iakovos*: 216; *Kalopsidha*: 69–70; *Enkomi I*: 225; *Enkomi III*: Pl. 56:1–3, 6, 8; *Stephania*: 49).[4] Monochrome and Base Ring I imports are found in Israel in LB I-IIA contexts (Amiran 1969:173, Pl. 54:1–8, Pl. 55:3, 10), but they are more common in LB I contexts (Dothan 1973:8, Fig. 4:5–7, Tel Mor Stratum 11; *Enc. Arch. Exc. III*: 889; *Ashdod II-III*: 79, Stratum 5; *Lachish II*: Pl. XLIV: 168, Fosse Temple I; *Lachish IV*: Pl. 81:869; Hankey 1981:108, Taanach). Although Base Ring II ware started on Cyprus in Late Cypriote IB, it is diagnostic of Late Cypriote II (*Enkomi I*: 242). In Israel it appears sporadically in Late Bronze Age I and becomes popular in Late Bronze Age II (Amiran 1969:173, Pl. 54:10–12, 18–19; *Ashdod II-III*: 82, Stratum 4; *Lachish IV*: Pl. 81:870).

Because of the lack of suitable chronological data, it is impossible to ascribe the Monochrome and Base Ring I-II wares from Tel Michal to specific phases of the Late Bronze Age.

B. Aegean Ware

A fragment of a cup decorated with a spiral (Pl. 58:7) is the only Aegean vessel recorded at Tel Michal. Stratigraphically it is out of context, since it was uncovered on the southern slope. It belongs to a well-known type of Late Minoan IA or Late Helladic I teacup. Three intact cups of this type were found at Ayia Irini in northwest Cyprus (Pecorella 1973:20, Nos. 1–3; Vermeule and Wolsky 1978:298–299, Fig. 2). Fragments of six other Aegean cups decorated in the same fashion were found in Toumba tou Skourou, situated several kilometers south of Ayia Irini (Vermeule and Wolsky 1978:303–307, Nos. 4–5, 8–11). Enkomi, on the eastern part of the island, yielded the fragments of two cups and an Aegean alabastron (*Enkomi I*: 229–230, Frontispiece 1–3; *Enkomi II*: 445, Pl. 304:1–3; *Enkomi III*: Pl. 58:26, 27, 27a, 28).

The origin of the Aegean cups found on Cyprus is still debated among scholars. The cups from Toumba tou Skourou originated in a tomb that yielded an intact Late Minoan I jug and fragments of at least four other Minoan vessels (Vermeule and Wolsky 1978:299–301, Nos. 1–3, 305: Nos. 6–7). Vermeule (1980:24) believes that the cups, like other Aegean imports found in the same tomb, are of Minoan workmanship. Pecorella (1973:21) tends to regard those of Ayia Irini as products from mainland Greece; Dikaios cannot decide whether the Enkomi cups are to be labeled Late Minoan IA or Mycenaean I (*Enkomi II*: 230, n. 186). Other scholars consider "Aegean" rather than "Minoan" or "Mycenaean" to be the better label for these ceramic exports to the Levant in that period (Kemp and Merrillees 1980:276). However, the presence of Cypriote imports on "Crete and the islands in the Cretan orbit, and their lack on the mainland. . ." (Cadogan 1972:12; cf. Holmes 1975:93)[5] seem to support the assumption that the "Aegean" cups found on Cyprus came either from the Cyclades or most probably from Crete (Åström 1973:307; Muhly 1980:29). This applies also to the cup fragment from Tel Michal, the earliest Late Minoan I import so far recorded from the southeastern Mediterranean (cf. Hankey 1973:107; 1981:108, 115; Merrillees and Evans 1980:7ff.; Kemp and Merrillees 1980:253–276).

5.3. SUMMARY AND CONCLUSIONS

The Middle Bronze Age repertory of the first occupational phase at Tel Michal is quite homogeneous. It includes a large number of vessels imported from Cyprus during the Middle Cypriote III period. Of special interest are Red-on-Red bowls and White Painted V amphorae, which appear elsewhere in Israel in Middle Bronze Age IIB-C contexts (see 5.1.2.1, 3). The absolute chronology of Middle Cypriote III is still inconclusive; Saltz (1977:59, 66) has recently noted that at present it is impossible to offer more than the general equation MC III = MB IIB-C. Examination of the local ware seems to indicate that the assemblage as a whole belongs to the Middle Bronze Age IIC rather than to the Middle Bronze Age IIB. This assumption is based mainly on several typological features. First, slip and burnishing are rare on bowls, jugs, and juglets, thereby indicating that they are comparatively late in the series (see 5.1.1.1, 2, 7).

Second, the texture and shapes of various carinated bowls and pedestal bowls (or chalices) are diagnostic of the latest phase of Middle Bronze Age II (see 5.1.1.2). Third, there are several transitional MB-LB shapes among the cooking pots, storage jars, and lamps (see 5.1.1.5–6, 8).

The closest parallels to the MB IIC repertory of Tel Michal appear at Stratum X at Megiddo, the fill of the east gate at Shechem, the lowest level of Area G at Ashdod, and the earliest stratum at Tel Mor, which date from the middle of the 17th to the middle of the 16th centuries B.C.E.

The LB repertory at Tel Michal indicates that the second occupational phase at the site, which occurred in Late Bronze Age I, was far more prosperous than the third phase. It is difficult to determine whether the latter covers the entire duration of Late Bronze Age II, since no Mycenaean imports were found at the site. However, several Cypriote White Slip bowls and a fragment of local painted ware portraying the palm-tree motif indicate that the third occupational phase at Tel Michal continued well into the 13th century B.C.E. (see 5.2.1.B7). Parallels from elsewhere suggest that the bulk of local painted ware, including a large variety of decorated kraters and "domestic jars," belongs to Late Bronze Age I rather than II (see 5.2.1.B4–5).

The rich repertory of LB I ware includes a large number of Cypriote vessels. Of special interest is a series of early specimens of White Slip bowls, a few Bichrome ware sherds, and a single fragment of a Late Minoan IA cup (see 5.2.2.A1–2; 5.2.2.B). These early Cypriote and Aegean imports support the assumption that the first occupational phase of Tel Michal was followed immediately by the second phase. Furthermore, both phases seem to represent an uninterrupted cultural unity extending from the late 17th to late 15th centuries B.C.E.

The huge amount of Cypriote imports, including Middle Cypriote III and Late Cypriote IA fabrics, indicates that connections with the island of Cyprus itself were the raison d'être for the occupation of the site from the late 17th century B.C.E. onward. Tel Michal is the only MB IIC site known so far on the southern coast of the Sharon (Gophna and Ayalon 1980:149). Recent studies have shown that several coastal settlements (both urban and rural) existed at that date in other parts of Israel as well (Gophna and Beck 1981:75–77). New ports were founded at Tel Mor and probably also at Achzib (Dothan 1973:14; Kempinski 1974:116–117), and older harbors, like those of Jaffa and Yavneh Yam, were rebuilt (Kaplan and Kaplan 1976:539; Kaplan 1978:1218; Gophna and Beck 1981:77).

It is tempting to suggest that the maritime activities that took place on the coastal plain in the late 17th century B.C.E. correspond to the founding of the first harbor towns (such as Enkomi) in eastern Cyprus. The identity of the initiators of these activities is still open to speculation (Dothan 1973:15–17; Kempinski 1974:VIII-X, 127–130). There is no doubt, however, that the new pattern of coastal sites established at the close of the Middle Bronze Age II opened a new era of extensive trade with Cyprus that continued to flourish during the Late Bronze Age.

NOTES

1. Four bowls diagnostic of this ware were found at Tel Michal. Since all of them came from mixed deposits of later periods (Reg. Nos. 2517/1, 6674/1, 8414/1, 8431/6), they were excluded from our study.

2. There are indications that Bichrome ware appears in Israel and Cyprus at the end of the Middle Bronze Age II/Middle Cypriote III (Epstein 1966:124–125, 130; *Enkomi II*: 442; Saltz 1977:66) and prevails mainly during the Late Bronze Age I/Late Cypriote I (Amiran 1969:154; Merrillees 1971:74; Åström 1972:47; Artzy et al. 1976:20). Archaeological data from the Levant and Cyprus accord with the chronology of Bichrome ware in Egypt, since excavations at Tell ed-Da'ba in the eastern Delta show that this ware ranges from the latter part of the Second Intermediate period to the early days of the New Kingdom (Bietak 1970:31–34).

3. For the east Cypriote origin of clays of this ware, see Artzy et al. 1981:46–47; cf. Chap. 24b, Samples 4–5.

4. Analysis of samples from Ugarit and various sites in eastern Cyprus indicates that a particular type of Cypriote clay originating in the Troödos Mountains is common to vessels of these wares; see Artzy et al. 1981:40–44; cf. Chap. 24b, Sample 3.

5. The lack of Cypriote imports on the mainland, in contrast to the vast amount of LH IIIA-B wares in Cyprus, Syria-Palestine, and Egypt, raises a question that is beyond the scope of this paper (cf. Cadogan 1972:12 and, recently, Kemp and Merrillees 1980:247, 282).

REFERENCES

Amiran, R. 1969. *Ancient Pottery of the Holy Land*. Jerusalem.

Amiran, R., and Eitan, A. 1964. A Krater of Bichrome Ware from Tel Nagila. *IEJ* 14:219–231.

Artzy, M., Perlman, I., and Asaro, F. 1976. Wheel-Made Pottery of MC III and LC I Periods in Cyprus Identified by Neutron Activation Analysis. *RDAC*: 20–28.

Artzy, M., Perlman, I., and Asaro, F. 1981. Cypriote Pottery Imports at Ras Shamra. *IEJ* 31:37–47.

Åström, P. 1972. Some Aspects of Late Cypriote I Period. *RDAC*: 46–57.

Åström, P. 1973. Discussion following Prof. Pecorella's and Prof. Vermeule's Papers. Page 307 in: *Acts of the International Archaeological Symposium "The Mycenaeans in the Eastern Mediterranean."* Nicosia.

Bietak, M. 1970. Vorläufiger Bericht über die dritte Kampagne der Osterreichischen Ausgrabungen auf Tell ed Da'ba in Ostdelta Ägyptens (1968). *MDIK* 26:15–42.

Cadogan, G. 1972. Cypriote Objects in the Bronze Age Aegean and Their Importance. *Praktika*: 5–13.

Courtois, J. C. 1978. Corpus céramique de Ras Shamra-Ugarit. Pages 191–370 in: *Ugaritica VII*.

Courtois, L. 1969. Le mobilier Funeraire céramique de la Tombe 4253 du Bronze Récent (Ville sud d'Ugarit). Pages 120–137 in: *Ugaritica VI*.

Dever, W. G. 1974. The MB IIC Stratification in the Northwest Gate Area at Shechem. *BASOR* 216:31–52.

Dothan, M. 1973. The Foundation of Tel Mor and of Ashdod. *IEJ* 23:1–17.

Eisenberg, E. 1976. The Middle Bronze Age Temples at Tel Kittan. (Hebrew) *Qadmoniot* 9:106–109.

Epstein, C. 1966. *Palestinian Bichrome Ware*. Leiden.

Gittlen, B. M. 1975. Cypriote White Slip Pottery in Its Palestinian Stratigraphic Context. Pages 111–128 in: *The Archaeology of Cyprus*. N. Robertson, ed. Park Ridge, New Jersey.

Gophna, R., and Ayalon, E. 1980. Survey of the Central Coastal Plain, 1978–1979: Settlement Pattern of the Middle Bronze Age IIA. *Tel Aviv* 7:147–151.

Gophna, R., and Beck, P. 1981. The Rural Aspect of the Settlement Pattern of the Coastal Plain in the Middle Bronze Age II. *Tel Aviv* 8:45–80.

Hankey, V. 1973. Late Minoan Finds in South Eastern Mediterranean. Pages 104–111 in: *Proceedings of the Third International Cretological Congress, Rethymnon*. Athens.

Hankey, V. 1981. Imported Vessels of the Late Bronze Age at High Places. Pages 108–115 in: *Temples and High Places in Biblical Times*. A. Biran, ed. Jerusalem.

Holmes, Y. L. 1975. The Foreign Trade of Cyprus during the Late Bronze Age. Pages 90–110 in: *The Archaeology of Cyprus*. N. Robertson, ed. Park Ridge, New Jersey.

Kaplan, H., and Kaplan, J. 1976. Jaffa. *Enc. Arch. Exc. II*: 532–541.

Kaplan, J. 1978. Yavneh-Yam. *Enc. Arch. Exc. IV*: 1216–1218.

Kaplan, M. F. 1980. *The Origin and Distribution of Tell el-Yehudiyeh Ware*. (SIMA 62) Göteborg.

Kelley, A. L. 1976. *The Pottery of Ancient Egypt*. Toronto.

Kemp, B. J., and Merrillees, R. S. 1980. *Minoan Pottery in Second Millennium Egypt*. Mainz am Rhein.

Kempinski, A. 1974. *Canaan (Syria-Palestine) during the Last Stage of the MB IIB (1650–1550 B.C.)*. (Hebrew with English summary) Ph.D. dissertation. Hebrew University, Jerusalem.

Merrillees, R. S. 1968. *The Cypriote Bronze Age Pottery Found in Egypt*. (SIMA 18) Lund.

Merrillees, R. S. 1971. The Early History of Late Cypriote I. *Levant* 3:56–79.

Merrillees, R. S., and Evans, J. 1980. An Essay in Provenance: The Late Minoan IB Pottery in Egypt. *Berytus* 28:1–45.

Muhly, J. D. 1980. Metals and Metallurgy in Crete and the Aegean at the Beginning of the Late Bronze Age. *Temple University Aegean Symposium* 5:25–36. Philadelphia.

Negbi, O. 1978. Cypriote Imitations of Tell el-Yahudiyeh Ware from Toumba tou Skourou. *AJA* 82:137–149.

Pecorella, P. E. 1973. Mycenaean Pottery from Ayia Irini. Pages 19–24 in: *Acts of the International Archaeological Symposium "The Mycenaeans in the Eastern Mediterranean."* Nicosia.

Saltz, D. L. 1977. The Chronology of the Middle Cypriote Period. *RDAC*: 51–70.

Seger, J. D. 1974. The Middle Bronze IIC Date of the East Gate at Shechem. *Levant* 6:117–130.

Stern, E. 1976. A Late Bronze Age Temple at Tel Mevorakh. (Hebrew) *Qadmoniot* 9:109–111.

Stern, E., and Saltz, D. L. 1978. Cypriote Pottery from the Middle Bronze Age Strata of Tel Mevorakh. *IEJ* 28:137–145.

Toombs, L. E., and Wright, G. E. 1963. The Fourth Campaign at Balatah (Shechem). *BASOR* 169:1–60.

Vermeule, E. 1980. Minoan Relations with Cyprus: The Late Minoan I Pottery from Toumba tou Skourou, Morphou. Pages 22–24 in: *Temple University Aegean Symposium* 5. Philadelphia.

Vermeule, E., and Wolsky, F. 1978. New Aegean Relations with Cyprus: The Minoan and Mycenaean Pottery from Toumba tou Skourou, Morphou. *Proceedings of the American Philosophical Society* 122:294–317.

6a

Iron Age Stratigraphy and Architecture (Strata XIV-XII)

by Shmuel Moshkovitz

Remains of the Iron Age were found not only on the high tell but also on the three low hillocks to the east, marking the first time that settlement at Tel Michal extended beyond the mound itself. Iron Age remains belong to three occupational phases (Strata XIV-XII): Strata XIV-XIII date to the 10th century B.C.E. and Stratum XII to the 8th century B.C.E.

6a.1. HIGH TELL

Preservation of the Iron Age deposits is very poor, mainly due to erosional forces during prolonged occupational gaps following both the 10th- and 8th-century settlements. A gap of about 150 years separated Strata XIV-XIII from Stratum XII, and another long period of abandonment intervened between the end of Stratum XII and renewal of occupation in the Persian period. Persian period settlers further damaged Iron Age strata, especially by constructing the massive fortress of the earliest Persian occupation (Stratum XI) at the northern end of the tell, digging deep pits at the southern end, and laying the deep foundations of the Stratum VII structure in the center.

When the first Iron Age settlers arrived at Tel Michal in the 10th century B.C.E., the mound had already assumed the "stepped" profile it was to maintain throughout the following millennia: a lowered terrace covering the northern half and an upper terrace, about 2 m higher at the south, where the earthen platform of the Middle Bronze Age II had once stood. The newcomers leveled off the surface of the upper terrace, filling in depressions and dumping debris down the slopes, as demonstrated by huge quantities of Late Bronze Age pottery found spilling down the southern slope.

We found remains of the earliest Iron Age phase (Stratum XIV) all over the high tell (Fig. 6.1), but those of Stratum XIII were preserved mainly on the upper terrace. During the hiatus that followed Stratum XIII, the structures eroded severely because of the lack of solid foundations. The preservation of Stratum XII, the final phase, was even worse, and nothing but scattered sherds could be attributed to it.

6a.1.1. Stratum XIV

Upper Terrace

Structure 1522 (Fig. 6.2). This free-standing house at the northern corner of the terrace was mostly robbed out or eroded, leaving only the walls of its northeast corner. The northern wall (L1317), about 1 m wide, was robbed on the west (Robbers' Trench 1526), and most of its eastern wall (L1320), about 85 cm wide, was also missing (Robbers' Trench 1520). The straight edge of stone-paved Floor 1523 and another robbers' trench parallel to it indicated the western wall of the house. Accordingly, Structure 1522 measured about 8 m from east to west and at least 6 m from north to south. Inside the preserved corner was an oven, sunk 20 cm into the floor. Storage jars, bowls, kraters, and a juglet (Fig. 7.1:1, 6–7, 14, 18–20) were recovered from a thick layer of ashes and fallen brick debris on Floor 1514. South of the oven was Silo 1529, built of mudbrick and measuring 1.5 m in diameter; it was sunk about 60 cm below the level of Floor 1522 and covered by a layer of burnt debris. (The eastern half of the silo and the western half of the oven are still unexcavated since they lie under a wall of the Roman fortress.) The conflagration was strong enough to have burnt the sun-dried mudbrick of the silo to a deep red. Under this destruction layer, we recovered large quantities of charred grape seeds (see Chap. 19), indicating that the silo was used to store grapes or raisins. Floor 1523 was apparently cleaned before laying Floor 1510 of the overlying house of Stratum XIII.

By analogy with Structure 423 (see below), we conjecture

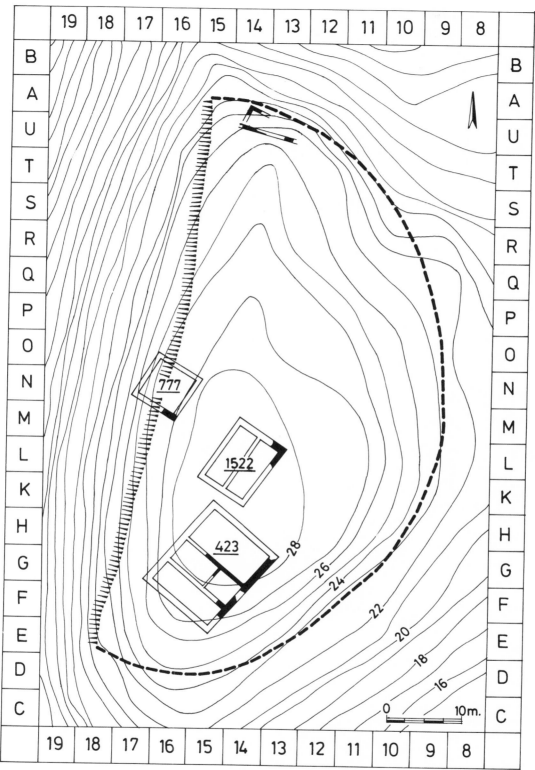

Figure 6.1. Iron Age structures on high tell (stratum XIV).

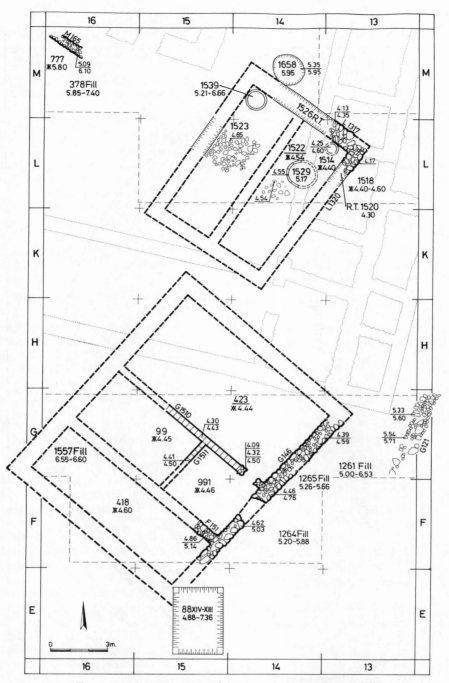

Figure 6.2. Structures 1522 and 423 on upper terrace (Stratum XIV).

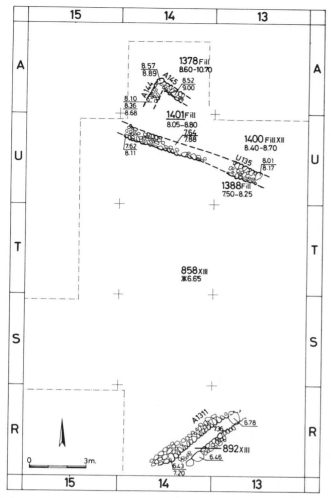

Figure 6.3. Structure 1401 on lower terrace (Stratum XIV); Walls U135 and drainage channel (Locus 893, Stratum XIII).

mudbrick (without stone foundations), whereas the door-jambs are built of *kurkar* stones. Room 991 is almost square, measuring 3.40 m × 8.85 m. Only a short segment of its southern stone wall (F151) survives. A brick wall (G1511) separates Rooms 99 and 991. The latter room is badly eroded, as is the whole western corner of the house. All that remains of the southern part of the building (Room 418) are a few patches of flooring, found tilting at a downward angle as a result of the slumping of the southern slope; our reconstruction of the southwestern sector of this house is therefore conjectural. Our tentative reconstruction of this building shows a rectangular house of about 12 m × 15 m, with a front courtyard and two rows of rooms behind it. The beaten-earth floors of the house, all at the same level, were covered with a layer of ashes and destruction debris.

A retaining wall was built about 3.5 m east of the house (G121), and Fills 1261 and 1264 were laid against it to support the house on its eastern side.

Lower Terrace

On the lower terrace about 7 m west of Structure 1522 stands the remains of another Iron Age building, consisting of Wall M165, running in almost the same direction as Wall L1317 and preserved to a height of about 1 m; its floor (Locus 777) is at level 5.80 m, which is about 1.25 m lower than the floors of Structure 1522. A rich collection of pottery vessels was found in Fill 378 underneath Floor 777 (Fig. 7.1:2, 9–10, 13, 15–16, 19).

At the northern end of the mound we found only a few fragmentary walls. Our attribution of these remains to Stratum XIV instead of XIII is based more on assumption than hard facts. Walls A144 and A145 form the outer corner of Structure 1401, which was erected on the slope of the Late Bronze Age earthen rampart (Fig. 6.3). To compensate for the steep incline here, a fill of ash and sand layers about 2.50 m thick (Locus 1378) was laid under the building. When this fill collapsed, most of the walls were carried away with it. The function of this structure, standing so close to the northern tip of the mound, was undoubtedly (like the forts later built on the same spot) connected with the need to control the path leading up the hill from the beach (and anchorage?) below.

South of these remains, nothing of this stratum is preserved on the lower terrace, mainly because of the major construction works carried out in the earliest Persian stratum (XI).

6a.1.2. Stratum XIII

Upper Terrace

Structure 1513 (Fig. 6.4). The remnants of this house, overlying Structure 1522 of the earlier Iron Age stratum, include two parallel walls (M146 and M147), about 2.70 m apart from each other, and Wall M149, perpendicular to them. In the southern part of the building, stone-paved Floor 1510 lies 30 cm above Floor 1523 of Stratum XIV. A

that a thin, brick partition wall may have divided the dwelling space (Room 1523) from the courtyard or working area (Room 1522).

Outside the house, next to Robbers' Trench 1526, was Pit 1658, apparently used for refuse, since it was filled with ashes, bones, and broken pottery vessels.

Structure 423 (Fig. 6.2). An unexcavated area 10 m wide separated Structures 1522 and 423, but their walls are on the same alignment and at the same level. Larger than its neighbor, Structure 423 is divided into at least four units. The stone foundation of its outer wall (G146) is 90 cm wide and preserved to a height of two courses. The fallen brick debris found inside the house indicates a superstructure built of mudbrick.

The northern unit (Room 423), which presumably served as a courtyard, is 5 m wide and at least 7 m long, although its northwestern corner lies beyond the excavated area. A doorway at the eastern end of Wall G1510 led into Room 991. This wall, only 40 cm wide, is made of *ḥamra*

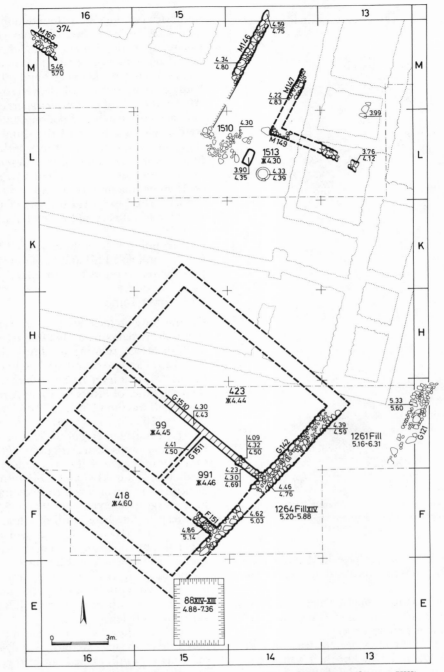

Figure 6.4. Structure 1513 and reused structure 423 on upper terrace (Stratum XIII).

rectangular ashlar (45 cm × 85 cm) found lying on its long side (Pl. 14) on the southern side of Room 1513 probably served as a roof-supporting pillar. An oven (70 cm in diameter) stood on beaten-earth Floor 1513. This structure may be tentatively reconstructed as a "four-room house," with Unit 1513 serving as the central courtyard, 1510 as a broadroom at the rear, and additional rooms located on each side of the courtyard.

Structure 423. This house was reused in Stratum XIII almost without changes except for blocking the opening between Courtyard 423 and Room 991. The blocking, which covered the ashy destruction layer, was done with the same type of *ḥamra* mudbricks used for Wall G1510, indicating that it was either repaired or partially rebuilt at this time.

Since the Stratum XIV floors were reused in this phase, we have assigned all the pottery from them to Stratum XIII,

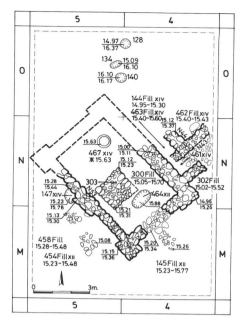

Figure 6.5. Cultic building on eastern hillock (Strata XIV–XIII).

although a black juglet, an iron sickle-blade, and a bronze arrowhead that may belong to Stratum XIV came from the fill beneath the floor of Room 991.

The pottery from this house constitutes the largest Iron Age assemblage found at Tel Michal. The floor of Courtyard 423 yielded several restorable vessels: a storage jar, a holemouth jar, a burnished jug, an oil lamp, and a redslipped bowl (see Chap. 7), as well as a basalt grinding stone and a bronze fibula. On Floor 99 we found a jug containing a number of small objects. This little collection included seven courie shells with their backs removed, three beads of bone or faience, two knobbed gaming pieces of faience, and a fragment of a bone handle with the iron rivet still preserved in one of its attachment holes (Pl. 79:2). On the tilted floor of Room 418 were four juglets (two of them intact), a stone weight, and a basalt grinder with pierced handle.

A complete storage jar and fragments of cooking pots and hand-burnished bowls were recovered from a deep probe (Locus 88) cut into the southern slope, at a level about 1.50 m lower than that of the nearby floors. This material was apparently dumped outside the house, either when the settlers of the second Iron Age phase cleaned its floors for reuse or sometime later during their occupancy. This group of pottery (Fig. 7.2) has therefore been assigned to Strata XIV-XIII.

Lower Terrace

This terrace continued to be occupied in Stratum XIII. At the west, Wall M166 (Fig. 6.4) was built over Floor 777 of the previous stratum and parallel to Wall M165.

At the northern end of the lower terrace, we exposed a stretch of wall (U135) about 8 m long and 80 cm wide (Fig. 6.3); apparently it served as the outer wall of a structure of Stratum XIII, the rest of which was completely destroyed by later constructions, particularly the Stratum XI fort. Surprisingly, a patch of floor (Locus 858) was preserved at level 6.65.

Close to the southern limit of the lower terrace, we uncovered a well-constructed water channel (Locus 892), unfortunately missing most of its capstones. Judging by its size (inner width about 50 cm) and solid construction, we presume that it drained a rather large structure that still lies buried in the unexcavated area farther south.

6a.1.3. Stratum XII

Although no architectural features attributable to this stratum were found on the high tell, the presence of numerous potsherds (Fig. 7.4) in later fills attests to its existence. In one case, Stratum XII pottery was found mixed with Persian period pottery on a Stratum X floor (Locus 1501). Remains of this phase may still lie in the unexcavated portions of the mound, but otherwise we must assume that they suffered total dismantling or erosion.

6a.2. THE EASTERN HILLOCK

The two Iron Age phases uncovered on this small hillock are contemporary to Strata XIV and XIII on the high tell.

6a.2.1. Stratum XIV

This stratum marks the first occupation of the sandy hillock. The architectural remains are extremely scanty since they were almost completely dismantled by the builders of Structure 300 of Stratum XIII, who left only a few northern walls: i.e., the stone foundations of Walls N43 and N44, at right angles to each other (Fig. 6.5). A stone pavement (Locus 461) joined Wall N43 on the southeast. Part of an oven and the fenestrated foot of a chalice (Fig. 7.5:7) were found in Locus 467 west of these walls. Several pits (Loci 128, 134, 139, and 140) dug into the sandy virgin soil on the northern and eastern sides of the hillock contained a considerable number of vessels, including two intact chalices (Fig. 7.5:5–6) and the foot of a third one (Fig. 7.5:8). The chalices in particular tend to support our hypothesis that these pits were the *favissae* of a cultic building already erected on this hillock in the earliest Iron Age stratum (see below). However, because of the lack of stratigraphic proof, we attributed the *favissae* to Strata XIV-XIII.

6a.2.2. Stratum XIII

In this phase, a single building (Structure 300) occupied the center of the hillock on the same spot and with the same orientation as the walls of the previous stratum (Fig. 6.5; Pl. 16). The northeastern part of the building has not been

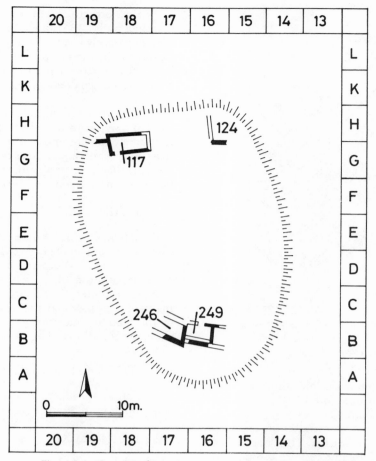

Figure 6.6. Remains of Iron Age structures on southeastern hillock.

preserved. The walls are ornamented with buttresses: two flanking the entrance at the corners of the facade, and the third projecting from the southwestern wall (N53). If we assume that the building was symmetrical, the third buttress was at the midpoint of the southwestern wall, whose original length was about 7 m, and two buttresses may be reconstructed at the corners of the rear wall. The southeastern side has a monumental entrance through Wall M41 and a sloping, paved path that leads to it. Opposite the entrance, but slightly off center, is a low platform measuring 1.60 m × 1.70 m (Locus 303) made of roughly hewn, medium-size *kurkar* stones and preserved to the height of a single course. Three goblets were discovered on the floor next to it (Fig. 7.5:15–17).

Our presumption that this building had a cultic function is based on the following considerations: (1) the structure's plan, consisting of a single room with a central platform; (2) the platform itself, which could have been either the base of an altar or an offering table; (3) the unusual use of ornamental buttresses on the outer faces of the walls; (4) the orientation of the corners of the building to the four points of the compass, which may reflect a religious belief (see Yadin 1972:104–105, n. 4); (5) the unusually wide en-

trance (1.50 m), which is almost half the length of the facade (3.50 m), and the paved path leading to it; and (6) the pottery repertory—mainly goblets and chalices—found in and around the building.

Among the other cultic buildings of this period is the contemporary temple of Stratum IX at nearby Tell Qasile (*Tell Qasile*: 50, Fig. 51), which also consists of a single rectangular room without internal partitions; in plan, it is a direct continuation of its Stratum X predecessor. However, the Tell Qasile temple, which measures 7.5 m × 13.4 m, is much larger than ours and its entrance layout (indirect axis) is different. Unlike the temple at Tel Michal, it is not an isolated building standing outside the settlement, but an integral part of it. A similar bent-axis entrance is seen in Shrine 1 at Sarepta (Pritchard 1975: Fig. 2), which dates to a much later period but has a stone platform at the rear. The best parallel to our temple is the "high place" excavated by Avigad (1961:98) on the northeastern hillock some 400 m north of Structure 300. It is the only building on its hillock and also has a central platform. The main difference between the two is that Avigad's "high place" is square (10 m × 10 m), whereas Structure 300 is (according to our reconstruction) oblong; also, the "high place" lacks

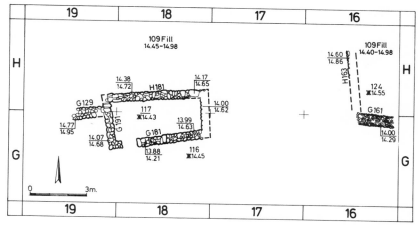

Figure 6.7. Structures 117 and 124 on southeastern hillock.

the ornamental buttresses of our building. Avigad interpreted his building as an open-air shrine, whereas ours could be reconstructed as a roofed shrine or temple.

6a.2.3. Stratum XII

No architecture was attributable to this phase, which is represented by sporadic sherds and three storage jars (Fig. 7.5:18–20). The complete jar came from Pit 464, which cut through the deposits of Stratum XIII near Platform 303.

6a.3. THE SOUTHEASTERN HILLOCK

Since only one 10th-century B.C.E. phase was found here, we attributed it to Strata XIV/XIII.

6a.3.1. Strata XIV/XIII

Remains of four structures, the first to be erected on the southeastern hillock, seem to belong to a string of houses that encircled an open courtyard (Fig. 6.6). The outer diameter of this compound measures approximately 32 m. We excavated the hillock at its northern and southern ends and also observed probes dug here by Avigad in 1960.

Two units were exposed at the north: Structures 117 and 124 (Fig. 6.7). The first of these measures 3.00 m × 5.50 m, with an entrance through its long wall (G181), close to the corner (Pl. 17). The beaten-earth floor was devoid of finds. Wall G129, which abuts onto the western wall of Structure 117, indicates the continuity of a ring of interconnected houses in this direction. Only a small part of central Courtyard 116 was exposed. The same walls were apparently reused in the Persian period.

The Persian occupation almost completely destroyed Structure 124, at the eastern end of the compound. A 10th-century black juglet (Fig. 7.5:22) found lying on a patch of flooring somehow escaped destruction. The open space between the two houses may have served as the entrance to the compound.

At the southern end of the hillock another two houses (Structures 246 and 249) were partially excavated (Fig. 6.8). The eastern one consists of two rooms (246 and 238). Room 249, measuring 2.20 m × 3.20 m, has benches along both of its long walls. A brick wall of the Persian period cut the connecting points between Structure 249 and adjacent Structure 246 on the west. The long walls of the latter have been mostly robbed (Robbers' Trenches 230 and 240). Plastered benches were found along Wall B173 and Robbers' Trench 230. Apart from an iron blade in Room 246, neither room yielded any finds.

6a.4. SUMMARY AND CONCLUSIONS[1]

Tel Michal, like Tel Poleg to the north, was not occupied during Iron Age I in the 12th-11th centuries B.C.E. This gap clearly marks the northern boundary of Philistine settlement at Tell Qasile and Tel Gerisa.

Strata XIV-XIII indicate the first period that the three hillocks east of the high tell were settled. On the high tell, isolated houses stand on both the upper and lower terraces. On two of the eastern hillocks, remains of cult places were uncovered. An open-air "high place" occupied the northeastern hillock (Avigad 1961), and remains of what was probably a roofed-over chapel (Structure 300) were found on the eastern hillock. The buildings on the third, southeastern hillock may have served as a subsidiary unit for these religious edifices.

The presence of complete vessels in pits and silos of Stratum XIV and the traces of burning suggest that a sudden catastrophe, perhaps an earthquake, brought this settlement to an end. The subsequent Stratum XIII represents an attempt to rebuild the site, probably abandoned after a brief duration. Strata XIV and XIII are both dated to the second half of the 10th century B.C.E.

Archaeological evidence from the same period has been reported at several sites in the coastal plain: an administrative building of Stratum VII at Tel Mevorakh (*Tel Mevorakh I*: 77–78) and small settlements at Tel Poleg

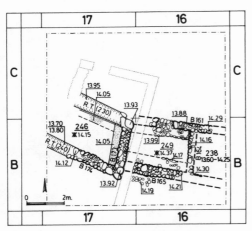

Figure 6.8. Structures 246 and 249 on southeastern hillock.

(Chap. 35) and at Tell Qasile (Strata IX and VIII, *Tell Qasile*: 11). To the south, Jaffa was unoccupied, or at least unimportant at this time (Kaplan and Kaplan 1976:539).

The renewed settlement of the coastal plain to the north of the Yarkon River should be linked with Biblical references to King Solomon's commercial and maritime contacts with Phoenicia. The sites of Tel Michal, Tel Poleg, and Tel Mevorakh may therefore be considered as trade stations along the maritime route. There is no clear indication regarding the ethnic affiliation of the inhabitants of these sites, whether Israelite, Phoenician, or mixed population. The assumption that Tell Qasile was still Philistine but under the political hegemony of the United Monarchy (Mazar 1977:343) may also fit the northern sites with Phoenician settlers under Solomonic suzerainty. The contemporaneous existence of two different cultic practices on the eastern hillocks may represent two different deities, a custom quite common among the Phoenicians.

Stratum XII is represented only by scattered sherds found in several places on the site. No structures could be related to this phase, which dates to the 8th century B.C.E.

NOTE

1. Section 6a.4 was rewritten by Z. Herzog because of the untimely death of Shmuel Moshkovitz.

REFERENCES

Avigad, N. 1961. Excavations at Makmish, 1960. *IEJ* 11:97–100.

Kaplan, Ḥ., and Kaplan, J. 1976. Jaffa. *Enc. Arch. Exc. II:* 532–541.

Mazar, A. 1977. *The Temples of Tell Qasile*. (Hebrew) Ph.D dissertation. Hebrew University, Jerusalem.

Pritchard, J. B. 1975. *Sarepta*. Philadelphia.

Yadin, Y. 1972. *Hazor*. The Schweich Lectures of the British Academy, 1970. London.

6b

A Complex of Iron Age Winepresses (Strata XIV-XIII)

by Ze'ev Herzog

A new complex of winepresses was discovered at Tel Michal after the completion of the scheduled excavation seasons. While quarrying sand in the area east of Tel Michal in 1982, bulldozers gradually exposed a layer of red sandy soil that had been covered by sand dunes about 2 m deep. In the red sand layer were remains of plastered structures. An archaeology enthusiast, Yehuda Friedman of Givatayim, discovered the partially exposed remains while hiking and informed us about them. A salvage excavation was carried out on behalf of the Israel Department of Antiquities and Museums and the Institute of Archaeology of Tel Aviv University.[1]

The rescue excavation, directed by the author, led to the exposure of two unique winepress complexes located about 180 m east of the high tell and about 100 m northeast of the eastern hillock (Area I). No additional building remains were found in the immediate area.

The winepress complexes, each measuring about 5 m × 7 m, lie 10 m apart. Since they were dug and constructed in the ground, their outer limits are not straight. Their general plan and internal divisions are similar and attest to a considerable degree of technical uniformity despite some differences in dimensions (Fig. 6.9).

The two complexes are not in the same state of preservation: the central part of the complex lying to the northeast (No. 2900) is badly damaged, but its complete plan can be restored on the basis of the southwestern complex (No. 2910) described below (Pl. 18).

6b.1. COMPLEX 2910

The sides and internal divisions of the installation were constructed of *ḥamra* bricks and *kurkar* stones. The whole structure was coated with a thick layer of chalky plaster containing a considerable amount of shell fragments (as much as 50 percent of the material). In this respect, the plaster differed completely from that covering the other winepresses at Tel Michal.

The plan of each complex structure consists of three main components: two winepresses at either end and an elongated rectangular basin (Locus 2911) in the middle. Each winepress (2910 and 2906) has a treading surface and two receiving vats. The dimensions of the treading floors in complex 2910 are 2.10 m × 2.70 m (Floor 2910) and 2.30 m × 3.50 m (Floor 2906). Each of these surfaces is connected by two channels to two round receiving vats of differing size. The larger vats (2907 and 2913) have diameters of 1.50 m and 1.10 m and are 1.50 m and 1.30 m deep, respectively. The smaller vats (2908 and 2916) have diameters of 0.90 m and 0.75 m and are 0.50 m and 0.80 m deep, respectively. At various points in the sides of the larger vats are three or four plastered ledges to facilitate descent and ascent from the vat (Pl. 19). In the wall that separates the two vats from the treading surface of each winepress, there is a protrusion in the plaster with a shallow depression in the center that seems to have supported round-based jars into which the new wine was poured. A small hollow in the bottom of each receiving vat collected the last drops of wine, thus facilitating the emptying of the contents.

Between the two winepresses is the third part of the complex, a rectangular basin (2911) measuring 1.00 m × 3.50 m. A plastered channel connects it to the treading surfaces on both sides. Since no receiving vat is directly connected to the basin, it cannot be an additional small winepress. It is preferable to interpret it as a bin to store the grapes brought from the vineyard before treading. A certain amount of juice ran out of the piled-up grape bunches, and this too was collected via one of the channels leading to the treading surface.

The fact that the two receiving vats of each press are not joined to each other by a channel, although they are both connected to the treading surface, indicates that the complex was designed to allow maximum flexibility of operation by the blocking or opening of channels as needed. It was possible to use both vats together, or separately to tread a limited quantity for collection in the small vat (less than 0.5 m^3) or a larger quantity for collection in the large vat (about 2.5 m^3).

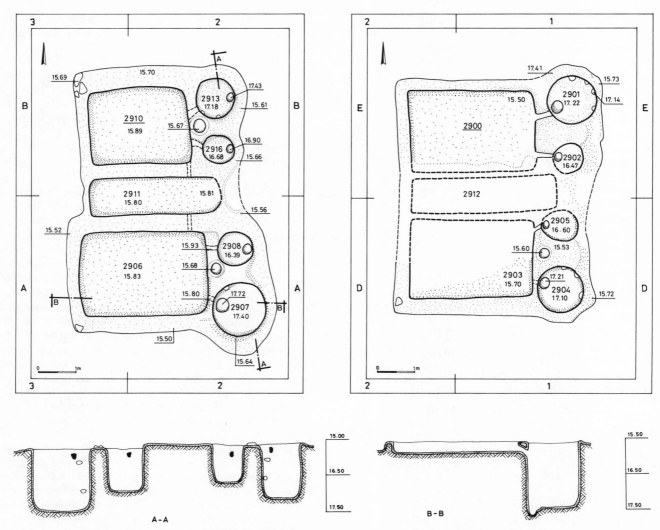

Figure 6.9. Two Iron Age winepress complexes. Complex 2900 is located about 10 m northeast of complex 2910.

6b.2. OPERATION OF THE WINEPRESSES

There were thus four separate winepresses in the two complexes. The fact that the planners preferred this arrangement to one large vat suggests that the winepresses were also constructed for farmers who owned small vineyards and processed and marketed their own produce individually. The construction of four winepresses so close together undoubtedly attests to the intensity of viticulture in the region.

Another explanation for the presence of four identical winepresses is based on the assumption that the preliminary fermentation process took place in the receiving vats themselves (Etam 1980:91). According to the Talmud (Massekhet Terumot), fermentation took about 3 days. If this was indeed done in the vats instead of jars, we may speculate that the four winepresses were operated in turn. Grapes were trodden in one press and the new wine re-

mained in the receiving vat to ferment for the following 3 days, during which time additional batches of grapes were trodden in the other three winepresses. On the fourth day the fermented wine in the first press was emptied into jars and the cycle was repeated.

6b.3. DATING THE WINEPRESSES

Since the winepresses lie beyond the borders of the Tel Michal settlement, it is not possible to date them stratigraphically. Although very few pottery sherds were found in and around the winepresses, all are from the Iron Age. It is important to note this, since the dominant pottery collected from the surface on all parts of the hill dates from the Persian, Hellenistic, and Roman periods. This later material is totally absent from the winepresses, probably because they were already filled with drifting sand and buried before the Persian period. The latest date that can be given to the sherds found is Iron Age II (10th-9th centuries B.C.E.). Since the winepresses were constructed adjacent to the settlement of Tel Michal, they were most likely in use at the same time the tell was occupied; in the 9th century there was a gap in settlement, so it may be concluded that the winepresses were constructed in the 10th century B.C.E., which was also the time when the nearby eastern hillock was first occupied (Chap. 6a).

Two additional types of evidence support this dating. First, these winepresses are completely different from those belonging to the Persian and Hasmonean periods at Tel Michal. Significant differences include the absence of sedimentation vats, the circular rather than square shape of the receiving vats, the pretreading storage basins, the ledges in the vats for footholds, and the hollowed stands to hold the wine jars. Second, there are several similarities between our winepresses and those in the Ephraim hills, which were dated to the Iron Age on the basis of their presence within settlements of that period (Etam 1980:37–93). Although "construction" technique in the hill country involved rock hewing rather than digging into the soil and building lime-plastered walls (as required in the plains), the winepresses have some similar features. In both cases, the receiving vats are round and not square. In both cases, they have footholds instead of stairs, although in the hill country these were depressions hewn into the rock, rather than ledges, since it is obviously easier to cut into the rock than to leave ledges protruding from it.

Our Tel Michal presses may possibly have another feature that is known in the hill country. A huge limestone rock, whose nearest possible origin must be the Samarian hills, was dug up by the same bulldozer that exposed our winepresses. It is 3 m long, weighs more than 2 tons, and has two holes of different sizes bored into it (Pl. 20). When the stone was found, remains of plaster rich in shell fragments, similar to that covering our winepresses, still adhered to its surface. A similar stone, found in a hill country site called Qala' 2 (Etam 1980:37–63), was interpreted as a base into which a horizontal beam was inserted. Etam suggests that treaders clung to ropes tied to the beam so as not to slip (as depicted in Egyptian frescoes). We suggest, however, that the stone was used to support a beam that exerted pressure on the grapeskins to squeeze out the last drops (similar to equipment for pressing olives). If our limestone rock is indeed connected with the Iron Age winepresses at Tel Michal, it may have stood in the northern complex (No. 2900), which is totally destroyed in the center.

6b.4. SUMMARY

The almost certain dating of the winepresses at Tel Michal to the 10th century B.C.E. can provide the "missing link" from the Iron Age in the chain of wine production in the Sharon. Early examples of winepresses are at present known only from Tel Aphek in the Late Bronze Age (Kochavi 1981:81). There is an almost unbroken chain in the Persian and Hellenistic periods at Tel Michal itself (see Chaps. 8 and 12) as well as in the Roman and Byzantine periods at many sites in the vicinity, such as Tell Qasile and Apollonia (Roll and Ayalon 1981). There is no doubt that the production of wine was a very important factor in the economy of the Sharon.

NOTE

1.My thanks to the director of the Department of Antiquities and Museums for permission to publish the results of the excavation.

REFERENCES

Etam, D. 1980. *The Production of Oil and Wine in the Ephraim Hills in the Iron Age*. (Hebrew) Master's thesis. Tel Aviv University.

Kochavi, M. 1981. The History and Archaeology of Aphek-Antipatris. *BA* 44:75–86.

Roll, I., and Ayalon, E. 1981. Two Large Wine Presses in the Red Soil Region of Israel. *PEQ* 113:111–125.

7

Iron Age Pottery (Strata XIV-XII)

by Lily Singer-Avitz

Settlement at Tel Michal was renewed during the Iron Age following a gap of some 400 years. For the first time in the history of the site, occupation spread beyond the high tell to include the three eastern hillocks (Areas B, C, and Avigad's excavation).

Three stages of settlement at this period were noted: Strata XIV and XIII, both dated within the 10th century B.C.E. and separated by a gap of some 150 years from the third stage (Stratum XII), which is recognized by pottery alone since no architectural remains have survived (see Chap. 6a).

A sequence of strata that would have enabled us to build a typological sequence is lacking. Furthermore, pottery assemblages could not always be ascribed to a particular stratum. Our main goal is therefore to try to integrate the Tel Michal Iron Age settlement into the chronological framework of this period. The ceramic analysis deals first with the three strata of the high tell and then with the eastern hillocks. Since most of the loci are poor in pottery remains, the vessels are presented according to types (rather than as separate assemblages), arranged in the customary typological sequence from open to closed vessels.

7.1. HIGH TELL

7.1.1. Stratum XIV

Architectural remains of this stratum, characterized by free-standing, isolated structures, were noted all over the high tell. The ceramic assemblages, however, are not very rich.

Bowls

The hand-burnished bowl (Fig. 7.1:1) with two horizontal handles attached to the rim is decorated with two brownish black stripes painted below the rim and on the handles. This bowl is a Cypriote import, apparently of Black-on-Red (BoR) I(III) ware. According to Gjerstad, the walls of the bowls of this ware are less rounded than those of the BoR

II(IV) ware (*SCE IV, 2*: 70) and the rims are not inverted. Furthermore, BoR I(III) ware bowls are burnished, whereas the BoR II(IV) ware bowls are not (*SCE IV, 2*: 68–69).

This type of bowl was common in northern Israel and along the Syrian-Lebanese coast in the 10th century B.C.E. (*Hazor III-IV*: Pls. CLXXIV:9, CCCLV:5), Tel 'Amal Stratum III (Levy and Edelstein 1972:361, Fig. 15:10–11), Tell Keisan Stratum 8b (*Tell Keisan*: Pl. 56:1), Beth-shan Stratum V (*Beth-shan 1966*: Fig. 63:22), Megiddo Stratum VA (*Megiddo I*: Pls. 30:140; *Megiddo II*: Pl. 90:1–2), Tell Abu Hawam Stratum III (*TAH*: 6, Fig. 8), Tel Mevorakh Stratum VII (*Tel Mevorakh I*: Fig. 17:4–7), Tell el-Far'ah (N) Stratum 3 (de Vaux and Steve 1952: Fig. 6:16), and Al Mina Stratum VIII (du Plat-Taylor 1959:75–76).

In view of these analogies, it seems that the dates given by Gjerstad (*SCE IV, 2*: 421–427) to BoR I(III) ware (850–700 B.C.E.) are not compatible with the strata in which it appears in Israel (the same applies to the rest of the types belonging to this family) and that it should be antedated to the 10th century. According to Birmingham (1963:33), who reexamined the Cypriote pottery groups, these bowls first appear in Cyprus around 925 B.C.E. and are present until the end of the 8th century.

The repertoire of local bowls is quite uniform in nature. These bowls feature red slip and hand burnishing both inside and out, usually horizontal on the upper part of the body and from the point of carination downward either chordal or vertical on the interior. The red-slipped and hand-burnished bowl of Figure 7.1:2, which has relatively thin walls, is carinated near the base. Similar bowls were found in Taanach Period IIB (*Taanach I*: Fig. 48:7–14) and Tel 'Amal Stratum III (Levy and Edelstein 1972: Fig. 15:3). This type of bowl, which appears throughout the Iron Age, is very common in the 8th century, although by then wheel burnishing replaces hand burnishing, as in Beer-sheba Stratum II (*Beer-sheba I*: Pl. 59:39–40) and Lachish Stratum III (*Lachish III*: Pl. 79:16). A bowl with a thickened inverted rim, grooved on its outer side (Fig. 7.1:3), is also red slipped and burnished. These bowls, common during the 10th century, were found in Tell Qasile Stratum IX

(Mazar 1977: Fig. 56:2) and Gezer Stratum VIIA (Gitin 1979 II: Pl. 10:14).

Kraters

All kraters are of the closed, carinated type, with a thickened rounded rim, a pair of loop handles drawn from the rim to the carination, and a ring base. They are all red slipped and hand burnished, both inside and out. Some of them are small (Fig. 7.1:4–5; Pl. 59:1) and some are quite large (Fig. 7.1:6–7). They are typical of Strata XI-VIII at Tell Qasile (Mazar 1977:286, Figs. 57:7–12, 58:8–13). Further analogies come from Gezer Stratum VIIA (Gitin 1979 II: Pl. 11:3), Lachish Stratum V (*Lachish V*: Pl. 41:10; *Lachish III*: Pl. 105:8), and Tel Esdar Stratum II (Kochavi 1969: Fig. 5:5). This type was also found in Syria in the cremation burials at Hama, Periods I-II (= Stratum F on the tell, dated 1200–925 B.C.E.; *Hama II, 3:* Fig. 61).

Cooking Pots

The cooking pots in this stratum are wide and shallow, with a carinated body, an externally concave, triangular rim, and a pair of loop handles (Fig. 7.1:8–9). This type of pot was very common during the 11th-10th centuries B.C.E., and it is difficult to distinguish any chronological development in it. According to Mazar's observations at Tell Qasile (1977:291–292), the main criterion is the addition of handles from the 10th century onward and a tendency for the rim to become more elongated: the rims in Strata XII-XI at Tell Qasile are relatively short, becoming longer in Strata X-IX, even though their basic shape remains the same (Mazar 1977: Fig. 57:21–22, Stratum IX, Fig. 58:20–21, Stratum VIII). Further examples were found at Taanach Period IIA (*Taanach I*: Fig. 29:1–5), Period IIB (*Taanach I*: Fig. 49:1–3), and Tell Keisan Stratum 8 (*Tell Keisan*: Pl. 55:1–3).

The cooking pot of Figure 7.1:10 has a convex rim and its body is rounded and less carinated. This is not a common type, but a close parallel was found at Taanach in Period IIA (*Taanach I*: Fig. 21:5).

Storage Jars

The most common type of storage jar at Tel Michal has a sloping shoulder that makes a sharp angle with the wall of the jar and a body fairly wide at the shoulder, narrowing down toward the base. Rims are very short (Fig. 7.1:17–18). Parallels from other sites are relatively scarce: Arad Stratum XI (Aharoni 1981: Fig. 9:5), Grave No. 21 at Tell er-Reqeish (Culican 1973: Fig. 4), Ashdod, Area M, Strata 11-10 (*Ashdod IV*: Figs. 3:17–18, 9:1–3), and Tell Keisan Stratum 7, first half of the 9th century (*Tell Keisan*: Pl. 50:5).[1]

Two other profiles are present: the storage jar of Figure 7.1:19 has a rounded shoulder and a short rim. The jar of Figure 7.1:20, which has a rather plump body and an erect, straight rim, is paralleled in Hazor Stratum X (*Hazor III-IV*: Fig. CLXXII:14).

Jugs

The small jug of Figure 7.1:11 has a globular body, round base, and narrow neck. Since part of the rim is missing, it is not clear whether it was pinched or not.

Juglets

The dipper juglets with rounded base and wide neck (Fig. 7.1:12–14) will be discussed together with the assemblage of Stratum XIII, since no complete examples were found in this stratum. The juglet neck (Fig. 7.1:15) is Black-on-Red ware. On complete specimens, the handle extends from the ridge in the center of the neck to the body. This is the most common juglet of this ware found in Israel, particularly in the north (and along the Syrian-Lebanese coast) and in the coastal plain, although it also occurs farther inland and in the south. In Cyprus it was classified by Gjerstad as Black-on-Red I(III) and II(IV) and dated to the 9th-7th centuries B.C.E. (*SCE IV, 2:* 421–427). However, further studies indicate that this type should be antedated in Cyprus to the second half of the 11th century and that its origin may even be Phoenician. Its distribution in the 11th century is relatively limited, and it becomes more and more common in the 10th century B.C.E. (Birmingham 1963:36, Ill. 1:20).

Lamps

The lamps of Stratum XIV are large with rounded bases (Fig. 7.1:16). Further examples come from Hazor Strata X-IX (*Hazor III-IV*: Fig. CLXXVII:17), Tel 'Amal Stratum III (Levy and Edelstein 1972: Fig. 14:1), Megiddo Stratum V (*Megiddo I*: Pl. 37:17), and Tell Keisan Stratum 8 (*Tell Keisan*: Pl. 56:10).

7.1.2. Iron Age Strata XIV-XIII

This assemblage came from ash and *hamra* layers on the southern slope (Locus 88) that could not be stratigraphically attributed either to Stratum XIV or XIII.

Bowls

As in Stratum XIV, all bowls are red slipped and hand burnished. The carinated bowl with slightly everted rim of Figure 7.2:1 has vertical burnishing below the keel. A similar bowl was found in Taanach Period IIB (*Taanach I*: Fig. 46:11). A small red-slipped and hand-burnished bowl (Fig. 7.2:2) with rounded sides also came from this locus. The burnishing is horizontal halfway down the sides and vertical from the middle downward. This bowl, which has a relatively wide distribution, can be seen in Megiddo Stratum VA (*Megiddo II*: Pl. 89:11), Taanach Period IIB (*Taanach I*: Fig. 48:15–19), Tell Qasile Stratum VIII (Mazar 1977: Fig. 59:4), and Tel Dan Stratum IV (Biran 1982: Fig. 24:16).

Kraters

The thick-rimmed, red-slipped, and hand-burnished kraters (Fig. 7.2:3–5) resemble those from Stratum XIV.

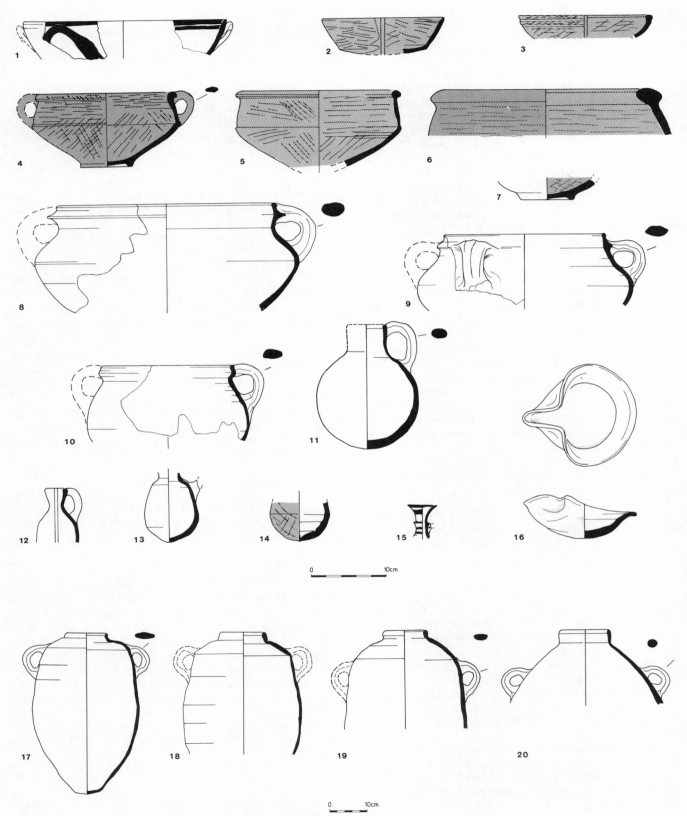

0   10cm.

0   10cm.

Figure 7.1. Pottery of Stratum XIV (High tell).

Legend for Fig. 7.1

No.	Type	Reg. No.	Locus	Description	Pl.
1	Bowl	9551/1	1522	Brown (brown); hand burnish, brownish-red slip, brown-black decoration.	
2	Bowl	2218/1	378	Brown (gray), small white grits; hand burnish, red slip.	
3	Bowl	5736/1	1388	Brown (brown), small white grits; hand burnish, red slip.	59:1
4	Small krater	10466/1	1658	Dark brown (dark gray), small white grits, hand burnish, red slip.	
5	Small krater	9740/1	1557	Brown (gray); hand burnish, red slip.	
6	Krater	9549/2	1522	Brown (brown), small white grits; hand burnish, red slip.	
7	Krater	9549/3	1522	Brown (brown), small white grits; hand burnish, red slip.	
8	Cooking pot	8479/1	1264	Brown-black (brown-black), small white grits.	
9	Cooking pot	2232/1	378	Brown-gray (black), small white and gray grits.	
10	Cooking pot	2201/3	378	Brown (gray), small white grits.	
11	Jug	9520/2	1514	Dark gray (dark gray), small white and gray grits.	
12	Juglet	9555/1	1514	Brown (brown), small white grits.	
13	Juglet	2222/1	378	Brown (black), small and large white grits.	
14	Juglet	9562/1	1522	Brown (brown), small white grits; hand burnish, red slip.	
15	Juglet	2207/1	378	Pink (pink-gray); black decoration.	
16	Lamp	2208/1	378	Brown-red (dark brown).	
17	Storage jar	9520/1	1514	Brown (gray), small gray and white grits.	
18	Storage jar	9595/2	1522	Brown (brown), small white and gray grits, few large white grits.	
19	Storage jar	2201/4	378	Brown (gray), small gray and white grits.	
20	Storage jar	9549/1	1522	Brown (dark gray), small white grits, few large white grits.	

The krater of Figure 7.2:4, with a grooved, thickened rim, is paralleled at Tell Qasile Stratum VIII (Mazar 1977: Fig. 58:11) and at Tell el-Far'ah (N) Stratum 3 (de Vaux and Steve 1957: Fig. 17:2). The krater of Figure 7.2:5 has the same type of grooved rim but also possesses a bar handle. These handles were quite common in the 10th century, but very few were found at Tel Michal. A similar krater came from Taanach Period IIB (*Taanach I*: Fig. 47:1).

Cooking Pots

Two types of cooking pots were found in this locus: wide, shallow pots (Fig. 7.2:6–7) resembling those from Stratum XIV and closed vessels with an incurving rim and one loop handle (Fig. 7.2:8). Although this type is shaped like a jug, it is made of the same kind of clay as the others and traces of soot testify to its use over the fire. We have therefore called it a "cooking jug." This is a very common vessel (often unnoticed since it is usually included among the jugs) that began to appear in Iron Age I (e.g., Tel Masos Stratum II; Kempinski et al. 1981: Fig. 9:13) and continued into Iron Age IIC (e.g., Beer-sheba Stratum II; *Beer-sheba I*: Pl. 61:98), exhibiting very few typological variations throughout the centuries. Close parallels to our specimens came from Taanach Period IIB (*Taanach I*: Fig. 50:1–3) and Tell Abu Hawam Stratum III (*TAH*: 22, Fig. 80).

Storage Jars

The ovoid storage jar (Fig. 7.2:11; Pl. 59:13) has a slightly emphasized, rounded shoulder; a straight neck ending with a plain, rounded rim; a round base; and a pair of loop handles, oval in section and without ridges, on the shoulder. These jars are most common in Strata XI-IX at Tell Qasile. Identical vessels were found in levels of the 11th-10th

centuries in central and southern Israel, whereas they are relatively rare in the north (Mazar 1977:294–295).

Juglets

The pointed base of a black-burnished juglet (Fig. 7.2:9) is the only example from this locus. It belongs to the group of "black juglets" found in many Iron Age II sites, such as Megiddo Strata V-IV (*Megiddo I*: Pl. 5:124–127), Taanach Period IIB (*Taanach I*: Fig. 40:4–6), Tell Abu Hawam Stratum III (*TAH*: Pl. XIII, No. 91), Tell el-Far'ah (N) Stratum 3 (de Vaux and Steve 1951: Fig. 10:2; 1952: Fig. 6:1; 1955: Figs. 16:5, 17:3–4), and Beer-sheba Stratum VI (*Beer-sheba II*: Fig. 30:6, 7).

Lamps

As in Stratum XIV, the lamps are large and round based (e.g., Fig. 7.2:10).

7.1.3. Stratum XIII

Most of the pottery in this stratum came from Structure 423 on the upper terrace (which had also been used during the previous stratum) and from Structure 1513, which was built over the ruins of Structure 1522.

Bowls and Kraters

The carinated bowl (Fig. 7.3:1) has a plain rim and a small disk base. It is completely red slipped internally, but it is red slipped externally only down to the keel. The slip bears traces of hand burnishing. A similar bowl was found in Tell Abu Hawam Stratum III (*TAH*: Pl. XIII: 68).

The closed krater (Fig. 7.3:2), hand burnished both inside and out, with a pair of handles, a thickened rim, and

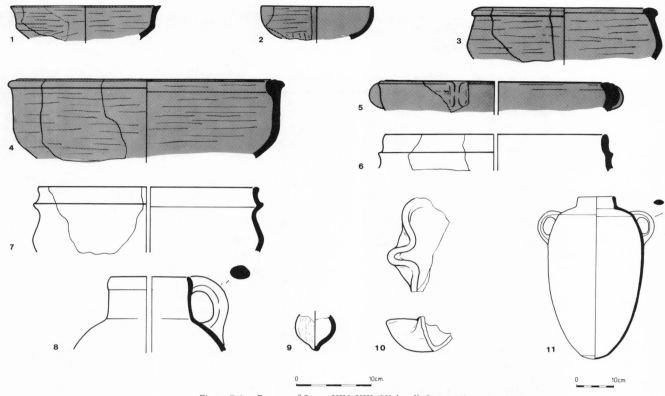

Figure 7.2. Pottery of Strata XIV–XIII (High tell, Locus 88).

Legend for Fig. 7.2

No.	Type	Reg. No.	Description	Pl.
1	Bowl	480/3	Brown (brown); hand burnish, red-brown slip.	
2	Bowl	475/1	Brown (brown), small white grits; hand burnish, red slip.	
3	Krater	497/2	Brown (gray), small white grits; hand burnish, brown slip.	
4	Krater	497/1	Brown (brown-gray), small white grits; hand burnish, red slip.	
5	Krater	497/3	Brown (brown-gray); hand burnish, red slip.	
6	Cooking pot	491/2	Brown (brown), small white grits.	
7	Cooking pot	497/5	Dark brown (black), small white grits.	
8	Cooking pot	497/6	Brown (black), small white and gray grits.	
9	Juglet	491/1	Black (black), small white grits; vertical slip.	
10	Lamp	470/1	Brown (brown).	
11	Storage jar	496/1	Brown (gray), small and large white grits.	59:13

a ring base, is closely related to those of the previous stratum. A parallel was found in Ashdod, Area D, Stratum 4, although the latter is decorated with stripes of black paint in a style characteristic of what the excavators term "Ashdod ware" (*Ashdod I*: 131–132, Fig. 36:13).

Storage Jars

The storage jar with sloping shoulders and the type with swollen body from the preceding stratum (Fig. 7.1:17–18, 20) both continue in Stratum XIII (Fig. 7.3:14–15; Pl. 59:14).

A new vessel in this stratum is the holemouth jar (Fig. 7.3:16; Pl. 59:15), with a thickened rim and a body that

swells out from the rim and then tapers to a rounded base. Such jars begin to appear toward the end of the 10th century B.C.E.—for example, in Gezer Stratum VIIa (Gitin 1979: Pl. 9:3–7), in Arad Stratum XI (Aharoni 1981: Fig. 10:8), and in Taanach Period IIB (*Taanach I*: 35:2).[2]

Jugs

The spherical jug with ring base (Fig. 7.3:3; Pl. 59:7) has a long neck with a handle drawn from just below the mid-neck ridge to the shoulder. It is decorated with black and red concentric circles. Parallels were found in Tell Abu Hawam Strata IV-III (*TAH*: Figs. 52, 152) and Megiddo Stratum VA-IVB (*Megiddo II*: Pl. 88:15), as well as in

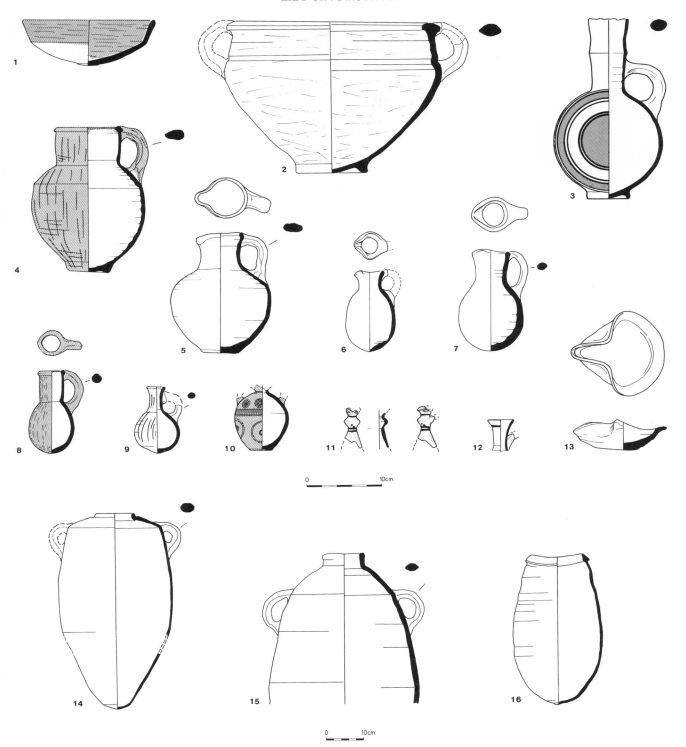

0   10cm.

0   10cm.

Figure 7.3.   Pottery of Stratum XIII (High tell).

81

Legend for Fig. 7.3

No.	Type	Reg. No.	Locus	Description	Pl.
1	Bowl	2542/1	423	Brown-red (dark brown), small black and white grits.	
2	Krater	4986/1	1510	Brown (gray), small white grits; hand burnish.	
3	Jug	553/1	99	Red-brown (red-brown), small gray grits; red slip, black decoration.	
4	Jug	2559/1	423	Light brown (brown), small white grits; vertical burnish, red slip.	
5	Jug	5813/1	858	Light brown (gray), small and large white grits.	
6	Juglet	2508/1	418	Orange (gray), small gray grits.	
7	Juglet	2524/1	418	Brown (brown), small white and gray grits, large white grits.	59:11
8	Juglet	2512/1	418	Brown-red, small white grits; vertical burnish, red slip.	59:12
9	Juglet	6463/1	99	Black (black); vertical burnish.	
10	Juglet	2552/1	418	Buff (buff), small gray grits; horizontal hand burnish, red slip, black decoration.	
11	Juglet	6411/1	423	Red-orange (gray); vertical burnish, black decoration.	
12	Juglet	2573/1	423	White (white); black decoration.	
13	Lamp	2558/1	423	Brown (brown).	
14	Storage jar	2554/1	423	Brown (gray); small white and gray grits, large white grits.	
15	Storage jar	9486/2	1510	Brown (gray), small white grits, many large white grits.	59:14
16	Holemouth jar	2548/1	423	Brown (brown), small white grits.	59:15

Cyprus and along the Lebanese coast (Chapman 1972:71–73, 152, 185; Birmingham 1963:37, Ill. 1:29; *Tyre*: Pl. XXV, Stratum X2). Most of the parallels show that this vessel did not appear before the 10th century B.C.E., perhaps not until late in that century, and that it continued into the 9th century (Birmingham 1963:37). The red-slipped, hand-burnished globular jug (Fig. 7.3:4; Pl. 59:8) has a thickened rim and ring base. In profile it resembles the jugs used for cremation burials in sites of the southern Shephelah, such as Tell er-Reqeish (Culican 1973: Fig. 2:R10) and Tell el-Far'ah (S), Tomb 215 (*CPP*: 34V2), although the latter vessels are somewhat larger. The same types were also found in architectural contexts in sites such as Ashdod Stratum 3a, Area D (*Ashdod I*: Fig. 38:1–2; *Ashdod II-III*: 99, Figs. 42:1–2, 46:1–4, 51:1–2). The jug of Figure 7.3:5 (Pl. 59:9) has a globular body, flat base, and trefoil rim. Such rims are quite common on Iron Age jugs, both in northern and southern assemblages. Analogies come from 'En Gev Stratum III (Mazar et al. 1964: Fig. 6:2) and Tel Dan Stratum IV (Biran 1982: Fig. 27:3).

Juglets

This stratum yielded a number of locally made dipper juglets and small "black juglets," as well as a group of imported juglets of Black-on-Red ware (Fig. 7.3:10–11) and White Painted ware (Fig. 7.3:12).

The dipper juglets (Fig. 7.3:6–8; Pl. 59:11–12) have a cylindrical body, rounded base, wide neck, and pinched rim. Although typical of Iron Age II, they are a continuation of the Iron Age I tradition. Similar vessels were found at Tell Keisan Stratum 8 (*Tell Keisan*: Pl. 56:6–7), Taanach Period IIB (*Taanach I*: Fig. 40:7, 11), Tell Abu Hawam Stratum III (*TAH*: Figs. 57–58), Megiddo Stratum V (*Megiddo I*: Pl. 5:141–142), Tel 'Amal Stratum IV (Levy and Edelstein 1972: Fig. 13:5–6), Beer-sheba Stratum IV (*Beer-sheba I*: Pl. 55:14), Tell el-Far'ah (S) Tomb 225 (*CPP*: 45J2), Tell Beit Mirsim Stratum B3 (*TBM I*: Pl. 51:12), and Beth-shemesh Stratum IIA (*Ain Shems IV*: Pl.

LXIV). The juglet of Figure 7.3:8 (Pl. 59:12), with its thickened rim, is rather different; this type was found mainly in sites of the southern Shephelah such as Gezer (*CPP*: 52M2), Tell el-Far'ah (S) (*CPP*: 52M3), and Lachish Stratum V (*Lachish V*: Pl. 42:10).

The black-burnished juglet (Fig. 7.3:9) has a rounded body and a handle extending from just beneath the rim to the body, whereas the handles of "black juglets" common in the 10th century issue from the center of the neck (Amiran 1969: Pl. 87:3) and the 8th-century types have a small, flattened body and a handle starting at the rim (Amiran 1969: Pl. 89:22). The Tel Michal juglets may represent an intermediate stage; they are rather small but not yet as tiny as the 8th-century specimens. Their handles have started to "climb" up the neck but have not yet reached the rim. Parallels come from Arad Stratum XI (Aharoni 1981: Fig. 7:15), Tomb 9 at Tell er-Reqeish (Culican 1973: Fig. 13:29a, Photo 479), and Tell en-Nasbeh (*TN II*: 851–854).

The juglets of Figure 7.3:10–11 are Black-on-Red II(IV) ware. Birmingham calls no. 10 (1963: Pl. 1:17) a two-handled flask. Number 11 has a long neck, swollen at midpoint where the handle is attached. For comparisons, see *SCE IV, 2*: Fig. XXXIX:9, 18.

The juglet of whitish clay, decorated with black paint (Fig. 7.3:12), is of White Painted II ware – a type of Cypriote ware found in a large number of sites in Israel, mainly in the north and the coastal plain, whereas it is rare in the interior (*Tel Mevorakh I*: 57–59).

Lamps

Several fragments of large, round-based lamps, resembling those of the preceding stratum, are not illustrated. The small flat-based lamp (Fig. 7.3:13) is paralleled in Megiddo Stratum V (*Megiddo I*: Pl. 38:18).

7.1.4. Stratum XII

No floors or occupational surfaces belonging to this stratum

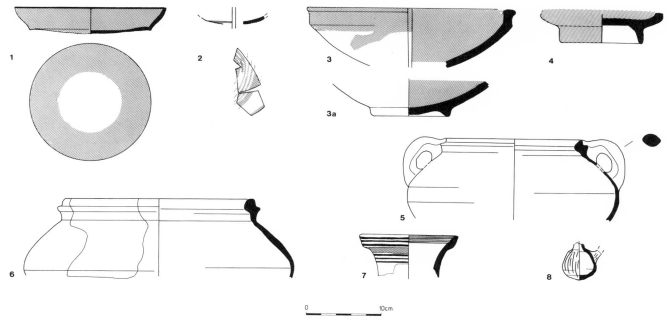

Figure 7.4. Pottery of Stratum XII (High tell).

Legend for Fig. 7.4

No.	Type	Reg. No.	Locus	Description
1	Bowl	8892/1	1400	Brown (brown); wheel burnish, red slip, black decoration.
2	Bowl	10345/4	1641	Yellowish (buff); wheel burnish, red decoration.
3	Bowl	8890/1	1400	Buff (buff), small white grits; red slip.
3a	Bowl	8890/1	1400	Buff (buff), small white grits, red slip.
4	Bowl	10345/5	1641	White (white); wheel burnish, red slip.
5	Cooking pot	9451/3	1501	Brown-red (brown-gray), small white grits.
6	Cooking pot	9541/1	1514	Brown (brown), small white grits.
7	Jug	8410/4	1259	Buff (buff); black and red decoration.
8	Juglet	7299/1	1069	Black (black); vertical burnish.

were distinguished, all the illustrated sherds coming from fills and sorted on typological grounds only. The little pottery there was, however, includes locally made vessels, "Samaria bowls," and Cypriote imports of Bichrome ware.

Bowls

Figure 7.4:1 shows a carinated bowl with very thin walls and flattened base, red slipped on the interior and exterior (except the base), and covered with closely spaced wheel burnishing. The rim is decorated with a black stripe. This vessel belongs to the "thin Samaria bowl" category, dated to the first half of the 8th century B.C.E., found in Samaria Period IV (*Samaria-Sebaste III*: Fig. 18:7), Hazor Strata X-IX (*Hazor I*: Pl. XLV:12–13), Tell Keisan Stratum 5 (*Tell Keisan*: Pl. 40:12a), and Tyre Strata III-II (*Tyre*: Pl. XI:12–14). The base of the bowl of Figure 7.4:2 also belongs to this group. It is red slipped on its interior and exterior and covered with continuous wheel burnishing. Its base is decorated with red and yellow concentric circles, formed by grooves in the slip that permit the natural yellow color of

the clay to show through. Similar decoration appears on bowls from Hazor Stratum V (*Hazor I*: Fig. LIV:6), Megiddo Strata V-III (*Megiddo I*: Pl. 25:1), Samaria (*Samaria-Sebaste III*: Figs. 9:2, 19:3–4), Tyre Stratum I (*Tyre*: Pl. I:2), and Tell Keisan Stratum 5 (*Tell Keisan*: Pl. 40:12a, b, c).

The carinated bowl of Figure 7.4:3 apparently belongs to the ring base of Figure 7.4:3a, although the joining piece is missing. It is red slipped and bears traces of burnishing. Based on its shape and yellowish "soapy" fabric, it is probably one of the "thick Samaria bowls." A similar vessel was found in Hazor Stratum VIII (*Hazor II*: Pl. LV:22). The trumpet base of Figure 7.4:4 is of the same ware (Amiran 1969: Pl. 67:14).

Cooking Pots

The two-handled cooking pots with thick, ridged rim of Stratum XII (Fig. 7.4:5–6) are the open type common all over the country from the second half of the 9th century through the 8th century B.C.E. For a comprehensive discussion, see Type 105 at Gezer (Gitin 1979,III: 230–235).

Jugs and Juglets

The red-and-black painted jug with everted rim, although found in an LB fill (Fig. 7.4:7), is of Cypriote Bichrome IV ware (*SCE IV, 2*: Fig. XXXIII:9); further examples come from sites along the northern coast, such as Al Mina Stratum VIII (du Plat-Taylor 1959: Fig. 2:4) and from the Middle Iron Age stratum (850–700 B.C.E.) at Tarsus (*Tarsus III*: Fig. 126:563, 606–608). Hanfmann (*Tarsus III*: 51–55) believes that some of these jugs were produced in Tarsus itself and some were imported from Cyprus.

The "black juglet" (Fig. 7.4:8) is burnished horizontally. Such juglets are known in Beer-sheba Stratum II (*Beer-sheba I*: Pl. 62:126–128), Lachish Stratum III (*Lachish III*, Pl. 88:309), Tell Beit Mirsim Stratum A (*TBM I*: Pl. 68:31), and Megiddo Stratum III (*Megiddo I*: Pl. 2:49).

7.2. EASTERN HILLOCK (AREA C)

Since most finds from Area C came from the *favissae* near the cult building (Structure 300), they could not be attributed to either of the two Iron Age strata and consequently were assigned to Strata XIV/XIII. Only one vessel, the foot of a chalice (Fig. 7.5:7), can be assigned to Stratum XIV. Three goblets (Fig. 7.5:15–17) are clearly from Stratum XIII. The pottery was very poorly preserved, apparently because of the high salinity of the soil; the clay was friable and crumbly, making reconstruction of the vessels extremely difficult.

7.2.1. Strata XIV/XIII

Bowls

The bowl of Figure 7.5:1 (Pl. 59:3) is large and round, its shape resembling the Black-on-Red bowl of Stratum XIV on the high tell (Fig. 7.1:1). However, its clay is coarser, it was turned on a wheel, and has a red-painted, pierced bar handle. The bowl is painted both inside and out with bands of black. The only analogies come from Tell Abu Qudeis Stratum IV (Stern and Beit-Arieh 1979: Fig. 9:8) and Tel Mevorakh Stratum VII (*Tel Mevorakh I*: Fig. 17:12–13, Pl. 33:9–10); there do not seem to be any such bowls in Phoenicia or Cyprus. Considering the coarse clay, Stern (*Tel Mevorakh I*: 54) regards this type as a local imitation of the Black-on-Red ware, an argument supported by the presence of bar handles (common on local bowls) instead of horizontal ones.

The red-slipped and hand-burnished carinated bowl with simple rim and small disk base (Fig. 7.5:2; Pl. 59:2) was discovered in situ covering the mouth of a cooking pot (Fig. 7.5:9; Pl. 59:6); it is identical to the carinated bowl (Fig. 7.3:1) of Stratum XIII on the high tell. The thick-walled bowl (Fig. 7.5:3), made of very coarse and crumbly clay, bears traces of red slip; it is difficult to determine whether it was burnished. The ring base of Figure 7.5:4 is

red slipped and hand burnished and seems to have belonged to a bowl or small krater like those found on the high tell (Fig. 7.1:4–5; Pl. 59:1).

Chalices

These were found only on the eastern hillock. The bowl element is carinated with a flaring rim (Fig. 7.5:5–8; Pl. 59:4–5); the high foot is either straight or stepped, and one of them has triangular fenestrations (Fig. 7.5:7; Pl. 59:4). Mazar (1977:228) has tried to follow the chronological development of such chalices from Tell Qasile according to the depth of the bowl (theorizing that the shallow bowl of Stratum XI becomes progressively deeper in later strata); however, the paucity of specimens has led him to express some reservations about his conclusions. Similar chalices were found in numerous sites throughout Israel, the shapes varying considerably in the 11th- and 10th-century assemblages (Mazar 1977:435, n. 937). Only rarely does this type of chalice appear after the 10th century B.C.E.

Cooking Pots

As on the high tell, the cooking pots in Area C are of two types: wide mouthed (Fig. 7.5:9–10; Pl. 59:6) and narrow mouthed, i.e., "cooking jugs" (Fig. 7.5:11). Both types also occur in the repertory of the "high place" excavated by Avigad (1961: Fig. 1:C-D).

Jugs and Juglets

The globular jug (Fig. 7.5:12) with long neck and ridged, trefoil rim is red slipped and hand burnished. Parallels were found in Tel 'Amal Stratum IV (Levy and Edelstein 1972: Fig. 11:7), Tel Mevorakh Stratum VII (*Tel Mevorakh I*: Fig. 16:1, Pl. 31:5), and Lachish Stratum V (*Lachish V*: Pl. 42:7). Another globular jug (Fig. 7.5:13) has a ring base and wide neck; although part of the rim is missing, it appears to have been of the trefoil type. Parallels come from Taanach Period IIB (*Taanach I*: Fig. 37:2) and Hazor Stratum VIII (*Hazor II*: Pl. LVIII:13–14).

The cylindrical dipper juglet with rounded base (Fig. 7.5:14; Pl. 59:10) has a wide neck and pinched rim. Traces of red slip are discernible. Similar juglets were found on the high tell in Stratum XIV (Fig. 7.1:12–14) and Stratum XIII (Fig. 7.3:6–7; Pl. 59:11).

7.2.2. Stratum XIII

The three goblets from Structure 300 (Fig. 7.5:15–17) are the only vessels attributable to this stratum. These goblets, present only on the eastern hillock, have a small globular body and a tall base. Such small goblets were not common in Iron Age II, and perhaps they go back to a prototype first appearing in the 13th century B.C.E. (*Megiddo II*; Pl. 72:14–15). This shape, with or without decoration, is common in Iron Age I (12th-11th centuries), for example, in Megiddo Strata VIIA, VIB, and VIA, the Beth-shan temples, and Tell Qasile Strata XII-X (Mazar 1977: Figs. 15:22, 23:43, 34:2, 36:7–11, 38:16, 44:13–14). Because this type

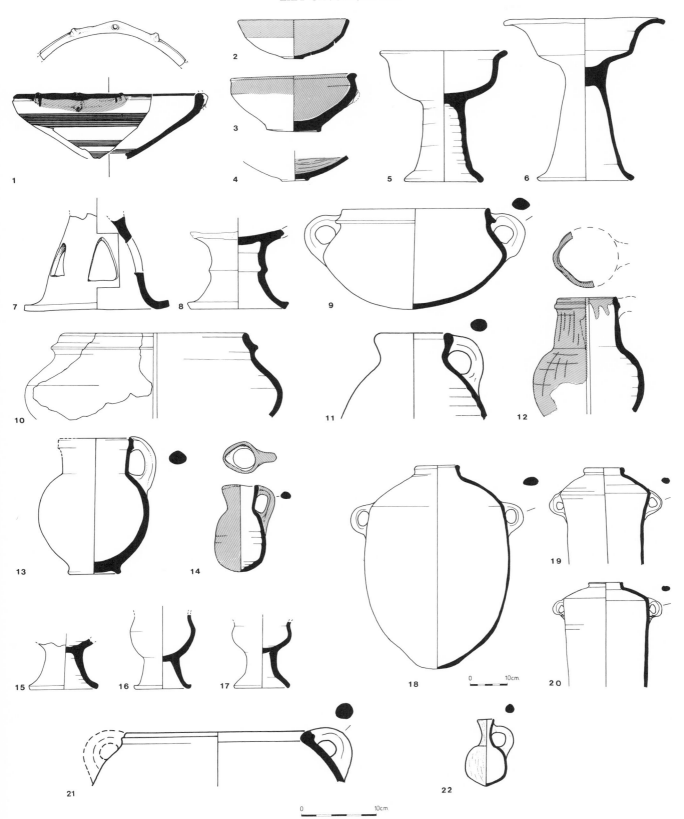

Figure 7.5. Pottery of eastern and southern hillocks (Areas C and B), Strata XIV–XII.

IRON AGE POTTERY

Legend for Fig. 7.5

No.	Type	Reg. No.	Locus	Description	Pl.
				Stratum XIV (No. 7) and Strata XIV/XIII, Area C	
1	Bowl	943/1	140	Light brown (brown); horizontal burnish, black and red decoration.	59:3
2	Bowl	947/1	140	Brown-red (brown-red), small white grits; hand burnish, red slip.	59:2
3	Bowl	949/1	128	Brown (black), small white grits; red slip.	
4	Bowl	943/2	140	Brown-gray (gray), small white grits; hand burnish, red slip.	
5	Chalice	921/1	128	Brown (gray), small white grits.	
6	Chalice	882/1	128	Brown (gray), small white and gray grits.	59:4
7	Chalice	954/1	467	Brown (brown), small white grits.	59:5
8	Chalice	937/1	140	Brown (black), small white grits.	
9	Cooking pot	947/2	140	Brown-red (gray-black), large and small white grits.	59:6
10	Cooking pot	916/1	128	Dark brown (gray), large and small white grits.	
11	Cooking pot	976/1	139	Brown (black), large and small white grits.	
12	Jug	903/1	128	Brown (gray), small white grits; hand burnish, red slip.	
13	Jug	3335/1	471	Brown (black), small white grits.	
14	Juglet	919/1	128	Light brown, small white grits; red slip.	
				Stratum XIII, Area C	
15	Goblet	1008/1	300	Brown (gray), small white grits.	
16	Goblet	3278/1	300	Brown (brown), small white grits.	
17	Goblet	3227/1	300	Brown (gray), small white grits.	
				Stratum XII, Area C	
18	Storage jar	3288/1	464	Buff (buff), large and small white grits.	59:16
19	Storage jar	975/1	454	Orange (orange), small white grits.	
20	Storage jar	3229/1	454	Orange (orange), few large grits.	
21	Cooking pot	984/1	145	Brown (gray), small white grits.	
				Strata XIV/XIII, Area B	
22	Juglet	701/1	124	Black (black); vertical burnish.	

of goblet was found in temples in all three of these sites, Mazar (1977:229) assumes that it (as well as its LB prototypes) was used in rituals. The Tel Michal goblets are much smaller than the other examples, but a similar vessel was found in Tyre Stratum XIII-1 (*Tyre*: Pl. XXXIII:23). Another parallel came from Megiddo Stratum III (*Megiddo I*: Pl. 33:3), but this late example seems to be a chance occurrence.

7.2.3. Stratum XII

The plump-bodied, round-based storage jar (Fig. 7.5:18; Pl. 59:16) came from Pit 464 near the platform of Structure 300. Made of light-colored clay, it has a slightly rounded rim and a ridge at the base of the neck. Such ridge-necked jars are known in the northern part of the country from the 10th to 6th centuries B.C.E. (*Taanach I*: 27), but the earlier types were heavier and reddish brown, whereas the later ones were made of light-colored clay, like our specimen. Furthermore, the ridge on the earlier jar is usually midway up the neck, as in Taanach Period IIB (*Taanach I*: Pls. 33, 34:1–3) or Tel Dan Stratum IV (Biran 1982: Fig. 26:3–4), whereas the ridge on later specimens is at the base of the neck, as in Megiddo Strata IV-III (*Megiddo I*: Pl. 14:70), Hazor Stratum VI (*Hazor III-IV*: Pl. CLXXXV:19), and Gezer Stratum VIA (Gitin 1979, II: Pl. 18:3, 4). Hence it seems that our specimen should be assigned to Stratum XII.

The cylindrical storage jars with pronounced shoulder (Fig. 7.5:19–20) have a short rim, almost square in profile. This type of jar made its first appearance in the 9th century, was very common in the 8th-7th centuries, and continued into the Persian period. It has been broadly discussed by Sagona (1982:75–78). These vessels, used extensively in maritime trade, were apparently produced in the Israelite kingdom, most likely at Hazor (Geva 1982:44–45).

The cooking pot with a thick, ridged rim (Fig. 7.5:21) resembles those of Stratum XII (Fig. 7.4:5–6) on the high tell.

7.3. SOUTHEASTERN HILLOCK (AREA B)

As on the eastern hillock, it was difficult to distinguish between Strata XIV and XIII. The pottery is poorly preserved and the assemblage meager. The black juglet assigned to Strata XIV/XIII (Fig. 7.5:22) is identical to that found in Stratum XIII on the high tell (Fig. 7.3:9).

7.4. CONCLUSIONS

The analysis of Iron Age pottery at Tel Michal shows the assemblage of the two earlier strata (XIV and XIII) to be similar, and one may assume them to be close in date.[3] The comparisons, chiefly with assemblages from the coast and northern part of Israel, provide a date in the second half of the 10th century B.C.E.

The assemblage correlates with the chronological range

of the following strata: Megiddo VA-IVB, Tell Abu Hawam III, Tel ʻAmal IV-III,[4] Taanach IIB, Hazor X, Tel Dan IV, Tel Mevorakh VII, Tell el-Farʻah (N) 3, Tell Qasile IX-VIII, Tell Keisan 8, and Gezer VIIA (according to Gitin's enumeration). The repertoire is not varied, the most conspicuous vessels being red-slipped, hand-burnished bowls and kraters. Certain vessels, like the Black-on-Red ware bowls and juglets and the Bichrome jug, show ties with the north, whereas others, like the carinated-shouldered storage jars and holemouth jars, have links to the south. In general, the pottery fits well with the assemblages of other coastal sites of Israel and was mostly locally produced. Along the Syro-Lebanese coast there are several sites rich in imported wares, but very few 10th-century sites in Israel, either coastal or inland, have yielded imported material in any quantity, the exception being Tel Mevorakh (*Tel Mevorakh I*: 52). This dearth of imports at Tel Michal corresponds with the stratigraphic-architectural evidence that the site was sparsely settled during the Iron Age, compared with the preceding Late Bronze Age and following Persian periods, which were both characterized by abundant imports.

Although the ceramic repertoire of Stratum XII is especially meager, comparative analysis shows that it should be dated to the 8th century B.C.E. The few finds there were may indicate some link with the northern part of the country, as reflected by the Samarian and Bichrome IV wares.

NOTES

1. These jars seem to be the forerunners of a type that became predominant later in the Iron Age, as seen in the 9th century B.C.E., for example, in Beer-sheba Stratum IV (*Beer-sheba I*: Pl. 55:19), and particularly in the 8th century—e.g., Beer-sheba Stratum II (*Beer-sheba I*: Pl. 57:1-3), Lachish Stratum III (*Lachish III*: Pl. 94:472), Tell er-Reqeish (Culican 1973: Fig. 1:R1), Gerar (*Gerar*: Pl. LV), Tell el-Farʻah (S) (*CPP*: 46:D, PI), Ashdod Stratum 3b, Area D (*Ashdod II-III*: Fig. 38:4)—and the 7th century—e.g., Lachish Stratum II (*Lachish V*: Pl. 49:18-19). These jars are common mainly in the Shephelah sites. Slight typological developments in this type of jar enable us to make a clear chronological distinction: the 8th-century specimens are wider than the earlier ones and their bases are shorter, whereas the 7th-century jars have a longer, truncated base (*Lachish V*: Pl. 54, Type SJ 250).

2. Holemouth jars become common throughout the southern part of the country: Beer-sheba Stratum II (*Beer-sheba I*: Pl. 58:17-28), Lachish Stratum III (*Lachish III*: Pl. 90:392), Tell Beit Mirsim Stratum A (*TBM I*: Pl. 52:6), and Beth-shemesh (*Ain Shems IV*: Pl. LXV:27); in the 7th

century, Lachish Stratum II (*Lachish III*: Pl. 97:537-541), Ramat Raḥel (*Ramat Raḥel II*: Fig. 21:1-12), and En-gedi Stratum V (*En-gedi 1966*: Fig. 21:1-2), albeit with minor changes, mainly in the shape of the rim.

3. The pottery published by Avigad from the northeastern hillock (1961: Fig. 1:b, c, d) is identical to that found in both strata.

4. Although Stratum IV at Tel ʻAmal is dated by the excavators to the first half of the 10th century B.C.E., Rast (*Taanach I*: 26) considers it to be closer to Stratum III.

REFERENCES

Aharoni, M. 1981. The Pottery of Strata 12-11 of the Iron Age Citadel at Arad. (Hebrew) *EI* 15:181-204.

Amiran, R. 1969. *Ancient Pottery of the Holy Land*. Jerusalem.

Avigad, N. 1961. Excavations at Makmish, 1960. *IEJ* 11:97-100.

Biran, A. 1982. The Temenos at Dan. (Hebrew) *EI* 16:15-43.

Birmingham, J. 1963. The Chronology of Some Early and Middle Iron Age Cypriot Sites. *AJA* 67:15-42.

Chapman, S. 1972. A Catalogue of Iron Age Pottery from the Cemeteries of Khirbet Silm, Joya, Qrayè and Qasmieh of South Lebanon. *Berytus* 21:55-194.

Culican, W. 1973. The Graves at Tell er-Reqeish. *Australian Journal of Biblical Archaeology* II, 2:66-105.

de Vaux, R., and Steve, A. M. 1951. La troisième campagne de fouilles à Tell el-Farʻah, près Naplouse. *RB* 58:393-430; 566-590.

de Vaux, R., and Steve, A. M. 1952. La quatrième campagne de fouilles à Tell el-Farʻah, près Naplouse. *RB* 59:551-583.

de Vaux, R., and Steve, A. M. 1955. Les fouilles de Tell el-Farʻah, près Naplouse. *RB* 62:541-589.

du Plat-Taylor, J. 1959. The Cypriot and Syrian Pottery from Al Mina, Syria. *IRAQ* 21:62-92.

Geva, S. 1982. Archaeological Evidence of Trade Relations between Israel and Tyre? (Hebrew) *EI* 16:44-46.

Gitin, S. 1979. *A Ceramic Typology of the Late Iron II, Persian and Hellenistic Periods at Tell Gezer*, I-III. Ph.D. dissertation. Hebrew Union College, Cincinnati, Ohio.

Kempinski, A., Zimhoni, O., Gilboa, E., and Rösel, N. 1981. Excavations at Tel Masos: 1972, 1974, 1975. (Hebrew) *EI* 15:154-180.

Kochavi, M. 1969. Excavations at Tel Esdar. (Hebrew) *ʻAtiqot* 7:14-48.

Levy, S., and Edelstein, G. 1972. Cinq années de fouilles à Tel ʻAmal (Nir David). *RB* 79:325-367.

Mazar, A. 1977. *The Temples of Tell Qasile*. (Hebrew) Ph.D. dissertation. Hebrew University, Jerusalem.

Mazar, B., Biran, A., Dothan, M., and Dunayevsky, I. 1964. Ein Gev Excavations in 1961. *IEJ* 14:1-49.

Sagona, A. G. 1982. Levantine Storage Jars of the 13th to 4th Century B.C. *Opuscula Atheniensia* 14:73-110.

Stern, E., and Beit-Arieh, Y. 1979. Excavations at Tel Kedesh (Tel Abu Qudeis). *Tel Aviv* 6:1-25.

8

Persian Period Stratigraphy and Architecture (Strata XI-VI)

by Ze'ev Herzog

8.1. STRATIGRAPHY

Remains of the Persian period are the most extensive at Tel Michal and appear in every area of the excavation (Fig. 1.2). Since all parts of the site were not occupied during the same time periods, different stratigraphic sequences developed in separate areas. On the high tell, six strata were observed, but only three exist on the northern hill and only one on each of the three eastern hillocks. Furthermore, the duration of occupational stages is not assumed to be the same length; there were relatively more frequent rebuildings on the high tell. Since there is no direct contact between the separate areas, it was necessary to establish a correlation based on typological and chronological considerations.

8.1.1. High Tell

In contrast to the earlier Bronze and Iron Age strata, which were reached in limited areas, the Persian period settlements were unearthed over most of the high tell. However, the final sequence of strata was determined only during the fourth and last excavation season, when the deepest deposits of this period were excavated at the center of the tell. This sequence includes six occupational phases, Strata XI-VI, each of which is represented by new constructions. The total accumulation of debris from these strata was close to 2 m.

The appearance in the fourth season of clear evidence for the existence of the lowest Stratum XI led to a reevaluation of stratigraphic conclusions concerning both the northern and southern ends of the high tell. Structure 872 at the northern end had been attributed previously to the Iron Age mainly because its fragments were situated above Structure 873 of the Late Bronze Age and below walls of Stratum X, then believed to be the lowest Persian stratum. Furthermore, at the end of the fourth season, a Persian

lamp was found under the northern wall of the building. Now it seems more appropriate to date these remains to Stratum XI.

A similar situation occurred in the southern part of the high tell. Pits 415 and 420, previously assigned to Stratum X, are now related to Stratum XI, since this stratum is characterized by pits, and in view of the early Eastern Greek pottery found in them.

Once the stratigraphic sequence in various parts of the high tell was established, a clear topographic differentiation arose between an upper terrace at the center and southern parts of the tell and a lower area at the north, the same configuration observed in the Iron Age (Chap. 6a). The differences in elevation (Table 8.1) demonstrate a step of 2.30–2.72 m.

Despite lower elevation, the main structure was located at the northern end of the high tell during all six phases of the Persian period. These buildings, interpreted as administrative headquarters or military forts, were probably located at this point because of its strategic advantage in controlling the ascent from the beach and the anchorage.

The uppermost Persian stratum, Stratum VI, was considerably disturbed by the construction of the Hellenistic fortress of Stratum V. Overall preservation of Persian period walls and intact floors is very poor, resulting in fewer objects in well-stratified contexts and the necessity of relying heavily on material found in fills and pits. The plans of forts and dwellings, when they include suggested reconstruction, should be regarded only as ideational suggestions rather than as precise outlines.

8.1.2. Northern Hill

Expansion of occupation over the northern hill took place for the first time during the Persian period. Because of very shallow and weathered remains, excavations on the north-

Table 8.1. Floor Elevation in Main Structures
on Upper and Lower Terraces of High Tell

Stratum	Upper Terrace		Lower Terrace		Difference in Elevation m
	Locus	Elevation m	Locus	Elevation m	
XI	1504	4.21	872	6.65	2.44
X	1506	4.00	717	6.35	2.35
IX	1308	3.60	339	5.90	2.30
VIII	1300	3.43	340	6.00	2.57
VII	940	3.03	343	5.75	2.72
VI	369	2.85	322	5.53	2.37

ern hill were limited to a small fraction (5 percent) of the original (estimated) size of the settlement. Several probes on the perimeter of the hill helped determine the extent of occupation and revealed data on nonhabitational activities such as pottery production and winepressing. The three Persian period occupational phases on the northern hill are assumed to be contemporary with the last three phases of this period on the high tell and are accordingly termed Strata VIII, VII, and VI. A wider chronological range without inner subdivisions is applied to the cemetery (Area E), whose tombs are assigned to Strata XI/VI (Chap. 11; Pl. 36). On typological grounds, the pottery kilns are assigned to Stratum IX or VIII.

The poor preservation of structures on the northern hill is a result of both discontinuity of occupation in most of the area and climatic destructive processes. In addition, the builders of the huge Hellenistic winepress (Stratum V) destroyed all the walls under it and leveled off the walls around it.

8.1.3. Eastern Hillocks

All three eastern hillocks were settled for the first time in the Iron Age and resettled in the Persian period, after a gap

of at least 300 years. Architecturally, one main occupational stratum in the Persian period exists on each of the hillocks, with scanty evidence of secondary use. It is possible that they were occupied already in Stratum VII, but the pottery is most similar to that of Stratum VI of the high tell. The stratigraphy of the two hillocks excavated by us (Areas B and C) corresponds exactly to that of the northeastern hillock excavated previously by Avigad (Chap. 1.2.2).

8.1.4. Excavated Area and Range of Occupation

Table 8.2 summarizes the different units used at Tel Michal in the Persian period with emphasis on their total area, the scale of excavations over the area, and the chronological range of settlements within each unit.

8.2. STRATUM XI

Building remains of Stratum XI were recorded solely at the northern end of the high tell, and this also was possible only after reevaluation of the evidence, as noted above (Section 8.1.1.). The rest of the tell was apparently covered with pits, ovens, and huts (Fig. 8.1).

8.2.1. Structure 872 at Northern End of High Tell

The main feature at the northern end of the high tell is Wall S144, constructed of light-yellowish sandy bricks laid on foundations made of two parallel rows of stones. The space between the rows of stones was filled with soil (Locus 701). At least one room (Loci 866 and 874) is evident from the fragmentary remains of Walls T148 and U1412.

The reconstructed plan of Structure 872 (Fig. 8.2) uses the southeastern side as a basic measure. We cannot determine whether more rooms existed around the central court-

Table 8.2. Total and Excavated Areas and Range of
Occupation in the Persian Period

Area	Location	Total Area m²	Excavated Area m²	Excavated Area %	Range of Occupation XI X IX VIII VII VI
A	High tell	1,600	750	47	——————
B	Southeastern hillock	1,000	250	25	———
C	Eastern hillock	625	200	32	———
D	Northern hill	13,000	600	4.6	———
E	Cemetery	7,500	750	10	——————
Total: Tel Michal expedition		24,125	2,550	10.5	
Northeastern hillock (Makmish)		1,000	200 ?	20 ?	

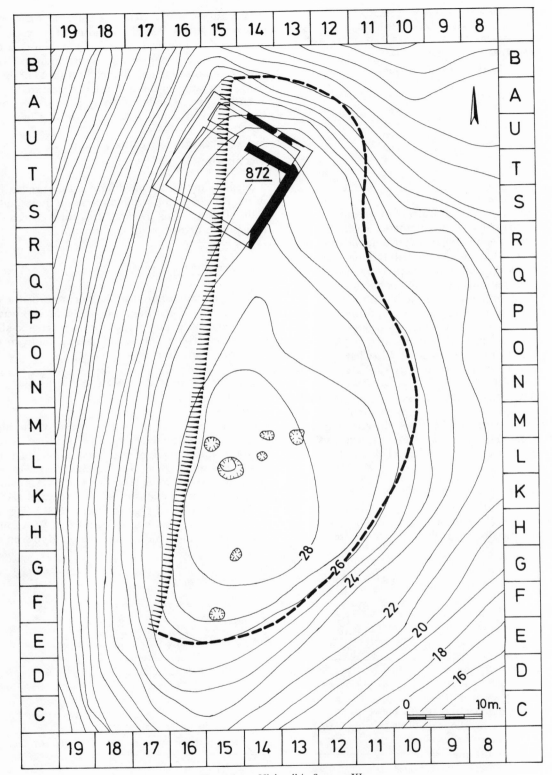

Figure 8.1. High tell in Stratum XI.

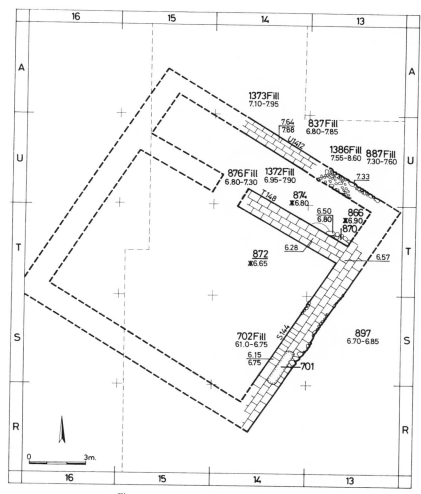

Figure 8.2. Structure 872 of Stratum XI.

yard because the southern side was destroyed by later construction and the western side is completely eroded.

8.2.2. Pits and Ovens

Wherever Stratum XI was reached south of Building 872, the only structures found were pits and ovens (Fig. 8.3; Pls. 21; 22) embedded in a thick layer of ashy soil (Locus 1500), which accumulated continuously. The pits were filled with ashes, bones, and pottery sherds. Presumably, their original function was storage, and after they were emptied of the stored commodities they were converted to waste disposal. This process was repeated several times; a good illustration appears in Stratum XI in Silo 1503, which cuts into Pit 1519.

The two southernmost pits (415 and 420) contained quantities of Eastern Greek and Cypriote pottery sherds, fragments of local vessels, an iron knife, and an alabaster vase.

The concentration of ovens (Loci 1504, 1505, 1507) in

one spot (Fig. 8.3) indicates that this was a communal cooking area. Like the pits, the ovens were not all used contemporaneously, as is apparent from their different elevations.

8.2.3. Conclusions

The settlement of Stratum XI is characterized by Structure 872, which served as administrative headquarters, and by the pits and ovens that we interpret as remains of a military depot. Whereas the camp commander and staff dwelt in Fort 872, we assume that the troops were quartered in tents or huts. The pits probably contained grain for the Persian army on its campaigns against Egypt (Chap. 2).

The average diameter of a pit is 2 m and the depth 1.5 m, which results in a capacity of 4.7 m³ for each granary, or almost 33 m³ for the seven pits that we exposed. If we estimate the total storage area as 10 times greater than that of the excavated areas, we come up with the considerable amount of 330 m³ of grain. Such quantities were probably transported to the site by ship.

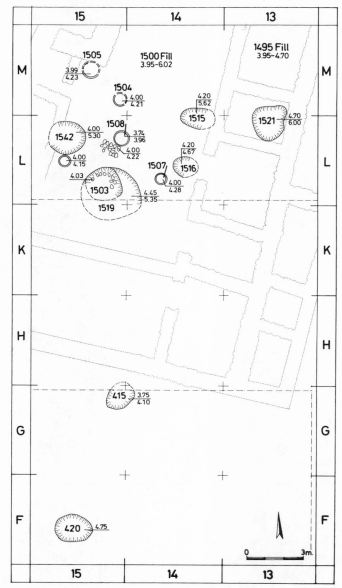

Figure 8.3. Pits and ovens in central and southern sectors of high tell, Stratum XI.

8.3. STRATUM X

The main difference in Stratum X (Fig. 8.4) is the introduction of houses that replace the previous (Stratum XI) pits and ovens in the center of the high tell.

8.3.1. Building Remains at the Northern End of the High Tell

The remains of Stratum X are relatively well preserved on the northern end of the high tell. However, the narrow strip on which they were preserved and the assumed large scale of the structure (or structures) that stood here make it impossible to reconstruct an overall layout (Fig. 8.5).

Wall R132 is the most substantial element, 1.5 m wide, but preserved to a height of only 0.5 m. Most of the area north of Wall R132 is occupied by Courtyard 856. The bodies of five pottery vessels, their bottoms either broken or intentionally removed, were sunk some 30–35 cm into the gray floor of the courtyard (Pl. 23). These vessels are found in a limited area and probably served as some kind of drainage installation. Three cooking ovens were found west of the installation, and a cylindrical stone roller of the type used for rolling plastered roofs was found nearby. Pits 864 and 1385 were cut for dumping garbage. The area east of Courtyard 856 was divided by Walls S135 and T132 into three spaces.

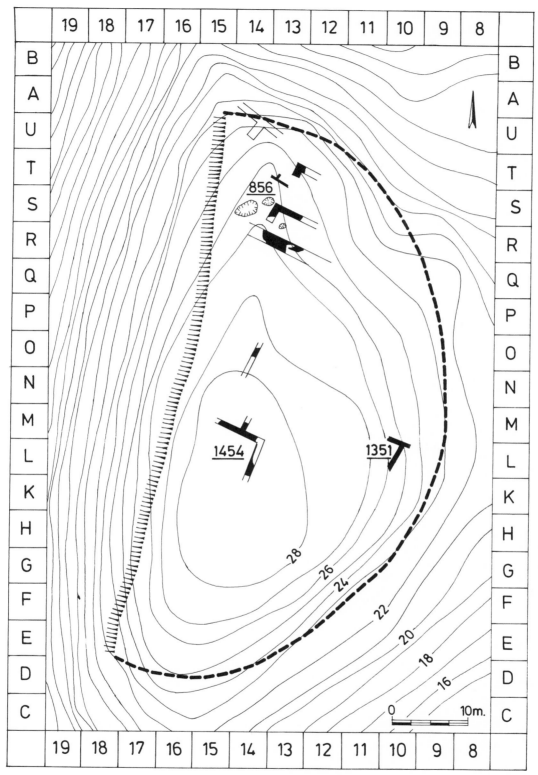

Figure 8.4. High tell in Stratum X.

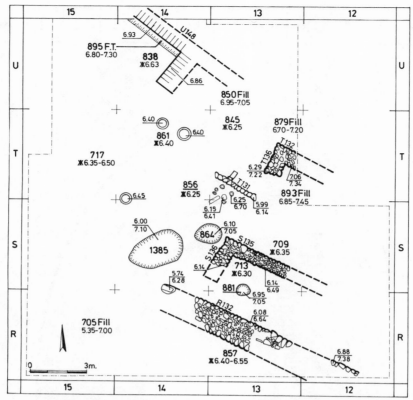

Figure 8.5. Courtyard 856 and surrounding structures, Stratum X.

The width of Wall R132 and the large Courtyard 856 support the assumption that a public building, possibly a fort, was located in Stratum X at the northern end of the high tell (as was true for all other phases of the Persian period).

8.3.2. Center of the High Tell

Sporadic remains of three structures are presented in Figure 8.6. The largest unit includes Courtyard 1454, with a partially paved floor of *kurkar* pebbles. In the unpaved northern part of the courtyard were two ovens, indicating a cooking function. Another oven and paved areas (Loci 1501 and 1509) were found east of Wall L147.

On a much lower elevation, hence on the lower terrace, fragments of two additional structures (1351 and 1656) were unearthed. The only other evidence from this stratum comes from fills (Fig. 8.6).

8.3.3. Conclusions

Construction of houses in the center of the high tell points to two functional changes in the site: first, it serves as evidence of permanent occupation; second, it illustrates the diminishing (or discontinuity?) of the storage function.

8.4. STRATUM IX

Remains of Stratum IX include stone-built structures found all over the high tell (Fig. 8.7). As in other phases of the Persian period, an upper terrace (Structures 412, 1308, and 1483) is distinguished from the rest of the mound. Several pits and silos appear at the southern end.

8.4.1. Building 344 and Its Vicinity

No significant wall appears at the northern end of the high tell in Stratum IX to indicate the existence of a main structure. Judging from the earlier and later character of this part of the site, we tentatively combined Walls S145 and R139 into Structure 344 (Fig. 8.8). The resulting hypothetical structure is composed of Courtyard 344 (with an oven), small Chamber 1909 in the center, and large storage Pit 840 on the eastern side.

Floors 339 and 839 presumably belong to open space that separated Structure 349 from Structure 898. The latter is also tentatively reconstructed on the basis of fragments of Walls R155 and R148. West of the two structures, a large Pit 721 was used for dumping refuse.

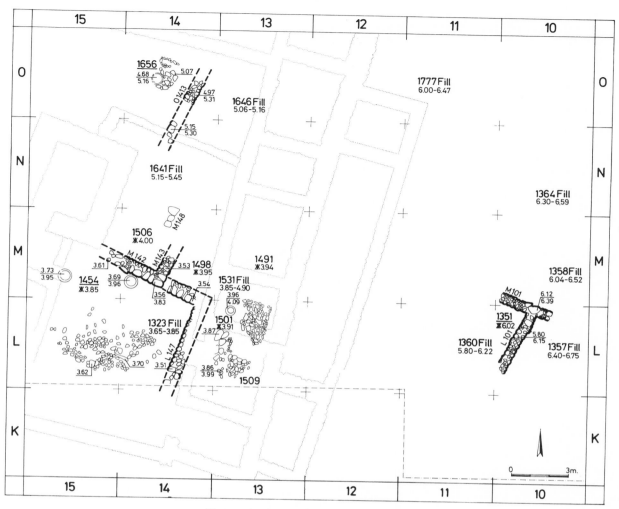

Figure 8.6. Center of high tell, Stratum X.

8.4.2. Central and Southern Sectors of the High Tell

Remains of several structures are present at this part of the tell. The two better-preserved areas were on the upper terrace: Structures 1308 and 412 (Fig. 8.9).

Structure 1308 is roughly square (7.5 m × 8.5 m) and includes an L-shaped courtyard (Loci 1308 and 1453) with stone pavement. It is not clear whether the courtyard was closed on its northern side. A small Chamber 1322 (2.2 m × 2.6 m), also with stone pavement, is located at the northwestern corner of the building. A doorway with raised threshold, 1.5 m wide, connected the courtyard and what is evidently an additional (unexcavated) part of the building on the south.

Structure 412 is reconstructed from several poorly preserved walls. The room could have served as a central unit for several stone-lined silos (Loci 997, 1251, and 410) and larger pits (Loci 985 and 988). The storage area was bolstered on the east by a series of retaining walls (F142, F143, and F144).

On the lower terrace, poorer building remains are discernible. Structure 1771 on the east contained at least two rooms. The northern part of Figure 8.9 includes several wall fragments with no clear layout.

8.4.3. Conclusions

It seems reasonable to attribute to Structure 344 the function of an administrative center for the small settlement. However, the homogeneous nature of structures over the high tell may point to a decrease in the role of central authority and the development of a local, more independent community.

8.5. STRATUM VIII

Stratum VIII marks the start of a flourishing period in the history of Tel Michal. In addition to the occupation on the high tell (Fig. 8.10), we also assign to this stratum the first activity on the northern hill.

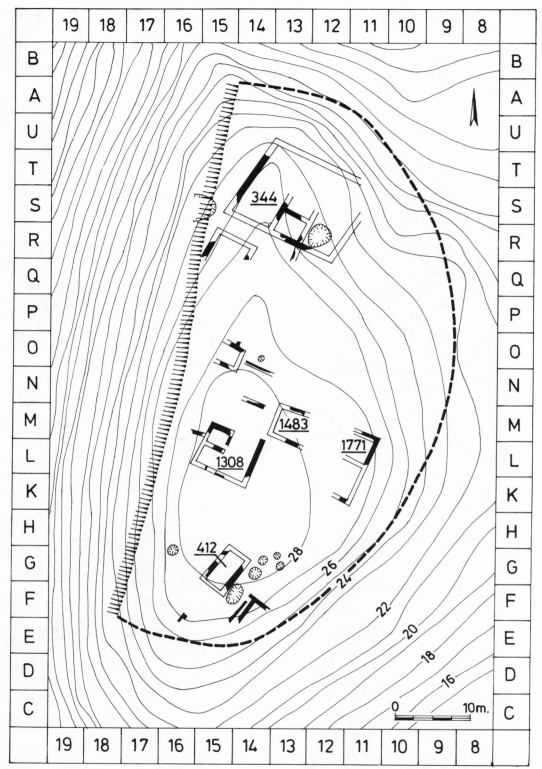

Figure 8.7. High tell in Stratum IX.

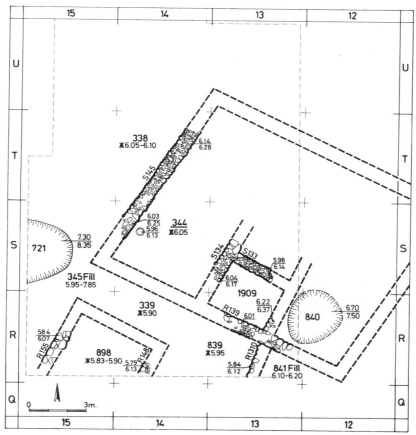

Figure 8.8. Structure 344 on northern end of high tell, Stratum IX.

8.5.1. Fort 340 at the Northern End of the High Tell

Although largely reconstructed, our suggested layout of Fort 340 is supported by the width of the main walls, by their orientation, and above all by monumental Stairway 859 that led into the courtyard (Fig. 8.11). Courtyard 340 is reconstructed by assuming an entrance in the center of Wall T145; accordingly, the courtyard measures 11 m × 11 m. It had a beaten-earth floor, and an oven was found next to Wall S142. Stairway 859 is 1.60 m wide and each step was 20–25 cm high. This was apparently the main entrance into Fort 340.

The general plan of the fort is unknown; however, it is clear that a room or rooms were located on the northwestern side (Locus 342). Two rooms (one numbered 830) that were annexed to the fort on its northern side probably served as watchtowers controlling both the stairway and the approach from the beach.

Three wall segments (R134, R138, and R145) were discovered in the courtyard at asymmetric angles. They may be inner partitions for Locus 722A, which perhaps served as an enclosure for donkeys or horses.

8.5.2. Remains in the Central and Southern Sectors of the High Tell

On the upper terrace of Stratum VIII, two main structures – 1304 and 89 – were unearthed (Fig. 8.12). Retaining Wall F151 supported the raised elevation of this terrace on its southwestern side. On the lower terrace, there were remains of several more fragmentary structures.

Structure 1304 is basically a revised phase with some internal alterations of Structure 1308 (Stratum IX). A small room (948) is now separated in the southern corner, whereas the rest of the area is reserved for Courtyard 1304. East of Structure 1304, two rooms (1490 and 1499) may have belonged to the same building, but the connection is missing.

The southern end of the high tell is relatively well preserved, for two reasons: the area was supported by retaining Wall F151, which was about 4.00 m wide, and the unusually rich collection of pottery vessels found in Room 92 in a burnt destruction level must have resulted from a local fire (no other buildings in the settlement were similarly burnt). The western side, however, suffered strong erosion.

The existing part of Structure 89 includes Courtyard 89 and Room 92. The courtyard, which is quite small (3.00 m × 3.50 m), was entered from the north, via Lane 405 (see

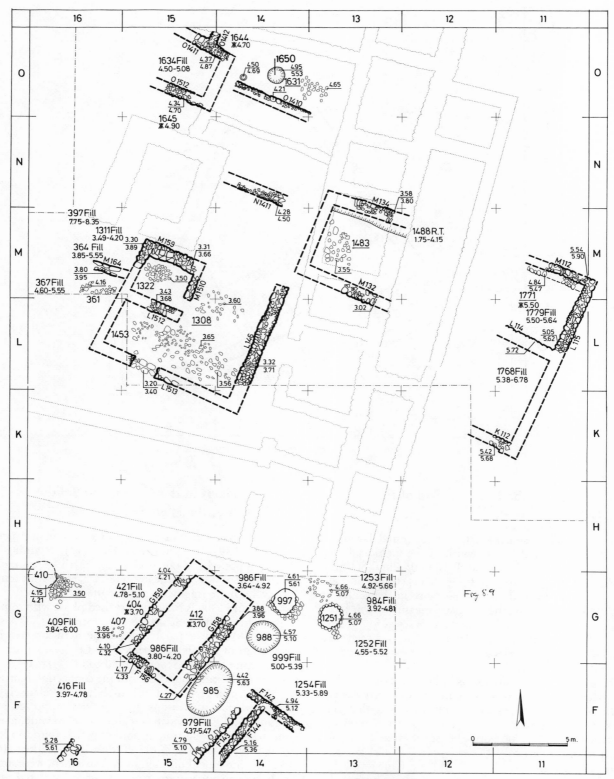

Figure 8.9. Central and southern sectors of high tell, Stratum IX.

98

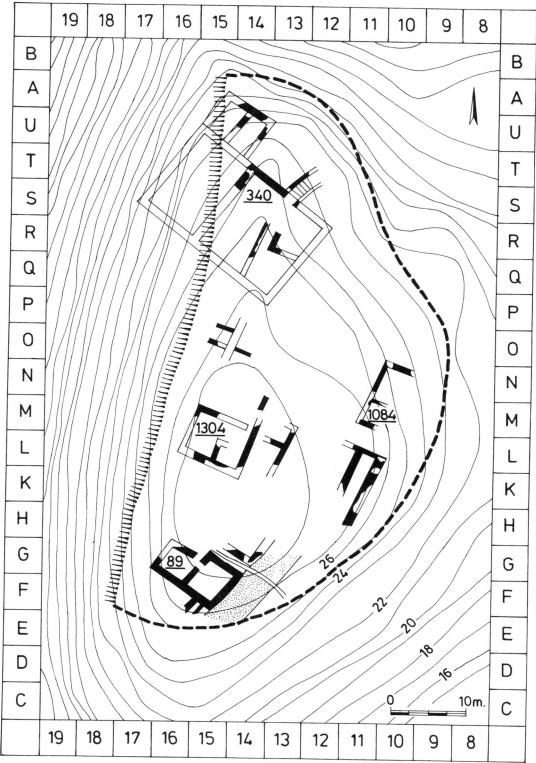

Figure 8.10.   High tell in Stratum VIII.

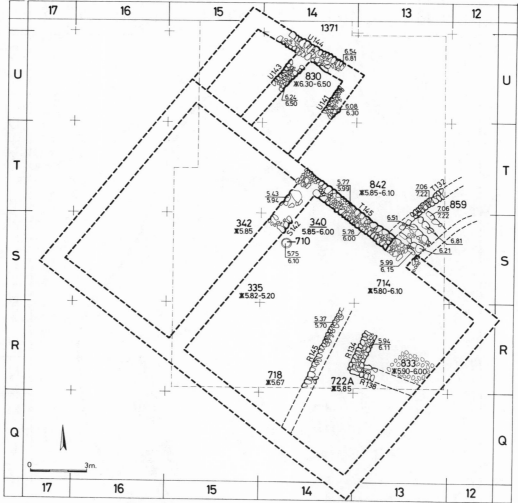

Figure 8.11. Fort 340 on northern end of high tell, Stratum VIII.

below). Another doorway connected the courtyard with Room 92 (3.60 m × 4.25 m), which was found packed with a thick layer of burnt bricks mixed with broken pottery vessels. The 1.00-m-wide walls of Room 92, made of *kurkar* stones (Pl. 24), were preserved to a height of 1.5 m, unusual at Tel Michal. The *ḥamra* brick superstructure had collapsed into the room, forming a layer of debris about 60 cm deep.

In the southwestern corner of Room 92, a semicircular, stone-lined silo (Locus 93) contained two intact storage jars (Pl. 25). When the broken vessels from the main part of Room 92 and from Silo 93 were restored, 27 storage jars came to light (Figs. 9.4; 9.5; 9.6). Such a concentration of storage jars in a rather small room clearly points toward its function as a storeroom, probably a wine cellar. The full wine jars occupied most of the room, whereas the stone-lined silo in the corner was presumably used to stack empty jars.

Stubs of Walls F153 and F154 suggest that more rooms (or structures) existed in Stratum VIII south of Structure 89,

but they were entirely eroded, together with the southern end of retaining Wall F151.

Only a fraction of a house (Wall G144) to the north of Structure 89 fell within the excavated area. The two houses were separated by Lane 405, 1.20 m wide. Under the floor of the lane ran Drain 413, which conducted rainwater below retaining Wall F151 and outside the settlement. The drain, which was 40 cm wide, was covered with flat *kurkar* slabs.

Several structures were partly uncovered on the lower terrace, but there were insufficient data for a detailed analysis (see Structures 1032, 1084, and 1069 on Fig. 8.12).

8.5.3. Northern Hill (Areas D and E)

The earliest occupational level in Area D is correlated to Stratum VIII on the high tell. In the central part of the northern hill, this level consisted of an accumulation 2 m thick of ashes mixed with small stones, animal bones, and quantities of pottery sherds (see Loci 1113 and 1128 on Fig. 8.21).

Figure 8.12. Center and southern end of high tell, Stratum VIII.

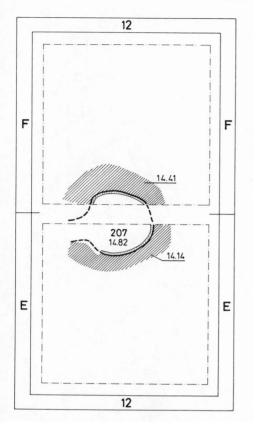
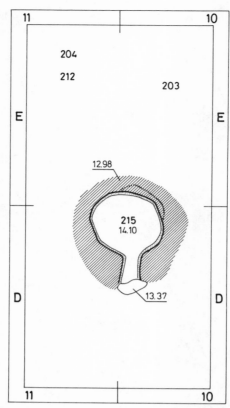
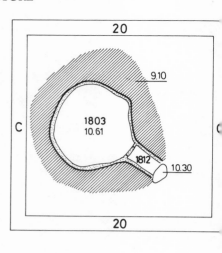

Figure 8.13. Pottery kilns on northern hill (Area D).

Remains of industrial installations were found on the periphery of the northern hill. On the eastern side, a small winepress (Locus 510) was identified. It consisted of a plastered pressing floor (80 cm × 80 cm) and a circular vat about 70 cm in diameter. Wall fragments and floor patches around the installation indicate that the area was also inhabited (Pl. 33).

On the southern and western sides of the hill, remains of three pottery kilns were discovered (Fig. 8.13; Pls. 30; 31). The best preserved is Kiln 1803, which undoubtedly collapsed at the end of a firing process and was then abandoned. In the debris of the kiln, parts of five storage jars (Fig. 9.12:6–10) were found mixed with the clay and bricks of its superstructure (Pl. 32). The opening for feeding the fire chamber of the kiln was still blocked. The shape of the lower part is roughly circular, 2.20–2.40 m in diameter. The walls of the kiln were constructed with square *hamra* bricks laid against the pit in which it was built. The kiln was plastered several times on the inside; in some cases, the plaster overheated and was transformed into a melted, slaglike glazed clay. Figure 8.14 shows an attempt to reconstruct the shape of the kiln, based on the evidence described above. The pottery vessels lay on an intermediate floor supported by small brick-built columns.

Two similar but slightly smaller kilns were uncovered on the southwestern side of the northern hill (Kilns 215 and 207; Fig. 8.13; Pl. 34). Interestingly, despite their spatial proximity, the ventilation (and fuel-feeding) openings are oriented in a different direction in each of the three kilns. Perhaps they were coordinated with the prevailing winds (southeast, south, and southwest) during different parts of the day or in different seasons of the year.

8.5.4. Conclusions

Stratum VIII illustrates the climax of a process of development at Tel Michal that started with Stratum XI as a military post and grew into a multifunctional military-commercial and civilian village. Fort 340 continued to fulfill an administrative and military role, but Structure 89 may already represent a local wine merchant. The emerging "lower city" on the northern hill emphasizes a variety of light industries: winepressing, pottery production, and possibly metal forging, which may be deduced from the many metal objects uncovered on the northern hill and the slags collected on its southern slope (Chap. 25b.9). The growth of population and stability of occupation are further reflected by intensified usage of the northern slope as a graveyard.

8.6. STRATUM VII

Stratum VII marks a powerful increase in the size and quality of construction: both Fort 329 and Structure 1013

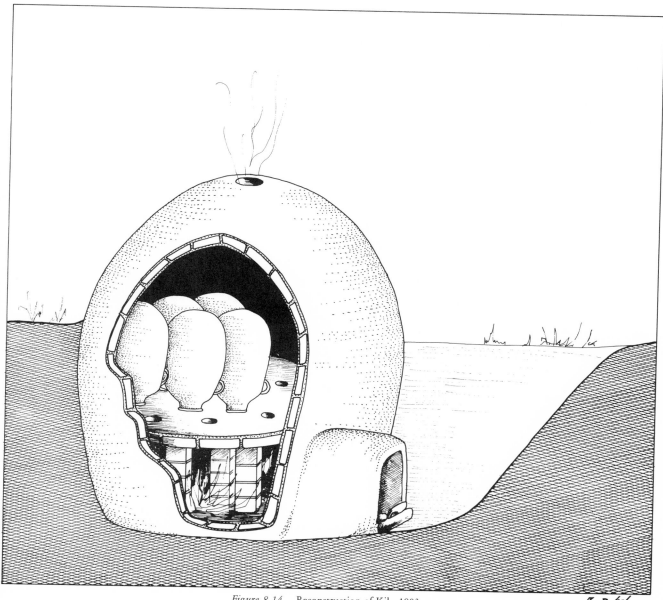

Figure 8.14. Reconstruction of Kiln 1803.

J. Dekel

demonstrate such achievements (Fig. 8.15). In this phase we also see the first use in the Persian period of the three eastern hillocks. The detailed description of these remains will, however, be incorporated into the discussion of Stratum VI, since the single occupation phase on the eastern hillocks covers the period of both Strata VII and VI on the high tell. Clear continuity between Strata VII and VI is marked also by the reuse of Fort 329 in Stratum VI (Fort 324).

8.6.1. Fort 329

Only a narrow ridge remained of the original northern part of the mound, but it contains the substantial Wall S141, which clearly belongs to a public building, interpreted by us as Fort 329 (Fig. 8.16). Wall S141, 1.40 m wide, is constructed of dark clay bricks laid over *kurkar* stone foundations. Two sections of roughly perpendicular walls (T142 and R153), 12 m apart, form the framework to inner Courtyard 329. The white chalk floor of the courtyard joined Wall S141 at its stone foundation by means of a slanted step that contained a channel for a water drain. Drain 704 drew runoff water eastward from Courtyard 329, through Wall S141 and under Structure 341 (Pl. 26). The channel was 40 cm wide and covered by squared *kurkar* capstones laid well above the floor surface.

At the northern end of Wall S141 there was a stone threshold of well-hewn chalk stones, belonging to the main

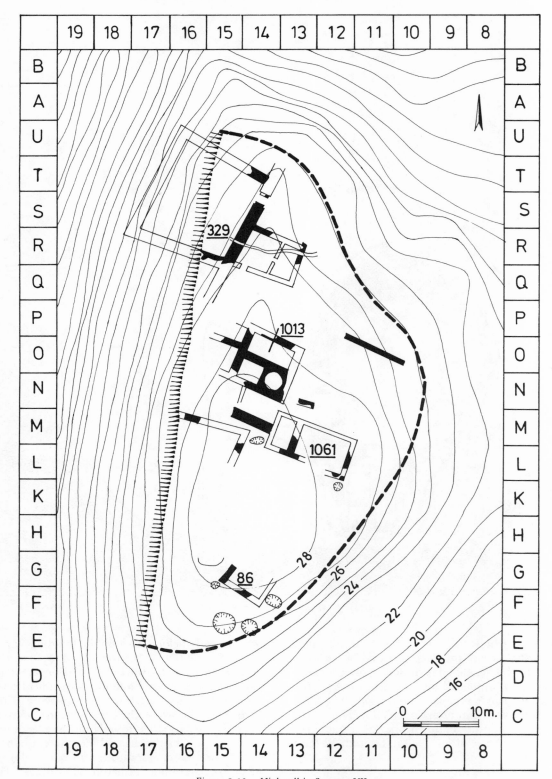

Figure 8.15. High tell in Stratum VII.

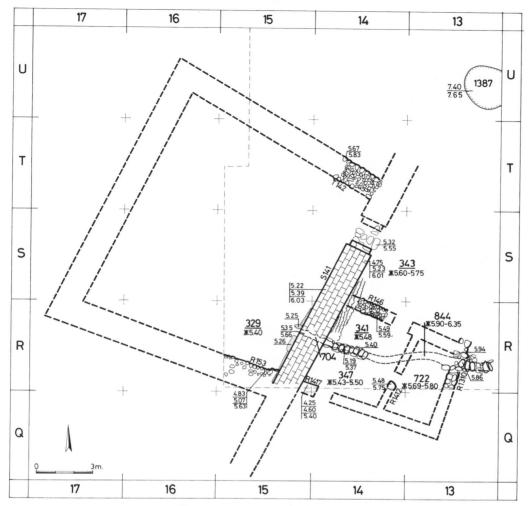

Figure 8.16. Fort 329 of Stratum VII.

entrance into Fort 329. No evidence is available on the rooms that presumably abutted the central courtyard because of the limit of excavations on the south and the severe erosion on the west and north.

Structure 341 is annexed to Fort 329 on the east. Its almost completely reconstructed layout contains two rooms. The location of Structure 341 next to the entrance into the fort suggests that it served as a guardroom for the gatekeepers, a function similar to that of the annexed rooms of Stratum VIII Fort 340 (Fig. 8.11).

8.6.2. Structure 1013 and Structures to the South

In contrast to the previous strata, the upper terrace of the high tell has no structure of any significance, and the most important one is Structure 1013 on the lower terrace (Fig. 8.17). The separation between the two terraces is marked in Stratum VII by retaining Wall M141, which supported the structures to its south on a higher elevation.

Structure 1013 contains five units, but more rooms could have existed both on the western and northern sides. Room 1013 measures 2.40 m × 5.60 m and was filled with a deposit 80 cm deep of disintegrated mudbricks. Under the debris, a large amount of pottery vessels, an iron blade, and an oven were found, suggesting that Room 1013 had been a small courtyard.

The parallel southern part, separated by Wall 0134, was divided into two parts, one round and one square (Rooms 1029 and 1022), both surrounded by brick walls. Excavations in Room 1029 revealed that its floor was sunk about 2.00 m lower than the floor level in the rest of the building. This fact, in addition to the circular shape of the room, tends to indicate its use as a public silo for grain storage (Pl. 27). The upper half-meter of its walls curves inward, showing that the silo had a domed roof. The entrance into the silo had to be located in the upper (mostly missing) part, since no other opening into Room 1029 was observed. Several pottery vessels (Fig. 9.8:1–13) found at the bottom of the silo must have been discarded after the silo was emp-

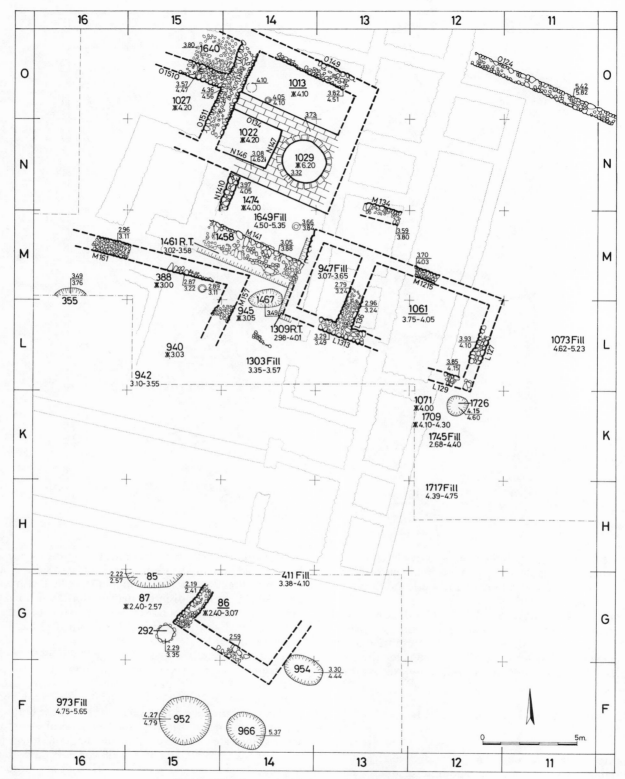

Figure 8.17. Center and southern end of high tell, Stratum VII.

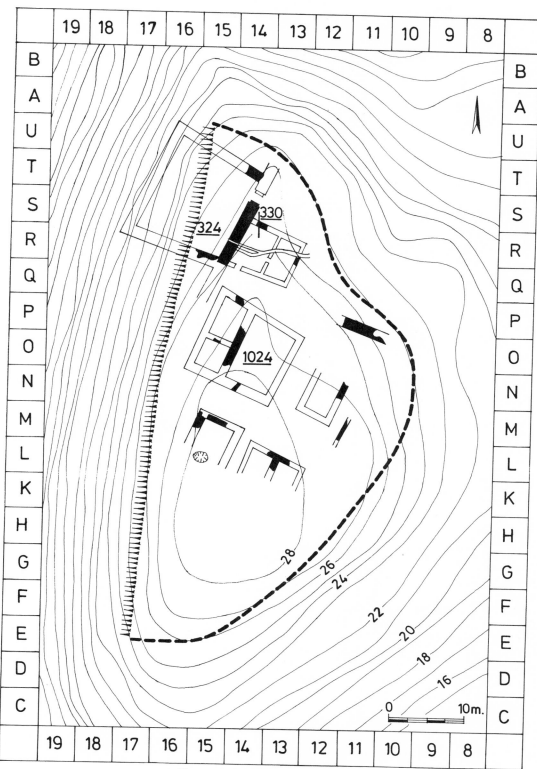

Figure 8.18. High tell in Stratum VI.

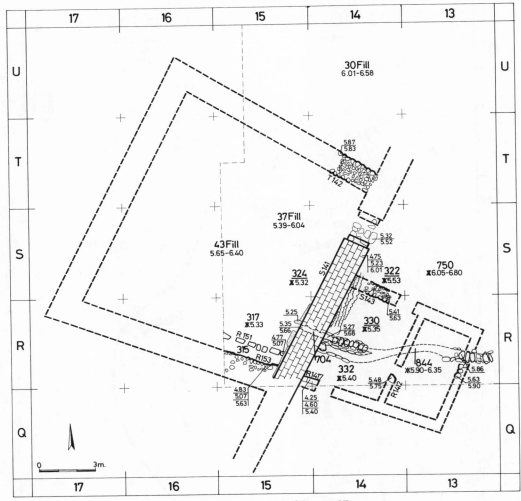

Figure 8.19. Fort 324 of Stratum VI.

tied with no intention of reuse. In Room 1022, the bricky debris goes down more than 1 m; a Persian mortarium and part of a storage jar were found in it (Figs. 9.9:1, 4).

The two western units, Rooms 1027 and 1640, are only partially preserved; the latter was paved with small pebbles. Structures 1061 and 388 are fragmentary, and it is difficult to reconstruct a meaningful plan.

In the southern sector of the high tell, Room 86 was centered in a group of pits and silos. The pits vary in size (1.50 - 3.20 m in diameter). Pit 954 is about 1 m deep, and the rest were eroded. It may be assumed that the pits were originally silos, like Silo 292, and later were reused for dumping refuse.

8.6.3. Northern Hill and Eastern Hillocks

Stratum VII is represented on the northern hill only by fragmentary walls and pavements. It appears that, in this phase, the area was still used mainly for light industry and that construction of actual buildings only began in Stratum VI.

The three eastern hillocks may well have come into use in Stratum VII, but as only one phase was observed the detailed description is presented under Stratum VI.

8.6.4. Summary and Conclusions

The division of the high tell into a fort on the north, dwellings in the center, and storage facilities on the south is maintained in Stratum VII, but with some alterations. Structure 1013, with its large silo, was obviously not a private dwelling but was used for administrative and economic purposes. This interpretation is supported by the clay bulla found in the fill of Silo 1029. The bulla, which bears two different seal impressions, probably to seal a commercial document (see Chap. 28a: No. 7; Pl. 74:3) indicates that this building had an official function. This is an interesting change from the more monumental scale of construction, previously restricted to a military fort. Additional storage capacity was provided in the concentration of storage pits at the south of the high tell.

As suggested above (8.1.3), it is quite possible that occu-

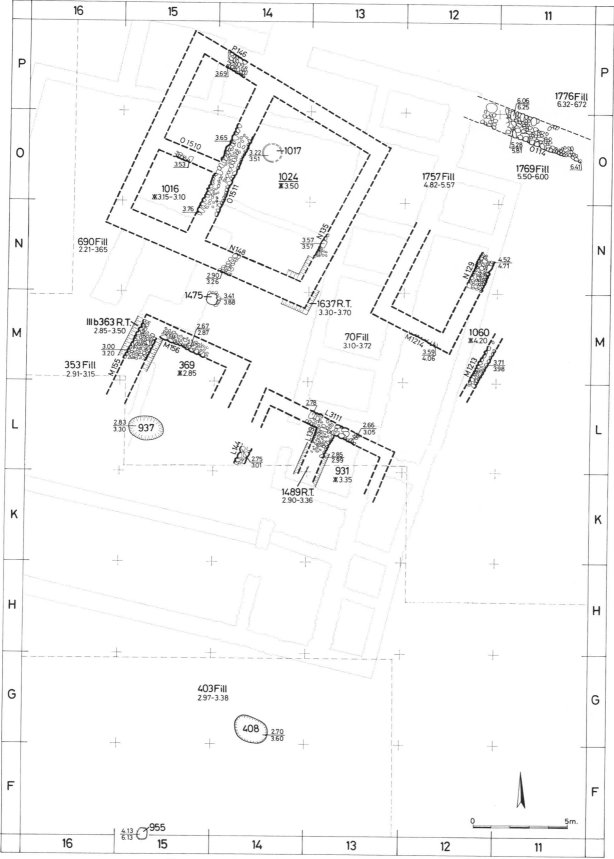

Figure 8.20. Center and southern end of high tell, Stratum VI.

pation of the eastern hillocks started in this stage. The Phoenician chapel on the northeastern hillock (known as Makmish) is dated to the same general period (Avigad 1977:768–770). Its distance from the high tell (about 400 m) and its close association with the cemetery on the northern hill may be an indication of social (and/or ethnic) divergence between the inhabitants on the peripheral mounds and the political and military administration on the high tell. Social stratification may also be deduced from the different types of burials and especially from the contrast between the stone-built cist graves and the more simple types (see Chap. 11).

8.7. STRATUM VI

In most respects, Stratum VI is simply a continuation of Stratum VII: the plan of Fort 324 follows that of Fort 329 (Fig. 8.18). The only important change is the discontinuation of Structure 1013 of Stratum VII, which is replaced by Structure 1024.

On the eastern hillocks only one building phase was found. It is assumed that it correlates to Strata VII-VI on the high tell, without any destruction between the two strata. The majority of the finds, of course, date to the latest of the two strata (VI).

8.7.1. Fort 324

Fort 324 is a reuse, with slightly raised floors (Fig. 8.19), of Fort 329, which was then still standing. The only alteration is a line of ashlar *kurkar* stones (Wall R151) built only 50 cm away from Wall R153. The fact that the stones do not lie on the floor but on a higher level (together with the large intervals between individual blocks) may indicate that this is not their original position. They may have fallen from an upper part of the fort.

Minor changes were introduced in Guardhouse 330, which replaced former Structure 341. An additional channel now joined Drain 704 in Room 330. A coin of Alexander the Great was found stuck into the floor of Entryway 322, and a second one was found in Locus 750, slightly down the slope (see Chap. 27: Nos. 28, 32).

8.7.2. Buildings in the Center and South of the High Tell

Remains of four structures covering most of the center of the high tell (Fig. 8.20) are so fragmentary that nothing certain can be said about their layout or size. It is clear, however, that Structure 1013 was no longer in use and that the new structure in Stratum VI (Structure 1024) did not have the public nature of its predecessor. According to our hypothetical reconstruction, Structure 1024 contains a large courtyard (6.10 m × 8.60 m) with Oven 1017, and at least two rooms on the west. The other structures at the center of the tell suffered in later construction processes that also tended to rob earlier walls. This damage is demonstrated by Robbers' Trenches 363, 1489, and 1637 (Fig. 8.20) and 935 (Fig. 12.7).

Two silos (Loci 408 and 955) in the southern sector are related to Stratum VI, so they mark the continuity of use for storage of this end of the high tell. Four storage jars, a large jug, and a juglet (Fig. 9.10:1–6) found in Silo 955 are evidence for this.

8.7.3. Settlement on the Northern Hill (Area D)

An extensive area was exposed on the eastern side (Fig. 8.21), and smaller probes were cut on the southern side and in the northwest corner of the northern hill. Before these excavations, bulldozers had to remove overlying sand dunes that were up to 2 m high. In spite of the sand protection, the architectural and artifactual remains are very poor. The reasons for such poor preservation are trifold: first, the latest Persian period settlement was not destroyed but abandoned, and the houses were emptied of their valuables; second, most of the architectural remains were dismantled by builders of Winepress 566, who leveled off all the area around it (Pl. 35); and, finally, erosion after the Hellenistic period and before the accumulation of the dunes added to the destruction. Consequently, only a single foundation course was preserved in most cases, and an intact floor level is seldom noted. Only fragmentary, scattered pottery was found in the area (Fig. 9.13; Pl. 28).

The resulting plan (Fig. 8.21) of Stratum VI is difficult to interpret in terms of separate buildings or internal divisions. However, two characteristics are obvious: settlement limits and common orientation. Most of the walls on the northern hill are similarly oriented to the northeast or to the northwest, which suggests an attempt at planning. An even stronger point for planning is the straight and continuous line of Wall G151, which borders the settlement on its southeast side. Since the wall is only 70–80 cm wide, it was probably not a fortification wall but simply a kind of stone fence to demarcate the settlement.

8.7.4. Eastern Hillock (Area C)

Part of a brick structure (Fig. 8.22) was uncovered on the eastern hillock (Structure 143). Its continuation to the southeast was destroyed by Hellenistic Silo 135 (Pl. 29). Room 143 contains a plastered bench along Wall N51; the white plaster continues from the bench down to the floor. Two parallel drainage channels (Locus 137), plastered and lined with sherds, run southeast of the building. On the northern side of Room 143 are scattered stones, probably from an open space or courtyard (Locus 129). In the debris north and east of Building 143, vast quantities of shells and large chunks of white lime indicate that shell and bones were burnt to produce lime for plaster.

In the vicinity of Structure 143, several pits contained a hoard of seven unused oil lamps (one too fragmentary to illustrate) (Fig. 9.11:3–8; Pl. 64:10), two fragments of incense altars (Fig. 31.6:7–8), a hoard of five coins inscribed to Alexander the Great (Chap. 27), and a silver signet ring (Chap. 28a: No. 5; Pl. 74:1). These fine objects strongly

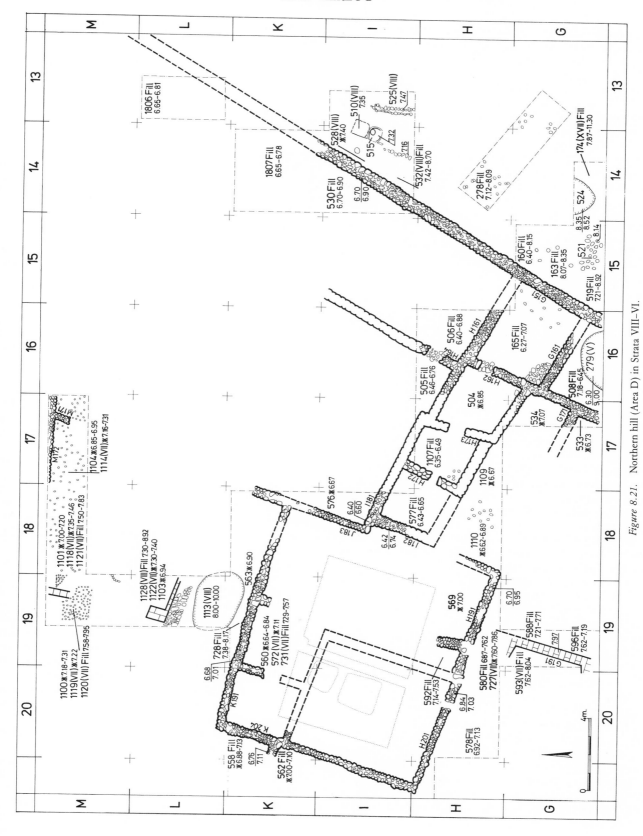

Figure 8.21. Northern hill (Area D) in Strata VIII–VI.

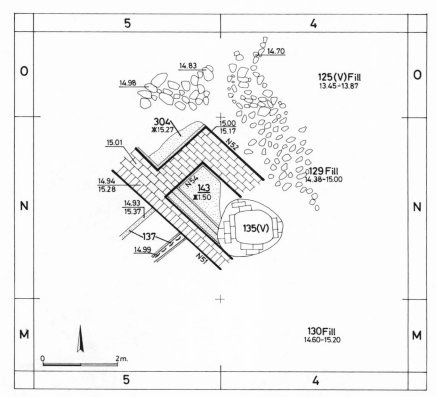

Figure 8.22. Structure 143 (Strata VII–VI) and Silo 135 (Stratum V) on eastern hillock (Area C).

suggest that Structure 143 had a religious function and that the pits were *favissae* for the offerings brought to it.

8.7.5. Southeastern Hillock (Area B)

Persian period occupation here (Fig. 8.23) generally follows the Iron Age layout: a circular arrangement of units around an open courtyard (Chap. 6a.3.1). In some cases (Structure 112), the very foundations of an Iron Age house (117) were reused.

On the southern part of the hillock, a single structure (237) was found, almost totally eroded. It was constructed over a layer of gray fill (Locus 241). The shape of the building is rectangular (3.20 m × 8.80 m), with entrance on the short northern side (Wall C172). A small patch of raised floor may indicate a second phase of use in the Persian period.

On the northern side of the hillock, two rooms are attributed to Stratum VI. Room 112 (at the west) was constructed over the foundations of Room 117 of Stratum XIV. Structure 108 (at the east) consists of trapezoid Room 108, with a stone pavement in its eastern half and adjacent brick Platform 110. South of the two buildings was an open courtyard, partly paved with stone (Loci 103, 104). The area was partially excavated during Avigad's expedition to Makmish (Loci 101, 106).

8.8. SUMMARY AND CONCLUSIONS

The results of our excavations of the Persian period remains at Tel Michal show a peculiar dichotomy: the quantity of material is overwhelming, but the picture of particular structures or strata is mostly incomplete because of accumulated destructive processes. With the given preservation conditions, only a method of extensive exposure as applied by our expedition could produce the large inventory of pottery, metal, glass, stone, and bone artifacts analyzed throughout this volume.

The chronological framework for the division into six phases of the relatively short period was achieved through independent studies by Anson F. Rainey of the history of the region (Chap. 2) and by Ronald T. Marchese of the Greek imported wares (Chap. 10). Conclusions were confirmed by the study of local pottery by Lily Singer-Avitz (Chap. 9) and, for the later phases, by the numismatic study of Arie Kindler (Chap. 27).

The overall picture of the six phases reflects a process of development in the site from a military station in Stratum XI to an extended settlement in Stratum VI (Table 8.3). This process is attested to in the northern hill, where a settlement estimated as covering an area of thirteen hectares shows clear signs of planning. It was probably smaller but similar to the site of Tel Megadim, a northern neighbor in the Persian period (Broshi 1977). A well-planned city of the

Table 8.3. Summary of the Persian Occupation at Tel Michal

	High Tell	Type of Settlement		Cultural and Historical Correlations	Approximate Dates[a] (B.C.E.)
		Northern Hill	Eastern Hillocks		
XI	Fort 872; granaries and ovens	. . .	. . .	Eastern Greek and Cypriot wares. Cambyses invades Egypt 525 B.C.E.	525–490
X	Courtyard 856 (in fort?); dwellings	. . .	. . .	Egypt revolts after 460	490–450
IX	Fort 344; dwellings and granaries	. . .	. . .	Eshmunezer is given the mighty lands of grain in Sharon	450–430
VIII	Fort 340; dwellings and Storehouse 89	Kilns, small winepress, and refuse pits	. . .	Sharon plain firmly in Phoenician control	430–400
VII	Fort 329; Storehouse 1013; dwellings and granaries	Planned settlement	Sanctuaries at Makmish and Building 143 on eastern hillock; farmstead on southeastern hillock	Coins of 'Abd-'ashtart (378–358 B.C.E.)	400–350
VI	Fort 324; dwellings	Planned settlement	Same as above	Persian pottery and coins of Alexander the Great. Ptolemy occupies Syrian coast (301 B.C.E.)	350–300

[a] For dates, see also Chap. 2.

same period is now being uncovered at Tel Dor (Stern 1983), with strong evidence for regularity in planning.

The founding of a military depot at Tel Michal in the third or last quarter of the 6th century B.C.E. is clearly related to the invasion of Egypt by Cambyses in 525 B.C.E. The absence of a settlement on the site rules out Stager's assumption that the storage pits in the Persian period served to store a surplus during the seasons of plenty (Stager 1971:88), as well as the hypothesis by Goffer et al. (1983) that such pits were intended for the preparation of compost to fertilize cultivated fields. The sandy soil around Tel Michal is not arable, and the grain to fill the silos and granaries in Stratum XI and subsequent phases had to be brought either by ship or overland from the fertile eastern part of the Sharon, or even farther away.

The development of the site was supported by the only agricultural product that may be raised on the sandy coastal soil—grapes. Evidence for earlier winepresses is described in Chapter 6b. To the small Winepress 510 in Area D we may add a larger one, located between Areas B and C, that was cleaned by Avigad's expedition and contained Persian period material (M. Megiddon, personal communication).

An important economic factor was the local production of pottery vessels (Kiln 1803), which may have supplied the storage jars found in the wine cellar of Structure 89 in Stratum VIII.

The prosperity of the site is well attested by the rich repertory of imported vessels (Chap. 10) and the large quantities of metal objects (Chaps. 25a and 25b). The large concentration of metal artifacts on the northern hill, the evidence of forging of ferrous metals (Chap. 25b.9), and the abundance of metal offerings in the cemetery reflect both the wealth of the population and the work of local metalsmiths.

The sea was surely an important source of subsistence. Fishing is evident from bones as well as from lead fishing weights (Chap. 25a: Nos. 153–160). Trade relations with Greece, Cyprus, Egypt, and Persia are well documented through finds of pottery, alabaster, jewelry, glass, coins, and metals.

This large range of contacts makes it difficult to ascertain the kind of population that lived at the site. The dominant group seems to be the Phoenicians (Chap. 2); however, a seal from the cemetery, found by Avigad, is inscribed with Palaeo-Hebrew script that shows a number of special traits in common with the Samaritan seals from Wadi ed-Daliyeh (Cross 1966:209, n. 26). This may point to a mixed population of Phoenicians and Samaritans (and Jews?) on the site.

Tel Michal was not destroyed during the campaign of Alexander the Great; like some other sites (Shiqmona and Tel Ṣippor; Stern 1982:255), it continued to exist undisturbed until the end of the 4th century B.C.E.

REFERENCES

Avigad, N. 1977. Makmish. *Enc. Arch. Exc. III*: 768–770.

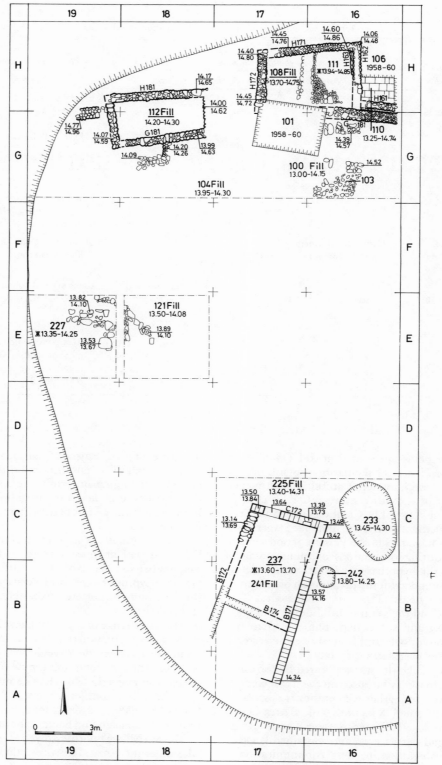

Figure 8.23. Structures on southeastern hillock (Area B).

Broshi, M. 1977. Megadim. *Enc. Arch. Exc. III*: 823–826.

Cross, F. M. 1966. Aspects of Samaritan and Jewish History in Late Persian and Hellenistic Times. *HTR* 59:201–211.

Goffer, Z., Molcho, M., and Beit-Arieh, I. 1983. The Disposal of Waste in Ancient Beer-sheba. *JFA* 10:231–235.

Stager, L. E. 1971. Climatic Conditions and Grain Storage in the Persian Period. *BA* 34:86–88.

Stern, E. 1982. *Material Culture of the Land of the Bible in the Persian Period, 538–322 B.C.E.* Warminster.

Stern, E. 1983. Notes and News: Tel Dor, 1983. *IEJ* 33:259–261.

9

Local Pottery of the Persian Period (Strata XI-VI)

by Lily Singer-Avitz

9.1. Introduction

Remains of the Persian period were found at Tel Michal in all areas of excavation: the high tell, the northern hill (Areas D, E, and F), the two small hillocks to the east (Areas B and C), and the hillock in the northeast excavated in 1958 and 1960 (Avigad 1977). On the tell itself there were six strata of the Persian period (Strata XI-VI), reflecting continuous occupation throughout the period, whereas in Areas B, C, D, and F most of the pottery came from the final phase. The cemetery (Area E), although unstratified, seems to cover the entire period.

The assemblage of Persian period pottery is rich and varied and includes a large repertory of imported wares (see Chap. 10). The purpose of this study, however, is to trace the internal typological evolution and chronological sequence of locally produced pottery. (In an attempt to determine whether certain vessels of dubious origin were locally produced, we submitted 16 samples to petrographic analysis, the results of which appear in Chap. 24c.)

Our typological study is based primarily on material found on the floors or recovered from well-stratified pits and silos of the six Persian strata on the high tell, producing a basic scheme with which the pottery of the northern hill and the small hillocks can be correlated and supplemented by comparative material from contemporaneous sites. Some of the available comparative material has not been used at all, particularly that derived from sites where stratigraphic continuity is lacking for the Persian period or where the period is represented only by nonstratified pits or by a stratum that was roughly assigned to the 5th-4th centuries B.C.E. on the basis of its Attic ware or coins. In many such sites, the evaluation of the pottery—as S. Gitin (1979, III:12) so aptly puts it—is often based "on the intuitive skills of the excavator and not on hard evidence."

There are two works summarizing the ceramic data of this period. The first (Stern 1982) is a comprehensive study of all facets of the Persian period, with a chapter on the pottery covering all the published—and much of the unpublished—material excavated before 1978. The second is by Lapp (1970), who attempted to put the typological development of the pottery into a chronological framework. However, his classification of the ceramic material into five successive chronological groups was based on assemblages that to a large extent are unstratified, and he also failed to take regional variations into account. Our comparisons are therefore drawn mainly from well-stratified sites such as Akko, Shiqmona, Tell Abu Hawam, Tel Megadim, and Tel Mevorakh that—like Tel Michal—are situated on the Mediterranean coast.

The assemblages are presented typologically (from open to closed vessels), stratum by stratum, whereas loci rich in material are treated as separate units. Pottery from fills or other loci of dubious stratigraphic attribution has been excluded from this report. Vessels of particular interest are discussed in detail under the stratum in which they first appear in quantity. For types that have been dealt with extensively by Stern (1982), the reader is referred to his bibliography. The typological charts (Figs. 9.16–9.17) are intended to help the reader follow the development of the individual types or the presence (or absence) of a diagnostic vessel in a particular stratum.

Absolute dates (B.C.E.) for each of the six Persian strata on the high tell have been determined by the imported Eastern Greek, Cypriote, and Athenian wares (Chap. 10), as well as by historical considerations as follows (for a more detailed dating scheme, see Chap. 2):

Stratum XI: 525–490
Stratum X: 490–450
Stratum IX: 450–430
Stratum VIII: 430–400

Stratum VII: 400–350
Stratum VI: 350–300

When referring to comparative material, I have followed the excavators' dates for the relative sites with two exceptions. First, for Tell Keisan, the transition from the Iron Age to the Persian period that falls between Strata 4 and 3 is dated by the excavators to 580 B.C.E., and the transition between the Persian and Hellenistic periods (between Strata 3 and 2) is dated to 380 B.C.E. (*Tell Keisan*: 27). Neither date is acceptable on historical grounds. The beginning of Stratum 3 should be lowered to the end of the 6th century and that of Stratum 2b (Early Hellenistic, according to the excavators, and dated by them to 380–312) should be added to the Persian period for the following reasons: (1) Stratum 2b includes Loci 111 and 113, which contain storage jars of definite Persian type (*Tell Keisan*: Pl. 7:1, 1a, 4) that do not exist in the Hellenistic repertory. (2) In Stratum 2a there is a significant architectural change: the building of Stratum 2b ceases to exist, and there are only pottery deposits (*Tell Keisan*: 113, Fig. 30). (3) The pottery of Stratum 2a seems to be a mixture of Persian period and Hellenistic wares. Consequently, Stratum 2b is still Persian, perhaps ending with the conquest of Akko by Ptolemy I in 312 B.C.E. (*Tell Keisan*: 113). Second, for Tell Abu Hawam we have followed Stern (1968), who dates Stratum IIA to 538–385 B.C.E. and Stratum IIB to renewal shortly after 385 until 332 B.C.E.

9.2. HIGH TELL

9.2.1. Stratum XI

The earliest Persian period stratum is characterized by silos and cooking ovens. The largest ceramic assemblage came from Pit 415 on the southern slope, which penetrated into the Iron Age stratum and was sealed by a floor of Stratum IX. In addition to the local ware (Fig. 9.1:4, 8–9, 11, 14), this pit contained a varied collection of imported East Greek and Cypriote wares (Chap. 10; Fig. 10.1:1–3, 6).

Bowls (Fig. 9.1:1–2)

The only type of bowl from this stratum is popularly called a "mortarium," a large, heavy vessel with an externally thickened rim, rippled outer surface, and thick ring base. The clay is coarse and poorly levigated. Number 1 is of yellowish clay, and No. 2 is of brown clay. This vessel, so ubiquitous throughout the Persian period that it has become known as the "Persian bowl," is discussed at length by Stern (1982:96–98).

Cooking Pots (Fig. 9.1:3–4)

The Persian period cooking pot continues the tradition of its late Iron Age predecessor, but its body is now more globular and it has developed a short neck with a ridge at the bottom and a triangular, everted rim. Two handles extend from rim to shoulder. Parallels come from a Persian

fortress near Ashdod, a single-period site dated to the 5th century B.C.E. (Porat 1974: Fig. 4:13), and from Stratum 2b at Tell Keisan (*Tell Keisan*: Pl. 2:9, 9a).

Storage Jars

Fragments of the five most common types of storage jars of this period at Tel Michal already appear in Stratum XI. Jar Type 1, elongated with narrow body, rounded rim, short neck, thick walls, and two shoulder handles (Fig. 9.1:10) is made of greenish white clay (see Section 9.2.4). The Type 2 storage jar (Fig. 9.1:11) is characterized by a bag-shaped body and a very short neck. Although present in Strata XI–X, this type is more common in Stratum IX (Section 9.2.3). The flat-shouldered jar (Type 3; Fig. 9.1:12) is discussed in Section 9.2.3. The amphora Type 4 (Fig. 9.1:13) has an externally thickened rim, a narrow ridge at midneck, and two rounded handles. In Cypriote terminology, this amphora belongs to Type VI Plain White ware (Gjerstad 1960: Fig. 16:2). Its widespread distribution includes mainland Greece, Rhodes, Cyprus, and the eastern Mediterranean coast. According to Stern (1982:114), it is of Eastern Greek origin.

The basket-handled jar, classified as Type 5, has an elongated body narrowing down diagonally at midpoint to a pointed base. The two handles rise high above the rim.

The jar is widely distributed along the eastern Mediterranean coast from Al Mina in the north to Naukratis in the south. In Israel it is found mainly in coastal sites, less frequently in the hinterland (Stern 1982:111). Many of these jars have been recovered from the sea (Barag 1961: Pl. 7:6; Zemer 1977: Pl. 8:24), and it seems that they were used extensively in the flourishing maritime trade of the period.

There are three variants of this type. Variant A (Fig. 9.15:1–2) has a relatively long neck, rounded rim, and narrow ridge at the base of the neck. Variant B (Fig. 9.15:3–5) also has this ridge but a much shorter neck and an everted rim. On Variant C the ridge is missing and there is no neck at all, the everted rim issuing directly from the shoulder (Fig. 9.1:14–15).

The last is the only variant that was found on the high tell and in Area D; the best preserved specimens came from Strata XI–IX, although there were still numerous sherds in Strata VIII–VI. In the cemetery, however, the basket-type jars were all either Variant A or Variant B.

Judging by the contexts in which these jars have been found, we see that they seem to appear at the end of the Iron Age, namely at Meṣad Ḥashavyahu (Naveh 1962: Fig. 6:13, upper fragment, neck missing) and Tell Keisan (*Tell Keisan*: Pls. 23–24). At the latter site the shape differs from that of the Persian period: the body is shorter and more squat, the neck is even longer than that of Variant A, and there is a depression in the lip suitable for holding a lid. At Shiqmona it was noted that the basket-handled jars of the Babylonian period had a relatively long neck (*Shiqmona I*: 60); although none were illustrated, we assume that they resemble those of Tell Keisan. Apparently Variant A (with neck) existed in Israel only at the beginning of the Persian period as a continuation from the Iron Age, since it has

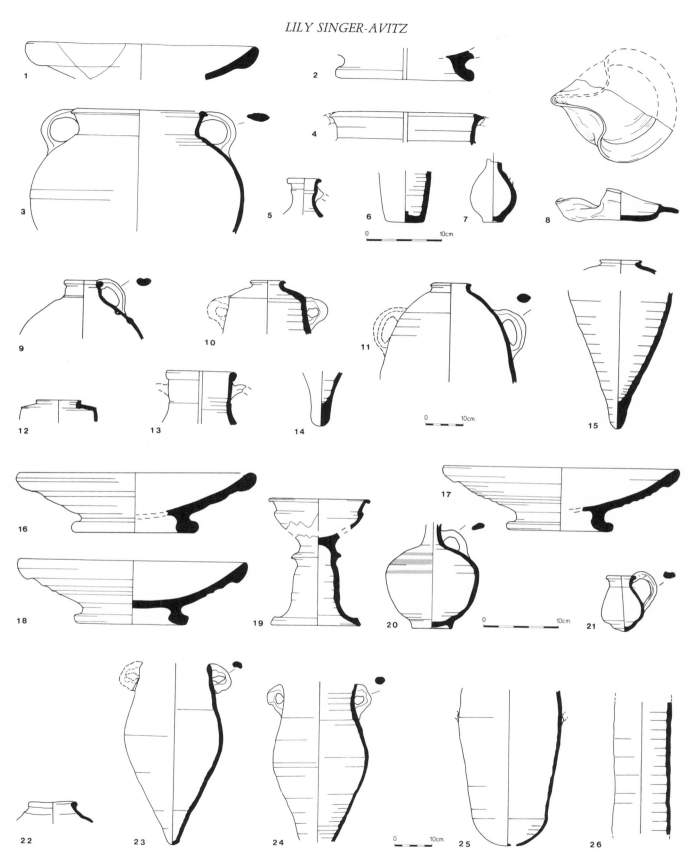

Figure 9.1. Pottery of Stratum XI (Nos. 1–15) and Stratum X
(Nos. 16–26).

Legend for Fig. 9.1

No.	Type	Reg. No.	Locus	Description
1	Bowl	9459/3	1500	Buff (buff), small white and gray grits.
2	Bowl	9631/1	1515	Brown (gray), small gray grits.
3	Cooking pot	10402/1	1666	Brown (brown), small white grits.
4	Cooking pot	2498/1	415	Brown (brown), small white and gray grits.
5	Decanter	9621/2	1500	Buff (buff), small gray grits.
6	Juglet	9543/1	1519	Buff (brown), small white grits.
7	Juglet	10413/1	1666	Light brown (brown), small white and gray grits.
8	Lamp	2522/3	415	Pink-orange (pink), few small white and gray grits.
9	Jug	2522/2	415	Light brown (light brown), small white and gray grits, large white grits.
10	Storage jar	9621/1	1500	Buff (buff-gray), small white grits.
11	Storage jar	2513/1	415	Brown-pink (gray), small white and gray grits, large white grits.
12	Storage jar	9620/2	1500	Orange (orange), small white grits.
13	Amphora	9631/2	1515	Brown (brown-red), small white and gray grits.
14	Storage jar	9459/2	1500	Brown (brown-gray), small white and gray grits.
15	Storage jar	2522/1	415	Orange (gray), small white grits, large white grits.
16	Bowl	9430/1	1454	Buff (buff), small gray grits.
17	Bowl	5856/1	881	Light brown (light brown), small gray grits.
18	Bowl	5954/1	857	Brown (brown), small black grits.
19	Chalice	5403/1	713	White (white), small white and gray grits.
20	Jug	10448/1	1656	Brown (brown), small white and gray grits; horizontal burnish; red decoration.
21	Cup	5779/1	864	Brown (brown), small white grits.
22	Storage jar	9451/1	1501	Brown-pink (light gray), small white grits.
23	Storage jar	9462/1	1501	Orange (orange), small gray grits; horizontal burnish.
24	Storage jar	5697/1	856	Orange (orange), small white and gray grits.
25	Storage jar	9467/1	1501	White (white), small gray grits.
26	Drainage pipe	5681/1	856	Brown-red (brown-red), small white and gray grits.

been found only in 5th-century sites at the Persian fort near Ashdod (Porat 1974: Photo 4:14) and at Tell Abu Zeitun (Stern 1982: Photo 156). Variant C (neckless) persisted throughout the entire period, judging by its presence in Megiddo Stratum I (*Megiddo I*: Pl. 12:64); Tel Megadim (Stern 1982: Photo 157); Shiqmona, in both Persian period strata (*Shiqmona I*: Pls. XLIX: 91, LVIII: 137, 138); and in most of the strata at Tel Michal.

The origin of the basket-handled jar is still somewhat obscure and the evidence conflicting. Stern (1982:111) assumed that it was of Eastern Greek (Rhodian) origin. However, Sagona (1982:90) points out that at Ialysos (Rhodes) there are only three examples (all used for infant burials), tenuously dated to the 5th century B.C.E. In Cyprus these jars are more abundant and appear in many variations. There they were classified by Gjerstad (1960: Fig. 15:5–7) according to body shape: Plain White wares V, VI, and VII (a classification system that is not very practical for the Israeli archaeologist, since very few complete vessels were found in Israel). No differentiation according to the neck/rim criterion was made in the studies of the Cypriote wares. However, at Salamis, two types seem to be present among the Plain White V ware. Variant A (necked) is the most common (*Salamis II.4*: Pl. XLIX:1, 4, 5), whereas Variant C (neckless) is represented by one example (*Salamis II.4*: Pl. CCVII:3). All of the basket-handled jars at Salamis were used for infant burials, usually set into shallow pits in the fill of the dromos of the tombs (*Salamis II.4*: 221). Since infant burial in storage jars is not very common in Cyprus,

this practice, better known in the Greek world (Kurtz and Boardman 1971:72), apparently became popular in Cyprus under Greek influence. At Tel Michal these jars were also used for infant burials (see Section 9.5).

From petrographic analysis of the Tell Keisan jars that date to the end of the Iron Age, it seems that these specimens were imported; petrographically and typologically they resemble those found in Tomb 79 at Salamis, but they were not a local product at this site either (*Tell Keisan*: 359–360).

The petrographic analyses of jars from Tel Michal show that the clay for Variant A (Chap. 24b, Sample 6) came from a source close to the sea, possibly the Carmel region. Samples 5 and 7 (both Variant C) were made of the same material as vessels produced at Tel Michal itself (Chap. 24b, Sample 16). From this we assume that these jars were apparently produced in cities engaged in maritime trade and that, although originally imported, at some stage they began to be manufactured locally. Buhl (*Sukas VII*: 113) came to a similar conclusion with regard to Class VIII 2E of the basket-handled jars from Tell Sukas (here Variant C).

Jug

The upper half of the large globular jug (Fig. 9.1:9) has a wide, cylindrical neck, rounded rim, and single handle extending from rim to shoulder. Its light brown clay is full of air bubbles (see discussion of Stratum VI [Section 9.2.6], where this jug type was most common).

Decanter (Fig. 9.1:5)

The decanter has a narrow ridged neck, triangular rim, and loop handle extending from neck ridge to shoulder. This type of vessel, well known from the end of the Iron Age, is not particularly common in the Persian period, although it continued to exist—mainly in the southern part of the country—throughout the 6th and the beginning of the 5th centuries B.C.E. (Stern 1982:116).

Juglets

The dipper juglet fragment (Fig. 9.1·6) has a flat base and elongated, cylindrical body. Complete specimens have a wide neck, everted rim, and loop handle from rim to shoulder. The type is very common in Cyprus, where it is found in assemblages dating from the 6th century to the end of the Persian period; it is known there as Type V-VII Plain White ware (Gjerstad 1960: Fig. 9:10, 12, 14). In Israel it also began to appear in 6th-century assemblages: e.g., in Stratum XI at Tel Michal and Stratum II at Gil'am (Stern 1970: Fig. 14:7) and at Shiqmona (Stern 1982: Photo 179). It is widely distributed in the coastal zone, but only a few isolated specimens have been recorded in the hinterland. A sample of a similar vessel was submitted to thin-section analysis (Chap. 24c, No. 10), which confirmed that the clay was most likely not of local origin.

The oval juglet (Fig. 9.1:7), by analogy to complete vessels, has a narrow handle from rim to shoulder. Such juglets were found at En-gedi (Stern 1982:124, Photo 190); in Stern's opinion, they are most characteristic of the hill country.

Lamps

The large open lamp (Fig. 9.1:8) with its flat base, wide rim, and pinched mouth continues the Iron Age tradition. It is made of pinkish orange clay, but in the same locus (415) were several sherds of other open lamps (not illustrated) made of whitish clay.

9.2.2. Stratum X

The remains of this stratum, encountered in most areas of the high tell, included a large structure, perhaps a fort, at the northern end and several private dwellings in the center. There was very little pottery; what was there is similar to that of Stratum XI.

Bowls

Of the three mortaria from this stratum, one (Fig. 9.1:16) is made of greenish clay and the other two (Fig. 9.1:17–18) of light brownish clay. The number of ripples on the outer walls of these three specimens varies from two to six.

Chalice

The bowl and pedestal of the chalice (Fig. 9.1:19) do not join, but since they came from the same locus and are made of the same yellowish white clay, they undoubtedly belong to each other. The rim of the bowl is sharply everted; both the bowl element and the high pedestal are carinated. This is the only Persian period chalice found on the site, and, indeed, chalices were very rare in the Persian period; of the few specimens found elsewhere (e.g., *Shiqmona I*: Figs. 130, 183), none resembles our vessel.

Cooking Pots

The few, small sherds of cooking pots from this stratum (not illustrated) resemble those of Stratum XI.

Storage Jars

The Type 2 storage jar (Fig. 9.1:22) is characterized by a bag-shaped body, very short neck, narrow ridge at the shoulder join, and two shoulder handles. The clay is pinkish brown. Although present in Strata XI-X, this type is more common in Stratum IX.

In Room 1501 at the center of the tell, several storage jars were found inserted into the floor. Most of them lacked shoulders (and the shoulder breaks were smoothed over); some lacked bases as well. Two of the better preserved specimens are seen in Figure 9.1:23 and 25; the latter had a hole drilled through its base. It is obvious that these jars were broken deliberately for a specific purpose. In Room 856 at the northern end of the tell a similar installation was found, consisting of a baseless, neckless jar (Fig. 9.1:24) and a clay pipe (Fig. 9.1:26). A stone roller was lying nearby (Pl. 23). Apparently, in both of these rooms the jars (and pipe) were used as conduits for liquids in some kind of installation, but its function is not clear. (For the typology of the jars, see Sections 9.2.3 and 9.2.4.)

Jug

A globular jug with a cylindrical neck has a ring base, a loop handle extending from midneck to shoulder (Fig. 9.1:20), and three horizontal stripes painted across the shoulder. This was a popular jug type throughout the Persian period (Stern 1982: Photo 175).

Cup

The little bag-shaped cup (Fig. 9.1:21) has a very short neck, externally thickened rim, convex base, and large loop handle extending from rim to midbody. Two similar cups with flat bases came from Stratum II at Hazor (*Hazor III-IV*: Pl. CXCI:13, 14). Since this vessel only appears sporadically, it is difficult to establish its temporal or geographic range, but apparently it existed in both the 5th century (Tel Michal) and 4th century B.C.E. (Hazor).

9.2.3. Stratum IX

The two largest assemblages in this stratum came from Pits 985 and 997.

Bowls

The mortarium continues to be the predominant bowl

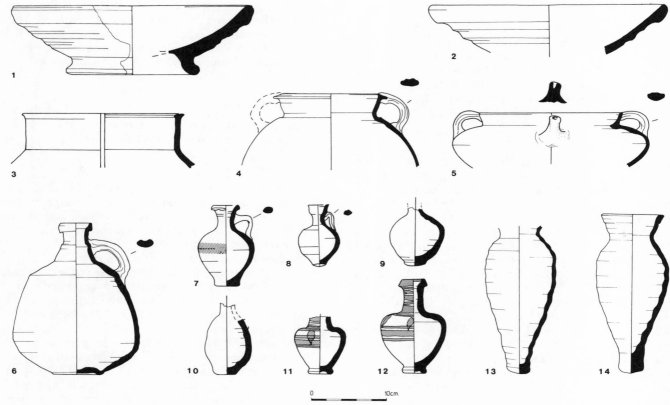

Figure 9.2. Pottery of Stratum IX.

Legend for Fig. 9.2

No.	Type	Reg. No.	Locus	Description	Pl.
1	Bowl	1955/1	339	Buff (brown), small white grits.	
2	Bowl	5577/1	840	White (light gray), small white and gray grits.	
3	Krater	2435/2	404	Buff (buff), small gray grits.	
4	Cooking pot	6624/1	985	Dark brown (dark brown), small white and gray grits.	
5	Cooking pot (chytra)	543/1	404	Orange (orange), small white grits.	
6	Decanter	6616/1	985	Light brown (gray), small white grits.	60:3
7	Juglet	10368/1	1644	Brown (brown), small white and gray grits; red decoration.	
8	Juglet	10294/1	1631	Buff (buff), small white and gray grits.	
9	Juglet	10340/1	1634	Brown (brown), small white grits.	
10	Juglet	10383/1	1631	Buff (gray-buff), small white grits.	
11	Bottle	1777/1	323	Light brown; red decoration.	
12	Bottle	6645/1	997	Light brown; red decoration.	60:2
13	Bottle	6644/1	997	Brown-buff (brown buff).	
14	Bottle	6646/1	997	Buff (buff).	60:1

type; those illustrated here (Fig. 9.2:1–2) are made of yellowish white clay.

Krater

The globular krater (Fig. 9.2:3) with wide mouth and everted rim most likely had two vertical rim-to-shoulder handles. Kraters are relatively rare at Tel Michal. A similar vessel comes from Samaria (Stern 1982: Fig. 124).

Cooking Pots

The cooking pots of this stratum (Fig. 9.2:4) are like those of Strata XI-X. In addition to the local types, however, there is an imported chytra (Fig. 9.2:5) that has a wide mouth, depressed-ovoid body, pair of loop handles, and unpierced spout; it is made of well-levigated, brownish orange clay. The chytra is known in Greece in the 5th century B.C.E. Most of those from the Athenian Agora have two horizontal handles (*Agora XII*: 221–226, Fig. 18, Pl. 94:

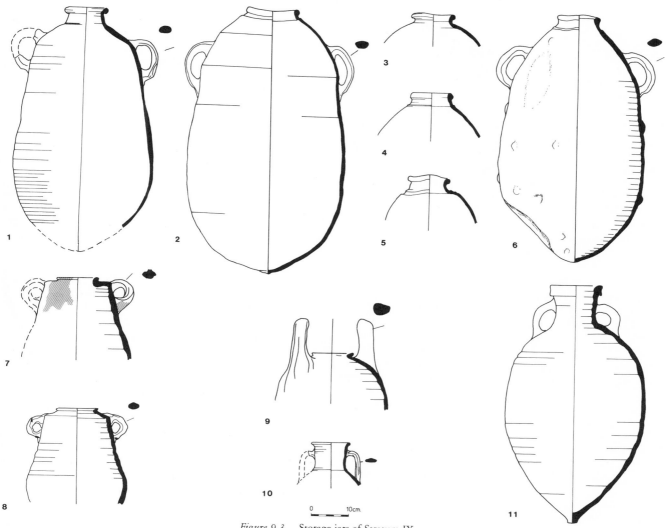

Figure 9.3. Storage jars of Stratum IX.

Legend for Fig. 9.3

No.	Type	Reg. No.	Locus	Description	Pl.
1	Storage jar	6638/1	997	Light brown (brown), small white grits.	
2	Storage jar	5580/1	840	Light brown (light brown), small white grits.	60:10
3	Storage jar	5589/1	840	White (gray-brown), small white and gray grits.	
4	Storage jar	537/1	98	Buff (light gray), small white and gray grits.	
5	Storage jar	10410/1	1650	Light buff (dark gray), small white and brown grits.	
6	Storage jar	6571/1	979	Light brown (gray), small and large white grits.	
7	Storage jar	2557/1	421	Orange (orange), small white and gray grits; red paint.	
8	Storage jar	6319/1	1308	Light brown (orange), small white and gray grits.	
9	Storage jar	6537/1	985	Buff (brown-gray), small white and gray grits.	
10	Amphora	2435/1	404	Pink (pink), few white grits.	
11	Amphora	11008/1	1771	Buff (brown-red), small white grits.	60:9

Nos. 1947, 1949–1955), but there is one example with loop handles (*Agora XII*: Pl. 94: No. 1944). The spout, when pierced, was used either for pouring or to release steam. From the petrographic analysis of a fragment of the chytra (Chap. 24c, Sample 1), it is clear that it was not locally made. There is one entirely different kind of cooking pot in the Athenian Agora (*Agora XII*: Pl. 94: No. 1946) that is an import from Palestine, showing that even the commonest types of kitchenware found their way into the international trade of the period, albeit in very limited quantities.

Storage Jars

The elongated jar (Fig. 9.3:1) has an externally thickened rim, short neck, and two shoulder handles (Type 1; for discussion, see Section 9.2.4).

The bag-shaped jars (Fig. 9.3:2–6; Pl. 60:10) are often misshapen and their rims are irregular (perhaps warped in firing). They have short necks with a ridge at the base, sloping shoulders, a pair of shoulder handles, and rounded bases that are slightly pointed at the very bottom. The clay is light colored and friable. Classified as Jar Type 2, they already appear in Strata XI-X (Fig. 9.1:11, 22). They are rather rare at other sites, with parallels coming from the Persian stratum at Tell en-Nasbeh, dated to 575–450 B.C.E. (*TN II*: Pl. 18:34). Although this type is most common at the beginning of the Persian period at Tel Michal, there is one specimen at Tel Mevorakh in Stratum IV (*Tel Mevorakh I*: Pl. 25:1); perhaps, therefore, Type 2 jars continued for some time, and it is only by chance that no later examples were found at Tel Michal.

The flat-shouldered jar (Type 3) has either a horizontal shoulder that makes a right angle with the body (Fig. 9.3:7) or a diagonally slanted shoulder (Fig. 9.3:8). The body widens out at midpoint, then narrows down to a pointed base. The clay is usually orange. These jars are neckless, the erect rim issuing directly from the shoulder, with the two shoulder handles usually distorted or twisted. Although they give the impression of poor workmanship, Artzy (1980) has come to the conclusion after extensive study that they were purposefully "twisted" to make them easier to lift and transport.

One of the jars (Fig. 9.3:7) has splashes of red color on its upper part, a phenomenon that was observed on a specimen at Tel Mevorakh (*Tel Mevorakh I*: Fig. 6:4). Stern notes that painted decoration is rare on jars of this type and that apparently the painted specimens are confined to the northern coastal plain (*Tel Mevorakh I*: 34). (None have been published so far.)

The flat-shouldered jar first appears in the 8th-7th centuries B.C.E. and continues to flourish throughout the Persian period. It is widely distributed along the Phoenician coast, Cyprus, Rhodes, and the Punic settlements in the western Mediterranean (Stern 1982:109; *Tyre*: 67; Sagona 1982:80–82). The main type of container used to transport goods in the Mediterranean, it comprises about half the jars recovered from the sea off the coast of Israel (Barag 1961: Pl. 4:7; Zemer 1977: No. 25). There are several theories as to its origin. Stern (1982:110) is of the opinion that this type of jar originated in Rhodes. However, in the light of its early appearance on the Levantine coast, it is more likely to be Syro-Phoenician (Gjerstad 1960:113; *Tyre* 1978: Pl. IV:1). According to petrographic analysis (Chap. 24c, Sample 2), it may have been produced in a locality where the hills are close to the sea, like the Carmel coastal plain.

The complete amphora from this stratum (Fig. 9.3:11; Pl. 60:9) has an oval body, sloping shoulders, two rounded handles from midneck to shoulder, and button base (Jar Type 4). It is made of light greenish-white clay. In Cypriote typology, it belongs to Type VI Plain White ware, dated by Gjerstad to 475–400 B.C.E. (1960: Fig. 16:2). There was also an upper body fragment of a smaller amphora of the same type of ware (Fig. 9.3:10), but of pinkish fabric (cf. Gjerstad 1960: Fig. 16:5). Petrographic analysis shows that this vessel was imported (Chap. 24c, Sample 4).

The basket-handled jar (Fig. 9.3:9) is similar in every respect to the specimen from Stratum XI (Fig. 9.1:15).

Bottles

Two almost identical bottles (Fig. 9.2:13–14; Pl. 60:1) came from Pit 997. Both have elongated pyriform bodies, thickened stump bases, flaring necks, and everted rims. Although no close parallels are available, these bottles seem to carry on the Assyrian tradition of the 8th-7th centuries B.C.E. (e.g., *Tell Halaf IV*: Tafel 56:13). The sample submitted to petrographic analysis (Chap. 24c, Sample 9) was manufactured in a region deficient in quartz sand and rich in limestone, possibly the hill regions of Israel.

From the same pit came an entirely different type of bottle (Fig. 9.2:12; Pl. 60:2) with a long, thin neck, thickened everted rim, bulbous body, and small ring base. It is decorated in red with horizontal stripes and vertical leaves. A similar bottle (Fig. 9.2:11) was found in Locus 323, an ash fill of Stratum V. Other examples come from Tel Zeror (Stern 1982: Fig. 195a), Gezer (*Gezer II*: Pl. 179:2), Lachish (*Lachish III*: Pl. 103: No. 673), and Sheikh Zuwaid (*Anthedon*: Pl. 57:62S).

Stern (1982:125, Fig. 195) suggests that this bottle is a forerunner of the unguentaria that arrived in Palestine at the end of the Persian period and that it is of western origin. This, however, is unlikely since these vessels are found mainly in local excavations and are hardly known in Cyprus or Greece. In any case, the petrographic analysis shows that the material of our bottle is local (Chap. 24c, Sample 15).

Decanter

The sack-shaped decanter (Fig. 9.2:6; Pl. 60:3) has a concave base, narrow ridged neck, molded triangular rim, and single loop handle from neck ridge to shoulder. A similar decanter was found in Stratum XI (Fig. 9.1:5).

Juglets

The globular juglet (Fig. 9.2:7) has a flaring neck, ring rim, thick disk base, handle from midneck to shoulder, and horizontal, red-painted stripe around its widest girth. It is a type that is found mainly in the coastal zone in 5th- to 4th-century contexts (Stern 1982:123–124). The other two juglets from Stratum IX (Fig. 9.2:9–10) are paralleled in Stratum XI (Fig. 9.1:7).

9.2.4. Stratum VIII

A rich assemblage of some 20 reconstructable storage jars, mostly elongated Type 1, was found in Storeroom 92 (Figs. 9.4; 9.5:1–10; Pls. 61; 62:1–4), and another 7 of the same type (Fig. 9.6:1–7; Pl. 62:5–8) were found in stone-lined Silo 93 in the southwest corner of the room. Together with

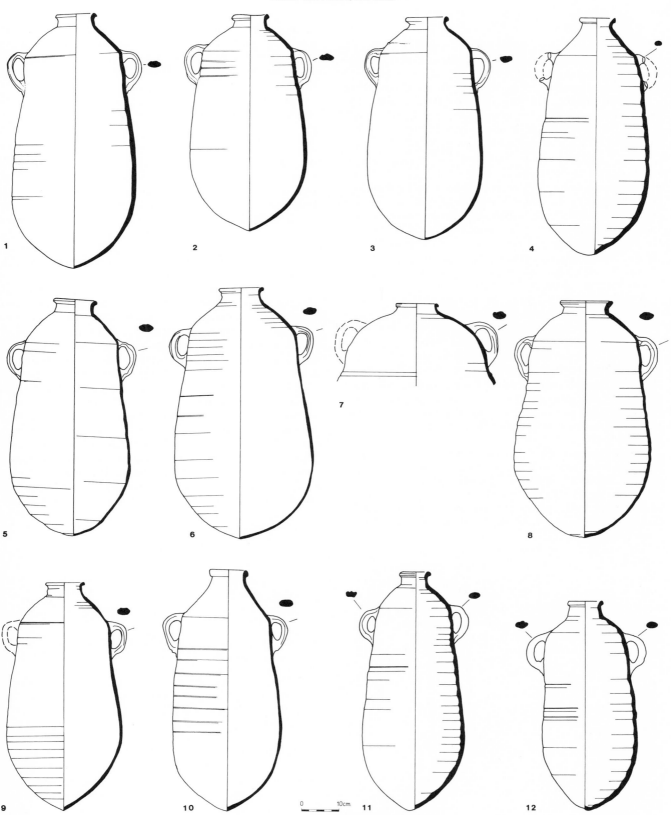

Figure 9.4. Storage jars of Locus 92, Stratum VIII.

123

Legend for Fig. 9.4

No.	Type	Reg. No.	Description	Pl.
				61:1
1	Storage jar	517/2	Buff (gray), small white and gray grits.	
2	Storage jar	520/2	Buff (brown), small white and gray grits.	
3	Storage jar	517/3	Buff (brown), small white grits.	61:2
4	Storage jar	520/8	Buff-gray (light gray), small white and gray grits.	61:3
5	Storage jar	520/9	Buff (buff-light brown), small white and gray grits.	61:7
6	Storage jar	527/1	Buff (brown), small gray and red grits.	61:4
7	Storage jar	533/1	Brown-gray (gray), small white and gray grits, large white grits.	
8	Storage jar	520/10	Buff (buff), small white and gray grits.	61:6
9	Storage jar	520/14	White-gray (gray-brown), small white and gray grits.	61:5
10	Storage jar	529/1	Buff (buff), small white and gray grits.	
11	Storage jar	520/7	Buff (buff), small white and gray grits.	61:8
12	Storage jar	520/5	Buff (light gray), small white grits.	61:9

the jars in Storeroom 92 were a few small vessels (Fig. 9.5:11–16) and some sherds of black-glazed Attic ware.

Bowls

As in the previous strata, the only type of bowl found here was the ubiquitous mortarium (Fig. 9.7:1–2).

Cooking Pots

This stratum was a transitional period for the cooking pots. The type with everted rim (Fig. 9.5:11–12) continues to appear alongside a new type (Fig. 9.7:3) that dominates in the next two strata (see Section 9.2.5).

Storage Jars

The most common storage jar in this stratum is Type 1, found in the storeroom and silo mentioned above. This type has a convex, slightly pointed base, rounded rim, short neck, and pair of shoulder handles (Figs. 9.4:1–12; 9.5:1–8; 9.6:1–7; Pls. 61; 62:1–3, 5–8). The clay is usually greenish yellow and well fired. Several of the jars are grooved where ropes were tied around them before firing, either between and under the handles (Fig. 9.4:2, 6; Pl. 61:4) or farther down on the body (Figs. 9.4:1, 4, 10–12; 9.5:1–4; 9.6:1–4; Pls. 61:1, 3, 8–12; 62:5–6). The body shape varies from long and narrow (Figs. 9.4:10–12; 9.5:1–2; Pl. 61:8–10) to ovoid (Fig. 9.4:1–8; Pl. 61:1–4). There are also slight variations in the rims, which are usually rounded (Figs. 9.4:2–7, 9–12; 9.5:5–8; Pls. 61:2–4, 6–10; 62:1–3) but sometimes squared (Fig. 9.5:2–4; Pl. 61:10–12), recalling to a certain extent the jars of the Hellenistic period (Lapp 1961: Type 11.2, B-E). Nevertheless, the group as a whole is homogeneous. Since jars of the same type were found in the pottery kiln on the northern hill (Fig. 9.12:6–10; Pl. 63:1–5), we may presume that they were all manufactured at Tel Michal. They are apparently a continuation of the tradition of Stratum IX (Fig. 9.3:1), differing from their forerunners mainly in profile, which became narrower and more cylindrical as time went on.

Jars of the same type are known in sites dated to the end of the Persian period – e.g., Cave I in Wadi ed-Daliyeh (Lapp and Lapp 1974: Pl. 18.1) and in Cistern 7, Strip 1, at Samaria (*Samaria 1924*: Fig. 165:2A).

There is one jar in this assemblage (Fig. 9.5:9; Pl. 62:4) that is a variant of the flat-shouldered storage jar (see Section 9.2.3). This variant (Jar Type 3a) has a sharply slanted shoulder, and its greatest circumference is at the lower third of the body. Its clay is invariably white. This variant is found at Tel Michal only in Stratum VIII. At Tel Mevorakh it is confined to Stratum IV (*Tel Mevorakh I*: Fig. 6:8, 10–12), at Akko to Stratum 4 (Dothan 1976: Fig. 27:4), and at Gil'am to Stratum II (Stern 1970: Fig. 8:12–14). The only site at which it might occur earlier is Shiqmona, where it appears in Room PG3 of the "Persian Stratum" (*Shiqmona I*: Pl. XLIX:92). However, since the floors of the later Stratum B penetrated into the "Persian Stratum," the excavator was not certain that all of the vessels shown in Pl. XLIX could be attributed to it (*Shiqmona I*: 36); hence this vessel may come from Stratum B, where several others of this type were found (*Shiqmona I*: Pls. LIX:139, LX:143–144). Consequently, it seems that this variant of the flat-shouldered storage jar began to appear at the end of the 5th century B.C.E. and continued in production until the end of the Persian period.

Along with this variant, the common Jar Type 3 (Fig. 9.7:9) continues. A few bases and rims of basket-handled jars (Fig. 9.5:10) continued to appear in this stratum (see Section 9.2.2).

Amphoriskos

This has a rounded body, concave disk base, flaring neck, everted rim, and two horizontal handles (Fig. 9.7:4). Although the neck and body do not join, there is no doubt that they belong to the same vessel, since the orange, well-levigated clay is of a most unusual composition. No parallels for this vessel are known to me. According to the petrographic analysis (Chap. 24c, Sample 8), it was an import.

Juglets

The flat-based dipper juglet (Fig. 9.5:14) has an elongated

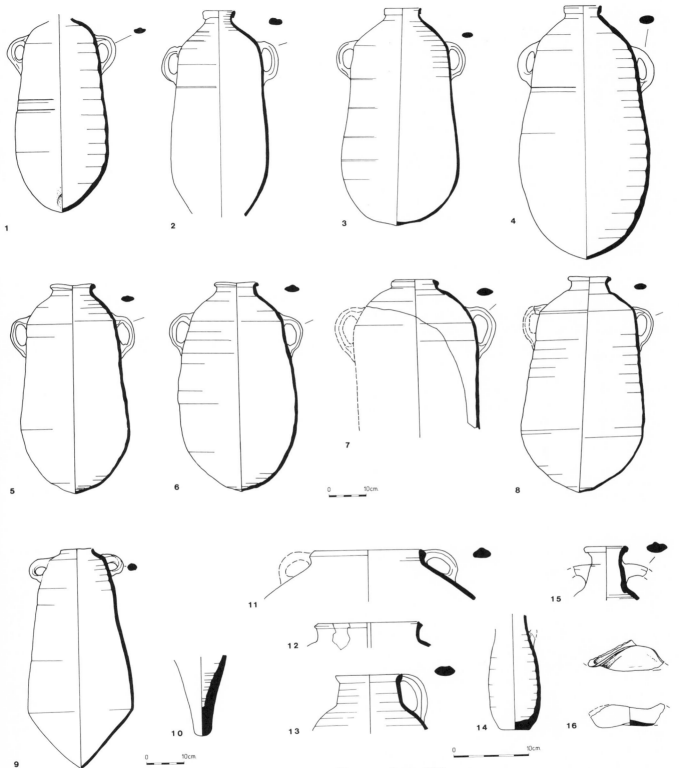

Figure 9.5. Pottery of Locus 92, Stratum VIII.

Legend for Fig. 9.5

No.	Type	Reg. No.	Description	Pl.
1	Storage jar	520/6	White (white), large white grits.	
2	Storage jar	520/12	Buff (buff), small white and gray grits.	61:10
3	Storage jar	520/13	Light brown (brown), small white and gray grits.	61:11
4	Storage jar	520/4	Buff (buff), small white grits, large gray grits.	61:12
5	Storage jar	512/1	White (white), small gray and brown grits.	62:1
6	Storage jar	512/2	Buff (light brown), small gray and brown grits.	62:2
7	Storage jar	539/2	Brown (gray), large and small white grits.	
8	Storage jar	520/16	Buff (buff), small gray grits.	62:3
9	Storage jar	520/1	White (white), small white grits.	62:4
10	Storage jar	493/2	Brown-red (brown-gray), small white grits.	
11	Cooking pot	520/15	Brown-red (brown-red), small white and gray grits.	
12	Cooking pot	502/1	Brown (brown), small gray grits.	
13	Jug	493/3	White (pink), small white grits.	
14	Juglet	532/1	Orange (orange).	
15	Flask	533/2	Brown (gray), small white and gray grits.	
16	Lamp	493/1	Pink (pink), small gray and red grits.	

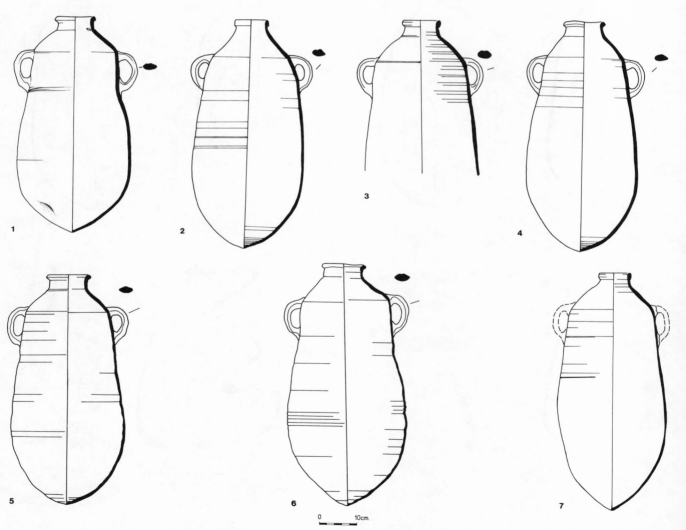

Figure 9.6. Storage jars of Locus 93, Stratum VIII.

LILY SINGER-AVITZ

Legend for Fig. 9.6

No.	Type	Reg. No.	Description	Pl.
1	Storage jar	464/1	Buff (light brown), small white and gray grits.	
2	Storage jar	501/1	Buff (light brown), small white and gray grits.	62:5
3	Storage jar	506/1	Buff (buff), small gray grits.	
4	Storage jar	505/1	Buff (light brown), small white and gray grits.	62:6
5	Storage jar	506/2	Buff (light brown), small gray and brown grits, large black grits.	
6	Storage jar	464/3	Buff (buff), small gray grits.	62:8
7	Storage jar	464/2	White (light brown), small red grits.	

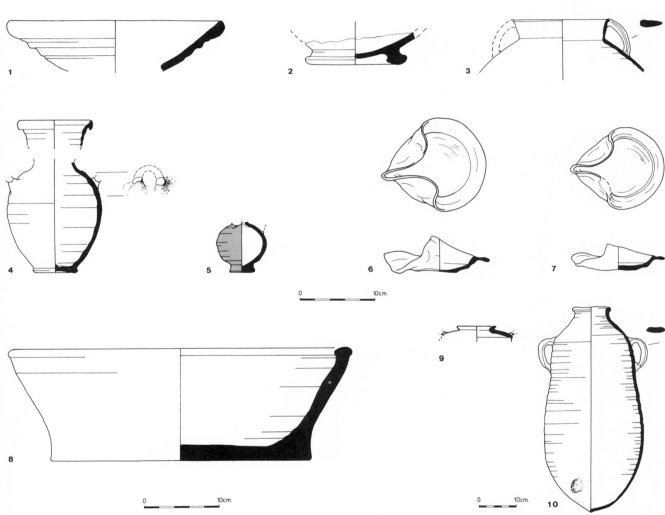

Figure 9.7. Pottery of Stratum VIII.

127

Legend for Fig. 9.7

No.	Type	Reg. No.	Locus	Description	Pl.
1	Bowl	9335/1	948	Buff (buff-gray), small white and gray grits.	
2	Bowl	550/2	405	Buff (brown-pink), small gray grits.	
3	Cooking pot	7203/1	1076	Brown (brown), small white grits.	
4	Amphoriskos	2443/1	405	Orange-brown (orange-brown), small gray grits.	
5	Juglet	6987/1	1028	Light brown (light brown); red slip.	
6	Lamp	1884/1	340	Orange (orange), small white grits.	
7	Lamp	2442/1	405	Pink-orange (pink-orange), small gray grits.	
8	Basin	8315/1	1033	Brown (brown); handmade.	
9	Storage jar	5500/2	830	Orange (orange), small brown grits.	
10	Storage jar	3861/1	1033	Light brown (light brown), small white and gray grits.	62:9

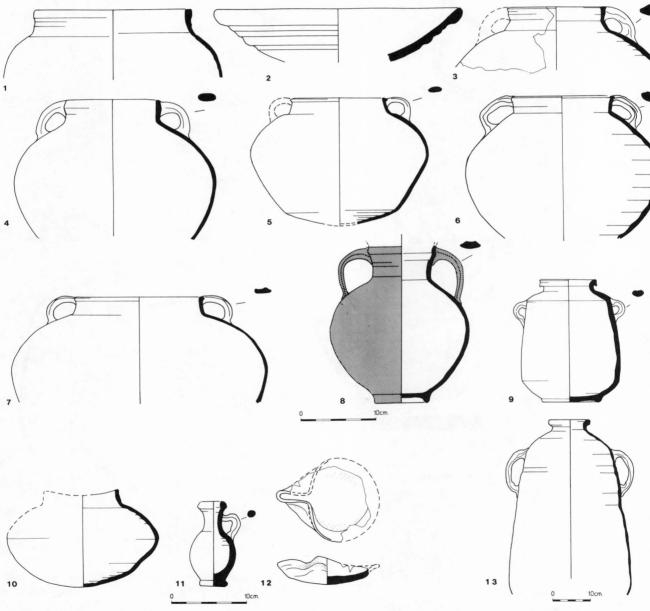

Figure 9.8. Pottery of Locus 1029, Stratum VII.

128

Legend for Fig. 9.8

No.	Type	Reg. No.	Description	Pl.
1	Krater	10371/1	Light brown (light brown), small white and gray grits.	
2	Bowl	8345/8	Buff (buff), small white and gray grits.	
3	Cooking pot	8345/7	Dark brown (black).	
4	Cooking pot	10323/3	Dark brown-gray (dark brown-gray), small white and gray grits.	
5	Cooking pot	10323/2	Brown-red (brown), small white and gray grits.	
6	Cooking pot	8345/6	Dark brown (dark brown), small white grits.	
7	Cooking pot	10323/4	Dark brown (brown), small white grits.	
8	Amphora	10356/1	Buff (buff), small gray grits; red slip.	60:4
9	Amphoriskos	8344/1	Light brown (light brown), small gray grits.	60:5
10	Jug	8345/5	Brown (gray-black), small gray grits.	
11	Juglet	10306/1	Brown-orange (gray), small white and gray grits.	
12	Lamp	8345/3	Brown-red (brown-red), small and large white grits.	
13	Storage jar	8345/4	Buff (buff), small gray grits.	

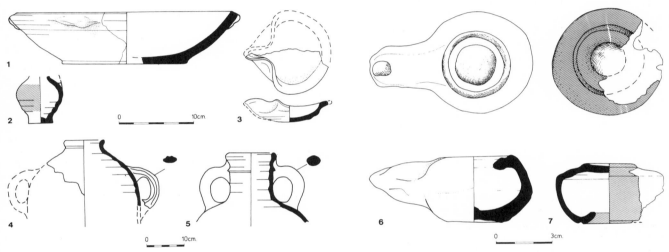

Figure 9.9. Pottery of Stratum VII.

Legend for Fig. 9.9

No.	Type	Reg. No.	Locus	Description	Pl.
1	Bowl	9656/1	1022	Brown (brown).	
2	Juglet	10203/1	1640	Light brown (light brown); red decoration.	
3	Lamp	6991/1	1640	Pink (pink), small white and gray grits.	
4	Storage jar	6953/1	1022	Brown-orange (gray), small white and gray grits.	
5	Amphora	9236/1	1458	Brown (brown), small white grits.	
6	Lamp	6449/1	966	Buff (buff).	60:8
7	Lamp	2431/1	86	Orange (orange); red slip.	

cylindrical body and wide neck. It resembles the juglet from Stratum XI (see Fig. 9.1:6 and discussion in Section 9.2.1). The globular juglet (Fig. 9.7:5) with high disk base is red slipped and burnished.

Flask

The upper part of the large flask (Fig. 9.5:15) has a rounded rim and two handles extending from the ridged neck to the shoulder. Flasks were generally common in the south of the country and rarely found in the north (Stern 1982:115).

Lamps

The large, open lamps (Figs. 9.5:16; 9.7:6–7) have a flat base and pinched mouth. They are made of orange clay.

Basin

A large and irregularly shaped, round clay basin (Fig. 9.7:8) was found in Room 1033. Made of red *ḥamra* brick material, it has a flat base and inward folded rim.

9.2.5. Stratum VII

During the lifetime of this stratum, a large structure with thick, mudbrick walls stood in the center of the tell. One of its rooms was taken up completely by a cellar or sunken silo (Locus 1029) about 3 m deep and apparently covered by a domed roof. This locus yielded a rich assemblage of both local (Fig. 9.8:1–13) and imported wares (Fig. 10.2:10, 23).

Bowls

The usual type of mortaria persisted in this stratum (Fig. 9.8:2), but it was joined by a flat-based variant with unrippled walls and two small lug handles made of reddish brown, poorly levigated clay (Fig. 9.9:1). This variant appears solely in Stratum VII. Parallels come from Tel Mevorakh Stratum IV (*Tel Mevorakh I*: Fig. 4:21), Tel Megadim Stratum II (Stern 1982: Photo 120), Tel Dor (Stern 1985: 423, Fig. 3), the Persian fort near Ashdod (Porat 1974: Fig. 4:3, Pl. XII:2), and Gezer Stratum IV (Gitin 1979 II: Pl. 30:2). These lug-handled mortaria apparently span the mid-5th to mid-4th centuries B.C.E.

Krater

The krater of Figure 9.8:1 resembles that of Stratum IX (Fig. 9.2:3).

Cooking Pots

The cooking pots of Stratum VII (Fig. 9.8:3–7) differ from their predecessors and begin to take on the attributes of their Hellenistic successors. The clay is well levigated, the walls are thinner, the firing is better, and the clay has a metallic ring. The rim is usually straighter and thinner, although otherwise the profile has not changed significantly. This chronological distinction may also be seen in the cooking pots from the Persian fort near Ashdod (Porat 1974: Fig. 4:13) dated to the 5th century and from Stratum 3b at Tell Keisan (*Tell Keisan*: Pl. 21:9, 9a), which resemble ours from Strata XI–IX, whereas the later types from Stratum II at Hazor (*Hazor I*: Pl. LXXX:23–27) are analogous to the Tel Michal pots of Strata VIII–VI.

Storage Jars

The elongated type of storage jar (Figs. 9.8:13; 9.9:4) that predominated in Stratum VIII (Fig. 9.4:1–12; Pl. 61:1–9) continued to be produced in Stratum VII.

The neck and shoulder of the Type VI Plain White ware amphora (Fig. 9.9:5) are covered with marine encrustations. This is the type known in Stratum IX; apparently the jar was recovered from or thrown up by the sea long after it had gone out of fashion.

The small jar with straight walls, ring base, sloping shoulders, very short neck, triangular-sectioned rim, and two shoulder handles (Fig. 9.8:9; Pl. 60:5) is rare at other sites. The closest parallel is from the "Persian Stratum" at Shiqmona (*Shiqmona I*: Pl. LVIII:87). At Tel Mevorakh, a ring base was found that could have belonged to such a jar (*Tel Mevorakh I*: Fig. 8:20).

The small, two-handled amphoriskos (Fig. 9.8:8; Pl. 60:4) is red slipped. A similar vessel (but without slip) was found at Shiqmona (*Shiqmona I*: Pl. XXXII:4). According to the petrographic analysis (Chap. 24c, Sample 12), the amphoriskos could have come from the hill regions.

Juglets

The small, rounded juglet with stump base (Fig. 9.9:2) is similar to those of Stratum VIII (Fig. 9.7:5). Another juglet (Fig. 9.8:11) has an oval body, narrow neck, ring rim, and handle from midneck to shoulder. This type, apparently a local product, is found mainly in coastal sites dating to the 5th–4th centuries B.C.E. (Stern 1982:124).

Lamps

The flat-based lamps with pinched lip (Figs. 9.8:12; 9.9:3) are smaller than their forerunners (Figs. 9.1:8; 9.7:6), although they have the same profile. The closed lamp with raised spout, made of light-colored (unglazed) clay (Fig. 9.9:6; Pl. 60:8), is apparently a local imitation of the black-glazed Attic ware. At Tel Michal the closed lamp makes its first appearance in Stratum VII. At Shiqmona it is found only in Stratum B (*Shiqmona I*: Nos. 135–136, 186). In the Athenian Agora it is dated from the mid-5th century to the second quarter of the 3d century B.C.E. (*Agora XII*: Nos. 70–71). Stratum VII yielded another lamp with a slightly different profile (Fig. 9.9:7) covered with red slip. It has a close parallel at Hazor (*Hazor I*: 60–61, Pl. LXXXII:1–2), where it is dated by analogy with the Greek lamps to somewhere between the first half of the 4th century and the first quarter of the 3d century B.C.E.

9.2.6. Stratum VI

In this stratum, a large fort was built at the northern end of the high tell, private dwellings at its center, and silos at the south. The ceramic assemblage comes mainly from Locus 955, an oval, stone-lined silo.

Bowls

The mortarium, which so predominated in the first five Persian period strata, is no longer present. Neither does it exist in Stratum B at Shiqmona, which is dated to the end of the 4th century B.C.E. (*Shiqmona I*: 60).

Two new types of bowls appear in this stratum. The first has a horizontal rim and ring base (Fig. 9.10:7) and is made of coarse brown unslipped clay, apparently a copy of the Attic fish plate. Such plates are more common in the Hellenistic period, when they are fashioned of well-levigated, pinkish clay and covered with a red slip (see Chap. 13). The imported black-glazed fish plates began to appear already in the first half of the 4th century at Tel Michal (Fig. 10.2:4, 13), Stratum 4 at Akko (Dothan 1976: Fig. 27:6), and Samaria (*Samaria-Sebaste III*: Fig. 52:38a). The locally produced, Persian period copies at Tel Michal are confined to Stratum VI.

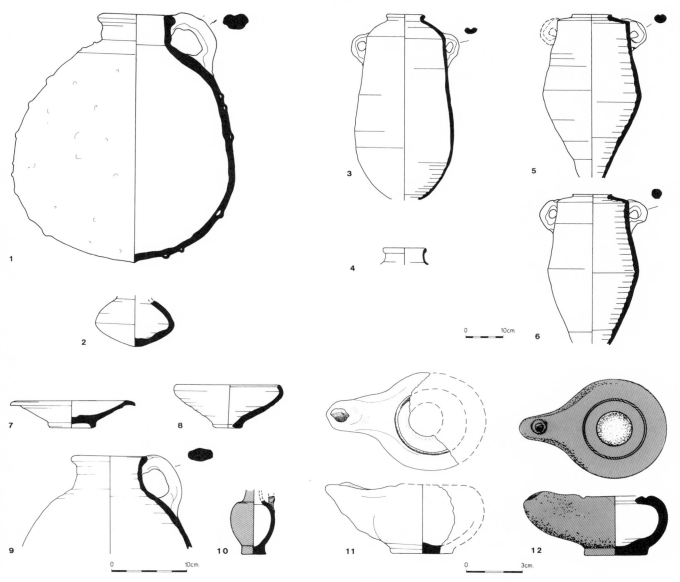

Figure 9.10. Pottery of Stratum VI.

Legend for Fig. 9.10

No.	Type	Reg. No.	Locus	Description	Pl.
1	Jug	6439/1	955	Brown-buff (brown-gray); small white grits.	60:7
2	Juglet	6640/1	955	Buff (buff).	
3	Storage jar	6439/2	955	Brown (brown), small white grits.	62:10
4	Storage jar	6439/4	955	Buff (buff), small gray grits.	
5	Storage jar	6439/3	955	Brown (brown), small white grits.	62:11
6	Storage jar	6418/1	955	Orange (orange), small white and gray grits.	62:12
7	Bowl	103/1	43	Brown (gray), small white grits.	
8	Bowl	5578/1	836	Orange (gray-brown), small white grits.	60:6
9	Jug	5573/1	836	Brown-orange (brown-orange), small white and gray grits.	
10	Juglet	6966/1	1024	Light brown (light brown); horizontal burnish; red slip.	
11	Lamp	6761/1	690	Orange (orange).	
12	Lamp	10272/1	690	Light brown (light brown); traces of red slip.	

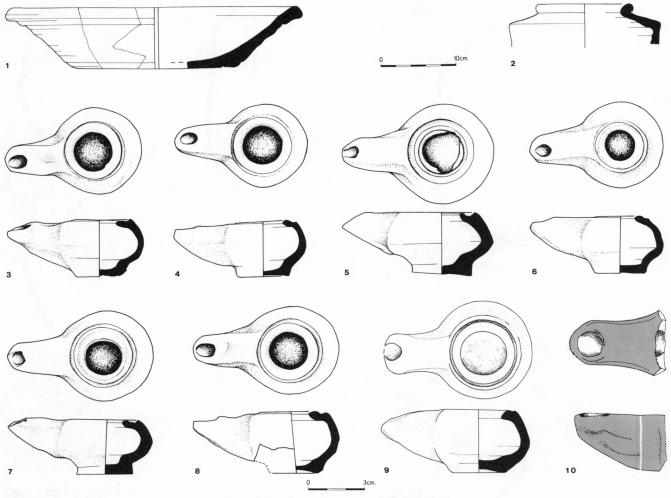

Figure 9.11. Pottery from eastern hillock (Area C).

Legend for Fig. 9.11

No.	Type	Reg. No.	Locus	Description	Pl.
1	Bowl	3250/1	453	Buff (buff).	
2	Storage jar	3286/1	453	Brown-orange (brown-orange), small red and white grits.	
3	Lamp	3210/1	129	Buff, few small white grits.	64:10
4	Lamp	3207/1	129	Pink, small white grits.	64:10
5	Lamp	3209/1	129	Buff, small white grits.	64:10
6	Lamp	3205/1	129	Light pink, small white grits.	64:10
7	Lamp	3208/1	129	Buff, small and large white grits.	64:10
8	Lamp	3206/1	129	Light brown (light brown), few small white grits.	64:10
9	Lamp	3267/1	453	Buff.	
10	Lamp	3219/1	453	Orange (orange); red slip, burnished.	

The second new type of bowl is small with incurving rim and has a string-cut flat base (Fig. 9.10:8; Pl. 60:6); this particular specimen may have served as a funnel, since it has a hole drilled through its bottom. In profile it resembles the small, curved, black-glazed Athenian bowls (*Agora XII*: 131, Fig. 8: Nos. 825–842, Pl. 33) that appear there in the 4th century B.C.E. This bowl also continues in the Hellenistic period (Fig. 13.2:1–5).

Storage Jars

The elongated storage jar (Fig. 9.10:4) carries on the tradition of this Type 1 jar from the previous two strata, both in fabric (light colored) and shape. The jar of Figure 9.10:3 (Pl. 62:10), which is practically neckless and made of brownish clay, may represent a new variant. The two flat-shouldered jars (Fig. 9.10:5–6; Pl. 62:11–12) are Type 3, which is present in all six Persian period strata.

Jugs

The large globular jugs (Fig. 9.10:1, 9; Pl. 60:7) have a wide cylindrical neck, rounded rim, and thick rim-to-shoulder handle. The clay is full of air bubbles, particularly evident in Figure 9.10:1 (Pl. 60:7). A shoulder of this type of jug was already found in Stratum XI (Fig. 9.1:9), and body sherds with air bubbles from Stratum VIII could represent additional vessels. However, the type is most common in Stratum VI. It was apparently produced throughout the Persian period but became more popular toward its closing phases, a conclusion borne out at other sites: Stratum V-IV at Tel Mevorakh (*Tel Mevorakh I*: Fig. 9:2–3); Tomb L23B at Atlit (Johns 1933: Fig. 71), which yielded Sidonian coins of the first half of the 4th century B.C.E.; a stone-lined pit of Period VIB at Taanach, dated 425–400 B.C.E. (*Taanach I*: Fig. 83:4–5), and Cistern 7, Strip 1, at Samaria (*Samaria 1924*: Fig. 167:4a, 4b).

Juglets

The small rounded juglet (Fig. 9.10:10) with narrow neck and stump base is covered with red slip. The squat biconical juglet (Fig. 9.10:2), found only in Stratum VI, resembles a juglet from Stratum IV at Tel Mevorakh (*Tel Mevorakh I*: 38, Fig. 9:14, Pl. 28:2) with a single handle and a wide ring rim. In both sites it appears toward the close of the Persian period, perhaps as an imitation of the Athenian *lagena* (e.g., *Shiqmona I*: Pl. 57:133).

Lamps

Although the two closed lamps depicted here (Fig. 9.10:11, 12) came from a disturbed context, it is very likely that they originated in Stratum VI and represent a continuation of the lamps of Stratum VII.

9.3. EASTERN HILLOCK (AREA C)

The principal architectural feature unearthed in this area was a bench-lined structure that may have had a cultic function. The main pottery deposits of the Persian period were recovered in the sand surrounding this structure. The assemblage of Locus 129 included a hoard of seven small, closed lamps and a black-glazed Attic sherd decorated with a rouletted floral design (Fig. 10.2:7). The seven lamps, six of which are illustrated (Fig. 9.11:3–8; Pl. 64:10), are all similar in profile and fabric. Since none of them bore any traces of soot, we assume they had never been used. These lamps, which are paralleled on the high tell in Strata VII-VI, may be local imitations of imported Attic lamps of the second half of the 4th century B.C.E. According to the petrographic analysis of one of these lamps (Chap. 24c, Sample 11), they could have been produced in the hill regions.

A similar small lamp and the red-slipped spout of another (Fig. 9.11:9–10) were found in Locus 453, together with a flat-based mortarium (Fig. 9.11:1). The latter vessel was horizontally grooved on the exterior, whereas the bottom of its base had a single groove around its circumfer-

ence. A similarly grooved mortarium base came from stone-lined pit 27 of Stratum VIB at Taanach (*Taanach I*: Fig. 86:1).

The fragment of a flat-shouldered jar (Fig. 9.11:2) resembles the jars of this type in Stratum VI on the high tell (Fig. 9.10:5–6; Pl. 62:11–12). A hoard of five coins of Alexander the Great and a coin of Ptolemy I were also found in this locus.

On the basis of the numismatic evidence and the ceramic analogies with Stratum VI, the occupation of this hillock was apparently confined to the end of the Persian period.

9.4. NORTHERN HILL (AREA D)

Although three building phases could be traced in Area D, only the latest, Stratum VI, had enough ceramic material to correlate it with the stratigraphy of the high tell. Except for two relatively large deposits (one from the pottery kiln and the other from Floor 610), the finds were sporadic, although there was a large quantity of Attic ware (Chap. 10) in addition to the local pottery.

9.4.1. Pottery Kilns

Remains of five complete storage jars of the same type and ware (Fig. 9.12:6–10; Pl. 63:1–5) were found on the floor of the pottery kiln (Locus 1803). The kiln evidently collapsed just after this batch of vessels was fired (Pl. 32). The results of thermal analysis carried out by Netta Halperin in the laboratories of the Tel Aviv University Institute of Archaeology showed that the firing temperature reached 750°-800° C. The same results were obtained upon firing similar storage jars taken as a control sample from Storeroom 92 of Stratum VIII on the high tell. The storage jars are all Type 1, represented by numerous complete specimens and hundreds of sherds, especially in Strata IX-VI. The wide-bottomed specimens from the kiln correspond best to the shape of the jars from Stratum IX (Fig. 9.3.1) and Stratum VIII (Figs. 9.4:5–8; 9.5:8). One of the jars from the kiln was used as the control sample in the petrographic analyses (Chap. 24b, Sample 16).

The intact mortarium (Fig. 9.13:1) was found near another kiln in Area F (Herzog et al. 1978:119–120).

9.4.2. Stratum VI

Bowls

Throughout Area D the bowls were all from the latest phase of the Persian period. Most have rounded walls, incurving rim, and ring base; they are covered with a grayish black or reddish black, mottled slip both inside and out (Figs. 9.12:1; 9.13:3–6). These bowls, which only began to appear in the 4th century B.C.E., are apparently a local imitation of black-glazed Attic originals (*Agora XII*: Pl. 33, Fig. 8: Nos. 825–842). Their appearance seems to coincide with that of the closed lamps, which are also copies of their Attic originals.

The two miniature "votive bowls" (Fig. 9.13:7–8) were

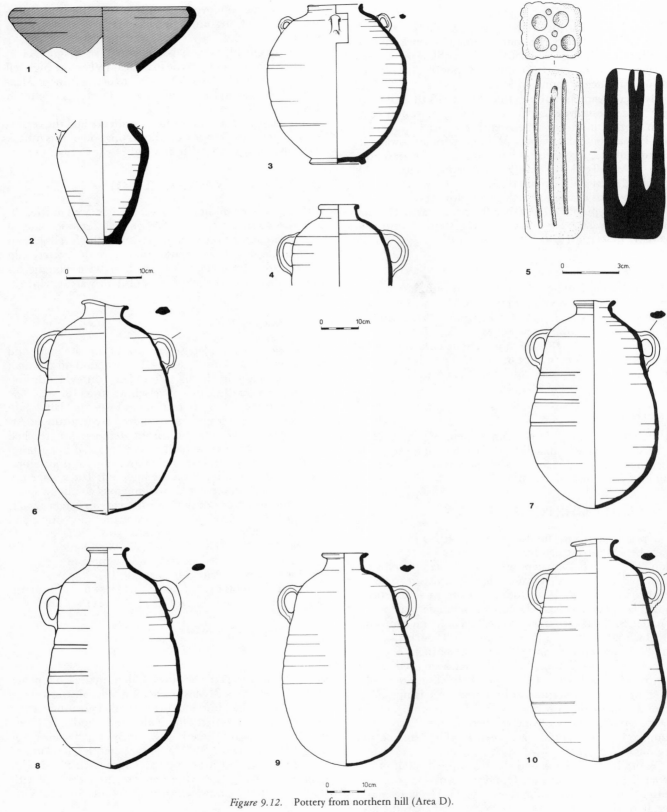

Figure 9.12. Pottery from northern hill (Area D).

Legend for Fig. 9.12

No.	Type	Reg. No.	Locus	Description	Pl.
1	Bowl	4456/1	610	Orange (orange); red slip.	
2	Amphoriskos	4538/2	610	Buff (buff), small gray grits.	
3	Storage jar	4538/1	610	Buff (buff), small white and gray grits.	63:6
4	Storage jar	4508/1	610	Buff (buff), small gray grits.	
5	Kohl tube	4471/1	610	Orange (orange).	
6	Storage jar	11251/3	1803	Buff (brown), small gray and brown grits.	63:1
7	Storage jar	11251/2	1803	Buff-gray (light gray), small white and gray grits.	63:2
8	Storage jar	11251/1	1803	Buff-gray (light gray), small white and gray grits.	63:3
9	Storage jar	11251/4	1803	Buff (light gray), small white and gray grits.	63:4
10	Storage jar	11251/5	1803	Buff (light gray), small white and gray grits.	63:5

not found in clear stratigraphic context but can be attributed to this stratum, although such bowls are also known in the Hellenistic period (e.g., the Hellenistic temple at Beersheba, unpublished).

Mortaria practically cease to exist in this stratum. The few sherds belonging to bowls of this type (Fig. 9.13:2) came from fills (e.g., Locus 1120) whose pottery contents may have originated in earlier strata.

Storage Jars

Another example of the Type 1 elongated jar is seen in Figure 9.12:4. The storage jar of Figure 9.13:17 is very rare in the Persian period; typologically it could be ascribed to the Hellenistic period. Nevertheless, it was found in situ in a Persian period structure (Room 504) together with a 4th-century B.C.E. Sidonian coin (Chap. 27, No. 2).

Also found together with a 4th-century B.C.E. (Greco-Phoenician) coin (Chap. 27, No. 14) were the basket-handled storage jars of Locus 728 (Fig. 9.13:18–19; Pl. 63:7), thereby supporting our assumption that this jar—although most common in Strata X-VIII and poorly represented in later strata—continued to be produced until the end of the Persian period.

The jar with four tiny shoulder handles, ring base, and extremely short neck (Fig. 9.12:3; Pl. 63:6) is very rare in the Persian period. The closest analogy is found in the "plain pottery" repertory at Tarsus (*Tarsus III*: Pl. 142: No. 1279), where it is dated to the 6th century B.C.E. (*Tarsus III*: 149).[1]

The small jar with ovoid body, disk base, and two (broken) horizontal handles (Fig. 9.12:2) is made of an extremely coarse and crumbly fabric. When unearthed, it was stuck into the mouth of the four-handled storage jar described above. This jar is not common in the Persian period, although a similar vessel (but of a different clay) was found in Stratum VIII on the high tell (Fig. 9.7:4).

The above three vessels (Fig. 9.12:2-4), together with the bowl of Figure 9.12:1, were found in Locus 610 with two coins of Alexander the Great (Chap. 27, Nos. 25, 31), confirming a 4th-century B.C.E. date for their appearance. The kohl container from this locus (Fig. 9.12:5; Pl. 77:3) is discussed in Chap. 31.

Juglets

The globular juglet (Fig. 9.13:11) with high disk base and triangular handle from neck to shoulder is typical of the Persian period and is widely distributed (Stern 1982: Photo 188). Another globular juglet (Fig. 9.13:10) with rounded bottom and rim-to-shoulder handle has very thin, delicate walls. Although unparalleled in the Persian period repertory, it was found in situ in Room 504 together with a 4th-century B.C.E. coin of Sidon (Chap. 27, No. 2).

Bottle

The pyriform bottle has a high stump base, thick walls, and is made of a coarse, friable clay (Fig. 9.13:12). In profile it recalls the bottles of Stratum IX (Fig. 9.2:11–12; Pl. 60:2), although it lacks their painted decoration.

Unguentaria

The necks of the two unguentaria are missing. One has a low stump base (Fig. 9.13:13), whereas the second has a much higher, string-cut base (Fig. 9.13:14). Although the unguentarium is better known in the Hellenistic repertory, it began to appear already at the end of the Persian period, both in Palestine and neighboring countries: Greece, Egypt, and Cyprus (Kahane 1952:131–139).

Flask

The flask has a narrow neck and two handles from midneck to shoulder (Fig. 9.13:16; Pl. 63:8). Its swollen body is made of two unmatching halves, held together by a wide, flat band. Parallels are found at En-gedi (*En-gedi* 1966: Fig. 32:1), erroneously attributed to the Iron Age in the Clark collection, and in Stratum I at Lachish (*Lachish III*: Pl. 92: No. 436).

Lid

The conical lid (Fig. 9.13:15; Pl. 63:9) with knob handle is made of the same metallic ware as the cooking pots of the late Persian period. In the Athenian Agora, cooking pot lids were first noted in 5th-century contexts (*Agora XII*: 228); the description that best suits our lid is for a 4th-century example: "The knob is minute and the top surface

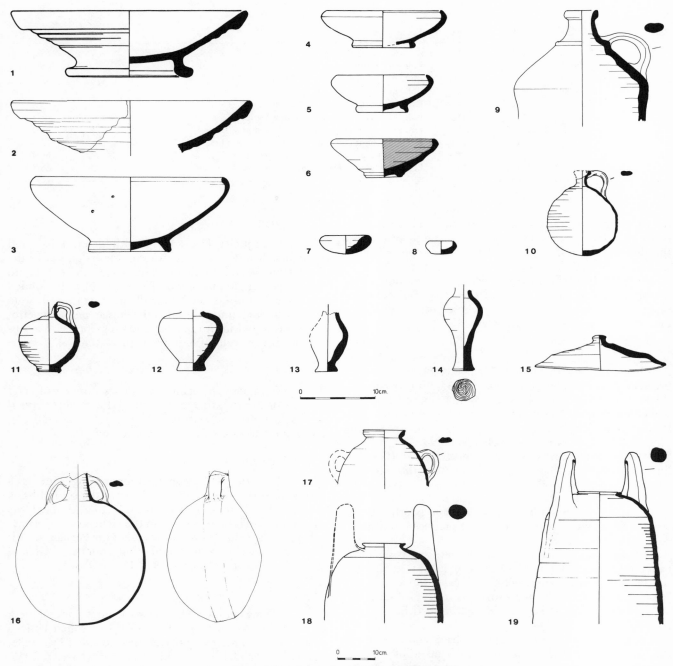

Figure 9.13. Pottery from Northern Hill (Area D).

of the lid is neatly decorated with wheelrun grooves and ridges" (*Agora XII*: 228, Pl. 95: No. 1981).

The coins and pottery repertory of Area D show that Stratum VI of the lower city is to be dated to the end of the 4th century B.C.E. and that it is contemporary with Stratum VI of the high tell. A few sherds of uncertain stratigraphic attribution may have originated in earlier phases of the Persian period. These include the mortarium (Fig.

9.13:2) from the ashy fill of Locus 1120 (from Stratum VII), the decanter shoulder from Locus 1815 (Fig. 9.13:9), and some of the Eastern Greek sherds of Locus 1814. In correlation with the stratigraphic evidence from the high tell, such sherds could not belong to Stratum VI, but there is nothing to prevent their attribution to one of the two earlier architectural phases in Area D that is lacking in pottery deposits.

Legend for Fig. 9.13

No.	Type	Reg. No.	Locus	Description	Pl.
1	Bowl	1507/1	219	Buff (buff), small gray grits.	
2	Bowl	7461/1	1120	Light brown (light gray), small white and gray grits, large white grits.	
3	Bowl	4438/1	602	Pink (pink); black slip.	
4	Bowl	4435/1	602	Pink (gray); black-brown slip.	
5	Bowl	11207/1	1803	Pink (pink), few small white and gray grits; red-black slip.	
6	Bowl	1143/1	278	Brown-pink (brown-pink); red slip.	
7	Bowl	3747/1	519	Brown-orange (brown-orange), small white grits.	
8	Bowl	1090/1	165	Brown-red (gray), small white grits.	
9	Decanter	11291/1	1814	White (gray), small white grits.	
10	Juglet	3640/1	504	Buff (buff).	
11	Juglet	3714/1	521	Buff (light brown), small white grits.	
12	Juglet	4439/1	602	Light brown (light brown), small white grits.	
13	Unguentaria	11275/1	1809	Orange (orange), small red and white grits.	
14	Unguentaria	7442/1	728	Brown-red (brown).	
15	Lid	7390/1	1101	Brown-red (brown-red), few small white grits.	63:9
16	Flask	4498/1	612	Brown-red (brown-red), small white grits.	63:8
17	Storage jar	3641/1	504	Brown-buff (brown-buff).	
18	Storage jar	4294/1	728	Buff-orange (light brown), small and large white grits.	
19	Storage jar	4294/2	728	Buff-orange (orange), small and large white grits.	63:7

Much of Area D seems to have been devoted to industry. There is a small press for making wine, kilns for firing pottery, and, judging by the numerous lumps of metallic slag lying about, perhaps also some metal-working installations. Although the building complex of Strata VII-VI in the lower city is divided into rooms and courtyards of a seemingly domestic nature, they did not yield any ordinary household objects such as cooking pots, jugs, or lamps. Perhaps part of this structure was occupied by workshops and light industry of the Persian period settlement on the tell above.

9.5. CEMETERY (AREA E)

In the Persian period cemetery on the northern hill at Tel Michal there were three main types of graves: pit burials, jar burials, and cist burials (Chap. 11). The 27 jar burials scattered throughout the cemetery were, with one exception, all interments of infants or children under the age of four. Only 17 of these burial jars are illustrated here since the rest of them crumbled to powder when unearthed and it was impossible to reconstruct them. However, most of the jar types could be identified in the field. The neck or base of many of the jars is missing, apparently having been deliberately broken off in order to create an aperture wide enough to receive the body. The jars used for these burials fall mainly into the three most common categories encountered on the high tell: bag shaped (Fig. 9.14:1–5; Pl. 64:1–3), elongated (Fig. 9.14:6–9; Pl. 64:4–6), and basket handled (Fig. 9.15:1–6).

The bag-shaped jars (Type 2) begin to appear in Stratum XI (Fig. 9.1:11) and are most common in Stratum IX on the high tell (Fig. 9.3:2–6; Pl. 60:10); they are discussed in Section 9.2.3. One of the examples from the cemetery was neatly severed just above the handles (Fig. 9.14:5; Pl. 64:3).

The elongated jars (Type 1) begin to appear in Stratum XI, are present in Stratum IX (Fig. 9.3:1), are most common in Strata VIII-VII (Figs. 9.4:1–12; 9.5:1–8; 9.6:1–6; 9.8:13; Pls. 61; 62:1–3, 5–8), but still appear in small quantities in Stratum VI (Fig. 9.10:4).

The basket-handled jars (Type 5) differ from those on the high tell and lower city. As described in Section 9.2.1, these jars come in three variants; those of the high tell are all Variant C (neckless), whereas two of the burial jars (Fig. 9.15:1–2) have the relatively long neck, rolled rim, and neck ridge of Variant A, and the other three have the short neck, everted rim, and neck ridge of Variant B (Fig. 9.15:3–5). Variant A was apparently more common at the beginning of the Persian period.

There were also a few examples of other jar types in the cemetery. One of these is a flat-shouldered jar (Fig. 9.14:10; Pl. 64:7) with an everted, ledgelike rim that does not appear on any of the other flat-shouldered jars at Tel Michal. A similar vessel came from Atlit (Johns 1933: Pl. XIX, No. 399).

Unique in the cemetery is the amphora of Plain White VI ware (Fig. 9.15:7; Pl. 64:8) dated to 475–400 B.C.E. (Gjerstad 1960:121); it is similar, however, to the amphorae recovered from the high tell, mainly in Stratum IX. Its handle is stamped with a Greek monogram (Chap. 28b). According to the petrographic analysis (Chap. 24c, Sample 3), it was imported.

Most of the burial offerings in all three types of graves were articles of personal adornment such as jewelry or, rarely, weapons. Only in two of the cist burials were there pottery offerings. In Cist Burial 1178 there was a juglet (Fig. 9.15:9) with narrow neck, everted rim, sloping shoulders, and sack-shaped body having its widest circumference near its flat base (Stern 1982: Photo 187). Another juglet/bottle that came from Cist Burial 1881 (Fig. 9.15:10) is similar to those in Stratum IX (Fig. 9.2:11–12; Pl. 60:2) but is un-

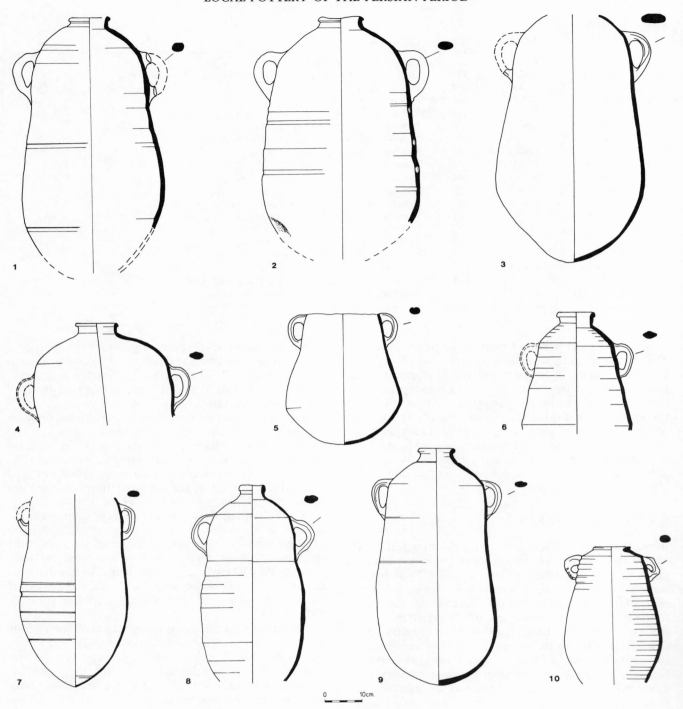

Figure 9.14. Storage jars from cemetery.

decorated. In addition to these juglets and the burial jars themselves, there was a complete mortarium that could not be associated with any specific grave (Fig. 9.15:8; Pl. 64:9).

The range of the ceramic assemblage indicates that the cemetery served the population of Tel Michal during all phases of the Persian period.

9.6. SUMMARY

The typological charts (Figs. 9.16–9.17) covering the six strata of the high tell are designed to help the reader follow the use span of the various vessels. The vessels selected are mainly those that can be traced through several successive

Legend for Fig. 9.14

No.	Type	Reg. No.	Locus	Description	Pl.
1	Storage jar	11625/1	1859	White (gray), small white grits.	64:1
2	Storage jar	11608/1	1852	White (gray), small white and gray grits.	64:2
3	Storage jar	4815/1	654	Buff (buff), small white grits.	
4	Storage jar	1254/1	176	Light brown (brown).	
5	Storage jar	7697/1	1187	Buff (light gray), small white grits.	64:3
6	Storage jar	4809/1	652	Buff-orange (buff-orange), small white grits.	
7	Storage jar	11670/1	1868	White (light brown), small white and gray grits.	64:6
8	Storage jar	7705/1	1188	Buff (buff), small white grits.	64:5
9	Storage jar	4804/1	651	Buff (buff), small white and gray grits.	64:4
10	Storage jar	4808/1	652	Orange (orange), small white and red grits, few large white and black grits.	64:7

strata, whether they evidence typological changes or not.

Three basic clay compositions are discernible in the local Persian period pottery found at the site. The first is white or yellowish with a greenish cast, the second ranges from reddish brown to orange, and the third is light brown or buff. Because of the fragmentary nature of the loci in which the pottery was found, usually patches of floors, pits, or fills rather than complete rooms, no attempt was made to arrive at a quantitative distinction between the clay types, since no accurate results could be expected from any such study. There seems to be no chronological or other significance to these different wares, since in many cases the same type of vessel, often from the same stratum or even from the same locus, occurs in different compositions. This observation is particularly relevant to the mortaria, basket-handled jars, and lamps – both open and closed types.

One characteristic of Persian period pottery frequently encountered in several types of vessels is the air bubbles that result from insufficient kneading of the clay and from improper firing. At Tel Michal, this trait was observed in only two types of vessels: the large globular jugs (Figs. 9.1:9; 9.10:1, 9; Pl. 60:7) and two of the bag-shaped storage jars (Figs. 9.3:6; 9.14:2; Pl. 64:2).

Paint was applied to only a very few types, mainly juglets, which were decorated with bands of brownish red. Burnishing was discerned only on a few isolated sherds of open lamps from Stratum XI. Impressed decoration typical of the Persian period (Stern 1982: 133–136), made with a triangular wedge and/or rounded cane, was found on only two objects at Tel Michal: a wedge-impressed, unstratified sherd (not illustrated) and a cane- and wedge-impressed band on a small clay altar (Fig. 31.6:11), also unstratified.

Bowls (Fig. 9.16:1–4)

The dominant bowl at Tel Michal throughout the first five Persian period strata is the so-called mortarium with high ring base, thick ring rim, and rippled outer surface (Fig. 9.16:1). Sometimes it is made of greenish yellow clay and sometimes of brownish red/orange clay. It continues un-

changed from Stratum XI to Stratum VII, where it is joined by a lug-handled variant (Fig. 9.16:2). In Stratum VI the mortarium is no longer in evidence.

Small bowls are completely absent, making their first appearance only in Stratum VI. One of these is the fish plate (Fig. 9.16:3), apparently an imitation of the black-glazed Attic original. Bowls with incurving walls (Fig. 9.16:4), evidently also copies of the widely dispersed Attic originals, likewise appear only in Stratum VI.

Cooking Pots (Fig. 9.16:5)

The cooking pot continues in the tradition of its Iron Age precursor, although it becomes more rounded and develops a neck. In Strata XI-IX the rim is triangular in section and there is a narrow ridge at the base of the neck. In Stratum VIII there are a few survivals of this cooking pot, but at the same time a new type appears. The general profile remains unchanged but the rim becomes straighter and thinner. The clay is well levigated, the walls are thin, the firing is good, and the vessel has a metallic ring to it. This type continues in Stratum VII, and (although no cooking pots were found in Stratum VI) it may be assumed that they had the same features. In Stratum IX there was a single specimen of the imported chytra.

Storage Jars (Fig. 9:17)

Five principal types of storage jars were distinguished (Fig. 9:17).

1. Elongated (Fig. 9.17:1)

This jar has an externally thickened rim, short neck, convex base that is slightly pointed at the very bottom, and two shoulder handles. It is usually made of greenish white clay. Rope impressions can be seen around the circumference on many specimens. Apparently this type evolved from the storage jars produced around the turn of the 7th century B.C.E. at En-gedi, Meṣad Ḥashavyahu, and Tel Masos (Aharoni and Aharoni 1976:86, Fig. 6:5). Since five com-

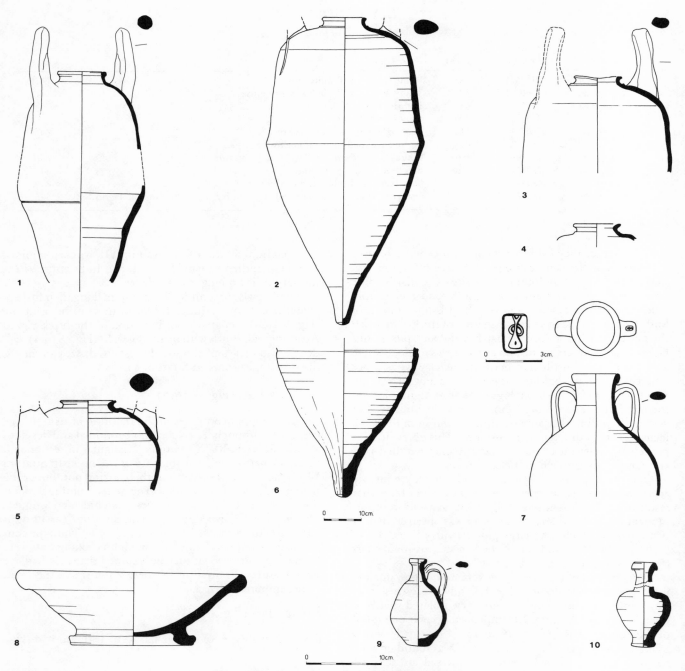

Figure 9.15.   Storage jars and other vessels from cemetery.

Legend for Fig. 9.15

No.	Type	Reg. No.	Locus	Description	Pl.
1	Storage jar	11632/1	1858	Brown (brown), small white and gray grits, large white grits.	
2	Storage jar	1292/1	190	Pink (pink), large and small white and gray grits.	
3	Storage jar	11657/1	1864	Brown (brown), small white grits.	
4	Storage jar	4836/1	665	Brown (brown), small white grits.	
5	Storage jar	11657/2	1864	Brown (brown), small white and gray grits.	
6	Storage jar	11632/2	1858	Orange (orange), small white and gray grits, small white grits.	
7	Amphora	1286/1	189	Brown (brown).	64:8
8	Bowl	4854/1	176	Buff (buff), small gray grits.	64:9
9	Juglet	7679/1	1178	Buff (orange), small white grits.	
10	Juglet	11740/1	1881	Brown (gray), small white grits.	

140

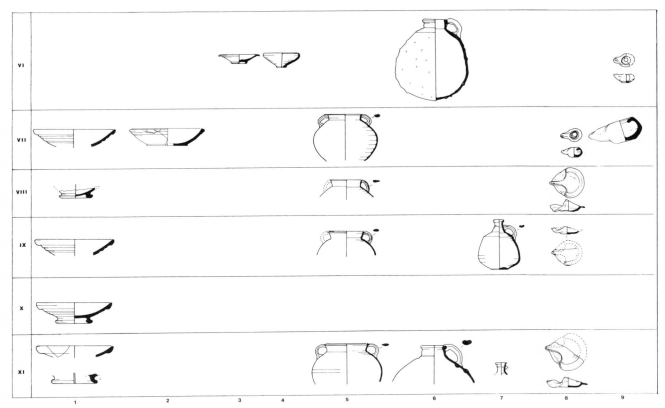

Figure 9.16. Comparative chart of Persian period vessel types by strata.

plete specimens of this type were found in the pottery kiln of the lower city, it is without doubt a local product. In Stratum IX the lower part of the body is fairly wide, but in Stratum VIII it becomes narrower and more cylindrical. In Stratum VII it retains the same profile. Although in Stratum VI it is represented only by rims and necks, it may be assumed that the complete jars resembled their Strata VIII-VII predecessors.

2. Bag Shaped (Fig. 9.17:2)

Both the body and rim of this type are often misshapen. It has a short neck with a ridge at the base and two shoulder handles. Present only in Strata XI-IX, it is apparently confined to the beginning of the period.

3. Flat Shouldered (Fig. 9.17:3)

The flat shoulder of this jar, sometimes horizontal, sometimes sloping, creates a sharp angle with its body. It has no neck, the thick rim issuing directly from the shoulder. The two shoulder handles are usually twisted slightly. The body widens in a straight line toward the center of the vessel and then narrows down again toward its pointed base. The clay is invariably orange brown. First appearing in the 8th-7th centuries B.C.E., this type persists throughout the Persian period. It is widely dispersed along the Phoenician coast,

Cyprus, Rhodes, and the Punic settlements of the western Mediterranean. At Tel Michal it is found in Strata XI-VIII and once again in Stratum VI; its absence in Stratum VII is apparently accidental. According to the petrographic analysis (Chap. 24c, Sample 2), it was probably produced in a locality where the hills are close to the sea, possibly the Carmel coastal plain.

A variant of this jar made of whitish clay (Type 3a) appears only in Stratum VIII. In addition to the color of the clay, it differs from the rest of the flat-shouldered jars since its widest circumference is not at midbody but at the lower third of the vessel.

4. Amphora (Fig. 9.17:4)

The amphora has an oval body, sloping shoulders, and a pair of rounded handles extending from midneck to shoulder. In Cypriote terminology, it belongs to Type VI Plain White ware and apparently is of Eastern Greek origin. The petrographic analyses indicate that the amphorae from Tel Michal were imported (Chap. 24c, Samples 3-4). At Tel Michal amphorae were found only in Strata XI-IX, with the exception of the barnacle-encrusted specimen of Stratum VII, which presumably originated in an earlier stratum.

141

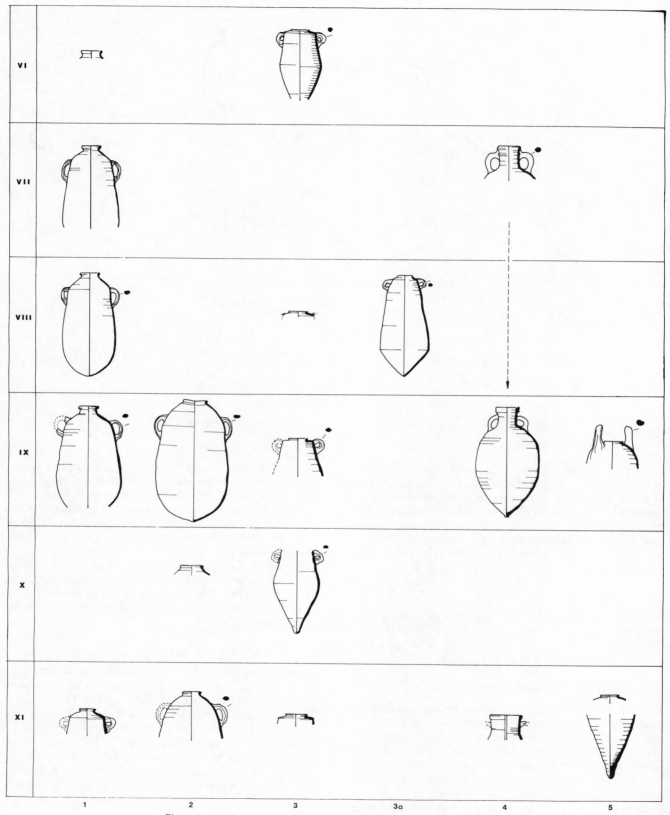

Figure 9.17. Comparative chart of Persian period storage jar types by strata.

5. Basket Handled (Fig. 9.17:5)

This type has rounded shoulders, elongated body ending in a pointed base, and two handles rising above the rim. Its neck comes in three variants: A) relatively long neck with rounded rim and neck ridge, B) very short with everted rim and neck ridge, and C) completely neckless, the rounded rim rising directly from the shoulder. Variant C was confined to the high tell and Area D, whereas the burial jars in the cemetery were either Variant A or B. The clay of all variants is coarse and either brownish orange or whitish green. Fairly complete specimens were found in Strata XI-IX, whereas in Strata VIII-VI this type is represented by only a few sherds. Three samples were submitted to petrographic analyses (Chap. 24c, Samples 5-7), and the results indicate that in all three cases the vessels could have been produced locally.

Jugs

The most common type of jug has a globular body, wide cylindrical neck, rounded rim, and rim-to-shoulder handle (Fig. 9.16:6). The clay is brown, often full of air bubbles. This type first appeared in Stratum XI, and some sherds were found in Stratum VIII, but it is most common in Stratum VI.

Decanters

The decanter has a sack-shaped body, concave base, narrow ridged neck, and loop handle extending from neck ridge to shoulder (Fig. 9.16:7). Present in Strata XI and IX, it is clearly a continuation of the late Iron Age decanter.

Juglets

Although juglets were not numerous at Tel Michal, several of the most popular types of the Persian period were found, usually globular or pyriform with high disk or stump base and handle from midneck to shoulder. Some are painted with horizontal bands or red slipped.

Lamps

The large open lamp with flat base, wide rim, and pinched mouth (Fig. 9.16:8), clearly a legacy from the Iron Age, flourished throughout Strata XI-VII. The clay is usually pinkish orange but occasionally is a light greenish-white. On a few of the Stratum XI specimens, burnishing is discernible. By Stratum VI this open lamp has completely disappeared, having been joined in Stratum VII by the closed type with raised spout (Fig. 9.16:9). Made of white or pink clay, the new lamp is a local product imitating the imported type in shape but lacking its typical black glaze. The petrographic analysis of one of these closed types (Chap. 24c, Sample 11) indicates that it could have been produced in the hill regions.

The ceramic developments of the six Persian period strata at Tel Michal may be summarized in terms of three phases. The first covers Strata XI-IX (circa 525-450 B.C.E.), the second Strata VIII-VII (circa 450-350 B.C.E.), and the third Stratum VI (circa 350-300 B.C.E.). The assemblages in the strata that make up each phase are not identical but have certain unifying features, and there is no sharp break between the phases.

At the beginning of the Persian period in the three earliest strata, the repertory is dominated by vessels having strong ties with the ceramic tradition prevailing at the end of the Iron Age. This is particularly apparent in the cooking pots, the decanters, and the open lamps. At the same time, Cypriote and eastern Greek imports, as well as copies of Cypriote wares (basket-handled jars), were very popular.

In the second phase, the cooking pot begins to show several traits typical of its Hellenistic successor: a straighter neck, thinner walls, and finer, better fired clay. The elongated storage jar that was somewhat "baggy bottomed" becomes more cylindrical, whereas its bag-shaped cousin disappears from the picture. The flat-shouldered storage jar is joined by a variant in white clay that has its greatest circumference at the lowest third of the body instead of at the midpoint. The amphora disappears and the basket-handled jar is represented by only a few isolated sherds. The open lamp is still present, but by Stratum VII it begins to face competition from the closed, spouted lamp, a copy of an Athenian import.

In the final ceramic phase the mortaria, which had persisted unchallenged for five strata, are no longer present. The influence of imports from the Greek mainland increases, the Attic vessels fostering many imitations in shape, although the decoration and finishing techniques were beyond the limited technical skill of local potters. Among the vessels copied were fish plates and small bowls with incurving walls. The only lamps were small, closed Attic types that, like so many other imitations of Athenian wares, were to dominate throughout the Hellenistic period.

NOTE

1. In the light of the imported Greek pottery found at Tarsus in the "Early Iron Age" stratum (Late Geometric) and in the "Middle Iron Age" stratum (Sub-Geometric), the date of these levels should be lowered by about 50 years (Snodgrass 1971:115, 126-127) and the date of the assemblages corresponding to the Persian period should be lowered accordingly. The presence of nonstratified Attic pottery on the mound shows that some kind of settlement existed in the 5th century and perhaps even in the 4th century B.C.E. (*Tarsus III*: 145).

REFERENCES

Aharoni, M., and Aharoni, Y. 1976. The Stratification of Judahite Sites in the 8th and 7th Centuries B.C.E. *BASOR* 224:73-90.

Artzy, M. 1980. The Utilitarian "Persian" Store Jar Handles. *BASOR* 238:69-73.

Avigad, N. 1977. Makmish. *Enc. Arch. Exc. III*: 768-770.

Barag, D. 1961. A Survey of the Vessels Recovered from the Sea off the Coast of Israel. *BIES* 25:231-238.

Dothan, M. 1976. Akko: Interim Excavation Report, First Season 1973/4. *BASOR* 224:1-48.

Gitin, S. 1979. *A Ceramic Typology of the Late Iron II, Persian and Hellenistic Periods at Tell Gezer I-III.* Ph.D. dissertation. Hebrew Union College, Cincinnati, Ohio.

Gjerstad, E. 1960. Pottery Types: Cypro-Geometric to Cypro-Classical. *Opuscula Athenensia* 3:105–122.

Herzog, Z., Negbi, O., and Moshkovitz, S. 1978. Excavations at Tel Michal, 1977. *Tel Aviv* 5:99–130.

Johns, C. N. 1933. Excavations at 'Atlit (1930–31). The South-Eastern Cemetery. *QDAP* 2:41–104.

Kahane, P. 1952. Pottery Types from the Jewish Ossuary Tombs around Jerusalem. *IEJ* 2:125–139.

Kurtz, D. C., and Boardman, J. 1971. *Greek Burial Customs.* London.

Lapp, P. W. 1961. *Palestinian Ceramic Chronology 200 B.C.-A.D. 70.* New Haven, Conn.

Lapp, P. W. 1970. The Pottery of Palestine in the Persian Period. Pages 178–197 in: *Archäologie und Altes Testament, Festschrift für Kurt Galling.* A. Kuschke and E. Kutsch, eds. Tübingen.

Lapp, P. W., and Lapp, N. L., eds. 1974. Discoveries in the Wâdī ed-Daliyeh. *AASOR* 41.

Naveh, J. 1962. The Excavations at Meṣad Ḥashavyahu: Preliminary Report. *IEJ* 12:89–113.

Porat, J. 1974. A Fortress of the Persian Period. (Hebrew) *'Atiqot* 7:43–55.

Sagona, A. G. 1982. Levantine Storage Jars of the 13th to 4th Century B.C. *Opuscula Atheniensia* 14:73–110.

Snodgrass, A. M. 1971. *The Dark Age of Greece: An Archaeological Survey of the Eleventh to the Eighth Centuries B.C.* Edinburgh.

Stern, E. 1968. The Dating of Stratum II at Tell Abu Hawam. *IEJ* 18:213–219.

Stern, E. 1970. Excavations at Gil'am. (Hebrew) *'Atiqot* 6:31–54.

Stern, E. 1982. *Material Culture of the Land of the Bible in the Persian Period, 538-332 B.C.E.* Warminster.

Stern, E. 1985. The Earliest Greek Settlement at Dor. (Hebrew, English summary 79*). *EI* 18:419–427.

Zemer, A. 1977. *Storage Jars in Ancient Sea Trade.* Haifa.

10

Aegean and Cypriote Imports in the Persian Period (Strata XI-VI)

by Ronald T. Marchese

Cross-cultural references abound during the Persian period for the area of Syria-Palestine (Perreault 1986). East Greek, mainland Greek, and Cypriote cultural zones interacted with both the coastal areas and the inner recesses of the Persian administrative system. Such interaction provides an excellent reference for the relatively homogeneous ceramic assemblages that existed in large areas of the Persian empire. Through the Phoenician cities, goods of relatively high value, although common in the areas where they were produced, found a wide distribution along the Levantine coast. This is especially evident in Palestine, where Greek and Cypriote imports and their local imitations were abundant. By the beginning of the Persian period, such imports were forcing out older wares and styles that had survived from the last phase of the Iron Age. Competing with these local assemblages, which had attained a high degree of functional uniformity, the imports influenced a steady transformation in ceramic types that is evident during the two and a half centuries of Persian rule. The appearance and extensive use of imports, therefore, provide a reference point for locally developing ceramic types. For Tel Michal, such datable remains determine the chronological divisions within the local ceramic assemblage as well as provide temporal limits of each Persian architectural phase at the site.[1]

Aegean and Eastern Mediterranean imports for Tel Michal can be divided into two main categories: Cypriote and, to a lesser extent, Eastern Greek; and those that belong exclusively to the Greek mainland. The former includes Cypro-Archaic and Classical varieties and a minor quantity of Eastern Greek Archaic types, whereas the latter is dominated by a wide variety of Athenian wares. Material ranges in date from the middle and late 6th century to the 4th century B.C.E. In addition to the Eastern Greek and Cypriote material, the assemblage includes a few pieces from Boeotia and Ionia. The greatest percentage, however, is strictly Athenian, quite typical of coastal sites in Syria-Palestine during the Persian period.

The imported pottery at Tel Michal is highly fragmentary and therefore difficult to identify. About 600 sherds were retrieved in the excavations, the majority of Athenian manufacture.

10.1. CYPRIOTE AND EASTERN GREEK IMPORTS

Cypriote imports are represented by a limited number of specimens. These consist primarily of body sherds, usually the upper shoulder and lower neck of the vessel. Most of the profiles indicate large to moderate-size storage vessels, most likely amphorae and hydriae. A few other shapes are also evident and reflect more specialized use. These include askoi (Fig. 10.1:8; Pl. 65:7) and Cypriote single-handled jugs (Fig. 10.1:2, 3; Pl. 65:2) decorated in horizontal bands and a wavy-line motif (cf. *Shiqmona I*: Pl. 68, No. 86; *SCE IV, 2*: Pl. IX:12/2). All are considered typical of Cypriote manufacture and had a wide distribution in Syria-Palestine during the 6th and 5th centuries B.C.E. (Amiran 1969: 286–290). There are also examples of banded White Slip (Fig. 10.1:11; Pl. 65:10), Bichrome (Fig. 10.1:9; Pl. 65:8), Black-on-Red (Fig. 10.1:10; Pl. 65:9), Bichrome Red (Fig. 10.1:2–3; Pl. 65:2), and, finally, White Slip banded types with a floral design. The latter was represented by only one example (Fig. 10.1:4; Pl. 65:3; cf. *SCE IV, 2*: 186–207, 253–320, Pl. XLIV:14).

Most of the material was decorated with horizontal bands of red to brown-black paint applied to a variety of surfaces but usually over a white or, to a lesser extent, red slip. Alternate motifs include a wavy line, usually placed on the upper shoulder; diagonal-to-vertical slashing haphazardly placed on the vessel; or a floral motif, again confined to the upper shoulder. Although common elsewhere, such

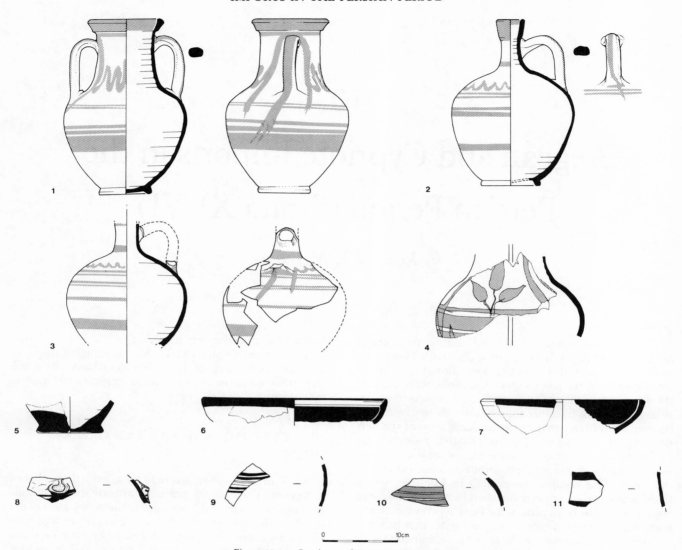

Figure 10.1. Cypriote and Eastern Greek imports.

examples are extremely rare at the site and appear only on a few types of sherds, mostly amphorae and jugs. The Cypriote material recorded at Tel Michal belongs primarily to the Cypro-Archaic IIB period (circa 550–475 B.C.E.) with survivals continuing into the Cypro-Classical IA-IB and early IIA sequences (circa 475–375 B.C.E.).[2] Examples of the latter, however, appear in unstratified deposits only.

The imported Greek pottery is highly fragmentary and not always easily identified. Examples that can be defined with any degree of certainty as Eastern Greek are extremely rare. Although a few sherds of Eastern Greek banded ware are evident (typical horizontal and less common horizontal and wavy-line types), they are far less frequent than the sherds of Cypriote manufacture.[3] Vessel shapes were similar to the Cypriote material, with the larger types predominating. These were represented by body sherds from the upper shoulder and neck of vessels. Only one example (Fig. 10.1:5; Pl. 65:4) was evident: the lower part of a vessel with

a flaring disk base, probably a squat amphora. (This intruded in an Iron Age locus.) Other types included shallow hemispherical bowls or one-handlers (Fig. 10.1:7; Pl. 65:6; cf. *Sukas II*: Fig. C, 136a) and "standardized" Ionian cups or bowls (Fig. 10.1:6; Pl. 65:5; *Sukas II*: Pl. V:105, 107), the latter also being a common type on Cyprus in the Cypro-Archaic IIB period. Each was represented by only one example and should therefore be considered as extremely rare at the site. Only one vessel was relatively well preserved. This was a moderate-size squat, strap-handled amphora (Fig. 10.1:1; Pl. 65:1). Generally, this is a common type in the eastern Mediterranean, although an exact parallel to this specimen is not available.

Eastern Greek examples are confined exclusively to the Archaic period. Although banded wares appear to be the most common type, alternate examples indicate a much wider assemblage. All are confined to the 6th century B.C.E. and were typical imports from the Eastern Greek

Legend for Fig. 10.1

No.	Type	Reg. No.	Locus	Stratum	Description[a]	Pl.
1	Squat amphora, Eastern Greek	2470/1	415	XI	Pale red; red to black horizontal bands with vertical slashing and wavy line applied over light buff to dull red surface.	65:1
2	Jug, Cypro-Archaic IIB/Classical IA	2470/2	415	XI	Pale orange to light brown; exterior matte to buff; dark red to brown-red horizontal bands on shoulder and neck; upper shoulder wavy line with vertical slash on handle.	65:2
3	Jug, Cypro-Archaic IIB/Classical IA	2470/3	415	XI	Same as above.	
4	Upper shoulder of amphora (?), Cypro-Archaic IIB	2574/1	420	XI	Buff orange slipped in matte white; thick-to-thin red horizontal bands crossed by leaves on upper shoulder.	65:3
5	Base of squat amphora, Eastern Greek	2201/2	378	XIV	Coarse to moderate grain; brown to pale pink clay; buff surface with unevenly applied black paint on lower part of base.	65:4
6	Bowl or cup, Eastern Greek (Ionian)	2522/2	415	XI	Pale red; interior slipped in dull black paint below rim, exterior slipped in brown-black paint, slightly striated and burnished below rim.	65:5
7	Hemispherical bowl or one-handler	5577/1	840	IX	Brown to dull red; interior slipped in brownish black, upper shoulder and rim in black over thin red exterior slip.	65:6
8	Shoulder of askoi, Cypro-Archaic IIB	8870/2	1387	VII	Pale red; buff to matte white with red to brown striated bands along shoulder.	65:7
9	Shoulder of vessel, probably jug, Cypro-Archaic IIB	8870/3	1387	VII	Pale red; black to red and matte white horizontal bands over natural buff-red surface (Bichrome).	65:8
10	Carinated shoulder of vessel, Cypro-Archaic IIB	11292/1	1814	VI	Pale red; red to black bands over natural surface (Black-on-Red).	65:9
11	Neck of jug, Cypro-Archaic IIB	8870/1	1387	VII	Pale red; red-brown striated horizontal bands on buff to matte white slip.	65:10

[a] All Cypriote and Eastern Greek wares are of a moderate grain structure and contain grit temper.

world with a wide distribution in Syria-Palestine (for discussion, see *Sukas II*). The moderate-size squat amphora is regarded as belonging to the stock of vases common all over Eastern Greece. This shape was also known in the Cypro-Archaic II period, with survivals existing in the Cypro-Classical I sequence on Cyprus. In shape and style this amphora also has strong connections with examples from Rhodes characterized by Fikellura ware of the mid-6th century B.C.E. Such material is usually contemporary with Ionian products. It must be noted that the only sherd of an Ionian cup (Fig. 10.1:6; Pl. 65:5) came from the same locus as the squat amphora (Locus 415 in Stratum XI).

The distribution of Cypriote and Eastern Greek wares was confined exclusively to the high tell, with only a few stray examples evident on the northern hill and eastern hillocks.

The Cypro-Classical IA-IB and IIA types soon disappeared, driven out by the rapid increase in Athenian products in the markets of Syria-Palestine. This is certainly evident by 475 B.C.E., if not earlier, when Eastern Greek and Cypriote types were no longer in vogue in this region (Perreault 1986). The influx of Athenian products quickly displaced the Archaic traditions of Eastern Greek and Cypriote potters. This is the case at Tel Michal, where a few Athenian products appeared as early as the last quarter of the 6th century and dominated the imported assemblages of the 5th and 4th centuries B.C.E.

10.2. ATHENIAN IMPORTS

The largest percentage of Persian period imports is of Athenian manufacture.[4] Appearing before the end of the 6th century, Attic ware became commonplace by the middle of the 5th century and is represented by a large variety of shapes and styles. These include typical Athenian bowls with thickened incurving rims (Fig. 10.2:3), the most common shape in the 4th century; bowls with tapered everted rims; bowls with rounded everted rims (Fig. 10.2:7); bowls with flat everted rims (Fig. 10.2:6), rare even in Athens and dated to the close of the 5th century; bowls with rounded and tapered rims (Fig. 10.2:5); and bowls with incurving and everted rims. Of the five types of salt cellars known in the Athenian assemblage, three are represented at Tel Michal: Fine type (Fig. 10.2:14), Concave wall, and Footed style. Other vessels include stemless cups (Fig. 10.2:22) and fish plates (Fig. 10.2:4), the latter represented by numerous examples from the 5th-4th centuries B.C.E. The lekythoi include black-bodied squat types, both fully glazed (Fig. 10.2:20–21; Pl. 66:6–7) and with running-dog motif (Fig. 10.2:18–19; Pl. 66:4–5); black-bodied elongated types with flaring disk base and reserve banding (Fig. 10.2:16; Pl. 65:11) or white paint (Fig. 10.2:17); and White Ground and banded types (Fig. 10.2:27; Pl. 66:10). There were also kantharoi and cup kantharoi; Attic Type A skyphoi (Fig. 10.2:8–9; Pl. 65:14), represented by numerous examples; Attic Type A Archaizing skyphoi (Fig. 10.2:15; Pl. 66:1), rare and dated to the mid-5th century in Athens; two types of bolsal, intentional or coral red (Fig. 10.2:12; Pl. 65:13),

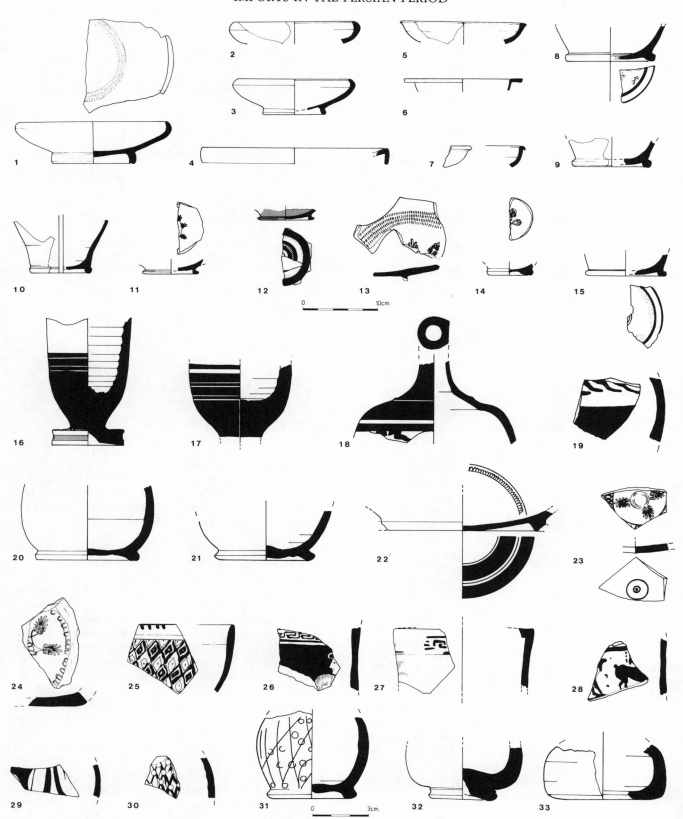

Figure 10.2. Athenian and miscellaneous imports.

Legend for Fig. 10.2

No.	Type	Reg. No.	Locus	Stratum[a]	Description[b]	Pl.
1	Bowl	550/1	405	VIII	Matte black to low luster interior and exterior; triple rows of rouletting on interior; bottom of base totally glazed.	
2	Bowl	4205/1	569	VI	Matte black interior and exterior glaze.	
3	Bowl	4453/1	602	VI	Ring base totally glazed, black to red-brown dull finish.	
4	Fish plate	1512/2	220	VIII/VI	Matte black interior and exterior.	
5	Bowl	5878/1	861	X	High lustrous interior and exterior.	
6	Bowl	6259/1	945	VII	Matte black to low luster glaze, unevenly applied.	
7	Bowl	6301/1	935	IIIa	Matte black to low luster.	
8	Attic Type A skyphos	1879/1	342	VIII	Interior and exterior low luster; bottom of base unglazed and signed: ΔΣ χΡ	65:14
9	Attic Type A skyphos	5569/1	840	IX	Same as above without inscription.	
10	Attic Type A skyphos	8345/2	1029	VII	Same as above.	66:2
11	Bolsal	8887/1	1386	XI	Totally glazed base; high lustrous black interior decorated with tight alternating lotus and palmette.	65:12
12	Bolsal, Type A variant	7487/1	1128	VIII	High lustrous black exterior, interior intentional or coral red; reserved underside with concentric circles.	65:13
13	Fish plate or bowl	853/1	129	VI	Matte black glaze; six rows of rouletting bordering linked palmettes.	66:3
14	Salt cellar (Fine Type)	6963/4	1024	VI	Interior impressed with tight palmette cross; thick matte black glaze.	
15	Attic Type A skyphos (Archaic Style)	10385/1	1032	VIII	Lustrous black glaze; reserve band above foot; thin concentric circles on underside of base.	66:1
16	Black-banded elongated lekythos	8764/1	1371	VIII	Lustrous red to red-brown banding on reserve surface.	65:11
17	Black-bodied elongated lekythos	1905/1	705	X	Black lustrous glaze with thin white ground banding.	
18	Black-bodied squat lekythos	7452/1	1113	VIII	Reserve banding on shoulder with running-dog motif; high lustrous black.	66:4
19	Black-bodied squat lekythos	6888/1	1013	VII	Same as above.	66:5
20	Black-bodied squat lekythos	8710/2	1371	VIII	High lustrous black glaze.	66:6
21	Black-bodied squat lekythos	8864/1	1385	X	Same as above.	66:7
22	Stemless cup	7453/1	1113	VIII	Lustrous black; parallel incised lines with small ovules; thick to thin concentric circles on underside of base.	
23	Base of stemless cup (?)	8345/1	1029	VII	Lustrous black; light palmettes around circle bordered by thin parallel incised lines with small ovules; base in reserve style with three red concentric circles.	
24	Base of stemless cup (?) or bolsal	4004/1	551	V–IV	Lustrous black; linked palmettes within border of parallel incised lines with small ovules.	
25	Cup skyphos (St. Valentine Group)	2506/1	409	IX	Lustrous black interior; exterior consisting of alternating white and black reserve diamond pattern on reserve surface.	66:8
26	Shoulder of Red Figure lekythos	9525/3	1500	XI	High lustrous black, Red Figure variety with beardless youth.	66:9
27	Shoulder of White Ground lekythos	4493/1	614	VII	Black Greek key and horizontal bands on white ground.	66:10
28	Bowl, or lekythos, Boeotian White Slip	6072/1	917	IIIb	Lustrous black on matte white. Two centaurs in Archaic style.	66:11
29	Shoulder of Red Figure lekythos	8756/1	1371	VIII	Thick lustrous black glaze on interior; exterior palmette leaves (probably palmette between figures).	66:12
30	White ground squat lekythos	4529/1	614	VII	White ground and reserve style with crossing black lustrous lines forming diamond pattern with white dots.	66:13
31	White ground squat lekythos	10430/1	1650	IX	Same as above.	
32	Attic Type 23A oil lamp	2417/1	89	VIII	High lustrous black.	66:14
33	Attic Type 23C oil lamp	6207/1	934	V	High lustrous black.	66:15

[a] A few Persian period sherds were found in Hellenistic fills.

[b] All Athenian wares are fine-grain types.

IMPORTS IN THE PERSIAN PERIOD

dated to the third quarter of the 5th century, and black-bodied varieties with impressed tight palmette and lotus (Fig. 10.2:11; Pl. 65:12), dated to the very end of the 5th century; one-handlers; squat-bodied amphorae dated to the last quarter of the 5th century; broad-rim plates; rolled-rim plates; and, finally, rilled-rim plates with molded foot.

The majority of vessels were fully glazed, with only a few examples bearing additional painted motifs. Typical impressed wares from the late 5th and 4th centuries included: bolsal with lotus and tight palmette (Fig. 10.2:11; Pl. 65:12); cup skyphoi with linked palmettes; palmette and ovules on small bowls or stemless cups (Fig. 10.2:22); salt cellar with palmette cross (Fig. 10.2:14), bowls with incurving rims (Fig. 10.2:1), and fish plates with rouletting and/or alternating palmettes (Fig. 10.2:13; Pl. 66:3); linked palmettes, floating palmettes, tight palmette cross and ovules (Fig. 10.2:23), linked palmettes and ovules (Fig. 10.2:24), and, finally, ovules and incised lines (see *Agora XII*: 22–23).

A full range of Attic ware is evident, with examples of all the major Athenian black-glazed types represented at the site. This is quite understandable, given the brisk trade along the Levantine coast (*Shiqmona I*: 42–46; Bailey 1940; Stern 1982, 1986; Elayi 1983; Perreault 1986). As a passive element in this coastal trade, the site received a large quantity of Athenian goods throughout the Persian period and especially after 480 B.C.E., when Athenian domination of the eastern Mediterranean markets was assured by the outcome of the Persian wars. The earliest stratified examples of Athenian material appear in Strata XI–IX and become common in Strata VIII–VI, a sequence that fits nicely into the chronology of Palestine during the early Persian period. This conclusion is supported by a similar situation at Akko and more importantly at Tel Dor (Marchese n.d.; Stern 1986), where the large influx of Athenian wares that appeared after 480 B.C.E. contains basically the same typological categories (i.e., Attic Type A skyphos, cup skyphos, stemless cup, kantharos, bolsal, lekythos, and salt cellar). Imported types at Tel Michal are the same as those found at other sites up and down the coast (Perreault 1986). Easily transported in bulk, Athenian vessels had a direct impact on the local ceramic industry and definitely fostered imitations. These, however, were in shape only, since the black glazing technique was beyond the abilities of the local potters. Such imitations were confined to bowls with incurving rim (*Agora XII*: 131), the predominant type at Tel Michal in the 4th century. The demand for this pleasant and utilitarian shape reached proportions not easily satisfied by imports. Except for local imitations of Athenian oil lamps, this was the only shape imitated at the site. In other communities, local potters tried unsuccessfully to produce more complicated shapes, notably lekythoi and skyphoi.

Distribution of the Athenian wares indicates limited dispersal over the site. Although present in most of the areas excavated, the greatest concentration was on the summit of the high tell and in and around the Persian period structures in the commercial and industrial areas immediately to the north. The highest ceramic concentration was in this northern area. However, very few imports were associated with the hundred or more graves in the cemetery of the Persian period adjacent to the commercial and industrial region of the site. Except for the storage jars used in the jar burials, there was also very little local pottery in the cemetery (see Chap. 11 tables).

The distribution of Athenian products at the site may reflect population clusters or concentrations or, more important, areas of social or ethnic differences (Stern 1986), since Athenian imports were prized possessions used only by those who had sufficient wealth to purchase them. Those objects that were comparatively rare – salt cellars, squat black-bodied and elongated lekythoi, bolsal, kantharoi, cup kantharoi, and rilled-rim plates – were found only on the high tell and the northern hill.

10.3. STRATIGRAPHIC PROGRESSION

Cypriote, Eastern Greek, and Athenian types are associated with all six Persian period levels (Strata XI-VI). Chronological considerations, which are based on type, style, and decoration, support the following division within the Persian period.

Stratum XI, the earliest Persian period stratum, dates from the beginning of the third quarter of the 6th century B.C.E. Eastern Greek banded wares on both a reserved and prepared surface are present in this stratum. Cypriote examples are common and include Cypro-Archaic IIB Bichrome and White Slip banded types. Athenian examples are also evident. A fragment of a Red Figure lekythos (Fig. 10.2:26; Pl. 66:9) and an Attic Type A skyphos are noted but are not common. We date their appearance to the end of Stratum XI, circa 500–475 B.C.E. Contemporary with the earliest recognizable Persian ceramic types, Stratum XI would tend to fall in the third quarter of the 6th to the end of the first quarter of the 5th centuries B.C.E.

Stratum X is very poor in imported pottery. The only items are black-bodied lekythoi, three types of bowls, and stemless cups, the latter a common Athenian product after 480 B.C.E. Stray examples of Cypro-Classical IA are also present. This stratum has a very narrow horizon dating from the end of the first quarter to the decade before the mid-5th century. After 450 B.C.E., Athenian wares, including a greater variety of types, increased rapidly at the site.

Stratum IX is confined to the mid-5th century, most likely between 460 and 430 B.C.E. Athenian goods are now quite common, whereas only one sherd from a Cypro-Classical IA vessel is evident. The stratum ends with the beginning of impressed Athenian wares, common after 430 B.C.E. Patterned skyphoi (circa 460 B.C.E. or perhaps a decade earlier), stemless cups, cup skyphoi, and Attic Type A skyphoi are common and tend to dominate the imported assemblage.

Stratum VIII falls in the last 30 years of the 5th century and the first decade of the 4th. During this 40-year span, impressed wares became the dominant type produced by Athenian potters. Before the middle of the 5th century, in-

150

cised patterns on fine ware appeared in limited number (*Agora XII*: 22–32). These are noticeably absent at the site since the types produced in Athens, in general, are rare. The initial attempt at incised patterning was quickly followed by a stamping and impressing technique. Adopted from metal work, such designs first made their appearance in combination with Red Figure decoration, usually on stemless cups. However, it is on black-glazed vases that impressions were chiefly used. Stamped decorations, appearing around 430 B.C.E., were mainly confined to a variety of drinking cups. Initially combined with the older tradition of incised lines, impressions became more complex at the close of the 5th century B.C.E. and began to appear on a greater variety of vessels, including mugs, one-handlers, acrocups, shallow stemless cups, small bowls, phiale, bolsal, cup skyphoi, kantharoi, rilled- and rolled-rim plates, salt cellars, and askoi.

At Tel Michal, however, impressed wares of the 5th and early 4th centuries are limited to bolsal, cup skyphoi, salt cellars, one-handlers, and bowls with incurving rims. Of these, the earliest stamped design is the palmette followed by the lotus (rarely used even in Athens and confined to the last quarter of the 5th century), ivy leaf (another short-lived pattern contemporary with the early palmette design), olive leaf, meander, boxed triangle, and diamond. Incising with stamp impressions covered the last thirty years of the 5th century, and the degeneration of the motif was complete within this period (*Agora XII*: 27). This technique gave way to mechanically produced ribbing or rouletting, a tradition that appeared after 390 B.C.E. and was confined to 4th-century fish plates, bowls with incurving rims, and bowls with rilled and rolled rims and molded bases. The predominant styles of the late 5th century (circa 430–400 B.C.E.) were linked palmettes within a border of ovules, palmettes on a circle, and palmette cross, the latter usually on bolsal (*Agora XII*: 29). Associated with the emergence of impressed designs was the appearance of deeper and narrower kantharoi and bolsal, which replaced stemless cups and cup skyphoi. Both were evident in the early 4th century, but the tradition certainly had antecedents in the 5th. The appearance of typical impressed wares and the emergence of more dominant Athenian types place Stratum VIII well within the confines of the late 5th century to the first decade of the 4th century B.C.E.

Stratum VII covers the late first quarter of the 4th and probably continues to the mid-4th century, perhaps no later than 340 B.C.E. Rouletting became common after 390 B.C.E., and the tradition matured and decayed within 40 years (*Agora XII*: 29). Rouletting is also associated with the appearance of a central nipple and totally black underside (except for the reserved or scraped resting surface of the foot). Free-floating palmettes were also common in the third quarter of the 4th century and not the middle (*Agora XII*: 30–32), thereby providing a break between Strata VII and VI. Along with the change in design, the most common shape in Strata VII and VI is the small bowl with incurving rim. This was the most popular Athenian import after 350 B.C.E. and the only example readily imitated by

local potters. The small bowl continued to the beginning of the 3d century, thereby providing a relatively long tradition for the period of Stratum VI (circa 340–300 B.C.E.). Stratum VI yielded only these small bowls.

Although Cypro-Archaic IIB, Cypro-Classical IA, and general Eastern Greek assemblages are represented in the early phases of the Persian period (primarily in Strata XI-X), black-glazed wares of Athenian manufacture are the dominant imports at the site, especially in the 5th-4th centuries. These vessels, mass-produced in standardized types of bowls, skyphoi, cup skyphoi, kantharoi, and plates with both plain and impressed decoration, did not serve as containers for Athenian goods but were imported for their own sake.

In black glaze, the overwhelming majority and the most common shape are bowls with incurving rims. Of the more specialized shapes, Attic Type A skyphoi are quite common. Lekythoi are the next most popular shape, both the elongated and squat black-bodied varieties. The latter consisted of totally glazed types as well as those bearing a running-dog motif. Fish plates are fairly well represented. Salt cellars and bolsal are relatively common. Other types are rare and usually represented by a few sherds only. Vessel shapes were confined to drinking cups, small bowls, and more specialized containers. Except for one moderate-size squat amphora, larger vessels are noticeably absent, a common phenomenon in Persian period sites in Israel. Easily transported, the smaller imported types predominated. The more utilitarian demand for larger vessels was completely dominated by local storage vessels.

Artistic masterpieces are almost completely absent. Only a few sherds of Red Figure (Fig. 10.2:26; Pl. 66:9) and White Slip (Fig. 10.2:28; Pl. 66:11) were unearthed, indicating a lack of the more delicate Athenian shapes and styles. Those found would not rank as the prime output of any Athenian workshop. They include a fragment from an elongated lekythos depicting a beardless youth (Fig. 10.2:26; Pl. 66:9), two fragments from a cup skyphos featuring a section of a palmette (Fig. 10.2:29; Pl. 66:12), a small fragment of a Boeotian bowl or lekythos with archaic centaurs (Fig. 10.2:28; Pl. 66:11), the lower part of a squat lekythos with a diamond and dot pattern (Fig. 10.2:30–31; Pl. 66:13), and the upper shoulder of a skyphos (Fig. 10.2:25; Pl. 66:8), also in a diamond motif. These are stray finds, usually appearing in fill deposits. Also present are a small number of Athenian oil lamps. These are confined to Attic Type 23A (Fig. 10.2:32; Pl. 66:14) varieties of the third quarter of the 5th to the early 4th centuries, and Attic Type 23C (Fig. 10.2:33; Pl. 66:15) samples (first and especially the second quarter of the 4th century B.C.E.). Both examples were extremely common and very popular at Athens (*Agora IV*: 56–59). Only a few were found at the site and were apparently not a popular item in the imported assemblage.

NOTES

1. A preliminary analysis of the material covered in this chapter appeared as "Chronological Implications of Aegean and Cypriote Imports in the Relative Dating of the Persian Period at Tel Michal, Israel," at the annual meeting of the American Schools of Oriental Research, Dallas, Texas, November 1980. I wish to thank Debora Sue Tommeraasen for her support in preparing this chapter and Beth Kwapick for help in the final typing of the manuscript, and I extend deep appreciation to Robert Wenning for his very helpful comments on the preliminary draft.

2. Cypro-Archaic IIB types are confined mostly to Bichrome and White Slip varieties. The examples fit nicely into the more common types of imported wares recorded at numerous sites in Israel.

3. Similarities exist with Tel Mevorakh (*Tel Mevorakh I*: 41, Fig. 10:9, 13–19, Pl. 30) and are considered common at several other sites. All examples indicate decoration over an unslipped surface.

4. Imported mainland types from 5th- and 4th-century strata are almost exclusively Athenian. Only one sherd is definitely Boeotian, although it is possible that Boeotian black-glazed wares were present in the Athenian assemblage. For a discussion of this ware, see Merker 1979:160–170.

REFERENCES

Amiran, R. 1969. *Ancient Pottery of the Holy Land*. Jerusalem.

Bailey, B. L. 1940. The Export of Attic Black Figure Ware. *Journal of Hellenic Studies* 60:60–70.

Elayi, J. 1983. L'importation de vases attiques en Phénicie à l'époque Perse. *Atti del I Congresso internazionale di studi fenici e punice Roma*. Rome.

Marchese, R. T. n.d. Athenian Imports at Tel Dor in the Persian Period.

Merker, G. 1979. Boeotian Pottery in Collections in Jerusalem. *IEJ* 29:160–170.

Perreault, J. 1986. Céramique et échanges: les importations attiques au Proche-Orient du VIe au milieu du Ve siècle, avant J.-C. Les données archéologiques. *Bulletin de Correspondence Hellenique* 110:145–175.

Stern, E. 1982. *Material Culture of the Land of the Bible in the Persian Period, 538–322 B.C.E.* Warminster.

Stern, E. 1986. On the Beginnings of the Greek Settlement at Tel Dor. *EI* 18:421–425.

11

Persian Period Cemetery (Strata XI-VI)

by LeGrande Davies, Katherine Kostamo, and Ronald Jyring

In the Persian cemetery at Tel Michal, located on the northern slope of the northern hill (Area E; Fig. 1.2), more than 100 burials were discovered during the four seasons of excavation. These were of three basic types: pit burials, jar burials, and cist burials, all of which were randomly scattered throughout the cemetery.

A total of 750 m² was excavated, consisting of a large area (20 m × 25 m) in the south and connected by a trench 2 m wide to a smaller area (10 m × 20 m) in the north (Figs. 11:1; 11:2; Pl. 36). Another 25 graves were uncovered on the eastern side of this slope in the previous excavations (Avigad 1977:770). If we assume that the cemetery occupied the entire northern slope and that the spacing of the graves was as dense throughout as it was in the excavated portion, we have probably dug only about 10 percent of the total number of graves.

Attempts were made in 1977 to determine the location of graves and the boundaries of the cemetery by means of an electric current resistivity survey (Herzog et al. 1978:118). This survey was unsuccessful, mainly because the resistivity unit that was used was more suitable for depths encountered in geological surveys than for those relevant to archaeological detection.

The environmental conditions of the cemetery were extremely detrimental to both the osteological material (see Pl. 38 for an attempt at skeleton preservation) and the grave constructions themselves. The soil is sandy and acidic, containing a high percentage of salts and salt components. Since the sand allowed rapid percolation of water, a high concentration of dissolved salts penetrated the bone material and then crystallized, causing expansion and breakage.

Many of the bones had deteriorated to a point where the remains were merely calcium-carbonate traces, white shadows in the soil, or sand-casts. Some of the skeletons, particularly those of the infants and children, had disintegrated to such an extent that only the teeth (protected by their enamel) remained. (See Chap. 21 for a full discussion of the skeletal remains.)

11.1. TYPES OF BURIALS

The 111 burials of the Persian period included 23 pit burials (Table 11.1), 27 jar burials (Table 11.2), and 51 cist burials of various types (Tables 11.3–11.5). Eight burials were too disturbed to be classified, and two are conjectured from the presence of concentrations of typical grave goods but no skeletal remains (Table 11.6). (For a comprehensive discussion of burial types of the Persian period, see Stern 1982:68–92.)

11.1.1. Pit Burials

Twenty-three pit burials, simple inhumations in the soil, were uncovered (Table 11.1). The graves were dug to a depth of at least 1 m, the corpse deposited and the grave filled up. The fill contained not only the original orange quartz sand but also a great deal of organic material, most likely the ground cover of the time. This is evidenced by the darker, slightly gray, striated sand that was seen directly above the graves in the balks. In most of the pit burials, the skeleton was placed upon the layer of heavy-grained calcarenite; apparently it was the start of this gravelly material that determined the depth to which the pits were dug. Because the ancient surface of the soil has changed with the shifting sands, the depths of the graves below the present-day surface vary greatly.

In all the pit burials, the skeleton was apparently placed in a basic extended position. This was discernible even in badly disturbed pits (Burials 185, 1181, 1880, 1886). All the skeletons lay flat on their backs. Most of the skulls faced upward; a few were tilted to the right or left, but this appeared to be the result of the settling of the soil when it was thrown back into the pit rather than a conscious effort to align the skull according to any specific orientation, and there was no radical twisting of the necks to make the skull face an absolute direction.

The arms of most of the skeletons were found in a relaxed, extended position at the sides or over the general pelvic area (Burials 180 and 181), but in a few of the burials

Table 11.1. Pit Burials

Locus	Angle of Burial (Degrees)	Sex	Age (Years)	Body Position or Remains	Arm Position	Grave Goods
180	293	M	Adult	Extended	(diagram)	
181	107	?	?	Extended	(diagram)	
185	108	?	?	Extended (legs only)		
189	?	?	?	?		Bronze cosmetic stick (Chap. 25a: 283); amphora (Chap. 28b)
1157	?	F	14?	Skull only		
1167	44	M	30	Extended	(diagram)	
1168	117	F	29	Extended	(diagram)	
1169	90	?	3; 5	Skulls only		
1181	265	F	35	Extended	(diagram)	
1185	105	F	30?	Extended	(diagram)	
1190	90	F	45 +	Extended?		
1191	70	?	?	Extended?		Bronze earring (Chap. 25a:180)
1850	180	M	29?	Extended?		
1853	?	?	2.5	Extended?		Bronze earring (Chap. 25a:179)
1854	135	M	25	Extended	(diagram)	Iron javelin point (Chap. 25a:32)
1860	90	?	30 +	Extended	(diagram)	
1863	276	F	30?	?	(diagram)	Bronze bracelet (Chap. 25a:219)
1877	92	?	2.5	Extended		
1878	68	?	32?	Extended	(diagram)	
1880	60	F	27	Extended		Silver ring (Chap. 25a:175)
1882	78	M	32	Extended	(diagram)	
1885	274	?	5	Extended	(diagram)	
1886	?			Skull only		

the arms and hands were arranged otherwise (Burial 1185: both arms folded across stomach; Burial 1878: right elbow bent and hand resting on neck, left hand across pelvic area; Burial 1882: right elbow bent at right angle, left arm lying straight at its side).

The declination of the pit burials (using the head as the point of reference) varies from 44 to 93 degrees. The majority had the head oriented to the eastern half of the compass, with more than half of these around 90 ± 20 degrees. There were four skeletons with heads in a westerly direction, close to 280 degrees (Burials 180, 1181, 1863, 1885). The head of one grave was oriented to 44 degrees (Burial 1167) and another to 180 degrees (Burial 1850). Two burials (1157 and 1886) consisted only of skulls lying in such a manner that determination of body angles was impossible.

11.1.2. Jar Burials

Twenty-seven jar burials were uncovered (Table 11.2). The jars were interred in the orange quartz sand either above or on the calcareous sandstone layer, then covered by orange quartz sand and the yellow blow-sand of the surface.

A storage jar burial involved breaking off one end of the vessel, sliding the body into the jar, and loosely capping the vessel with fragments of the same or another jar or jars or, in one case (Burial 190), unbaked clay (Pl. 40). Burial 1156 was covered with a *ḥamra* brick; a *kurkar* stone was used to

Table 11.2. Jar Burials

Locus	Jar Type	Angle of Burial (Degrees)	Skeletal Remains	Grave Goods
190	Basket handled (Fig. 9.15:2)		Disintegrated	
651	Elongated	95	Disintegrated	
652	One elongated, one flat shouldered (Fig. 9.14:6, 10)		Bone fragments	
654	One bag shaped (Fig. 9.14:3) one unidentified (in stone-lined cist; see under cist burials)	92	Newborn infant in semiflexed position	
662	Bag shaped (?), large fragments		Skull of 29-year-old; female?	
663	Basket handled	90	Infant of 18 months	Beads (Chap. 34:173–174)
665	Basket handled (Fig. 9.15:4)	97	Teeth only	
673	Fragments only (two or more jars)		Bone fragments	Bronze ring fragments
825	Basket handled		Bone fragments	Bronze bracelet (Chap. 25a:232)
826	Elongated	128	Infant in semiflexed position	Four bronze anklets (Chap. 25a:209–212); beads (Chap. 34:183–193)
828	Base of storage jar	0		
1156	One large sherd (robbed)			
1160	Fragments only (disturbed)			Stone bead (Chap. 34:194)
1163	Basket handled	90	Bone fragments	Two bronze anklets (Chap. 25a:214–215); beads, shells (Chap. 34:32–58)
1172	Bag shaped	95	Infant of 2 months	
1176	Fragments only (disturbed)			
1187	Bag shaped (Fig. 9.14:5)	90	Distintegrated	
1188	Elongated (Fig. 9.14:8)	275	Infant skull, ribs	
1852	Bag shaped (fragments of three jars; Fig. 9.14:2)	90	Adult; female?	
1858	Basket handled (fragments of three jars; Fig. 9.15:1, 6)	94	Two children of 2.5 and 3.5 years	Faience Horus eye (Fig. 29.1:9); two hair rings (Chap. 25a:202–203); serpentinite bead (Chap. 34:227)
1859	Bag shaped, badly disturbed (Fig. 9.14:1)			Beads (Chap. 34:228–230)
1864	Two basket handled; fragments placed end to end (Fig. 9.15:3, 5)	102		
1868	Elongated (Fig. 9.14:7)	110	Skull lines	
1870	Bag shaped	268		Two bronze earrings (Chap. 25a:189, 193); chert
1874	Unidentifiable (very friable)	90	Infant of 2 years	
1875	Basket handled (fragments of two jars)	96		Two bronze anklets (Chap. 25a:224–225); Horus eye; beads; shells (Chap. 34:127–133)
1879	Elongated	135	Bone fragments of infant	

close the open end of the jar of Burial 1187, whereas the jar of Burial 1875 was capped with a *ḥamra* brick, *kurkar* stones, and large potsherds from another basket-handled jar.

The types of vessels used for these burials were mainly large storage jars ranging from 55 to 150 cm in length, with an average length of about 80 cm. They may be classified into three main types (see Chap. 9): bag shaped (Jar Type

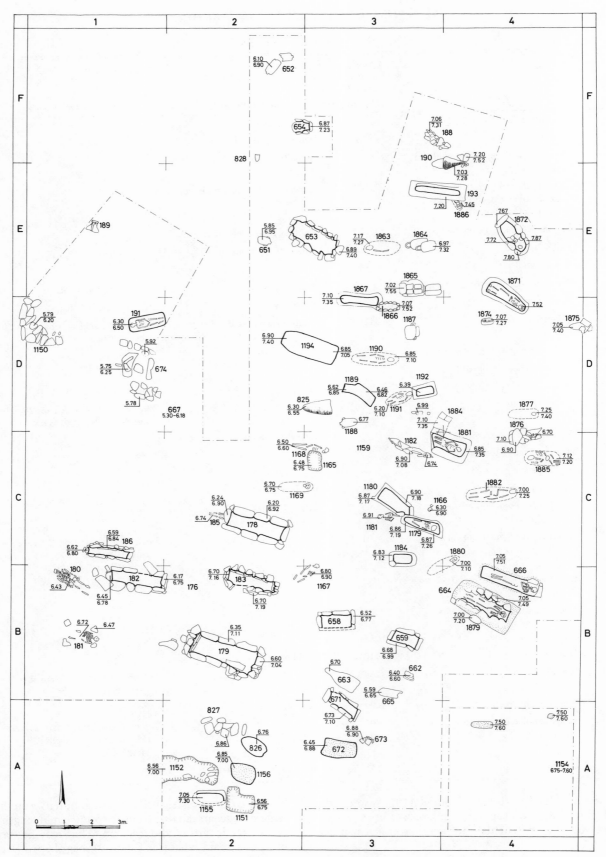

Figure 11.1.　Southern part of cemetery.

156

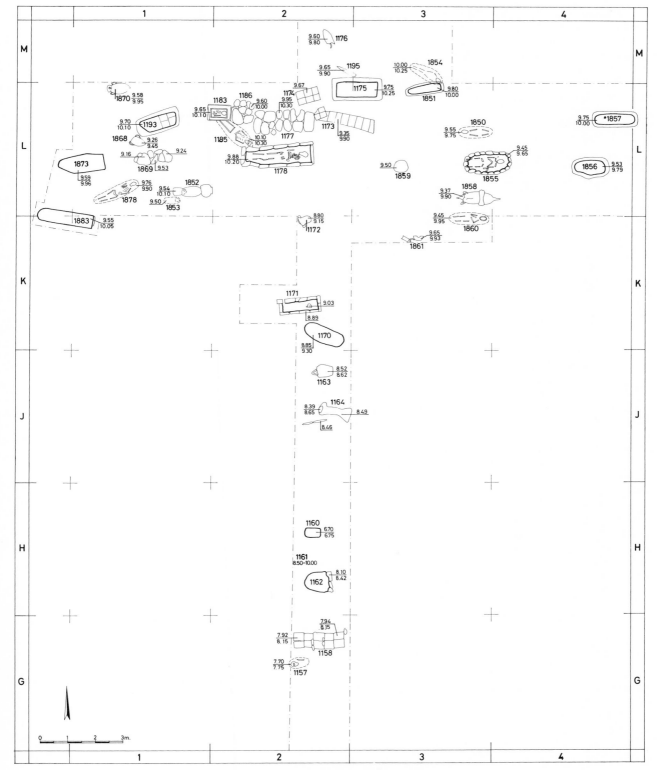

Figure 11.2. Northern part of cemetery.

2), elongated (Jar Type 1), and basket handled (Jar Type 5A-B).

In some cases, more than one jar was used for the burial. Burial 1858 consisted of three jars overlapping each other end to end. Together, these three jars covered the skeletons of two small children. Burial 1852 also consisted of large fragments of three jars, apparently covering a single female adult. Burials 673, 1864, and 1875 consisted of two burial jars each (plus additional jar fragments), each containing a single skeleton.

Except for two jars containing skeletons of adults, apparently females (Burials 662 and 1852), all the others contained the remains of infants or children under the age of four (Burial 663, 18 months; Burial 1172, 2 months; Burial 1858, two children, 3.5 and 2.5 years; Burial 1874, 2 years; Burial 1879, infant of undetermined age).

Because of the lack of solid skeletal material, it was difficult to determine the position of the infants within the jars, but the location of the head could usually be established according to the position of the teeth and a circle of calcium carbonate skull remains. In some cases, the presence of bronze anklets showed the location of the feet. By these means, the placement of the body within the jar could be either detected or deduced in eight of the jar burials. In four of these, the head of the infant—as well as the mouth of the vessel—pointed east. This was determined by skull and teeth (Burial 663), teeth alone (Burial 665), and placement of anklets (Burials 826 and 1875). In two jars, the head of the infant and the mouth of the vessel pointed west, as determined by the skull (Burial 1188) and placement of bronze hair rings (Burial 1870). In the remaining two jars with identifiable skeletal orientation, the mouth of the vessel pointed west and the head pointed east, as determined by anklets (Burial 1163) and skull lines (Burial 1868).

In most of the burials, the base of the vessel was broken off. The infant or child was then slid headfirst into the jar, or at least this seems to have been the case in six of the eight jars in which body position could be deduced. The declination of the jars ranged from 85 to 275 degrees. If the head pointed east, the average declination was 100 degrees; if it pointed west, the average declination was 271 degrees.

11.1.3. Cist Burials

In the 51 cist burials, the graves were dug down to the level of the gravelly calcarenite and then lined or covered by constructions of *ḥamra* mudbrick, stone, or wood or various combinations of these materials. These graves are of two basic types: (A) walled and (B) unwalled.

A. Walled Burials

In these graves, the sides of the pit were protected by walls, usually to a height of about 30 cm, built either of (a) *ḥamra* mudbrick or (b) stone.

(a) Mudbrick-Walled Cist Burials (Table 11.3). The graves constructed of *ḥamra* mudbrick used three kinds of coverings: brick, stone, or wood, or a combination of these materials.

Sixteen brick-covered graves have walls ranging from 10 to 20 cm in width. The length of the individual bricks varied between 20 cm (Burial 1183) and 40 cm (Burial 1179). The brick coverings came in two styles: corbeled (Burials 1158, 1183, 1865, and 1883) and flat topped (Burials 191, 1162, 1171, 1174, 1179, 1184, 1193, 1194, 1856, 1857, 1867, and 1881). The corbeling effect was obtained by leaning two bricks diagonally against each other to form a gable. Burial 1183, a superb example of corbeling, was the best preserved. The brick covering seems to have been strengthened at intervals by stones or sherds set in an upright position. The gable of Burial 1158 was strengthened with stones. In Burial 1193, the bricks were laid in two parallel rows across the top of the tomb walls. The upper bricks were 10 cm thick by about 25 cm^2. All other examples of the flat-laid brick construction were affected by the adverse soil conditions. Some of the bricks were "dissolved" to such an extent that the lines between the individual bricks were obliterated—e.g., Burials 1162 and 1171.

Two stone-covered graves (Burials 1175 and 1177) were found in the northern sector of the cemetery. The walls were the same width (10–20 cm) and height (30 cm) as those covered with mudbrick. The covering stones were of flat, unworked *kurkar* varying in diameter from 10 to 40 cm, laid flat and overlapping like shingles. Both of these burials cut earlier graves.

There were nine brick-walled, wood-covered graves (Burials 193, 666, 1155, 1178, 1180, 1192, 1851, 1871, and 1884). Conclusive evidence to explain the construction of the wooden covers was found in Burials 664 and 1178, the former a stone-walled grave (see Table 11.4). Both of these graves contained large bronze nails, lying in such a way as to indicate that thick wooden planks had once covered them. The position of the nails suggests that two planks held together by two wooden crossbars were laid lengthwise across the grave. The heads and upper shanks of the nails of both loci retained remnants of wood (identified as *Cupressus sempervirens*), but no other remains of the wooden covers survived.

These graves had two other characteristics that made it possible to identify additional examples of wood-covered graves. Around the edges of Burial 664, an extra layer of mudbrick was found on top of the stone and *ḥamra* walls. This apparently held the "lid" down tightly over the grave. Burial 1178 had a large *ḥamra* brick at its western end, which apparently also served to hold the cover in place. This "sealing" allowed only fine-grained sand to filter into the grave, in contrast to the coarse orange quartz sand that filled the other graves. Burials 193, 666, 1178, 1180, 1192, 1851, 1871, and 1884 all displayed these two characteristics: a brick layer around the edges plus very fine, filtered sand inside the grave (Pl. 39). Even though no nails were found on these graves, all other characteristics of the two wood-covered graves were evident. Most of the brick-walled graves are no more than 65 cm wide and could easily be spanned by two or three planks 30 cm wide and 2 m long. There was no need to nail these planks together, since they were held in place by the additional *ḥamra* mudbricks. Al-

158

Table 11.3. Cist Burials, Type A(a): Mudbrick Walled

Locus	Description	Size (cm)	Angle of Burial (Degrees)	Sex	Age	Body Position or Remains	Arm Position	Grave Goods
	Brick covered							
191	Flat	110 × 50				Extended?		
1158	Corbeled	200 × 65	95	M	36 years?	Extended		
1162	Flat	80 × 70	85					Bronze earring (Chap. 25a:182)
1171	Flat	170 × 54	76	M?	13 years	Extended		
1174	Flat	110 × 50	60					Two bronze earrings (Chap. 25a:183–184)
1179	Flat	160 × 50	105	?	1 year	Extended		Four bronze earrings (Chap. 25a:185–187, 191); beads (Chap. 34:195–206)
1183	Corbeled	85 × 60	90	?	6 months	Extended		Bronze fragments; ivory pendant and beads (Chap. 34:207–214)
1184	Flat	90 × 50	90	?	6 months	Extended		Two bronze bracelets (Chap. 25a:234–235); beads (Chap. 34:97–126)
1193	Flat	160 × 75	73	?	4 years	Extended		Two bronze earrings; silver earring, silver bracelet (Chap. 25a:188, 195–196, 231); beads (Chap. 34:215–219)
1194	Flat	205 × 80	115			Extended?		Six bronze plaques with rivets; folded sheet metal with rivets (Chap. 25a:139–144, 146); ostrich egg fragment; *Murex* shell
1856	Flat	100 × 57	288	?	2 months	Extended?		
1857	Flat	136 × 60	88		5 months	Extended		Earring fragments; bronze bracelet (Chap. 25a:238)
1865	Corbeled	135 × 50	180	F	Elderly	Extended		
1867	Flat	140 × 50	98	?	2 years	Extended		Blue faience beads; (Chap. 34:236–237); chert
1881	Flat	? × 95	115	F	27 years	Lower legs folded back		Clay juglets (Fig. 9.15:10); alabastron (Fig. 30.1:14)
1883	Corbeled	200 × 50	96	M	32 years	Extended		
	Stone covered							
1175	Flat *kurkar* stones (two skeletons)	170 × 70	85	F ?	29 years 30 months			
1177	Flat *kurkar* stones	200 × 62	85	F	37 years	Extended		
	Wood covered							
193	(See text)	200 × 60			Adult			
666		230 × 50	109	F	28 years	Extended		Beads and pendants (Chap. 34:59–96); bronze pendants (Chap. 25a:204–206)
1155			79	M				
1178	Four bronze nails with wood attached	270 × 70	80		31 years			Four bronze nails; bronze bowl; silver ring (Chap. 25a:94–97, 162, 176); clay juglet (Fig. 9.15:9)

Table 11.3. **Continued**

Locus	Description	Size (cm)	Angle of Burial (Degrees)	Sex	Age	Body Position or Remains	Arm Position	Grave Goods
						Skeleton		
1180		?	123			Teeth and bone fragments		Bronze bracelet (Chap. 25a:233)
1192		100 × 65	265			Skull fragments		
1851		125 × 50	80		2.5 years	Extended		Silver hair ring; two bronze bracelets (Chap. 25a:203, 236–237); beads and shells (Chap. 34:220–226)
1871		170 × 70	112	F	20 years	Extended		Bronze cosmetic stick (Chap. 25a:287); chert; beads (Chap. 34:134–172)
1884		50 × 50	105					Iron signet ring (Chap. 25a:172)

though the position of the nails makes it obvious that long planks were used for Burials 664 and 1178, the boards of the other graves may have been placed crossways like the stone slabs of tombs at other sites. Either way, the evidence for the use of wood as a grave cover is very strong, since none of the other brick-walled graves had this extra heavy layer of mudbrick, nor were they filled with the fine sand of the wood-covered graves.

(b) Stone-Walled Cist Burials (Table 11.4). The walls of 14 burials were built of stone (Pl. 37). The stones of the larger graves were well hewn, measuring about 65–70 cm × 19–24 cm × 32–35 cm. They were laid in two courses, bringing the depth inside the grave to about 65 cm. Usually three stones were used for each side and one at each end, so that the large cut-stone graves were approximately 2.5 m long and 1.10 m wide overall. The smaller tombs of hewn stone were about 1.20 m long and 0.75 m wide and were built of one (Burial 1866) or two courses (Burials 183 and 653), usually using a flatter type of *kurkar* stone. Sometimes the gaps were filled in with uncut stones, as in Burial 659.

Five of the stone-walled burials also used stone for the covering (Burials 182, 183, 186, 1866, and 1872). Burial 182, although disturbed, seems to have been covered with flat stone slabs, found lying crisscross on and around the grave. Burials 183 and 186 were covered with rough fieldstones. Burial 1866 was lined with six thin *kurkar* stones standing vertically side by side. It was covered with a massive construction of flattish fieldstones and *ḥamra*, which increased its outer dimensions to 70 cm × 100 cm, whereas its interior measured only 30 cm × 75 cm.

Burial 1872, measuring 75 cm × 180 cm, was built of large friable *kurkar* stones set on end upon the *kurkar* bedrock. The covering was made of the same type of stones, laid flat with dark *ḥamra* between them. A partition of stone seemed to divide the grave into two chambers, but

this might have been a "pelvic support" like that noted by Johns at Atlit (1933:58).

Only a few of the wood-covered, stone-walled burials display proof of their wood coverings. Because the planks were completely decayed, remnants of wood were preserved only where they were attached to the metal nails driven into the coverings and coffins as attested in Burial 664 (see above). (If wooden dowels had been used, probably no traces of the wood would have remained.) Burial 178 is the only one of the stone-walled graves that provided direct evidence of wood use (identified as *Cupressus sempervirens*). However, all nine graves of this type were filled with the same lighter, finer sand that had sifted in through the wooden planks in the brick-walled, wood-covered burials.

Burials 653 and 1855 were built of large, unhewn *kurkar* stones laid in one or two courses. These stones were about 50 cm long and standing on their ends with smaller stones lying on top, apparently to hold the wooden cover in place. Burials 658 and 671 were of smaller hewn-stone construction but basically were the same as the larger ones.

Two of the stone-walled burials are unique. Burial 654 was constructed of flat *kurkar* stones set on end like those of Burial 1866. Inside the grave was a jar that served as a coffin for a newborn infant. The top of the jar was broken off and its opening was sealed by the stones of the grave.

Burial 659, measuring 75 cm × 120 cm, was built of one course of hewn stone interspersed with rough fieldstones. Seventeen iron nails or fragments thereof, each about 6 cm long, were found inside the grave, two at each of the eight "corners" of a wooden coffin (and one lying beside it) that—if preserved—would have measured about 40 cm × 80 cm. Attached to the heads of the nails were small pieces of wood, identified as *Cupressus sempervirens*.

B. Unwalled Cist Burials

The unwalled cist burials, which make up about 20 percent

Table 11.4. Cist Burials, Type A(b): Stone Walled

Locus	Description	Size (cm)	Angle of Burial (Degrees)	Sex	Age	Body Position or Remains	Arm Position	Grave Goods
						Skeleton		
	Stone covered							
182	Hewn stone walls; stone slab covering	220 × 104	100					
183	Unhewn stone walls and covering	210 × 110	105					Bronze bowl (Chap. 25a:161)
186	Hewn stone walls and covering	185 × 80	99					
1866	Unhewn stone and *ḥamra* gable	75 × 30	88			Bone scraps		Two bronze anklets (Chap. 25a:220–221); beads (Chap. 34:234–235)
1872	Unhewn stone; "pelvic support"	180 × 75	146	F				Bronze ring; bronze cosmetic stick (Chap. 25a:168, 290); blue glass seal (Fig. 28.1:3); Persian bowl sherd; beads (Chap. 34:238–239)
	Wood covered							
178	Hewn stone walls (nail with wood attached)	260 × 110	108					
179	Hewn stone walls	270 × 130	110			Skull only		
653	Unhewn stone walls	210 × 100	123					Bronze Phoenician coin (Chap. 27:13); folded sheet with rivets; tweezers (Chap. 25a:145, 276)
654	Stone-walled jar burial	60 × 40	92		Newborn	Semiflexed		
658	Hewn stone walls (robbed)	120 × 100	87					
659	Hewn stones with coffin (iron nails)	120 × 75		?	11 months	Teeth only		Nails (e.g., Chap. 25a:112)
664	Stone and *ḥamra* walls (seven bronze nails)	250 × 70	120	M	32 years	Extended	Ⴠ	Javelin head; four knives; seven nails; signet ring; tweezers (Chap. 24a:31, 49, 54–56, 85–91, 173, 277); beads? (Chap. 34:175–182)
671	Hewn stone walls	130 × 50	133			Bone fragments		Metal fragment; sherds
1855	Unhewn stone walls	177 × 74	90	F	32 years	Extended	Ⴠ	Iron ring (Chap. 25a:178)

of the total number of cist burials, were covered either with stones or with *ḥamra* mudbricks, or sometimes with a combination of these materials (Table 11.5).

Four of these burials had stone covers, each of them unique. In Burial 1182 the stone covering formed a gentle curve 1.70 m long, ranging in height from level 6.75 at the east to level 7.15 at the west. The flattish *kurkar* stones were placed over the burial horizontally, vertically, and at various angles in between, and the stones incorporated a chunk of a gray cementlike substance mixed with shell and plaster on one side, perhaps remains of a floor. The whole construction seems to have been held together by red *ḥamra*. This strange method of construction was apparently used

because the pit was very narrow, causing the covering stones to form a somewhat vertical configuration. The human remains, consisting of the lower part of a skull, jawbone, and several teeth, were found directly south of the structure.

Burial 1869 was apparently constructed in a similar manner; it was covered with three large stones laid vertically. Large pottery sherds were placed on top of this construction where the stones joined. Burial 1186, covered horizontally with flat, overlapping *kurkar* stones, was mostly destroyed by Burial 1177 (a brick-walled, stone-covered grave). For that reason, only an arm with a bronze bracelet remained in it. Burial 1876 appears to be a combination of the two previous ones; it had both vertical and horizontal stones,

Table 11.5. Cist Burials, Type B: Unwalled

Locus	Description	Size (cm)	Angle of Burial (Degrees)	Sex	Age (Years)	Body Position or Remains	Arm Position	Grave Goods
1182	Horizontal and vertical stones with ḥamra	170 × ?	112	F	40 +	Skull?		
1186	Flat overlapping stones (robbed)	185 × 80	?			Arm only		Bronze bracelet (Chap. 25a:216)
1869	Horizontal and vertical stones + pottery sherds	130 × ?	90	?	6	Extended	⚥	Bronze earring; two bronze anklets (Chap. 25a:190, 222–223); beads (Chap. 34:1–31)
1876	Vertical and flat stones	125 × 66	68		1	Teeth		Pottery bases; cowrie shells
	Brick covered							
672	Flat	130 × 55	98					
1164	Flat with jar fragments	?	87			Bone fragments		
1170	*Ḥamra* brick ("melted")	?	115					
1173	*Ḥamra* clay over skeleton	?	95	M	32	Extended	⚥	Bronze coin of Alexander the Great (Chap. 27:30); iron ring fragment
1189	Flat (disturbed)	?	125			Bone fragments		
1873	Corbeled	165 × 60	89	F?	27?	Extended	⚥	Bronze bracelet (Chap. 25a:218)

and possibly two side walls. Only traces of the skeleton and some teeth of a 1-year-old child were found in it.

The six brick-covered graves (Burials 672, 1164, 1170, 1173, 1189, and 1873) vary in condition from Burials 1173 and 1873, which are very well preserved, to Burial 1170, which yielded only a light red substance that appeared to have seeped through the soil. Apparently these graves were originally corbeled with *ḥamra* mudbricks, although the moisture in the soil has rendered many of the original structures flat. There were only two graves with skeletons, and these were so impregnated by *ḥamra* that preservation was poor and excavation difficult. Grave goods were rather rare. Burial 1173, however, provided two helpful objects for dating: an iron ring with flat bezel and a coin of Alexander the Great.

It was possible to determine or deduce the orientations of nearly all of the cist burials (Tables 11.3–11.5). Most of the heads pointed east, usually within 20 degrees of true east-west. The heads of the others seem to have pointed west, or at least within 20 degrees of a true east-west axis. The full significance of this orientation is not yet fully understood.

In all but one of the cist burials, the skeletons were laid in an extended position on their backs (except in Burial 1881, where the knees were folded underneath the body). In 15 of the 51 cist burials the placement of the hands was discernible. Unlike the burials at Atlit and other Persian period sites, the arms were seldom laid straight along the sides of the body. Of the 15 hand positions encountered, only 2 were alike: those of Burials 1171 and 1881, which were in a relaxed position over the pelvic area. Otherwise, the hands appear up near the head, crossed at the chest, crossed over the pelvic area, one arm straight down and one raised, or in a variety of intermediate angles. The significant point is that the arms appear to have been placed randomly in relaxed positions, rather than in any specific ritualistic manner.

In the 51 cist burials unearthed, only 28 contained identifiable skeletons or skeletal material. The rest either had no skeletal material at all or it was in such a poor state of preservation that not even age or sex could be determined. Fourteen of the identifiable skeletons were of children less than 6 years of age, nine were 30 years or older, five were in the 20–30 age group, and only one was a juvenile. The scarcity of individuals in the 7–20 age group is curious. One explanation may be that since the bones of adolescents are not yet well solidified, they may simply have disintegrated, like those of the infants in the jar burials. Several of the 24 cist burials lacking identifiable skeletal material were of an appropriate size for this age group. Another possibility may be that those individuals who survived infancy lived to reach full adulthood.

Examination of the distribution of the sexes in either walled or unwalled graves shows that in all identifiable cases

Table 11.6. Undeterminable Burial Types

Locus	Description	Angle of Burial (Degrees)	Sex	Skeleton Age (Years)	Remains	Grave Goods
176	Scattered grave goods in sand					Arrowhead; knife; finger ring; three bronze bracelets (Chap. 25a:13, 60, 170, 239)
674	Stones (robbed)			Adult	Incisor	
827	Stones (robbed)	101		Child?		Pottery fragments
1159	Scattered grave goods in sand					Copper nail; finger ring; silver pendant; bronze bracelet (Chap. 25a:103, 167, 207, 217); beads (Chap. 34:240–241)
1161	Pit burial?		F	20 +	Bone scraps	
1165	Pit burial?		F?	10–15	Teeth only	
1166	Cist? (robbed)			Adult	Skull and teeth	
1195	Red *ḥamra* line (robbed)					
1861	Jar burial? (disturbed)	90		3	Teeth, bones	Bronze earring fragment; beads; mother-of-pearl Horus eye (Chap. 34:231–233)
1862	Pit burial?			4	Bone scraps	

the ratio of males to females was approximately equal, indicating that the choice of a walled or unwalled grave was a matter of personal preference rather than gender.

In only one cist grave was there evidence of a multiple burial. There were two occupants in Burial 1175, a 29-year-old female and a 30-month-old infant, probably mother and child.

11.2. GRAVE GOODS

Although a great deal of material was retrieved from the cemetery, very few of the individual burials were particularly rich in grave goods. Grave offerings were found in only 6 of the 23 pit burials (Table 11.1). Burial 189 contained an amphora and a cosmetic stick. Burial 1191 contained a bronze loop earring. Burial 1853, the grave of a 30-month-old infant, also had a bronze earring. Burial 1854, that of a 25-year-old male, contained an iron javelin point placed next to the left leg, perhaps indicating that he was connected to the military. Burial 1863 contained a bronze bracelet on the right arm of the poorly preserved skeleton of a female of about 30 years of age. Burial 1880, the grave of a 27-year-old female, contained a silver ring with a flat bezel and a star design.

Only in 10 of the 27 jar burials were there any grave goods (Table 11.2). In seven of them there were beads, mostly of frit but a few of semiprecious stone such as carnelian or serpentinite. In four of the burials bronze anklets or bracelets were found, three with plain ends (Burials 826, 1163, 1875) and one with zoomorphic terminals (Burial 825). Cowrie shells were found in two of the jars (Burials 1163 and 1875), most likely strung as beads. Three metal rings were found, one made of bronze (Burial 673) and the other two of silver, apparently hair rings (Burial 1858). Horus eyes were present in two of the jar burials. One was fa-

ience (Burial 1858) and the other mother-of-pearl (Burial 1875). A set of bronze loop earrings was recovered from Burial 1870. Perhaps the 10 burials containing articles of personal adornment belonged to small girls, but this is impossible to prove skeletally.

No pottery other than the jars themselves was found in or around these jar burials. There were no lamps or other types of vessels, either personal or votive, nor any tools or utensils. Apparently such objects were not buried with infants or children at Tel Michal.

Nor were grave goods particularly abundant in the cist burials (Tables 11.3–11.5). Other than a few articles of personal adornment, only two brick-walled graves (Burials 1178 and 1881) and two stone-walled burials (183 and 664) contained tools, weapons, or vessels: a javelin point, iron knives, bronze bowls, clay juglets, and an alabastron. Articles such as rings, bracelets, anklets, earrings, and beads seem to be present mainly in graves of females.

11.3. STRATIGRAPHY AND DATING OF THE CEMETERY

The cemetery has 12 examples of burials that were either cut through by other graves or else covered by them. (1) Pit Burial 185 consisted solely of the long bones of the legs protruding beyond Burial 178 (a stone-walled cist burial), the torso obviously having been removed when the latter grave was dug. (2) The *ḥamra* bricks of Burial 193 were found lying over the lower part of the skeleton of Pit Burial 1886. (3) Burial 1158, a brick-walled, corbeled grave, cut into Pit Burial 1157. (4) Brick-walled Cist Burial 1175 destroyed most of brick-walled Burial 1195, leaving only a thin line of reddish *ḥamra* from its northern wall. (5) Burial 1177, a brick-walled, stone-covered burial, cut Burial 1186, an unwalled, stone-covered grave, leaving only 40 cm of it intact and reusing most of its stones. (6) The feet of Pit Burial 1185 were covered by Cist Burial 1183, a small brick-walled, corbeled grave, although the skeleton was not disturbed. When Cist Burial 1179, a *ḥamra* mudbrick grave, was dug, it cut through (7) Cist Burial 1180, another brick-walled burial, and through (8) Pit Burial 1181, displacing the lower half of the skeleton and pushing some of its bones across the torso. (9) Cist Burial 1867, a large brick-walled grave, was cut by a small stone-covered, stone-lined grave (Cist Burial 1866). (10) Cist Burial 1881 incorporated the southern stone wall of Cist Burial 1884 into its northern wall. (11) The northeast corner of Cist Burial 1851, a brick-walled grave, covered the skull of Pit Burial 1854, although it did not disturb the skeleton. (12) Cist Burial 1855, a stone-walled grave, was lying on top of a very disturbed grave (Burial 1861) consisting of large fragments of two different jars and one red *ḥamra* brick (listed under undeterminable burial types, Table 11.6). No skeletal remains were found in it.

It would seem that the pit burials were the graves most frequently disturbed by others. At least 6 of the 23 pit burials were cut or covered by other interments, mainly the brick-walled and stone-walled cist graves; these specific pit burials are obviously earlier than the other types, but that does not prove that as a class they are all earlier. Nor is it possible to determine how much earlier; the few grave offerings associated with the pit burials are of the same 6th- to 4th-century B.C.E. horizon as those associated with the rest of the burials. It is also interesting that the brick-walled graves were sometimes cut by other brick-walled graves and sometimes by stone-walled ones. The only kind of grave that was not cut is the stone-walled cist category. In one case, a jar burial was integrated into the side of a stone-walled grave, but apparently the latter (Burial 664) was contemporary with the former (Burial 1879).

The grave goods in the burials, whether they cut or cover other burials or are themselves cut or covered, all belong to the Persian period. Two of the three types of storage vessels used for the jar burials are paralleled by stratigraphic finds on the high tell from all six Persian period strata (Chap. 9). The bag-shaped jars were most common in Strata XI-IX (Fig. 9.14:1–5), and the elongated type (Fig. 9.14:6–9) predominated in Strata VIII-VI. Two variants (A-B) of the basket-handled jars (Fig. 9.15:1–6) were not paralleled on the tell, whereas another variant of the same type (C) was found mainly in Strata XI-IX of the high tell but did not appear in the cemetery at all. In addition, there was one restorable specimen of an amphora from the cemetery that was not connected directly to any burial (Locus 189), and that is paralleled on the tell in Stratum IX.

Two coins from the burials supply absolute dates, at least for these two graves. The first is a 4th-century B.C.E. coin from Tyre that came from Burial 653 and the second is a coin of Alexander the Great from Burial 1173. Another coin from Tyre that was unearthed in A. Kempinski's previous excavations of the cemetery is dated to 359 B.C.E. (Stern 1982:72, 264, n. 19).

11.4. CONCLUSIONS

Because of the adverse soil conditions, the skeletons were badly preserved, particularly the soft bones of the infants in the storage jar burials and perhaps also those of the juveniles, whose remains are conspicuously absent. Nevertheless, enough skeletal material remained to determine that the adults, whether interred in pits (Table 11.1) or cist burials (Tables 11.3–11.5), were generally laid in extended position, flat on their backs, with their arms relaxed. In most cases their heads pointed east, usually within a few degrees of a true east-west axis. Similarly, in four of the eight jar burials in which the orientation of the body could be determined, the heads (as well as the mouth of the jars) also pointed east (Table 11.2). The significance of this orientation is not fully understood, but two possibilities arise. The first may have been a religious belief that made the west an important direction for the dead to face. The other—which may or may not be connected with the first—involves the precession of the heavens and the changing angles of the sun throughout the seasons, the time of year when a person died determining the angle of burial.

A rather surprising phenomenon is the uniformity of the cultural and socioeconomic status of the deceased. It was suggested that the general scarcity of grave offerings in the pit burials (less than 25 percent of which had any grave goods at all) indicates that their occupants were of a poorer class than those of the cist burials (more than 50 percent of which had associated grave goods). However, considering the great number of graves of all categories without any grave goods, it would be speculative to draw such a conclusion. It is more likely that the cemetery at Tel Michal was of a people who did not regularly bury "things" with their dead (or that the funeral offerings were of a perishable nature, such as grains, fruits, articles of cloth or wood, etc.).

A few items, such as a Persian period mortarium, were found in the soil of the cemetery but could not be related to specific graves. These may have held offerings or been offerings themselves; in general, however, the archaeological evidence shows that the people of Tel Michal were of uniform social status, of a pragmatic attitude regarding their dead, and with few superstitions about the afterlife, other than those reflected in the practice of burying the dead to face either the rising or setting sun.

REFERENCES

Avigad, N. 1977. Makmish. *Enc. Arch. Exc. III*: 768–770.

Herzog, Z., Negbi, O., and Moshkovitz, S. 1978. Excavations at Tel Michal, 1977. *Tel Aviv* 5:99–130.

Johns, C. N. 1933. Excavations at 'Atlit (1930–31). The South-Eastern Cemetery. *QDAP* 2:41–104.

Stern, E. 1982. *Material Culture of the Land of the Bible in the Persian Period, 538–332 B.C.E.* Warminster.

12

Hellenistic Stratigraphy and Architecture (Strata V-III)

by Ze'ev Herzog

Four phases of occupation in the Hellenistic period were recognized at Tel Michal. However, a full stratigraphic sequence was obtained only on the high tell. The two earlier stages (Strata V and IV) contain a large fortress and a few additional houses (Figs. 12.1; 12.6). The later part of the period saw the construction of a small fort, utilized twice, which we have assigned to phases a and b of Stratum III (Fig. 12.9).

The function of the northern hill changed drastically: instead of the extensive Persian period settlement of Strata VIII-VI, the area was occupied by a large winepress (used only in Strata V-IV). On the northeastern hillock, an open cultic structure continued the sacred tradition of this locale (Avigad 1977:770). Only a silo was preserved in the eastern hillock (Area C), but it yielded an important hoard of Ptolemaic silver coins (Kindler 1978).

Hasmonean occupation was even more limited. Apart from the fort on the high tell, only a small winepress was found, about 200 m south of the southeastern hillock.

12.1. STRATUM V

12.1.1. Fortress 806 on the High Tell

Remains of Stratum V consist of sections of solid walls (0.80–1.0 m wide) running parallel to each other (Fig. 12.2). The main feature is Wall L128, preserved to a length of more than 25 m, which obviously served as the eastern limit of the structure. The corner with Wall O127 forms the basic frame to Fortress 806. The southern closure (Wall G154) is less clear, mainly because of its slight shift in angle and the lack of direct contact. But since the northwestern corner is also not a right angle, we are probably correct in our reconstruction.

Wall O159 was presumably the western side of the fortress. This assumption is supported by its reinforcement with ashlar blocks laid as headers; such strengthening of the wall suits its position on the vulnerable western side of the tell (Pl. 41).

According to the proposed reconstruction, Fortress 806 is 34 m long and 24 m (mean) wide. The internal divisions in the northern half are clearer (mainly because the southern half was not completely excavated). Wall L1311 indicates division of the inner area into two main units. In the northern unit, Locus 806 was a small courtyard (6.8 m × 10.0 m) affording access to the surrounding rooms. Most likely the main gateway into the fortress was through the northern side of this Courtyard 806.

West of Courtyard 806 are two rows of rooms, separated by Wall O146. The row next to the courtyard contained at least three rooms of differing sizes. The northern narrow chamber (for storage?) presumably was entered through Room 694, which measures 3.70 m × 4.40 m and has a beaten-earth floor. Through Wall O147 runs a drain section made of reused *kurkar* blocks, each with a channel hewn along its long axis. Room 694 was entered from the courtyard. To the south, it opened into the third room through a doorway with ashlar door jambs; only the southern one is preserved.

The second row contained two or three rooms. Room 1025 was an almost square chamber (2.70 m × 2.80 m). The floor of Room 1014 was covered with a hard, gray, cementlike surface. It was in this room that a hoard of five silver tetradrachms of Ptolemy II and III was found in a small fusiform unguentarium. Since the area south of Room 1014 underlies the Roman period (1002) tower, we decided not to excavate it (Pl. 42).

On the east side of Courtyard 806, walls of Stratum V (and IV) are preserved only east and below the outer limit of the Roman fortress (Stratum II). Most of the inner walls were dismantled during the Roman period construction. The low elevation of the foundation for Wall L128 (4.68 m

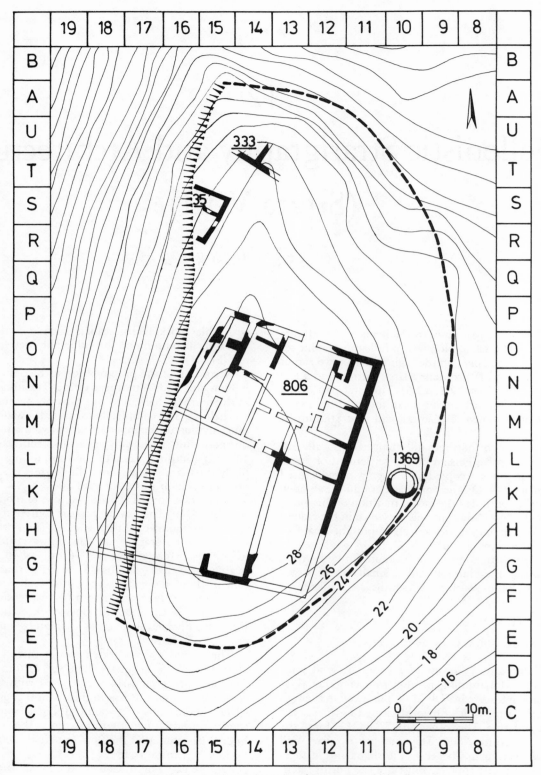

Figure 12.1. Architectural remains of Stratum V on high tell.

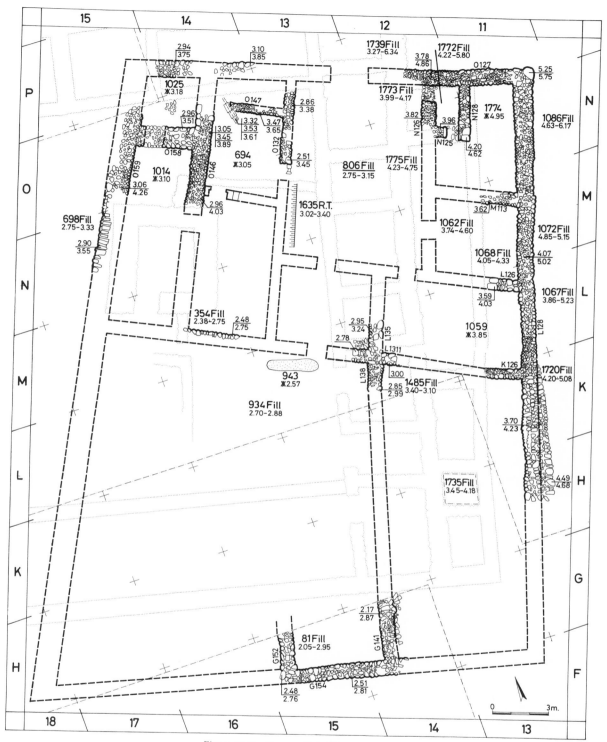

Figure 12.2. Fortress 806 of Stratum V.

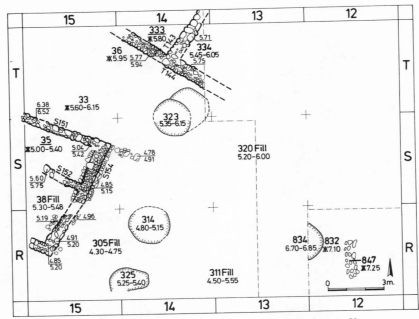

Figure 12.3. Buildings at northern end of high tell, Stratum V.

in the south end and 5.75 m in the northeast corner) indicates that the eastern side of the fortress was constructed on a lower terrace here. The floor level of Room 1774 (4.95 m) indicates that it was a basement, since it is about 2 m below the floor level of the western part. The foundations of Room 1772 are slightly higher than the floor level; perhaps this small chamber (1.20 m × 2.30 m) enclosed a staircase leading into the basement. Rooms 1774 and 1772, like most of the eastern part of Fortress 806, were reused without alterations in Stratum IV.

Room 1062 contained fills up to level 3.74 m, and no floor was encountered. The southernmost room (1059) has a floor at level 3.85 m. The finds on this floor belong to its second phase in Stratum IV.

Very little is known of the southern part of Fortress 806. Presumably, it also consisted of an arrangement of rooms around a central courtyard. The elevations of Walls G154, G152, and G141, as well as Fill 81, indicate that this part of the fortress was constructed on a higher elevation of the high tell.

To the east of Fortress 806, a large kiln (1369) with walls preserved to a height of 2.50 m was partially excavated (Fig. 12.1). No clear evidence pointed to its function. It seems too large for pottery; perhaps it was a calcination kiln for the lime of the floors, walls, and roofs of Fortress 806. It was probably used in both Strata V and IV.

12.1.2. Buildings North of Fortress 806

The area north of Fortress 806 was occupied in Strata V-IV by smaller structures, probably dwellings (Figs. 12.3; 12.8). Two buildings were found in Stratum V: Structure 333 on the north and Structure 35 to the south, with an open space (Courtyard 33) in between and to the east. Because of the topography of the tell, the whole area was about 3 m lower than the fortress and could be approached independently. Both structures suffered from severe erosion, mainly on the western side. The strong westward tilt of Wall S154 indicates ground sinkage, caused either by erosion or earthquake.

A gray surface at level 5.80 m was discovered in Room 333; the rest of the structure to the north and east was completely eroded away. Only the eastern wall and two sections of cross-walls are preserved in Structure 35, the southern building. Several refuse pits were cut into the open courtyard (Pits 314, 323, and 325).

12.1.3. Winepress on the Northern Hill

Construction of Winepress 556 on the northern hill was accompanied by drastic changes to the remains of the previous settlement. Some walls were reused in the framework around the winepress, but most of them were razed and their stones laid as an additional protective zone beyond the stone-walled frame, perhaps to decrease the amount of sand and dust in the vicinity.

The reuse of segments of earlier walls may have caused the discrepancy in orientation between the outer irregular frame and the fine rectangular winepress itself. The width of the stone pavement around the press varies from 1.0 m on its west side to 2.75 m on its north (Fig. 12.4; Pl. 44).

The plastered winepress, which measures 6.05 m × 9.20 m, is sunk about 30 cm lower than the stone pavement around it. Its components consist of Treading Floor 556 (5.25 m × 6.05 m), separated by Wall I191 from the two deep vats to its west. Although the plastered area of the

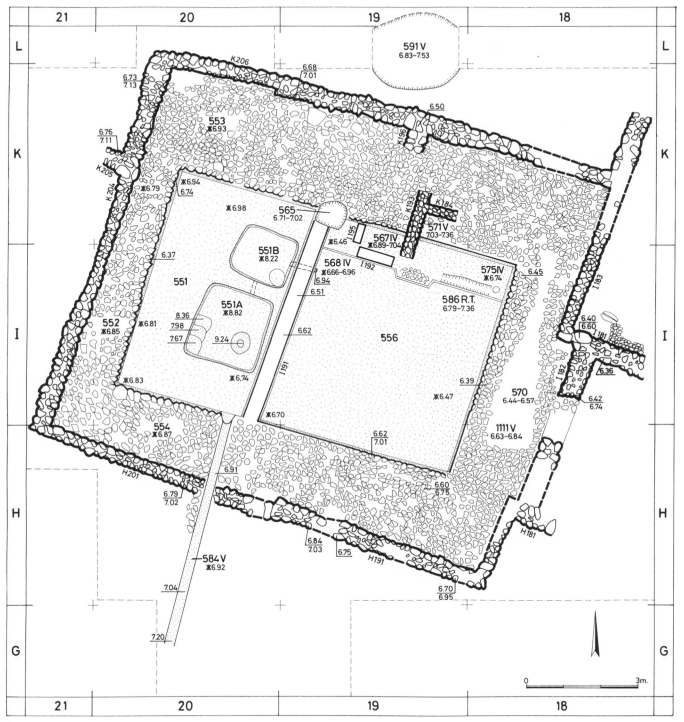

Figure 12.4. Winepress on northern hill, Strata V–IV.

winepress is almost a perfect rectangle, this wall is not parallel to the eastern and western sides, nor are the vats themselves completely regular in shape.

Vat 551B, which was filled by a pipe from Floor 556, has rounded corners and measures 1.40 m × 1.55 m with a depth of 1.24 m. A second pipe connects Vat 551B with Vat 551A (Pl. 46), which is much larger (1.90 m × 2.00 m, depth of 1.90 m). Three steps lead down into the latter vat. Both vats had a bowllike depression at the bottom for collecting the last drops of the precious wine.

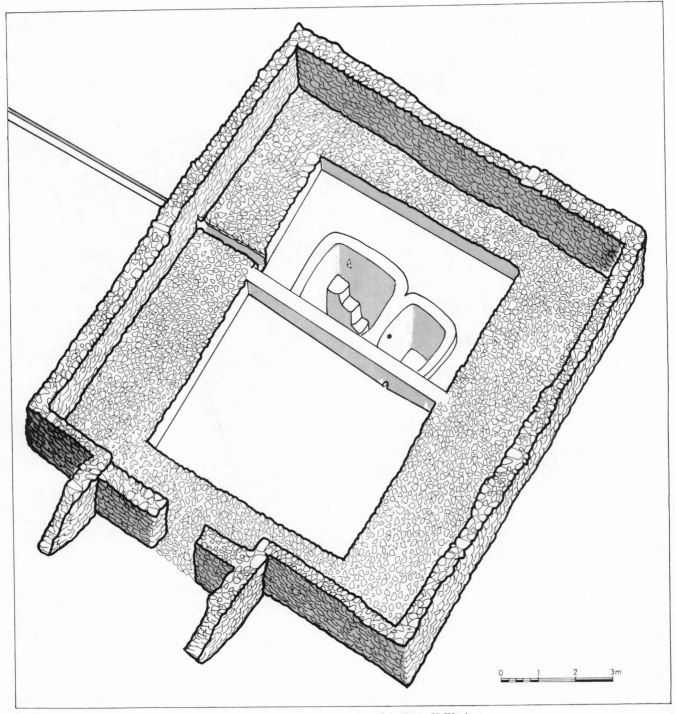

Figure 12.5. Isometric reconstruction of the Strata V–IV winepress.

The surfaces of the winepress were plastered with several coats of a lime composition, with a fine outer surface. The winepress was probably unroofed, since no signs of supporting pillars were found inside and the framework walls were too far apart, too low, and too poor in construction to carry a roof.

The winepress was used in both Strata V and IV, but a few alterations were made north of Floor 556 in Stratum IV. Whereas in Stratum V all of the treading floor was utilized (and Compartment 571 was attached to it at the north), it seems that at some time the northern side of Floor 556 sank below the level of the pipe that led into Vat 551B (as the

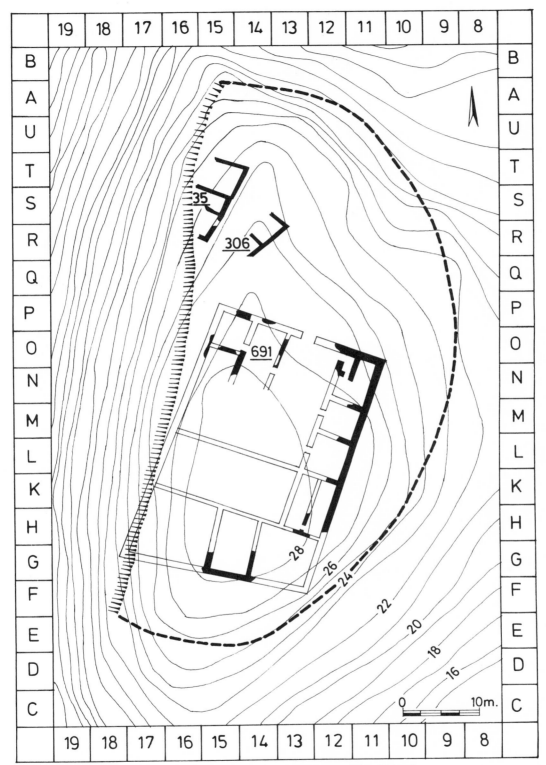

Figure 12.6. Architectural remains of Stratum IV on high tell.

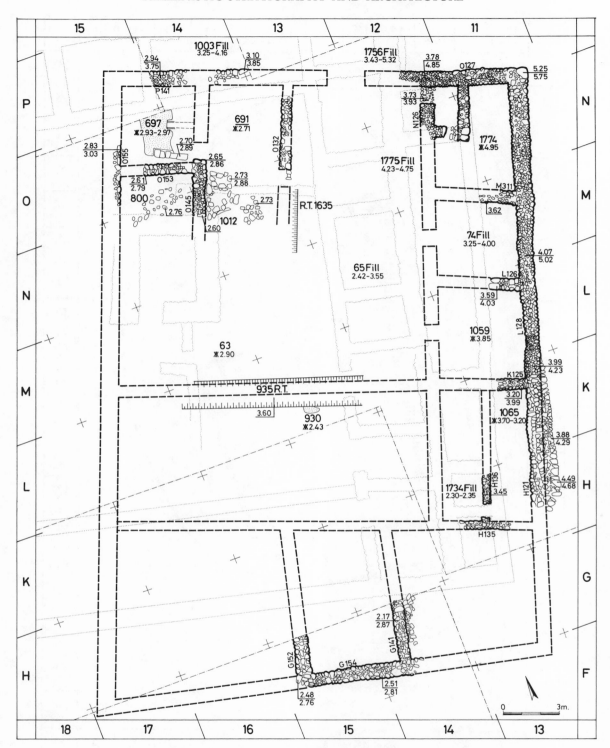

Figure 12.7. Fortress 691, Stratum IV.

result of an earthquake?), rendering this part of the treading floor unusable. The problem was solved by decreasing the size of the floor and constructing new compartments on it. These were made of ashlar blocks laid on the original (sunken) floor and plastered on their southern sides (Walls I192 and I195). However, most of Wall I192 was robbed during a later period.

In our reconstruction of the winepress, we have assumed that it was entered from the east. Grapes brought from the vineyard were stacked on the stone pavement around Treading Floor 556 until their turn to be pressed. Then they were spread on the floor and trod by barefoot workers. The must (new wine) drained into Vat 551B.

The pipe connecting Vat 551B with 551A is 1.0 m above floor level. It therefore had to fill up to this height before the wine could flow into Vat 551A. The capacity of the latter was 7,000 liters (1,840 gallons). It is not clear whether the wine remained in Vat 551A to ferment there or was removed immediately and fermented in jars. In any case, the stairs in Vat 551A were used by workers when they climbed in and out to fill the jars. Above the top step was a triangular foothold cut into the wall to help the workers climb out (see Fig. 12.5).

A channel 25 cm wide, running in the pavement and under the outer southern wall, was most likely to drain off the water used to wash Vat 551A before processing a new batch of grapes.

The purpose of the compartments on the northern side of the treading floor is unknown. They may have been installations for additional pressing of the grapeskins after the initial treading.

12.1.4. Silo 135 on the Eastern Hillock (Area C)

The only construction from the Hellenistic period found on this hillock was a silo built of red *hamra* bricks (Silo 135; Fig. 8.22; Pl. 29). Its top was at surface level. Partial (intentional?) firing occurred on one side of the silo. Not far from the silo, a rich hoard of Ptolemaic tetradrachms was found "floating" in the sand (Herzog et al. 1978; Kindler 1978). It is most unlikely that the silo and cache were isolated features on this hillock. Possibly a structure of some importance was located here, but no evidence of it was preserved.

12.1.5. Summary

Stratum V represents a new aspect of settlement at Tel Michal: occupation by a central authority. A large fortress dominates the high tell with practically no civilian area. Economic centralization is clear also in the large size of the winepress and the capacity of its vats. Obviously, the wine was not intended solely for consumption by the occupants of the fortress, but was traded outside. Prosperity and commercial contacts are demonstrated by the imported pottery (Chap. 13) and the numismatic assemblage (Chap. 27). They all point to a date in the 3d century B.C.E. under Ptolemaic suzerainty. The centralization brought to Tel

Michal by the Ptolemys continued under the Seleucid, Hasmonean, and Roman governments (Strata IV-II).

12.2. STRATUM IV

Stratum IV mainly reuses Stratum V structures, with minor alterations. Historically, this phase correlates with Seleucid rule in Israel in the 2d century B.C.E.

The general shape of the fortress is similar to that of Stratum V, but some walls are rebuilt on different lines (Figs. 12.6; 12.7). West Wall O154 is replaced by Wall O155 with a slightly different orientation. Wall K125 now partitions the center of the fortress. Although mostly robbed out (in Stratum IIIb), Robbers' Trench 935 clearly indicates its location. A patch of white plaster (Locus 930) is all that remains from the area south of the robbers' trench.

Room 691 was partially paved with stone at level 2.68–2.73 m. Adjoining it to the west was Room 697, taken up mostly by a plastered installation built of hewn stones in secondary use. The floor of the installation was carefully made from a layer of shells overlaid by about 5.5 cm of red soil and coated with a thick lime plaster. In Room 800, a patch of stone paving was unearthed at level 2.76. The pavements and plastered installation in the northeast corner of Fortress 691 may indicate that the room was used for some kind of light industry.

The southeast corner was also modified. Walls H135 and H136 were first constructed in Stratum IV. The main entrance and the row of rooms on the eastern side were reused without change.

In Stratum IV, Room 32 was added to Structure 35 and a new building (Structure 306) was erected (Fig. 12.8; Pl. 43). The minor changes in Winepress 551 are also attributed to Stratum IV.

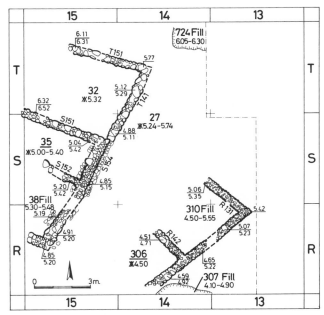

Figure 12.8. Buildings on northern end of high tell, Stratum IV.

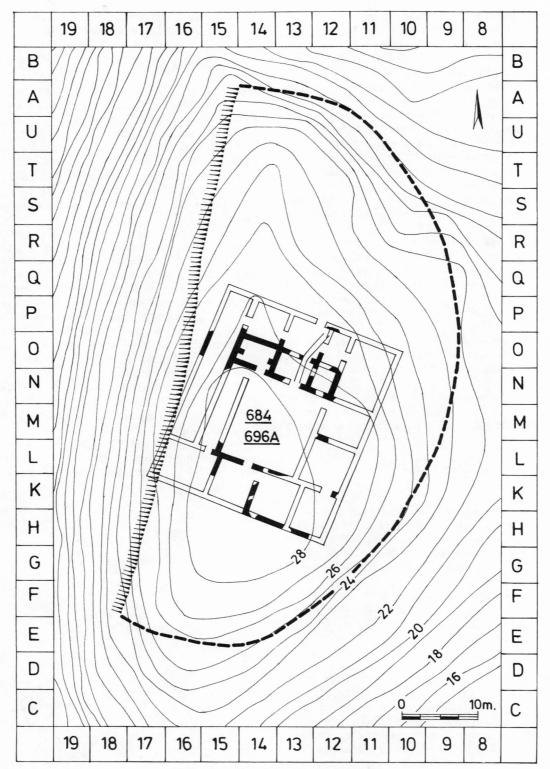

Figure 12.9. Forts 696A/684 of Strata IIIb/IIIa.

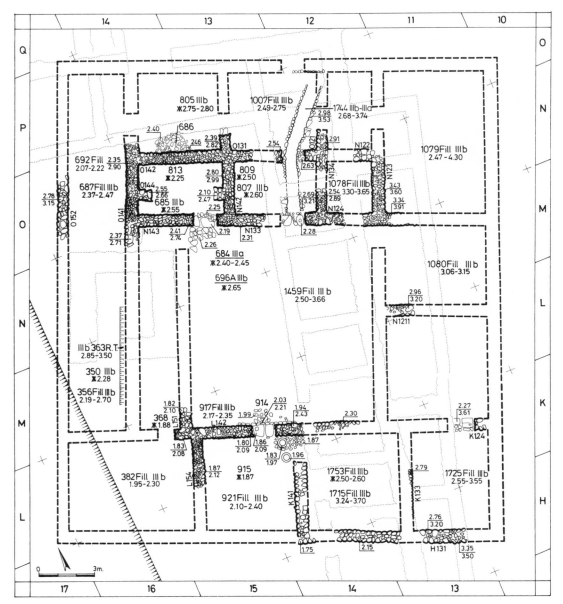

Figure 12.10. Detailed plan of Forts 696A/684 of Strata IIIb/IIIa.

12.3. STRATUM III

12.3.1. Fort 696A (IIIb) and 684 (IIIa)

Stratum III marks the last part of the Hellenistic period at Tel Michal and dates to the Hasmonean Kingdom, when only a simple structure, Fort 696A (Figs. 12.9; 12.10), existed at the site. A few raised floors within the fort indicate a second building phase in Stratum IIIa (Fort 684).

Fort 696A (earlier phase) is a well-built, compact structure. Only the southern end is reasonably assured, yet its general layout and inner division seem quite clear. Outer dimensions are 24 m × 27 m. The fort contains a central courtyard (Locus 696A) measuring 10 m × 11 m, with two

rows of rooms on the north and west and a single row on the east and south. Walls were laid in parallel lines and doorways had ashlar thresholds with door sockets. Four such thresholds were found in situ at the entrances to Rooms 685, 807, 921, and 1725. Similar thresholds were found in secondary use in the Roman fortress of Stratum II.

Courtyard 696A was drained by Drain 1744 (60 cm wide), which ran under the threshold into Room 807, under Wall O131, and then bent to the right toward the northeastern slope (Pl. 49). The main entrance to the fort is reconstructed through Rooms 1007 and 807 over the drain, which originally was covered.

Room 685 had a hard-packed gray floor at level 2.55 m.

In phase IIIa (Room 813), the floor was raised and two buttresses were added on the west and east sides, projecting about 50 cm into the room and presumably supporting an arch (Pl. 48). Room 915, on the south end of Courtyard 696A, had two ovens in its northeast corner, which actually blocked the doorway into Room 1753. The explanation for such a strange arrangement may be that only one oven was in use during each of the two phases of Stratum III and enough space was available to pass next to it.

According to the numismatic evidence (Chap. 27), Stratum IIIb dates to the days of Alexander Jannaeus in the first half of the 1st century B.C.E. It was most likely part of the defense system set up along the Yarkon River at this time (Kaplan 1972:89–90). Modifications in the fort (Stratum IIIa) were made during the same period. About a half-century passed before the site was reoccupied by a Roman fortress (Chap. 14).

12.3.2. Winepress 255

In a survey conducted south of Tel Michal, S. Lev Yadon identified a small winepress embedded in the sand dunes. The cleaning of the winepress yielded two coins of Alexander Jannaeus (Chap. 27: Nos. 145, 146). Winepress 255 (Fig. 12.11; Pl. 47) consists of a square pressing floor, shallow sedimentation basin, and square collecting vat. This small winepress concludes the sequence of such installations at Tel Michal, which first appeared in Iron Age II (Chap. 6b) and continued to be built and used in the Persian (Chap. 8) and Hellenistic periods.

REFERENCES

Avigad, N. 1977. Makmish. *Enc. Arch. Exc. III*: 768–770.

Herzog, Z., Negbi, O., and Moshkovitz, S. 1978. Excavations at Tel Michal, 1977. *Tel Aviv* 5:99–130.

Kaplan, J. 1972. The Archaeology and History of Tel Aviv-Jaffa. *BA* 35:66–95.

Kindler, A. 1978. A Ptolemaic Coin Hoard from Tel Michal. *Tel Aviv* 5:159–169.

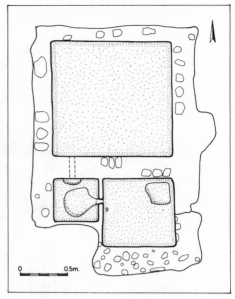

Figure 12.11.   Hasmonean winepress south of high tell.

13

Hellenistic Pottery (Strata V-III)

by Moshe Fischer

The Hellenistic pottery of Tel Michal offers the classical archaeologist dealing with Palestinian pottery a good opportunity to make use of a well-defined stratigraphic sequence. The four strata of this period on the high tell form the framework for this chapter. It should be emphasized, however, that even though the material is reasonably well preserved and there are at least a few representatives of most of the different types of vessels and wares, I have not tried to form "groups" or to present a corpus of the Hellenistic pottery of the site. The compilation of such groups from a single site, even a well-stratified one like Tel Michal, seems premature at this stage. Only the expansion of a corpus such as Lapp's (1961) (which brought together material from as many different sites as were available at the time) can make a significant contribution to the clarification of problems concerning the origin, development, and dating of the Hellenistic period local pottery. At present, however, the strictly stratigraphic material available for this purpose is insufficient. Perhaps a regional study of the pottery would be a useful first step. For example, coastal towns might be considered to form a region with common features, foreign influences, and interrelations, as suggested by the ceramic material from Ashdod, Caesarea, Dor, Shiqmona, Akko, and their hinterland counterparts, such as Tel Mevorakh and Tell Keisan. I hope that the material published here from Tel Michal will contribute to such a study and eventually be incorporated into an expanded corpus.

The four Hellenistic strata on the high tell have been defined by the excavators as follows:

Stratum V: Early Hellenistic (Ptolemaic), 3d century B.C.E.

Stratum IV: Late Hellenistic (Seleucid), 2d century B.C.E.

Stratum IIIb: Early Hasmonean (Alexander Jannaeus), 1st century B.C.E.

Stratum IIIa: Late Hasmonean (post-Jannaeus), 1st century B.C.E.

In addition to this stratified material, there were also scattered remains on the eastern hillock (Area C); only one fragment is included here (see Section 13.2.1 below). The northern hill (Area D) was mainly occupied during this period by a winepress and its adjacent auxiliary units. The pottery here correlates with that of Strata V/IV on the high tell. Since it is difficult to attribute it to one or the other of these strata, it is treated here as a single group.

13.1. STRATIFIED POTTERY FROM THE HIGH TELL

13.1.1. Stratum V (Early Hellenistic)

Bowls

The bowl of Figure 13.1:1 represents a homogeneous group of small, incurving bowls with string-cut, flattened, or disk base. The ware is coarse. The most common type of locally manufactured bowl in the Hellenistic period, it occurs in different variations in most of the sites referred to here, persisting even into the Roman period. The more carinated examples appear at Ashdod and Shechem in the second half of the 3d century B.C.E. (*Ashdod II-III*: Fig. 10:3; Lapp 1964:18, Fig. 1b:35). The rounded V-shaped specimens are well known from the 2d century B.C.E. at Ashdod, Beth-zur, and Tirat Yehuda (*Ashdod I*: 22–24, Figs. 4:1, 5:7, 10:1–4; *Ashdod II-III*: 173, Fig. 98:16; *Beth-zur 1933*: Pl. 13:18–21; Yeivin and Edelstein 1970: Fig. 9:2–3). At Tell Keisan they occur during the 3d and 2d centuries B.C.E. (*Tell Keisan*: 110). At Qumran they are dated from the end of the 1st century B.C.E. to 50–68 C.E. (Lapp 1961: Type 51.1:D, L). At Tel Michal they become very common in Stratum IV (Section 13.1.2).

The four small bowls with inverted rim, ring base, and brown-to-red wash (Fig. 13.1:2–5) are a legacy of the older Hellenistic tradition and a local imitation of the glazed bowls (Lapp 1961: Type 151.1). The ware is quite coarse, the workmanship crude, and the slip poor. By far the most popular bowls of Hellenistic Palestine, they are also well dated. In Stratum III at Samaria, this pottery was called "household ware" (*Samaria-Sebaste III*: 265). This "Late

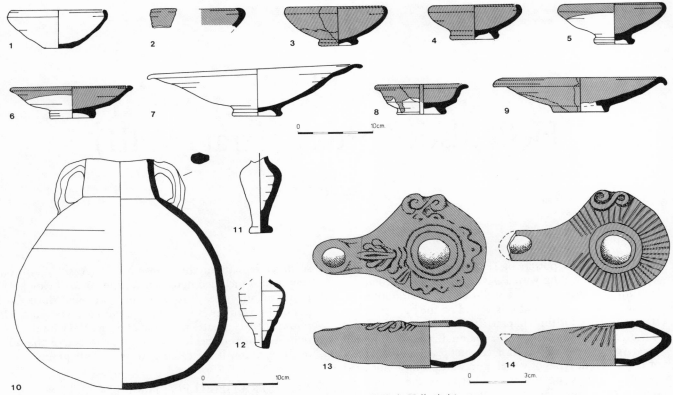

Figure 13.1. Pottery of Stratum V (Early Hellenistic).

Legend for Fig. 13.1

No.	Type	Reg. No.	Locus	Description	Pl.
1	Bowl	126/1	33	Orange (orange), small white grits.	
2	Bowl	5264/1	694	Brown (light brown); gray slip.	
3	Bowl	84/1	36	Brown (brown-black); red slip.	
4	Bowl	1702/1	314	Light brown (light brown), small white grits; black-brown slip.	
5	Bowl	122/1	33	Brown (brown), small white grits; red slip.	
6	Bowl	5590/1	847	Brown-pink (brown-pink); red slip.	
7	Bowl	97/1	33	Brown (brown), small white and gray grits.	
8	Bowl	1732/1	33	Brown-orange (brown-orange), few small black grits; red slip.	
9	Fish plate	1954/1	320	Brown-orange (brown-orange), small white grits; red slip.	
10	Cooking pot	1795/1	323	Brown (brown), small white and gray grits.	67:5
11	Unguentarium	11047/1	1739	Brown-orange (brown-orange), small gray grits.	
12	Unguentarium	6856/1	1014	Brown (brown), small white and gray grits.	
13	Lamp	7252/1	1086	Brown-gray (gray), small white grits; red slip.	
14	Lamp	86/1	36	Light gray (gray); red slip.	67:9

Hellenistic homemade ware" should be carefully differentiated from what is called "Late Hellenistic Red Ware" by Roller (1980:36, n. 1), since the latter is basically an imported ware. At Ashdod, Antioch, En-gedi, Samaria, Tel Mevorakh, and Tell Keisan, these bowls occur in the 3d-2d centuries B.C.E. (*Ashdod II-III*: Fig. 98:7; Waagé 1948:15, shape V, Pls. II-III; *En-gedi 1966*: Fig. 25:2; *Samaria-Sebaste III*: Fig. 38:1-4, 6; Rosenthal 1978:23, Fig. 3:10-12; *Tell Keisan*: 109, Pl. 13.1, etc.). At Akko and 'Arqa, bowls of this ware were especially common in the 2d century B.C.E., disappearing at 'Arqa around the end of that century (Dothan 1976:30, Fig. 30:4-6; Thalman 1978:56, 58, Fig. 43:1-5). At Samaria they occur at the end of the 2d century (Lapp 1961: Type 151.1:A, E). Some fragments from Caesarea with a less inverted rim were included with the "Late Hellenistic Red Ware" (Group V) and dated from the late 2d through the 1st century B.C.E. (Roller 1980:40, Nos. 23-25).

Another well-known type of the 3d-2d centuries is the small shallow bowl with flaring rim and more-or-less carinated belly (Lapp 1961: Type 151.3:B, C), which is represented by our bowl of Figure 13.1:6. This type is found at

Ashdod and Samaria from the end of the 3d to about the middle of the 2d centuries B.C.E. (*Ashdod II-III*: Fig. 14:11–12; *Samaria-Sebaste III*: 223, 233, Fig. 37:15–16, Fig. 48:7–8). Variants of different depths were dated at Akko and 'Arqa to the 2d century B.C.E. (Dothan 1976:30, Fig. 30:7, 9; Thalman 1978:57, Fig. 43:19–20); the same dating, by comparison with Tarsus and Samaria, was suggested for similar vessels from Dura Europos (*Dura Europos IV*: 7, nn. 36–37, 25). Our less carinated variant (Fig. 13.1:7) seems to be closer to the "homemade" Samarian examples (*Samaria-Sebaste III*: Fig. 54:7, 13). The deeper, more carinated example (Fig. 13.1:8) more closely resembles a bowl from Akko (Dothan 1976: Fig. 30:8).

Fish Plate

The fish plate is one of the hallmarks of the Hellenistic period. Lapp (1961) classifies the local variants as Type 153.1 and dates them to 200–100 B.C.E. Our Stratum V example (Fig. 13.1:9), a local imitation of the widespread Hellenistic type, has an everted drooping rim and a protruding ring around the central cup. At Tirat Yehuda this type came from the Early Hellenistic level (Yeivin and Edelstein 1970: Fig. 9:14–18) and at Samaria from a stratum dated to 200–150 B.C.E. (*Samaria-Sebaste III*: Figs. 37:12, 54:18). At Ashdod it occurs in Stratum 3b, dated to the 2d century B.C.E. (*Ashdod I*: 21–22, Fig. 2:1). It was probably around the beginning of the 2d century B.C.E. that this vessel began to be produced in a red-glazed ware instead of the former Attic black-glazed ware (see *Ashdod II-III*: 52–53). The rim of the later version tends to be more "droopy." At Tell Keisan it is dated to the 3d-2d centuries B.C.E. (*Tell Keisan*: 109, Pl. 13:12a-b, 15, 16), whereas at Akko, 'Arqa, and Tel Mevorakh the dating is close to the 2d century (Dothan 1976:31, Fig. 30:2–3; Thalman 1978:57, Fig. 43:13; Rosenthal 1978:23, Fig. 3:13–15). Fragments of fish plates were also present in the later Stratum IV at Tel Michal (Fig. 13.2:15–16). This popular Hellenistic vessel is completely absent in Roller's (1980) preliminary study of the Hellenistic pottery from Caesarea Maritima.

Cooking Pot

The isolated example of an amphoralike cooking pot (Fig. 13.1:10; Pl. 67:5) resembles a 3d-2d century specimen from En-gedi (*En-gedi 1966*: Fig. 25:3). The body shape is reminiscent of an example from Tel Yoqne'am (Ben-Tor et al. 1983: Fig. 7:10), which was dated to 175–100 B.C.E. A Late Persian specimen from Wadi ed-Daliyeh points toward the possible origin of this kind of cooking pot (Lapp and Lapp 1974: Pl. 23:3). A similar vessel may indicate the existence of a Late Hellenistic stratum at Gezer (Gitin 1979: Vol. II: Pl. 37:19).

Unguentaria (Fig. 13.1:11–12)

The lower parts of two spindle-shaped bottles (fusiform unguentarium) seem to belong to the earlier type, which is "heavier" and more compact, as pointed out by Kloner (1980:106–107, Fig. 2:2–3). At Ashdod and Beth-zur it oc-

curs in mid-2d-century contexts (*Ashdod II-III*: Fig. 18:10; *Beth-zur 1933*: Pl. X:14). It is also found at Tell Keisan in 2d-century strata, although Briend points out that this type must be earlier, by comparison with the finds from Tarsus and the fact that "la partie utile se réduire à une bulbe" (*Tell Keisan*: 111, Pl. 14:19). The various types have been classified by Lapp (1961) as Type 91.1:A-S.

Lamps (Fig. 13.1:13–14; Pl. 67:9)

Both lamps from Stratum V represent the well-known Hellenistic molded lamp of the "delphiniform" group, very common in the Eastern Mediterranean and generally dated to the 2d-1st centuries B.C.E. (Rosenthal and Sivan 1978:13). The decoration of each is different. The first has a palmette on its nozzle, a motif that occurs on a similar lamp from Ashdod dated to the 2d-1st centuries B.C.E. (*Ashdod I*: Fig. 8:5). Curled palmettes are seen on lamps from Tel Anafa from the 2d- to 1st-century stratum (Weinberg 1971:104, Pl. 18B, upper row) and on two lamps from Shiqmona (*Shiqmona II*: 28, Nos. 209–210). The second lamp has radial lines around the filling hole and an S-coil on one shoulder, common during the later Hellenistic period. The nozzle was generally undecorated, as on the 1st-century B.C.E. examples from the Jerusalem citadel, Samaria, 'Arqa, and Shiqmona (Johns 1950: Fig. 14:6; *Samaria 1924*: Fig. 194:II, 1a; Thalman 1978:66, Fig. 41:4; *Shiqmona II*: 39, No. 267).

13.1.2. Stratum IV (Late Hellenistic)

Bowls (Fig. 13.2:1–14)

The small V-shaped bowl with sharply inverted rim and flat to disk base is by far the most common type of bowl in the Late Hellenistic period. One example appeared already in Stratum V (Fig. 13.1:1), but by Stratum IV the type is represented by a group of five (Fig. 13.2:1–5; Pl. 67:1–3). Generally speaking, these are a continuation of the earlier examples, although the rims and bases are slightly different. As noted above (Section 13.1.1), these crudely made bowls are called "household ware" at Samaria (*Samaria-Sebaste III*: 265, Fig. 56.11). Lapp (1961) has presented a series of this unglazed type (Type 51.1) dated from 200 B.C.E. to 68 C.E. Additional examples were found at Tirat Yehuda in a 2d-century B.C.E. context (Yeivin and Edelstein 1970: Fig. 9:2–4) and at the citadel in Jerusalem in a 1st-century B.C.E. stratum (Johns 1950: Fig. 14:3). The latter has a disk base.

Two large black-glazed bowls (Fig. 13.2:6–7) are local imitations of the Early Hellenistic bowl classified as Type D in the excavations of the Athenian Agora and spread from there all over the eastern Mediterranean (Thompson 1934; *Samaria-Sebaste III*: 224–251). They represent one of the latest reminiscences of the Attic black-glazed bowls of the 4th century and are common in Israel in the 2d-century B.C.E. (*Ashdod II-III*: Figs. 8:13, 9:9–10), whereas at Samaria they are considered local products of the 3d-2d centuries B.C.E. (*Samaria-Sebaste III*: 250, Fig. 49:7).

There are two bowls in Stratum IV with flaring walls and

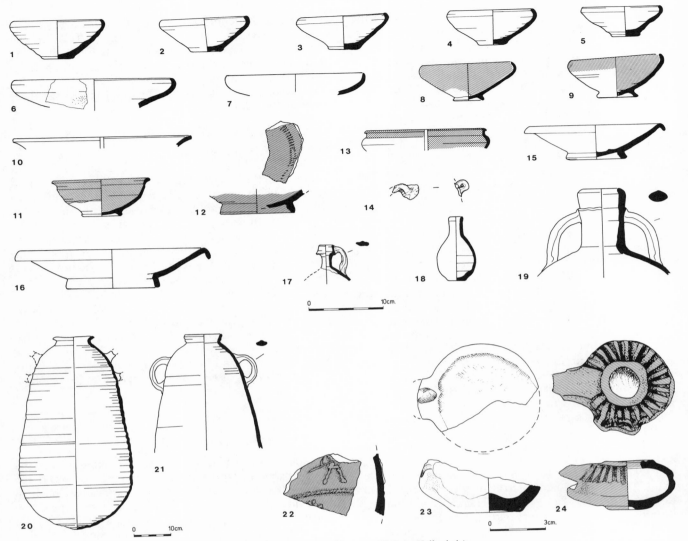

Figure 13.2. Pottery of Stratum IV (Late Hellenistic).

slightly carinated rims (Fig. 13.2:8–9; Pl. 67:4) of local red-slipped (glazed) Hellenistic ware (cf. Fig. 13.1:2–4). They were found on a floor together with two Seleucid coins (of Antiochus III and Demetrius II; see Chap. 27), which provide a terminus post quem for the end of Stratum IV in the last quarter of the 2d century. However, these bowls have good parallels at Samaria (*Samaria-Sebaste III*: Fig. 49:12; Zayadin 1966: Pl. 29:58), En-gedi (*En-gedi 1966*: Fig. 25:2), and Akko (Dothan 1976: Fig. 30:4), all from contexts of the 3d to 2d centuries. The less carinated wall and the flaring ring base of the second of these bowls perhaps point to an earlier date; as noted above, at 'Arqa this type had disappeared by the beginning of the 1st century B.C.E.

The flared, rounded rim of Figure 13.2:10 is similar to those of the shallow bowls of the 1st century B.C.E. (Lapp's Type 53:H). Parallels come from Jason's tomb in Jerusalem, Beth-zur, and the Jerusalem citadel (Rahmani 1967:80, Fig. 10:4; *Beth-zur 1933*: Pl. XIII:14; Johns 1950: Fig. 14:3).

The bowl with everted rim, slightly carinated belly, and ring base (Fig. 13.2:11) seems to be a continuation of the more carinated type of Stratum V (Fig. 13.1:8). This may be Lapp's Type 151.3:F (= *Samaria-Sebaste III*: Fig. 43:6), from the second half of the 2d century B.C.E.

One of the most common fine bowls of the Late Hellenistic period is red slipped (glazed), with inverted or everted rim, a ring base, and stamped decoration on the interior. On our specimen (Fig. 13.2:12), the decoration consists of rouletting. In general, our bowl is close to Lapp's Type 253.1. As pointed out by Kenyon, such bowls belong to the category of Eastern Terra Sigillata A (*Samaria-Sebaste III*: 283–284); a similar bowl at Samaria (*Samaria-Sebaste III*: Fig. 49:5), which was considered a non-Athenian import, was dated to the second half of the 2d century. At 'Arqa, Shiqmona, and Caesarea, it occurs in very late 2d-century and in 1st-century B.C.E. contexts (Thalman 1978: Fig. 43:4; *Shiqmona II*: No. 300; Roller 1980:41, No. 33).

Legend for Fig. 13.2

No.	Type	Reg. No.	Locus	Description	Pl.
1	Bowl	7049/1	1065	Light brown (brown), small white grits.	
2	Bowl	7107/1	1065	Light brown (light gray), large white grits.	67:2
3	Bowl	7059/1	1065	Light brown (gray).	67:1
4	Bowl	7117/1	1065	Light brown (light gray), small white grits.	67:3
5	Bowl	5149/1	697	Brown-orange (brown).	
6	Bowl	6095/4	930	Light gray (light gray); black glaze.	
7	Bowl	335/1	63	Pink (pink); black glaze.	
8	Bowl	72/1	32	Pink (pink); red slip.	67:4
9	Bowl	11016/1	1756	Brown (brown), small white grits; red slip.	
10	Bowl	5251/2	697	Brown (brown); brown slip.	
11	Bowl	5232/1	697	Light brown (light brown); red glaze.	
12	Bowl	5251/1	697	Light brown (light brown); brown-red slip.	
13	Bowl	5254/2	697	Light brown (light gray); gray slip.	
14	Bowl	5180/1	697	Light brown (light brown); red and black slip.	
15	Fish plate	5229/1	697	Brown (brown); black-red slip.	
16	Fish plate	1658/1	307	Light brown (light brown); black slip.	
17	Juglet	5221/1	697	Brown (brown).	
18	Bottle	342/1	74	Orange-brown (pink).	
19	Flask	11101/1	1744	Buff (gray), small gray grits.	
20	Storage jar	7053/1	1059	Brown-red (brown-red), small white grits.	
21	Storage jar	5241/1	697	Pink-buff (light gray), small and large white grits; yellow wash.	
22	Megarian bowl	6854/1	800	Brown (brown); red-black slip.	67:6
23	Lamp	1676/1	306	Brown (brown).	
24	Lamp	1733/1	32	Light brown (light brown), small brown grits; red slip.	67:10

Two fragments of a common type of deep bowl with profiled rim (Fig. 13.2:13–14) were found in Stratum IV (Lapp's Type 151.4). Although such bowls may sometimes be handleless, they usually have two pinched handles (Lapp's Type 151.4:A = *Samaria-Sebaste III*: Fig. 39:5). Our Figure 13.2:14 is a fragment of such a handle. This type of bowl dates to the mid-2d century B.C.E. at Ashdod, Shiqmona, and Caesarea (*Ashdod I*: Fig. 5:1–3; *Ashdod II-III*: Fig. 9:15; *Shiqmona II*: No. 243; Roller 1980:38, No. 12).

Fish Plates (Fig. 13.2:15–16)

The two fish plates from Stratum IV with drooping rims and raised ridge around the cup are similar to that of Stratum V (Fig. 13.1:9). Number 15 has close parallels in 2d-century B.C.E. contexts at Samaria, Tirat Yehuda, and Shiqmona (*Samaria-Sebaste III*: 262, Fig. 54:5; Yeivin and Edelstein 1970: Fig. 9:5–6, 9–10; *Shiqmona II*: No. 276).

Juglet (Fig. 13.2:17)

This is an example of one of the most common juglet types of the 1st century B.C.E.-1st century C.E., apparently a forerunner of the Herodian juglet (Lapp's Type 31.1, seriated from 200 B.C.E. to 70 C.E.). Our juglet is closely paralleled by a 2d- to 1st-century B.C.E. specimen at En-gedi (*En-gedi 1966*: Fig. 26:15).

Bottle (Fig. 13.2:18)

Such bottles were common in the Jewish tombs of Jerusa-

lem and vicinity during the 2d-1st centuries B.C.E., whereas at Tirat Yehuda they are found in pure 2d-century contexts (Yeivin and Edelstein 1970: Fig. 7:11, 14, 19). An example from Giv'at Shaul dates to the 1st century B.C.E. (Tzaferis 1974: Fig. 3:4), whereas another one from the French Hill in Jerusalem seems to be Herodian (Strange 1975: Fig. 15:20).

Flask (Fig. 13.2:19)

This is the upper part of a large flask with slightly twisted handles that may be dated from the Early Hellenistic period onward (Lapp's Type 29:A-C, from Samaria and Beth-zur). There is a parallel in the Hasmonean stratum at En-gedi (*En-gedi 1966*: Fig. 26:14). A similar vessel but without handles from Tell Keisan (called a "carafe" by the excavators) was compared to other Hellenistic material (*Tell Keisan*: 107, Pl. 10:20).

Storage Jars (Fig. 13.2:20–21)

Both storage jars from Stratum IV are Lapp's Type 11.3, which became popular in the second half of the 1st century B.C.E. They are elongated, bag-shaped vessels with short neck and rounded rim. The body is largely ribbed. At Tell Keisan they occur in the 3d century B.C.E. (*Tell Keisan*: 105: Pl. 8:3, 6–7). In the 2d century B.C.E. they are common at Ashdod, Shiqmona, and Tirat Yehuda (*Ashdod I*: Fig. 7:8; *Ashdod II-III*: Fig. 100:2; *Shiqmona II*: Nos. 212, 268–269; Yeivin and Edelstein 1970: Fig. 6:4).

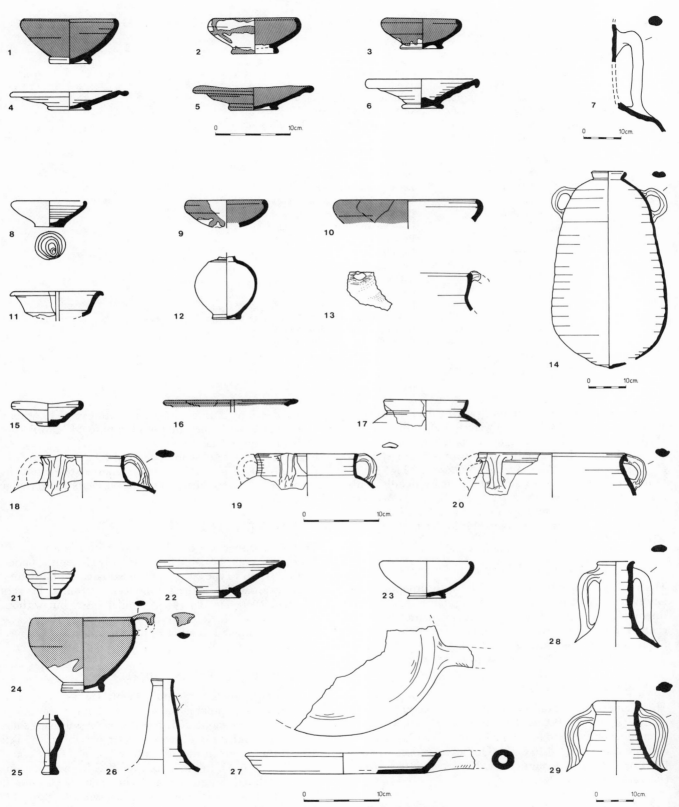

Figure 13.3. Pottery of Strata V/IV, IIIb, and IIIa.

Legend for Fig. 13.3

No.	Type	Reg. No.	Locus	Description
				Strata V–IV (Hellenistic) from High Tell
1	Bowl	11074/3	1766	Brown (brown), small white grits; red slip.
2	Bowl	7270/1	1354	Light gray (light gray); red slip.
3	Bowl	7249/1	1354	Brown (brown); red slip.
4	Fish plate	11074/1	1766	Light brown (pink).
5	Fish plate	11074/2	1766	Light orange (light orange); red slip.
6	Fish plate	10953/1	1766	Brown-red (black), small white grits.
7	Amphora	7270/2	1354	Buff (light orange).
8	Bowl	9268/1	1354	White (light gray), small white grits.
				Stratum IIIb (Early Hasmonean) from High Tell
9	Bowl	5152/1	687	Light brown (light brown); red slip.
10	Bowl	5138/2	697	Light brown (light brown); red-gray slip.
11	Bowl	5236/2	805	Light brown (brown); black glaze.
12	Aryballos	5148/1	685	Brown-orange (brown orange), small white grits.
13	Cooking pot	5236/1	805	Brown (brown-red).
14	Storage jar	10972/1	1766	Brown (brown), small white and gray grits.
				Stratum IIIa (Late Hasmonean) from High Tell
15	Bowl	6046/1	914	Orange (orange), small white grits.
16	Fish plate	5124/2	692	Light brown (brown); red slip.
17	Cooking pot	5124/1	692	Brown (brown-red).
18	Cooking pot	6067/1	914	Brown (brown).
19	Cooking pot	6067/2	914	Brown (brown).
20	Cooking pot	6067/3	914	Brown (brown); small gray grits.
				Strata V–IIIa from Various Areas
21	Juglet	852/1	125	Pink, (pink), small white grits.
22	Fish plate	4033/2	553	Orange (orange), small white grits.
23	Bowl	7508/2	570	Brown (gray).
24	Skyphos	4289/1	591	Light brown (light brown), small gray grits; black slip.
25	Unguentarium	4108/1	570	Light orange (light orange).
26	Lagynos	4033/1	553	Buff (buff), small gray grits.
27	Frying pan	7385/1	591	Brown (brown-black), white and mica grits.
28	Amphora	4303/1	585	Orange (brown-red), small white and gray grits, large white grits.
29	Amphora	7508/1	570	Brown (brown), small white grits.

Megarian Bowl (Fig. 13.2:22; Pl. 67:6)

The dating of the Megarian bowls is based upon the evidence from the Athenian Agora, as pointed out by Thompson (1934) and recently corrected and revised by Rotroff (*Agora XXII*). Lapp (1961) tried to bring Thompson's typology and chronology into agreement with the finds from Samaria. The Megarian bowls found in Israel seem to be late 2d-century types. The relief of a man holding a spear on our fragment also occurs at Samaria (*Samaria-Sebaste III*: Fig. 62:10). Megarian bowls with battle scenes were also popular at Shiqmona (*Shiqmona II*: Nos. 325–326).

Lamps (Fig. 13.2:23–24; Pl. 67:10)

The lamp of Figure 13.2:24 (Pl. 67:10) is quite similar to one of Stratum V (Fig. 13.1:14; Pl. 67:9). Another lamp fragment (Fig. 13.2:23) might be compared to a lamp from the Schloessinger collection (Rosenthal and Sivan 1978: No. 328), which has been dated to the 1st century B.C.E.-1st century C.E.

13.1.3. Strata V/IV (Early/Late Hellenistic)

The following vessels were found on the high tell, but the excavators were unable to determine from the architectural evidence whether they belonged to Stratum V or IV.

Bowls (Fig. 13.3:1–3)

The deep bowl with ring base (Fig. 13.3:1) may have evolved from the popular type with flaring walls seen in Stratum V (Fig. 13.2:8–9; Pl. 67:4), but it is deeper and its body approaches a hemispheric shape. This type occurs occasionally from the 2d century onward, for example, at Ashdod (*Ashdod II-III*: 54, 142, Figs. 15:20, 78:12) and Tirat Yehuda (Yeivin and Edelstein 1970: Fig. 9:1) but seems to have been more common at the end of the Hellenistic period (see Lapp's Type 52.2:F, from Qumran, dated 50–31 B.C.E.).

The two fine red-slipped bowls (Fig. 13.3:2–3) are similar to those of Stratum V (Fig. 13.1:3–5).

Fish Plates (Fig. 13.3:4–6)

The first two are similar to those of Stratum V (Fig. 13.1:9). The third (Fig. 13.3:6), which is of crude workmanship with pronounced internal ribbing and an accentuated internal cup, resembles more the fish plates of Stratum IV (Fig. 13.2:15–16). Closer analogies come from Ashdod

(*Ashdod II-III*: Figs. 9:13, 14:26).

Amphora (Fig. 13.3:7)

This high-neck and elongated neck-to-shoulder handle probably came from an amphora. The exact type is impossible to determine, but it seems to be one of the popular Hellenistic kinds (e.g., Grace 1934:306, Pl. II, 3d century B.C.E.; Baly 1962: Type 126). Quite possibly it is what has been called a "table amphora" at Tel Yoqne'am (Ben-Tor et al. 1983: Fig. 7:15).

13.1.4. Stratum IIIb (Early Hasmonean)

Bowls (Fig. 13.3:8–11)

The first of these (Fig. 13.3:8) has a string-cut base and inner ribbing, features that occur at the end of the Hellenistic period at Ashdod (*Ashdod I*: Fig. 10:12). Two of them (Fig. 13.3:9–10) are variants of the well-documented Hellenistic red-slipped ware (cf. Fig. 13.2:8–9; Pl. 67:4). The small incurving type (Fig. 13.3:9) of the late 2d century B.C.E. occurs at Ashdod, En-gedi, and Samaria (*Ashdod II-III*: Figs. 8:16, 98:7–9; *En-gedi 1966*: Fig. 15:2; *Samaria-Sebaste III*: 223, Fig. 38:1–4, 6–7, 9–10). A larger example of the same type (Fig. 13.3:10) is perhaps paralleled at Caesarea in the 2d-1st centuries B.C.E. (Roller 1980: Nos. 23, 25). The bowl of Figure 13.3:11 is a coarser example of the fine type of deeper bowls with carinated body (cf. Fig. 13.1:8); its yellowish clay and black glaze with greenish tinges indicate crude workmanship and poor firing. However, the type and ware are close to some specimens from Samaria and Ashdod (*Samaria-Sebaste III*: Fig. 43:5; *Ashdod II-III*: Fig. 14:12; see also Lapp's Type 151.3:E).

Aryballos (Fig. 13.3:12)

This aryballos, with spherical body and low ring base, seems to be a local imitation of an Attic type that occurs at Samaria and Tell Keisan in the 2d century B.C.E. (*Samaria-Sebaste III*: 270, Fig. 43:5; *Tell Keisan*: Pl. 9:12–13) and at Ashdod between 50 B.C.E. and the end of the era (*Ashdod II-III*: Fig. 17:3).

Cooking Pot (Fig. 13.3:13)

The rim of this pot is similar to those of the Late Hasmonean period (see below).

Storage Jar (Fig. 13.3:14)

This elongated bag-shaped jar with ribbed body is known from a number of sites during the 3d and 2d centuries B.C.E. There were two specimens in Stratum IV at Tel Michal (Fig. 13.2:20–21).

13.1.5. Stratum IIIa (Late Hasmonean)

Bowl (Fig. 13.3:15)

This is one more example of the small V-shaped bowls typical of the last decades of the Hasmonean period and persisting into the Roman period (Lapp 1961: Type 51.1:H, M, from the first half of the 1st century C.E.). Its irregular shape is paralleled by 1st-century B.C.E. examples from Ashdod (*Ashdod I*: Fig. 10:3–4; *Ashdod II-III*: Fig. 78:11).

Fish Plate (Fig. 13.3:16)

This sherd is probably the convex rim of a fish plate type known in the second half of the 2d century B.C.E. at Ashdod (*Ashdod II-III*: Fig. 78:6), Beth-zur (*Beth-zur 1933*: Pl. XIII:1), and Samaria (*Samaria-Sebaste III*: Fig. 37:4).

Cooking Pots (Fig. 13.3:17–20)

These globular cooking pots are variants of Lapp's Type 71.1, although our No. 17, with concave lip for holding a lid, is perhaps closer to Lapp's Type 71.2 from Beth-zur and Samaria (cf. *Samaria-Sebaste III*: Fig. 41:12, mid-2d century B.C.E.). This rim occurs also at Tell Keisan (*Tell Keisan*: Pl. 11:5a-b), Tirat Yehuda (Yeivin and Edelstein 1970: Fig. 8:2), Ashdod (*Ashdod II-III*: 61, Fig. 24:1), and the Jerusalem citadel (Johns 1950: Fig. 14:2a), all dated to the 1st century B.C.E. Numbers 18–19 are the popular Hellenistic type with globular body, high neck, slightly outcurved rim, and twisted handles (Lapp's Type 71.1:A-C). Analogies come from Ashdod and Tell Keisan (*Ashdod II-III*: 48, 144, Figs. 10:7, 80:3–4; *Tell Keisan*: 110, Pl. 11:3), dated to the 2d century B.C.E., and from the French Hill in Jerusalem (Kloner 1980: Fig. 2:13), dated to the 1st century B.C.E. At Akko our No. 17 has a parallel (with handles) attributed to the Late Hellenistic period (Dothan 1976: Fig. 30:14).

Cooking pot No. 20 is an outstanding example of a krater or casserole-like neckless vessel with thickened, drooping rim. It is a continuation of Lapp's Type 72.1:H. According to Kenyon, its ancestry is Israelite (*Samaria-Sebaste III*: 220, Fig. 41:7). This type occurs at Machaerus "agli ultimi anni della fortezza erodiana" (Loffreda 1980:398, Pl. 96:29); according to evidence from the Athenian Agora and Tel Mevorakh, it is also common in the 2d century C.E. (*Agora V*: 42, Nos. G:194–196; Rosenthal 1978:15, Fig. 2:6).

13.2. POTTERY FROM OTHER AREAS OF THE SITE

13.2.1. Southeastern Hillock (Area C)

Juglet (Fig. 13.3:21)

This juglet base contained a hoard of 47 Ptolemaic silver tetradrachms, which were buried in the hillock around 240 B.C.E. (Kindler 1978). The juglet, whose original height was probably about 10 cm, is apparently the common type with rounded body, high neck, and one handle that occurs at Samaria, Shiqmona, and Tell Keisan (*Samaria 1924*: Fig. 183:29a; *Shiqmona II*: No. 304; *Tell Keisan*: Pl. 14:27). At Tel Michal the coins date it to the second half of the 3d century B.C.E., corresponding to Stratum V on the high tell.

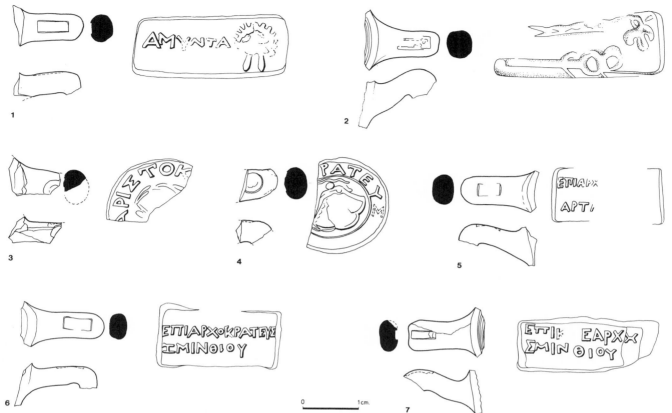

Figure 13.4. Hellenistic stamped handles.

Legend for Fig. 13.4

No.	Reg. No.	Locus	Stratum	Pl.
1	4243/1	575	IV	68:1
2	7294/1	1369	V	68:2
3	7030/1	74	IV	68:3
4	5239/1	696A	IIIb	68:4
5	1102/1	279	V	68:5
6	11213/1	1805	Unstratified	68:6
7	10225/1	684	IIIa	68:7

13.2.2. Northern Hill (Area D)

Bowl (Fig. 13.3:23)

This type of bowl is well represented on the tell itself (see Figs. 13.3:1; 13.2:8–9; Pl. 67:4).

Fish Plate (Fig. 13.3:22)

This deep fish plate of coarse "homemade" ware is typologically related to those from Stratum IV (Fig. 13.2:15–16).

Skyphos (Fig. 13.3:24)

This type of skyphos (Lapp's Type 151.5A) is paralleled at Samaria in the first half of the 2d century B.C.E. (*Samaria-Sebaste III*: Fig. 39:4); a similar example from 'Arqa was

dated to the end of the 4th and beginning of the 3d centuries B.C.E. (Thalman 1978:58, Fig. 43:7).

Unguentarium (Fig. 13.3:25)

This unguentarium, with a high foot and rounded body, is Kloner's Type 2, dated to the late 2d-early 1st centuries B.C.E. (Kloner 1980:107). It occurs at Samaria in a level dated 75–25 B.C.E. (*Samaria 1924*: Fig. 178:1; see also Lapp 1961: Type 91.2:B).

Lagynos (Fig. 13.3:26)

In Athens this vessel was common during the 2d century B.C.E. (Thompson 1934:450–451). Our lagynos with its conical neck is best compared to an example from the Athenian Agora dated to the first quarter of the 1st century B.C.E. (*Agora V*: Pl. 2:F67).

Frying Pan (Fig. 13.3:27)

An almost identical frying pan from Samaria was ascribed to the early 3d century B.C.E. (*Samaria-Sebaste III*: Fig. 41:23; see also Lapp's Type 78:B). This type occurs also in Level 2 of the Hellenistic period at Tell Keisan (*Tell Keisan*: Pl. 11:4).

Amphorae (Fig. 13.3:28–29)

The first of these, a rare local imitation of the common Hellenistic amphorae, has very few parallels, although

185

there are specimens at Ashdod and Tirat Yehuda (*Ashdod II-III*: Figs. 25:3, 100:1; Yeivin and Edelstein 1970: Fig. 7:22). The shape of the neck of the second fragment is comparable to that of a "table amphora" from Tel Yoqne'am (Ben-Tor et al. 1983: Fig. 7:15).

13.3. STAMPED HANDLES

Five of the seven handles presented here came from the Hellenistic/Hasmonean strata and two were surface finds.

No. 1 (Fig. 13.4:1; Pl. 68:1); rectangular; wreath with stripes at right.

Ἀμύντα[ς]

Amyntas was the eponym of Knidos during the years 166–146 B.C.E. (Grace and Savvatianou-Petropoulakou 1970: No. E62, E66). For Amynta as the name of the fabricant on stamped Samarian handles, see *Samaria 1924*: 18, 311, No. 6, here with laurel wreath on right. Another similar example was found at Marissa (Macalister 1901: No. 20, Fig. 4). The wreath occurs during the 2d and 1st centuries B.C.E. on Knidian handles (Grace and Savvatianou-Petropoulakou 1970: No. E92).

No. 2 (Fig. 13.4:2; Pl. 68:2); rectangular; anepigraphic; first line: unidentified symbol plus vine leaf; second line: caduceus facing right.

This stamp seems to be Rhodian, not earlier than mid-2d century B.C.E. (Grace 1962:115, Pl. 36:7; Grace and Savvatianou-Petropoulakou 1970: E7, E8, E60); for a caduceus combined with a grape cluster, see Grace and Savvatianou-Petropoulakou 1970:303, first half of 2d century B.C.E.; for years 160–146 B.C.E., ibid.: E60. This type also occurs at Salamis (Calvet 1972:31, No. 56, periods IV and V, end of 2d century B.C.E.). See also an example from Shiqmona with caduceus and vine leaf (Landau 1974: No. 347, dated 146–108 B.C.E.). The caduceus was quite popular on Knidian handles (see Grace 1956:157, Nos. 121–122, 124, 128–130, 145, 155) from the late 2d to the beginning of the 1st centuries B.C.E.

No. 3 (Fig. 13.4:3; Pl. 68:3); round; rose in center.

Ἀριστοκ[ράτευς]

Aristokrates was a well-known Rhodian fabricant (Nilsson 1909: No. 101; Grace 1934: No. 52; cf. Grace 1974:199, dated 208–199 B.C.E.). He is also represented at Salamis (Calvet 1972:25, Nos. 37–38) and Tell Keisan (Halpern-Zylberstein 1980: No. 41, Pl. 85:44, rectangular). At Samaria there are five specimens with his name (*Samaria 1924*: 311, No. 25).

No. 4 (Fig. 13.4:4; Pl. 68:4); round; rose in center.

[Δαμοκ]ράτευς

Since the first half of the inscription is missing, there are at least ten possibilities of restoring it; for example, Epikrates, Polykrates, Eukrates, Sokrates. However, on the basis of typologic and paleographic parallels, I prefer Damokrates. At least five Rhodian fabricants bore this name (see Landau and Tzaferis 1979: No. 36, Damokrates V; cf. Grace and Savvatianou-Petropoulakou 1970:307, E18, for Damokrates III). Round stamps with a central rose bearing the name of this fabricant are quite popular, especially during the second half of Grace's Period III (Grace 1974: years 210–175 B.C.E.; see also Grace and Savvatianou-Petropoulakou 1970:295, n. 1, regarding a fabricant named Damokrates who used rose types about 188 B.C.E., e.g., ibid.: 305, No. E14). His name appears four times at Marissa (Macalister 1901: Nos. 76–79), three times at Samaria (*Samaria 1924*: 311, No. 25), and three times at Salamis (Calvet 1972:26, Nos. 40–42). At Tell Keisan this fabricant is represented by a group of round and rectangular stamps (Halpern-Zylberstein 1980: Nos. 45–46, round, Pl. 85:42–43; Nos. 44 and 47, rectangular, Pls. 85:41, 86:77).

No. 5 (Fig. 13.4:5; Pl. 68:5); rectangular.

Ἐπὶ Ἀρχοκρ[ὰ
[τευς]
Ἀρτα[μιτίου]

Archokrates is a Rhodian eponym of Grace's Periods II-III (Grace 1934:219, Period III, 220–180 B.C.E.; Grace and Savvatianou-Petropoulakou 1970:378, s.v. Archokrates, Period II; compare, however, Grace 1974, where Period II is dated to 240–210 B.C.E.). For other examples, see Nilsson 1909: No. 137. At Tell Keisan, Archokrates is represented by two rectangular stamps attributed to Grace's Period II (Halpern-Zylberstein 1980: Nos. 9–10, Pls. 84:21, 85:30; cf. Grace 1953, No. 61, s.v. Archokrates). His name also appears on a stamp at Samaria (*Samaria 1924*: 313, No. 15).

No. 6 (Fig. 13.4:6; Pl. 68:6); rectangular.

Ἐπὶ Ἀρχοκράτευς
I(sic) μινθίου

This clear and well-preserved stamp impression bears the name of the same Archokrates as No. 5; only the month differs. In the spelling of the Rhodian Σμινίου, the first letter was mistakenly written as I (iota). For parallels and dating, see No. 5.

No. 7 (Fig. 13.4:7; Pl. 68:7); rectangular.

Ἐπὶ Κλέαρχ<χ>(ου)
Σμινθίου

This inscription is quite clear except that the right side was double stamped, thereby creating the duplication of X (chi) and Y (upsilon). Klearchos is a Rhodian eponym of Grace's Period II, years 240–210 B.C.E. (see also Nilsson 1909: No. 272; Grace 1953: No. 106). Klearchos is also represented by two handles at Marissa (Macalister 1901: Nos. 134–135, Fig. 48).

Although not all of these stamped handles were found in stratigraphic contexts, they are one of the most important ceramic finds of the Hellenistic period at Tel Michal, since they are proof of the widespread commercial connections of the settlement with important Hellenistic trade centers during this period.

13.4. SUMMARY

The assemblages of the four Hellenistic strata at Tel Michal include the principal types of locally produced Hellenistic wares. Although there are a number of imported specimens (plates, lamps, stamped amphorae), the bulk of the material is of local manufacture, particularly the bowls, which I have called "Late Hellenistic homemade ware." In many cases it is impossible to draw exact parallels to vessels from others sites — especially in respect to everyday vessels such as cooking pots and jugs. This fact points toward the existence of localized pottery workshops, even though the prototypes came mostly from larger, universal centers (Athens, Pergamon, etc.) or from the older local ceramic tradition. On the other hand, skyphoi, lagynoi, and especially lamps of different sites have more features in common. Presumably these were manufactured in regional centers and had a broader diffusion. The comparisons cited for the vessels found at Tel Michal show that although there are some types that can be securely dated by analogies from other sites, the dating of others will have to be postponed until a chronological framework is worked out. Even though most vessels came from stratified contexts, it is difficult to devise such a scheme for them. All this emphasizes the necessity for thorough publication of Hellenistic material wherever it is encountered — particularly in well-stratified sites such as Tel Michal — to facilitate typological comparisons and eventually to establish a chronological sequence for the pottery of this period.

REFERENCES

Baly, T. J. C. 1962. Pottery. *Nessana I*: 270–303.

Ben-Tor, A., Portugali, Y., and Avissar, M. 1983. The Third and Fourth Seasons of Excavations at Tel Yoqne'am, 1979 and 1981. *IEJ* 33:30–54.

Calvet, Y. 1972. *Salamine de Chypre III: Les timbres amphoriques (1965–1970)*. Paris.

Dothan, M. 1976. Akko: Interim Excavation Report, First Season. 1973/4. *BASOR* 224:1–48.

Gitin, S. 1979. *A Ceramic Typology of the Late Iron II, Persian and Hellenistic Periods at Tel Gezer*. Ph.D. dissertation. Hebrew Union College, Cincinnati, Ohio.

Grace, V. 1934. Stamped Amphora Handles Found in 1931–1932. *Hesperia* 3:196–310.

Grace, V. 1953. The Eponyms Named on Rhodian Amphora Stamps. *Hesperia* 22:116–128.

Grace, V. 1956. Stamped Wine Jar Fragments. Pages 113–189 in: *Small Objects from the Pnyx II (Hesperia* Suppl. 10). L. Talcott et al., eds. Princeton, N.J.

Grace, V. 1962. Stamped Handles of Commercial Amphoras. *Nessana I*: 106–130.

Grace, V. 1974. Revision in Early Hellenistic Chronology. *Mitteilungen des Deutschen Archäologischen Instituts Abteilung Athen* 89:193–200.

Grace, V., and Savvatianou-Petropoulakou, M. 1970. Les timbres amphoriques grecs. Pages 277–382 in: *Exploration archéologique de Délos XXVIII: L'îlot de la maison de comédiens*. Paris.

Halpern-Zylberstein, M. 1980. Timbres amphoriques. *Tell Keisan*: 243–255.

Johns, C. N. 1950. The Citadel, Jerusalem. *QDAP* 14:121–190.

Kindler, A. 1978. A Ptolemaic Coin Hoard from Tel Michal. *Tel Aviv* 5:159–169.

Kloner, A. 1980. A Tomb of the Second Temple Period at French Hill, Jerusalem. *IEJ* 30:99–108.

Landau, Y. 1974. Stamped Handles. *Shiqmona II*: 62–64.

Landau, Y., and Tzaferis, V. 1979. Tel Istabah, Beth Shean: The Excavations and the Hellenistic Jar Handles. *IEJ* 29:152–159.

Lapp, N. R. 1964. Pottery from Some Hellenistic Loci at Balatah (Shechem). *BASOR* 175:14–26.

Lapp, P. W. 1961. *Palestinian Ceramic Chronology, 200 B.C.–A.D. 70*. New Haven, Conn.

Lapp, P. W., and Lapp, N. R., eds. 1974. Discoveries in the Wâdī ed-Dâliyeh. *AASOR* 41. Cambridge, Mass.

Loffreda, S. 1980. Alcuni vasi datati della fortezza di Macheronte. *Liber Annuus* 30:377–402.

Macalister, R. 1901. Amphora Handles with Greek Stamps from Tell Sandahannah. *PEFQSt*: 25–43, 124–144.

Nilsson, M. 1909. *Timbres amphoriques de Lindos: Exploration archéologique de Rhodos V*. Copenhagen.

Rahmani, L. Y. 1967. Jason's Tomb. *IEJ* 17:61–100.

Roller, D. W. 1980. Hellenistic Pottery from Caesarea Maritima: A Preliminary Study. *BASOR* 238:35–42.

Rosenthal, R. 1978. The Pottery. *Tel Mevorakh I*: 14–19, 23–33.

Rosenthal, R., and Sivan, R. 1978. *Ancient Lamps in the Schloessinger Collection*. (Qedem 8) Jerusalem.

Strange, J. F. 1975. Late Hellenistic and Herodian Ossuary Tombs at French Hill, Jerusalem. *BASOR* 219:39–67.

Thalman, J. P. 1978. Tell 'Arqa (Liban Nord), Campagnes I–III (1972–1974), Chantier I., Rapport préliminaire. *Syria* 55:51–66.

Thompson, H. A. 1934. Two Centuries of Hellenistic Pottery. *Hesperia* 3:311–480.

Tzaferis, V. 1974. A Tower and Fortress near Jerusalem. *IEJ* 24:84–94.

Waagé, F. O. 1948. *Ceramics and Islamic Coins. Antioch-on-the-Orontes. Part I*. Princeton.

Weinberg, S. S. 1971. Tel Anafa: The Hellenistic Town. *IEJ* 21:86–109.

Yeivin, Z., and Edelstein, G. 1970. Excavations at Tirat Yehuda. (Hebrew) *'Atiqot* 6:56–69.

Zayadin, F. 1966. Early Hellenistic Pottery from the Theatre Excavations at Samaria. *ADAJ* 11:53–64.

14

Roman Fortress (Stratum II)

by Steven Derfler

The Roman fortress at Tel Michal is situated on the high tell (Area A) immediately beneath the remains of the Early Arab watchtower. During the long occupational gap at the site between the mid-1st and 9th centuries C.E., the process of erosion took its toll and many of the stones of the fortress were robbed. In addition, construction of the Early Arab watchtower, with floors at about the same level as those of the Roman structure, caused further damage to its remains. The western third of the fortress is entirely missing because of severe erosion on that side and also desertion of the site after the 10th century C.E. Most of its southern wing lies beyond the limit of excavation.

In the existing part of the structure, most of the walls are only foundations below floor level, although in a few places an intact threshold is preserved.

The proposed reconstruction of the fortress (Figs. 14.1; 14.2) shows a rectangular structure, estimated at 37.5 m north to south and about 30.5 m west to east, surrounding a central courtyard measuring 17.5 m × 22 m. In the center of the courtyard stood a massive rectangular tower, measuring 5.6 m × 6.0 m externally, with a slightly different orientation than the enclosing courtyard walls.

14.1. ARCHITECTURE

It appears that two sets of rooms surrounded the central courtyard on its eastern and northern sides. The western side of the fortress is entirely missing, and most of the southern wing was not excavated. No remains occur south of the partly unearthed southern wall (H141). We therefore assume that it served as an outer wall and that only one row of rooms bounded the fortress here. The inner curtain of this wing was not found because of the limits of the excavated area and the penetration of Early Arab graves cut along the western side of Wall M131. Judging by the proximity of the western side to the edge of the hill, we may assume that on this side also there was only one row of casematelike rooms. The entrance to the fortress is at the northeastern corner, the easiest approach up the hill.

14.1.1. Courtyard 812 and Tower 1002

Tower 1002 stands in the center of the courtyard. The massiveness of its foundations, which average 1.4–1.5 m in width, suggests that the tower had more than one story and rose high above the casemate fortress, whose walls were only about 85 cm thick. The entrance to the tower was in its southwestern corner. In its western half, a stone paving at 2.38 m was preserved. Along the northern wall (N153) was a narrow bench made of roughly squared stones. A coin of Valerius Gratus dated to 19 C.E. and a spout of an oil lamp (Fig. 14.3:14) were found in the tower. Two thin walls (about 50 cm wide) adjoining the tower and extending to its east and south are evidence that the courtyard was partitioned. These walls (N143 and N152) enclosed a rectangular area (Locus 907) of 7.5 m × 16 m on the eastern side of the courtyard. (Wall N143 is built directly over Wall N133 of the Hasmonean fort.) The entrance to this partitioned courtyard was south of Tower 1002.

In the northern part of Locus 907 we found a deep fill (Locus 66) reaching down to level 3.00 m. Composed of layers of ashy and stony soil, it was laid on top of the remains of Stratum VII. It seems that in their search for stones the builders of the Roman fortress robbed every earlier wall they came across—for example, the continuation of Wall L151 of the Hasmonean fort. Locus 66 is actually the fill of the robbers' trenches and pits dug beneath the courtyard floor. Only patches of this floor were preserved (at level 1.78 m). In the niche between partition Wall N143 and tower Wall N153, a small, ash-filled pit (Locus 682) was uncovered. To the east, another, larger pit, also filled with ash (Locus 696), was dug down to 2.65 m. These pits were probably used for garbage disposal by the occupants of the fortress. South of Tower 1002 we found a coin of the Julio-Claudian dynasty on a patch of white lime pavement (Locus 61) at level 2.35 m.

14.1.2. Eastern Wing

The eastern side of the citadel contains a double row of

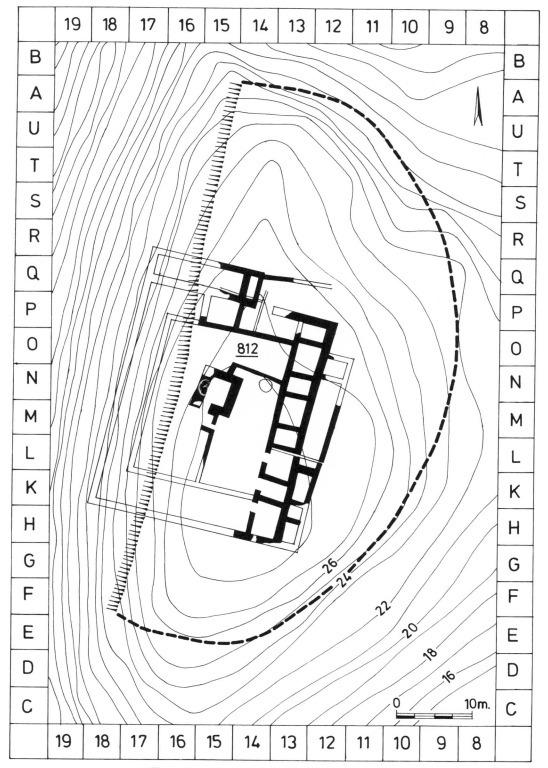

Figure 14.1. Location of Roman fortress on high tell.

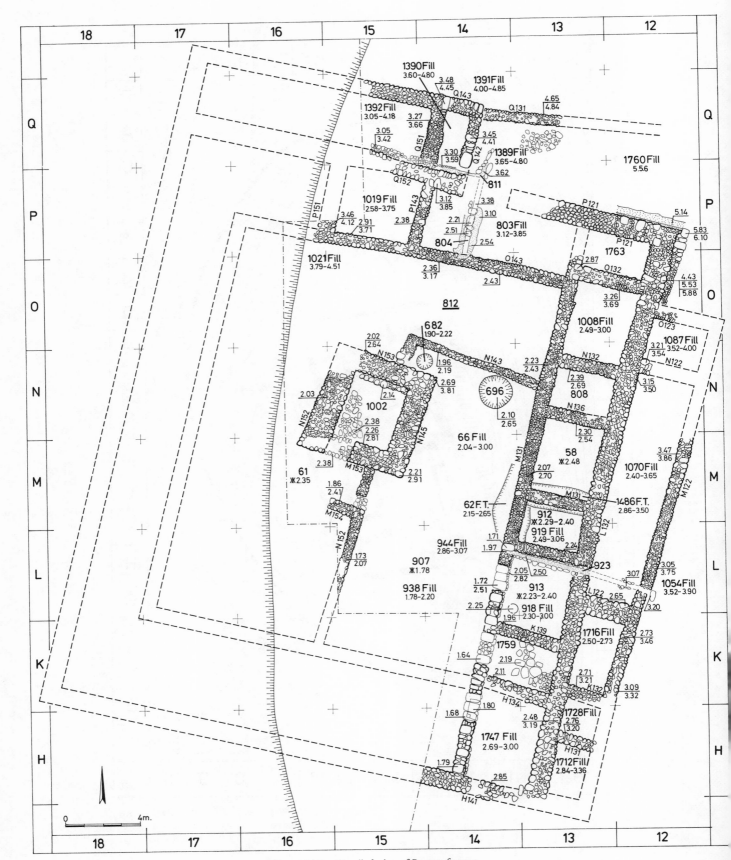

Figure 14.2.   Detailed plan of Roman fortress.

190

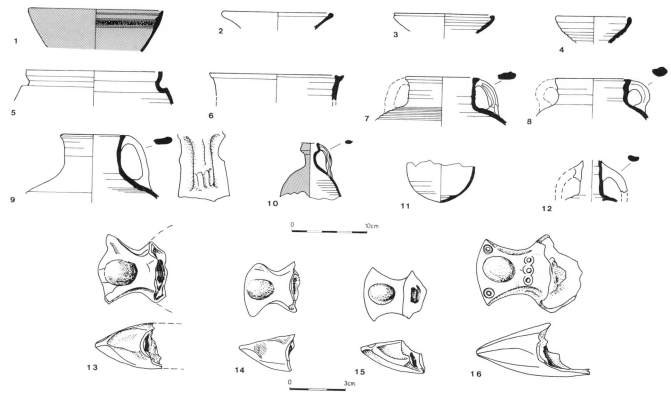

Figure 14.3. Roman period pottery.

Legend for Fig. 14.3

No.	Type	Reg. No.	Locus	Description
1	Bowl	6196/1	918	Light brown (light brown); red slip.
2	Bowl	5258/1	696	Orange (orange).
3	Bowl	6056/1	912	Light brown (light brown), small white grits.
4	Bowl	6086/1	919	Brown-orange (brown-orange), small white grits.
5	Cooking pot	6241/1	944	Brown (gray-brown), small white grits.
6	Storage jar	424/1	66	Brown (brown).
7	Cooking pot	6111/1	919	Brown (gray), small white grits.
8	Cooking pot	6223/1	938	Brown (gray), small white grits.
9	Jug	6099/1	918	Brown (gray).
10	Juglet	6329/1	944	Brown (gray), small white grits; red slip.
11	Juglet	6929/1	1019	Brown (gray), small white grits.
12	Flask	6377/1	66	Buff (gray), small gray grits.
13	Lamp	6758/2	1002	Buff (buff).
14	Lamp	6100/1	919	Gray (gray), small white grits.
15	Lamp	6056/4	912	Orange (orange).
16	Lamp	6056/4	912	Light gray (gray), small white grits.

rooms. The inner row is built more regularly, with better attention paid to parallel walls and right-angled corners. It consists of seven rooms, alternately large and small. The outer row of rooms is less regular, the outer eastern wall (M122) measuring only 0.75 m wide, whereas the central wall (L132) is 1.10 m wide.

The northern room (Locus 1008) is 3.2 m × 4.1 m, whereas the second room (Locus 808) is only 2.1 m × 3.2 m. A coin of Valerius Gratus was found in Room 1008.

Since no floors with intact finds nor even entrances were preserved in these rooms, it is difficult to determine their function. It seems that Room 808 could not be entered directly from the courtyard because Wall N143 abutted onto it, so presumably Rooms 808 and 1008 were interconnected and were both entered through Room 1008. This unit could have served as the commander's billet, often located at the corner of a Roman fortress (Gichon 1976:191, n. 5).

The next unit consists of Rooms 58 and 912. Room 58 is 3.1 m × 4.0 m with an earthen floor resting on stony fill at 2.48 m. A coin of the 1st century C.E. minted in Alexandria was found on the floor. Room 912 is 2.2 m × 3.1 m, and its floor is at level 2.29–2.40 m. Fragments of several pottery vessels were found on the floor (Figs. 14.3:3, 13, 16). Possibly these two rooms had some sort of official function, either as offices or adjoining chambers (praetorium) for the commander—or perhaps as the sacellum, the shrine of the fortress (Gichon 1976:192).

The three southern rooms of the eastern wing (Rooms 913, 1759, 1747) yielded the only preserved thresholds, made of three kurkar slabs set side by side (Pl. 50). A posthole 20 cm square was carved into the southern slab. The total width of the slabs is 1.50 m, but the doorway itself was 90–100 cm wide, according to the niche cut in the slabs. The doors could only open inward.

The threshold into Room 913, which measures 3.4 m × 4 m with beaten earth floor at level 2.23–2.40 m, was about 50 cm higher than the inside floor level. Remains of an oven and a basalt grinding stone were found in the southwestern corner of the room.

A plastered drain (Channel 923) ran eastward and downward along the northern side of Room 913. Apparently the drain started in the courtyard (Locus 907) and passed through Walls M131, L132, and M122, proving their contemporaneity. The preserved segment of the channel is 8 m long and measures 20 cm × 25 cm internally. The side walls are constructed of kurkar stones coated with plaster; the top of the drain was covered by flat kurkar slabs. The drain declined eastward at a gradient of 9 degrees and apparently drained a smaller area than the one at the north (Channel 804; see below). A coin of Marcus Ambibulus was found in the western end of the channel.

In the next room south (Room 1759), a stone pavement of large, flat kurkar stones was preserved at level 2.19 m. The room measures 2.3 m × 3.40 m and was devoid of finds.

Room 1747 was the largest in the eastern row, 3.4 m × 4.8 m. According to our reconstruction, it was entered from a room in the southern wing and not from the central courtyard. Only the fill beneath floor level was preserved.

The outer row of rooms in the eastern wing was badly damaged. Both corners were completely missing, and no floors or entrances were found. The outer wall (M122) is only 0.75 m wide, whereas its inner wall (L132) is 1.10 m wide. Nor is the orientation of Wall M122 parallel to that of Wall L132. In addition, the inner room divisions are less well organized than those of the inner row of the same wing. We assume therefore that the outer row of rooms played a secondary role in the activities of the fortress. The outer rooms could have been used for storage, and probably the floors and roofs were lower than those of the inner row.

The first room on the north (Room 1087) is bounded on the north by Wall O123, constructed 4.5 m south of the northeastern corner of the fortress. Most of the room was eroded down the slope; its reconstructed size is 2.3 m × 2.9 m. Next comes Room 1070, about 12.5 m long and 3 m wide. Its floor is not preserved, but it must have been above the top of Channel 923, at a level of about 2.8 m. The next three rooms are smaller. Room 1716 measures 2 m × 4 m, Room 1728 is only 1.8 m × 2 m, and Room 1712 is 1.7 m × 3 m. These last two are badly eroded.

14.1.3. The Northern Wing and Gateway

The gateway, consisting of the gate approach (Ramp 1760) and entry hall (Room 803), occupied most of the uncovered area at this end of the fortress. Instead of an outer row of rooms at the northeast corner, a long approach ramp (1760) ran parallel to the northern wall (P121). The northeastern corner of Walls L132 and P121 was sunk into the ground to a depth of about 3.5 m (down to level 6.10 m) and had unusually wide and solidly built foundations. The approach ramp was plastered with a thick lime composition, which abutted onto Wall P121 and curled up against it. The preserved stretch of plaster paving allows us to calculate an east-to-west gradient of 12 degrees for the approach. The ramp was made of Fill 1389, large quantities of stones mixed with earth. At the north a retaining wall (Q131) supported the approach ramp. To enter the citadel one had to turn left into the entry hall (Room 803). The entrance itself, reconstructed through Wall P121, was probably closed off by a door. The average measurements of Room 803 are 3 m × 8 m. The inner entrance, which may also have had a door, was not found, since Wall O143 was destroyed beneath the threshold.

The reconstruction of the gate passage is based on the assumption that it was directly above Channel 804. This channel, which drained Courtyard 812, was integrated into Wall O143. Traceable to a length of 3.1 m, it has a gradient of 15 degrees, sloping downward and curving slightly to the east. Characteristically, its exterior is roughly constructed, but its interior (25 cm deep and 30 cm wide) is very neatly finished. Four of its capstones remained intact, bonded with plaster to the channel; two were of hewn and two of unhewn kurkar. Another drainage channel (Locus 811) abutting the outer (northern) face of Wall Q152, and sloping downward from west to east, appears originally to have joined Channel 804, but the connecting segment was robbed together with the missing part of Wall Q152.

East of the entry hall is a small chamber (Room 1763) measuring 2.1 m × 3.2 m. Its location next to the gateway suggests that it served as a guardroom; therefore, we reconstructed an entrance into it from Room 803. West of Room 803 is Room 1019, measuring 3.6 m × 3.9 m. Its northwestern corner was not excavated. Two rooms (Loci 1392 and 1390) are the only remains of the second (northern) row of rooms. Room 1390 is a very small chamber (1.2 m × 3 m) that could have served as a staircase to the roof of the fortress, providing quick access for soldiers protecting the approach ramp. The function of the western room (1392) cannot be determined.

14.1.4. Constructional Methods

The stone foundations of all the walls were sunk about 1 m

beneath floor level. They were made of medium-size un-worked *kurkar* stones, usually laid in two rows intersticed with smaller stones and mud. In each superimposed course, about 30 cm high, the builders took pains to create a horizontal surface before adding the next course, even though the courses were composed of stones of varying sizes. The base of the foundations, on the other hand, is not even, and is somewhat higher wherever solid walls of earlier strata were encountered. The superstructure was built of large, roughly squared *kurkar* blocks, measuring 30 cm × 45 cm × 80 cm, which are particularly well preserved in the southern half of Wall M131. Such solid blocks were also incorporated in the foundations at some strategic points, such as the gateway.

The northern end of Wall L132 was built especially thick because of its location near the approach up the hill. The wall here is 1.8 m wide and set about 3.5 m below floor level; above it are narrower foundations about 1.3 m wide.

14.2. POTTERY

Very few floors of the fortress were preserved, and these were almost completely devoid of finds. The pottery repertoire therefore consists merely of sherds of vessels that had been broken before the evacuation of the fortress.

14.2.1. Pottery Types

Bowls

There is one fragment of Eastern sigillata A (Fig. 14.3:1). The fabric is homogeneous, well fired, and covered with an orange-red slip, burnished both inside and out. The rim is straight and internally ridged. Just below the rim is a molded pattern of circles with dots inside, under which are two parallel ridges. Similar vessels were found in Greece.

The bowls of Figure 14.3:2–4 seem to be locally made kitchenware of common utilitarian types. The shallow bowl (Fig. 14.3:2) is similar to some specimens from Qumran and the Jerusalem citadel (Lapp 1961: Type 53 H-J). The bowls with incurved rim (Fig. 14.3:3–4) continue the shape of such earlier vessels (Lapp 1961: Type 51.1 D, L).

Cooking Pots

Two different types of cooking pots are represented here: with "lid device" (Fig. 14.3:5–6) and without (Fig. 14.3:7–8). Of the first type, No. 5 is extremely angular, apparently in imitation of a metal vessel. It belongs to Lapp's "type with shoulder" (Lapp 1961: Type 72.2). The neck and body of the second type (Fig. 14.3:7–8) are finely ribbed (Lapp 1961: Type 71.1K).

Jugs (Fig. 14.3:9)

This one is poorly and unevenly fired, and the strap handle is not well fashioned (cf. Lapp 1961: Type 21.1 P, R).

Juglets (Fig. 14.3:10–11)

These two examples of globular juglets are very thin, finely made, round-bottomed vessels. Number 10, which is covered with a slightly burnished orange-red slip, has a crude strap handle that was obviously not in a leather-hard state before firing, as it has noticeably sagged before firming up (cf. Lapp 1961: Type 31.1 E).

Pilgrim Flask (Fig. 14.3:12)

The fragment may be compared to Lapp's Type 29 G.

Oil Lamps (Fig. 14.3:13–16)

The four lamp fragments are all in the Herodian style (Rosenthal and Sivan 1978), which dates predominantly from the last half of the 1st century B.C.E. to the middle of the 2d century C.E. The clays range from orange red to gray green in color. All pieces are well levigated, evenly fired, and show signs of use. Number 16 is decorated with two concentric circles stamped on the bow beyond the spout hole. A faint line of stamped dots separates a row of three more concentric circles from the spout hole. The other three spouts are undecorated.

14.2.2. Dating

The pottery assemblage falls within the chronological framework indicated by the Roman coins found on the tell (see Chap. 27). Accordingly, the fortress existed during the first half of the 1st century C.E.

14.3. CONCLUSIONS

The basic layout of the fortress is a square courtyard surrounded by casemate rooms. The double rows of rooms on the east and north were erected on those sides of the tell where the slope was not steep enough or sufficiently close to provide natural protection. If reconstructed symmetrically, the fortress could have housed 23 rooms in the internal casemates and another 9 rooms in the outer rows.[1]

Each of the larger rooms could have billeted a squad of about 10 men (see Gichon 1976:189), and the adjacent smaller room might have accommodated their commander. Assuming that there were 10–12 such double units, we may calculate a garrison of more than 100 soldiers, or a Roman maniple of 120 men.[2]

The tower in the center of the courtyard (for which we can find no parallel in Israel) undoubtedly served as a watchtower guarding the coast, and perhaps as a lighthouse at times of bad visibility.

The erection of the fortress at this spot in the beginning of the 1st century C.E. was surely connected with the Roman shipping of corn from Egypt. The Jewish fleet operating out of the port of Jaffa (Joppa), ever since its conquest by Simeon the Hasmonean in 142 B.C.E. (1 Macc. 14:5), was considered a threat to this maritime commerce (Gichon 1981:47–48, n. 40–41). Apparently the Romans found it necessary to establish a fortress on the coast at the closest possible anchorage north of the Yarkon River to control Jewish naval attacks as well as to provide services for their own ships anchoring there. They built their fort at Tel Michal on top of the ruins of the Hasmonean fort, which was probably deserted some time in the second half of the 1st century B.C.E.

The Roman fortress does not seem to have been destroyed by violence but was simply evacuated. This is another reason (in addition to stone robbing and erosion) why so few finds could be collected from its excavated areas. The abandonment of the fortress no doubt resulted from the conquest of Jaffa, first by Cestius Gallus in 66 C.E. and then by Vespasian 2 years later (*Jos. War* 3:9, 3). After the Romans had built a military camp over the ruins of Jaffa (*Jos. War*: 3:9, 4), there was no longer any justification for an independent fortress at nearby Tel Michal.

NOTES

1. In a previous publication (Herzog 1980: Fig. 13), a more schematic reconstruction (with two rows on each side) was suggested. However, the uncovering of outer Wall H141 does not allow a second row of rooms to be reconstructed in the southern wing.

2. A Roman century = 60–100 men; a maniple = two centuries.

REFERENCES

Gichon, M. 1976. Excavations at Mezad-Tamar, 1973–1974. *IEJ* 26:188–194.

Gichon, M. 1981. Cestius Gallus's Campaign in Judaea. *PEQ* 113:39–62.

Herzog, Z., ed. 1980. Excavations at Tel Michal 1978–1979. *Tel Aviv* 7:111–151.

Lapp, P. W. 1961. *Palestinian Ceramics Chronology, 200 B.C.-A.D. 70.* New Haven, Conn.

Rosenthal, R., and Sivan, R. 1978. *Ancient Lamps in the Schloessinger Collection.* (Qedem 8) Jerusalem.

15

Early Arab Occupation (Stratum I)

by Fredric R. Brandfon

15.1. ARCHITECTURE

The main evidence for occupation during the Early Arab period at Tel Michal came from a single structure at the summit of the high tell (Area A). Because of the erosion of the western slope, only the eastern part of this structure (Locus 50) was preserved. In addition, most of its walls were robbed for their stones following the abandonment of the site. The fragmentary remains therefore consist mainly of thick foundations, patches of plastered floors, and some plastered basins (Fig. 15.1). The only other remains of the Early Arab period were some plastered installations and floor uncovered in Area C on the eastern hillock (Herzog et al. 1978:113–114, Fig. 8).[1]

Wall M151, the only wall of the Early Arab structure still standing on the tell, is preserved only below floor level. About 1.10 m wide, it was constructed on top of Wall M153 of Roman Tower 1002. Basin 683 cuts the northwestern corner of this tower. The floor patches were scattered around the structure at levels 1.75–1.95 m, very close to the floor levels of the Roman fortress.

The eastern end of Wall M151 joins concrete foundation M150, made of fieldstones sunk into thick layers of white concrete, forming a solid block about 1.70 m × 2.30 m. The top of the block was flattened, presumably as preparation for an ashlar superstructure. The deep trench left by the robbers of these ashlars (Robbers' Trench 60) reached the base of foundation M150. In this trench we found pottery sherds of the Early Arab period (Fig. 15.2), together with fragments of stucco with relief decoration (Herzog et al. 1978: Pl. 35:1).

Robbers' Trench 373 probably indicates the location of the southern wall of Structure 50. Like Wall M151, it joins a massive concrete foundation (L150) measuring 1.90 m × 2.50 m at the east (Pl. 52). The plaster curling upward toward Robbers' Trench 370 is probably a remnant of a floor laid against the robbed wall. Since this floor is aligned with the eastern wall of the structure, it was very likely the entranceway between the two towers or buttresses built upon the concrete bases. A large triangular ashlar that may have served as the keystone of an arched entrance was found just opposite these buttresses.

The preserved remains of Structure 50 may be reconstructed as a square tower measuring about 7.30 m on each side, with four corner buttresses projecting about 60 cm beyond the line of the walls.

Arab methods of constructing concrete foundations are well known, but unlike the foundations of this period excavated in Jerusalem (Ben-Dov 1973:83–84), the concrete at Tel Michal does not contain much ash and its color is white rather than gray. Concrete foundations were used only for the corner buttresses, whereas Wall M151 was based on the remains of Roman Wall M153. Patches of white lime plaster paving were found sporadically around Structure 50, at levels ranging from 1.75 m (in the south) to 1.90 m (in the north), indicating that the entire area was plastered and served as an open courtyard.

Next to the northern face of Wall M151, a plastered installation (Locus 54) was uncovered. It was composed of two basins, each about 25 cm deep, surrounded by a line of stones. A straight row of stones bounded this area on the east. At a distance of 4 m north of Structure 50 was a larger basin (Locus 683), measuring about 1.70 m × 2.00 m and about 50 cm in depth (Pl. 53). It was lined with stones laid in concrete similar to that used for the foundations of the buttresses. There were three layers of white plaster in the basin; in one of them two clear footprints could be seen, suggesting that the basin was used to prepare lime plaster for the floors of this period.

The Early Arab architectural remains suggest a single structure standing on the summit of the mound and surrounded by an open courtyard.

15.2. POTTERY

A substantial number of homogeneous sherds were found in Structure 50 and the adjacent courtyard. There were no complete vessels. The pottery was uniformly unglazed, belonging to what Lane has termed "the ceramic

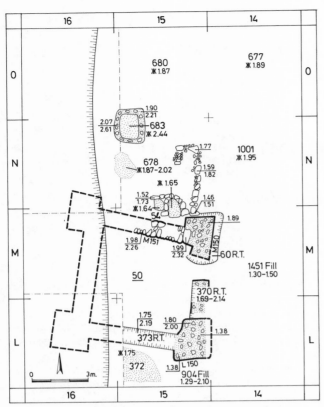

Figure 15.1. Early Arab remains on high tell.

underworld of Islam" (Lane 1953:25). Most of the sherds fall into the category called "white pottery" or "white-slipped pottery" by de Vaux and Steve (1950:127). There were also several lamp fragments.

Of the white pottery, the most common form at Tel Michal was a pitcher or jug with a flat base (Fig. 15.2:3, 4) and a simple rim. The rim often has parallel horizontal, incised bands beneath the lip (Fig. 15.2:2; cf. de Vaux and Steve 1950: Pl. XVI). Some of the white pottery was cast in a mold that produced impressed designs of elaborate geometric shape (Fig. 15.2:1). These pieces were also pitcher fragments (cf. Baramki 1944: Fig. 14:2, 3, 5). Decorative motifs included overlapping lozenges and ovate "leaves" with a herringbone pattern. A similar vessel was found on the northern Syrian coast at Al Mina (Lane 1953: Pl. 36:3).

The second type of jug features thick ribbing below the rim (Fig. 15.2:5), known on both pilgrim's flasks and jugs (Baramki 1944: Figs. 5:10, 15:5, 6).

A number of lamp fragments were found with similar molded designs (Fig. 15.2:7–9) and the typical thick vertical handle (Fig. 15.2:8). In one of them (Fig. 15.2:7), two birds flank a herringbone design that leads from the rim to the spout. The birds face away from the herringbone midrib toward circular designs that enclose a series of smaller circles. A floral motif is above each bird's head. An almost identical piece was found at Abu Ghosh (de Vaux and Steve

1950:35, Fig. 33:7), although here the birds are depicted somewhat differently.

Cooking pot lids are not unknown from the Early Arab period (Baramki 1944: Fig. 13:17–21; de Vaux and Steve 1950: Pl. B:15, 16). Such lids were also found at Tel Michal (Fig. 15.2:6), the best parallel coming from Khirbet el-Mefjer (Baramki 1944: Fig. 13:17).

Several pottery fragments may be of the type that de Vaux and Steve (1950:125) call "red pottery." Our red pottery falls into their fine ware category, decorated either with incised wavy lines (de Vaux and Steve 1950: Pl. B:29; Baramki 1944: Figs. 12:4, 14:6) or with molded decorations similar to those found on the white pottery.

15.3. CONCLUSIONS

The Early Arab pottery from Tel Michal is for the most part a homogeneous assemblage of plain, white sherds. Lane (1953:11–12) dates this pottery to the 9th–10th centuries C.E.

Although Khirbet el-Mefjer is mainly an 8th-century C.E. site, its major occupation occurring before or immediately after the earthquake of 746 C.E., it was partially cleared and reoccupied shortly thereafter (Baramki 1944:65, 74). Baramki concurs with Lane that the creamy white pottery of Khirbet el-Mefjer (his ware No. 20; our Plain White ware) is dated to the 9th–10th centuries C.E. Furthermore, he dates his ware No. 6, paralleled at Tel Michal by the jug rims with thick ribbing (Fig. 15.2:5), to the same period. The Early Arab occupation at Tel Michal must therefore be placed in the 9th–10th centuries C.E.

Regarding the function of this structure, its small size and the poor quality of the pottery and architecture preclude the likelihood that it was a mosque or other edifice with fine appointments. It is more tempting to look upon it as one of the lookout towers established "along the coast of Filastin" in order to announce the sighting of approaching ships. According to the 10th-century Arab geographer Mukaddasi:

> From every watch station on the coast up to the capital there are built, at intervals, high towers in each of which is stationed a company of men. On the occasion of the arrival of the Greek ships, the men, perceiving these, kindle the beacon on the tower nearest to the coast station and then onto that lying above it, and onwards one after another, so that barely an hour elapsed before the trumpets are sounding in the towers calling the people down to the watch stations by the sea. (LeStrange 1890:23)

Although Mukaddasi does not list any watchtower between the ports of Jaffa and Arsuf, there is no doubt that the high tell at Tel Michal was an excellent location for one of the lookout towers in this network of relay stations.

* * *

Evidence for post-10th-century C.E. activity at Tel Michal comes from three disturbed graves of the Mameluke period, two of which are jar burials and one a stone-lined cist tomb. Three coins (see Chap. 27) date this phase to the 12th–14th centuries C.E.

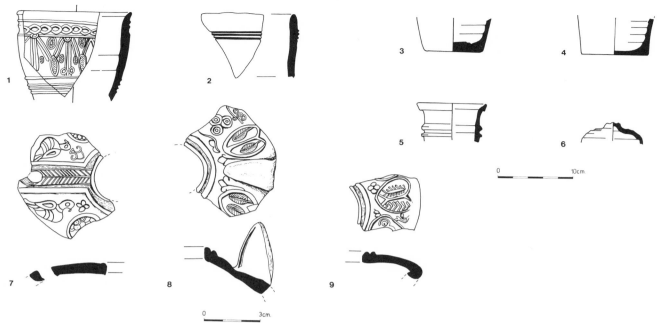

Figure 15.2. Early Arab pottery (Locus 60).

Legend for Fig. 15.2

No.	Type	Reg. No.	Description
1	Jug	2001/8	Buff
2	Bowl	2156/2	White
3	Jug	271/1	White
4	Jug	2148/2	White
5	Jug	2001/7	White
6	Lid	9203/1	White
7	Lamp	2001/5	White
8	Lamp	2001/3	White
9	Lamp	2001/4	White

NOTE

1. I would like to thank Rebecca Friedman, a graduate student at the University of Pennsylvania, for her valuable help in researching this article.

REFERENCES

Baramki, D. C. 1944. The Pottery from Khirbet el Mefjer. *QDAP* 10:65–103.

Ben-Dov, M. 1973. Building Techniques in the Ommayad Palace near the Temple Mount, Jerusalem. (Hebrew) *EI* 11:75–91.

de Vaux, R., and Steve, A. M. 1950. *Fouilles à Qaryet el-'Enab: Abu Ghosh, Palestine.* Paris.

Herzog, Z., Negbi, O., and Moshkovitz, S. 1978. Excavations at Tel Michal, 1977. *Tel Aviv* 5:99–130.

Lane, A. 1953. *Early Islamic Pottery.* London.

LeStrange, G. 1890. *Palestine under the Moslems.* London. Reprinted in 1965, Beirut.

16

Regional Geology

by Natan Bakler

The sequence of Late Quaternary sediments cropping out of the escarpment along the Tel Michal segment of the coastline of Israel provides a good opportunity for a detailed stratigraphic study of the Late Pleistocene and Holocene sediments of the Sharon plain. This sequence has been subdivided in previous works on the basis of European Pleistocene chronostratigraphy (Avnimelech 1952). Horowitz (1979) summarized these earlier studies and also suggested a chronostratigraphic table of his own (Horowitz 1979: Table 5.1). However, because of the problems involved in dating these sedimentary units and their correlations among the different coastal regions of Israel, application of this overall scheme to the limited area of the Sharon coastal plain seems to require further refinement of lithographic terms.[1]

A revised schematic profile along the coastal cliffs of our region has therefore been prepared (Fig. 16.1). The terminology for each of the stratigraphic units incorporates the names of their type localities (Gavish 1978), some of which have been more precisely localized than in our former study (Bakler 1978). The former (E. Gavish and N. Bakler, in press) and revised terminology are correlated in the accompanying list.

Hadera dune bed	Rishon LeZion sand
Ta'arukha *hamra* bed	Nof Yam sand
Tel Aviv *kurkar* bed	Beit Yanai *kurkar*
Netanya *hamra* bed	Netanya *hamra*
Upper part of Dor *kurkar* bed ⎫	
Tel Barukh *hamra* bed ⎬ Wingate *kurkar*	
Lower part of Dor *kurkar* bed ⎭	
Nahsholim *hamra* bed	
(café au lait)	Ga'ash *hamra*
Ramat Gan *kurkar*	Giv'at Olga *kurkar*

16.1. STRATIGRAPHY

16.1.1. Giv'at Olga *Kurkar*

The oldest and lowest exposed unit of the coastal cliffs is the Giv'at Olga *kurkar* bed. This unit forms typical dunal (bar-

khans) morphology, with a pronounced asymmetry to the northeast. The amplitude of the undulations can reach 20 m, and wavelengths within the dunes are close to 100 m. In some places (for example, at Giv'at Olga and Apollonia) the crests of the dunes are exposed, but sometimes the bottom may be partially or completely buried beneath the present-day surface. Around Tel Michal this *kurkar* makes up the basal unit of the coastal cliffs (Gvirtzman et al. 1983–84).

The unit is composed of the thick, cross-bedded lenses characteristic of eolian dunes, within which well and poorly cemented thin layers (laminae) alternate more or less parallel to each other. These give the unit its distinctive layered appearance, which is particularly obvious on eroded surfaces. From the northeast orientation of these dunes, we may deduce that the dominant winds during the time of deposition were from the southwest and that the climate was an arid one, probably interpluvial or interglacial.

Giv'at Olga *kurkar* is composed (in order of decreasing abundance) of quartz sand grains, calcareous cement, calcareous sand grains, and shell fragments. The size of the quartz grains ranges from medium to fine sand (0.12 mm); the grains are relatively well rounded, well sorted, and smaller than the carbonate grains. Most of the rock, however, is calcareous because of the cement that fills the spaces between the sand grains and shell fragments. The shells are of the same species found on the beach today. The cement consists of minute calcite crystals. Detailed studies prove that it was derived from the aragonite and high-magnesium calcite of the marine carbonate, which were diagenetically converted into calcite under freshwater (meteoric) environments (Gavish and Friedman 1969).

16.1.2. Ga'ash *Hamra* (café au lait)

In the vicinity of Tel Michal, the Giv'at Olga *kurkar* bed is overlain by the Ga'ash *hamra* unit, a dark-gray-to-brown sandy soil layer 1–2 m thick. Its thickness varies somewhat with the topography. The lower contact of this unit is gradual, whereas its upper contact is smooth and well

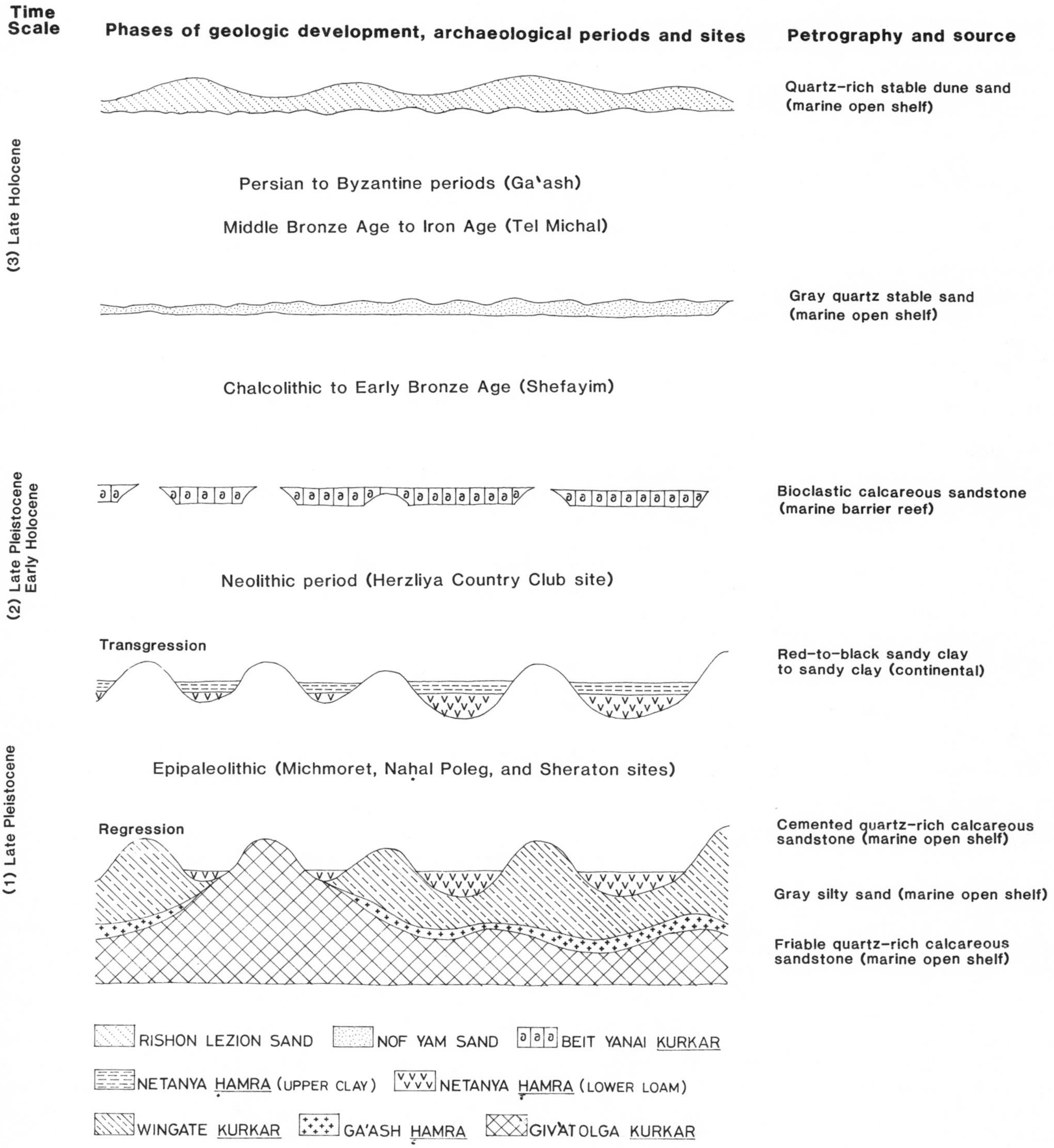

Time Scale	Phases of geologic development, archaeological periods and sites	Petrography and source

Quartz-rich stable dune sand (marine open shelf)

(3) Late Holocene

Persian to Byzantine periods (Ga'ash)

Middle Bronze Age to Iron Age (Tel Michal)

Gray quartz stable sand (marine open shelf)

Chalcolithic to Early Bronze Age (Shefayim)

(2) Late Pleistocene Early Holocene

Bioclastic calcareous sandstone (marine barrier reef)

Neolithic period (Herzliya Country Club site)

Transgression

Red-to-black sandy clay to sandy clay (continental)

Epipaleolithic (Michmoret, Nahal Poleg, and Sheraton sites)

(1) Late Pleistocene

Regression

Cemented quartz-rich calcareous sandstone (marine open shelf)

Gray silty sand (marine open shelf)

Friable quartz-rich calcareous sandstone (marine open shelf)

RISHON LEZION SAND   NOF YAM SAND   BEIT YANAI KURKAR

NETANYA HAMRA (UPPER CLAY)   NETANYA HAMRA (LOWER LOAM)

WINGATE KURKAR   GA'ASH HAMRA   GIVAT OLGA KURKAR

Figure 16.1. Schematic reconstruction of Sharon coastal cliffs (north-south).

defined, although tilted according to the morphology of the fossilized dune. This unit is uniformly overlain by Wingate *kurkar*. The sand-size grains are similar to those of the underlying Giv'at Olga *kurkar*. In addition, the soil contains a small percentage of silt and up to 10 percent calcium carbonate in the form of shell fragments of terrestrial snails. This unit is partially exposed to a height of about 1.0 m on the hillock south of Tel Michal.

16.1.3. Wingate Kurkar

This unit overlies the Ga'ash *hamra* unconformably, filling the interdune troughs. It is exposed at the bottom or in the middle of the coastal cliffs and forms most of the coastal scarp in many places. Its thickness varies from a few meters or less along the fringes of the troughs to more than 20 m at their centers. This sand unit is gradually enriched upward with red clay particles.

In general appearance, Wingate *kurkar* is similar to Giv'at Olga *kurkar*, since they both consist of typical cross-bedded eolian sand lenses containing alternating laminae of cemented and uncemented sand. However, the cross-strata of Wingate *kurkar* are only of medium to small scale, and they appear to be much less consolidated and cemented. The uncemented sand between the cemented laminae contains no more than 15 percent calcareous material. A comparison between thin sections of Wingate *kurkar* and Giv'at Olga *kurkar* shows that whereas the composition, size, and sorting of both are similar, Wingate *kurkar* contains less carbonate. Apparently, the recrystallization of the carbonate fraction was less complete than in the Giv'at Olga *kurkar*, since it is still possible to identify a small percentage of aragonite and high-magnesium particles within this *kurkar*.

Wingate *kurkar* is exposed north and south of Tel Michal and as a thick layer at the foot of the western scarp of the high tell. Because of its unconsolidated nature, this *kurkar* has a greater tendency to collapse and slump toward the beach than the underlying Giv'at Olga *kurkar*.

16.1.4. Netanya Hamra

Netanya *hamra* is a Mediterranean soil sediment locally called simply *hamra*. It is a red-brown to black loam consisting of sand, silt, and clay. Its bottom contact with the Wingate *kurkar* is transitional, whereas its upper contact is distinct. The upper part of the unit is often characterized by laminations of sand and black clay and sometimes by thick layers of black clay alone. This latter component is very plastic and contains some organic matter, although no fauna have been found in it. It is therefore considered an aquatic swamp deposit. Lateral changes to red-brown clay are often observed in zones where the paleotopography was higher during deposition, whereas the *hamra* in the lower part of the unit is always red.

The sands of Netanya *hamra* are similar in grain size and shape to those of Wingate *kurkar*, but it contains a negligible amount of carbonate. The fine-grained constituents of this soil are silt and clay.

Not only the composition of this unit but also its thickness vary in accordance with the paleomorphology of the Wingate *kurkar*. At topographic lows, it is usually a few meters thick and contains a high proportion of dark brown silt and clay, whereas on topographic highs it is relatively thin (no more than a few centimeters) and is a lighter shade of brown. The present-day elevation of this horizon varies from a few meters to 30 m above sea level.

This unit is exposed north of Tel Michal (along the banks of Nahal Gelilot), south of the site, and immediately to its east, and it was undoubtedly a major source for the material used so extensively to stabilize the Middle and Late Bronze Age ramparts (Chap. 4) and the *hamra* mudbricks used for construction throughout the occupancy of the site.

16.1.5. Beit Yanai (Calcarenite) Kurkar

This is the uppermost and youngest *kurkar* unit of the Sharon coast (known as *plata* in the local idiom); its contacts with both the underlying Netanya *hamra* and the overlying clayey sand dunes are always sharply demarcated. This unit appears as a homogeneous lithologic layer, its thickness varying from 1 to 5 m and sometimes even more. In many places it forms the top of the coastal cliffs and is not covered by younger sediments. It can be followed along its relatively horizontal layer for distances of hundreds of meters, its horizontal appearance being particularly obvious when viewed from offshore. In some places, however, it undulates appreciably, following the upper morphology of the Netanya bed, and perhaps also as the result of neotectonic activity.

The structure of Beit Yanai *kurkar* is much more uniform than that of the older *kurkars*. Medium- to small-scale cross-stratification can be recognized above the lowest layer of the unit, although it is usually difficult to distinguish the individual laminae since they are more uniformly cemented than in the older *kurkars*. Many of the large sandstone blocks found today at the foot of the cliffs—a well-known phenomenon along the Netanya-Yanai beach—were split off from this unit.

The constituents of Beit Yanai *kurkar* are calcareous particles of organic origin and quartz grains, in about equal proportions, with some calcite cement. The quartz grains are of similar or smaller size than the sands in the older *kurkar* units, and their sorting is better. The calcareous grains come from fragmented marine pelecypods, calcareous algae, and microfauna, as well as from land snails. Petrographically, Beit Yanai *kurkar* is defined as a biocalcarenite because of its typical bioclastic composition of sand-size particles. The mineralogic composition of the bioclastic materials is still the original aragonite and magnesium calcite; the cement is calcite. This indicates that the cementation took place under continental conditions but that fresh water did not yet affect the aragonite.

According to Neev and Bakler (1978), the bioclastic bank of Beit Yanai *kurkar* was deposited in a shallow marine beach environment. This theory is based on the widespread occurrence in the lower part of this bank of uniform horizontal layers. Moreover, the abundant presence of burrowers' traces, mostly in the biostrome-like lenses within the lower layer of this bank, strongly supports a marine (beach) environment of deposition. Gavish (1978), on the other hand, considers Beit Yanai *kurkar* to be a beach-dune eolian deposit in view of its uniform grain-size distribution, the presence of cross-stratification, and the abundance of land snails found within it. Beit Yanai *kurkar* was traced up to a few hundred meters east of the coastal cliff at Tel Michal and the immediate vicinity.

16.1.6. Sand Units (Rishon LeZion and Nof Yam Sands)

These sands unconformably overlie the Beit Yanai *kurkar* unit (or where it is absent, the Netanya *hamra* bed). They frequently cover the coastal cliff and part of the first *kurkar* ridge at its east, up to a depth of several meters. Deposited during the past 4,000 years, these sands create a complex of layers and dunes that is only partially preserved today. In the Sharon, most of this sand cover has been stabilized by vegetation, and a moderate amount of gray soil has started to form on it.

The active and stabilized sands are similar in structure and grain characteristics. Where cross sections of dunes are exposed, eolian cross-bedding typical of that seen in *kurkars* is evident. The amount of carbonate in these dunes is very low (less than 10 percent) compared with the amounts in *kurkars*, and no cementation is discernible. The carbonate comes from marine and terrestrial bioclastic material in varying proportions. The marine constituents, which consist of aragonite and high-magnesium calcite, have not undergone a process of mineralogic alteration. The average grain size and sorting of these sands are generally similar to those of the *kurkars* and the Ga'ash *hamra* bed. These sand deposits are stratigraphically divided into two subunits.

Nof Yam Deposit

This subunit, the older of the two, is found in various locales between Tel Aviv and Netanya. Its color is dark gray, similar to that of young sandy soils. The gray color, the presence of small amounts of organic material, and the lack of visible cross-bedding suggest an aquatic swamp origin of deposition, sometimes called the Shefayim swamp unit. Although there are other gray horizons above this deposit, they are localized and much less distinct. Above this gray horizon of the Nof Yam sands (4000–3000 B.P.) are the recent eolian sands deposited during the past 3,000 years, most of them fairly recently.

Rishon LeZion Deposit

This sand covers most of the ancient sites along the coastal cliffs, with deposits varying from 10 to 20 cm. Barkhans undulating morphology is dominant, although cross-bedding is typical. Only the very top of this sand is sufficiently stable to have produced a soillike gray color. The contact between this stable unit and the active sands of today is not clearly defined.

16.2. DEVELOPMENT OF THE SHARON COASTAL CLIFFS FROM LATE PLEISTOCENE TO RECENT TIMES

The southern segment of the Mediterranean coastline of Israel, which extends from the Mount Carmel block to Rafah (as defined by Neev and Ben-Avraham 1977), is characterized by a continuous linear cliff 10–50 m high, reaching its greatest height south of Netanya (the Sharon Escarpment). This scarp is breached by several rivers old enough to have created extensive inland floodplains.

A rocky *kurkar* strip extends from the present beach zone to a distance of a few hundred meters westward into the sea. This sandstone formation has been abraded to form patches of sea-level terraces. In some places, mainly opposite the estuaries of river channels (for example, at the mouth of Nahal Gelilot north of Tel Michal), these sandstone rock formations have disappeared, probably from erosion by winter flooding (A. Raban and Y. Turcaspa, personal communication).

Recently, several archaeological sites have been surveyed or excavated along the Sharon Escarpment. The data from these excavations, together with our detailed geologic studies, have helped us to decipher and date both the geologic and settlement histories of this zone since the Late Pleistocene or Early Holocene (Fig. 16.1). The chronology may be divided into three stages:

1) *Late Pleistocene regression.* This stage is represented by the Wingate *kurkar* bed and the Paleolithic culture. Because of this regression, the sea level dropped to more than 100 m below its present level (Fairbridge 1961; Milliman and Emery 1968). The eolian sands that penetrated inland before this regression had by then become lithified. At this stage, Pleistocene rivers cut their present channels across the existing sandstone ridges.

2) *Late Pleistocene–Early Holocene transgression.* The Epipaleolithic, Neolithic, Chalcolithic, and Early Bronze Age cultures belong to this period. With the accelerated sea-level rise that reached a maximum rate about 12,000 years ago, the drainage pattern clogged up and clay deposits filled the interridge troughs. Lagoons, swamps, and freshwater lakes dominated the coastal plain (Nir and Bar-Yosef 1976). The people of the Epipaleolithic culture inhabited the *hamra* (red loam) floodplains in the coastal zone, as evidenced by the quantities of flint implements found within the Netanya *hamra* unit, for example, at the sites at Nahal Poleg (Nir and Bar-Yosef 1976: Fig. 36) and the Sheraton Hotel beach.

Little human activity between 10,000 and 4000 B.P. has been recorded archaeologically, although small hunters' colonies apparently did exist here and there in swampy environments, for example, at the Herzliya Country Club site (Nir and Bar-Yosef 1976: Fig. 54). In the middle of this phase, the coastline was submerged by the sea and the Beit Yanai calcarenite bank was deposited (Avnimelech 1962). At the end of this transgression, seaborne sand covered the coast smoothly and stabilized. On this surface, Chalcolithic and Early Bronze Age agricultural societies were established and developed (Gophna 1978).

3) *Late Holocene*. During this stage, the Sharon coastal cliff attained its present basic morphology. Settlements from the Middle Bronze Age to the present developed without major geologic interruptions.

The phenomena observed at Tel Michal at the end of the Middle Bronze Age IIB and on a smaller scale at the end of the Late Bronze Age I when sizable masses of earth broke away from the western scarp of the high tell (see Chap. 4.1.4; 4.2) were probably caused by a rejuvenation of tectonic activity along the coastal fault system (Neev and Bakler 1978).[2] No further indications were noted at Tel Michal of the recurrence of catastrophic events of similar magnitude.

The Rishon LeZion sand deposit that covered the region at the end of this period up to present times overlies the archaeological remains at Tel Michal from the Persian period onward.

NOTES

1. This chapter was translated from the Hebrew by Zvi Erel of Everyman's University, Tel Aviv.

2. The editors are aware that the authors of Chaps. 17 and 18 hold somewhat different views concerning the detailed stratigraphy and erosional history of the tell.

REFERENCES

Avnimelech, M. 1952. Late Quaternary Sediments of the Coastal Plain of Israel. *Research Council of Israel Bulletin* 2:51–57.

Avnimelech, M. 1962. The Main Trends in the Pleistocene-Holocene History of the Israelian Coastal Plain. *Quaternaria* 6:479–495.

Bakler, N. 1978. Geology of Tel Michal and the Herzliya Coast. *Tel Aviv* 5:131–135.

Fairbridge, R. W. 1961. Eustatic Changes in Sea Level. Pages 99–185 in: *Physics and Chemistry of the Earth*, vol. 4. R. W. Fairbridge, ed. Oxford.

Gavish, E. 1978. Post Congress Excursion 45. Pages 226–231 in: *Sedimentology in Israel, Cyprus and Turkey. Guidebook, Part 2*. D. Yaalon, ed. Tenth International Congress on Sedimentology, 1978. Jerusalem.

Gavish, E., and Bakler, N. In press. The Sharon Coastal Strip: Geomorphologic and Sedimentological Causes and Processes. In *The Sharon Book*. (Hebrew) A. Shmueli, ed. Tel Aviv.

Gavish, E., and Friedman, G. M. 1969. Progressive Diagenesis of Quaternary to Late Tertiary Carbonate Sediments: Sequence and Time Scale. *Journal of Sedimentary Petrology* 39:980–1006.

Gophna, R. 1978. Archaeological Survey of the Central Coastal Plain, 1977. Preliminary Report. *Tel Aviv* 5:136–147.

Gvirtzman, G., Shachnai, E., Bakler, N., and Ilani, S. 1983–84. Stratigraphy of the Kurkar Group (Quaternary) of the Coastal Plain of Israel. Pages 70–82 in: *Geological Survey of Israel Current Research*. Jerusalem.

Horowitz, A. 1979. *The Quaternary of Israel*. New York.

Milliman, J. D., and Emery, K. O. 1968. Sea Levels during the Past 35,000 Years. *Science* 162:1121–1123.

Neev, D., and Bakler, N. 1978. Young Tectonic Activities along the Coasts of Israel. Pages 9–30 in: *Collection of Papers on Coast and Sea*. (Hebrew) Tel Aviv.

Neev, D., and Ben-Avraham, Z. 1977. The Levantine Countries: The Israeli Coastal Region. Pages 355–377 in: *The Ocean Basins and Margins*, vol. 4A. E. M. Nairn, W. H. Kanes, and F. G. Stehli, eds. New York.

Nir, D., and Bar-Yosef, O. 1976. *Quaternary Environment and Man in Israel*. (Hebrew) Tel Aviv.

17

Paleogeography of the Central Sharon Coast

by John A. Gifford and George Rapp, Jr.

As noted more than 80 years ago (Smith 1895), the Levantine coast south of Mt. Carmel does not favor maritime development because of its low, sandy morphology and lack of natural sheltered anchorages. This is particularly true of the Sharon coastline of Israel. Karmon (1956) discusses the history of the coastal plain in terms of its geography and points out that the area was historically the eastern margin of the Mediterranean rather than the western fringe of southwest Asia, as a result of maritime trading contacts that persisted despite the lack of harbors.

Aside from Joppa (only a small part of which has been excavated) and Dor (also only partially excavated), the Sharon coast lacks major port sites of antiquity. Small settlements of many historical and prehistorical periods remain unexcavated along the coastline, but it is interesting to examine the possibility that the oldest ports may have been eradicated by coastal erosion over the millennia, thus contributing to a skewed interpretation of the settlement pattern over the plain during those times.

We have attempted to study the nature and rate of coastal change between Tel Aviv and Netanya by core sampling the recent sedimentary sequences at several localities and interpreting the successive depositional environments using standard geologic approaches (see Kraft et al. 1977; Kraft et al. 1982). Our objective was to understand better the geography of the coastline north and south of Tel Michal during the periods of its occupation and to determine where vessels might have been harbored at the site.

17.1. GEOMORPHOLOGY OF THE COASTAL ZONE

In considering how the shoreline of the central Sharon plain may have changed during the past few thousand years, some general description of its geomorphology will help to set the stage.

The Sharon plain is the central sector of the accretionary coastal plain stretching from the eastern margin of the Nile Delta north-northeast to the Mt. Carmel promontory. It is a product of Plio-Pleistocene sedimentation from two major sources: Nile River sediments carried northward by longshore currents (Avnimelech 1962) and alluvium transported seaward from the Mesozoic limestone foothills of Samaria to the east. Only about half of the coastal plain is presently above sea level, with the submerged portion forming a uniform, low-angled continental shelf off the Israeli coast. This low-angled bottom extends into the nearshore zone along most of the coast, with bottom slope angles averaging about half a degree in depths from 0 to 25 m.

Two to five subparallel eolianite sandstone (*kurkar*) ridges are the dominant topographic elements of the Sharon plain; the intervening valleys were swampy (until drained in the 19th century) because the ridges blocked the flow of several ephemeral streams (Horowitz 1979:13). Since the *kurkar* ridges represent coastal sand dunes deposited and lithified during periods of lower Quaternary sea levels, it is not surprising to find remnants of at least two more ridges partially buried by recent marine sediments on the Israeli continental shelf (Hall and Bakler 1975). Both the terrestrial (red loam) and paludal (black clay) varieties of *hamra*-type soil sediments have also been sampled beneath marine sediments in the interridge swales seaward of the present coastline (e.g., in 7 m of water off Tel Barukh, immediately south of Tel Michal; see Bakler 1976:24). That early settlements existed on these interridge swales during lower stands of sea level is proved by the accidental exposure in 1968 of a 6th-millennium B.C.E. village site in the nearshore zone at Newe Yam, some 10 km south of Haifa (Wreschner 1983). Two other discoveries of this period, located several kilometers south of Haifa, are also described by Raban (1981:288). A Pottery Neolithic site contemporary with Newe Yam was discovered a few hundred meters southeast of Tel Michal, in the interridge swale just landward of the modern shoreline (see Chap. 18).

Newe Yam and similar Neolithic-Chalcolithic sites submerged in the nearshore zone along the coast of Israel are evidence of submergence due to the Flandrian sea-level transgression. In their compendium of Israel's coastal archaeological sites, Flemming et al. (1978) found that the

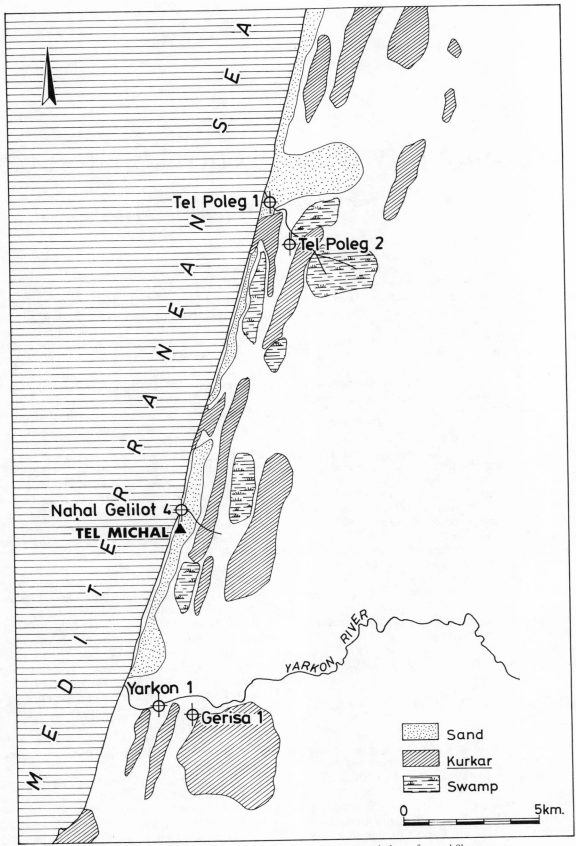

Figure 17.1. Locations of four coring localities and gross geomorphology of central Sharon coast.

204

Table 17.1 Stratigraphy of Five Cores at Locations Noted on Figure 17.1

Tel Poleg 1 (120 m inshore from swash zone, just west of standing water in stream channel; map ref. 13471/18562, elevation 0.96 m):

+0.96 m to +0.53 m — medium sand (10 YR 7/3), showing sand-filled burrows, sharp color[a] change at base;

+0.53 m to −0.16 m — coarse sand (10 YR 5/2), poorly sorted;

−0.16 m to −0.32 m — muddy sand (10 YR 5/2), articulated *Cerastoderma edule* shells at base of stratum;

−0.32 m to −1.11 m — moderately well-sorted sand (10 YR 6/2), very homogeneous, darkening to 10 YR 5/2 at base (with increasing mud content);

−1.11 m to −1.18 m — transition zone of very poorly sorted muddy sand with articulated *Cerastoderma edule* shells, C-14 date on shell material is 6520 ± 140 B.P. (UCR-1134);

−1.18 m to 1.61 m — sandy mud (10 YR 3/1) with micromolluscs.

Tel Poleg 2 (north end of freshwater pond between MB IIA site and highway, elevation 6.35 m):

+6.35 m to +3.85 m — brown muddy sand (10 YR 4/3), probably slope wash;

+3.85 m to +2.85 m — alternating sandy mud and mud strata;

+2.85 m to +1.15 m — poorly sorted muddy sand (10 YR 7/3).

Naḥal Gelilot 4 (parking lot, midchannel, approximately 100 m from shore; map ref. 13115/17463, elevation 4.02 m):

+4.02 m to +0.88 m — modern fill;

+0.88 m to −1.22 m — medium, slightly muddy sand with friable zones;

−1.22 m to −1.40 m — muddy, medium sand (10 YR 7/2) with clay lenses, pebble-size well-rounded *ḥamra* fragments at −1.25 m;

−1.40 m to −4.00 m — sandy mud (10 YR 6/6), with laminae of muddy sand throughout the section.

Yarkon 1 (north bank of river, 200 m west of Haifa road bridge; map ref. 13048/16720, elevation 0 [M̄S̄L̄]):[b]

0.00 m to −1.68 m — muddy sand (10 YR 4/2), lenses of sandier clay scattered throughout;

−1.68 m to −1.88 m — muddy sand (10 YR 7/2);

−1.88 m to −2.22 m — dense, sandy mud (10 YR 3/1);

−2.22 m to −2.33 m — lenses of muddy, medium sand (10 YR 7/2);

−2.33 m to −2.52 m — dense, homogeneous mud (10 YR 3/1);

−2.52 m to −2.56 m — lenses of medium sand (10 YR 7/2);

−2.56 m to −3.12 m — dense, homogeneous mud (10 YR 3/1), sharp contact with

−3.12 m to −3.25 m — coarse quartz sand (10 YR 5/2), sharp contact with

−3.25 m to −3.44 m — slightly gravelly mud (10 YR 3/2), less dense than overlying strata.

Gerisa 1 (at water level on Ayalon tributary adjacent to Tel Gerisa; map ref. 13198/16704, elevation 0 [M̄S̄L̄]):

0.00 m to −0.53 m — muddy, sandy gravel with fragments of plastic sheeting, grading to muddy sand at base (both 10 YR 3/1);

−0.53 m to −0.84 m — sandy mud (10 YR 3/2) with lenses of muddy sand and plant fragments;

−0.84 m to −0.96 m — slightly muddy, medium sand;

−0.96 m to −1.04 m — dense clay (10 YR 4/2);

−1.04 m to −1.52 m — muddy, gravelly sand with fragments of *Mya* shell;

−1.52 m to −1.82 m — well-sorted, medium sand (10 YR 6/4);

−1.82 m to −2.06 m — poorly sorted, gravelly muddy sand with pebbles up to 4 cm in diameter, including an abraded ceramic vessel handle (possibly of Persian date);

−2.06 m to −2.13 m — sandy mud (10 YR 4/3);

−2.13 m to −2.28 m — muddy, sandy gravel with marine pelecypod shells (including articulated *Mya*), gastropod shells, and small abraded pottery fragments);

−2.28 m to −2.45 m — mud (10 YR 3/2), with a large burned bone fragment and small wood charcoal fragments;

−2.45 m to −2.79 m — clay (10 YR 3/1), with lighter colored subangular rock granules.

---

[a] All colors refer to moist sediment.

[b] M̄S̄L̄ = mean sea level.

vast majority of post-Early Bronze Age sites correlate to within 1 m of present sea level, indicating minimum eustatic sea-level change and tectonic activity during the past 4,000 years. Their conclusions in respect to neotectonics directly oppose those of Neev et al. (1973; 1978), who postulate downwarping and subsequent partial upfaulting of the coast of Israel in the historical past.

This "coastal neotectonics" controversy has momentous implications for the correct interpretation of all coastal archaeological sites in Israel, including Tel Michal; it revolves around (1) artificial vs. natural deposition of elevated pelecypod shell beds and (2) depositional environments of various recent coastal sediments vis-à-vis their present elevation above sea level. Along the present shoreline at Tel Michal and at Tel Poleg, both of which we investigated thoroughly, no *Glycymeris* shell beds nor post-2000 B.P. marine deposits were noted at elevations above present sea level. Further, there is no expression of marine erosion in the form of abrasion/solution notches or platforms along the channel mouth banks of either the Nahal Poleg or the Nahal Gelilot (immediately north of Tel Michal). We believe that Ronen (1980) has explained more plausibly the origin of the raised pelecypod beds, and we see no substantive geologic evidence at the above-mentioned localities for the neotectonic events postulated by Neev et al. (1973; 1978).

17.2. SUBSURFACE STRATIGRAPHY OF THE CENTRAL SHARON COASTLINE

Figure 17.1 illustrates the locations of our four major coring localities, as well as the gross geomorphology of the central Sharon coast; Table 17.1 presents summary core logs for each locality.

17.3. INTERPRETATION OF COASTAL PALEOGEOGRAPHY

The Yarkon and Gerisa cores, taken at the present base level of deposition, both represent sequences of alluvial muds and sands. The coarser sediments with their marine fauna may have been deposited during summer periods of no freshwater runoff, when the lower Yarkon channel becomes a narrow estuary. Not enough organic material in a reliable stratigraphic context was recovered from either of the two cores to allow radiocarbon dating; only a questionable Persian period ceramic sherd indicates an earliest possible date for the level at −2 m in the Gerisa core. It is known from coring by the Geological Survey of Israel (N. Bakler, personal communication, 1978) that about 30 m of alluvium fills the river bedrock channel near our Yarkon 1 coring locality. Thus, the Yarkon has been the major drainage in the central Sharon plain at least since the Late Pleistocene-Early Holocene, and presumably always would have allowed ship traffic access inland as far as channel depth and vessel draft permitted (possibly at or near Tel Gerisa). It is unlikely that vessels would have ascended farther upstream on the higher water levels of the winter runoff maximum, as summer was the normal sailing season of antiquity.

A major MB IIA fortified settlement existed at Tel Poleg on the second *kurkar* ridge inland from the modern shoreline. In addition, a contemporaneous settlement—Tel Ashir—was located on the northern end of the first *kurkar* ridge overlooking Nahal Poleg (Gophna and Ayalon 1980). When corrected by the calibration table of Klein et al. (1982), our shell sample from 1.15 m below sea level in the Poleg 1 core produces a date of about 3550 B.C.E. Thus, a marine embayment existed at the mouth of the Nahal Poleg in the mid-Chalcolithic, and possibly into the Bronze Age. A gap of several hundred meters (north-south) exists in the coastal *kurkar* ridge at the mouth of the Poleg stream, eroded by the meandering channel during lower sea level. As it rose during the Holocene, the sea would have flooded this indentation, creating a natural harbor and a logical place for a port settlement. With continued sedimentation (by alluviation and longshore currents), the indentation would have filled in. According to A. Raban (who developed this theory), by the early 1st millennium B.C.E. all such natural harbors along the Levantine coast would have been rendered useless for anchorage, and it was left to the Phoenicians to develop the artificially excavated harbor design known as a *cothon*.

Our second core at Tel Poleg, located several hundred meters upstream at the foot of the fortification on the second *kurkar* ridge, did not penetrate below present sea level and represents alluvium and colluvium that may postdate the Flandrian transgression. Marine conditions could have extended inland as far as Tel Poleg in the 3d and 2d millennia, depending on the rate of sedimentation.

Figure 17.2 graphically presents the subsurface stratigraphy from core Gelilot 4, in a north-south cross section through the channel of Nahal Gelilot immediately north of Tel Michal. Coring here penetrated some 5 m below present sea level, and whereas the stratigraphy is relatively uniform, the laminae of muddy sand suggest deposition in a subaerial or very shallow marine environment where wave energy was not able to carry the mud into deeper water. At about −1.5 m the laminae disappear, which may indicate permanent flooding of the ancestral Gelilot channel by rising sea level. Assuming no local tectonics or subsidence between Nahal Gelilot and Nahal Poleg, 12 km to the north, the time of this hypothesized sea-level position can be estimated from the Poleg 1 radiocarbon date at about 5200 B.C.E. Our probing transect along the modern beach seaward of Nahal Gelilot (Chap. 18) shows that its channel is cut to about 6 m below the beach surface at this elevation (1 m), which equals the maximum depth of core Gelilot 4. Therefore, at any reasonable stream gradient, a water depth of 1 or 2 m would have existed in the ancestral Gelilot channel some 100 m or so seaward of the present channel mouth. This area would have been the most likely natural anchorage for the MB IIB settlement at Tel Michal.

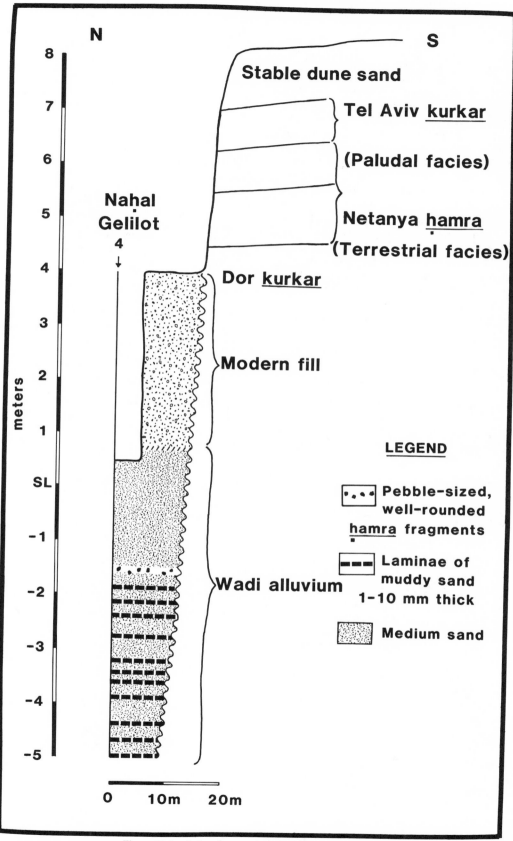

Figure 17.2. Subsurface stratigraphy from core Gelilot 4.

207

17.4. DISCUSSION

Because neither the Tel Michal-Naḥal Gelilot nor the Tel Poleg coastline contains *kurkar* bedrock outcrops, it was not possible to identify definitively any sea-level stands higher than modern sea level. Archaeological evidence for a high stand of + 1 m at 1500 years B.P. has been reported recently from the site of Dor, 13 km north of Caesarea (Sneh and Klein 1984). These authors also describe both geomorphologic and archaeological evidence from Dor for a low stand of − 1 m centered at 800 years B.P. However, their dating of the archaeological installations is very general, and none of their data points for the last 4,000 years are based on a radiocarbon date. Although our evidence from Tel Michal and Tel Poleg is ambiguous concerning historical-period high and/or low sea-level stands, we believe that the probability of large-scale, fault-controlled vertical movements of the central Sharon coast during this period is minimal. Recently Oleson et al. (1984:283, n. 4) have suggested that the conspicuous major subsidence of Roman breakwaters of the Sebastos harbor at Caesarea may be attributable not to neotectonism but rather to simple sediment failure through liquefaction.

REFERENCES

Avnimelech, M. 1962. The Main Trends in the Pleistocene-Holocene History of the Israelian Coastal Plain. *Quaternaria* 6:479–495.

Bakler, N. 1976. *Calcareous Sandstones and Sands of the Israel Mediterranean Offshore Aggregate Reserves.* U.N. Development Program/GSI Offshore Dredging Project, Summary Report. Geological Survey of Israel. Tel Aviv.

Flemming, N. C., Raban, A., and Goetschel, C. 1978. Tectonic and Eustatic Changes on the Mediterranean Coast of Israel in the Last 9000 Years. Pages 33–94 in: *Progress in Underwater Science*, vol. 3. J. C. Gamble and R. A. Yorke, eds. London.

Gophna, R., and Ayalon, E. 1980. Survey of the Central Coastal Plain, 1978–1979: Settlement Pattern of the Middle Bronze Age IIA. *Tel Aviv* 7:147–151.

Hall, J. K., and Bakler, N. 1975. *Detailed Bathymetric and Shallow Seismic Surveys at Five Locations along the Mediterranean Coast of Israel.* U.N. Development Program/GSI Offshore Dredging Project, Report No. 1. Geological Survey of Israel. Tel Aviv.

Horowitz, A. 1979. *The Quaternary of Israel.* New York.

Karmon, Y. 1956. Geographical Aspects in the History of the Coastal Plain of Israel. *IEJ* 6:33–50.

Klein, J., Lerman, J. C., Damon, P. E., and Ralph, E. K. 1982. Calibration of Radiocarbon Dates. *Radiocarbon* 24:103–150.

Kraft, J. C., Aschenbrenner, S. E., and Rapp, G., Jr. 1977. Paleogeographic Reconstructions of Coastal Aegean Archaeological Sites. *Science* 195:941–947.

Kraft, J. C., Kayan, I., and Erol, O. 1982. Geology and Paleogeographic Reconstructions of the Vicinity of Troy. Pages 11–41 in: *Troy: The Archaeological Geology.* G. Rapp, Jr., and J. A. Gifford, eds. Princeton, N.J.

Neev, D., Bakler, N., Moshkovitz, S., Kaufman, A., Magaritz, M., and Gophna, R. 1973. Recent Faulting along the Mediterranean Coast of Israel. *Nature* 245:254–256.

Neev, D., Shachnai, E., Hall, J. K., Bakler, N., and Ben-Avraham, Z. 1978. The Young (Post Lower Pliocene) Geological History of the Caesarea Structure. *Isr. J. Earth* 27:43–64.

Oleson, J. P., Hohlfelder, R. L., Raban, A., and Vann, R. L. 1984. The Caesarea Ancient Harbor Excavation Project (C.A.H.E.P.): Preliminary Report on the 1980–1983 Seasons. *JFA* 11:281–306.

Raban, A. 1981. Recent Maritime Archaeological Research in Israel. *International Journal of Nautical Archaeology* 10:287–308.

Ronen, A. 1980. The Origin of the Raised Pelecypod Beds along the Mediterranean Coast of Israel. *Palaeorient* 6:165–172.

Smith, G. A. 1895. *The Historical Geography of the Holy Land.* London.

Sneh, Y., and Klein, M. 1984. Holocene Sea Level Changes at the Coast of Dor, Southeast Mediterranean. *Science* 226:830–831.

Wreschner, E. E. 1983. The Submerged Neolithic Village 'Newe Yam' on the Israeli Mediterranean Coast. Pages 325–334 in: *Quaternary Coastlines and Marine Archaeology.* P. M. Masters and N. C. Flemming, eds. New York.

18

Site Geology

by John A. Gifford, George Rapp, Jr., and Christopher L. Hill

Archaeological survey and excavation in the coastal plain of Israel depend to a great degree on understanding the recent geologic history of the region. Little bedrock crops out along the coastal plains, and even that is relatively friable. Microenvironments of erosion, deposition, and soil formation produce a complex mosaic of sedimentary units despite the generally subdued areal topography.

In this chapter we summarize our observations on the geologic aspects of Tel Michal and its immediate surroundings as an aid to understanding some of the natural and artificial phenomena that are recorded in the archaeological record of the site.

18.1. NATURAL ENVIRONMENT OF TEL MICHAL

The high tell is a promenance on the westernmost of a series of three to four subparallel rock ridges that extend along and inland of the present shore zone. Such elongated ridges (and their intervening swales) are physiographic elements characteristic of the entire coastal zone of Israel. In the central (Sharon) coastal plain, the westernmost ridge forms a discontinuous sea cliff rising to 40 m or more above present sea level. The Geologic Map of Israel (northern sheet, scale 1:250,000) identifies these as "*kurkar* ridges of the Upper Pleistocene Era."

The *kurkar* ridges are fossil dune deposits (eolianites) cemented by the ubiquitous mineral calcium carbonate. Generally, the sediment of the ridges is a poorly consolidated, medium-to-fine sand, white to buff or gray in color. Filling the swales between these ridges (and, in the case of the westernmost ridge, interstratified therein) is the other basic sediment type of the coastal plains—a sandy loam of various shades of red, locally termed *ḥamra*. (According to the U.S. Department of Agriculture Soil Taxonomy System, most *ḥamras* would be classified as calcic rhodo-Xeralfs.) In the historical and prehistoric past, both sediments represented major sources of building materials, as discussed below (Section 18.3).

The coast of Israel has been a transport route for Nile River sediments moving northward under the influence of predominant winds and currents (Emery and Neev 1960). The longest-period waves impinge upon the coastline out of the west (280 degrees), which is the greatest possible fetch direction, and longshore currents generally set to the northeast. Locally the current direction may be reversed close inshore, with sufficient velocity to transport fine sand. Along the Sharon coast, sand beaches are uniformly narrow (less than 100 m) and low angled, without well-defined berms and backbeach zones. Thus high-energy winter storm waves easily reach and undercut the friable *kurkar* foundations of the coastal ridge, producing vertical sea cliffs up to 10 m high. Such a cliff exists at the base of the highest promenance of the Tel Michal site. The modern beach sediment, as shown by Sample 7 (Table 18.1), consists of a poorly sorted medium sand.

Wind directions measured at Tel Aviv from 1940 to 1947 show that the predominant wind is out of the west (41.4 percent), with greater than 10 percent at force 6–7. The second most common winds come from the southwest (39.8 percent), with greater than 10 percent at force 6 (Yaalon and Laronne 1971). These strongest winds occur between January and April. Along the coast of Israel, the prevailing winds are also the dominant ones.

Dominant west winds of force 6 and greater presently transport sand from the beaches over the coastal *kurkar* ridges and up to a kilometer inland (as at Ziqim and Hadera), forming a discontinuous sand blanket inland from the present shore. East of Tel Michal these dunes have an average relief (where undisturbed) of 3–4 m from crest to blowout floor; they are typically semistabilized by the *Artemesia monosperma* and *Cyperus mucronatus* plant association (Zohary 1962:117), a *batha* community of the coastal zone characterized by the dominance of psammophytes (Fig. 18.1). On flatter areas of the coastal ridge with less sand cover, the vegetation is a *Poterium spinosum* and *Thymelaea hirsuta* association. Along the steep west slopes of the high tell and the ridgetops to the north and south, the association is *Sporobolus* and *Lotus*.

Table 18.1. Basic Grain-Size Parameters of Tel Michal Sediment Samples

Sample	Description	M_Z[a]	σ_I	Sk_I	K_G	Sand (%)	Silt (%)	Clay (%)
	Ḥadera Dune Samples							
1	From E slope of high tell	2.47	0.81	0.63	3.26	86.8	8.8	4.4
1A	Sandpit 300 m E of high tell, top of section	2.45	1.14	0.62	5.61	89.5	6.0	4.5
1B	Area C, Locus 129, Reg. No. 893: "white sand"	2.50	0.60	0.56	1.75	92.4	5.8	1.8
1C	Area C, Locus 129, Reg. No. 894: "NW bottom sand"	2.70	1.78	0.75	4.90	86.5	6.8	6.7
1D	Sandpit 300 m E of high tell, layer 1, "Upper Dunes"	2.10	0.44	-0.21	1.48	97.9	1.6	0.5
1E	Area C, Locus 129, Reg. No. 891	2.38	0.37	0.38	1.48	98.5	1.5	0
	Tel Aviv **Kurkar** *samples*							
2	Naḥal Gelilot, S bank, Section 78/1	2.27	1.93	0.22	5.65	92.9	0.6	6.5
2A	High tell, Area A: below LB wall	2.22	0.64	0.15	1.46	95.1	1.4	3.5
2B	High tell, Area A: thin stratum with MB IIB sherds	2.22	1.52	0.37	3.94	92.4	1.8	5.8
2C	High tell, W slope: red-brown sand below MB IIB ash	2.34	0.92	0.31	2.29	92.5	3.8	3.7
2D	400 m SE of high tell: sand containing PN artifacts	2.28	1.35	0.44	4.24	92.3	1.3	6.4
2E	Sandpit 300 m E of high tell, layer 3, unit above base of section	2.18	0.47	-0.05	1.10	98.1	1.1	0.8
2F	High tell, sand fill of Rampart 1701	2.12	0.52	-0.08	1.08	97.9	0.9	1.2
2G	High tell, sand layer of Rampart 1722	2.32	0.46	-0.05	1.08	99.1	0.9	0
2H	High tell, Area A, Locus 1767, Reg. No. 10993: sand fill in ḥamra quarry	2.29	0.50	-0.02	1.12	96.6	1.5	1.9
	Dor **Kurkar**							
3	High tell, SW flank, Section 77/1	2.33	0.44	0.20	2.00	96.9	2.6	0.5
3A	Hillock S of high tell, friable *kurkar*	2.36	0.38	0.18	1.69	98.5	1.2	0.3
	Netanya **Ḥamra**							
4	Bulldozed pit 400 m E of high tell, above Dor *kurkar*	3.25	2.28	0.69	6.60	80.3	7.2	12.5
4A	Area D, bottom of deep test pit	5.37	3.83	0.86	1.05	64.9	10.3	24.8
4B	High tell, SW flank, Section 78/2	5.13	3.75	0.82	1.87	67.5	14.3	18.2
4C	Area C, Locus 130, Reg. No. 899: bottom sand	5.16	3.76	0.84	1.78	69.2	9.0	21.8
4D	Area C, Locus 129, Reg. No. 895: upper sand	2.47	0.40	-0.09	0.95	98.3	1.7	0
4E	Area C, Locus 302, Reg. No. 1005: hard-packed gray floor	3.23	2.20	0.69	4.10	79.6	6.9	13.5
4F	Hillock S of high tell, N slope, Section 79/1	5.63	4.09	0.84	0.57	56.1	14.9	29.0
4G	Hillock S of high tell, N slope, Section 77/1	5.61	3.99	0.79	0.60	56.5	14.5	29.1
4H	Area C, Locus 130, Reg. No. 996: brick debris	5.45	4.02	0.87	0.59	61.5	10.3	28.2
4I	Area D, Square G16, bottom of test pit	5.28	3.87	0.89	1.23	65.0	10.4	24.6
	Naḥsholim **Ḥamra**							
5	Hillock S of high tell, W slope, Section 79/1	2.96	1.58	0.57	6.95	87.1	6.6	6.3
5A	Hillock S of high tell, W slope, Section 79/1	3.04	1.72	0.64	5.99	85.1	6.5	8.4
	Ramat Gan **Kurkar**							
6	High tell, beach cliff, uncemented stratum	3.12	0.61	0.36	1.63	86.3	9.7	4.0
	Modern Beach							
7	Swash zone W of high tell	2.40	1.58	0.57	7.49	90.7	0.5	8.8

[a] M_Z = graphic mean, σ_I = graphic standard deviation, Sk_I = inclusive graphic skewness, and K_G = graphic kurtosis.

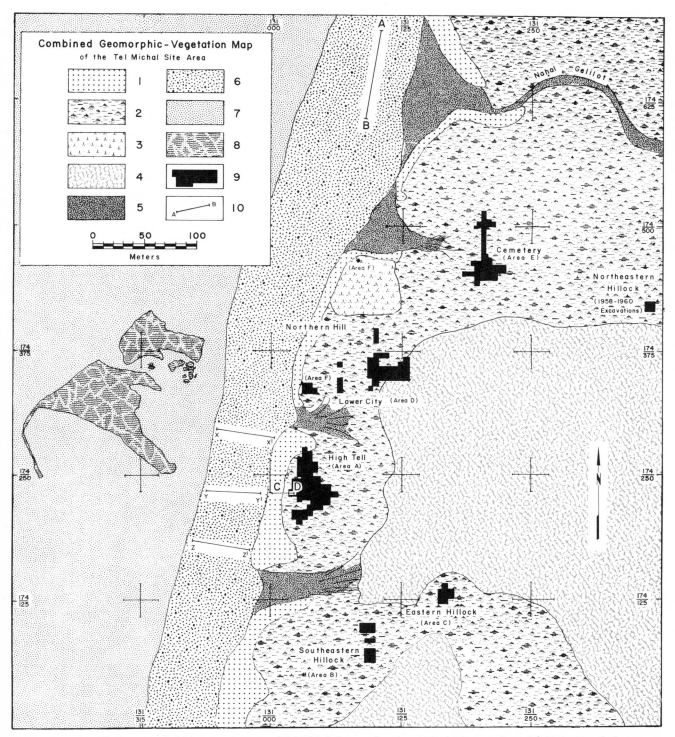

Figure 18.1. Combined geomorphologic-vegetation map of Tel Michal site area, based on 1948 air photography and field checking during excavation period (1977–80). Legend: (1) actively eroding coastal scarp slopes with little or no sediment cover, sparse vegetation cover of *Sporobolus-Lotus* association; (2) low angle slopes (less than 10 degrees) with Hadera dune sand cover of 0.2- to 0-m thickness and the *Artemesia-Cyperus* plant association; (3) flat ridge crest with sediment cover less than 0.2 m thick and a *Poterium-Thymelaea* association; (4) inland Hadera dune field with sand thickness greater than 2 m, *Artemesia-Cyperus* plant association; (5) alluvial and colluvial sands of slope-wash channels and of Nahal Gelilot, transported to beach during winter rains; (6) low-angle beach; (7) nearshore (less than 2 m deep) medium sand cover; (8) rock substrate of fossil *Vermetus* reef protruding through sand cover; (9) excavation areas; and (10) transect and cross section locations: probe transect perpendicular to Nahal Gelilot (A-B), cross section on high tell (C-D) (see Fig. 18.3), and three transects perpendicular to cliff face of high tell (X-X', Y-Y', Z-Z').

Before extensive commercial development along the Israel coastal zone (beginning around 1948), a small wadi (el-Gharbi) drained the swale inland of Tel Michal (or Makmish); it emptied into the Mediterranean immediately north of the flat ridgetop containing excavation areas D and E (Fig. 18.1). Now the ephemeral winter discharge of this drainage (renamed Naḥal Gelilot) has been channeled in a subsurface culvert and the wadi bed itself has been graded and straightened to provide vehicular access to the beach. It appears that the premodern wadi bed followed an artificial channel cut in Roman (or earlier) times to drain both the swale east of the coastal ridge and the one east of the next kurkar ridge inland. In antiquity, low interridge areas were often either artificially drained for agriculture or dammed (as at Zikhron Ya'aqov) for mariculture or salt pans (Rim 1950).

Winds play the dominant role in controlling patterns of erosion (deflation) and deposition (dune formation) on the sand blanket inland from Tel Michal, but there is also localized erosion by running water on and around the coastal kurkar ridge, where base level is the Mediterranean. Light to moderate rains falling on the thicker sand deposits (greater than 20 cm or so) are probably absorbed with little or no erosive effect. Heavy or prolonged winter rains engender sheet wash of sand, which is diverted around the north and south ends of the high tell to produce ephemeral shallow, braided channels. In this way, significant quantities of sand are transferred westward to the backbeach zone, though some of this redeposited sand is subsequently remobilized by the west wind and returned to the inland sand blanket, known as the Hadera dune bed. There is probably a net addition of sand, with constant reworking of the blanket to several meters in depth. Along the western slopes of the kurkar ridge (the high tell and ridgetops to the north and south), no permanent sand cover exists; unconsolidated to semiconsolidated archaeological and geologic strata there are subject to net erosion (by sheet flow and rill formation, as well as by wave undercutting of the basal kurkar unit) and mass movement (soil creep and microslumping) of the upper strata (discussed below). On the high tell, the western slope angle was measured as 40 degrees above the kurkar cliff, somewhat steeper than average natural slopes in semiarid climates (Ritter 1978:165). Slope evolution may take place through parallel retreat if the unconsolidated sedimentary units are homogeneous throughout the interior of the high tell.

Some observations concerning the nature of mass movement on the west slope of the high tell were made possible by the stepped stratigraphic trench (Fig. 4.3; Pl. 5), of which the lowest locus (929, at 19.8 m above sea level or 10.2 m below datum) rests on natural undisturbed Dor kurkar overlying Ramat Gan kurkar. In the south face of the stepped trench (Plate 81), it appears that erosion begins within the strata—about 1.5 m in from the slope surface—by stepped microslumping along high-angle (70–90 degree) planar slip surfaces. This slumping initiates soil creep downslope to maintain equilibrium with the back-eroding, vertical kurkar cliff at the west base of the tell. A second ero-sional process operates simultaneously on the outermost 30–40 cm of slope sediments: this material is homogenized by root action, shrinkage/swelling, and slope wash to produce a characteristic mixed zone (Locus 906). Implications of all these long-term erosional phenomena for the evolution of the high tell will be considered below.

A series of three east-west probing transects (X-X', Y-Y', and Z-Z') across the width of the beach west of the high tell (see Fig. 18.1 for location) showed a maximum of 1.8–2.0 m of sand at the kurkar cliff foot, thinning to 0.5–1.0 m at the swash zone 40 m away. Allowing for the average beach slope of 1° 40', these transects indicate that a subhorizontal wave-cut platform exists on the Ramat Gan kurkar. The platform also underlies the mouth of the sand-filled gulley immediately south of the high tell, confirming that this feature has not eroded bedrock below the present base level and is therefore of recent origin.

Beneath the modern beach at the mouth of Naḥal Gelilot, however, a probing transect (A-B) revealed a buried channel cut to approximately 6 m below the backbeach surface (for details of the subsurface stratigraphy of Naḥal Gelilot, see Fig. 17.1). This channel has no surface expression in the sandy nearshore zone.

Northwest of the high tell and the northern hill, a sinuous line curving out from the swash zone marks the eroded seaward trace of the kurkar ridge's bedrock foundation. Between this line and the beach, a discontinuous, irregular area of hard bottom projects through the sand cover. The hard bottom represents a dead vermetid gastropod (Dendropoma pretraeum) reef, its surface now about 1.5 m below sea level. Since the upward growth of D. pretraeum is limited by mean sea level (Safriel 1974), and radiocarbon analysis of a whole-rock sample of the reef surface shows it to be 495 ± 70 years old (UCR-11249), some local subsidence in this vicinity is indicated for the historical past. As demonstrated by underwater sampling of its core, the Dendropoma reef off Tel Michal developed on a hard substrate of Ramat Gan kurkar.

Roughly 500 m farther offshore, air photos show another kurkar ridge in 7 m of water (N. Bakler, personal communication). There probably exists an interridge swale (locally termed a marzeva) between the present shoreline and this submerged ridge, as is the case off Tel Barukh, 2 km south of Tel Michal (Bakler 1976:24; Hall and Bakler 1975).

18.2. SEDIMENTARY UNITS OF TEL MICHAL

All of the geologic units underlying and surrounding Tel Michal date to the Late Quaternary (Pleistocene and Holocene) epoch and have been assigned most recently (Horowitz 1979:113) to the Ruhama Loess member of the Gaza formation. Ronen (1983) presents a more detailed composite section of coastal ridge stratigraphy in the Sharon plain, comprising 10 sedimentary cycles of kurkar-hamra development that subsume the eight units identified by Horowitz and by Bakler (Bakler 1976:132). In the following subsec-

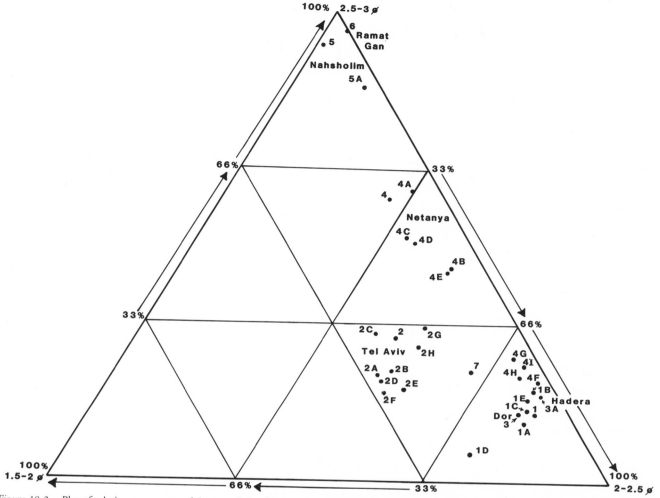

Figure 18.2. Plot of relative percentages of three sand-size fractions from Tel Michal sediment samples. All samples are identified and characterized more completely in Table 18.1. Hadera dune sand and Dor *kurkar* samples are predominantly composed of grains in 2–2.5 φ size fraction, whereas Nahsholim and Ramat Gan sediments are relatively finer, and Netanya *ḥamra* samples are intermediate.

tions, descriptions and interpretations are presented of all units identified in exposures of the coastal cliffs, in the Nahal Gelilot channel, in commercial sand pits dug east and southeast of Tel Michal, and in the soundings of the excavation itself. The description proceeds in stratigraphic order from the lowest (oldest) unit upward.

18.2.1. Ramat Gan *Kurkar*

The basal eolianite of the coastal ridge, this friable, quartz-rich calcareous sandstone is well exposed in a 3- to 4-m-high vertical scarp at the western base of the high tell. The exposure reveals typical low-angled (0–30 degrees), undulating eolian cross-bedding sets that represent vertical sand accretion beneath a vegetative cover (Yaalon and Laronne 1971). This unit is thickest under the northern hill, thinning out southward as it passes beneath the high tell; it probably continues below the present beach surface in front

of the hillock immediately to the south.

Several theories have been proposed for the lithification of *kurkar* (e.g., Yaalon 1967), but none adequately explains the commonly observed rhythmic alteration of friably cemented strata with completely uncemented ones. Grain-size analysis of a pure sample of unconsolidated Ramat Gan sediment shows it to be a moderately sorted muddy fine sand with a graphic mean of 3.1 φ.[1]

Most of the information that allows the granulometric characterization of sedimentary units from Tel Michal is contained in the weight percentages of the 1.5–2 φ, 2–2.5 φ, and 2.5–3 φ size fractions relative to one another. A ternary plot of the percentages of these three size fractions for a number of samples (Fig. 18.2) separates them into well-defined fields. The Ramat Gan sediment (Sample 6) is the finest of all those plotted, and it acts as a fine-grained diluent to modern beach sand when cliff erosion introduces it into the shore zone (Fig. 18.2, Sample 7).

18.2.2. Naḥsholim *Ḥamra*

This sandy loam crops out in the vicinity of Tel Michal only on the seaward slope of the hillock south of the high tell. The 1.5–3 φ size fractions of two samples of this unit are comparable in their mineralogy and proportions to the Ramat Gan sediment, suggesting its derivation from the latter by addition of silt-clay size fractions. An eolian transport mechanism for these fine fractions in Israel's *ḥamras* is likely, since there are insufficient aluminosilicates in the *kurkar* sands to weather into an iron-rich fine fraction (Farrand and Ronen 1974). At issue is the source area for the fines – either the Negev (Karmeli et al. 1968) or the exposed Mediterranean continental shelf during the last pleniglacial (Ronen 1983). The latter seems more probable in light of the prevailing winds, and the similarity of coastal plain *ḥamra* clay mineralogy (Singer and Shachnai 1969) to that of the western Nile Delta sediments (Weir et al. 1975) supports this provenance.

18.2.3. Dor *Kurkar*

A section of this unit 3 m thick is exposed on the southwest downslope of the high tell and at the bottom of the deep test trench of Area D on the northern hill. It is a well-sorted, unconsolidated sand with a dry color of 7.5 YR 5/6 (strong brown), often showing rhizoconcretions. About 95 percent of the 1.5–3 φ size fraction consists of subround to round quartz grains (the more round are also polished), all slightly stained by iron oxide. Four percent of these size fractions comprises rounded and polished biogenic carbonate grains, and the remaining 1 percent comprises rounded and polished, dark sedimentary rock fragments. The 1.5–3 φ size fractions of two Dor *kurkar* samples are plotted in Figure 18.2. They show a distribution very similar to that of the Ḥadera dune samples (Section 18.2.6).

18.2.4. Netanya *Ḥamra*

This is the best developed of the several rhodo-Xeralf units of the coastal ridge. Farrand and Ronen (1974), in their reconstruction of the geologic history of the Carmel coastal plain, state that the correlative Netanya unit there began to form during the maximum regression of the last glacial (ca. 18,000 years B.P.); Epipaleolithic (17,000–11,000 years B.P.) stone tools are often found within this unit all along the Israeli coast. Ronen (1983) identifies the source of the iron-rich silt-clay fraction of *ḥamras* in general as the fine-grained continental shelf sediments below 35 m.

Both terrestrial (containing oxidized iron minerals) and paludal (with reduced iron) facies of the Netanya *ḥamra* crop out in natural and artificial exposures around Tel Michal. Several samples (4–4I) from geologic and archaeological contexts are plotted in Figure 18.2. Their 1.5–3 φ size fractions are intermediate between the fine Ramat Gan and Naḥsholim sediments on the one hand and the coarser Dor sands on the other, suggesting that the Netanya sand fractions may be a mixture of these two sources through redeposition.

18.2.5. Tel Aviv *Kurkar*

This unit is of limited distribution around Tel Michal, with a maximum observed thickness of about 2 m along the course of the Naḥal Gelilot; it quickly thins and intermixes with the underlying Netanya *ḥamra* to the east and south of the tell.

Tel Aviv *kurkar* is unique in its high percentage of biogenic carbonate grains: 51 percent of the 1.5–2 φ fractions of samples from Naḥal Gelilot is composed of cemented fecal pellets, micromollusc shell fragments, worn echinoid spines, polished *Halimeda* plates, foraminifera tests, and bryozoan fragments, all indicating derivation from a hard-bottom community in nearby shallow marine water. The balance of these samples comprises subround to round and polished quartz grains lacking any iron oxide coating, which explains the relatively light color of this unit in exposures. Grain-size analysis shows the Tel Aviv *kurkar* to be a poorly sorted sand with a graphic mean of about 2.3 φ (Table 18.1). The more common large carbonate grains in the 1.5–2 φ fraction account for its coarseness relative to the sand fractions of the other units (Fig. 18.2).

Horowitz (1979) states that the Tel Aviv *kurkar* was deposited during a stillstand of the Versillian Transgression that was 2–3 m higher than present sea level, and Bakler et al. (1972) also conclude that this unit represents a shallow marine deposit. But Ronen (1983) places it with all the other terrestrial (continental) deposits of the coastal plain, and we concur with this identification. The unit as exposed along Naḥal Gelilot (Plate 82) shows low-angle eolian cross-bedding, exhibits rhizoconcretions penetrating the underlying Netanya *ḥamra*, and also contains infilled insect burrows and snail shells, 90 percent of which are the land species *Xeropicta vestalis* (Heller and Tchernov 1978).

Ronen (1983) obtained six radiocarbon dates on this unit (his No. 4); they equal an average age of 6,135 ± 41 years B.P. (5568 half-life), or 5,290–4,915 calendric years B.P. using the correction tables of Klein et al. (1982).

To the east of Tel Michal, the Tel Aviv *kurkar* grades laterally into a calcarenitic *ḥamra*. Within this facies, a bulldozed area 400 m southeast of the high tell revealed an in situ deposit of worked stone and pottery fragments: flint scrapers, one coarsely denticulated sickle blade, one small winged arrowhead, retouched flint flakes and debitage, and friable fragments of a coarse-ware vessel. The arrowhead and pottery were dated to the Pottery Neolithic (PN) by E. Ayalon (Museum Haaretz).

18.2.6. Ḥadera Dune Bed

Deposition of this unit has occurred from the cessation of the influx of carbonate-rich Tel Aviv sediment in post-Pottery Neolithic time up to the present, since it represents the constant eolian transport of Mediterranean beach sand eastward. Human activities of construction, agriculture, and herding during the occupation of Tel Michal modified this unstable sand surface on a small scale, but natural erosion and dune movement have more effectively homogenized the archaeological stratigraphy over the past

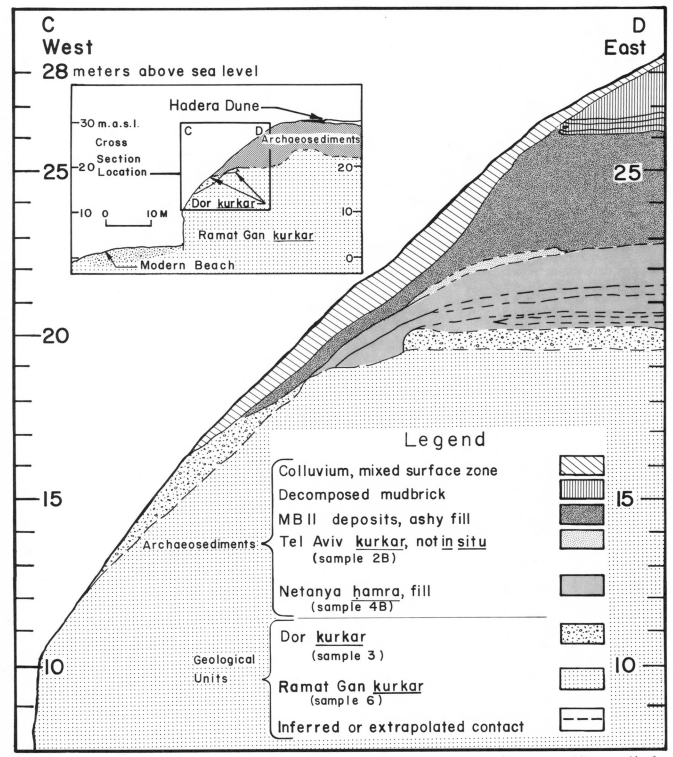

Figure 18.3. Schematic east-west cross section illustrating stratigraphic relationships of geologic and archaeosedimentary materials on west side of high tell (see Fig. 18.1, section C–D). Representative samples (see Table 18.1) of stratigraphic sequence are indicated in legend. Ramat Gan *kurkar* is oldest unit in the sequence. Sediments representative of Naḥsholim *ḥamra* were observed only on western slope of hillock to south of high tell and are not shown in this diagrammatic stratigraphic section.

Remaining units are archaeosediments or reworked (not in situ) geologic deposits. Netanya *ḥamra* is represented as fill. Tel Aviv *kurkar* was observed on high tell as thin, reworked stratum associated with MB materials. Other archaeosediments on high tell include MB II ashy fill, decomposed mudbrick, and mixed zone of colluvium on surface of tell. Inset diagram shows location of section C–D.

two millennia. The net process here is considered to be one of deposition.

The 2–2.5 φ size fraction of a sample from the base of a 4-m-high sandpit scarp 300 m east of the high tell shows about 70 percent subangular to subround quartz grains (the rounded grains with more surface frosting), with the remaining 30 percent a biogenic carbonate composed of fecal pellets, *Halimeda* plates, foraminifera, and shell fragments. The biogenic fraction decreases upsection, reaching 5–10 percent at the modern surface.

Almost all the Iron Age, Persian, and Hellenistic features and artifacts at Tel Michal are buried under 0.5–2 m of Ḥadera dune sand. During the 1st millennium B.C.E., structures were built on (or in) this sediment and provisions were made to stabilize the sand surfaces around them by means of artificially laid *ḥamra* coatings. Postoccupation erosional and depositional processes have mixed the stratigraphy on the northern hill and eastern hillocks so that excavated artifacts of different periods often were found "floating" at the same level in the Ḥadera dune sand. There is probably almost no original stratigraphy in these areas, except perhaps beneath undisturbed features.

18.3. CONSTRUCTION MATERIALS (ARCHAEOSEDIMENTS)

The geologic materials at Tel Michal were used by occupants of the site for construction purposes and appear in the stratigraphic record as archaeosediments. On the high tell, leveling platforms composed of Netanya *ḥamra* and Tel Aviv *kurkar* sand were constructed during the Middle Bronze Age. On these *ḥamra* and sand fills, occupants erected walls of *ḥamra* or of Ramat Gan *kurkar* cobbles and small boulders collected from the beach. At the northern end of the high tell, a Middle Bronze Age *ḥamra* wall 3.4 m high was found to rest on alternating layers of *ḥamra* and sand fill. In the stratigraphic trench on the western slope, the leveling platforms were observed to lie directly on a thin, incipiently developed stratum of Netanya *ḥamra*, at an elevation 18 m above sea level (12 m below datum). Figure 18.3, which illustrates the relationships of geologic and archaeosedimentary units on the high tell, represents Netanya *ḥamra* as a fill resting above the Ramat Gan *kurkar* and the Dor *kurkar*. Other archaeosedimentary deposits on the high tell include Tel Aviv *kurkar*, ashy fill, decomposed mudbricks, and a mixed surface zone (Fig. 18.3). Occupation debris (mostly ash) and rebuilding in later phases contributed to net accretion on the high tell while these construction materials (particularly the *kurkar* building stones) were constantly reused. Tel Aviv *kurkar* sands appear to be confined to the Middle Bronze Age strata and are replaced by Ḥadera sands in the Late Bronze Age and subsequent layers; this suggests that the Tel Aviv sands were still common surface sediments until the mid-2d millennium B.C.E. However, in the Persian period cemetery (Area E), tombs were cut into the Tel Aviv *kurkar* unit and were built up of Ramat Gan *kurkar* blocks and occasionally of Netanya

ḥamra mudbricks; the whole area eventually was buried underneath the Ḥadera dune sand (Plate 83). There has doubtless been a continuous overturning of the unstable Ḥadera dune sand covering Area E and the other outlying areas during the past 2,500 years.

Sample 4H (Fig. 18.2) illustrates the correlation of mudbrick sediment from Persian period strata with outcrop samples of the Netanya *ḥamra* from immediately south of the high tell.

Besides consolidated and unconsolidated natural sediments, another common inorganic building material utilized at Tel Michal was artificial lime plaster. Microscopic examination of several Persian period lime-plaster samples often showed fragments of partly burned marine mollusc shells (?*Glycymeris*), plus some bone fragments. Beach shells and large mammal bones were calcined and slaked to produce the plaster.

18.4. ACCRETION AND EROSION OF THE HIGH TELL

At the midpoint of the west slope of the high tell, *kurkar* bedrock was reached at 18 m above mean sea level. On the downslope at the northern end, this same contact exists at about 15 m above mean sea level; on the downslope of the southern end, it exists about 16 m above mean sea level. Thus the MB IIB *ḥamra* platform was centered on a preexisting high point of the coastal ridge (Fig. 18.4). This core of Ramat Gan *kurkar* already had been significantly eroded on the west by sea-level transgression and wave abrasion. However, it is not unlikely that in the mid-2d millennium B.C.E. the vertical backbeach cliff was still some 20 m west of its present position, or about half the width of the modern beach. Since then, far less erosion has occurred on the north and south flanks of the high tell, and least of all on the eastern slope.

Vertical and horizontal accretion of the original Middle Bronze Age platform on the high tell very likely proceeded in pulses of artificial sediment deposition from destruction and rebuilding events superimposed on a continuous addition of some beach sand by eolian transport. At the same time, erosion of the western slope probably always pressed later construction eastward, down the more gentle and weather-protected landward slope. Most of the coarsest stone building material—cobbles and small boulders of *kurkar*—would have remained near the high tell crest as recycled wall blocks, whereas sand and finer-size sediments would have been continually lost, necessitating frequent replacement. With the end of occupation on the high tell in the 8th century of this era, artificial addition of sediment ceased there, as did vertical and horizontal growth of the tell, so that erosion of the west slope by natural processes emerged as the dominant ongoing geologic process.[2]

Figure 18.4 is a schematic east-west cross section through the high tell that attempts to summarize the evolution of its deposits from the first habitation in the Middle Bronze Age up to the present.

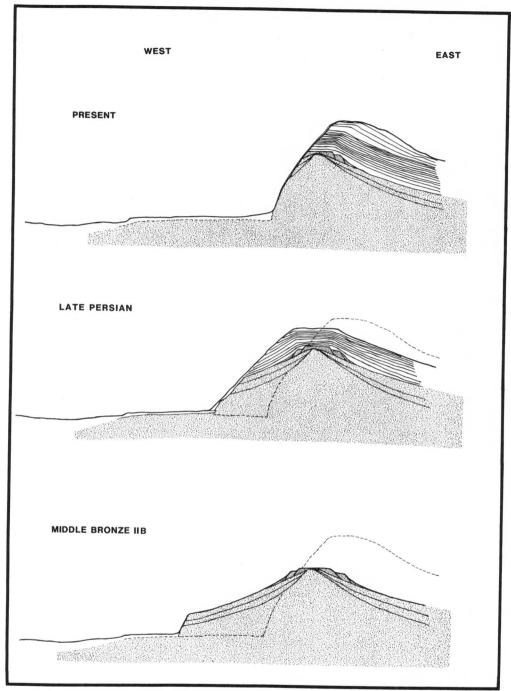

Figure 18.4. East-West diagrammatic cross section through high tell at about position of stratigraphic trench on western slope. Three stages in evolution of high tell are schematically portrayed, based on geologic and archaeological data. In Middle Bronze IIB, artificial platforms were built on ridge crest of Ramat Gan *kurkar* bedrock covered by strata of Dor *kurkar* and Netanya *ḥamra*. West slope of tell extended some 20 m farther toward shore than at present. By (approximately) Late Persian period, continued Late Bronze Age, Iron Age, and Persian occupations had extended cultural strata upward and outward, while shore processes continued to erode west slope. Upper surface of high tell may have achieved its maximum areal extent at this time. Since abandonment of high tell, erosion has predominated and continues to undercut and bring down sediments of both natural and cultural strata. Modern-day outline profile of high tell is shown as dashed line.)

NOTES

1. The data obtained from grain-size analysis may be presented in several different ways. Here, the phi scale (φ) is used for diameters of sediment grains; it has significant computational advantages over a simple expression in micrometers of the diameter. Important size-class boundaries in this scale are from -1 to $+4\ \varphi$ (the sand size range), from $+4$ to $+8\ \varphi$ (the silt size range), and from $+8$ to $+14\ \varphi$ (the clay size range).

Descriptive statistical parameters (measures of average grain size, uniformity of grain size, asymmetry, and peakedness of the grain-size distribution) here follow the formulae of Folk (1974), which are standard for most American sedimentologic analyses. However, instead of presenting the usual graphics of histograms or cumulative distribution curves, Figure 18.2 only plots the relative percentages of three size fractions (1.5–$2\ \varphi$, 2–$2.5\ \varphi$, and 2.5–$3\ \varphi$) in the medium- to fine-sand range that most characterize each of the different sedimentary units around Tel Michal. All of the grain-size statistics for each sample are presented in Table 18.1.

2. For a detailed stratigraphic description of construction and destruction processes during the Middle and Late Bronze Ages, see Chap. 4. Tectonic activities are considered by the author of Chap. 4 as one of the major forces that caused the drastic changes in the topography of the tell.

REFERENCES

Bakler, N. 1976. *Calcareous Sandstones and Sands of the Israel Mediterranean Offshore Aggregate Reserves*. U.N. Development Program/GSI Offshore Dredging Project, Summary Report. Geological Survey of Israel. Tel Aviv.

Bakler, N., Denekamp, S., and Rohrlich, V. 1972. Sandy Units in the Coastal Plain of Israel: Environmental Interpretation Using Statistical Analysis of Grain-Size Data. *Isr. J. Earth* 21:155–178.

Emery, K. O., and Neev, D. 1960. Mediterranean Beaches of Israel. *Bulletin of the Geological Survey of Israel* 26:1–22.

Farrand, W. R., and Ronen, A. 1974. Observations on the Kurkar-Hamra Succession on the Carmel Coastal Plain. *Tel Aviv* 1:45–54.

Folk, R. L. 1974. *Petrology of Sedimentary Rocks*. Austin, Tex.

Geological Survey of Israel. 1975. Geological Map, Northern Sheet (1:250,000). Jerusalem.

Hall, J. K., and Bakler, N. 1975. *Detailed Bathymetric and Shallow Seismic Surveys at Five Locations along the Mediterranean Coast of Israel*. U.N. Development Program/GSI Offshore Dredging Project, Report No. 1. Geological Survey of Israel. Tel Aviv.

Heller, J., and Tchernov, E. 1978. Pleistocene Landsnails from the Coastal Plain of Israel. *Isr. J. Zool.* 27:1–10.

Horowitz, A. 1979. *The Quaternary of Israel*. New York.

Karmeli, D., Yaalon, D. H., and Ravina, I. 1968. Dune Cycles and Soil Stratigraphy in the Quaternary Sedimentary Cycles of the Sharon Coastal Plain. *Isr. J. Earth* 17:45–53.

Klein, J., Lerman, J. C., Damon, P. E., and Ralph, E. K. 1982. Calibration of Radiocarbon Dates. *Radiocarbon* 24:103–150.

Rim, M. 1950. Sand and Soil in the Coastal Plain of Israel. *IEJ* 1:33–48.

Ritter, D. F. 1978. *Process Geomorphology*. Dubuque, Iowa.

Ronen, A. 1983. Late Quaternary Sea Levels Inferred from Coastal Stratigraphy in Israel. Pages 121–134 in: *Quaternary Coastlines and Marine Archaeology*. P. M. Masters, and N. C. Flemming, eds. New York.

Safriel, V. 1974. Vermetid Gastropods and Intertidal Reefs in Israel and Bermuda. *Science* 186:1113–1115.

Singer, A., and Shachnai, E. 1969. The Micromorphology and Clay Mineralogy of Sandy Paleosols from the Coastal Plain of Israel. In *Études sur le Quaternaire dans le monde*. INQUA, 8th Congress. Paris.

Weir, A. H., Ormerod, E. C., and el-Mansey, I. M. I. 1975. Clay Mineralogy of Sediments of the Western Nile Delta. *Clay Minerals* 10:369–386.

Yaalon, D. H. 1967. Factors Affecting the Lithification of Eolianite and Interpretation of Its Environmental Significance in the Coastal Plain of Israel. *Journal of Sedimentary Petrology* 37:1189–1199.

Yaalon, D. H., and Laronne, J. 1971. Internal Structures in Eolianites and Paleowinds, Mediterranean Coast of Israel. *Journal of Sedimentary Petrology* 41:1059–1064.

Zohary, M. 1962. *Plant Life of Palestine: Israel and Jordan*. New York.

19

Botanical Remains

by Nili Liphschitz and Yoav Waisel

Information regarding the climatic and botanical history of the Sharon plain is very limited and pertains mainly to the last 200 years. The data available are based on meteorologic records for the last 60–70 years and on reports of various travelers (Thomson 1859; Tristam 1865; Wilson 1880; etc.). Information regarding the flora of the Sharon during ancient times from the beginning of the Early Bronze Age through the Late Bronze Age, Iron Age, and Classical period is available for one site only, Tel Aphek. Some data regarding the coastal Sharon were obtained from neighboring Apollonia, but this information is confined to the Byzantine and Early Arab periods.

As assumed in previous dendroarchaeological investigations (Liphschitz and Waisel 1973–78), timber for everyday use was usually taken from the immediate environment, so its composition represents the type of vegetation and the ecological conditions that prevailed during the relevant periods. Dendroarchaeological analysis of Tel Michal contributes, therefore, to the knowledge and understanding of the botanical history of the region.

The average annual rainfall at Tel Michal is 550 mm. The mean annual temperature is 19°C (12°C in January and 26°C in July). The present shrub and tree flora of the region includes *Retama roetam* and *Pistacia lentiscus* on the sand dunes and *kurkar* ridges, *Quercus ithaburensis* on the sandy loam plains, and *Pistacia palaestina* together with *Quercus calliprinos* on the Samarian foothills in the east.

19.1. MATERIALS AND METHODS

Samples of about 1–1.5 cm^3 were taken from the carbonized wood retrieved from the excavations. The samples were aspirated in absolute alcohol for 90 minutes, dipped in methyl-benzoate-celloidin solution for 24 hours, transferred to benzene for 20 minutes, and, finally, to 50°-55°C paraffin for 48–96 hours. Blocks were prepared and sections 12 μ thick were made with a microtome. Cross sections as well as longitudinal, tangential, and radial sections were prepared by means of the usual techniques. After 24 hours, the sections were deparaffinated and mounted in Canada balsam. The anatomical description of the wood was made from these sections.

Fruits and seeds were identified to the species level by comparison with modern-day fruits and seeds (Table 19.1). Samples taken from live trees were used to identify the wood species (Table 19.2).

Table 19.1. Fruits and Seeds

Species	Reg. No.	Locus	Stratum
Juglans regia	5196	689	I
Lens sp.	5133	1002	II
Olea europaea	9747	1556	XVI
	9764	1559	XVI
	9758	1559	XVI
	9754	1558	XVI
	9742	1556	XVI
	9802	983	XVI-XV
	10707	1701	XV
	10796	1744	IIIa
	5133	1002	II
	5204	689	I
	5196	689	I
	5114	678	I
	5125	683	I
Vicia sp.	9611	1529	XIV
	5133	1002	II
Vitis vinifera	9611	1529	XIV
	5133	1002	II

19.2. RESULTS

The most common seeds retrieved in the excavations were from olives (Table 19.1). Grape (*Vitis vinifera*) and vetch (*Vicia*) seeds were also present. The Eurasian (or Circassian) walnut (*Juglans regia*) and lentil (*Lens*) were represented by one specimen each.

BOTANICAL REMAINS

Table 19.2. Wood Samples

Species	Reg. No.	Locus	Stratum	Species	Reg. No.	Locus	Stratum
Cupressus sempervirens	1261	178	XI-VI	*Quercus calliprinos*	5893	876	XI
	4830	659	XI-VI	(continued)	5622	701	XI
	4834	659	XI-VI		5432	713	X
	7674	1178	XI-VI		5448	713	X
	6689	997	IX		5451	713	X
	6378	1317	VIII		5445	713	X
Olea europaea	5481	723	XVII		5755	713	X
	5912	885	XVI		5741	861	X
	5897	885	XVI		5860	857	X
	8845	873	XVI		5959	879	X
	5905	877	XVI		5589	840	IX
	9756	1559	XVI		5603	840	IX
	9802	983	XVI-XV		10393	1631	IX
	10370	1641	X		10315	1631	IX
	3247	453	VI		5526	840	IX
	376	61	II		6358	1300	VIII
Pinus halepensis	10754	1709	VII		10323	1029	VII
	10257	1635	V		10276	1029	VII
	5505	832	V-IV		10298	1029	VII
	11069	1775	V-IV		3286	453	VI
	6815	685	IIIb		6888	1024	VI
	359	66	II		6891	1014	V
	6730	811	II		6861	694	V
	5133	1002	II		6907	697	IV
Pistacia lentiscus	552	99	XIII		6788	692	IIIa
Pistacia palaestina	9758	1559	XVI	*Quercus ithaburensis*	9742	1556	XVI
	559	99	XIII		8711	1372	XI
	5790	870	XI		5656	339	IX
	5717	857	X		5757	898	IX
	1863	339	IX		10299	1634	IX
	5682	722	VII		517	92	VIII
	359	66	II		10812	1709	VII
	5231	689	I		155	36	V
Pistacia sp.	9764	1559	XVI	*Quercus* sp.	5780	873	XVI
	5794	873	XVI		6747	694	V
	983	147	XIV		5534	832	V/IV
	10420	1661	XIV		6828	1012	IV
	5815	866	XI	*Retama roetam*	1150	174	XVII
	7670	1161	XI-VI		9611	1529	XIV
	6698	999	IX		9777	1261	XIV
	5620	842	VIII		3327	471	XIV-XIII
	10226	696A	IIIb		2548	423	XIII
Quercus calliprinos	9782	1558	XVI		9452	1500	XI
	9754	1558	XVI		9478	1500	XI
	9747	1556	XVI		6666	984	IX
	2237	378	XIV		6687	1251	IX
	3342	471	XIV-XIII		10389	1645	IX
	9486	1510	XIII		517	92	VIII
	5679	858	XIII		8340	1029	VII
	5829	872	XI		4509	611	VII
	5843	876	XI		5729	347	V-IV

Table 19.3.   Abridged Key for Identification of Tree Species

1.	Wood consisting of tracheids without vessels.	2
—	Wood with vessels.	3
2.	Resin ducts present regularly in each growth ring.	*Pinus halepensis*
—	Resin ducts absent in wood.	*Cupressus sempervirens*
3.	Vessels arranged mainly in dendrite shape, radially alternating with xylem rays. Rays are of two types: multiseriate and uniseriate.	4
—	Vessel arrangement not as above. Rays are of one type only.	5
4.	Vessels arranged only in dendrite shape.	*Quercus calliprinos*
—	Vessels arranged in a dendrite shape, in addition to a ring porous appearance of the wood.	*Quercus ithaburensis*
5.	Diffuse porous wood.	6
—	Ring or semi-ring porous wood.	7
6.	Parenchyma storied.	*Retama roetam*
—	Parenchyma nonstoried.	*Olea europaea*
7.	Ring porous wood.	*Pistacia palaestina*
—	Semi-ring porous wood.	*Pistacia lentiscus*

Eight species of trees were found at Tel Michal (Table 19.2): *Cupressus sempervirens* (cypress), *Olea europaea* (olive), *Pinus halepensis* (Aleppo pine), *Pistacia lentiscus* (lentisk), *Pistacia palaestina* (terebinth), *Quercus calliprinos* (Calliprinos oak), *Quercus ithaburensis* (Tabor oak) (Pl. 69:1–4), and *Retama roetam* (white broom). A dichotomic key for the identification of these eight species was prepared based on the anatomical features of each. An abridged version of this key appears as Table 19.3.

Half the wood samples were collected from strata dating to the Persian period. The other half came from strata belonging to the Middle Bronze Age, Late Bronze Age, and Iron Age and from the Hellenistic, Roman, and Early Arab periods (Table 19.4).

Quercus calliprinos constituted 33 percent of the total number of wood samples and 42 percent of the samples collected in Persian period strata. *Retama roetam* constituted 13 percent of the total number of wood samples and 15 percent of the samples found in Persian period strata. All the other species were found in small percentages.

Cupressus sempervirens is an evergreen tree indigenous to the temperate regions and high mountain ridges of the Mediterranean. It appears today in this region in natural stands only in the high mountains east of the Jordan, in Edom, and in southern Sinai. Around the Mediterranean, it appears on different rock types and on various soils. The species has two varieties—horizontal and pyramidal—both of which are widely used today as ornamental trees or in afforestation projects. Cypress wood was commonly used for construction in the past.

Olea europaea is a long-lived evergreen tree typical of the Mediterranean climate; cultivation of this species dates back many thousands of years. Wild olive trees thrive on Mt. Carmel and in the Galilee, but most populations are either domesticated or escapes. Olive trees grow to old age and develop thick trunks, yielding useful timber of hard and durable wood.

Pinus halepensis is a Mediterranean evergreen tree native to the central and northern parts of Israel. In the past, pines were probably much more common in Judea, Samaria, and the soft limestone hills of Galilee. Because *Pinus halepensis* has been extensively felled and used throughout the ages, its native distribution has declined. It is a fast-growing species with moderate ecological requirements. The trunk may reach a diameter of 1 m.

Pistacia lentiscus is a large evergreen shrub or small tree of the Mediterranean woodlands. It is a leading species in maquis and garigue communities in the warm, lower sections of the Mediterranean hill regions of Israel, and it occupies stable sand dunes and calcareous sandstone in the Tabor oak and carob communities of the coastal plain. Since the plant is resistant to saltwater spray, it can grow close to the seashore. It reaches a height of 3–4 m and forms numerous trunks but rarely develops into a true tree.

Pistacia palaestina is a deciduous tree of the Mediterranean maquis and a major component of the *Quercus calliprinos* and *Pistacia palaestina* association. The tree can attain an age of several hundred years and may grow 5–10 m high, with a single trunk.

Quercus calliprinos is an evergreen tree. It is one of the dominant arboreal species in Israel and, together with *Pistacia palaestina*, leads the maquis plant associations that characterize the Mediterranean hill belt from the upper Galilee to Judea. The tree may attain large dimensions and develop a thick trunk.

Quercus ithaburensis is a deciduous forest tree. It is a leading member of the Tabor oak and storax association. At one time, such forests covered large areas from the foot of

Table 19.4. Chronological Distribution of Wood Samples

Species	MB	LB	Iron	Persian	Hellenistic	Roman	Arab	Total
Cupressus sempervirens				6				6
Olea europaea	1	6		2		1		10
Pinus halepensis				1	4	3		8
Pistacia lentiscus			1					1
Pistacia palaestina		1	1	4		1	1	8
Pistacia sp.		2	2	4	1			9
Quercus calliprinos		3	4	23	4			34
Quercus ithaburensis		1		6	1			8
Quercus sp.		1			3			4
Retama roetam	1		4	8	1			14
Total	2	14	12	54	14	5	1	102

Mt. Hermon to the coastal plain. Today only remnants of such forests survive. A notable group occurs in the Cherquas grove in the Sharon. The climatic and soil conditions under which the Tabor oak thrives indicate that the tree is native to the transitional zone between the Mediterranean and steppe belts (400–500 mm annual rainfall). It usually does not grow beyond 500 m above sea level. The tree can reach an age of hundreds of years and a diameter of several meters, and its wood is valuable for building and furniture construction.

Retama roetam is a large desert shrub that has penetrated into the sandy habitats of the coastal plain. Its wood and thick roots serve as fuel.

19.3 DISCUSSION

The botanical material in Israel's coastal region is rather poorly preserved because of the relatively wet climatic conditions. Only small pieces of wood were preserved at Tel Michal. Nevertheless, the present investigation leads us to conclude that the same vegetation that covers the area around Tel Michal today covered it also in ancient times.

Retama roetam and *Pistacia lentiscus* grow today in the vicinity of the tell on the sand dunes and the *kurkar* ridges. *Quercus ithaburensis* is found in areas of sandy red soils. Today there are very few Tabor oaks in the region, but before World War I forests of them covered the Sharon to the banks of the Yarkon River (Eig 1934). The *Quercus calliprinos* and *Pistacia palaestina* plant communities today inhabit the foothills in the east, but their remnants can be found in protected locales of the *kurkar* hills (Zohary 1955; Waisel et al. 1978). The ecological requirements of *Pinus halepensis*, *Cupressus sempervirens*, and *Olea europaea* enable them to grow in this district.

Remnants of six of these species—*Cupressus sempervirens*, *Olea europaea*, *Pistacia lentiscus*, *Pistacia palaestina*, *Quercus ithaburensis*, and *Retama roetam*—were also found in neighboring Apollonia, though in later strata of the Arab period (Liphschitz and Waisel 1978). Remnants of seven of these species—*Cupressus sempervirens*, *Olea europaea*, *Pinus halepensis*, *Pistacia lentiscus*, *Pistacia palaestina*, *Quercus calliprinos*, and *Quercus ithaburensis*—were found in Tel Aphek in the Sharon in strata dating back to the Early, Middle, and Late Bronze Ages and the Hellenistic and Roman periods (Liphschitz and Waisel 1973–78).

The stability of vegetation in this region suggests either that macroclimatic changes have not occurred since the Bronze Age or that their magnitude was too small to affect the plant cover.

REFERENCES

Eig, A. 1934. A Historical Phytosociological Essay on Palestinian Forest of *Quercus aegilops* L. ssp. *ithaburensis* (Desc.) in Past and Present. *Beiheft Botanisches Zentralblatt* Part B 51:225–272.

Liphschitz, N., and Waisel, Y. 1973–78. *Dendroarchaeological Investigations in Israel: Tel Aphek.* (Hebrew) Mimeographed reports 12, 18, 33, 42, 49, and 64. Tel Aviv University.

Liphschitz, N., and Waisel, Y. 1978. *Dendroarchaeological Investigations in Israel: Apollonia.* (Hebrew) Mimeographed reports 60 and 80. Tel Aviv University.

Thomson, W. M. 1859. *The Land and the Book.* New York.

Tristam, H. B. 1865. *The Land of Israel: A Journal of Travel in Palestine.* London.

Waisel, Y., Pollak, G., and Cohen, Y. 1978. *The Ecology of the Vegetation of Israel.* (Hebrew) Tel Aviv University.

Wilson, C. W. 1880. *Picturesque Palestine, Sinai and Egypt.* London.

Zohary, M. 1955. *Geobotany.* (Hebrew) Tel Aviv.

20

Paleobotany from Phytoliths

by Margaret Thomson and George Rapp, Jr.

Phytoliths, which are microscopic-size particles of silica that are deposited in and around the cells of plants, are most common in species of the grass family. When the plant material dies and decays, phytoliths are left behind in sediments as a type of microfossil. Although some phytoliths fall into the range of fine to very fine sand-size particles (250 μ down to 60 μ in length or diameter) (Rovner 1971), the average size of most phytoliths released into sediments seems to fall into the range of silt-size particles (about 60 μ to about 2 μ in length or diameter) or of clay-size particles (less than 2 μ in length or diameter) (Wilding and Drees 1971; 1974).

Phytolith studies were undertaken at Tel Michal to assist in reconstructing the vegetational and agricultural components of the paleoenvironment. Decisions to include plants in the plant phytolith reference collections for Tel Michal were based on the present and possible past sedimentary environments around Tel Michal; which plants occurred naturally in the different kinds of sedimentary environments now or once present around Tel Michal; which plants had value to ancient people as food sources, building material, etc.; and which plant species or groups are known to accumulate silica in large enough quantities to form phytoliths.

Detailed descriptions of present and possible past microenvironments of the Tel Michal region are presented in Chaps. 3 and 16–18. Briefly, the present regional environments include (1) the surf zone; (2) the sand dunes and sand sheets covering the coastal cliff (including Tel Michal) and extending into the coastal plain; (3) the *marzeva* zone, a trough or swale of alluvial clay between the coastal cliff and (4) the first *kurkar* ridge, which lies about 1.5 km inland; and (5) the Sharon plain.

In the past, there was also a small river channel, known as the Wadi Gelil or Naḥal Gelilot, which existed just north of Tel Michal. Naḥal Gelilot may have had a seasonal or year-round flow of fresh water, thus providing an environment that allowed the growth of hydrophytic vegetation.

Vegetation in Israel, especially on the coastal plain, has been so altered by human processes that it is difficult to reconstruct the natural vegetation of ancient environments of the coastal plain. Nevertheless, Zohary (1962; 1973), through intensive study of the remnants of untouched vegetation in Israel, has written in-depth geobotanical studies that include discussions of the naturally occurring climax and degraded vegetation of the coastal plain.

At present, the sandy clays of the Sharon plain and northern Philistia have a prairielike vegetation cover that includes a species of bunch grass and other herbs, annuals, and perennials (Zohary 1962). The original Mediterranean oak forests of the Sharon contained *Quercus ithaburensis* as the dominant species (also recovered in the excavations; see Chap. 19) and a wide variety of herbs, annuals, and perennials (Zohary 1973).

Zohary (1973) is of the opinion that most of the current vegetation on the *kurkar* ridges and consolidated dunes of the Sharon plain near the seashore does not represent the normal climax vegetation for this particular sedimentary environment. The climax vegetation in many of these places probably consisted of carob (*Ceratonia siliqua*) and lentisk (*Pistacia lentiscus*) trees (one sample of the latter was recovered in the excavations), as well as a variety of herbs, annuals, and perennials, and this particular type of vegetation probably had a savanna-like appearance.

The hydrophytic vegetation originally present near streams and on seasonally inundated areas of the Sharon plain probably consisted of the same types of vegetation found in various undisturbed habitats near freshwater sources and in seasonally inundated areas of Israel today. Low banks of permanent rivers and streams and periodically submerged swamps are dominated by tall grasses, such as *Phragmites australis*, *Saccharum ravennae*, and *Arundo donax*; by sedges and rushes; and by lower-growing grasses and other plants that prefer wet habitats. Elevated banks of permanent or ephemeral rivers are occupied by willows, sedges, grasses, and other perennials and annuals. Areas that flood in winter but dry up in summer are dominated by annuals, such as *Juncus acutus*, sedges, *Cynodon dactylon*, and other relatively low-growing plants.

Among all the naturally occurring vegetation types that

might have been present around Tel Michal in the past, about 190 species of plants are listed by Zohary (1962; 1973) as commonly present. This author stresses that the traditions surrounding the current use of wild plants by people in the Near East for food, medicine, oil, basketry, etc., indicate their possible utilization in antiquity as food, medicines, and building materials.

Plant specimens were obtained by collecting plants from around Tel Michal and from habitats that might once have existed around Tel Michal (for example, at Tel Poleg, at the mouth of the Poleg River, and at the Tel Aviv University botanical gardens); and by obtaining specimens of out-of-season plants from the Tel Aviv University herbarium and from researchers at Tel Aviv University who were working with specific groups of plants. In total, 163 species of identified plants were obtained from Israel.

The phytolith research reported here involved the study of a limited number of plant phytolith assemblages from a few of the plants collected from the above sources and an examination of the phytolith assemblages contained in a limited number of the sediment samples collected from Tel Michal. The objectives in studying the sediment phytolith assemblages were to gain an understanding of the variety of phytoliths occurring in the chosen sediment samples, to gain an understanding of the origin of the sediment phytolith assemblages, and to examine the implications of the origin of the sediment phytolith assemblages.

Two sediment samples collected from the high tell during the 1979 and 1980 field seasons were selected: (1) Reg. No. 9757; Locus 1559; level 6.10 m: Late Bronze Age ashy fill with carbonized seeds and fish bones. This was one of the fills used to build up Rampart 1562. (2) Reg. No. 6103; Locus 922; level 9.50 m: Middle Bronze Age IIB fill from platform with carbonized seeds. These samples were selected because they originated in two of the earliest strata at Tel Michal and because the presence of carbonized plant material in both these loci indicated that they might contain the remains of cooking fires and hence phytoliths from ashed plant material.

Four plant samples were selected for examination of the phytoliths occurring in the leaves. The examination was carried out in the Archaeometry Laboratory of the University of Minnesota at Duluth.

1. Lab. No. 10091. *Agropyron junceum*, leaf; Tribe Triticeae—silica bodies oblong to elliptical in shape;
2. Lab. No. 10100. *Agropyron junceum*, leaf 2; Tribe Triticeae—silica bodies oblong to elliptical in shape;
3. Lab. No. 10307. *Triticum dicoccoides*, leaf; Tribe Triticeae—silica bodies oblong to elliptical in shape; and
4. Lab. No. 10430. *Aegilops longissima*, leaf 2; Tribe Triticeae—silica bodies oblong to elliptical in shape.

Agropyron junceum and *Aegilops longissima* are common members of the plant communities found on the coastal plain of Israel today, and they thus may have been available in the past as fuel, animal fodder, or building material. *Triticum dicoccoides*, wild emmer wheat, grows wild in northeastern Israel, and its cultivated variant, *Triticum*

dicoccum, may have originated somewhere in the southwestern portion of the Fertile Crescent (northeastern Israel, southeastern Lebanon, and southwestern Syria), the center of distribution of *Triticum dicoccoides* (Feldman and Sears 1981). Therefore, wild emmer wheat, or more likely a domesticated variant, may have been a food crop cultivated on the Sharon plain during the early occupation of Tel Michal.

Careful examination of the phytoliths from the selected plant specimens demonstrated characteristics that help distinguish one plant phytolith assemblage from another. Measurement of the basal length of the short trapezoids proved that determining the size distribution of phytolith types other than crosses may be an important part of defining a phytolith assemblage (Pearsall 1979). Each plant specimen we examined exhibited a different size distribution of the basal length of the hats. In addition, the long trapezoids in *Aegilops longissima*—leaf (10430) had a slightly different shape and size than the long trapezoids in *Agropyron junceum*—leaf (10091 and 10100). Finally, the phytolith assemblage of *Triticum dicoccoides*—leaf (10307) contained several types of phytoliths (a cone, a plate, and a silicified stomate) not observed in *Aegilops longissima*—leaf or in *Agropyron junceum*—leaf.

Because this study was limited in scope, only a qualitative comparison was made between the quantitative data generated from counting the phytolith types in the reference plants and the data acquired from counting the phytolith types in the sediments. Several observations resulted from this comparison. First, the range of phytolith types present in the sediments was quite limited. If the full range of grasses currently found around Tel Michal had contributed phytoliths to the archaeological sediments, one would expect to find more dumbbell, saddle, and long-trapezoid phytoliths than were actually present in the sediments.

However, the lengths of the short trapezoids in the sediments ranged from approximately 9 μ to 20 μ, a size distribution much greater than that observed in any of the reference plants. This fact strongly suggests that more than one type of plant or plant part is represented by the phytoliths in the archaeological sediments. Furthermore, the phytolith types present in the two Tel Michal sediment samples are usually found in all types of grass parts, including the inflorescences, suggesting that the phytoliths in the sediments represent a variety of plants or plant parts. However, the absence of a characteristic phytolith (cone, no papillae, blunt, asymmetrical) from the leaf of *Triticum dicoccoides* (10307) indicates that that plant part is definitely not represented in the Tel Michal sediments studied. Finally, a comparison of the phytolith types present in both the Tel Michal sediments showed that the two phytolith assemblages were basically the same except for differing proportions of a few phytolith types. Whatever mechanism resulted in phytolith deposition, the variety of plants contributing the phytoliths probably remained the same over the time span represented by the two archaeological sediments studied.

Fire might well have been the agent responsible for the addition of phytoliths to the Tel Michal sediments. Carbonized plant material present in Locus 922 and Locus 1559 indicates that these loci may contain remnants of material from fires. The phytoliths in the sediments might represent the remains of fuel or of a plant(s) processed near the fire and accidentally ashed in it.

Two possible sources of fuel must be considered. Large quantities of animal dung would have been available as fuel. Studies of plant material digested by ruminants have shown that phytoliths survive passage through the digestive tracts of animals (Smithson 1958) and can be identified readily when extracted from animal dung. Fuel for fires might also have been taken from the vegetation around Tel Michal, although available wood probably would have been preferred to grasses and scrub vegetation.

It is also possible that the occupants of Tel Michal utilized wild plant foods from the neighborhood and processed these by parching portions of plants to release seeds or some other edible part.

Therefore, it is likely that the phytoliths observed in the Tel Michal sediments represent some aspect of the vegetation present around Tel Michal in the past. If the phytoliths represent only the grasses, then a limited conclusion might be drawn that the Bronze Age vegetation around Tel Michal contained fewer and different species than at present, and possibly included large tracts of grasses that have since disappeared.

REFERENCES

Feldman, M., and Sears, E. R. 1981. The Wild Gene Resources of Wheat. *Scientific American* 244:102–112.

Pearsall, D. M. 1979. *The Application of Ethnobotanical Techniques to the Problem of Subsistence in the Ecuadorian Formative.* Ph.D. dissertation. University of Illinois, Urbana-Champaign.

Rovner, I. 1971. Potential of Opal Phytoliths for Use in Paleo-Ecological Reconstruction. *Quatern. Res.* 1:343–359.

Smithson, F. 1958. Grass Opal in British Soils. *Journal of Soil Science* 9:148–155.

Wilding, L. P., and Drees, L. R. 1971. Biogenetic Opal in Ohio Soils. *Soil Science Society of America, Proceedings* 35:1004–1010.

Wilding, L. P., and Drees, L. R. 1974. Contributions of Forest Opal and Associated Crystalline Phases to Fine Silt and Clay Fractions of Soils. *Clay and Clay Minerals* 22:295–306.

Zohary, M. 1962. *Plant Life of Palestine: Israel and Jordan.* New York.

Zohary, M. 1973. *Geobotanical Foundations of the Middle East.* Stuttgart.

21a

Human Skeletal Remains

by Michele Hogan and Sara C. Bisel

The Persian period cemetery at Tel Michal was located on the northern hill, a sandy hillock with no remarkable geologic characteristics. The excavated portion of the cemetery yielded more than 100 burials (see Chap. 11; Pls. 36–40). The conditions of the terrain, mainly the acidity of the soil, as well as the presence of roots and burrowing land snails, rendered the skeletal material friable, fragmentary, and unmeasurable once removed from the site. Documentation was established with approximate in situ measurements, photographs, and collection of bones and teeth whenever possible. Individuals were present in various states of preservation from full skeleton to bone scraps. The skeletal material of only 67 individuals was sufficiently well preserved to be submitted for analysis.

The available material lent itself to three methods of analysis: (1) demographic, using sex and age at death; (2) dental, based on lesions of teeth and alveolae; and (3) bone mineral, using chemical analysis of bone. The first two methods are discussed in this chapter, the third in Chaps. 21b and 21c. Pathological analysis for illness, trauma, and genetic anomaly was inconclusive because of the fragmentary condition of the material. The analysis carried out, however, was helpful in characterizing the population and allowing some sociological insight. Interpretations must be viewed in light of the condition of the material and the small population size.

21a.1. DEMOGRAPHY

For our demographic study, all individuals were aged and sexed. Age was assessed using epiphyseal closure (McKern and Stewart 1957), tooth development and eruption (Logan and Kronfeld 1933; Schour and Poncher 1940), general appearance of the bones, and skull suture closure (Todd and Lyon 1924).

Sex was assessed using traits of the pelvis and skull and the general appearance of the bones (Keen 1950; Stewart 1979). The 67 individuals excavated are listed in Table 21.1. There were 8 infants (0–1 year), 15 children (1–10 years), and 3 youths (10–15 years). Gender could not be

reliably determined for individuals who had not reached puberty. Of the 34 adults (over 15 years of age), 8 were male, 12 were female, and 14 were too fragmentary for gender to be determined.

The frequencies of death in each age group at Tel Michal are summarized in Table 21.2 and Figure 21.1. These show the high mortality rate for infants and young children, perhaps due to acute infection and/or malnutrition. Malnutrition and acute infection in young children are so interrelated that it is impossible to determine which is the principal cause and which the effect. Undoubtedly, both are factors. Adult female deaths peaked in the late twenties.

Average age at death of this population was lower than that of other populations of the same period, perhaps at least partly because of selective preservation. The fragmentary skeletons may have been those of older individuals whose thinner bones decayed more rapidly. Maternal deaths during childbirth also caused a lowering of average age at death. Further, deaths of mature males may have occurred in places other than Tel Michal through war and accidents at sea and in overland travel.

Average age at death for the Persian period population at Tel Michal, excluding those not socially adult (under 15 years), was 30.6 years for males ($N = 7$, S.D. = 2.57) and 29.3 for females ($N = 9$, S.D. = 4.97). Compare this with Hellenistic Athenians: males at 49.9 years ($N = 7$) and females at 44.3 years ($N = 15$) (Bisel 1980). The lower average age at death at Tel Michal may, of course, be a result of selective preservation.

21a.2. DENTAL ANALYSIS

Twenty-six adults had teeth and/or alveolae available for dental analysis. Because evidence for this study was incomplete, conclusions were tentative. The mean number of teeth or alveolae present per mouth was 19.038 (S.D. = 9.013). That an average of 13 teeth or alveolae were missing indicated that our statistics were not entirely accurate, leaving the trends elicited open to question.

Table 21.1. Catalog of Skeletal Material

Burial	Sex	Age[a]	Burial	Sex	Age
180	...	Adult	1850	M	29***
181	...	? (Human)	1851	...	2.5
185	...	Adult	1852	...	Adult
193	...	Adult	1853	...	30 months
654	...	Newborn	1854	M	25
659	...	11 months	1855	F	32
662	F**[b]	29	1856	...	2 months
663	...	1.5	1857	...	5 months
664	M	32	1858a	...	3.5
666	F	28	1858b	...	2.5
674	...	Adult	1860	***	30-35***
1157	F***	14**	1861	...	3
1158	M***	36**	1862	...	<4
1161	F*	20 +	1863	F***	30***
1165	F***	10-15	1865	F***	Adult
1166	...	Adult	1866	...	
1167	M	30	1867	...	2
1168	F	29	1869	...	6
1169a	...	3-4	1871	F	20
1169b	...	5	1872	F***	***
1171	F**	13	1873	F**	27***
1172	...	2 months	1874	...	2
1173	M	32	1876	...	1
1175	F***	29	1877	...	2.5
1177	F	37	1878	***	32***
1178	M	31	1879	Infant or child	
1179	...	1	1880	F	27
1181	F	35	1881	F	27
1182	F***	40 + **	1882	M	32
1183	...	6 months	1883	M	32
1184	...	6 months	1884	...	(Human)
1185	F***	30**	1885	...	5
1190	F***	45 +			
1192	...	(Human)			
1193	...	4			

[a] Numbers represent years unless otherwise stated.
[b] * = Information reliable enough to be included in statistical analysis, although reservations still exist; ** = limited reservations still exist concerning accuracy of determination, but information considered reliable enough to be included in statistical analysis; and *** = reservations exist strong enough to exclude data from statistical analysis.

Table 21.3. Individuals in the Dental Analysis

Burial	Sex	Age (Years)	Total No. of Teeth or Alveolae	Ante-mortem Loss	Caries	Dental Index[a]
662	F**[b]	29	14	0	1	.071
664	M	32	32	0	0	0
666	F	28	32	0	0	0
1158	M***	36***	20	4	0	.050
1165		10-15	16	0	2	.125
1167	M	30	23	0	0	0
1168a	F	29	24	0	4	.167
1173	M	32	14	0	0	0
1175	F***	29	29	0	0	0
1177	F	37	9	0	0	0
1178	M	31	21	0	0	0
1181	F	35	26	1	0	.038
1182	F***	40 + ***	11	0	0	0
1185	F***	30***	4	0	0	0
1190	F***	45 +	5	0	2	.400
1850	M***	29***	25	0	0	.120
1854	M	25	30	0	0	0
1855	F	32	12	0	1	.077
1860		30-35	26	0	2	.077
1863	F***	30***	18	0	1	.056
1865	F***	Elderly	5	0	0	0
1871	F	20	30	0	0	0
1873	F*	27***	19	0	0	0
1878		32***	28	0	2	.071
1880	F	27	17	0	1	.059
1882	M	32	5	0	0	0

[a] Dental Index = number of caries + antemortem loss + abscesses/ number of teeth and/or alveolae present.
[b] * = Information reliable enough to be included in statistical analysis, although reservations exist; ** = limited reservations still exist concerning accuracy of determination, but information considered reliable enough to be included in statistical analysis; and *** = reservations exist strong enough to exclude data from statistical analysis.

Table 21.2. Death Frequencies of Persian Period Population

Sex	<1	>1-5	6-10	11-15	16-20	21-25	26-30	31-40	41+	Adult	Human	Total
M	...	...	...	...	0	1	1	5	0	0	...	7
F	...	...	...	...	1	1	5	3	0	0	0	10
?	9	15	1	3	0	0	3	4	1	7	7	50
Total	9	15	1	3	1	2	9	12	1	7	7	67

Individuals in the dental analysis are listed in Table 21.3. Lesions present were reported as antemortem loss or caries; abscesses were not observed. Dental index was calculated as the number of lesions divided by the total number of teeth or alveolae present. As shown in Table 21.4, analysis was continued by correcting the absolute dental index to age 40.8 years in order to compare the "younger" Tel Michal people with the "older" Athenians. The correction was obtained using the equation $Y = -0.48399514 + (0.58206327)X$, where Y = dental lesion index and X = age in years. This linear curve was determined to be the best fit of the data from a previous study using 166 individuals over 18 years of age from analogous ancient sites (Bisel 1980). Mean age was 40.875 years.

These data indicated that the people buried in the Persian period cemetery at Tel Michal had better teeth than the Athenian people of a slightly later period. The differences in absolute dental indices between the two populations were, of course, much greater than the differences in the age-corrected indices. The latter indices were more meaningful because of the great difference in average age at death between the two populations. The age-corrected indices showed that Tel Michal adults of both genders considered together had only 41.7 percent of the lesions of

Table 21.4. Dental Analysis Means for Tel Michal (Persian Period) and Athens (Hellenistic Period)

Site	Sex	N	Average Age	Dental Index[a] Mean	S.D.	Age-corrected Dental Index Mean[b]
Tel Michal	F	8	30.125	.052	.057	.115
	M	6	30.33	0	0	0
	All	26	31.38	.050	.086	.105
Athens	F	12	44.3	.354	.300	.308
	M	6	49.9	.204	.227	.139
	All	18	46.2	.305	.276	.252

[a] Dental index = number of caries + antemortem loss + abscesses/number of teeth and/or alveolae present.

[b] Age-corrected dental index: corrected to age 40.9 years.

Athenian adults of both genders. This difference was significant but difficult to explain. Possibly, the texture of food at Tel Michal was rougher than that at Athens. Rough texture would wear away teeth and eliminate caries as they formed. Both sites show males with fewer lesions than females, which was again difficult to explain. However, it

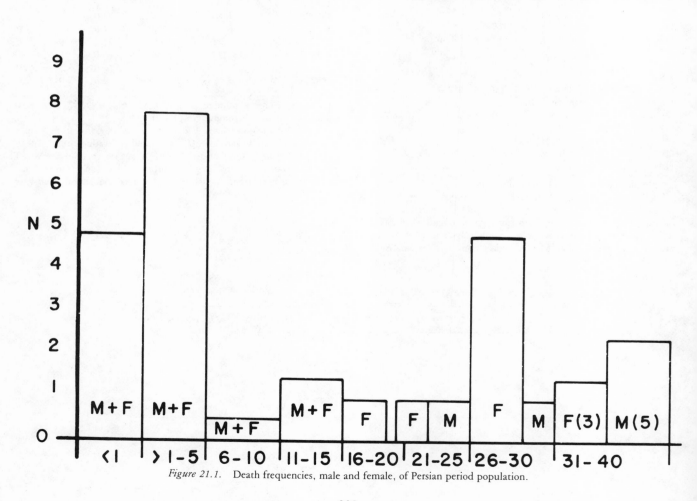

Figure 21.1. Death frequencies, male and female, of Persian period population.

should be noted that both sexes at both sites had much better teeth than modern industrialized populations.

Third molars ("'wisdom" teeth), which may be unstable, were present with no apparent anomalies in the skulls that were not fragmented. Third molars were present in 10 burials; in 8, they were fully developed. There was no evidence of genetic anomalies such as peg teeth or extra cusps. Nor was there any evidence of artificial deformation of teeth, such as filing of the incisors for religious or cosmetic purposes.

No cusp patterns have been established for the Persian period. Dahlberg (1951:165) designates the following maxillary cusp divisions: 4+ for well-defined cusps, 4– for hypocene small cusps, 3+ for no hypocene but a cuspule, 3– for no hypocene or cuspule. In addition to these patterns, cusp divisions can be Y shaped or plus (+) shaped. A 4+ shaped like a Y has been designated 4Y+; a 4+ shaped like a + has been designated +4+. Mandibular patterns are designated +4, Y4, +5, and Y5 (fossil man).

Only 10 of the adult dentitions were evaluated for cusp patterns. Loss of crowns, lack of molars, and wear prevented a larger sample size. The patterns are compared with those of other societies in Table 21.5. The distribution of maxillary cusp patterns is shown in Table 21.6.

Another observation made from the intact skulls was the consistently excellent occlusion of both deciduous and permanent teeth. Perfect or nearly perfect occlusion is common in ancient populations because of better development of the mandible and maxilla bony structure. This is probably the result of more rigorous chewing and consequent strengthening of the jaws of ancient people as opposed to those of modern Western societies.

Table 21.5a. **Percentage Distribution of Patterns on Lower First Molars**[a]

Group	No. of Individuals	Y5	+5	Y4	+4
Tel Michal, Persian period	10	10	Indeterminate		50
Ancient European, white[b]	54	83	0	11	6
Chicago, white[c]	75	84	2	8	2

[a] Some percentages do not total 100 because of missing teeth.
[b] Helman (1928).
[c] Dahlberg (1975).

Table 21.5b. **Percentage Distribution of Patterns on Lower Second Molars**[a]

Group	No. of Individuals	Y5	+5	Y4	+4
Tel Michal, Persian period	10	1	1	30	61
Ancient European, white[b]	54	2	11	9	77
Modern European, white[b]	110	0	1	5	94

[a] Some percentages do not total 100 because of missing teeth.
[b] Helman (1928).

Table 21.5c. **Percentage Distribution of Patterns on Lower Third Molars**

Group	No. of Individuals	Y5	+5	Y4	+4	Irregular
Tel Michal	10	6	31	25	32	6
Ancient European, white[a]	54	6	34	11	49	
Modern European, white[a]	110	4	34		62	

[a] Helman (1928).

Table 21.6. **Percentage Distribution of Maxillary Cusp Patterns**

Molar	4+	4-	3+	3	Irregular or missing
M_1	53	6	12		29
M_2	30	10	5	5	50
M_3	0	10	20	20	50

REFERENCES

Bisel, S. 1980. *A Pilot Study in Aspects of Human Nutrition in the Ancient Eastern Mediterranean, with Particular Attention to Trace Minerals in Several Populations from Different Time Periods.* University Microfilms. Ph.D. dissertation. University of Minnesota, Minneapolis.

Dahlberg, A. A. 1951. The Dentition of the American Indian. Pages 138–176 in: *The Physical Anthropology of the American Indian.* New York.

Dahlberg, A., ed. 1975. *Dental Morphology and Evolution.* Chicago.

Helman, M. 1928. Racial Characteristics in Human Dentition. *Proceedings of the American Philosophical Society* 2:157–174.

Keen, J. A. 1950. A Study of the Differences between Male and Female Skulls. *American Journal of Physical Anthropology* 8:65–79.

Logan, W. H. G., and Kronfeld, R. J. 1933. Development of the Human Jaws and Surrounding Tissue from Birth to Age of 15 Years. *Journal of the American Dental Association* 20:379–427.

McKern, T. W., and Stewart, T. D. 1957. *Skeletal Age Changes in Young American Males, Analyzed from the Standpoint of Age Identification.* Quartermaster Research and Development Command, Environmental Protection Division, Technical Report EP-45. Natick, Mass.

Schour, I., and Poncher, H. G. 1940. *Chronology of Tooth Development.* Evansville, Ind.

Stewart, T. D. 1979. *Essentials of Forensic Anthropology.* Springfield, Ill.

Todd, T. W., and Lyon, D. W. 1924. Endocranial Suture Closure, Its Progress and Age Relationship. Part 1: Adult Males of White Stock. *American Journal of Physical Anthropology* 7:325–384.

21b

Nutritional Chemistry of the Human Bones

by Sara C. Bisel

Chemical analysis of human bone can be used to demonstrate nutritional and sociological patterns in ancient populations. Human bones from the Persian period cemetery at Tel Michal were analyzed for calcium, phosphorus, strontium, magnesium, copper, and zinc. Animal bones were analyzed as controls.[1]

Bone samples of approximately 0.5 g, most frequently from the tibial crest, were weighed to 10^{-4} g. These samples were dissolved in 3 ml of concentrated hydrochloric acid. Further dilutions were made, and values were determined by atomic absorption spectroscopy. Table 21.7 shows the dilutions and wavelengths used (Perkin-Elmer Corporation 1972). Phosphorus was analyzed by spectrophotographic methods, using a total dilution of 1:3,000. Two milliliters each of the standard phosphorus reagents aminonaphtholsulphonic acid and ammonium molybdate were added to 1 ml of dilute sample. Values were read at a wavelength of 630 nm on a spectrophotometer (Fiske and Subbarow 1925).

Table 21.7. Specifications for Atomic Absorption Spectroscopic Analysis of Bone Mineral

Mineral	Total Dilution	Wavelength (nm)
Ca	1:75,000	422.6
Sr	1:150	460.7
Mg	1:500, 1:7,500	285.2
Zn	1:150	213.8
Cu	1:9	324.7

Soil samples from assumed agricultural strata were analyzed to indicate soil mineral in the food chain. Ten grams of soil were weighed to 10^{-4} and shaken for 2 hours with 20 ml of extractant consisting of 0.005M DTPA (diethylenetriaminepentaacetic acid), 0.1M triethanolamine, and 0.01M calcium chloride and corrected to a pH of 7.3. Zinc and copper values were read by atomic absorption spectroscopy (Lindsay and Norvell 1978). For determination of calcium, magnesium, and strontium, 0.5 g of soil sample was weighed to 10^{-4} g and shaken with 5 ml of 1N ammonium acetate for one half hour. Further dilutions were made: 1:500 for calcium, 1:50 and 1:500 for magnesium, and no dilution for strontium. Values were read by atomic absorption spectroscopy (U.S. Soil Conservation Service 1979:24).

Bone minerals are reported in Tables 21.8 and 21.9 as absolute values and as ratios with calcium. The latter method corrects for differential leaching and also for weight contamination of extraneous materials in the bone. In addition, human strontium is reported as a ratio of Sr/Ca with the site-specific sheep/goat Sr/Ca so that strontium in human bone could be compared from site to site.

Table 21.10 compares bone mineral from Tel Michal with that from Late Bronze Age Nichoria, Hellenistic period Athens and Dhema (Bisel 1980; forthcoming), and modern United States (Zipkin 1970; Janes et al. 1975). Nichoria is located in the southwestern Peloponnesus and Dhema in the highlands of Phokis, mainland Greece. Table 21.11 compares available mineral in the soil from Tel Michal, Athens, and Nichoria.

Calcium and phosphorus values of the ancient bones are about what we would expect from archaeological material. The organic collagen portion of the bone has disappeared, leaving the calcium and phosphorus to assume a relatively larger proportion of the remaining bone.

Since soil containing strontium supplies it to plants, strontium analysis can be used to assess the quality of protein ingested by archaeological populations (Brown 1973; Schoeninger 1979). Animals low on the food chain—herbivores—have relatively high levels of strontium in their bones but little or none in their flesh. Omnivores, feeding on plants and animal flesh, have relatively less strontium in their bones. Carnivores, feeding largely on flesh, have the lowest bone-strontium levels. However, human bone from different soil systems cannot be compared unless a site cor-

Table 21.8. Bone Mineral of Human Bone from the Persian Period Cemetery

Burial	Sex	Age (Years)	Ca (mg/g)	P (mg/g)	Ca/P	Sr (µg/g)	Sr/Ca	Site-corrected Sr/Ca	Mg (mg/g)	Mg/Ca	Zn (µg/g)	Zn/Ca	Cu (µg/g)	Cu/Ca
662	F**a	29	249.74	145.40	1.85	235.78	.944	.229	1.42	.0057	89.97	.360	6.887	.0276
664	M	32	276.81	135.31	2.05	630.10	2.276	.553	1.32	.0048	52.00	.188	6.974	.0252
666	F	28	292.62	82.61	3.54	310.65	1.062	.258	1.04	.0035	44.38	.152	5.991	.0205
1157	F***	14**	269.39	141.11	1.91	547.12	2.031	.494	1.41	.0052	66.65	.247	6.999	.0260
1158	M***	36**	290.65	139.12	2.09	326.61	1.124	.276	1.52	.0052	104.87	.361	6.292	.0216
1165	F***	10-15	284.22	108.20	2.63	276.25	.972	.236	1.82	.0064	53.12	.187	6.056	.0213
1167	M	30	271.00	154.05	1.76	461.27	1.702	.414	1.54	.0057	63.42	.234	6.400	.0236
1168	F	29	381.76	109.85	3.48	317.67	.832	.202	1.73	.0045	78.02	.204	6.186	.0162
1171	F**	13	285.34	153.16	1.86	495.15	1.735	.422	1.78	.0062	72.73	.255	4.700	.0165
1173	M	32	259.91	140.43	1.85	221.00	.850	.207	1.48	.0058	130.73	.503	5.790	.0223
1175	F***	29	322.95	138.93	2.32	446.94	1.384	.336	1.52	.0047	83.62	.259	5.882	.0182
1177	F	37	269.34	154.03	1.75	330.36	1.226	.298	1.66	.0061	92.26	.342	5.179	.0192
1178	M	31	269.35	148.65	1.81	226.25	.840	.204	1.64	.0061	75.42	.280	5.333	.0198
1181	F	35	272.16	134.19	2.03	309.34	1.137	.276	1.35	.0050	77.33	.284	7.317	.0269
1182	F***	40+**	288.68	107.48	2.69	765.01	2.650	.644	1.35	.0047	46.19	.160	6.582	.0228
1185	F***	30*	259.11	130.42	1.99	309.22	1.193	.290	1.38	.0053	94.48	.365	6.184	.0239
1190	F***	45+	285.71	116.88	2.44	428.57	1.500	.365	1.52	.0053	78.17	.274	6.631	.0232
1852		Adult	288.98	127.88	2.26	601.79	2.082	.506	1.23	.0044	59.58	.206	5.005	.0173
1854	M	25	269.94	144.37	1.87	258.57	.958	.233	1.52	.0056	110.82	.411	8.183	.0303
1855	F	32	260.11	125.14	2.08	420.49	1.616	.393	1.40	.0054	61.99	.238	7.763	.0298
1860		30-35	241.94	93.46	2.59	243.44	1.006	.245	1.28	.0053	42.08	.174	6.131	.0253
1863	F***	30***	270.54	106.85	2.53	350.29	1.295	.315	1.54	.0057	50.04	.185	38.657b	.1429b
1865	F***	Adult	291.45	136.17	2.14	337.78	1.159	.282	1.14	.0039	53.81	.185	6.457	.0222
1871	F	20	247.87	100.21	2.47	329.58	1.330	.323	1.37	.0055	49.03	.198	5.883	.0237
1873	F*	27***	269.51	107.93	2.50	280.29	1.040	.253	1.26	.0047	52.36	.194	5.359	.0199
1877		2.5	270.59	156.37	1.73	487.34	1.801	.438	1.27	.0047	48.17	.178	6.290	.0232
1878	***	32***	287.58	136.68	2.10	532.33	1.851	.450	1.64	.0057	85.66	.298	5.140	.0179
1880	F	27	275.65	121.91	2.26	313.11	1.136	.276	1.58	.0057	66.90	.243	7.386	.0268
1881	F	27	248.14	91.72	2.71	370.05	1.491	.362	1.10	.0044	43.03	.173	4.303	.0173
1882	M	32	270.10	145.10	1.86	367.09	1.359	.330	1.20	.0044	50.74	.188	5.193	.0192
1883	M	32	237.56	108.34	2.19	209.61	.882	.214	1.10	.0046	69.87	.294	5.198	.0219

a * + Information reliable enough to be included in statistical analysis, although reservations exist; ** = limited reservations still exist concerning accuracy of determination, but information considered reliable enough to be included in statistical analysis; and *** = reservations exist strong enough to exclude data from statistical analysis.

b Burial 1863 has very high Cu value because of contamination by bronze bracelet; it has been excluded from statistics.

Table 21.9. Bone Mineral of Animal Bone from Tel Michal

Sample	Species	Ca (mg/g)	P (mg/g)	Ca/P	Sr (µg/g)	Sr/Ca	Mg (mg/g)	Mg/Ca	Zn (µg/g)	Zn/Ca	Cu (µg/g)	Cu/Ca
1	Sheep/goat	198.58	146.67	1.35	671.27	3.380	2.82	.0143	149.52	.7529	7.289	.0367
2	Sheep/goat	229.09	166.70	1.37	1,096.64	4.787	4.99	.0216	132.70	.579	19.379	.0846
3	Sheep/goat	290.35	170.19	1.71	1,101.62	3.794	3.68	.0125	136.64	.471	9.223	.0318
4	Cattle	316.04	119.81	2.64	901.92	2.854	4.07	.0129	77.62	.246	11.311	.0358
5	Cattle	276.58	151.59	1.82	676.76	2.447	1.70	.0065	61.80	.223	5.748	.0208
6	Sheep/goat	274.10	172.62	1.61	1,283.09	4.681	4.38	.0160	162.98	.594	16.535	.0603
7	Pig	240.14	162.86	1.47	927.01	3.860	6.57	.0274	131.69	.548	12.240	.0510
8	Sheep/goat	265.14	171.78	1.54	1,143.44	4.313	3.50	.0132	113.24	.427	20.714	.0781
Average sheep/ goat $\overline{X}$		257.45	165.59	1.52	1,059.21	4.114	3.87	.0150	139.02	.540	17.60	.0684
S.D.		31.11	10.82	.15	299.63		.85		18.67		3.60	

Table 21.10. Means and Standard Deviations of Human Bone Mineral from Tel Michal, Athens, Nichoria, Dhema, and the United States

Site, Period	Sex	N		Ca (mg/g)	P (mg/g)	Ca/P	Sr (µg/g)	Sr/Ca	Site-Corrected Sr/Ca	Mg (mg/g)	Mg/Ca	Zn (µg/g)	Zn/Ca	Cu (µg/g)	Cu/Ca
Tel Michal, Persian	M	7	x̄	264.95	139.46	1.90	339.13	1.34	.326	1.40	.0053	79.00	.298	6.153	.0232
			S.D.	13.06	14.94		159.28			.20		30.43		1.118	
	F	10	x̄	276.69	117.30	2.36	321.73	1.16	.282	1.39	.0050	65.52	.237	6.225	.0225
			S.D.	39.54	23.09		133.88			.21		22.27		1.108	
	M-F	31	x̄	276.09	127.16	2.27	378.67	1.37	.333	1.41	.0051	69.27	.251	6.12	.0221
			S.D.	26.37	21.62		133.88			.21		22.27		.92	
Athens, Hellenistic	M	24	x̄	264.45	153.21	1.73	114.80	.434	.533	2.75	.0104	167.73	.634	. . .	. . .
			S.D.	44.16	22.70		26.10			.89		60.16			
	F	18	x̄	294.60	146.40	2.01	112.67	.382	.487	2.48	.0084	140.05	.475	. . .	. . .
			S.D.	51.06	38.66		26.93			.51		26.61			
Nichoria, Late Bronze	M	12	x̄	311.7	145.52	1.73	70.8	.228	.581	.58	.0019	118.3	.381	. . .	. . .
			S.D.	18.4	18.4		16.4	.052		.16		17.0			
	F	14	x̄	319.0	164.7	2.01	66.2	.208	.530	.59	.0019	122.5	.382	. . .	. . .
			S.D.	27.1	51.6		11.8	.035		.10		44.1			
Dhema, Hellenistic	M	1	x̄	232.06	144.09	1.61	17.85	.077	.250	1.36	.0059	142.81	.615	. . .	. . .
	F	3	x̄	248.49	147.88	1.68	29.16	.118	.407	1.88	.0073	172.90	.695	. . .	. . .
			S.D.	9.86	16.20		13.30			.63		92.60			
United States modern	M-F	40	x̄	220.4	102.5	2.15	. . .	. . .	. . .	2.81	.0127	147.1	.671	5.94	.0270
			S.D.	30.7						.33		49.8			

Table 21.11. Available Minerals in Soil from Tel Michal, Athens, and Nichoria

Site, period	Sample	Ca (mg/g)	Sr (µg/g)	Sr/Ca	Mg (mg/g)	Zn (µg/g)	Cu (µg/g)
Tel Michal, Persian	1	3.040	26.78		.6081	1.4341	.6573
	2	3.564	26.73		.5494	.7197	.7597
	3	2.504	19.33		.5460	.7592	.6793
	x̄	3.036	24.28	8.00	.568	.971	.699
	S.D.	.530	4.29		.035	.402	.054
Athens, Hellenistic	1	4.417	6.8		4.620	.9377	2.2546
	2	4.000	6.7		5.000	.99	. . .
	x̄	4.209	6.75	1.60	4.810	.964	2.25
	S.D.	.295	.07		.269	.037	. . .
Nichoria, Late Bronze	1	4.650	6.3		.0455	1.24	. . .
	2	5.80	9.4		.0680	1.24	. . .
	x̄	5.235	7.85	1.50	.0568	1.24	. . .
	S.D.	.813	2.19		.016	0	

rection is made, a ratio of the human Sr/Ca value to the site-specific sheep/goat Sr/Ca value.

The human bones from the Persian period cemetery at Tel Michal had high absolute strontium values and high Sr/Ca ratios, a finding explained by the high strontium values of the soil. Nevertheless, examination of the site-corrected Sr/Ca ratio shows that the Tel Michal population was high on the food chain. A comparison of the Tel Michal population to Hellenistic Athenians and Dhemans, and to Late Bronze Age Nichorians, demonstrates that Tel Michal people were lowest in site-corrected Sr/Ca ratios. Therefore, they must have consumed relatively large amounts of terrestrial animal meat and relatively smaller amounts of vegetable protein.

Zinc levels at Tel Michal were the lowest for all groups in the comparison. Red meat is the best source of zinc in the diet; we have just demonstrated the high meat content of the Tel Michal diet. The zinc available in the soil at Tel Michal was equivalent to that at Athens, so zinc was significantly present in the food chain. Therefore, we must look to problems in human absorption of zinc as the cause of low bone-zinc levels. To corroborate, note that animal bone-zinc levels remain high. Poor absorption of zinc has been linked to use of unleavened bread and high-fiber cereal products, foods with a high phytate content (inositol hexaphosphate). Phytate binds zinc in the gut, interferes with its absorption, and results in low bone-zinc levels (Reinhold 1972; Prasad 1978). We can conclude that the Tel Michal people of the Persian period ate unleavened flatbread and unrefined cereals.

Copper values at Tel Michal are nearly equivalent to modern U.S. values. It is interesting to note that Burial 1863 (probably a female) has a copper level of 38.657 µg/g, more than six times the Tel Michal mean. The only bone available to sample was part of a forearm, which bore a bronze bracelet (see Chap. 25a:219). Obviously, the excess copper in the bone came from the bracelet as postmortem contamination.

Bone magnesium levels in the Tel Michal population were relatively low, about half that of the population of either the modern United States or Hellenistic Athens, but almost twice that of Nichoria. Bone magnesium levels corresponded to soil magnesium levels. Tel Michal soil is about one-eighth as rich in magnesium as Athens soil, and 10 times richer than Nichoria soil. The Tel Michal people probably did not suffer from the lack of magnesium but simply achieved physiologic equilibrium at a lower magnesium level. This situation illustrates both the dependence of human bone mineral on the soil that nourishes it and also the efficiency of the human body in conserving and utilizing available mineral, albeit in minimal supply. All people buried at Tel Michal have nearly equivalent bone-magnesium levels, suggesting that all may have been raised on Tel Michal soil with no immigration of adults.

CONCLUSIONS

Mineral analysis indicates a diet high in terrestrial animal meat, supplemented by coarse, unleavened bread and unrefined cereal products. By implication, the mineral analysis indicates the importance of herding in the economy (Chap. 22). Nearly uniform magnesium levels suggest that immigration of adults was not common.

NOTE

1. Thanks are due to the Trace Metal Laboratory, Mayo Clinic, Rochester, Minn., and to J. T. McCall, Head of Section, for the use of the laboratory, and to K. Kostamo for assistance in the analyses.

REFERENCES

Bisel, S. C. 1980. *A Pilot Study in Aspects of Human Nutrition in the Ancient Eastern Mediterranean, with Particular Attention to Trace Minerals in Several Populations from Different Time Periods.* University Microfilms. Ph.D. dissertation. University of Minnesota, Minneapolis.

Bisel, S. C. Human Bone Mineral and Nutrition in Late Bronze Age Nichoria and Athens, Using Analysis of Morphology and Trace Mineral Content of Human Bone. Chap. 6 in: *Excavations at Nichoria in Southwest Greece*, vol. 2. W. A. McDonald, ed. Minneapolis. Forthcoming.

Brown, A. F. B. 1973. *Bone Strontium Content As a Dietary Indicator in Human Skeletal Populations.* University Microfilms. Ph.D. dissertation. University of Michigan, Ann Arbor.

Fiske, C. H., and Subbarow, Y. 1925. The Colorimetric Determination of Phosphorus. *Journal of Biological Chemistry* 66:375–400.

Janes, J. M., McCall, J. T., and Kniseley, R. N. 1975. Osteogenic Sarcoma: Influence of Trace Metals in Experimental Induction. Pages 433–439 in: *Trace Substances in Environmental Health.* Columbia, Mo.

Lindsay, W. L., and Norvell, W. A. 1978. Development of a DTPA Soil Test for Zinc, Iron, Manganese, and Copper. *Soil Science Society of America Journal* 42:421–428.

Perkin-Elmer Corporation. 1972. *Analytical Methods for Atomic Absorption Spectrophotometry.* Norwalk, Conn.

Prasad, A. S. 1978. *Trace Elements and Iron in Human Metabolism.* New York.

Reinhold, J. G. 1972. Phytate Concentrations of Leavened and Unleavened Iranian Breads. *Ecology of Food and Nutrition* 1:187–192.

Schoeninger, M. J. 1979. *Dietary Reconstruction at Chalcatzingo, a Formative Period Site in Morelos, Mexico.* Technical Report 9, University of Michigan.

U.S. Soil Conservation Service. 1979. Soil Investigation Report 1, Method 5A6. Page 24 in: *Soil Survey Laboratory Methods and Procedures for Collecting Soil Samples.* U.S. Department of Agriculture, Washington, D.C.

Zipkin, I. 1970. The Inorganic Composition of Bones and Teeth. Pages 69–103 in: *Biological Calcification: Cellular and Molecular Aspects.* H. Schrar, ed. New York.

21c

Lead Analysis of the Skeletal Tissue

by Arthur C. Aufderheide, Jo Ann E. Wallgren,
and Michele Hogan

21c.1. LEAD PHYSIOLOGY

Lead is absorbed either through the gastrointestinal tract or the respiratory tract, and it is transported in the blood. Small amounts are excreted in the urine and feces. In greater amounts, lead is stored in body tissues, about 10 percent in soft tissues and 90 percent in the skeleton. It is deposited at whatever skeletal sites are most actively proliferating. During certain periods of childhood, therefore, lead may well be distributed throughout the skeleton in an irregular manner. In adults, our previous work has suggested that the skull or the cortex of a long bone generally yields lead concentrations equivalent to that of the mean lead concentration of the entire skeleton. Most of the bone samples from the Tel Michal Persian cemetery (Chap. 11) came from these two skeletal sites.

In natural liquids and foods, the concentration of lead is so low that even the rather feeble body excretory mechanisms are adequate to prevent accumulation in bone and soft tissue. Therefore, unless unusual quantities of lead have been ingested, the skeleton should contain no detectable quantities of lead.

21c.2. NONNATURAL EXPOSURE TO LEAD

Exposure to absorbable lead in amounts greater than those normally encountered under natural conditions usually results in the body's inability to excrete the absorbed lead, which leads to tissue deposition, primarily in skeletal tissues. In a previous publication (Aufderheide et al. 1981), we reported that skeletal lead concentrations reflect a lifetime exposure to excessive quantities of lead in a roughly quantitative fashion. Within certain populations, skeletal lead content reflected the social or occupational status of specific individuals. Sources of lead exposure among an-

cient peoples included food contamination (from storage or preparation containers, pewter tableware), contaminated liquids (lead pipes, stills, storage containers, additives), lead manufacture (mining, smelting, casting, pottery), and miscellaneous (cosmetics, etc.).

21c.3. ANALYTICAL METHOD

Lead analysis was carried out by drying and then ashing the specimen, dissolving 20 mg of bone ash in nitric acid, adding lanthanum (to suppress matrix effect), and analyzing directly in a flameless (graphite furnace) atomic absorption spectrometer. The precision of this procedure is approximately equal to ± 10 percent (one standard deviation), and the detection limit under the conditions of this analysis is approximately 1.2 µg of Pb/g of bone ash (Wittmers et al. 1981).

21c.4. RESULTS

Most of the 40 bones analyzed showed no lead at all or only trace amounts (Table 21.12). In modern living Americans aged 20–40 years, such values range from 20 to 50 µg of Pb/g of bone ash. The highest value found in the Tel Michal bones was 5.3 µg.

The detection limit is defined as the concentration of a solution required to produce a signal equal to twice the standard deviation of the background fluctuation. Under the described conditions, this is produced by a bone ash specimen containing 1.2 µg of Pb/g of bone ash. However, one can reduce to less than 1 percent the probability of background fluctuation being responsible for a determined value by doubling the 1.2 value. In the Tel Michal bones, values exceeding 2.4 µg of Pb/g of bone ash include those shown in the accompanying tabulation.

Burial	Lead (µg/g of Bone Ash)
654	2.8
1175	3.8
1178	2.8
1862	5.3
1879	3.9

The value of 5.3 µg of Pb/g of bone ash is more than six standard deviations above the background fluctuation and probably represents a very small quantity of lead stored in that person's bones during his or her life. For purposes of quantitative perspective, this amount can be compared with the values quoted above that are usually found in modern Americans. Most of the other values lie sufficiently close to the detection limits to make their significance questionable.

In summary, the bones from the Persian period cemetery at Tel Michal show either no lead at all or, at most, very slight traces. These values imply that, with the exception of Burial 1862, none of the individuals studied was exposed (by ingestion or inhalation) to amounts of lead greater than those from normal, natural sources.

REFERENCES

Aufderheide, A. C., Neiman, F. D., Wittmers, L. E., Jr., and Rapp, G. 1981. Lead in Bone II. Skeletal-Lead Content As an Indicator of Life-Time Lead Ingestion and the Social Correlates in an Archaeological Population. *American Journal of Physical Anthropology* 55:285–291.

Wittmers, L. E., Jr., Alich, A., and Aufderheide, A. C. 1981. Lead in Bone I. Direct Analysis for Lead in Milligram Quantities of Bone Ash by Graphite Furnace Atomic Absorption Spectroscopy. *American Journal of Clinical Pathology* 75:80–85.

Table 21.12. Lead Analysis Report of Skeletal Tissue from Persian Period Cemetery

Burial	Bone	Lead Concentration (µg/g of Bone Ash)
654	?	2.8
662	Skull	<1.2
663	Mandible	<1.2
664	Skull	<1.2
666	Skull	<1.2
1157	Skull	<1.2
1158	Skull	<1.2
1161	Femur	<1.2
1167	Skull	<1.2
1168	Skull	<1.2
1169a	Skull	<1.2
1171	Skull	2.1
1173	Skull	<1.2
1175	Skull	3.8
1177	Skull	1.8
1178	Skull	2.8
1179	Skull	<1.2
1181	Femur	<1.2
1184	Skull	<1.2
1185	?	<1.2
1190	Skull	<1.2
1850	Skull	<1.2
1852	Skull	<1.2
1853	?	<1.2
1854	Skull	<1.2
1855	Skull	<1.2
1858a	?	<1.2
1861	?	<1.2
1862	Skull	5.3
1863	Humerus	<1.2
1865	?	<1.2
1866	Skull	<1.2
1867	Long bone	<1.2
1869	Skull	<1.2
1871	Skull	2.4
1874	Long bone (child)	<1.2
1877	Skull	<1.2
1878	Skull	<1.2
1879	Long bone (infant)	3.9
1880	Skull	1.4

22

Animal Bones

by Salo Hellwing and Nurit Feig

Bone material was excavated from 1977 to 1980 at Tel Michal in strata ranging from the Middle Bronze Age IIB (beginning circa 1750 B.C.E.) to the Early Arab period (10th century C.E.). Bone fragments were collected from 737 loci in 2,193 baskets (Table 22.1). These figures include some mixed material that was treated separately or discarded in compiling the statistical tables. Bones from mixed contexts represent only 2 percent of the total.

The recording and chronological attribution of the loci and registration numbers are presented in Table 22.2, which shows that the total bone material consisted of 16,329 fragments, of which 5,435 could be identified. The total weight of the bones was 354.3 kg. Sixty percent of the bone material, 9,407 fragments in 1,199 baskets, came from 379 loci of the Persian period, whereas 1,692 bone fragments came from the Hellenistic period. The other periods yielded very little bone material, presumably because the earlier periods have not yet been dug extensively and because the site was occupied from the Hasmonean period onward by forts, fortresses, or watchtowers rather than by a large civil population.

Identification of material was based on comparisons with recent osteological collections in the Institute of Archaeology and the Zoological Museum of Tel Aviv University and from pertinent literature (Cornwall 1968; Schmid 1972). The bones were cleaned at the site or in the laboratory and then weighed and sorted according to species. Some bones had to be treated with acetic acid to remove sedimentary encrustations. State of preservation was recorded. Standard measurements were made according to von den Driesch (1976), and age estimations according to the criteria of Silver (1969). Specimens chosen for photography were marked. Estimates of the relative frequencies of animal species and the minimum number of individuals (MNI) were calculated according to Watson (1979).

Sieving was carried out only occasionally at the site; therefore, small mammals and birds are not represented in the material. Whenever possible, an attempt was made to distinguish between goat and sheep bones on the basis of

Table 22.1. Bone Fragments Collected from Tel Michal

Excavation Seasons	No. of Loci	No. of Baskets	Percentage of Loci
Tel Michal 1 (1977)	82	206	9.3
Tel Michal 2 (1978)	175	560	25.0
Tel Michal 3 (1979)	255	786	35.0
Tel Michal 4 (1980)	225	641	30.5
Total	737	2,193	

the differences in the distal metapodials (Boessneck 1969); otherwise, both species were treated as a single category: sheep and goat (*Ovis/Capra*). The cervids, which included two species (fallow deer and red deer), were identified according to Besold (1966).

22.1. THE FAUNAL ASSEMBLAGE

Table 22.3 is a complete list of identified species. Domestic mammals were represented by eight species and wild mammals by six. A few birds, turtles, fish, and molluscs were also present.[1]

Distribution of bone fragments according to species and periods is shown in Table 22.4. Sheep and goats were the most abundant (54.8 percent) throughout the periods studied, followed by cattle, which accounted for 34.0 percent of the total identified fragments. All other mammals, as well as birds, reptiles, etc., were poorly represented. Cervids accounted for 4.4 percent and dogs for 1.6 percent of the total analyzed fragments.

The numerical relationship between domestic and wild animals is presented in Table 22.5. Most of the bones (5,043) belonged to domesticated mammals, representing 92.7 percent of the total identified bone fragments, whereas hunted wild animals yielded only 7.2 percent, possibly indicating that of all meat consumed throughout the chronological periods less than 10 percent was of wild origin.

Table 22.2. Distribution of Loci, Baskets, and Bone Fragments According to Periods

Period	No. of Loci	%	No. of Baskets	No. of Identified Bones	%	No. of Unidentified Bones	Total Weight of Bones (kg)	Excavated Area (m²)
Middle Bronze Age IIB	14	1.9	40	110	2.0	308	8.465	1,000
Late Bronze Age	65	9.1	208	641	11.7	2,446	53.255	1,000
Iron Age	57	8.0	137	406	7.4	1,076	27.110	1,500
Persian	379	53.5	1,199	3,281	60.0	9,407	203.015	2,000
Hellenistic	76	10.7	249	527	9.6	1,692	31.400	1,000
Hasmonean	38	5.3	83	171	3.1	413	9.590	800
Roman	61	8.6	163	207	3.8	752	13.520	1,000
Early Arab	18	2.5	70	92	1.6	237	7.980	300
Total[a]	708		2,149	5,435		16,329	354.335	

[a] Excluding surface material.

Table 22.3. Faunal Assemblage

Domestic mammals
  Capra hircus (goat)
  Ovis aries (sheep)
  Bos taurus (cattle)
  Equus asinus (ass)
  Equus caballus (horse)
  Camelus sp. (camel)
  Sus scrofa (pig)
  Canis familiaris (dog)

Wild mammals
  Gazella gazella (gazelle)
  Cervidae (red deer and fallow deer)
  Capreolus capreolus (roe deer)
  Lepus sp. (hare)
  Rodentia (rodent)

Aves (birds)
  Struthio camelus (ostrich)
  Gallus domesticus (domestic fowl)
  Anser sp. (goose)

Reptilia (reptiles)
  Trionyx triunguis (soft-shelled turtle)

Pisces (fish)

Invertebrates
  Mollusca (molluscs)

Table 22.6 shows the composition of domestic animal stock in successive periods. Sheep and goats predominated, representing nearly 60 percent of the bones, with cattle accounting for 36.7 percent.

The minimum number of individuals according to animal species and periods is shown in Table 22.7, based on a total of 403 individuals including 187 caprovines (46.5 percent), 84 cows and oxen (20.8 percent), and 33 cervids (8.2 percent).

Table 22.8 shows the ratio of adult to young animals. Apparently, inhabitants of Tel Michal mostly slaughtered adult sheep, goats, and cattle. Pigs, on the other hand, were more frequently butchered when still young (16.6 percent). The highest percentage of young animals (6.1 percent) in the sample came from the Roman period. It is interesting to note that 18.3 percent of the dog remains also came from young animals. Only 6.9 percent of the hunted cervids were young individuals. From these data on the ages of slaughter, we can conclude that the inhabitants raised most animals to adulthood, mostly hunted adult animals (the mean percentage of young animals for all periods was 4.1 percent), and apparently had a sound knowledge of animal husbandry. The animals were exploited not only for their meat but also for their milk, wool, and hides and for their use as draft animals.

22.1.1. Description of Species

Vertebrates

Sheep and Goat (Ovis aries and Capra hircus). Sheep and goat represented 54.8 percent of the total animal remains (Table 22.4), with 2,980 identifiable fragments representing an MNI of 187 (Table 22.7). The large percentage of adult animals is striking: only 2.9 percent of the bones belonged to young specimens with unfused skeletal elements. The relatively small number of animals identified specifically as either sheep or goat does not permit a definite conclusion concerning their taxonomical status. (Only in the Persian period was the sample larger.) However, throughout the periods it appears that sheep were more common than goats. Of the 42 metapodials analyzed, 92 percent belonged to sheep and only 8 percent to goats.

Table 22.9 shows the distribution of skeletal elements according to periods. The most common bone elements of sheep and goat unearthed were mandibulae (402 fragments) followed by scapulae and humeri (257 and 232 frag-

Table 22.4. Distribution of Identified Bone Fragments According to Species and Periods

Period	Chelonia	Reptilia (Varia)	Pisces	Struthio camelus	Anser sp.	Gallus domesticus	Aves (Varia)	Lepus sp.	Rodentia	Capreolus capreolus	Cervidae	Camelus sp.	Gazella gazella	Canis familiaris	Sus scrofa	Equus asinus	Equus caballus	Bos taurus	Ovis/Capra	Total
Middle Bronze Age 11B	49	45	1	…	7	…	…	…	4	…	2	…	…	…	…	…	1	…	1	110
Late Bronze Age	289	258	…	2	2	12	3	…	40	…	1	…	12	…	1	…	21	…	…	641
Iron Age	239	123	…	…	3	5	2	1	25	…	3	…	2	1	…	…	2	…	…	406
Persian	1,799	1,136	10	32	12	51	13	21	149	…	18	1	29	…	…	1	7	1	1	3,281
Hellenistic	327	144	5	7	…	19	3	6	11	2	1	…	…	…	…	…	1	…	1	527
Hasmonean	111	46	…	1	2	…	4	1	4	…	…	…	2	…	…	…	…	…	…	171
Roman	114	65	1	…	4	…	…	1	9	…	9	…	2	2	…	…	…	…	…	207
Early Arab	52	36	…	…	…	…	…	1	1	…	1	…	1	…	…	…	…	…	…	92
Total	2,980	1,853	17	42	30	87	25	31	243	2	35	1	48	3	1	1	32	1	3	5,435
Percentage	54.8	34.0	0.31	0.77	0.55	1.6	0.45	0.57	4.4	0.03	0.64	0.01	0.88	0.05	0.01	0.01	0.58	0.01	0.05	…
Order of frequency	1	2				4			3											

Table 22.5. Distribution of Domesticated and Wild Animals According to Species and Fragment Counts

Animal	Domesticated	Wild
Ovis/Capra	2,980	
Bos taurus	1,853	
Equus caballus	17	
Equus asinus	42	
Sus scrofa	30	
Camelus sp.	31	
Canis familiaris	87	
Gazella gazella		25
Cervidae		243
Gallus domesticus	3	
Pisces		32
Aves		48
Total	5,043	392[a]
Percentage	92.7	7.2

[a] Not all wild species are included in this table.

ments, respectively). There were fewer bones from the posterior part of the skeleton. This numerical predominance of anterior skeletal elements may reflect inhabitants' preference for the forepart of the body. The same phenomenon is seen at Tel Aphek (Hellwing, in press), Nichoria (Sloan and Duncan 1978), and Tel Dan (Wapnish et al. 1977). Table 22.10 shows that about 60 percent of the bones compared came from the anterior part of the body, forelegs predominating: 257 scapulae versus 106 pelvic bones, 232 humeri versus 70 femora. According to Higgs (1968), the femur is less well represented because of differences in durability. In our samples, however, metacarpi outnumbered metatarsi. These two bones are similar in structure and durability.

For measurements of Ovis/Capra bones, see Table 22.11. Three common skeletal elements – astragalus, humerus, and phalanx I – were measured (126 bones). The results agree with the data published by Ducos (1968) for domestic animals in Palestine and are similar to those obtained by us from Tel Aphek.

Cattle (Bos taurus). Cattle were represented by 34 percent of the total remains of animal bones (Table 22.4), with 1,853 identifiable fragments representing an MNI of 84. Although the number of young specimens seems to be nearly double that of sheep/goat (5.0 percent cattle versus 2.9 percent sheep and goat), 95 percent of the cattle were slaughtered as adults. Table 22.12 shows that the most common cattle bones were mandibulae (148 fragments), followed by scapulae (141) and radii (97). As was the case with sheep and goats, there were more bones belonging to the foreparts (55 percent) than to the hindquarters (Table 22.13).

Table 22.14 gives the measurements of five common cattle bones. The measurements of phalanges I and II show that the cattle kept at Tel Michal were slightly larger than those at Tel Aphek (Hellwing, in press), Lachish, and Arad (Lernau 1975, 1978).

Pig (Sus scrofa). The percentage of pig remnants at the site was very small. Only 30 bone fragments were recovered from all the periods (Table 22.15); 12 fragments came from

Table 22.6. Composition of the Main Domestic Animal Stock in Successive Periods
(Expressed in Number of Fragments and Percentages)

Period	Ovis/ Capra	Bos taurus	Equus caballus	Equus asinus	Sus scrofa	Camelus sp.	Canis familiaris	Gallus domesticus	Total
Middle Bronze Age IIB	49	45	1	...	7	...	...	...	102
Late Bronze Age	289	258	...	2	2	...	12	...	563
Iron Age	239	123	...	...	3	1	5	1	372
Persian	1,799	1,136	10	32	12	21	51	...	3,061
Hellenistic	327	144	5	7	...	6	19	...	508
Hasmonean	111	46	...	1	2	1	...	...	161
Roman	114	65	1	...	4	1	...	2	187
Early Arab	52	36	...	...	...	1	...	...	89
Total	2,980	1,853	17	42	30	31	87	3	5,043
Percentage	59.09	36.7	0.33	0.83	0.59	0.61	1.72	0.05	...

Table 22.7. Minimum Number of Individuals

Period	Chelonia	Reptilia (Varia)	Pisces	Struthio camelus	Anser sp.	Gallus domesticus	Aves (Varia)	Lepus sp.	Rodentia	Capreolus capreolus	Cervidae	Camelus sp.	Gazella gazella	Canis familiaris	Sus scrofa	Equus asinus	Equus caballus	Bos taurus	Ovis/Capra	Total
Middle Bronze Age IIB	7	2	1	...	3	...	...	...	2	...	2	...	...	...	...	...	1	...	1	19
Late Bronze Age	16	10	...	1	2	3	2	...	3	...	1	...	4	...	1	...	1	...	...	44
Iron Age	18	8	...	...	1	1	2	1	3	...	1	...	2	1	...	...	1	...	...	39
Persian	96	44	1	3	5	7	4	4	16	...	2	1	4	...	...	1	4	1	1	194
Hellenistic	21	9	1	2	...	2	1	1	3	1	1	...	...	...	...	1	...	1		44
Hasmonean	11	3	...	1	1	...	2	1	2	...	...	...	1	...	...	...	...	...		22
Roman	11	5	1	...	2	...	...	1	3	...	1	...	1	1	...	...	...	...		26
Early Arab	7	3	...	1	...	...	...	1	1	...	1	...	1	1	...	...	...	...		15
Total	187	84	4	8	14	13	11	9	33	1	9	1	13	2	1	1	8	1	3	403
Percentage	46.5	20.8	0.99	1.98	3.4	3.2	2.73	2.23	8.2	0.24	2.23	0.24	3.23	0.49	0.24	0.24	1.98	0.24	0.72	...

Table 22.8. Ratio of Adult to Young Animals[a]

Period	Ovis/ Capra	Bos taurus	Equus caballus	Equus asinus	Sus scrofa	Canis familiaris	Gazella gazella	Camelus sp.	Cervidae	Capreolus capreolus	Ratio Adult/Young	Total Animals	Young (%)
Middle Bronze Age IIB	48/1	43/2	1/0	...	7/0	...	...	...	4/0	...	103/3	106	2.8
Late Bronze Age	276/13	246/12	...	2/0	2/0	12/0	3/0	...	32/8	...	573/33	606	5.4
Iron Age	232/7	118/5	...	...	2/1	5/0	2/0	1/0	25/0	...	385/13	398	3.2
Persian	1,743/56	1,078/58	10/0	31/1	9/3	48/3	12/1	21/0	141/8	...	3,093/130	3,223	4.0
Hellenistic	320/7	137/7	5/0	7/0	...	6/13	3/1	6/0	11/0	2/0	497/27	524	5.1
Hasmonean	111/0	46/0	...	1/0	2/0	...	4/0	1/0	4/0	...	169/0	169	...
Roman	111/3	58/7	1/0	...	3/1	...	...	1/0	8/1	...	182/12	194	6.1
Early Arab	50/2	33/3	...	...	...	...	...	1/0	1/0	...	85/5	90	5.5
Total	2,891/89	1,759/94	17/0	41/1	25/5	71/16	24/1	31/0	226/17	2/0	5,087/223	5,310	4.1
Young (%)	2.98	5.0	...	2.3	16.6	18.3	4.0	...	6.9	...			

[a] Based on bone fusion; not all species are included.

Table 22.9.   Distribution of Identifiable Fragments of Sheep and Goat (*Ovis/Capra*) According to Periods

Bone	MB IIB	LB	Iron Age	Persian	Hellenistic	Hasmonean	Roman	Early Arab	Total
Mandibula	8	31	35	244	39	18	13	12	402
Maxilla	...	1	6	33	3	5	...	1	49
Skull fragments	...	2	2	54	8	...	...	3	69
Horn core	7	4	10	20	3	2	1	1	48
Scapula	6	22	15	166	29	3	11	5	257
Humerus	2	26	24	135	23	8	11	3	232
Ulna	1	10	8	36	13	1	6	...	75
Radius	2	23	15	74	24	6	11	4	159
Metacarpus	1	13	14	72	7	4	4	1	116
Femur	1	8	5	44	5	3	2	2	70
Tibia	6	32	20	106	22	9	8	4	207
Metatarsus	2	13	15	50	3	3	3	...	89
Pelvis	1	15	5	67	7	5	4	2	106
Astragalus	2	5	9	64	11	2	2	1	96
Calcaneus	1	7	...	29	5	2	...	...	44
Metapodia	5	20	11	176	41	8	7	5	273
Phalanx I	2	14	6	78	6	5	5	1	117
Phalanx II	...	2	...	12	2	...	...	2	18
Phalanx III	...	1	2	6	...	1	1	...	11
Molars	1	39	34	269	67	22	21	3	456
Premolars	...	...	...	20	1	4	...	1	26
Incisors	...	1	2	5	...	...	2	...	10
Tooth fragments	...	...	...	4	...	...	...	...	4
Vertebrae	1	...	...	25	7	...	...	1	34
Ribs	...	...	...	2	...	...	...	...	2
Carpalia	...	...	...	...	1	...	...	...	1
Tarsalia	...	...	1	8	...	...	...	...	9
Total	49	289	239	1,799	327	111	114	52	2,980

Table 22.10.   Distribution of Six Skeletal Elements of the Anterior Part of *Ovis/Capra* versus Six Skeletal Elements of the Posterior Part

Bone	Number of Fragments
Anterior	
Horn core	48
Scapula	257
Humerus	232
Ulna	75
Radius	159
Metacarpus	116
Total	887
Percentage	59.1
Posterior	
Femur	70
Tibia	207
Pelvis	106
Astragalus	96
Calcaneus	44
Metatarsus	89
Total	612
Percentage	39.9
Total of all fragments	1,499

Table 22.11.   Measurements (mm) of Three Bones of *Ovis/Capra*

Bone	Number	Length/Height[a]	Width
Astragalus	52	Min. 28.5	Min. 16.0
		Max. 36.0	Max 23.5
		Mean 31.1	Mean 20.9
Humerus (distal)	55	Min. 13.0	Min. 27.2
		Max. 19.1	Max. 37.0
		Mean 16.5	Mean 30.8
Phalanx I	19	Min. 30.0	Min. 13.4
		Max. 38.5	Max. 22.0
		Mean 35.0	Mean 15.4

[a] Length shown for astragalus and phalanx I; height shown for humerus.

Table 22.12. Distribution of Identifiable Fragments of Cattle (*Bos taurus*) According to Periods

Bone	MB IIB	LB	Iron Age	Persian	Hellen-istic	Hasmonean	Roman	Early Arab	Total
Mandibula	4	20	9	102	6	2	2	3	148
Maxilla	···	6	···	9	7	2	···	1	25
Skull fragments	2	2	2	21	1	···	···	···	28
Horn core	1	3	···	15	3	2	1	···	25
Scapula	3	17	10	86	14	1	6	4	141
Humerus	4	14	10	50	7	3	3	3	94
Ulna	···	8	1	16	7	···	···	1	33
Radius	1	14	7	61	10	2	2	···	97
Metacarpus	1	11	3	40	5	2	2	3	67
Femur	1	5	6	36	2	···	2	1	53
Tibia	2	13	4	47	10	3	6	···	85
Metatarsus	4	6	6	39	2	1	1	···	59
Pelvis	1	7	11	30	2	1	2	1	55
Astragalus	1	7	5	36	4	1	···	···	54
Calcaneus	1	9	6	33	2	4	2	2	59
Metapodia	4	10	11	78	20	5	5	3	136
Phalanx I	2	26	9	112	10	8	1	5	173
Phalanx II	5	12	3	58	2	2	5	1	88
Phalanx III	2	11	4	28	3	···	···	1	49
Molars	5	21	9	147	21	5	21	5	234
Premolars	···	6	2	30	1	···	3	1	43
Incisors	···	8	2	19	3	1	···	···	33
Tooth fragments	···	···	···	1	···	···	···	···	1
Vertebrae	···	···	1	15	1	···	···	···	17
Ribs	···	···	···	2	···	···	···	···	2
Carpalia	1	10	1	15	···	1	1	···	29
Tarsalia	···	12	1	10	1	···	···	1	25
Total	45	258	123	1,136	144	46	65	36	1,853

Table 22.13. Distribution of Six Skeletal Elements of the Anterior Part of Cattle (*Bos taurus*) versus Six Skeletal Elements of the Posterior Part

Bone	Number of Fragments
Anterior	
Horn core	25
Scapula	141
Humerus	94
Ulna	33
Radius	97
Metacarpus	67
Total	457
Percentage	55
Posterior	
Femur	53
Tibia	95
Pelvis	55
Astragalus	54
Calcaneus	59
Metatarsus	59
Total	375
Percentage	45
Total of all fragments	832

Table 22.14. Measurements (mm) of Five Cattle Bones

Bone	Number	Length/Height[a]	Width
Astragalus	22	Min. 57.5	Min. 31.4
		Max. 74.0	Max 51.0
		Mean 64.2	Mean 41.0
Humerus (distal)	15	Min. 27.5	Min. 49.0
		Max. 35.0	Max. 72.3
		Mean 32.3	Mean 68.4
Phalanx I	71	Min. 48.0	Min. 27.0
		Max. 72.5	Max. 36.5
		Mean 64.7	Mean 33.5
Phalanx II	29	Min. 35.0	Min. 27.5
		Max. 45.0	Max. 37.0
		Mean 40.0	Mean 33.5
Phalanx III	3	Min. 43.0	Min. 33.5
		Max. 45.5	Max. 35.0
		Mean 45.3	Mean 34.0

[a] Length shown for astragalus and phalanges I–III; height shown for humerus.

Table 22.15. Distribution of Identifiable Fragments of the Pig (*Sus scrofa*) According to Periods

Bone	MB IIB	LB	Iron	Persian	Hasmonean	Roman	Total
Mandibula	2	...	1	4	...	1	8
Maxilla	1	...	1	1	...	...	3
Skull fragments	1	...	...	...	...	...	1
Humerus	1	1	1	2	...	1	6
Metacarpus	...	...	...	...	2	2	4
Tibia	...	...	...	1	...	...	1
Calcaneus	1	...	...	...	...	...	1
Astragalus	...	...	...	1	...	...	1
Metapodia	...	1	...	1	...	...	2
Pelvis	1	...	...	...	...	...	1
Phalanx I	...	...	...	1	...	...	1
Premolar	...	...	...	1	...	...	1
Total	7	2	3	12	2	4	30

Table 22.16. Distribution of Identifiable Fragments of the Ass (*Equus asinus*) According to Periods

Bone	LB	Persian	Hellenistic	Hasmonean	Total
Humerus	...	1	...	...	1
Scapula	...	2	...	...	2
Radius	...	2	1	...	3
Metacarpus	...	2	...	1	3
Femur	...	4	1	...	5
Tibia	...	1	1	...	2
Pelvis	...	1	...	...	1
Astragalus	...	2	1	...	3
Metapodia	...	3	2	...	5
Phalanx I	...	3	...	...	3
Phalanx II	...	1	...	...	1
Phalanx III	...	2	...	...	2
Molar	...	3	1	...	4
Incisor	2	5	...	...	7
Total	2	32	7	1	42

Table 22.17. Distribution of Identifiable Fragments of the Horse (*Equus caballus*) According to Periods

Bone	MB II	Persian	Hellenistic	Roman	Total
Maxilla	...	...	...	1	1
Ulna	...	...	1	...	1
Radius	...	...	1	...	1
Metacarpus	...	1	...	...	1
Metapodia	...	1	...	...	1
Phalanx I	...	2	...	...	2
Molar	...	3	1	...	4
Premolar	...	3	...	...	3
Centrocarpalia	1	...	2	...	3
Total	1	10	5	1	17

the skull and 10 from the forelimb (6 humeri and 4 metacarpalia).

*Horse and Ass (*Equus caballus *and* Equus asinus*).* The ass was represented by 42 bone fragments (Table 22.16) with an MNI of 8 (Table 22.7). The most common bones were femora and metapodia. There were only 17 horse bones, which came from four individuals (Table 22.17). From this data, we may assume that equids did not play an important role in the economy of the inhabitants.

Camel (Camelus sp.). Thirty-one fragments were recovered, representing an MNI of 9. Most of the bones belong to phalanges I and II (Table 22.18).

Dog (Canis familiaris). Dog bones representing 13 individuals (87 fragments) accounted for 1.6 percent of the total bones analyzed. The bulk of the dog bones came from the Persian and Hellenistic periods. Most frequent were humeri (24), followed by mandibulae and ulnae (Table 22.19). Sixteen bones were unfused, i.e., belonging to young animals (Table 22.8). The percentage of dog bones throughout all periods was very small, and no inference can be made as to the socioeconomic utilization of dogs. It is unlikely that herding dogs were used since, according to Higgs (1968), goats usually withstand the dog. Watchdogs may have been used, however.

Deer (Cervidae). In total, 243 bone fragments of cervids were recovered (MNI of 33) from all periods combined. The most frequent skeletal elements were lower jaws, humeri, metacarpi, metatarsi, and calcanei (Table 22.20). The bones found belong to two species, the red deer and the fallow deer, distinguished mainly by measurements of metapodia and phalanges. The data suggest that most of the measured bones (18) belong to the red deer. Only four fragments of antlers were recovered from the 33 specimens. For measurements of Cervidae bones, see Table 22.21.

Gazelle (Gazella sp.). Gazelles were very poorly represented at the site; only 25 fragments with an MNI of 9 were recovered from all strata. Most of the bone fragments were metapodia (Table 22.22).

Birds. A few bones of domestic birds, such as hen and goose, were identified, but apparently these fowl were not important in the economy of the inhabitants. It is worthwhile mentioning, however, the find of a humerus belonging to the ostrich (*Struthio camelus*).

Varia. Few remains of fish and reptiles were discovered, except those of soft-shelled turtles. Bone remnants of hare and roe deer were also found. Some skeletal elements that may have intruded into the excavation belong to the mole rat (*Spalax*), a rodent widely distributed in Israel at present.

Invertebrates

Mollusc shells unearthed during the first excavation season were analyzed and identified by E. Tchernov (Table 22.23). Seventeen species of Mollusca (mostly marine) were present, the most abundant types being *Glycimeris violacescens*, *Murex trunculus*, and *Thais haemostoma*.

Mollusca are useful in zooarchaeology because of their wide distribution, good state of preservation, and relative freedom from human influence. Some species may have

Table 22.18. Distribution of Identifiable Fragments of the Camel (*Camelus* sp.) According to Periods

Bone	Iron Age	Persian	Hellenistic	Hasmonean	Roman	Early Arab	Total
Mandibula	…	2	…	…	…	1	3
Maxilla	…	2	…	…	…	…	2
Phalanx I	…	7	5	…	…	…	12
Phalanx II	1	5	…	…	1	…	7
Metapodia	…	…	1	…	…	…	1
Molar	…	5	…	1	…	…	6
Total	1	21	6	1	1	1	31

Table 22.19. Distribution of Identifiable Fragments of the Dog (*Canis familiaris*) According to Periods

Bone	LB	Iron Age	Persian	Hellenistic	Total
Mandibula	3	…	6	1	10
Maxilla	…	…	1	3	4
Skull fragments	…	…	1	…	1
Scapula	…	1	3	1	5
Humerus	5	…	13	6	24
Ulna	…	1	7	1	9
Radius	2	1	3	1	7
Metacarpus	…	…	2	…	2
Femur	…	…	5	…	5
Tibia	…	2	4	…	6
Pelvis	…	…	3	1	4
Calcaneus	1	…	…	…	1
Metapodia	1	…	1	…	2
Phalanx I	…	…	1	…	1
Molar	…	…	1	…	1
Costae	…	…	…	5	5
Total	12	5	51	19	87
Percentage	13.7	5.7	58.6	21.8	

been eaten by the inhabitants at Tel Michal; others, such as the genus *Murex*, from which a purple dye used throughout the Middle East was extracted (Biggs 1963, 1969), probably had other types of economic value. The genera *Cardium* and *Glycimeris* (both marine bivalves) are known to have been used as fertility charms. However, since in many cases the valves of *Glycimeris* molluscs are punctured at the umbo by wave action, it is difficult to demonstrate that they were perforated by humans to produce decorative or religious objects.

22.1.2. Chronological Summary of Animal Remains (Tables 22.24–22.27)

Middle Bronze Age IIB

The samples studied from the Middle Bronze Age IIB consist of 110 identifiable bone fragments with an MNI of 19. Sheep and goat remains represented 44.5 percent and cattle remains nearly 41 percent. The distinctive feature of this period is the large number of domesticates (92.7 percent), whereas hunting supplied only a small proportion of the

Table 22.20. Distribution of Identifiable Fragments of Cervids According to Periods

Bone	MB IIB	LB	Iron Age	Persian	Hellenistic	Hasmonean	Roman	Early Arab	Total
Mandibula	…	3	2	17	2	…	…	1	25
Maxilla	…	1	3	…	…	…	1	…	5
Skull fragments	…	…	…	1	…	…	…	…	1
Antlers	…	…	…	3	1	…	…	…	4
Scapula	…	3	2	8	…	…	1	…	14
Humerus	1	5	1	8	…	…	…	…	15
Ulna	…	1	…	2	…	…	…	…	3
Radius	1	4	2	6	…	…	…	…	13
Metacarpus	…	1	2	10	…	…	…	…	13
Femur	…	…	1	4	…	…	…	…	5
Tibia	1	1	2	7	1	1	…	…	13
Metatarsus	…	1	…	10	2	…	…	…	13
Astragalus	…	2	1	2	…	…	1	…	6
Calcaneus	…	1	…	12	1	1	2	…	17
Metapodia	1	7	5	34	1	2	1	…	51
Pelvis	…	…	…	4	1	…	…	…	5
Phalanx I	…	5	3	8	…	…	1	…	17
Phalanx II	…	4	1	11	1	…	1	…	18
Phalanx III	…	1	…	…	1	…	1	…	3
Molar	…	…	…	2	…	…	…	…	2
Total	4	40	25	149	11	4	9	1	243

Table 22.21. Measurements (mm) of Cervidae Bones

Bone	Number	Length/Height[a]	Width
Cervus elaphus			
Phalanx I	8	Min. 46.5 Max. 57.5 Mean 50.1	Min. 20.0 Max. 31.8 Mean 25.6
Phalanx II	3	Min. 32.0 Max. 37.0 Mean 35.0	Min. 22.0 Max. 24.0 Mean 23.0
Metacarpus proximal	3	...	Min. 35.0 Max. 39.5 Mean 36.5
Metatarsus proximal	4	...	Min. 30.0 Max. 38.5 Mean 33.6
Dama dama mesopotamica			
Phalanx I	1	25.0	19.0
Humerus (distal)	2	Min. 25.0 Max. 27.3 Mean 26.1	Min. 45.0 Max. 48.0 Mean 46.5

[a] Length shown for metacarpus, metatarsus, and phalanges; height shown for humerus.

Table 22.22. Distribution of Identifiable Bone Fragments of Gazelles (*Gazella* sp.) According to Periods

Bone	LB	Iron Age	Persian	Hellenistic	Hasmonean	Total
Mandibula	...	...	1	...	...	1
Horn core	...	...	1	...	...	1
Humerus	...	...	1	1	...	2
Radius	...	...	1	...	2	3
Metacarpus	...	...	2	...	...	2
Tibia	1	...	...	1	...	2
Metatarsus	1	...	1	...	...	2
Astragalus	...	...	...	1	...	1
Metapodia	...	...	5	...	1	6
Phalanx I	1	2	1	...	1	5
Total	3	2	13	3	4	25

animal protein consumed. Another characteristic feature is the presence of a relatively large number of pigs (6.3 percent) and cervids (3.6 percent). The dog is strikingly absent.

Late Bronze Age

The sample of identifiable bones derived from the Late Bronze Age consists of 641 bone fragments representing 44 animals. Again, sheep, goats, and cattle represent the majority, accounting for 85 percent of all animal remains. During this period the share of pork products in the meat

Table 22.23. Distribution of Mollusca Species by Percentage

Name	No.	Percentage
Glycimeris violacescens	34	26.4
Murex trunculus	22	17.0
Thais haemostoma	20	15.5
Cyprea spurca	11	8.5
Murex brandaris	10	7.8
Phalium saburon	6	4.7
Spondylus gaederopus	6	4.7
Cardium tuberculatum	6	4.7
Dolium galea	2	1.5
Anomia ephippium	2	1.5
Petreus sp. (terrestrial)	2	1.5
Conus mediterraneus	2	1.5
Charonia nobilis	2	1.5
Donax politus	1	0.8
Dentalium sp.	1	0.8
Polynices josephinus	1	0.8
Nussa circimcincta	1	0.8
Total	129	100.0

diet may have decreased to 0.3 percent. Only 1.8 percent of all animal bones came from dogs. Hunting of wild animals is reflected in the remains of deer (6.2 percent). No horse bones were retrieved from the Late Bronze Age strata, although we found remains of a single donkey.

Iron Age

There were 406 animal bone remains, representing an MNI of 39. Compared with the Middle and Late Bronze Ages, sheep and goat (now 58.8 percent of all animal remains) had increased in importance at the expense of cattle (whose remains decreased to 30.2 percent). The percentage of hunted animals, however, stayed relatively high (6.1 percent). The distinctive feature of this period is the first occurrence at the site of the camel (*Camelus* sp.).

Persian Period

The bone samples for the Persian period are the largest group available for any of the periods analyzed at Tel Michal, totaling 3,281 fragments and representing an MNI of 194. The increase of sheep and goats, which started in the Iron Age, continued. Cattle were second in importance. Hunting supplemented animal protein in the diet, as reflected in the bone remains of cervids (4.5 percent) and a few gazelles. Noteworthy is the single ostrich bone (*Struthio camelus*), presumably imported from some distance, since the bird is generally found in the desert or the Arabah and formerly inhabited the Negev and Judean deserts.

Hellenistic Period

The sample comprises 527 bone fragments representing an MNI of 44. The share of sheep/goat in the domestic animal

Table 22.24. Chronological Distribution of Animal Bones (As Expressed in Fragments and Percentages)

Period	Chelonia	Reptilia (Varia)	Pisces	Struthio camelus	Anser sp.	Gallus domesticus	Aves (Varia)	Lepus sp.	Rodentia	Capreolus capreolus	Cervidae	Camelus sp.	Gazella gazella	Canis familiaris	Sus scrofa	Equus asinus	Equus caballus	Bos taurus	Ovis/Capra	Total
Middle Bronze Age IIB	49	45	1	…	7	…	…	…	4	…	2	…	…	…	…	…	1	…	1	110
%	44.5	40.9	0.9	…	6.3	…	…	…	3.6	…	1.8	…	…	…	…	…	0.9	…		
Late Bronze Age	289	258	…	2	2	12	3	…	40	…	1	…	12	…	1	…	21	…	…	641
%	45.0	40.2	…	0.3	0.3	1.8	0.4	…	6.2	…	0.1	…	1.8	…	0.1	…	3.2	…	…	
Iron Age	239	123	…	…	3	5	2	1	25	…	3	…	2	1	…	…	2	…	…	406
%	58.8	30.2	…	…	0.7	1.2	0.4	0.2	6.1	…	0.7	…	0.4	0.2	…	…	0.4	…	…	
Persian	1,799	1,136	10	32	12	51	13	21	149	…	18	1	29	…	…	1	7	1	1	3,281
%	54.8	34.6	0.3	0.9	0.3	1.5	0.3	0.6	4.5	…	0.4	0.03	0.8	…	…	0.03	0.2	0.03	0.03	
Hellenistic	327	144	5	7	…	19	3	6	11	2	1	…	…	…	…	…	1	…	1	527
%	62.0	27.3	0.9	1.3	…	3.6	0.5	1.1	2.08	0.3	0.1	…	…	…	…	…	0.1	…	0.1	
Hasmonean	111	46	…	1	2	…	4	1	4	…	…	…	2	…	…	…	…	…	…	171
%	64.9	29.6	…	0.5	1.1	…	2.3	0.5	2.3	…	…	…	1.1	…	…	…	…	…	…	
Roman	114	65	1	…	4	…	…	1	9	…	9	…	2	2	…	…	…	…	…	207
%	55.0	31.4	0.4	…	1.9	…	…	0.4	4.3	…	4.3	…	0.9	0.9	…	…	…	…	…	
Early Arab	52	36	…	…	…	…	…	1	1	…	1	…	1	…	…	…	…	…	…	92
%	56.5	39.1	…	…	…	…	…	1.0	1.0	…	1.0	…	1.0	…	…	…	…	…	…	

Table 22.25. Comparative Numbers of Bones of Domestic and Wild Animals According to Periods

Period	Domestic	Wild	Total	Domestic (%)	Wild (%)
Middle Bronze Age IIB	102	8	110	92.7	7.3
Late Bronze Age	563	78	641	87.8	12.2
Iron Age	372	34	406	91.6	8.4
Persian	3,061	220	3,281	93.2	6.8
Hellenistic	508	19	527	96.3	3.7
Hasmonean	161	10	171	94.1	5.9
Roman	187	20	207	90.3	9.7
Early Arab	89	3	92	96.7	3.3
Total	5,043	392	5,435		

Table 22.26. Comparative Numbers of Bones of *Ovis/Capra* and *Bos taurus* According to Periods

Period	Ovis/Capra	Bos taurus	Total	Ovis/Capra (%)	Bos taurus (%)
Middle Bronze Age IIB	49	45	94	52.1	47.8
Late Bronze Age	289	258	547	52.8	47.1
Iron Age	239	123	362	66.0	34.0
Persian	1,799	1,136	2,935	61.2	38.7
Hellenistic	327	144	471	69.4	30.6
Hasmonean	111	46	157	70.7	29.3
Roman	114	65	179	63.6	36.3
Early Arab	52	36	88	59.0	41.0
Total	2,980	1,853	4,833		

stock increased over that of the Persian period, constituting about 62 percent of the bones analyzed. Cattle herding seemed to decrease in importance (27.3 percent). The number of dog remains increased significantly (3.6 percent of the total, compared with 1.5 percent in the Persian period, 1.2 percent in the Iron Age, and 1.8 percent in the Late Bronze Age). Some horse and donkey remnants were also found. Pigs were absent.

Hasmonean Period

The bone sample for this period is relatively small, 171 fragments (MNI of 22). Trends continued toward caprovine prevalence and diminution of cattle. The number of pigs increased slightly (1.1 percent of the total compared with 0.0 percent in the Hellenistic period and only 0.7 and 0.3 percent in the Iron Age and Persian period, respectively). Hunting was not significant. No dog bones were found.

Table 22.27. Percentages of Four Main Domestic Animals in Three
Excavation Sites (Israel and Anatolia)

Site	Period	Sheep/ Goats	Cattle	Pigs	Donkeys/ Horses
Koruçutepe	Middle Bronze Age II	48	40	11	1
	Late Bronze Age	58	30	11	1
Tel Michal	Middle Bronze Age II	44	40.9	6.3	0.9
	Late Bronze Age	45	40.2	0.3	0.3
Tel Aphek	Middle Bronze Age II	52.6	29.9	7.1	2.5

Roman Period

This period is represented by 207 bone fragments, with an MNI of 26. The number of cattle bones increased slightly. The dog again was absent.

Early Arab Period

The samples analyzed included 92 bone fragments with an MNI of 15. The trend toward increased raising of cattle was notable. On the other hand, consumption of pigs declined; no pig bones were found at Tel Michal in the Early Arab stratum, perhaps because of religious or cultural factors. Hunting also decreased (3.3 percent). Dogs were absent entirely.

22.2. CONCLUSIONS

The bone remains from Tel Michal provide us with direct evidence of the economy, animal exploitation, and diet of the inhabitants from the Middle Bronze Age II until the Early Arab period.

The percentage of domesticated animals was high from the beginning of settlement, starting with 92.7 percent of the total remains in the Middle Bronze Age and reaching 96.7 percent during the Early Arab period. These percentages indicate that animal husbandry was practiced continuously throughout the periods of occupancy at Tel Michal and suggest a relatively stable ecological environment, with possible minor changes in the microclimate. (Determination of detailed climatic changes requires analyses of microfaunal skeletal elements, and very few of these were recovered from Tel Michal.)

As is characteristic of many Near Eastern sites, the subsistence economy was based mainly on the raising of sheep and goats, the main sources of meat at Tel Michal throughout all the periods of occupation. The same pattern was found at several other sites in Israel and at Heshbon in Jordan.

Sheep appear to have been more common than goats. A similar preference for sheep was found at Heshbon during all the periods of occupation there (LaBianca 1975). This phenomenon suggests that wool was an important by-product of sheep domestication (Redman 1978).

Numerically, cattle breeding took second place at Tel Michal but may have been of equal significance since cattle produce more meat per head than sheep or goats, and beef is highest in nutritional value. Similar data for the ratio of sheep and goats to cattle were obtained from Tel Aphek (Hellwing, in press) and from Koruçutepe in eastern Anatolia (Boessneck and von den Driesch 1975). It appears that cattle as sources of meat and milk and as beasts of burden were indispensable to early Near Eastern societies.

Since sheep, goats, and cattle were the main domestic animals raised at Tel Michal, we may conclude that terrestrial animal meat was a major source of protein in the diet of the inhabitants. This was chemically confirmed by Bisel (see Chap. 21b) in her analysis of human bone mineral. Comparing the strontium/calcium ratios in skeletal fragments, Bisel concludes that the settlers of Tel Michal mostly consumed meat of terrestrial animals and relatively less vegetable protein.

The diet of the inhabitants at Tel Michal was supplemented to an extent by the flesh of wild animals, mainly red deer and gazelles. Remains of horses, donkeys, and dogs were rare throughout the ages; apparently these animals played an insignificant role in the diet of the people and were kept for other purposes. Camels were very rare, their few bone fragments present only from the Iron Age onward.

Pig production, relatively high in the Middle Bronze Age II, decreased drastically during the Late Bronze Age and remained low during the subsequent periods of occupation. Pig bones were nonexistent in the material of the Hellenistic and Early Arab periods; their absence in the latter period may be related to the influence of Islam in the region. Pigs were often slaughtered young, indicating that they were raised mainly for their tender meat. Such a preference for the meat of young pigs has been noted by others (Higgs 1968; Boessneck and von den Driesch 1975; Hellwing, in press).

Since most of the sheep, goats, and cattle were slaughtered as adults at Tel Michal, we may assume that the animals were maintained for their milk, wool, meat, and for reproductive stock. The situation is similar at Heshbon, where 60–70 percent of the sheep and goat bones came from young adults (LaBianca 1975). At the Aegean site of Saliagos, on the other hand, 40.4 percent of the sheep/goats and 68.6 percent of the cattle bones belonged to immature animals, suggesting that they were valued more for their meat (Higgs 1968).

At Tel Michal there was a numerical predominance of bones belonging to the forepart of the skeletons (humeri, scapulae) of sheep, goats, and cattle. This phenomenon, which may have some social or cultic significance, was reported also for Tel Dan (Wapnish et al. 1977).

Molluscs and fish were apparently not important in the diet of the ancient settlers, notwithstanding the proximity of Tel Michal to the sea. Some species of molluscs, such as *Murex brandaris* and *Murex trunculus*, may have been eaten, as seems to have been the case at Saliagos (Shackleton 1968). *Glycimeris violacescens*, the dominant species at Tel

Michal, was recovered from Neolithic and Early Bronze Age levels at Jericho, where the shells were used in necklaces or similar articles (Shackleton 1968).

Only 32 fragments of fish bones were recorded at Tel Michal. It is possible that they are scarce because the bones of the smaller varieties of fish, after being softened by the cooking process, were simply ingested together with the edible part of the fish. Several worked and polished fish bones were recorded, however, indicating the likelihood that all fish bones of sufficient size were recovered. In contrast to the picture at Tel Michal, fish bones of several species were found at Saliagos, with an overwhelming preponderance of tunny fish that apparently were deliberately caught during seasonal fishing expeditions of the inhabitants (Renfrew et al. 1968).

In summary, the overall picture is that of a sedentary economy based mainly on agriculture and animal husbandry.

NOTE

1. We would like to express our thanks to Professor E. Tchernov for his assistance in the identification of the mollusc material and for his advice and criticism.

REFERENCES

Besold, K. 1966. *Geschlechts und Gattungsunterschiede an Metapodien und Phalangen mitteleuropäischer Wildwiederkäuer.* Ph.D. dissertation. University of Munich.

Biggs, E. J. 1963. On the Mollusca Collected during the Excavations at Jericho 1952–1958 and Their Archaeological Significance. *Man* 13:153.

Biggs, E. J. 1969. Molluscs from Human Habitation Sites and the Problem of Ethnological Interpretation. Pages 423–429 in: *Science in Archaeology.* D. Brothwell and E. Higgs, eds. London.

Boessneck, J. 1969. Osteological Differences between Sheep (*Ovis aries* Linné) and Goats (*Capra hircus* Linné). Pages 331–358 in: *Science in Archaeology.* D. Brothwell and E. Higgs, eds. London.

Boessneck, J., and von den Driesch, A. 1975. Tierknochenfunde vom Koruçutepe bei Elâzig in Ostanatolien. Pages 1–220 in: *Koruçutepe 1 (Studies in Ancient Civilization).* M. N. van Loon, ed. Amsterdam.

Cornwall, I. W. 1968. *Bones for the Archaeologist.* London.

Ducos, P. 1968. *L'origine des animaux domestiques en Palestine.* Publications de l'Institut de Préhistoire de l'Université de Bordeaux, Mémoire 6. Bordeaux.

Hellwing, S. In press. Animal Remains from the Early and Middle Bronze Age at Tel Aphek. In *Tel Aphek-Antipatris I.* P. Beck and M. Kochavi, eds. Tel Aviv.

Higgs, E. S. 1968. Saliagos Animal Bones. Pages 114–117 in: *Excavations at Saliagos near Antiparos.* J. D. Evans and C. Renfrew, eds. London.

LaBianca, Ø. 1975. Øystein and Asta Sakala. The Anthropological Work. Pages 235–247 in: *Heshbon 1973: The Second Campaign at Tell Hesbān.* R. S. Boraas, and S. H. Horn, eds. Berrien Springs, Mich.

Lernau, H. 1975. Animal Remains. *Lachish V*: 86–103.

Lernau, H. 1978. Faunal Remains, Strata III-I. Pages 83–111 in: *Early Arad: The Chalcolithic Settlement and Early Bronze City*, vol. 1. R. Amiran et al., eds. Jerusalem.

Redman, C. L. 1978. *The Rise of Civilization: From Early Farmers to Urban Society in the Ancient Near East.* New York.

Renfrew, J. M., Greenwood, P. H., and Whitehead, P. J. 1968. Appendix VIII: The Fish Bones. Pages 118–121 in: *Excavations at Saliagos near Antiparos.* J. D. Evans and C. Renfrew, eds. London.

Schmid, E. 1972. *Atlas of Animal Bones for Prehistorians, Archaeologists and Quaternary Geologists.* New York.

Shackleton, N. J. 1968. The Mollusca, the Crustacea, the Echinodermata. Pages 122–141 in: *Excavations at Saliagos near Antiparos.* J. D. Evans and C. Renfrew, eds. London.

Silver, I. A. 1969. The Ageing of Domestic Animals. Pages 283–303 in: *Science in Archaeology.* D. Brothwell and E. Higgs, eds. London.

Sloan, R. E., and Duncan, M. A. 1978. Zooarchaeology of Nichoria. Pages 61–77 in: *Excavations at Nichoria in Southwest Greece*, vol. 1. G. Rapp, Jr. and S. E. Aschenbrenner, eds. Minneapolis.

von den Driesch, A. 1976. *A Guide to the Measurement of Animal Bones from Archaeological Sites.* Peabody Museum Bulletins. Cambridge, Mass.

Wapnish, P., Hesse, B., and Ogilvy, A. 1977. The 1974 Collection of Faunal Remains from Tell Dan. *BASOR* 227:35–62.

Watson, J. 1979. The Estimation of the Relative Frequencies of Mammalian Species: Khirokitia 1972. *JAS* 6:127–137.

23

Computer Techniques and Analyses

by Debra F. Katz

Computer personnel investigated ways to incorporate computer technology into the excavation and analytical phases of the project. Computer efforts began during the summer of 1978; the on-site phase ran through the summer of 1979 and the off-site phase continued through 1980. The primary goal was to develop and evaluate nonstatistical computer applications for the Tel Michal project.[1]

The initial strategy for the project was to establish reasonable goals for the types of applications desired and to make these applications available to the archaeologists during the excavation and also later during postexcavation analyses. The applications were defined as follows: (1) Design a computer database to store all excavation data previously recorded on several different forms, thus reducing the amount of clerical work. (2) Determine which computer-assisted studies would be most valuable for the archaeologist. (3) Assist in excavation management by providing continuous data-retrieval services. (4) Assist in operations such as cataloging, preparing material for publication, and providing information to aid in planning the next excavation season.

23.1. DATABASE DESIGN

SYSTEM 2000[2] was the database management system selected to store specific archaeological information. This system is utilized worldwide; it can handle hierarchical data structures, textual and numerical data; and it provides easy and efficient updating and retrieval operations using an easy-to-understand language. The definition can be modified to store additional material or to restructure existing material at any time during the life of the database. The report-writer feature produces sophisticated formats of data output retrieved from the database.

An ideal database for postexcavation processing would produce a conceptual reconstruction of the site in three dimensions. To accomplish this ultimate goal, it was necessary to understand the specific objectives of the excavation, to determine the methods of acquiring material remains, to

identify the techniques for recording data (i.e., the required types, formats, and amount of data), and to define the criteria used for compilation and classification of the recorded data.

Excavation data at Tel Michal were recorded on locus cards by the area supervisor. Before their arrival in Israel, computer personnel—each focusing on a specific aspect of the excavation data—designed a preliminary database definition that incorporated all previous methods of recording excavation data. In refining the design, the group retained as much of the original terminology and format as possible.

A significant amount of redundancy was eliminated when the information was stored in the database. Any such computer application should allow for relative data independence among the physical storage layout, the input techniques, and the retrieval capabilities. By breaking down the various types of data into related groups of specific attributes, the database design allowed for a wide variety of retrieval and updating capabilities that could be selected and organized according to a number of different criteria.

The focus of the database is defined by the basic recording unit of excavation, an individual locus or feature and its associated data. For each locus or feature, about 125 distinct attributes (components) were identified to describe related information. These attributes included excavation history and artifact type, characteristics, provenance, location, chronological assignment, and related documented references.

The hierarchical structure of SYSTEM 2000 was well suited to the inherent hierarchical nature of the excavation and recording techniques. Basic information regarding a locus/feature, such as type, area, square, numerical designation, or location, was identified as occurring once per locus/feature and grouped together. Since some loci contained more than one descriptor for a particular attribute, groups of attributes were defined under a common component name, referred to as a *repeating group*. For example, within a locus each basket of material uncovered was described in terms of its location, contents, and numerical

System Release Number   **2.60F**
Database name is Michal
Definition Number 31
Database Cycle   **1**

1* Type entry (char x(25));
2* Locus number (integer number 9999);
3* Area (char x(5));
4* Square (char x(10));
5* Stratum (char x(10));
7* Area supervisor (char x(15));
8* Date opened (date);
9* Level opened (decimal number 999.99);
10* Date closed (date);
11* Level closed (decimal number 999.99);
12* Floor level (decimal number 999.99);
13* Final locus (integer number 9(7));
14* Wall number (char x(7));
15* Wall date (date);
17* Brief wall description (non-key char x(50));
19* Bricks top (non-key decimal number 999.99);
20* Bricks base (non-key decimal number 999.99);
21* Stones top (non-key decimal number 999.99);
22* Stones base (non-key decimal number 999.99);
23* Wall length (non-key decimal number 999.99);
25* Wall orientation (integer number 999);
32* Earth matrix sample (char x(10));
33* Scientific analysis ref (char x(10));
34* Source-code (char x);
35* Last-alteration (date);
36* Loci info (record);
    37* Type code (char x in 36);
    38* Loci-above-below (integer number 9999 in 36);
    39* Squares (char xxxx in 36);
40* Locus card (record);
    41* Full description (non-key char x(70) in 40);
    42* Notes (char x(50) in 40);
50* Photos-drawings (record);
    52* Photo-drawing number (char x(12) in 50);
60* Basket list (record);
    61* Basket number (integer number 9(5) in 60);
    62* Basket date (date in 60);
    63* Basket level (decimal number 999.99 in 60);
    64* Find description (char x(50) in 60);
    65* Provenance (char x (50) in 60);
    66* Status of find (char x in 60);
    67* New basket locus (integer number 9(7) in 60);
    68* Ceramic count of bases (integer number 9(7) in 60);
    69* Basket-stratum (char x(5) in 60);

70* Objects (record in 60);
    71* Registration number (char x(7) in 70);
    72* Object (char x(25) in 70);
    73* Object date/period-period of reign (char x(20) in 70);
    74* Period-stratum (char x(5) in 70);
    75* Ceramic type/ruler (char x(10) in 70);
    76* Material (char x(10) in 70);
    77* Clay/area (char x(6) in 70);
    78* Core/city (char x(6) in 70);
    79* Grits little/mint (char x(6) in 70);
    80* Grits big/diameter minimum (char x(6) in 70);
    81* Firing/diameter maximum (char x(10) in 70);
    82* Make acquired (char x(10) in 70);
    83* Burnish/location (char x(10) in 70);
    84* Slip/date of issue (char x(6) in 70);
    85* Decoration/denomination (char x(100) in 70);
    86* Ostracon/found (char x(200) in 70);
    87* Drawing/axis (char x(10) in 70);
    88* Photo number/weight (char x(10) in 70);
    89* Join. Bask./presented (char x (10) in 70);
    90* X location along southern balk (decimal number 9999.99 in 70);
    91* Y location along western balk (decimal number 9999.99 in 70);
    92* Level (decimal number 999.99 in 70);
    93* Share of (char x(25) in 70);
    94* Special/locus/sample (char x(20) in 70);
    95* Object square (char x(20) in 70);
100* Object notes (record in 70);
    101* Full object description (char x(50) in 100);
    102* Legend (char x(100) in 100);
110* Publication (record in 70);
    111* Author (char x(25) in 110);
    112* Title (char x(100) in 110);
    113* Journal name (char x(150) in 110);
    114* Page (integer number 9999 in 110);
    115* Figure (char x(5) in 110);
    116* Plate (char x(5) in 110);
120* Museum storage-analysis (record in 70);
    121* Type of analysis (char x(100) in 120);
    122* Location name (char x(100) in 120);
    123* Acquisition number (char x(10) in 120);
    124* Acquisition date (date in 120);
    125* Return date (date in 120);

Figure 23.1.   Database description for Tel Michal.

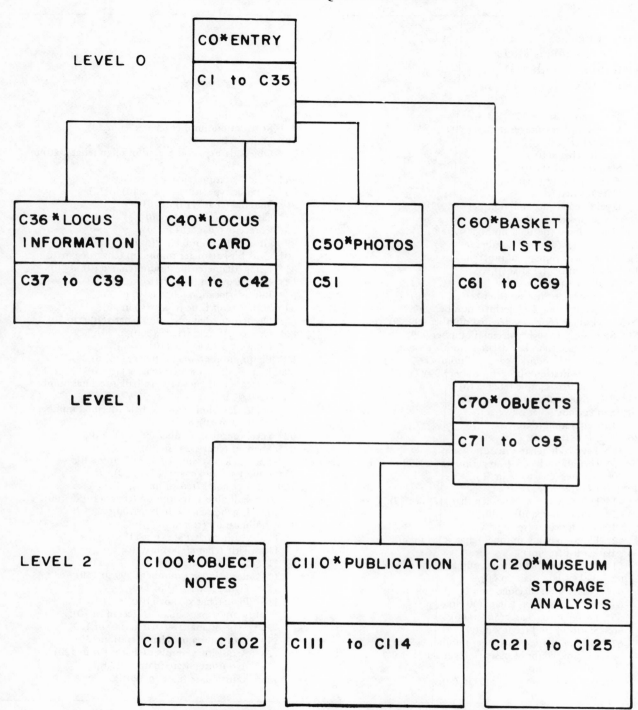

Figure 23.2. Graphic representation of Tel Michal database.

and chronological assignments. The database definition provided for the description of numerous baskets found within a single locus using component numbers 61 through 70, all part of the repeating group number 60* BASKET LIST. (The "basket" list includes all buckets of recordable material, numbered serially. The basket number is the primary retrieval unit. The registration numbers used in this volume consist of the basket number and suitable subnumbers, separated by a diagonal.)

Furthermore, within a basket, multiple objects to be cataloged and studied further were recorded under the repeating group 70* OBJECTS. The BASKET LIST (C60) and OBJECTS (C70) repeating groups contain all necessary data on each object recovered at the excavation, whereas the repeating group OBJECT NOTES (C100) allows for the storage of additional observations regarding a single object. Another repeating group, PUBLICATIONS (C110), contains references to any articles published about an object and serves as the beginning of a cross-index to future research of similar materials. The MUSEUM STORAGE ANALYSIS (C120) repeating group allows an archaeologist to keep track of specific objects once they leave the site for permanent storage, museum display, or further analysis. Other repeating groups include information on photo references, various loci above and beneath the locus recorded, and unedited and extensive field notes recorded by the excavator.

Once on site, the database was described and discussed with the archaeological staff and subsequently modified to address their particular concerns and expectations and the most crucial areas of computer assistance. The resulting definition is described in Figure 23.1 and represented graphically in Figure 23.2.

23.2. IMPLEMENTATION

For the Tel Michal project, SYSTEM 2000 was installed on a CDC 6600 series computer with a SCOPE operating system. The computer was located at the Tel Aviv University Computation Center in Ramat Aviv, about a half-hour drive from the site.

During the excavation seasons in 1978 and 1979, on-site duties consisted of data collection from each area on two of the seven existing forms used—locus cards and basket lists. A program was implemented to allow for those inexperienced with computers to perform data entry and modifications of general locus and basket information with ease. The program also contained error-checking routines to ensure more accuracy of data entered.

The necessary forms were collected daily by the computer staff and taken to the University of Tel Aviv Computation Center for data entry and retrievals. The type and format of data retrieval were produced according to the archaeologists' requests, and results were brought back to the site by late afternoon and reviewed with the area supervisors.

Initially, it was intended that all excavation data from the site be stored in the database and kept up-to-date. Un-

fortunately, the slow response time of the computer and a backlog of data from the previous season prevented the production of current material concerning all areas of the site. Therefore, data from only one area (Area C) was recorded to test the computer applications, to establish a methodology for computerized analysis of archaeological data, and to determine possible uses of the database when the area supervisors wrote end-of-season excavation reports. This also changed the focus of the project from an immediate system for on-site utilization to one that was more research oriented.

Predefined formatted reports were produced during the season using the report-writer facility of SYSTEM 2000, thus significantly reducing the time invested in clerical work.

Minnesota archaeological staff members experimented with retrieval operations from the database during the winter of 1978. Thus, goals more specific to problems encountered during the excavation were redefined for the 1979 season. The 1978 season revealed an urgent need to standardize rigorously the terms and descriptions used by the various area supervisors to provide for easier quantification of data at the site. Progress was made through the joint efforts of supervisory excavation staff and computer technical staff, although further refinement of the terminology was still an ongoing need.

A new area of study during the 1979 season involved the use of computerized graphic programs as an aid to archaeological analysis of the site. All artifacts recovered and cataloged from the excavation were presented spatially in a given locus or area: (1) in *plan* view, with X and Y coordinates measured from the southwest corner of a given square (Fig. 23.3); (2) in *section* view perspective with an east-west orientation (Fig. 23.4); and (3) in *section* view with a north-south orientation. The coordinates were entered in the database, and a program was written to produce a graph showing artifact distribution based upon any desired number of criteria, such as the chronological period of origin, specific artifact type or specific level, locus, or feature.

23.3. RESULTS

Two types of forms, locus cards and basket lists, were successfully developed through the use of a data entry program. This method of entry allowed for storage of all excavation data and for organized and rapid retrieval of data, thus reducing significantly the amount of paperwork required of each supervisor. Refinements continued throughout the project.

The database design allowed for a variety of retrieval operations. The reports produced lists of loci and walls, daily basket list forms, and locus card information.

Figure 23.5 is a reproduction of the locus card used at Tel Michal. It can be altered slightly to omit basket descriptions, thus reducing locus data to one or two lines rather than requiring an 8-by-11-inch form.

Lists were developed to report all details concerning a

SPECIAL FIND COORDINATES
ONE FIND PER BASKET

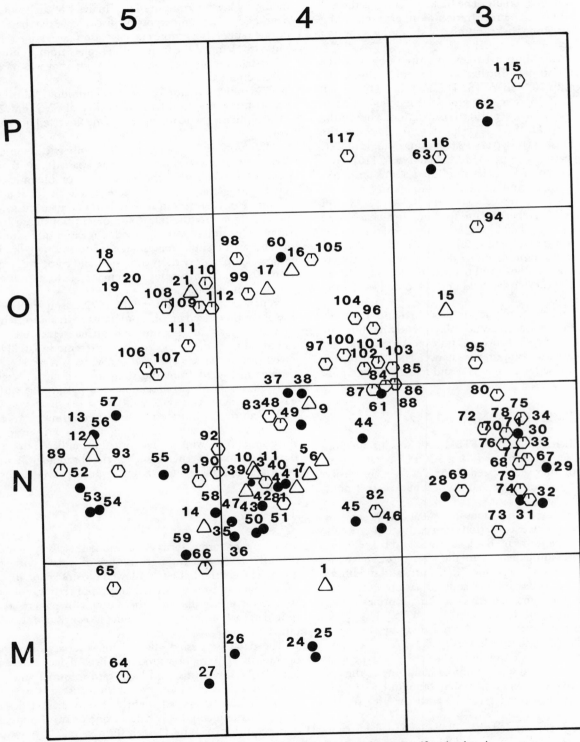

Figure 23.3. Graphic representation of distribution of Area C artifacts in plan view.

Legend for Fig 23.3

1△	984/1	COOKING POT RIM	78 ⊙	3268/50	PEBBLE
3△	855/60	IRON FRAGMENTS	79 ⊙	3271/50	FLINT TOOL
4△	853/50	TWO WORKED STONES	80 ⊙	3301/60	COIN
5△	862/50	FLINT IMPLEMENT	81 ⊙	857/50	STONE ALTAR
6△	888/50	GRINDING STONE (FRAGMENT)	82 ⊙	907/60	ARROWHEAD
7△	908/60	IRON FRAGMENT	83 ⊙	977/1	COMPLETE BOWL
8△	940/1	GEOMORPHIC FIGURINE	84 ⊙	3206/1	LAMP
9△	3275/60	IRON FRAGMENTS	85 ⊙	3208/1	LAMP
10△	969/50	FLINT IMPLEMENT	86 ⊙	3210/1	LAMP
11△	3252/1	BOWL (WITHOUT BASE)	87 ⊙	975/1	TOP PART OF JAR
12△	877/50	FLINT IMPLEMENT	88 ⊙	3283/60	IRON FRAGMENTS
13△	886/50	FLINT IMPLEMENT	89 ⊙	922/60	IRON TOOL FRAGMENT
14△	3296/1	DECORATED SHERD	90 ⊙	978/50	FLINT IMPLEMENT
15△	976/1	COOKING POT	91 ⊙	1008/1	CHALICE – SMALL & CLOSED
16△	909/1	CHALICE FRAGMENT	92 ⊙	3278/1	RIMLESS CHALICE
17△	916/1	COOKING POT FRAGMENT	93 ⊙	954/1	CHALICE BASE
18△	921/1	COMPLETE CHALICE	94 ⊙	918/60	FIBULA
19△	885/50	GRINDING STONE (FRAGMENT)	95 ⊙	933/60	BRACELET FRAGMENT
20△	943/1	BOWL FRAGMENT	96 ⊙	851/60	COIN
21△	957/50	GRINDING STONE	97 ⊙	852/60/1	COIN
24●	-59●	LAB SAMPLE	98 ⊙	903/1	JUG (UPPER PART)
60△		LAB SAMPLE	99 ⊙	919/1	COMPLETE JUGLET
61△		LAB SAMPLE	100 ⊙	850/50	ALTAR (FRAGMENT)
62△		LAB SAMPLE	101 ⊙	3205/1	LAMP
63△		LAB SAMPLE	102 ⊙	3207/1	LAMP
64 ⊙	3201/50	FLINT TOOL (FRAGMENT)	103 ⊙	3209/1	LAMP
65 ⊙	3229/1	STORAGE JAR – TOP HALF	104 ⊙	3211/60	IRON FRAGMENT
66 ⊙	3227/1	CHALICE (BASE)	105 ⊙	949/1	COMPLETE BOWL
67 ⊙	3218/50	FLINT TOOL?	106 ⊙	852/1	JUGLET – LOWER HALF
68 ⊙	3219/1	ATTIC LAMP	107 ⊙	866/60	BROKEN KNIFE
69 ⊙	3220/50	WEIGHT?	108 ⊙	878/60	IRON FRAGMENTS
70 ⊙	3222/50	GRINDING STONE (FRAGMENT)	109 ⊙	882/1	CHALICE
71 ⊙	3236/60	COIN	110 ⊙	883/60	IRON TOOL BROKEN
72 ⊙	3237/60	ARROWHEAD	111 ⊙	937/1	INCENSE BURNER
73 ⊙	3245/50	WORKED STONE?	112 ⊙	947/1	COMPLETE BOWL
74 ⊙	3246/1	COOKING POT (UPPER PART)	115 ⊙	3328/60	COPPER "KEY"
75 ⊙	3249/64	COIN	116 ⊙	3335/1	JUG
76 ⊙	3250/80	BEAD FRAGMENT	117 ⊙	3337/61	IRON FRAGMENT
77 ⊙	3267/1	LAMP			

particular artifact type, coordinates for selected data in a format utilized as input to graphics routines, forms to assist volunteers in recording coordinates for cataloged objects, and all geologic samples taken by the excavation staff.

The same reports were presented with the data re-sorted according to different criteria, which provided easier means for cross-referencing between the various existing forms. For example, basket lists were recorded according to the date of discovery and then rearranged numerically and by depth for a specific locus to give the excavator a better stratigraphic record.

Figures 23.3 and 23.4 are examples of the type of graphic representations designed to portray artifact distributions visually. Data were retrieved from the database for finds dated to the Persian and Hellenistic periods. Through stereographic reproduction, a three-dimensional representation is possible. Artifact types will eventually be delineated by their material through the use of different symbols to represent each type. On more sophisticated graphics terminals, the user can easily manipulate the view desired and get a three-dimensional perspective of the artifacts and their context and relationship to each other and to their assigned period.

23.4. CONCLUSIONS

The Tel Michal computer project confirmed the value of an on-site computerized recording system during archaeological excavation. Deficiencies in the existing system were recognized, and modifications were made to increase the potential of the system.

Further work needs to be done to standardize terminology and recording methods for obtaining coordinates of objects, features, and topographical data. Data recorded must also be reduced to the most significant attributes for analysis and interpretation. The use of key words to describe loci could reduce data entry time significantly: comparative studies can be extremely difficult without them.

Limitations in the database management system pre-

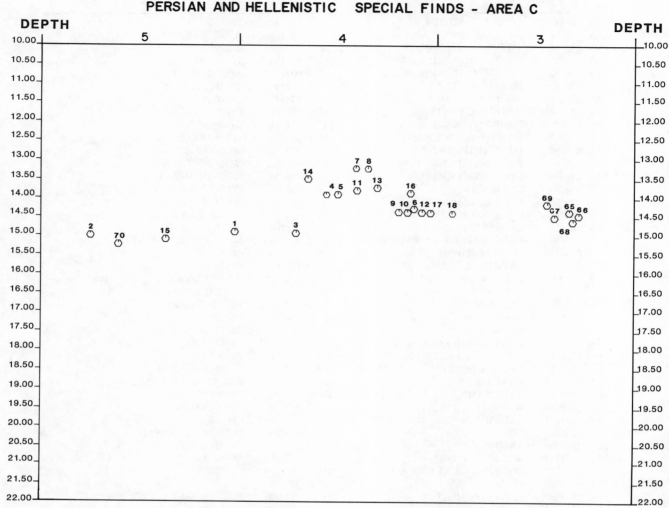

Figure 23.4. Graphic representation of Area C artifacts in section view.

vented many more potential applications. Since the implementation of the database, new features and enhancements to SYSTEM 2000 now meet some of the excavators' earlier needs. The system's capability to search for key words, phrases, or characters helps to locate similar data that were previously described in various terminologies.

Computer-plotted maps were not used at Tel Michal because maps had already been produced manually. However, the computer could produce a graphic visual representation of an excavated locus, square, area, or site, reducing it to a visually manageable size for the archaeologist's use in viewing artifact distributions and strata from a variety of new perspectives. Patterns in the data could be more easily recognized and strata and artifact assemblages could be more easily identified than with conventional archaeological techniques.

To explore the feasibility and benefit of computer-plotted maps and sections, the coordinates of cataloged objects were entered in the database. By specifying a subset

of data to be plotted, excavators then had greater flexibility in examining the various contexts and relationships among finds.

As yet, no simple method exists for graphic reproduction of architectural features such as wall structures and locus drawings. However, graphic programs can present schematic vertical geologic and archaeological sections, strata designations, contour maps of the site, and isometric drawings of artifacts.

A major feature of a computer database is its capacity for "instant" generation of formatted reports, charts, maps, and artifact-distribution printouts. The database can also provide references to particular objects and lists of the objects with some descriptive data.

The use of a computer for storing information from the archaeological site at Tel Michal provided a simple means of retrieving, processing, and handling a vast amount of data. More immediate benefits included the ability to check on a daily basis for errors in the recording and entry

Legend for Fig. 23.4

1	978/50	P	FLINT IMPLEMENT
2	975/1	P	TOP PART OF JAR
3	977/1	P	COMPLETE BOWL
4	853/1	P	ATTIC BOWL FRAGMENT
5	853/2	P	ATTIC BOWL FRAGMENT
6	3205/1	P	LAMP
7	3206/1	P	LAMP
8	3206/2	P	LAMP (FRAGMENTS)
9	3207/1	P	LAMP
10	3208/1	P	LAMP
11	3209/1	P	LAMP
12	3210/1	P	LAMP
13	850/50	HEL	ALTAR (FRAGMENT)
14	857/50	P	STONE ALTAR
15	866/60	P	BROKEN KNIFE
16	851/60	HEL	COIN
17	852/1	HEL	JUGLET—LOWER HALF
*18	852/60/1	HEL	COIN
65	3219/1	P	ATTIC LAMP
66	3246/1	P	COOKING-POT (UPPER PART)
67	3250/1	P	BOWL
68	3267/1	P	LAMP
69	3301/60	HEL	COIN
70	3229/1	P	STORAGE JAR—TOP HALF

*Items 19–64 are a group of Hellenistic coins that have been left out of this graphic representation.

LOCUS CARD: TEL MICHAL

Final—130 Old—130   **Area—C**   **Square—M04**

Type of Locus	Stratum	Date Opened	Level Opened	Date Closed	Level Closed	Floor Level	Locus Above	Locus Below
Not Specified P		05/07/77	14.60	28/07/77				
Basket No.	Basket Date	Level	+ −R	Find Description	15.20		127	148 146
00860	05/07/77	14.67	−					
03200	03/03/78	14.77	−	Sherds, Shells				
00868	07/07/77	14.86	+					
00861	06/07/77	14.95	+	Shell Object				
00873	08/07/77	15.03	−					
00899	12/07/77	15.03	+	Lab Sample				
03215	04/07/78	15.14	+	Persian Sherds				
00968	22/07/77	15.23	+	Bone				
03203	03/07/78	15.79	+	Sherds, Shells; Persian-Iron				

Description

This locus consisted of reddish sandy soil and fill.
Fired bricky debris, perhaps from kiln Locus 135, was discovered in small patches around 14.55. A few tumbled stones were also in evidence. However, no real architecture could be discerned. Sherds were of a mixed Persian and Israelite nature.
1978—removed N. balk
Photo references—Patchy bricky debris (#1)

Figure 23.5. Sample of computer-generated locus card.

of data, for consistency of recording methods and entry conventions, and for the location and movement of any item once it had been excavated and cataloged. Using the immediate results from the computer to explore emerging relationships among features and artifact types, excavators can augment and improve their excavation strategies.

NOTES

1. I would like to thank Control Data Corporation, Intel Corporation, the Tel Aviv University Computation Center, and the University of Minnesota Computer Center for their assistance. Thanks are also due to Steven Nachtsheim, assistant director of the University of Minnesota Computer Center, who wrote the data entry program, to Carol Moss, University of Minnesota, Duluth, who performed the data entry, and to Steve Reisman, who programmed the projections.

2. SYSTEM 2000 is a registered trademark of Intel Corporation.

REFERENCES

Aharoni, Y., Herzog, Z., Kochavi, M., Moshkovitz, S., and Rainey, A. F. 1976. Methods of Recording and Documenting. *Beer-Sheba I*: 119–131.

Control Data Corporation. 1975. *DDL Version 2 Reference Manual*. Sunnyvale, Calif.

Gaines, S. W. 1974. Computer Use at an Archaeological Field Location. *Am. Antiquit.* 39:454–462.

24a

Provenance of Three Categories
of Bronze Age Decorated Vessels

by Vanda Vitali, George Rapp, Jr., and Ora Negbi

The purpose of this study was to determine the provenance of certain unusual decorated kraters with a horizontal loop handle found at Tel Michal. These are quite rare in Late Bronze Age assemblages of Israel (Chap. 5.2.1.B4; Fig. 5.8.11–14). In addition, two other decorated wares found on the site were analyzed: Chocolate-on-White (Chap. 5.2.1.B1, n.1) and Bichrome ware (Chap. 5.2.2.A; Fig. 5.9:13–16). The origin of the former has hardly been studied before. Although Bichrome ware has been shown to be Cypriote in a number of neutron activation analyses, it is still problematic because some specimens may be local imitations (Artzy et al. 1973; 1976; 1981; see Chap. 24b, Sample 8).[1]

Such studies have shown that the chemical (elemental) composition of ceramic wares provides a sensitive means for distinguishing locally made Cypriote-style vessels from those that were actually made in Cyprus and imported to the Levant. Thus, it was decided that instrumental neutron activation analysis (INAA), a technique most frequently used in this type of study, should be performed on the three wares mentioned above to determine their origins. It was also decided that all three vessel types of unknown origin be principally compared with the Cypriote ceramics, since Cyprus is believed to be the source of almost all the imported pottery at Tel Michal.

The underlying concept in provenance determination based on the chemical composition of pottery is that the elemental content of pottery is characteristic of the clay from which the pottery is made. The composition of the clay in turn relates directly to the local geology of the site where the clay was formed. Therefore, in provenance studies, potsherds and clays of known origin are first analyzed so that the chemical concentration profiles characteristic of individual ceramic groups or sites can be defined. A comparison of these concentration profiles with the profile of a ceramic (or groups of ceramics) of unknown origin can then be performed to establish the likelihood of an unknown ceramic belonging to any of the known groups or to another group of unknown origin.

The ceramics selected for this study were as follows: (1) Local Canaanite ware, including undecorated bowls, cooking pots, and storage jars, which by their sheer quantities in every excavation are assumed to be of local manufacture, an assumption confirmed by petrographic analyses. Included in this group are some painted versions of the above. This group represents the general Late Bronze Age repertoire of local, domestic, everyday vessels. (2) Red-on-Black, White Painted, White Slip, Monochrome, and Base Ring wares. (3) Wares of "unknown" origin: decorated kraters, Chocolate-on-White, and Bichrome wares. Table 24.1 lists the types and numbers of samples for each of these groups. The size of the sample for each category is proportional to its representation in its respective group on the site.

The instrumental neutron activation analyses were done on a TRIGA-type reactor at the University of Wisconsin, Madison. The irradiation time was 2 hours in a neutron flux of 2×10^{13}. After 10 days of decay time, the samples were counted for 1 hour using an intrinsic germanium detector with an active volume of 117 cm^3; 1.85 KEV full-width, one-half maximum (FWHM) resolution; and a rated efficiency of 29 percent. The counting was done on a Tracor Northern TN11 unit.

The INAA was carried out as part of a long-term University of Minnesota-Duluth Archaeometry Laboratory investigation of the geologic/geographic provenance of native copper artifacts. The experimental conditions as well as the trace elements examined in this study were those selected for copper analyses and are not ideal for ceramics. Originally the ceramics were analyzed for twenty elements, namely As, Ba, Cd, Ce, Co, Cr, Cs, Fe, Hf, Lu, Ni, Sb, Sc, Se, Ta, Te, Th, W, Yb, and Zn. The element concentration data were then subjected to multivariate statistical analysis.

Table 24.1. Ceramics of Local, Cypriote, and Unknown Origin Used in the Instrumental Neutron Activation Analysis

Origin	Category	No. of samples analyzed	Illustration	Sample No. in Petrographic Analysis[a]
Group 1: Local	Undecorated bowls	10	Fig. 5.5:1-11	...
	Cooking pots	9	Fig. 5.6:1-10	21, 23
	Undecorated storage jars	10	Fig. 5.7:1-5	17
	Decorated bowls	2	Fig. 5.8:1-6	16
	Decorated storage jars and jugs	10	Fig. 5.9:1-11	13, 20
Group 2: Cypriote	Monochrome and Base Ring	5	Fig. 5.10:16-20	1, 2, 3, 22
	White Slip	9	Fig. 5.10:1-12	4, 5
	White Painted	9	Fig 5.4:5-16	7, 12
	Red-on-Black	3	Fig. 5.4:1-2	18
Group 3: Unknown	Decorated kraters	6	Fig. 5.8:11-14	6, 14, 19
	Bichrome	4	Fig. 5.9:13-16	8
	Chocolate-on-White	4	Not illustrated	9, 10, 11

[a] See Chap. 24b.

Provenance studies of various Cypriote style wares (Artzy et al. 1973; 1976; Bieber 1977; Courtois 1977; Artzy et al. 1981) have shown that, given the basaltic origin of most Cypriote clays, there exists a general compositional profile characteristic of Cypriote ceramics that distinguishes them from wares originating in Israel. Thus, it was decided that general elemental concentration profiles ("'fingerprints") be established that are characteristic of the local Canaanite and Cypriote wares, respectively. These profiles would then serve as a basis for the comparison and allocation of the samples of unknown origin and their allocation to either the Canaanite or the Cypriote group.

Classification and discriminant procedures were the techniques used for the statistical analysis of the compositional data. A detailed description of these methods is given in Cooley and Lohnes (1971). All statistical procedures were performed using SPSS Version 9 programs.

Vessels believed to be of local origin and those of Cypriote origin were first separated into their respective groups (Groups 1 and 2). These a priori groups formed the basis for comparison in the classification procedure. Before establishing the characteristic concentration profiles for each of the two groups and before initiating the classification procedure, the distribution properties of elemental concentrations for the measured elements of each group were examined and an investigation of the relationships between various elements was performed (CONDESCRIPTIVE and PEARSON CORR programs, respectively). On the basis of the results obtained, it was decided that raw data rather than log-transformed data would be used and that only eight elements—barium, cobalt, chromium, iron, hafnium, lutetium, scandium, and ytterbium—would be considered in the subsequent statistical analysis.

Assuming an approximate multivariate normal distribution with approximately equal variance-covariance matrices for the two groups, a characteristic concentration profile for each of the two groups was established using the classification function (Klecka 1975). Results of the subsequent discriminant analysis showed that on the basis of elemental composition, local and Cypriote ceramic groups can be distinguished from each other in a statistically significant manner. A histogram of the analyzed local and Cypriote samples along the linear discriminant function, which most successfully separates the two groups on the basis of their overall chemical composition, illustrates this finding (Fig. 24.1).

Individual samples of the vessels of unknown origin (Group 3) were then allocated to the two established groups, based on the value of the expected probability calculated for each sample for each of the groups (Tatsuoka 1971). This probability expresses the relative likelihood of an unknown ceramic belonging to each one of the known groups of ceramics.

The following results were obtained: all six samples of the decorated kraters and the four samples of the Chocolate-on-White ware (Group 3) were found to resemble the vessels of the local group (Group 1); three samples of "Bichrome ware" were attributed to the Cypriote group (Group 2); whereas the fourth sample was found to be closer in elemental composition to the vessels of Group 1, although it showed only a slightly greater expected probability of belonging to the local group than to the Cypriote group. Figure 24.2 illustrates these findings. However, it should be pointed out that most of the samples of unknown origin exhibited rather small conditional probability values for the groups to which they were allocated. This indicates that the chemical composition of these unknown ceramic samples is not very similar to that of the vessels in the groups to which they were assigned. Although this might be so, the small conditional probability values could also have resulted from the definition of the a priori groups by a broad selection of vessels represented by too few samples.

This study has shown that, in general, the local pottery excavated at Tel Michal can be distinguished chemically in

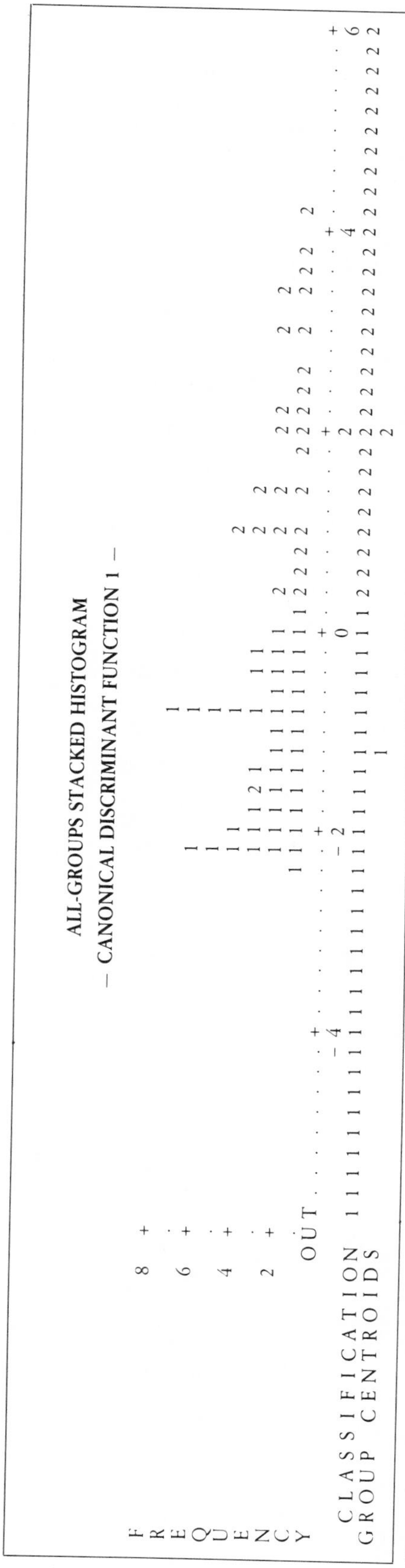

Figure 24.1. Histogram of analyzed local Canaanite (Group 1) and Cypriote (Group 2) pottery along linear discriminant function showing separation of two groups based on their chemical composition.

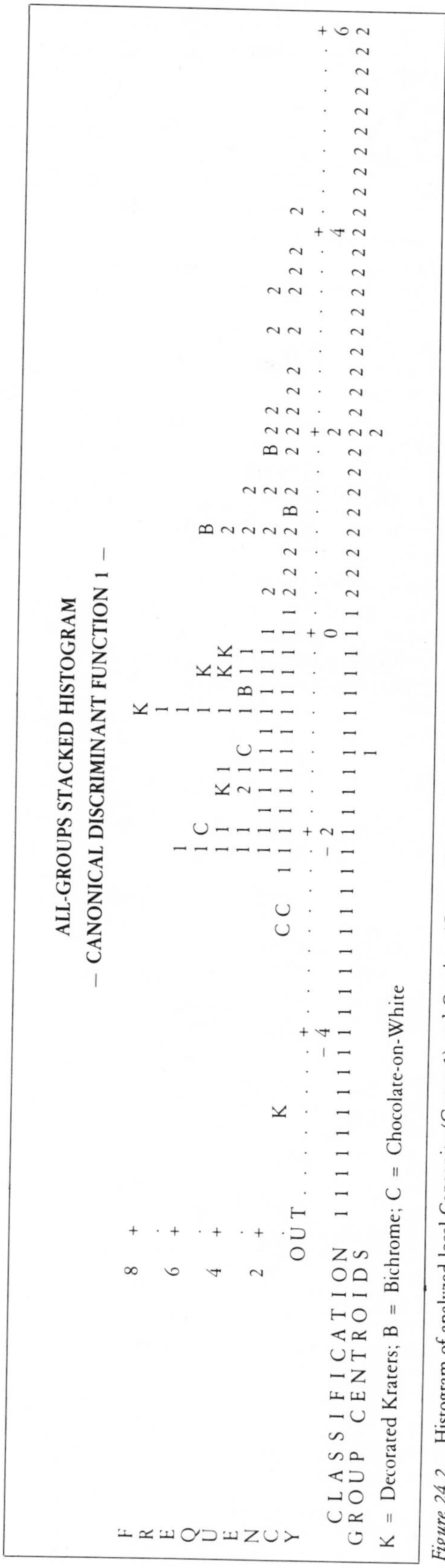

Figure 24.2. Histogram of analyzed local Canaanite (Group 1) and Cypriote (Group 2) wares showing allocation of samples of unknown origin.

K = Decorated Kraters; B = Bichrome; C = Chocolate-on-White

a statistically significant manner from the Cypriote wares found at the site. This finding was not unexpected. It was also shown that, among the specimens of unknown origin submitted for analysis (Group 3), only the Bichrome ware appears to be Cypriote. The decorated kraters—whose provenance was the motivation for this study—are most likely not of Cypriote origin, as their composition more closely resembles local wares than Cypriote wares. However, the question of their precise origin in the Levant remains open. The same applies to the origin of the Chocolate-on-White ware (see Chap. 24b, Samples 9–11, where they are shown to contain nonplastic inclusions typical of Nubian sandstone).

However, the results of the provenance determination of the selected vessels of unknown origin should be taken merely as an indication of the potential that exists for using a statistical approach to the chemical characterization and classification of the given ware type. In any further study, it would be necessary to refine the definition of the individual groups by using a much larger number of samples. It could also be valuable to compare the wares on a type and/or site basis rather than globally, as was done in this study. A more precise determination of the origin of the three categories of "unknown" wares could be accomplished by comparing the wares of interest with ceramics from a number of potential sources.

NOTE

1. James Allert, University of Minnesota, provided invaluable assistance in performing the statistical analysis for this study. Since 1972, the University of Minnesota-Duluth Archaeometry Laboratory neutron activation analyses have been supported, in part, by the Reactor Sharing Program under DOE contract E-(11–1)-2144 to the University of Wisconsin Reactor Facility, Richard Cashwell, Director.

REFERENCES

Artzy, M., Asaro, F., and Perlman, I. 1973. The Origin of the "Palestinian" Bichrome Ware. *JAOS* 93:446–461.

Artzy, M., Perlman, I., and Asaro, F. 1976. Wheel-Made Pottery of the MC III and LC I Periods in Cyprus Identified by Neutron Activation Analysis. *RDAC*: 20–28.

Artzy, M., Perlman, I., and Asaro, F. 1981. Cypriot Pottery Imports at Ras Shamra. *IEJ* 31:37–47.

Bieber, A. M. 1977. *Neutron Activation Analysis of Archaeological Ceramics from Cyprus*. Ph.D. thesis. University of Connecticut.

Cooley, W. W. and Lohnes, P. R. 1971. *Multivariate Data Analysis*. New York.

Courtois, L. 1977. Céramiques et métallurgie anciennes. *BASLS* 16:9–17.

Klecka, W. R. 1975. Discriminant Analysis. Pages 434–467 in: *Statistical Package for the Social Sciences*, 2d ed. N. H. Nie et al., eds. New York.

Tatsuoka, M. M. 1971. *Multivariate Analysis: Techniques for Educational and Psychological Research*. New York.

24b

Petrographic Analysis of the Bronze Age Pottery

by Jonathan Glass

Twenty-three samples of Middle Bronze Age II and Late Bronze Age pottery from Tel Michal were selected for petrographic analysis. These samples were drawn from a larger collection of more than 80 sherds that had been prepared previously for instrumental neutron activation analysis (INAA) (Chap. 24a; Table 24.1).[1] A broad range of representative sherds was selected for thin-section analysis by eye and by microscopic examination.

This chapter is intended to (1) give a petrographic description of the various MB II and LB pottery types from Tel Michal; (2) offer a workable classification system that might partially explain the nature of the material variations; (3) discuss the possible provenance of the different material groups; (4) provide an additional basis for the interpretation of the neutron activation data; and (5) delineate a framework for future detailed studies on selected problems related to the Tel Michal pottery.

Of the 23 samples analyzed, 13 distinct petrographic types were defined that probably represent 13 different pottery workshops in various geologic environments in or outside Israel. Three major provenance categories were distinguished. The *foreign pottery* category includes all the samples for which the petrographic analysis indicated geologic environments inconsistent with the general geologic features of central Israel. The *local (noncoastal) pottery* category includes all samples for which the petrographic analysis indicated general geologic features of Israel but inconsistency with the geology of the coastal plain. These, then, were apparently not manufactured at or near Tel Michal but could have originated in any other region that shared the same geologic features. The *local (coastal) pottery* category includes all the samples for which the petrographic analysis indicated geologic environments consistent with the geology of the coastal plain of Israel. These samples were probably manufactured in Tel Michal or in the nearby vicinity.

24b.1. FOREIGN POTTERY

The following 13 samples probably originated outside the Tel Michal area and are very likely of foreign manufacture.

Samples 1, 2, and 22

Samples 1 and 2 were classified by the excavators as Cypriote Monochrome ware, but without comparative material a positive determination could not be made. Petrographically, they were not of local origin. This conclusion is based primarily on the presence of tiny mica flakes that form an original constituent of the clay. In many details, Sample 22 (which came from a Base Ring I vessel) resembles Samples 1 and 2 and is probably of the same origin.

Sample 3

This sample came from a jug of Cypriote Base Ring ware. Although petrographic data are insufficient to prove foreign origin, the sample was rich in carbonate inclusions and micas were probably absent, indicating probable origin in a Cypriote environment dominated by carbonate lithologies.

Samples 4 and 5

These belong to the Cypriote White Slip ware, which consists petrographically of nonlocal elements. The nonplastic assemblage of these samples included various lithic and mineral fragments derived from altered basic igneous rocks of volcanic origin. Perhaps these samples came from the central part of Cyprus where such rocks were abundant.

Sample 7

This sample, which belongs to Cypriote White Painted

ware, was characterized by a silty clay with various silicates: hornblende, plagioclase, micas, and quartz. Sandy quartz and carbonate inclusions also occurred. The clay-rich groundmass was highly calcareous and microfossiliferous.

Samples 9, 10, and 11

All three samples, which turned out to be Chocolate-on-White ware, shared several petrographic features that indicated their probable common source. Their clay-rich groundmass was silty, free of carbonates, and fired to a light color. The coarser nonplastics were rounded quartz grains in a variety of light and dark shale fragments resembling (but not identical to) Midianite pottery. According to the petrographic data, this pottery was probably not of local Canaanite origin. These samples reflected a geologic environment like the Nubian sandstone terrain of Sinai, the southern Negev, and Transjordan.

Sample 12

The nonplastic assemblage of this sample, classified as Cypriote White Painted ware, included various mineral and lithic fragments: hornblende, epidote, rutile, biotite, highly altered feldspars, olivine, quartz, carbonates, serpentine, and lithic fragments of volcanic rocks. This assemblage reflects a geologic terrain dominated by basic and perhaps ultrabasic rocks consistent with the geology of the Troödos Mountains in central Cyprus. However, such rocks also originate in other Mediterranean countries such as Turkey, Syria, and Greece.

Sample 15

A highly calcareous and micaceous clay characterized this sample, which is classified as Cypriote Composite ware (see Chap. 5.1.2.2). The micas indicated foreign origin (not included in the INAA study).

Sample 18

This fine-grained sample is Black-on-Red ware. Nonplastics were almost absent down to the silt fraction. The sample was basically a very fine micaceous clay. Petrographically it was certainly not local, but comparative material is needed to make a more conclusive statement concerning its provenance.

24b.2. LOCAL (NONCOASTAL) POTTERY

Samples 6, 14, 16, 19, 20, and 23

This group of sherds was characterized by a large-volume proportion of coarse sand composed of three main ingredients: quartz, various carbonates, and flint splinters. The clay-rich groundmass was microfossiliferous and spotted with tiny iron oxide concretions. Clearly, such a clay and such an assemblage of coarse nonplastics did not come from the coastal plain of Israel, and it can therefore be stated safely that this pottery was not manufactured at Tel Michal or any other coastal site. Quartz, carbonates, and flint associated in a coarse sand have been found in Neogene deposits exposed along the eastern fringes of the southern coastal plain, but a more detailed study is needed to confirm this correlation.

Five of the samples (6, 14, 16, 19, and 20) belong to decorated kraters, bowls, and jugs, whereas the sixth (23) is a cooking pot.

Sample 8

This sample belonged to the so-called Bichrome ware for which a Cypriote origin has been suggested (see Chap. 5.2.2). The coarse nonplastics were dominated by rounded quartz grains, and the clay-rich groundmass was calcareous and rich in microfossils. Such a combination of materials could be of local origin, but since the Cypriote sites where this pottery was found occur on the northeastern part of the island where the lithology is basically similar to that of Israel, a definite conclusion cannot be reached.

Sample 13

The coarse, nonplastic assemblage of this sample (a locally produced decorated jug) was dominated by rounded quartz and chalky grains. The clay-rich groundmass was calcareous and contained microfossils.

24b.3. LOCAL (COASTAL) POTTERY

Sample 17

The coarse nonplastics here were dominated by rounded sandy quartz grains, and the clay-rich groundmass was silty (quartz) and very dark. Here the nonplastics were probably derived from inland sand dunes or *ḥamra*. (*Kurkar* grains were absent.) This sample was defined by the excavators as a locally produced storage jar.

Sample 21

This sample bore the most conclusive evidence of local production. The coarse nonplastics were mainly rounded grains of *kurkar* (local term for a quartz-rich sandstone cemented with carbonate). *Kurkar* is the typical hard rock of the coastal plain of Israel. Moreover, the fact that rounded grains of *kurkar* occur in this pottery points to the local narrow belt of beach sands. Therefore, it is more than likely that this pottery was manufactured at Tel Michal itself. The excavators identified the sample as part of a cooking pot.

24b.4. CONCLUSIONS

Ten of the petrographic samples listed in Group 1 (foreign) probably originated overseas. Some of the samples were Cypriote, such as the Base Ring (3, 22) and the White Slip wares (4, 5). Others may have been Cypriote, also (1, 2, 7,

12, 15, 18), but more data are needed for confirmation. Three others (9, 10, and 11) apparently came from southern Jordan, Sinai, or the southernmost tip of Israel.

As a working hypothesis, the pottery allocated to Group 2 (local, noncoastal) should be regarded as originating somewhere within the borders of Israel but not strictly in the coastal plain. Future studies should attempt a detailed correlation with additional ceramic material from other excavations. At this stage of research, a foreign origin should not be totally excluded.

The petrographic study indicates an origin in the coastal plain or the vicinity of Tel Michal for the pottery allocated to Group 3.

NOTE

1. The three groups into which the samples in the INAA study were classified by the excavators (namely, "local," "Cypriote," and "unknown") were not known to me before my analysis; a correlation of the results is shown in the final column of Table 24.1. One of the samples chosen by me (15) does not appear in this column because it was not included in the INAA study.

24c

Petrographic Analysis of
Persian Period Pottery

by Paul Goldberg, Lily Singer-Avitz, and Aharon Horowitz

Thin-section studies were carried out on 16 pottery samples taken from various types of Persian period vessels recovered from Tel Michal during the final excavation seasons. The samples were subjected to thin-section analyses to determine their microconstituents, the ultimate objective being to identify the source areas of the raw materials. The primary question, of course, was whether these vessels were brought to the site through trade with other localities, such as Cyprus or Greece, or whether they were locally manufactured.

Samples 1–11 were taken from vessels of plain ware, whereas Samples 12–15 came from decorated vessels. Sample 16 was included for comparative purposes, since it came from a storage jar found in a Persian period pottery kiln (Chap. 8; Pls. 30–32), and its microconstituents would therefore approximate those of locally produced ceramics.

Detailed descriptions and illustrations of the entire ceramic assemblage of the Persian period appear in Chap. 9 (local pottery) and Chap. 10 (imported pottery).

24c.1. MATERIAL AND RESULTS

1. Chytra, Stratum IX (Fig. 9.2:5)

The chytra was a popular vessel in Greece during the 5th century B.C.E. Our specimen has a wide mouth, depressed ovoid body, two loop handles, and an unpierced spout. It is made of well-levigated, brownish orange clay. (For further details and comparisons, see Chap. 9.2.3.)

The sample contains abundant and generally unweathered feldspars (mostly plagioclase) and basalt fragments, also relatively fresh. The matrix contains abundant weathered biotite.

2. Flat-Shouldered Storage Jar, Stratum IX (Fig. 9.3:7)

This storage jar (Type 3), well known in Israel from the 8th-7th centuries B.C.E., continued to be produced throughout the Persian period. It is widely distributed along the Phoenician coast, Cyprus, Rhodes, and the Punic settlements in the western Mediterranean. Its origin is not certain, but since it appeared early on the eastern Mediterranean coast, a local Syro-Phoenician origin (Section 9.2.3) seems likely.

The sample contains subrounded to rounded quartz sand, inclusions of some rounded pottery-tempering material, chert, and an abundance of calcite microfossils. One edge of the sherd has been decarbonated, although the matrix is generally calcareous. Chalk and iron-rich clay as well as a source of sand must have been located near the production center.

3. Amphora of Plain White VI Ware (Fig. 9.15:7)

This amphora, made of a greenish white fabric, was found in the Persian period cemetery (Chap. 11). Its shoulder is stamped with a Greek monogram (see Section 9.5). Of interest is the abundance of biotite, some muscovite, and clumps of sand-size, cream-colored material that could be either clay or ash. There is also a large amount of mica.

4. Amphora of Plain White VI Ware, Stratum IX (Fig. 9.3:11)

This amphora is made of a finer fabric than Sample 3, pinkish instead of greenish white (Section 9.2.3). It contains a relatively large amount of fine mica (muscovite?) and coarse basalt fragments within an originally calcareous matrix; only the core remains carbonated. The total absence of quartz sand and the homogeneity of the matrix suggest intentional sorting of the clay. The source requires abundant limey mud and mica.

5–7. Basket-Handled Jars

The following three samples were taken from basket-handled jars (Type 5), which come in three variants: A, B, and C (see Section 9.2.1). They are widely distributed along the eastern Mediterranean coast from Syria to Egypt; in Israel they are found mainly in coastal sites, seldom in the interior. Many of these jars have been recovered from the sea, and apparently they were used extensively in maritime trade. From petrographic analyses of a number of basket-handled jars from Tell Keisan dating to the end of the Iron Age, it seems that these particular specimens were imported. Petrographically and typologically, they resemble jars from Tomb 79 at Salamis in Cyprus, although they are not a local product at this site either (*Tell Keisan*: 359–360). These jars are generally assumed to be of Eastern Greek (Rhodian?) origin.

5. Basket-Handled Jar, Stratum X Fig. 9.1:15)

This is Jar Type 5, variant C (neckless), made of orange clay. It is the only variant that was found on the high tell and the northern hill. The best-preserved specimens came from Strata XI-IX, but numerous sherds were found in Strata VIII-VII.

The abundance of well-rounded quartz and feldspar in the sample points to a coastal source. The markedly red clay matrix could be due to the addition of *ḥamra*. Somewhat problematic is the presence of granules that appear to be marl; since the granules are well rounded, the material could have been derived from a local wadi.

6. Basket-Handled Jar (Fig. 9.15:2).

This sample, found in the Persian period cemetery, has a short neck, rolled rim, and a ridge at the base of the neck (variant A). It is extremely rich in calcite. It also contains a few heavy minerals that are not particularly common in the other samples: glauconite and garnet, as well as the more common hornblende and augite. The excellent rounding of the temper suggests a fluvial source associated with fine, calcareous sediments such as the reworked loesses in the lower Nahal Besor basin. The well-rounded quartz sand implies proximity to the beach.

7. Basket-Handled Jar, Stratum IX (Fig. 9.3:9)

This is variant C, similar to Sample 5 above, although its color is buff. Petrographic analysis shows a composition identical to that of No. 5.

8. Amphoriskos, Stratum VIII (Fig. 9.7:4)

This vessel, with two horizontal handles, is not common in the Persian period repertory. The matrix of the sample consists of homogeneous calcareous clay; coarse tempering material is virtually absent. There are traces of fresh mica. The presence of basic heavy minerals and some weathered basalt suggests the proximity of basaltic terrain.

9. Bottle, Stratum IX (Fig. 9.2:13)

Although no close parallels are known to us, this bottle carries on the Assyrian tradition (Chap. 9.2.3). It seems to be a peculiarly chaotic mixture of fine sand-size calcareous fragments intermixed with finer calcareous matrix. Coarser temper is lacking. It probably came from an area deficient in quartz sand but rich in limestone and foraminiferal chalk.

10. Dipper Juglet, Stratum IX; not illustrated but similar to Figs. 9.1:6 and 9.5:14

This is Type V-III Plain White ware, common in Cyprus (see Section 9.2.1). The sample contains basalt fragments, abundant heavy minerals, and biotite (volcanic ash?). The greenish, cloudy (isotropic) matrix could have been caused by reducing conditions during firing.

11. Lamp (Fig. 9.11:8)

This is one of seven lamps found in a deposit in Area C, all very similar in profile and fabric. The calcareous clay and foraminifera-rich (i.e., chalk) matrix strongly resemble a marl source such as the widespread Taqiye formation.

12. Red-Slipped Amphora, Stratum VII (Fig. 9.8:8)

The composition of this sample is the same as that of No. 11 above.

13. Strap-Handled Amphora, Stratum XI (Fig. 10.1:1)

On typological grounds, this decorated amphora probably came from an Eastern Mediterranean site (see Section 10.1). The green tinge of the matrix suggests reducing conditions. The matrix was originally calcareous, but only traces remain in the core; the edges are decarbonated. Although the source is indeterminate, the presence of mica and pottery temper may be significant.

14. Single-Handled Jug, Stratum XI (Fig. 10.1:3)

This jug, decorated in horizontal bands and wavy-line motifs, may come from a Cypriote source (see Section 10.1).

The sample is similar to No. 9, but has slightly coarser tempering material.

15. Small Bulbous, Decorated Bottle, Stratum IX (Fig. 9.2:11)

This sample seems to be a mixture of beach sand (rounded quartz grains), calcareous wadi fragments (rounded limestone grains), and marl matrix (fine-grained calcareous material). A coastal source seems likely.

16. Storage Jar (Fig. 9.12:6–10)

This sample is taken from one of five storage jars of the same type (Jar Type 1) and fabric found on the floor of the pottery kiln of the northern hill (Section 9.4.1). Since it is obviously of local origin, it serves as a comparative specimen. The composition of this sample is identical to that of Nos. 5 and 7 (basket-handled jar without neck), and it may be assumed that these jars are also local products, perhaps imitations of similar imported types.

24c.2. CONCLUSIONS

The 16 samples of pottery can be divided into five groups according to their constituents, as seen in the thin sections.

Samples 5, 7, and 16 are virtually identical, with well-rounded quartz grains and feldspar that indicate a coastal source. The red clay in the matrix may represent an addition of *ḥamra*, whereas the rounded granules of what appears to be marl could have originated from local wadi material. These wares have been produced locally. Sample 15 probably also belongs to this group.

Samples 1, 3, 4, 8, and 10 are characterized by their basaltic constituents. Rocks that could serve as raw material do not occur in the vicinity of Tel Michal, and the pottery is most probably imported. A likely source is one of the Greek islands, Greece itself, or Cyprus.

Samples 2 and 6 contain limestone, chalk, and subangular quartz sand and were probably produced in a locality where hills are close to the sea, possibly the Carmel coastal plain.

Samples 13 and 14 contain a green tinge to the matrix, limestone fragments but no microfossils, and mica, perhaps indicating a source close to metamorphic rocks. No locale in Israel fulfills such a requirement, and the ware may have been imported from Greece or Cyprus.

Samples 9, 11, and 12 are characterized by calcareous material, with little or no quartz; they might have come from the hilly regions of Israel.

25a

Metal Artifacts

by James D. Muhly and Polymnia Muhly

Tel Michal presents an interesting and important assemblage of metalwork, particularly for the Persian period. Of the more than 500 metal objects discovered there, some 70 percent came from Persian period strata. No major body of metalwork from the Persian period in Palestine has been published to date, and work in precious metals—chiefly silver—is known mainly from grave offerings found at Tell el-Far'ah (S) and from a group of five so-called Philistine tombs excavated by Macalister at Gezer (*Gezer I*: 289–297) that was soon properly dated to the Persian period by C. L. Woolley (1914–16:128). Very little analytical work has been done on any metal finds from this period, and throughout the whole Middle East metal analysis of objects from the Persian period has been confined to work in silver (for summary, see Reade 1986).

The goal has been to analyze as many of the Tel Michal metal artifacts as possible, whether made of copper, bronze, lead, or silver. No iron objects were analyzed because the chemical composition of a piece of iron, whether well preserved or corroded, reveals little regarding the nature of the metal, but one of the iron sickles (Cat. No. 64) was studied metallographically. Of the 341 objects cataloged, 57 were made of iron. Of the 18 silver objects, 16 were analyzed; of the 13 lead objects, 7 were analyzed. There were 253 cataloged artifacts made of copper or copper-based alloys; of these, 207 were analyzed. This is the largest body of metalwork, predominantly of the Persian period, ever to be analyzed in a systematic fashion. The only comparable analytical project would be that recently carried out on the metalwork from Sardis, published as part of the complete volume devoted to that material (Waldbaum 1983).

In attempting to understand the development of metalwork during the 1st millennium B.C.E., several bodies of material provide more or less fixed points. In each case, historical circumstances have created a terminus post quem, making it possible to state that nothing from the site should be later than the date of the historical event associated with the destruction of that site. The first of these collections of metalwork, that from the Median site of Tepe

Nush-i Jan in western Iran (*Nush-i Jan III*) is perhaps the least satisfactory of the group in this respect. Although the main occupation of the fort at Nush-i Jan came to an end circa 650 B.C.E., the site was reoccupied by squatters for an indefinite period thereafter, certainly at least well into the 6th century B.C.E., and much of the metalwork (apart from the silver hoard) seems to have come from the period of squatter occupation (Muscarella 1985). Nevertheless, the bulk of the metalwork from Nush-i Jan must date from before circa 550 B.C.E., and the lack of any connection with that from Tel Michal is one indication that the two sites are in no way contemporary.

More precisely dated is the large body of material from the Persian siege mound at Old Paphos in western Cyprus (*Paphos I*). Paphos was besieged and taken by the Persians during the course of the Ionian Revolt (499–494 B.C.E.), so nothing from the siege mound should be later than circa 497 B.C.E. The material that is published to date, chiefly arrowheads, represents what was in circulation during the second half of the 6th century B.C.E. and presents a number of parallels with comparable finds from Tel Michal.

A hoard of silver jewelry from Jordan was found together with some 90 coins that can be dated no later than circa 445 B.C.E. (Kraay and Moorey 1968). The various earrings from the hoard represent the silver jewelry in circulation during the first half of the 5th century B.C.E., and the close parallels with earrings in bronze and silver from Tel Michal certainly help to date the material from the latter site. On the other hand, the 78 coins found with a hoard of silver jewelry from the vicinity of Sinope, on the southern shore of the Black Sea, indicate a date of deposition in the late 5th century B.C.E. (Kraay and Moorey 1981). The three silver bracelets from this hoard again show parallels with those in bronze from Tel Michal.

This general date of the 5th century B.C.E. for much of the metalwork from Tel Michal is supported by the very detailed correspondences between the material from Tel Michal and that from two very important cemetery sites: Deve Hüyük in northern Syria, near Carchemish (Moorey 1980a), and Kamid el-Lōz in the Beqa'a of Lebanon

(*Kamid el-Lōz 2*). The circumstances of recovery were totally different: the material from the Deve Hüyük cemetery was looted just before the outbreak of World War I, and the bulk not thrown away was purchased by T. E. Lawrence and C. L. Woolley, whereas the Kamid el-Lōz cemetery was systematically excavated by a German expedition under the direction of Prof. Rolf Hachmann. Yet the two bodies of material are remarkably similar and share many close parallels with the metalwork from Tel Michal.

On the basis of associated finds, especially the imported Greek pottery, the period of use for both cemeteries can be put at circa 480–380 B.C.E. (Moorey 1980a:8). This refers only to the finds from the inhumation cemetery known as Deve Hüyük II, not the earlier cremation cemetery of Deve Hüyük I from which no metal finds seem to have survived, nor the later Deve Hüyük III that scarcely exists within the body of salvaged material. The pottery from Deve Hüyük II looks much like that from Kamid el-Lōz (Moorey 1980a:11). The finds from both of these cemeteries provide a detailed cross section of the type and range of metalwork in circulation throughout the Levant and the Middle East during the course of the 5th century B.C.E.

Moorey argued that the cemetery of Deve Hüyük II represented the burials of "a garrison of predominantly Iranian-speaking troops rather than local Syrians . . . " (Moorey 1975; Moorey 1980a:10), and the predominance of weapons and horse trappings found supports that supposition. Kamid el-Lōz, on the other hand, was a cemetery that included male, female, and child burials, where personal ornaments and toilet equipment predominated, where weapons were scarce and everything appeared to be of local manufacture. In all of these respects the situation at Kamid el-Lōz is much more like that at Tel Michal. Imported Attic pottery was, of course, found at Tel Michal (though not in the cemetery), and one intact Attic vase was found in Grave 1 at Kamid el-Lōz (*Kamid el-Lōz 2*: Pl. 1). On the basis of this and other evidence, Poppa argued that the cemetery at Kamid el-Lōz was in use over a period of two generations, from 450/40 to 370/60 B.C.E. (*Kamid el-Lōz 2*: 70). These dates are not far removed from the slightly higher chronology used in this report, based upon that proposed by Moorey.

It must be remembered that there are important differences between Tel Michal and Kamid el-Lōz, not entirely because material from the latter site comes only from a cemetery. At Tel Michal all 22 fibulae came from the settlement, with no examples found in the cemetery. In contrast, 18 of the burials at Kamid el-Lōz produced fibulae, with only one fibula in each grave (*Kamid el-Lōz 2*: 54). The pins from Tel Michal, 12 examples of copper/bronze and one of silver, all came from the settlement, whereas 12 of the burials from Kamid el-Lōz contained pins, some (7, 18, 29) producing more than one example.

The cemetery at Kamid el-Lōz strikes one as being a far richer cemetery than that at Tel Michal, containing a greater quantity of silver jewelry, especially earrings, with even a massive gold earring from Grave 73 (*Kamid el-Lōz 2*: 39–40). In contrast, the burials at Kamid el-Lōz tended to be simple burials in the shallow earth, whereas the cemetery at Tel Michal produced at least four different types of burials, including ones in cist tombs built of stone or of red *ḥamra* bricks as well as the jar burials known from a number of contemporary contexts, including that at Neirab near Aleppo (Abel and Barrois 1928:203, Fig. 7). Wooden coffins must have been used at both Kamid el-Lōz and Tel Michal; although no trace of the wood has survived, the three iron coffin nails from Grave 42 at Kamid el-Lōz (*Kamid el-Lōz 2*: 59, Pl. 17) are paralleled by the 17 copper examples (not all cataloged) from Tomb 659 at Tel Michal (85–91). The differences between Kamid el-Lōz and Tel Michal should not be allowed to obscure the major similarities in the metalwork from the two sites.

The bulk of the metalwork from Deve Hüyük II, Kamid el-Lōz, and Tel Michal reflects the metal industry of the 5th century B.C.E. For the following half century, one of the most important sites is that of Olynthus, on the mainland of the Chalcidic peninsula in northern Greece, destroyed by the Macedonian king Philip II in 348 B.C.E. What is important about Olynthus is that the American excavations at the site, under the direction of David M. Robinson, uncovered a large part of the 4th-century Greek city, producing a body of finds as remarkable for its variety as for its quantity. The metalwork from Olynthus was published by Robinson in a large volume that to this day remains an invaluable store of information on the material culture of the ancient world (*Olynthus X*). No scholar responsible for publishing the "small finds" from an excavation can afford to overlook Robinson on the finds from Olynthus.

To describe the metalwork from Tel Michal as belonging predominantly to the Persian period is not to imply that it was made or used by anyone of Iranian origin. The lack of direct evidence for the presence of Iranian elements in Palestine during the period of the Achaemenian Empire is a well-known problem. In 1980, Moorey stated that "material traces of the two hundred years of Persian rule in the Near East are still generally elusive" (Moorey 1980a:128), and archaeological work in the 1980s has produced nothing to alter that assessment.

The inhabitants of sites such as Kamid el-Lōz and Tel Michal most likely had no direct connection with Persia or with any official of the Achaemenian Empire. Things certainly were different at Samaria, the local capital of the Persian province, and the chance find of fragments of the bronze fittings from an Achaemenid throne from that site provides some indication of the metalwork produced under Persian supervision or at least under Persian influence (Tadmor 1974). The same could be said for the metalwork from the tomb near Shechem, where elaborate objects such as a bronze thymiaterion and a bronze lamp are virtually unparalleled anywhere in the Levant (Stern 1980).

The metalwork from Tel Michal, if not made at the site itself, is certainly of local origin. Some would argue that questions of provenance can be decided by the evidence from metal analysis and that the wealth of such analytical evidence from Tel Michal should provide an ideal opportunity for such a study. Unfortunately, there now exists overwhelming evidence to demonstrate the impossibility of establishing provenance on the basis of the chemical analysis of metal artifacts (Muhly 1973:339–342; Gale and Stos-Gale 1982:11–12).

What chemical analysis does best is to establish the types of alloys being used—whether unalloyed copper, arsenical copper, bronze or leaded bronze, whether unalloyed silver or sterling silver (alloyed with copper). Analysis of the metalwork from Tel Michal has revealed that for simple objects, such as nails, tacks, and needles, unalloyed copper was considered eminently suitable. Ladles, fibulae, and bracelets tended to be made from leaded bronze and earrings and finger rings were made of bronze, additions of lead being quite rare. The fibulae from Tel Michal present some remarkable alloys, a situation known from other sites as well.

Virtually all the silver artifacts from Tel Michal proved to have at least 1.0 percent copper, with one example (241) best described as a silver-copper alloy. The lead artifacts were made basically of pure lead, with No. 138 (having 1.12 percent tin) as the only significant exception. Number 331, having only 69.3 percent lead, was probably too corroded to give significant results.

The addition of lead as an alloying agent in copper is a practice once thought to exist no earlier than Roman Imperial times. We now realize that the practice had a long history, going back well into the Bronze Age, and was already widespread in the 1st millennium B.C.E. (Waldbaum 1983:171, with recent literature, n. 20). Many objects from the Persian period were made of leaded bronze. In addition to the Tel Michal examples discussed below, these include a lamp from Shechem (A. Lupu in Stern 1980:109; analysis incorrectly listed as being from the thymiaterion), a caryatid censer from Amman (Khalil 1986:108–109), and much contemporary metalwork from Etruria and southern Italy (Craddock 1986:221–231).

It could be that in many cases this lead was not added for any metallurgical purpose but simply to save money. Copper was always a rather expensive metal, tin even more so, and there was much metallic lead being produced, chiefly as a by-product of the extraction of silver from argentiferous galena. There were few practical uses for this lead, so the sensible thing was to mix it with copper in all those cases where the admission of lead would have no significant effect upon the properties of the artifact to be cast from the resulting alloy.

In the catalog that follows, no attempt has been made to include all the metal fragments found at Tel Michal. With a few exceptions, the material cataloged has been the objects thought worth drawing. The numbers used in the catalog are repeated in the figures. Thus every object cataloged keeps its same number if included in the figures. It is hoped that those who have fought their way through several recent French archaeological publications, trying to go from illustration to text, will appreciate this simple approach to the problem.

The objects in the catalog are grouped according to function—weapons, tools, etc.—and within each class according to type—arrowheads, swords, daggers, etc. Whenever possible, the material is further divided according to subtype and/or material, but fine typological distinctions have been avoided because the relatively small number of objects would make such subdivisions confusing. Within each group or subgroup, the objects are arranged chronologically beginning with the earliest. Short comments on typology, function, and technique are appended to each group.

Individual entries are given consecutive numbers that also identify the objects in the illustrations (Figs. 25.1–25.16). Unless otherwise noted, all entries are illustrated. Each entry is identified by the registration number, locus number, area, and stratum. (Strata separated by a hyphen indicate use in both strata; a slash between strata numbers gives the possible stratigraphic span.) An asterisk preceding the catalog number denotes that the object has been analyzed. The analyses are found in Table 25.12 of Chap. 25b.

Dr. P. R. S. Moorey studied the Tel Michal metalwork in November 1982 and graciously turned over his notes to us. We thank Dr. Moorey for making these notes available for use in preparing this catalog, as well as for much helpful advice in dealing with the archaeology of the Middle East during the Persian period.

WEAPONS

I.   ARROWHEADS OR JAVELIN HEADS
Ia.   Trefoil Socketed Arrowheads
        Copper or copper-based alloys
*1.   4530/60; 618; D; VII (Pl. 70:1)
*2.   6385/60; 1317; A; VIII (Pl. 70:2)
*3.   9328/60; 948; A; VIII
*4.   9624/60; 1500; A; XI (Pl. 70:4)
*5.   10314/60; 1639; A; VIII (Pl. 70:5)
*6.   11286/60; 1814; D; VI (Pl. 70:6)
*7.   6312/60; 947; A; VII
*8.   9225/60; 942; A; VII
*9.   1910/60; 329; A; VII
*10.   4451/60; 602; D; VI
*11.   10351/60; 1634; A; IX (not illustrated)
*12.   10380/60; 1645; A; IX (not illustrated)
*13.   1256/60; 176; E; XI/VI (Pl. 70:13)
*14.   1108/60; 165; D; VI
15.   1120/60; 279; D; V
*16.   1/63; 1; Unstratified
*17.   1/62; 1; Unstratified

All the socketed arrowheads are of the type classified in Cleziou 1977 as F17, except Nos. 12, 14, and 15, which are Type F3. (For recent discussions, see Stronach 1978: 180–181, 218–219, Fig. 94; Moorey 1980a:65; Stern 1982:154–155.)

Ib.   Tanged Arrowheads or Javelin Heads
        Copper or copper-based alloys
*18.   6434/60; 99; A; XIII (Pl. 70:18)
*19.   5910/60; 872; A; XI
*20.   10381/60; 1646; A; X
21.   9540/60; 1512; A; XV

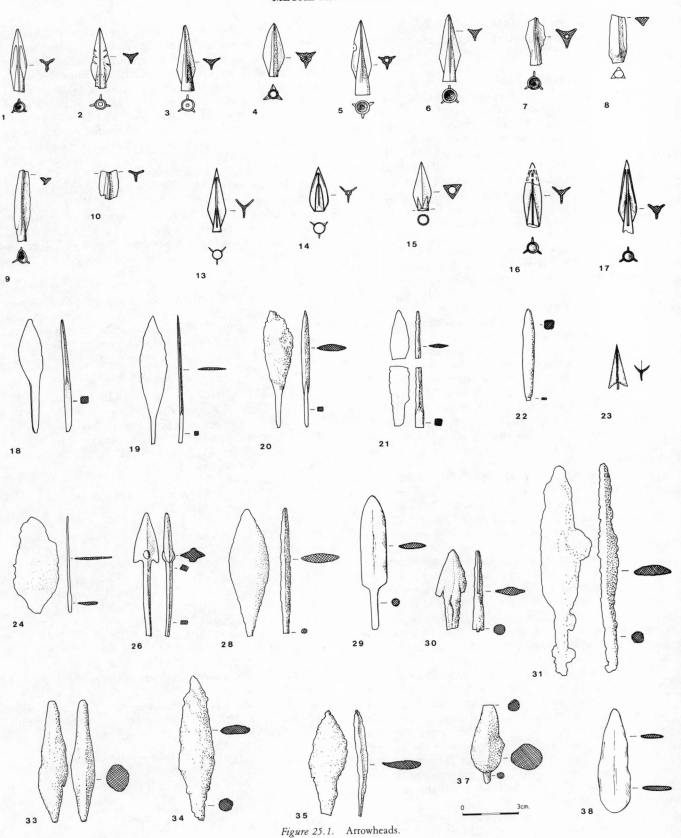

Figure 25.1. Arrowheads.

*22. 9629/60; 1515; A; XI
*23. 2433/60; 86; A; VII (Pl. 70:23)
 24. 9655/60; 1500; A; XI
*25. 9369/60; 1308; A; IX (not illustrated)
*26. 8920/60; 1391; A; II (Pl. 70:26)
*27. 1/61; 1; Unstratified (not illustrated)

Number 20 may have been a light javelin point. Number 21 is a simple type, noteworthy only because made of bronze(?), as opposed to iron, as is common in this period (cf. Stern 1982:156–157). This also pertains to No. 22, which is "bolt-shaped" (*Lachish III*: Pl. 60:8, of iron), and No. 23, which is of unusual shape with a tiny tang. Number 24, of sheet metal, has the beginning of a tang and may have been a simple arrowhead. Numbers 26–27 are of Greek type (cf. Stern 1982:156, Fig. 265).

The tanged arrowhead has a long history, having become the dominant type in Iran by the late 2d millennium B.C.E. (*Nush-i Jan III*: 27), with both socketed and tanged examples known from the Late Bronze Age Aegean (Avila 1983). Number 18, from the 10th century B.C.E., could be seen as the descendant of a type common in Greece during the 13th century B.C.E. (cf. Avila 1983: Pls. 28, 61B:Type 2b).

What is remarkable about the trefoil socketed arrowheads from Tel Michal is the large amount of lead they contain. For example, Nos. 12, 13, 16, and 17 contain from about 11 to 17 percent lead, Nos. 2 and 6 have over 30 percent lead, and Nos. 3, 5, and 7 really have more lead than copper (each having more than 50 percent lead). The addition of small amounts of lead would have aided in the casting of the complex shape of this type of arrowhead by increasing the fluidity of the metal, but such a high incidence of lead is more likely to be related to a desire to increase the weight of the arrowhead (see Rothenberg 1975:78–80).

The contemporary (6th-5th century B.C.E.) arrowheads from Sardis were also made of leaded bronze (Waldbaum 1983:33–34). Eight arrowheads were analyzed, using both emission spectrographic and atomic absorption analytical techniques (one, No. 20, was analyzed by both methods). Of the eight arrowheads (18–22, 29, 30, 34), only one (29) had less than about 3.0 percent lead; five had at least 6.0 percent lead (18, 19, 21, 22, 34), with one of these (19) having 15.0 percent lead (Waldbaum 1983:160–161, Table V.3, 172, Table V.4b).

Iron

28. 1856/60; 341; A; VII (Pl. 70:28)
29. 907/60; 129; C; VII/VI
30. 3237/60; 453; C; VI (Pl. 70:30)
31. 4877/66; 664; E; XI/VI
32. 11615/60; 1854; E; XI/VI (not illustrated)
33. 10407/60; 1649; A; VII
34. 9498/60; 1503; A; XI
35. 10346/60; 1639; A; VIII
36. 6688/60; 979; A; IX (not illustrated)
*37. 2/66; 1; Unstratified

This is a small group but of diverse shapes. Numbers 34–35 are simple, leaf-shaped arrowheads (cf. *Lachish III*:

Pl. 60); No. 31 is probably a javelin head (not unlike *Gezer II*: Pl. CCXV:27, of bronze). Of similar shape but surely an arrowhead is No. 29 (cf. *Gezer II*: Pl. CCXV:12, 59). Number 30 (Pl. 70:30) is of more-or-less triangular shape, with a midrib (cf. *Lachish III*: Pl. 60:13, of iron).

Ic. Leaf-Shaped Tangless Arrowheads
Iron
38. 1137/60; 174; D; XVII

Number 38 is of special interest because of its context; if securely dated to Stratum XVII, it would become perhaps the sole example of a Middle Bronze Age iron arrowhead. Unfortunately, Locus 174 is a fill with a few MB IIB sherds unearthed in a trial pit, so the actual stratigraphic context of No. 38 must remain in doubt. Moreover, the upper limit of the pit could not be distinguished from an intrusive Persian period pit (Locus 524).

Tufnell argued that iron arrowheads became common only at the end of the 10th century B.C.E. but then quickly replaced bronze, with iron being the dominant metal for arrowheads down to circa 600 B.C.E. (*Lachish III*: 385–386). The return to bronze was in turn seen as a response to a "growing shortage of iron" (*Lachish III*: 388). These conclusions have quite rightly been rejected (Rothenberg 1975:80; Moorey 1980a:65).

Bronze and iron arrowheads tended to remain in use throughout most of the 1st millennium B.C.E. The superior metallurgical properties of iron (and steel) arrowheads were often considered to be offset by the problems connected with their manufacture, the casting of multiple bronze arrowheads being so much easier than the forging of individual iron ones.

Iron arrowheads were unknown in Iran during the Iron I period (circa 1350–1000 B.C.E.), coming into use only during Iron II (circa 1000–750 B.C.E.) when the tanged iron arrowhead achieved a popularity that it maintained during the succeeding Iron III period (circa 750–550 B.C.E.) (*Nush-i Jan III*: 27). An iron arrowhead at Middle Bronze Age Tel Michal remains an unlikely possibility, even though the shape of No. 38 seems to be unparalleled at Tel Michal or at any other Iron Age site in the Middle East.

II. SWORDS
Iron
39. 5441/60; 713; A; X
40. 5441/61; 713; A; X

The iron swords of the Persian period that have been found in Israel, Syria, and the Egyptian Delta are not similar to the examples from Tel Michal.

Sword from Memphis: *Meydum and Memphis III*: Pl. XXXVIII:2 with scabbard, 29.1 inches long.

Sword from Tell Beit Mirsim (*TBM III*: 79: Pl. 61:12), 62.5 cm long, five rivets, "single edged." The shape is much more regular than that of the Tel Michal swords, widening toward the hilt (tang?).

Sword from Neirab: Carrière and Barrois 1927:209, Fig. 15A, about 50 cm long with five rivets and midrib.

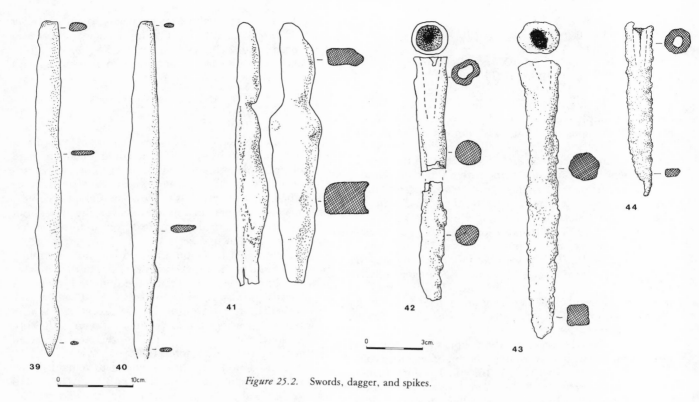

Figure 25.2. Swords, dagger, and spikes.

Swords from Deve Hüyük are of an entirely different type (Moorey 1980a:53).

The Tel Michal swords seem to be of local type (according to unpublished notes of P. R. S. Moorey).

Iron swords have a long history in Cyprus, going back to the 11th century B.C.E. (Snodgrass 1964:93–100; Snodgrass 1981). As late as circa 600 B.C.E., the Cypriotes were still using iron swords more than 90 cm in length, as we know from an example found in Tomb 3 at Salamis (Snodgrass 1981:133). For a contemporary iron sword of similar size from the site of Vered Jericho, see Shanks and Eitan 1986: 33, 35.

The two iron swords from Tel Michal, having a preserved length of about 47 cm, are to be compared to two iron swords from the Persian period cemetery at Tell el Mazar that seem to be of comparable length (*Tell el Mazar I*: 92, Nos. 117, 118).

III.   TANGED DAGGER
             Iron
41.   8445/60; 1251; A; IX

A rare example but with a good parallel in Tomb 96 at Gezer (*Gezer II*: Pl. XC:22), of somewhat greater length and with a shorter tang.

IV.   "SPIKES"
             Iron
42.   6518/60; 979; A; IX
43.   7453/60; 1113; D; VIII
44.   5608/60; 343; A; VII

It is not certain whether these objects should be classified as weapons since their function is unclear. Their shape suggests spear butts, but they do not seem large and sturdy enough to fulfill this function, and no iron spearheads have been found at Tel Michal. Examples found at other sites have been interpreted variously. Petrie considered them spear butts (*Beth-Pelet*: 9, Pl. XXVI:98 from Tomb 661, Pl. XXI:92 from Tomb 552), whereas Albright interpreted them as implements, possibly ox goads (*TBM III*: 78, Pl. 61:14). Small projectile points of similar shape and section have been found in the Persian siege mount at Paphos (*Paphos I*: 17–19), but larger versions that are very similar to the "spikes" from Tel Michal are of uncertain function (*Paphos I*: 19–20). See also Waldbaum 1983: No. 16 for a similar object dating to the 6th century B.C.E. and identified as a spear butt.

TOOLS AND IMPLEMENTS

V.   KNIVES
Va.   Curved-Backed Knives
             Iron
45.   2844/60; 246; B; XIV/XIII
46.   2498/60; 415; A; XI (not illustrated)
47.   3751/60; 519; D; VI (not illustrated)
48.   4233/60; 596; D; VI
49.   4877/65; 664; E; XI/VI
50.   6901/60; 1013; A; VII
51.   8420/60; 1251; A; IX

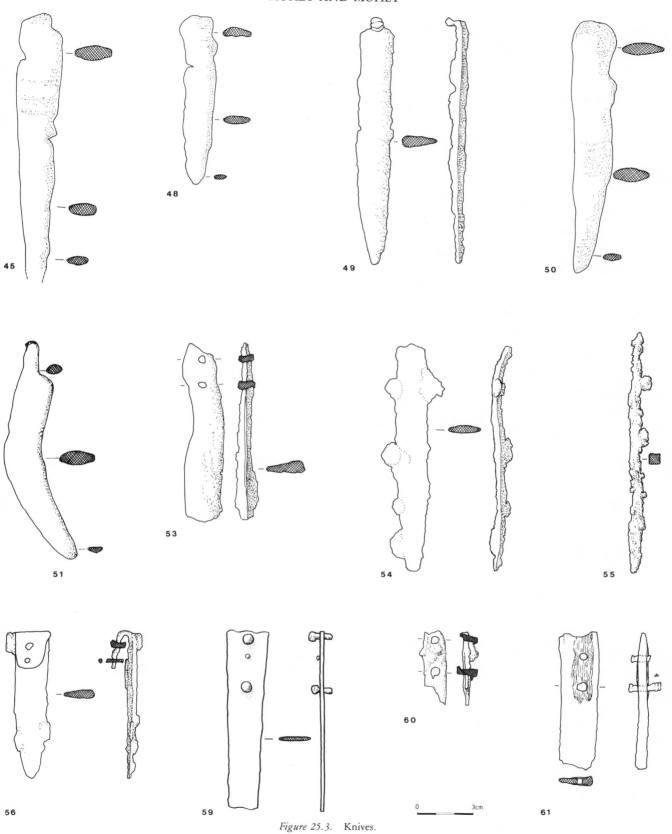

Figure 25.3. Knives.

52. 10303/60; 1631; A; IX (not illustrated)
53. 1915/60; 320; V (fragmentary)

Vb. Straight-Backed Knives
    Iron
54. 4877/60; 664; E; XI/VI
55. 4877/67; 664; E; XI/VI
56. 4877/64; 664; E; XI/VI
57. 4225/61; 594; D; VII (fragmentary; not illustrated)
58. 2330/60; 388; A; VII (fragmentary)
59. 1136/60; 279; D; V (fragmentary)
60. 9575/60; 1515; A; XI (fragmentary)
61. 6378/60; 1317; A; VIII (fragmentary)
62. 2065/60; 352; A; VIII (fragmentary; not illustrated)
63. 6689/60; 997; A; IX (fragmentary; not illustrated)

The inclusion of knives among the tool and implement category is somewhat arbitrary, since knives have many functions. In fact, certain knives listed above, especially some of the examples of Type Vb from Burial 664, are large enough to have been weapons rather than tools. Both types found at Tel Michal are common in this period, with good parallels at other sites of the eastern Mediterranean. For discussion and references, see Moorey 1980a:58. Numbers 51–52, however, may have had a specialized function. Their strongly curved shape may indicate that they were agricultural tools, perhaps pruning knives (cf. *Lachish III*: Pl. 59:3).

VI. SICKLES
    Iron
64. 540/60; 99; A; XIII (Pl. 70:64)
65. 11046/60; 1771; A; IX (not illustrated)
66. 10964/60; 1771; A; IX (not illustrated)

Number 64 is of a shape that occurs in much earlier tanged examples of bronze (Moorey 1971: Pl. XXIII:32–33), whereas examples from this period or later in Israel and Cyprus do not have the upward curving tip (cf. *Ain Shems IV-V*: 153, Pl. LIII:57 of the late 11th or 10th century; *TBM III*: Pl. 61:8–9, 13; *Paphos I*: Pl. XI:480).

Number 64 was examined metallographically by Prof. Robert Maddin in June 1978. His report states:

A section of the blade was removed, polished metallographically by standard techniques and observed with the optical microscope at low, intermediate and high magnifications in the polished, as well as the etched (3 percent nital- 3 percent nitric acid in ethyl alcohol) condition. No carbides could be observed in either the relic form or the surviving form; on the other hand, stringers of slag could be observed. I consequently conclude that the iron blade was made of wrought iron without any carburization.

Although carburized iron or steel was certainly being produced in Palestine by the 10th century B.C.E. (cf. Stech-Wheeler et al. 1981; Muhly 1982), it is not surprising to find this sickle made of wrought iron. A sickle required

no great structural strength, and similar sickles during the 2d millennium B.C.E. were made of unalloyed copper, not bronze (cf. Moorey 1971).

VII. PICK
     Iron
67. 8726/60; 1371; A; VIII

Iron picks were known in the land of Israel from at least the 11th century B.C.E., and such picks are mentioned in Neo-Assyrian royal inscriptions and from excavations at Neo-Assyrian sites (cf. Davis et al. 1985). The pick (Hebrew *qilšôn*) mentioned in 1 Sam. 13:21 is almost certainly an iron pick.

VIII. CHISEL
      Copper or copper-based alloys
*68. 3319/60; 466; C; VI

' The shape and the small size (length about 7.0 cm) of this object suggest its identification as an engraving tool. The arsenical copper used in making this tool (with 1.60 percent arsenic) would be a suitable alloy for such a tool, providing the necessary hardness and ductility. Unpublished examples of such engraving tools are known from sites in Palestine and Cyprus; no study has yet been made of this class of artifacts, however, and there are those who believe that the engraved decoration found on various copper and bronze objects could only have been made with iron (really steel) engraving tools (see Bouzek 1978).

IX. NEEDLES, AWLS, ETC.
    Copper and copper-based alloys
*69. 9768/60; 1558; A; XVI (Pl. 70:69)
*70. 10835/60; 1730; A; XVI
*71. 1/67; 1; Unstratified
*72. 5715/60; 861; A; X
*73. 2127/60; 357; A; VIII
*74. 6871/60; 698; A; V
*75. 377/60; 70; A; VI
*76. 1/67a; 1; Unstratified
*77. 6315/60; 947; A; VII
     Iron
78. 5712/60; 347; A; VII (fragmentary)
79. 6972/60; 1016; A; VI (fragmentary)

Plain and hook-headed needles, such as Nos. 69–71 and 72–74 respectively, are common at sites of this period (cf. *Kamid el-Lōz 2* passim). Numbers 75–76 are similar to the hooked type but are thicker, lack a pointed end, and are probably small hooks. Number 79 may be part of an awl, whereas Nos. 77–78 are possibly parts of bodkins (for examples of this type of tool, see *Olynthus X*: Pl. CXV: 1746–1749).

Of the 11 needles (and related artifacts) from Tel Michal, 9 were of copper, 2 of iron. All nine copper needles were analyzed. They were made of unalloyed copper with the exception of No. 70, a long needle having 1.91 percent arsenic and 1.63 percent iron. This is one of the few objects from Tel Michal that could properly be described as arsenical copper, having over 1.0 percent arsenic. Other examples

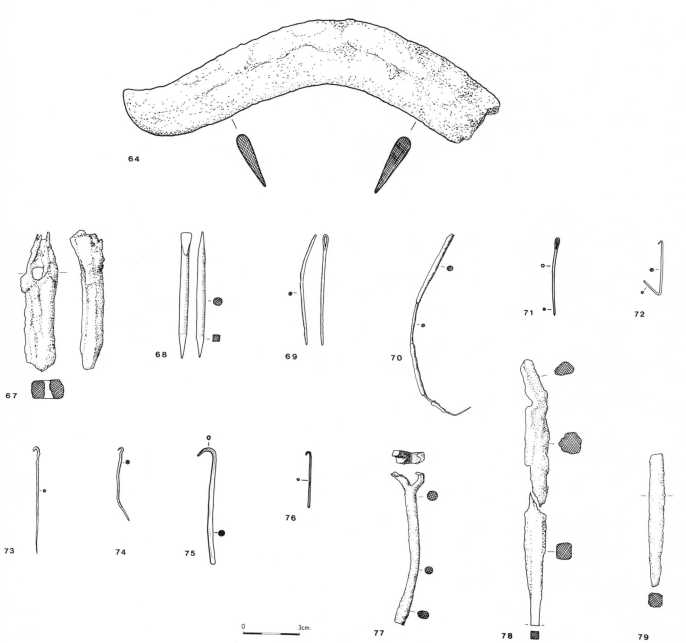

Figure 25.4. Sickles, pick, chisel, and needles.

include an arrowhead (No. 14: 1.17 percent arsenic) and a
chisel (No. 68: 1.60 percent arsenic).

STRUCTURAL FITTINGS

X.   NAILS
Xa.   Long Nails
          Copper and copper-based alloys
*80.   11062/60; 1772; A; V
*81.   3809/60; 519; D; VI
*82.   4166/60; 588; D; VI

*83.   4295/60; 731; D; VII
*84.   4503/60; 614; D; VII
*85.   4841/60; 664; E; XI/VI
*86.   4866/60; 664; E; XI/VI
*87.   4871/60; 664; E; XI/VI
 88.   4871/61; 664; E; XI/VI (Pl. 70:88)
*89.   4871/62; 664; E; XI/VI
*90.   4871/63; 664; E; XI/VI (Pl. 70:90)
*91.   4871/64; 664; E; XI/VI

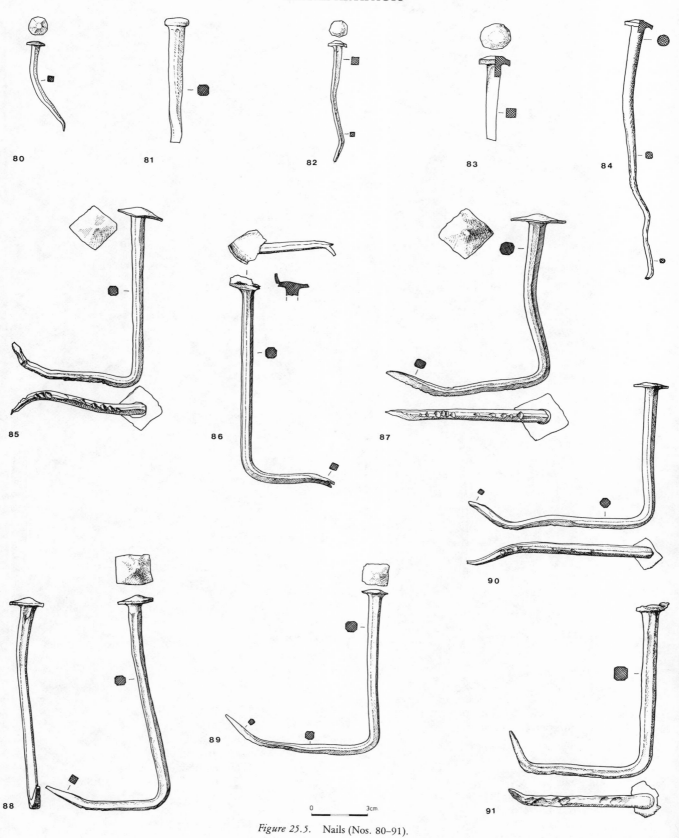

Figure 25.5. Nails (Nos. 80–91).

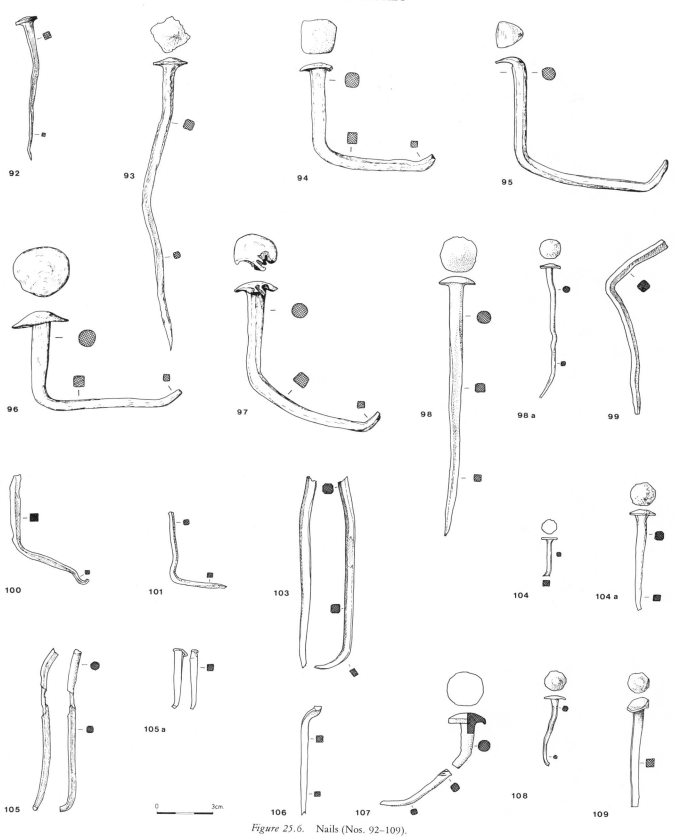

Figure 25.6. Nails (Nos. 92–109).

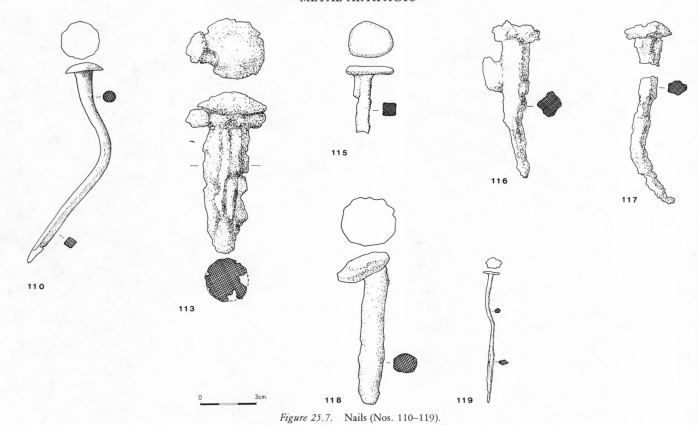

Figure 25.7. Nails (Nos. 110–119).

*92.	5644/60; 317; A; VI
*93.	5716/60; 704; A; VI (Pl. 70:93)
*94.	7661/60; 1178; E; XI/VI
*95.	7662/60; 1178; E; XI/VI
*96.	7674/60; 1178; E; XI/VI
*97.	7675/60; 1178; E; XI/VI
98.	8754/60; 1371; A; VIII
*98a.	5575/61; 842; A; VIII
*99.	7468/60; 1128; D; VIII (fragmentary)
*100.	10305/60; 1640; A; VII (fragmentary)
101.	10328/60; 1633; A; VIII (fragmentary)
102.	9366/60; 1308; A; IX (fragmentary; not illustrated)
*103.	11721/60; 1159; E; XI/VI (fragmentary)
*104.	4046/60; 551; D; V-IV
*104a.	5504/60; 832; D; V/IV
*105.	321/60; 63; A; IV (fragmentary)
*105a.	5202/60; 684; A; IIIa
*106.	4162/60; 579; D (unstratified; fragmentary)
*107.	6902/60; 693; A (unstratified; fragmentary)
*108.	6910/60; 693; A (unstratified)
*109.	11230/60; 500; D (unstratified)
*110.	2427/60; 89; A; VIII

Iron

111.	4295/61; 731; D; VII (fragmentary; not illustrated)
112.	4834/60; 659; E; XI/VI (not illustrated)

113.	10270/60; 1013; A; VII
114.	1701/60; 311; A; V (not illustrated)
115.	10801/60; 1720; A; V
116.	6949/60; 697; A; IV
117.	9248/60; 1459; A; IIIb
118.	6939/60; 1021; A; II
119.	2142/60; 50; A; I

Xb.   Tacks

Copper and copper-based alloys

*120.	535/60; 87; A; VII
*121.	4054/60; 560; D; VI
122.	4451/61; 602; D; VI
*123.	10283/60; 690; A; VI
*124.	8896/60; 1389; A; II
*125.	5457/60; 311; A; V
*126.	7127/60; 1072; A; V
*127.	4103/60; 570; D; V/IV
*128.	4108/60; 570; D; V-IV (Pl. 70:128)
129.	4103/61; 570; D; V-IV (not illustrated)
*130.	410/60; 63; A; IV
*131.	10733/60; 1710; A; VIII
*132.	4550/60; 500; D; Unstratified (Pl. 70:132)
133.	2/64; 1; Unstratified
134.	2/65; 1; Unstratified

Iron

135.	5203/60; 684; A; IIIa (not illustrated)

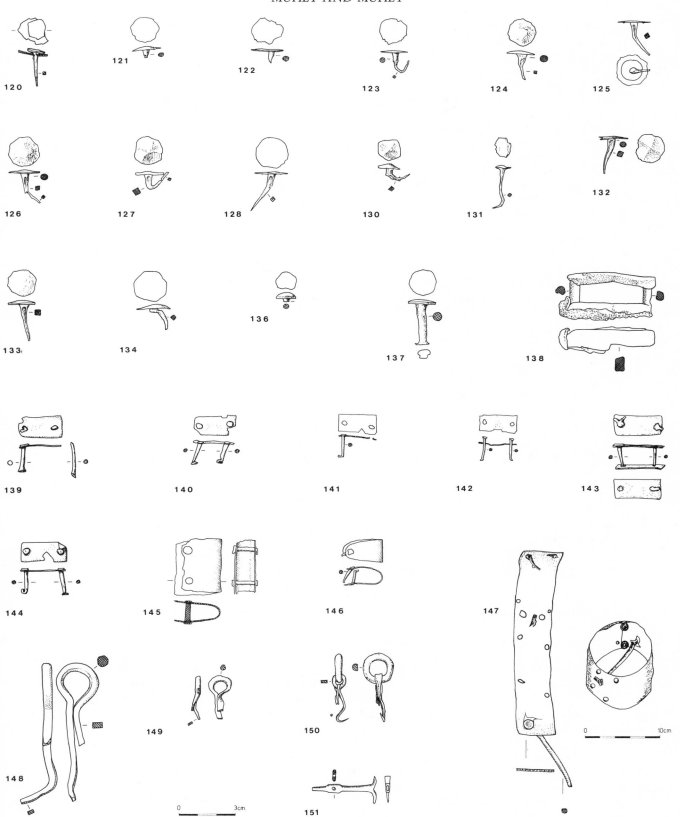

Figure 25.8. Tacks, clamps, and cotter pins.

279

The long nails (Type Xa) are of various sizes but essentially of the same type, with shanks of square section and in most cases with faceted heads. The coffin nails from Burial 664 (85–91) form a separate group. They have square-faceted heads, and their shanks are bent at a right angle. The nails from Burial 1178 (94–97) are similar but with circular heads. The iron nail (1 out of 17) from Burial 659 (112) is similar but shorter. The iron nails from Grave 42 at Kamid el-Lōz (Kamid el-Lōz 2: Pl. 78) are very similar and also bent at right angles. See also the copper nails from Tell el-Kheleifeh (Glueck 1941: Pl. 10:2).

The tacks (Type Xb) are all very similar with a short, thin shank and disproportionately large, circular heads, faceted or flat. The single iron example of this type (135) is very corroded.

Of the 34 copper nails from Tel Michal, 30 were analyzed. Of these 30, the copper content of five (80, 82, 103, 109, 110) does not seem to have been recalculated; the remaining 25 have a copper content of 98.9 percent. Obviously all the nails were made of unalloyed copper and could have been driven only into soft woods such as pine or fir.

Of the 15 tacks from Tel Michal, 11 were analyzed. Discounting the four examples (123, 124, 127, 131) that do not seem to have been recalculated, the remaining seven averaged 99.02 percent copper. Again, these tacks could not have been pressed into material of any hardness. On the Mohs hardness scale, copper has a value of 2–3, equal to materials such as gypsum and calcite.

XI.   RIVETS
Copper or copper-based alloys
*136.   4417/60; 602; D; VI (fragmentary)
 137.   28/61; 22; Unstratified

XII.   CLAMP
Lead
*138.   348/60; 65; A; IV
For similar clamps, see Olynthus X: Pls. 98–99:1567–1583; Waldbaum 1983: Pl. 20:292.

XIII.   RECTANGULAR PLAQUES WITH RIVETS
Copper or copper-based alloys
*139.   7703/60; 1194; E; XI/VI
*140.   7703/61; 1194; E; XI/VI
*141.   7706/61; 1194; E; XI/VI
*142.   7706/62; 1194; E; XI/VI
*143.   7709/60; 1194; E; XI/VI (Pl. 70:143)
*144.   7710/60; 1194; E; XI/VI

All of these plaques are from the same burial, and their function should be determined by the context. Similar plaques occur in burials at Deve Hüyük (Moorey 1980a: No. 158, used to repair No. 157), at Meqabelein (Harding 1950: Pl. XIV:17), and at Neirab (Abel and Barrois 1928: Pl. XVI.a).

All six of the plaques or clamps from Tel Michal were analyzed. The analysis of No. 140 was made on a very corroded sample and probably should be discounted. The other five plaques were all made of unalloyed copper, averaging 98.7 percent copper with no significant trace-element impurities. Clearly these objects were not designed to withstand force or strain.

XIV.   FOLDED SHEET METAL WITH RIVETS
Copper or copper-based alloys
*145.   4821/60; 653; E; XI/VI
*146.   7706/60; 1194; E; XI/VI

Both objects may have been fittings from the sheaths of weapons. An object almost identical to No. 145 was used to repair the chape of a dagger found at Deve Hüyük (see Stucky 1976: Fig. 7 for the best photograph of this object). For chapes, see Goldman 1957. For a possible parallel from Kamid el-Lōz, see Kamid el-Lōz 2: Pl. 5, Grave 4:4. Number 145 seems to have a very close parallel in iron from Stratum IV at Lachish (Rothenberg 1975: Pl. 37:6).

XV.   SHEET METAL SLEEVE
Copper or copper-based alloys
*147.   4497/60; 612; D; VI (Pl. 70:147)

It is possible that this was a join for two pieces of wood forming part of an object such as an oar or a plough.

The three examples of sheet metal from Tel Michal (145, 146, 147) were all analyzed and were all made of unalloyed copper, averaging 97.36 percent copper. See remarks on plaques above.

XVI.   CLASPS AND COTTER PINS
Copper and copper-based alloys
*148.   3328/60; 469; C; VI
*149.   4454/60; 610; D; VI
*150.   10282/60; 690; A; VI
*151.   2060/60; 63; A; IV

Number 149 may have been a cotter pin used on an object such as a box (cf. Waldbaum 1983: No. 412), whereas the larger size of No. 148 would render it suitable for a lynch pin. Number 150, a solid ring with a strap looped through it, may have been part of a leather belt or a wooden box. Number 151 is more problematic, but it may also have been part of a box lock.

All four of the clasps and cotter pins from Tel Michal were analyzed; each one was made of a distinctive alloy. Number 148 is unalloyed copper, having 98.18 percent copper; No. 150 is leaded copper with only 0.90 percent tin but 5.75 percent lead; No. 149 is a normal bronze, with 6.50 percent tin. The surprising piece proved to be No. 151, consisting of 78.08 percent copper, 5.53 percent tin, 2.82 percent lead, and 11.75 percent zinc. This is the only object from Tel Michal having more than 1.0 percent zinc. Objects of copper with a high zinc content, properly described as brass, are rare but not unknown in Iron Age and even Bronze Age contexts (Craddock 1978), and it probably is dangerous to use the presence of zinc as evidence against the authenticity of a particular object (as does Muscarella 1982). Nevertheless, a number of the early instances of brass found in the archaeological literature, including the examples from Macalister's excavations at Gezer, must be rejected (Craddock 1980:131–132).

There remains the MB I (MB IIA) duckbill axe from Tomb 92 at Beth-shan with 6.5 percent zinc (Oren

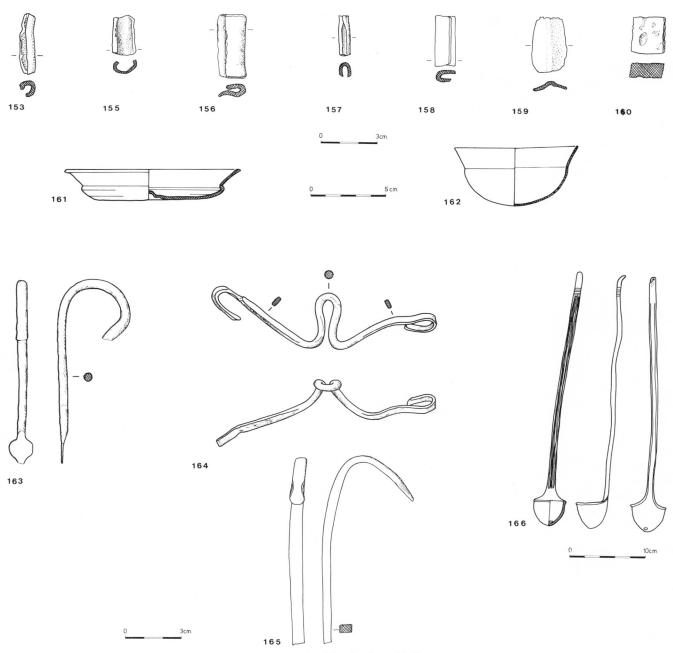

153   155   156   157   158   159   160

161   162

163   164   165   166

Figure 25.9. Weights, bowls, and ladles.

1971:128) and, from an Iron Age context, the two bowls from Neo-Assyrian Nimrud having 6.39 percent and 5.51 percent zinc (Hughes et al. 1981:144). Number 151 would then be another instance of the pre-Roman use of brass.

All of these early examples are probably accidental alloys, the zinc being present already in the copper ore. The actual production of brass as an intentional alloy, produced directly from copper and calcined zinc ore by the cementation process, is now thought to have been developed first in Anatolia at the end of the 2d century B.C.E. (Craddock et al. 1980).

WEIGHTS

XVIIa. Fishing Weights
Copper or copper-based alloys
*152. 2049/60; 363; A; IIIb (fragmentary; not illustrated)
153. 10305/61; 1640; A; VII (fragmentary)
Lead
154. 1109/60; 165; D; VI (fragmentary; not illustrated)
*155. 3740/60; 508; D; VI

281

156. 6888/60; 1024; A; VI
157. 6740/60; 694; A; V
158. 10941/60; 1739; A; V
*159. 5146/60; 686; A; IIIa

Very similar net weights of lead have been found at various Late Bronze Age sites in the Aegean (Iakovidis 1969–70:355 with references) and in the Cape Gelidonya shipwreck (Bass 1967:131).

XVIIb. Weights
        Lead
*160. 3815/60; 534; D; VI

Unmarked rectangular lead weights of similar dimensions have been found at Olynthus (*Olynthus X*: Nos. 2457–2459).

VESSELS AND LADLES

XVIIIa. Vessels
         Copper and copper-based alloys
*161. 1274/60; 183; E; XI/VI (Pl. 71:161)
*162. 7663/60; 1178; E; XI/VI (Pl. 71:162)

XVIIIb. Vessel Parts
         Copper and copper-based alloys
*163. 541/60; 404; A; IX
*164. 1/60; 1; Unstratified

Number 161 (Pl. 71:161) is a shallow example of the common omphalos bowl of this period (Stern 1982:144–145). Bowls such as No. 162 (Pl. 71:162), with decoration in separate overlay, are also fairly common (see *Beth-Pelet*: Pl. XXVIII:756; Moorey 1980a: No. 113). Number 163 is the handle of a jug, as the flattened lower part and notched upper end indicate. Number 164 is the handle of a cauldron or similar type of vessel.

The profile of bowl No. 162 is virtually identical to examples from accidentally discovered tombs near Khirbet Ibsam in Lower Galilee (Amiran 1972:135, Fig. 1) and near Shechem (Stern 1980:95, Fig. 6:3). In publishing the Shechem bowl, Stern argues that on the basis of the chemical analysis of the metal it can be shown that the bowl was made of local copper and was therefore the product of a local workshop (Stern 1980:101). Unfortunately, as we have pointed out above, chemical analysis has yet to provide the evidence necessary to support such claims. The bowl from Shechem was made of a high-tin bronze and the lamp from the same tomb was made of a leaded bronze, but nothing can be said as to the sources of the metals used in making these objects.

All four of the vessels and vessel parts from Tel Michal were analyzed. The handle (164) was made of unalloyed copper, consisting of 98.50 percent copper. The others were all made of bronze, with 5.55 percent (161), 7.38 percent (162), and 12.21 percent (163) tin. Like the bowl from Shechem, the two bowls contained virtually no lead. Could it be that leaded bronze, so ubiquitous an alloy in the metalwork of the Persian period, was not considered suitable for making carinated bowls? This would be in keeping

with the fact that such bowls were not cast but were hammered into shape by raising from a flat sheet of bronze.

The nearly contemporary (end of 4th century B.C.E.) manufacture of such a bowl is shown in one of the scenes carved on the walls of the tomb of Petosiris, near Hermopolis-West (Tuna el-Gebel) in Egypt (Lefebvre 1923: Pl. VIIb).

The 1911 excavations at Sardis produced a silver bowl very similar to Tel Michal No. 162 (Waldbaum 1983:146, No. 964), now in the Istanbul Archaeological Museum and dated to the 5th century B.C.E. Neutron activation of samples from this bowl (Waldbaum 1983:188–190, Tables V.7–8) gave 93.5 percent silver, 6.25 percent copper, and 0.28 percent gold (average of three analyses). Another Sardis example, now in the Metropolitan Museum of Art and also of silver, has a wider flaring rim (Waldbaum 1983:148, No. 974).

XVIIIc. Ladles
         Copper and copper-based alloys
*165. 7244/60; 1351; A; X (Pl. 71:165)
*166. 4418/60; 603; D; VII (fragmentary)

The ladles found in Israel have been discussed by Stern 1982:147, Fig. 244. The shape of No. 165 (Pl. 71:165) is defined by an incision running around the outer side of the lip and continuing along the back of the handle. The front of the handle is decorated with multiple vertical, incised lines terminating in a group of horizontal strokes that continue on the sides. The curved handle of the second ladle (166) has a rounded, flat terminal, reminiscent of a duck's bill, perhaps a simplification of the duck's-head terminal found in many such dippers.

Ladles often form part of wine-drinking sets that were very common in the period 600–300 B.C.E. (see Moorey 1980b; Chavane 1982:64–68; von Bothmer 1984). The finest examples of the ladle (Greek *kyathos*) are in silver and represent some of the most magnificent examples of metalwork to have survived from the ancient world (von Bothmer 1984:41f.). Examples in silver are known from the sites of Gezer and Tell el-Far'ah (S) in Israel (Stern 1982:146–147), the most remarkable being the ladle from Tell el-Far'ah with a handle formed by the outstretched body of a nude woman, a motif known best in a series of swimming-girl cosmetic spoons from New Kingdom Egypt (Brovarski et al. 1982:205–207).

The two ladles from Tel Michal were made of leaded bronze. Number 165 had 10.12 percent tin and 18.75 percent lead; No. 166 had 9.61 percent tin and 4.52 percent lead. No other ladles have been analyzed, so it is impossible to assess the significance (if any) of these variations. Detailed analyses were made on a silver ladle from Sardis, found in Tomb 100 in 1911 and now in the Istanbul Archaeological Museum (Waldbaum 1983:146–147, No. 965). The average of six analyses on samples taken from the handle and the rim of the bowl showed 97.34 percent silver, 2.34 percent copper, and 0.29 percent gold (Waldbaum 1983:188–190, Tables V.7–8).

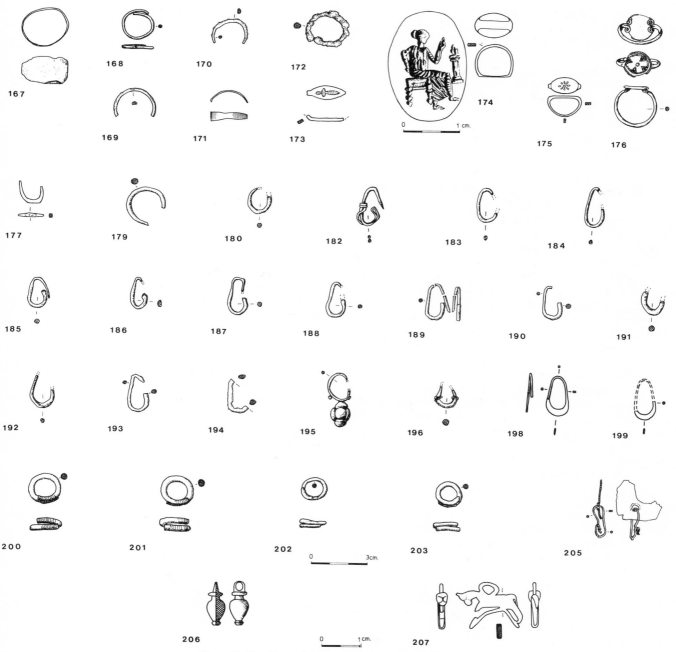

Figure 25.10. Finger rings, earrings, hair rings, and pendants.

JEWELRY AND OBJECTS OF PERSONAL USE

XIX. FINGER RINGS

XIXa. Simple Rings of Wire or Sheet Metal
Copper and copper-based alloys

*167. 7644/60; 1159; E; XI/VI

*168. 11706/60; 1872; E; XI/VI

*169. 7348/60; 1104; D; VI (fragment)

*170. 1273/61; 176; E; XI/VI (fragment)
Silver

*171. 4210/60; 580; D; VI (fragment)
Iron

172. 11726/60; 1884; E; XI/VI

For this simple type, see Moorey 1980a: Nos. 315–316; see also comments in *Lachish III*: 390 on the type with overlapping ends.

XIXb.   Rings with Bezel
               Copper or copper-based alloys
*173.   4879/60; 664; E; XI/VI
               Silver
*174.   3314/60; 466; C; VI (Pl. 74:1)
*175.   11720/60; 1880; E; XI/VI (Pl. 71:175)
*176.   7680/60; 1178; E; XI/VI (Pl. 71:176)
               Lead
*177.   7242/60; 1357; A; X (fragmentary)
               Iron
178.   11636/60; 1855; E; XI/VI (not illustrated)

The majority of these rings are of the most common type for this period, with oval bezels made in one with the flat hoops (cf. Moorey 1980a:85, Nos. 323–326). Numbers 173 and 175 have simple intaglio designs. In No. 176, a slight flattening of the hoop forms a rudimentary bezel defined as an oval by incision. Signet ring No. 174 is noteworthy for the depiction on the bezel of a seated woman before an incense altar. (The ring is discussed in detail in Chap. 28a; Fig. 28.1:4; Pl. 74:1.) The face and hair are summarily rendered, the folds of the dress are dry and schematic, and the composition is awkwardly fitted in the field of the bezel; there is no doubt, however, that the scene is modeled on a Greek motif, closely paralleling the design of a gold ring in the Ashmolean Museum (Richter 1968: No. 286) dated to the 5th or 4th century B.C.E.

Number 176 is of a different type than the rest, having a hoop with double-spiral terminals soldered on the underside of the circular bezel, which is decorated with granulation. This type of attachment occurs in rings with rectangular bezels from Atlit and Kamid el-Lōz (Johns 1933:54, Fig. 11; Kamid el-Lōz 2: Pl. 8, Grave 7:16). For No. 174, see comments in Boardman 1970:332.

The use of the finger ring with oval bezel and thin hoop in the Middle East coincided with the westward expansion of the Achaemenid Empire (Moorey 1980a:85). The type is a characteristic feature of jewelry of the Persian period, but its origins must lie in the Greek world.

Of the 12 rings from Tel Michal, 5 were bronze, 4 silver, 2 iron, and 1 lead. All were analyzed save for the two iron rings. The bronze rings were made of a normal tin alloy, with nothing unusual in the variation of tin concentration. All the silver rings had some copper, but No. 175 is unusual in having 13.9 percent copper. A silver finger ring from Tepe Nush-i Jan had 7.7 percent copper (M. J. Hughes in Nush-i Jan III: 58). The lead ring from Tel Michal (No. 177) was made essentially of pure lead (98.5 percent), with only 0.61 percent zinc and 0.54 percent copper.

XX.   EARRINGS
XXa.   Circular Earrings
               Copper and copper-based alloys
*179.   11606/60; 1853; E; XI/VI
*180.   7699/60; 1191; E; XI/VI (fragmentary)
181.   24a/61; Unstratified (not illustrated)
Numbers 179–180 correspond to Type 4 at Kamid el-

Lōz, No. 181, which is embellished with twisted wire, and to Type 5 (Kamid el-Lōz 2: 55).

XXb.   Ovate Earrings
               Copper and copper-based alloys
*182.   7636/60; 1162; E; XI/VI
*183.   7665/60; 1174; E; XI/VI
184.   7665/61; 1174; E; XI/VI
*185.   7690/60; 1179; E; XI/VI (Pl. 71:185)
*186.   7690/61; 1179; E; XI/VI
*187.   7690/63; 1179; E; XI/VI
*188.   7730/60; 1193; E; XI/VI
*189.   11672/60; 1870; E; XI/VI
*190.   11690/60; 1869; E; XI/VI
*191.   7690/62; 1179; E; XI/VI (fragmentary)
*192.   7694/60; 1159; E; XI/VI (fragmentary)
193.   1671/61; 1870; E; XI/VI
*194.   103/60; 43; A; VI (fragmentary)
*194a.   4859/60; 673; E; XI/VI (not illustrated)

With the exception of No. 182, the rest are of the simplest type made of bronze wire (Kamid el-Lōz 2: 54–55, Type I; cf. Moorey 1980a:4). Number 182 is also of a common but slightly more complex type, in which the wire is twisted back up around the lower half of the earring (Kamid el-Lōz 2: 55, Type 3).

Fourteen of the 17 bronze earrings from Tel Michal were analyzed. They are made of a basic tin alloy, with 4.0–9.0 percent tin. Only one (194) has any appreciable amount of lead (2.0 percent), whereas another (188) has 13.20 percent tin and 1.0 percent arsenic. Obviously a straightforward bronze alloy was considered suitable for making earrings. The exception is No. 194a, which has a very unusual 6.08 percent iron.

               Silver
*195.   7733/62; 1193; E; XI/VI (Pl. 71:195)
*196.   7733/60; 1193; E; XI/VI
*197.   4472/60; 610; D; VI (fragmentary; not illustrated)
*198.   1/64; 1; Unstratified
*198a.   9390/60; 1308; A; IX (not illustrated)
*199.   1/65; 1; Unstratified (fragment)

Number 195 is decorated with large pendant drops arranged in a symmetrical pattern. The type occurs in simpler (Lachish III: Pl. 54:1, 4–5) or more elaborate versions (Kamid el-Lōz 2: Pl. 5:10) enriched with granulation.

Only No. 198 is completely preserved. The form with a thickened lower hoop is best paralleled at Lachish (Lachish III: Pl. 55:43). Number 196 bears additional decoration of small granules in the lower part of the hoop. Number 198a is ovate, with wire wound around the lower edge as decoration.

The silver earring, either leech or boat shaped or in the form of a circular hanger adorned with cluster pendants, is one of the most common items in the repertoire of jewelry from the Persian period. The better examples also have granulations, and the finest pieces are superb products of court jewelry (McKeon 1973; Stronach 1978:176–177). The fine Neo-Assyrian examples are known more from depictions on Assyrian reliefs than from actual finds *in corpore* (Maxwell-Hyslop 1971:235–246). The best examples known from Palestine come from Tell el-Far'ah (S) and from Tell Jemmeh (Kraay and Moorey 1968:194–202; Moorey 1980a:82–83). As usual, the finds from Deve Hüyük and Kamid el-Lōz provide important parallels for the earrings from Tel Michal.

All six of the silver earrings from Tel Michal were analyzed. They are basically of silver with small amounts of copper added to harden the naturally soft silver metal. Copper was added to silver in all parts of the ancient world, going back in time at least to Predynastic Egypt (Gale and Stos-Gale 1981:114). The practice is, of course, still followed today; sterling silver is a silver-copper alloy of 0.925 fineness. By this definition, both Nos. 197 and 199 could be described as sterling silver. Number 198 has a slightly lower copper content (5.45 percent); Nos. 195 and 196 have a considerably lower copper content (1.03 and 1.54 percent, respectively), whereas No. 198a is unusual in being made of unalloyed silver (with only 0.56 percent copper).

Number 196 also has 1.02 percent arsenic, and Nos. 198 and 199 are surprising in having significant amounts of tin (2.72 and 2.25 percent, respectively). Could it be that in making the silver-copper alloy, the silversmith accidentally added bronze instead of copper? The earrings from the Jordanian silver hoard had a much lower copper content, with nothing over 1.0 percent copper (Kraay and Moorey 1968:229). One of the earrings in the hoard from Babylon, now in the British Museum, had only 0.14 percent copper (M. J. Hughes in *Nush-i Jan III*: 88). For a remarkable example in gold from Lachish, see Shea and Maxwell-Hyslop 1979.

XXI.   HAIR RINGS
Silver
*200.   11612/60; 1161; E; XI/VI
*201.   11613/60; 1851; E; XI/VI (Pl. 71:201)
*202.   11633/60; 1858; E; XI/VI
*203.   11633/61; 1858; E; XI/VI

All four are of the same form, except that the terminals of Nos. 200–201 are decorated with vertical incised strokes. Twisted rings of this type, probably worn in the hair above the ears, have been found in burials at Atlit and Deve Hüyük (Johns 1933: Fig. 5, Pl. XXV:640–641; Moorey 1980a:84, Nos. 312–313; see also Kraay and Moorey 1968:219–220).

There is some controversy regarding the identification of these objects as hair rings. In publishing the material from Kamid el-Lōz, R. Poppa maintained that (in the Iron Age?) hair was not fastened with any sort of metal implement or decorated with any kind of metal attachment. On the other hand, silver rings identified as hair rings go back into the Early Bronze Age in Cyprus (Karageorghis 1965), where a possible example in gold also was recently excavated at the Chalcolithic site of Sotira-Kaminoudhia (Karageorghis 1986:25).

Moorey identifies similar spiral rings from Deve Hüyük as hair rings (Moorey 1980a:79, Fig. 12:312–313), and the same identification should hold for those from Tel Michal. The silver used in the Tel Michal examples shows no apparent pattern. One of the rings (201) is made of a very pure silver, whereas another (203) has 3.3 percent copper. This variation in fineness is quite characteristic for silver of the Persian period (cf. M. J. Hughes in Reade 1986:88).

XXII.   PENDANTS
Copper and copper-based alloys
*204.   4845/60; 666; E; XI/VI (not illustrated)
*205.   5453/60; 713; A; X
206.   4845/61; 666; E; XI/VI (Pl. 71:206)
Silver
*207.   11645/60; 1159; E; XI/VI (Pl. 71:207)

Number 206, probably from an earring, is a very common shape in this period, occurring in various metals or in faience (for discussion and references, see Kraay and Moorey 1968:202–203). An example identical to No. 206 has been found at Kamid el-Lōz (*Kamid el-Lōz 2*: Pl. 10, Grave 10:2). Number 205 is a rather crude example of sheet bronze with a wire loop threaded through it; No. 207 may represent a leaping bull (or a horse) and is unusual.

Of the four pendants from Tel Michal, three were analyzed. The two bronze pendants had 9.97 percent (204) and 6.35 percent (205) tin. Number 204 also had 6.65 percent lead and should properly be called a leaded bronze. The silver pendant, No. 207, must be quite corroded, as analysis revealed only 73.98 percent silver, with 3.22 percent copper and no other element present in an amount greater than 1.0 percent.

XXIII.   DIADEM
Copper and copper-based alloys
*208.   1271/60; 1150; E; Unstratified

The diadem is a simple band tapering toward the perforated rounded ends. A thin incised line runs along its upper and lower edges. Contemporary cemeteries and settlements in Israel and Syria have not produced similar objects (for a general discussion of diadems, see Szilágyi 1957).

Analysis of the diadem showed it to be made of bronze with 82.72 percent copper, 13.97 percent tin, and only 0.18 percent lead. The high tin content might represent a deliberate attempt to give the diadem a yellowish color to imitate gold (cf. Cooney 1965:41).

XXIV.   BRACELETS OR ANKLETS
XXIVa.   Simple Bracelets with Overlapping Flattened Terminals
Copper or copper-based alloys
*209.   4881/60; 826; E; XI/VI
*210.   4881/61; 826; E; XI/VI
*211.   4881/62; 826; E; XI/VI
*212.   4881/63; 826; E; XI/VI (not illustrated)
*213.   5469/60; 344; A; IX (fragmentary; not illustrated)
*214.   7638/60; 1163; E; XI/VI
*215.   7638/61; 1163; E; XI/VI

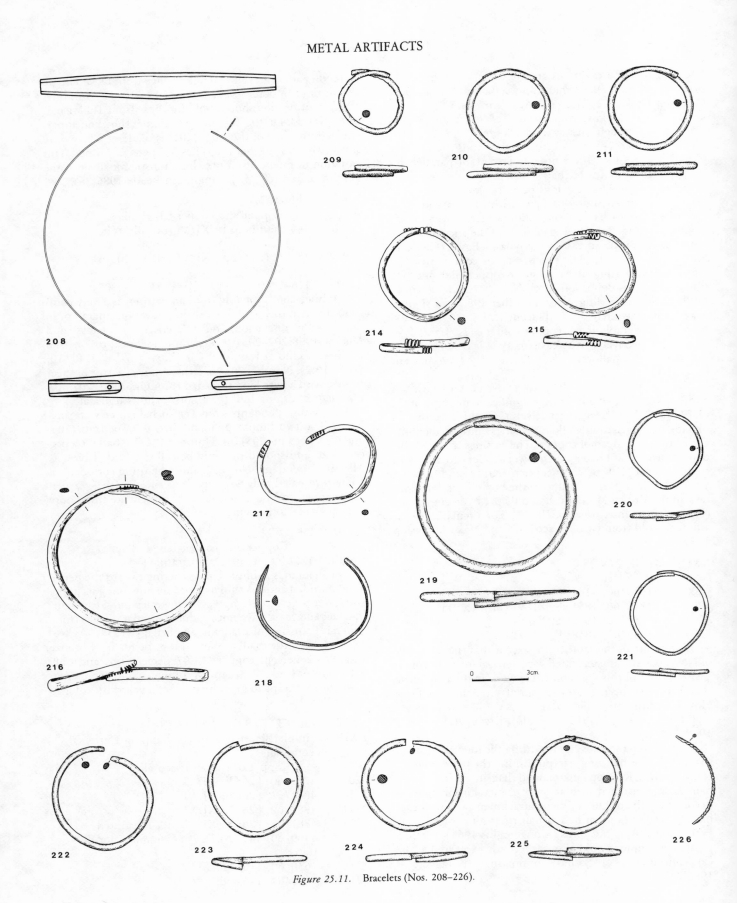

Figure 25.11. Bracelets (Nos. 208–226).

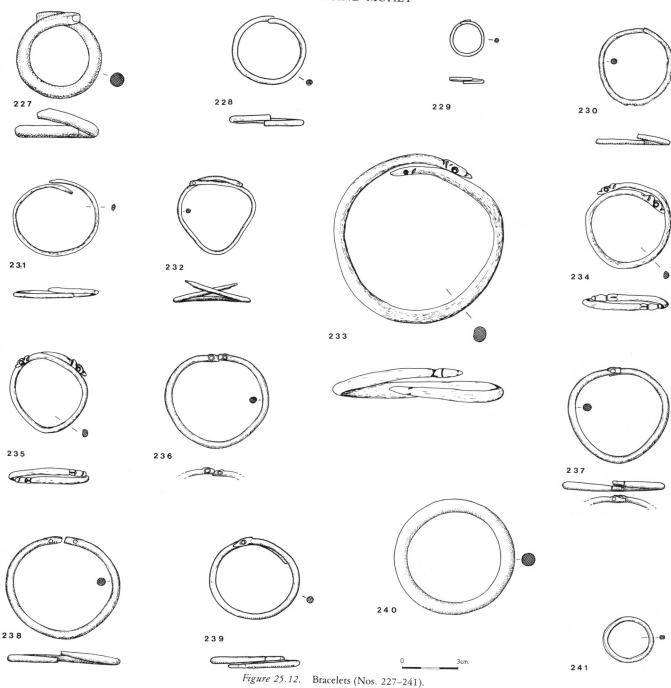

Figure 25.12. Bracelets (Nos. 227–241).

0 _____ 3cm.

*216. 7687/60; 1186; E; XI/VI
*217. 7698/60; 1159; E; XI/VI
218. 11727/60; 1873; E; XI/VI
219. 11656/60; 1863; E; XI/VI
*220. 11669/60; 1866; E; XI/VI
*221. 11669/61; 1866; E; XI/VI
*222. 11684/60; 1869; E; XI/VI
*223. 11684/61; 1869; E; XI/VI
*224. 11697/60; 1875; E; XI/VI
*225. 11697/61; 1875; E; XI/VI

*226. 4288/60; 588; D; VI (fragmentary; not illustrated)
227. 9490/60; 58; A; II
*228. 1266/61; 176; E; XI/VI
*229. 1273/60; 176; E; XI/VI
*230. 23/60; 1; Unstratified
        Silver
231. 7733/61; 1193; E; XI/VI

Four examples (214–217) have terminals decorated with vertical incised strokes; No. 226 is made of twisted wire. On

287

the question of function, see Moorey 1980a:74, 78 with references.

XXIVb. Bracelets with Zoomorphic Terminals
Copper and copper-based alloys
*232. 4874/60; 825; E; XI/VI
*233. 7676/60; 1180; E; XI/VI
*234. 7678/60; 1184; E; XI/VI (Pl. 71:234)
*235. 7678/61; 1184; E; XI/VI (Pl. 71:235)
*236. 11603/60; 1851; E; XI/VI
*237. 11603/61; 1851; E; XI/VI
*238. 11626/60; 1857; E; XI/VI
*239. 1266/60; 176; E; XI/VI

For the type, see Moorey 1980a:78 with references. The bracelets from Tel Michal range from examples in which the calf-head terminals are rendered in some detail (232, 235, 239) to very schematic versions (236–238).

XXIVc. Circular Bracelets
Copper and copper-based alloys
*240. 7105/60; 1065; A; IV
Silver
*241. 25/60; 2; Unstratified

According to Moorey (1980a:74), a width of 7.5 cm is the dividing point between bracelets and anklets. By that criterion, most of the examples from Tel Michal can properly be classified as bracelets, with only Nos. 216 (interior diameter of 7.6 cm), 219 (interior diameter of 7.8 cm), and 233 (interior diameter of 7.8 cm) to be considered as possible anklets, except in infant burials (see Chap. 11). According to the excavator, the distinction between bracelets and anklets was very clear at Tell el Mazar because all examples were found in position, on the arm and leg bones of the excavated skeletons (*Tell el Mazar I*: 93). Since the bracelets from Tell el Mazar had a diameter of about 4.5–5.0 cm and the anklets from 7.0–7.5 cm, this agrees reasonably well with the division suggested by Moorey.

The bracelet with calf-headed or ram-headed terminals can be considered one of the most characteristic, even ubiquitous, products of Achaemenid art. The presence of such bracelets at Tel Michal is probably the one thing that brings the site closest to the orbit of Persian civilization and the art of the "Achaemenid International Style" (for the phrase, see Moorey 1980a:129). Proper Persian examples of such bracelets should be made of silver, but examples are known even in gold, especially those from the Vouni palace in Cyprus (Amandry 1958). Most of the known examples unfortunately come from the antiquities market and are therefore without date or context, but the limited evidence available suggests that such bracelets were most prevalent during the 5th century B.C.E. (cf. Stronach 1978:173–176, 210–211, Fig. 90. Stronach's dates are certainly too low, but this is not the place to enter into a discussion of such problems as the date of the Oxus Treasure).

Twenty-eight of the 31 copper/bronze bracelets from Tel Michal were analyzed. With a few notable exceptions, they are made of bronze with 8.0–11.0 percent tin and no significant amount of arsenic. Several of them have up to 6.0 percent lead, most likely added as a separate material to improve the fluidity of the molten metal. Number 238 is unusual in having 8.0 percent tin and 10.52 percent lead, but strangest of all is No. 212 with 21.73 percent tin and 17.27 percent lead. It would have been easy to cast but difficult to hammer the metal made of such an alloy; it is possible that the lead was added to lower the melting point raised by the high tin content.

XXV. FIBULAE
XXVa. Bow Fibulae with Spring Catch
Copper and copper-based alloys
*242. 2551/60; 423; A; XIII (fragmentary)
*243. 6535/60; 984; A; IX (fragmentary)
*244. 1981/60; 344; A; IX (fragmentary; Pl. 71:244)
245. 6535/61; 984; A; IX (fragmentary; not illustrated)
*246. 8752/60; 1371; A; VIII (fragmentary)
*247. 5751/60; 334; A; V (Pl. 71:247)
*248. 4541/60; 618; D; VII (fragmentary)
249. 1152/60; 279; D; V
*250. 6266/60; 1309; A; VII (fragmentary)
*251. 8329/60; 1029; A; VII (fragmentary)
*252. 2077/60; 352; A; VIII (fragment)
253. 103/61; 43; A; VI (fragment)
*254. 7373/60; 728; D; VI (fragmentary)
*255. 4276/60; 594; D; VII (fragmentary)
*256. 1853/60; 323; A; V (fragmentary; not illustrated)
*257. 1152/60; 279; D; V (fragmentary; not illustrated)
*258. 7451/60; 1128; D; VIII (fragmentary)
*259. 6884/60; 1015; A; Unstratified (fragment)

Most of the fibulae have more or less elaborately beaded and/or ribbed bows (for the classification and distribution of these fibulae, see Moorey 1980a:85–86 with references). Numbers 250–251 and 256 belong to undecorated examples of the same type. Such plain fibulae, primarily with semicircular bows, occur at Lachish (*Lachish III*: Pl. 58:21, 22), Gerar (*Gerar*: Pl. XVIII:21–22), and Tell Zakariyeh (Bliss and Macalister 1902: Pl. 80:8). For Hellenistic and Roman examples, see *Samaria-Sebaste III*: Fig. 103:1. Examples similar to No. 244 are known as far south as Persian period sites in the central Negev (Meshel 1977:128, Fig. 8:11, Pl. 11:4) and in the Gulf of Aqabah (Glueck 1941: Pl. 9:1).

XXVb. Bow Fibulae with Riveted Bow
Copper and copper-based alloys
*260. 918/60; 129; C; VII/VI (fragmentary)
261. 8888/60; 1386; A; XI (fragmentary)
*262. 1802/60; 323; A; V (Pl. 71:262)
*263. 6825/60; 685; A; IIIb

The bronze fibula in *Lachish III* (Pl. 57:39) provides the best parallel for the earlier examples from Tel Michal. For a Hellenistic example, see *Samaria-Sebaste III*: Fig. 103:3.

Eighteen of the 22 fibulae were analyzed. They are made, for the most part, of bronze, often with a high tin content, frequently containing considerable amounts of

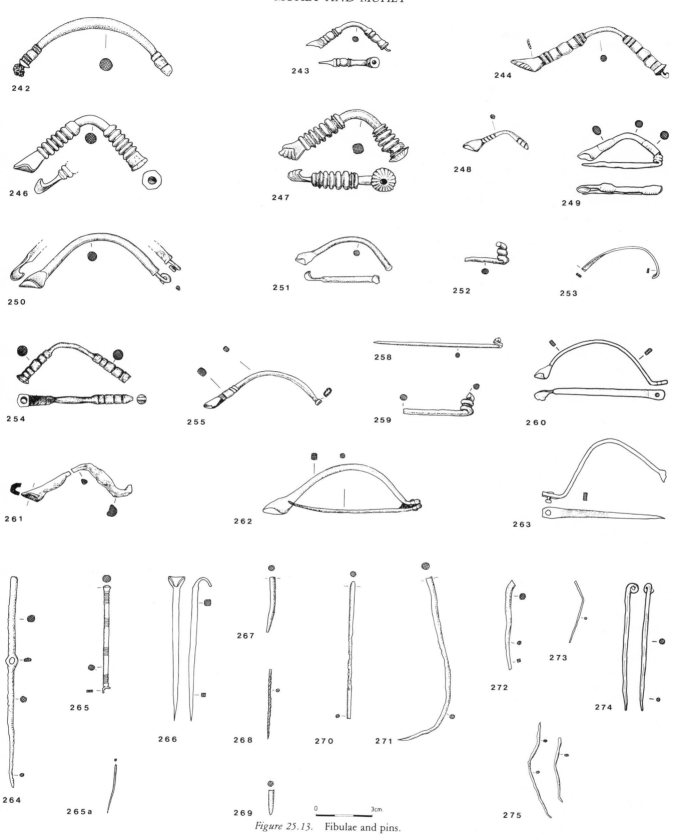

Figure 25.13. Fibulae and pins.

lead. Examples are Nos. 242 (with 74.02 percent copper, 7.46 percent tin, and 17.75 percent lead), 244 (with 80.16 percent copper, 13.20 percent tin, and 4.60 percent lead), 246 (with 74.2 percent copper, 11.45 percent tin, and 4.17 percent lead), and 256 (with 82.60 percent copper, 3.54 percent tin, and 9.97 percent lead). Both the tin and the lead must represent materials added separately to form a deliberate ternary alloy. This alloy greatly increased the fluidity of the molten metal to facilitate the casting of the intricate fibula shape and decoration and to aid in the finishing of the solidified casting. The different ratios of copper, tin, and lead may also have been designed to vary the color of the finished product, as was the case in the use of such a ternary alloy by the ancient Chinese (Chase 1983).

The only comparable body of analyzed fibulae is those of the Early Iron Age from the Toumba, Skoubris, and Palia Perivolia cemeteries at Lefkandi, on the island of Euboea, Greece (Jones 1980). The 67 X-ray fluorescence analyses published therein are most unusual because they present several fibulae (as well as several bracelets) made of an alloy containing 20 percent tin, 15–30 percent lead, and 15–30 percent iron (Jones 1980:452, Table 1b). It is not clear just how or why an ancient smith would have made a fibula with only some 20 percent copper, 20 percent tin, 30 percent lead, and 30 percent iron. Such an alloy would produce a metal so brittle that the fibula would break apart the first time it was used.

XXVI. PINS

Copper and copper-based alloys
264. 9748/60; 971; A; XV
265. 9662/60; 1530; A; XV (fragmentary)
*265a. 5486/60; 701; A; XI
266. 3378/60; 1114; D; VII
*267. 4449/61; 603; D; VII (fragment)
*268. 4464/60; 610; D; VI (fragment)
*269. 4523/60; 618; D; VII (fragment)
*270. 1864/60; 342; A; VIII (fragmentary)
271. 6893/60; 1022; A; VII (fragmentary)
*272. 1680/60; 38; A; V (fragment)
*273. 1748/60; 320; A; V (fragmentary)
*274. 1/66; 1; Unstratified

Silver
275. 11256/60; 1804; D; Unstratified (fragmentary)

This group consists primarily of fragments that may be pieces of pin shanks, but in some cases (e.g., 270 and 271) may be parts of kohl sticks. The complete example, No. 264, is a simple toggle pin; the upper half of another (265) is decorated with groups of incisions (cf. Beth-Pelet: Pl. XI:69, 70, 77, etc.). Numbers 266 and 274 are roll-headed. The type occurs at Deve Hüyük (Moorey 1980a: Nos. 355–358), but examples from Olynthus (Olynthus X: Pl. CX:1755–1762) are closer to No. 274.

Seven of the 12 copper/bronze pins from Tel Michal were analyzed. There is no obvious connection between object and alloy. Two of the pins (265a, 272) were made of unalloyed copper, one (274) of low-tin bronze, three of bronze with 5.0–8.0 percent tin (267, 268, 273), and one

of high-tin bronze, with 13.89 percent tin (269). The variation in tin content would have resulted in pins of different color, a contrast that the ancient metalworker probably found desirable.

XXVII. TWEEZERS

Copper and copper-based alloys
*276. 4822/60; 653; E; XI-VI (fragmentary)

Iron
277. 4876/60; 664; E; XI-VI (Pl. 71:277)

Tweezers of bronze are fairly common in the Persian period (cf. Lachish III: Pl. 54:27; Moorey 1980a: No. 384; Beth-Pelet: Pl. XXI:91), but the iron example, No. 277, is unusual. For another bronze example from Tell el Mazar, together with references to other known examples, see Tell el Mazar I: 101–102.

The tweezers from Tel Michal were made of low-tin bronze, having 96.62 percent copper and 2.9 percent tin. It is interesting, given the popularity of tweezers in the Middle East, to see that the only pair found at Sardis was in iron and from a very late (Byzantine?) context (Waldbaum 1983:108, No. 647).

XXVIII. COSMETIC STICKS

Copper and copper-based alloys
278. 9758/60; 1559; A; XVI (fragmentary)
*279. 6542/60; 956; A; XV
280. 9650/60; 1530; A; XV (fragmentary)
281. 9571/60; 1522; A; XIV (fragmentary)
*282. 2041/60; 352; A; VIII (fragmentary; not illustrated)
*283. 1288/60; 189; E; XI/VI
284. 4449/60; 603; D; VII
*285. 4522/60; 618; D; VII (not illustrated)
286. 5727/60; 702; A; XI
*287. 11678/60; 1871; E; XI/VI
*288. 6351/60; 1312; A; VIII
*289. 6893/61; 1022; A; VII (fragmentary)
*290. 11711/60; 1872; E; XI/VI
291. 5937/60; 837; A; XI (fragmentary)
292. 8814/60; 864; A; X (fragmentary)
293. 1864/61; 342; A; VIII (not illustrated)
*294. 6624/60; 985; A; IX (not illustrated)
*295. 10721/60; 1364; A; X (not illustrated)
*296. 1724/60; 311; A; V
*297. 11032/60; 1739; A; V
*298. 4108/61; 570; A; V-IV
*299. 6280/60; 935; A; IIIa (fragmentary)

All the sticks from Tel Michal are of simple types with rounded, beveled or straight-edged, simply incised terminals. For a recent discussion of similar material, see Moorey 1980a:98–99 with references. Fifteen of the 22 cosmetic sticks were analyzed. There is no obvious connection between object and alloy. Some of the sticks were made of essentially pure copper, with over 99 percent copper (especially 282, 289, and 296). Others were made of bronze, with varying amounts of tin, including Nos. 290 (5.34 percent tin), 287 (6.34 percent tin), 297 (8.0 percent tin), and 283 (10.70 percent tin). Number 297 also has 4.48 percent

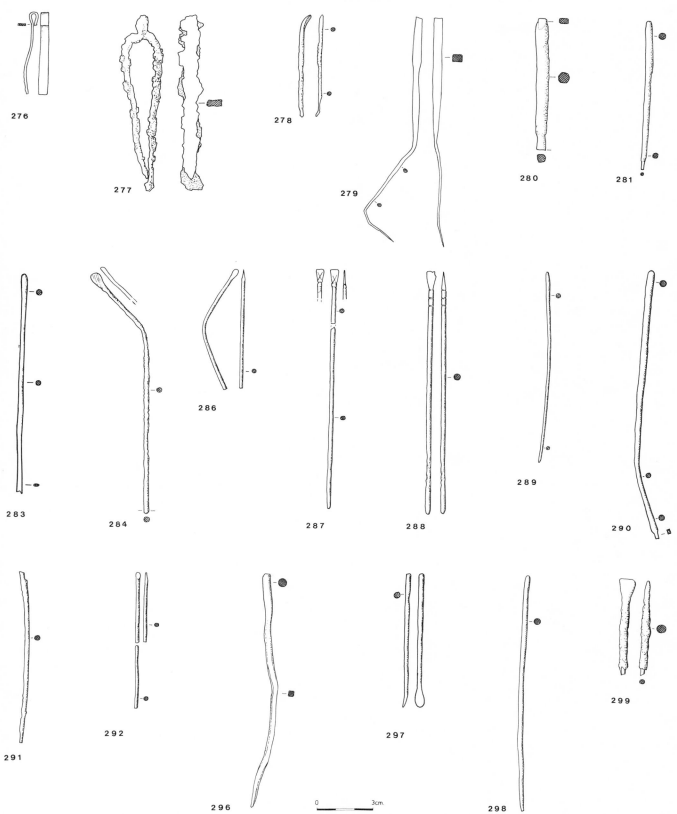

Figure 25.14. Tweezers and cosmetic sticks.

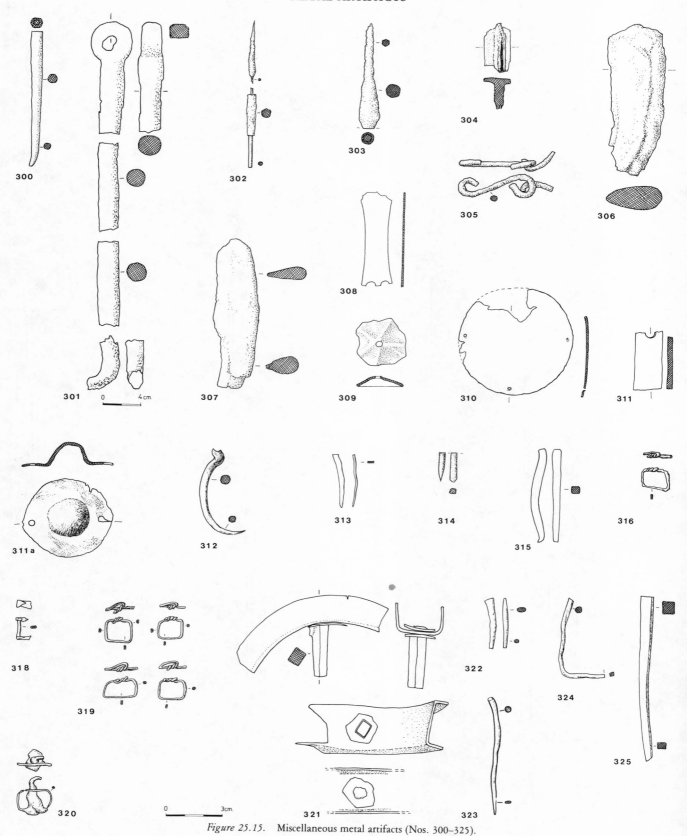

Figure 25.15. Miscellaneous metal artifacts (Nos. 300–325).

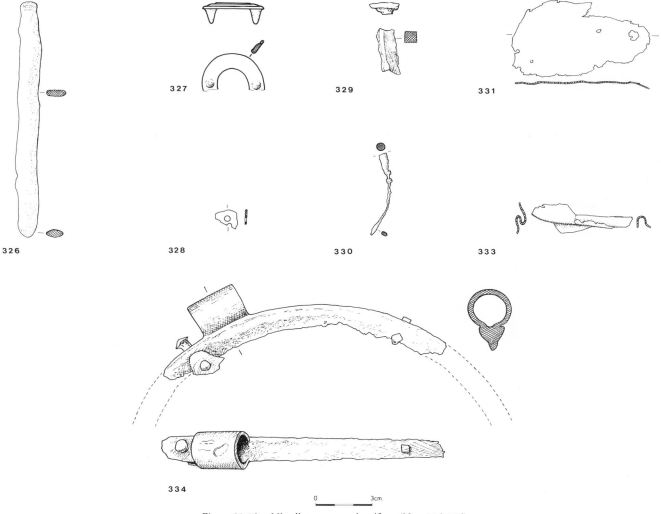

Figure 25.16. Miscellaneous metal artifacts (Nos. 326–334).

lead, whereas other examples—Nos. 285, 293, and 298—are best described as low-tin leaded alloys of copper.

MISCELLANEOUS
Copper and copper-based alloys

300. 9742/60; 1556; A; XVI
      Fragment of an awl?
301. 6461/60; 964; A; XV
      Fragmentary rod with a ring head
302. 9590/60; 1512; A; XV
      Arrowhead?
*303. 10478/60; 1659; A; XV
      Arrowhead?
*304. 2848/60; 240; B; XIV/XIII
      Unidentified fragment
*305. 6336/60; 948; A; VIII
      Chain links (cf. *Gezer II*: Pl. LXXXVI, from Tombs 65–73)

306. 10407/60; 1649; A; VII
      Unidentified fragment
307. 8850/60; 1387; A; VII
      Unidentified fragment
*308. 7369/60; 1101; D; VI
      Fragment of a small spatula?
*309. 3321/60; 466; C; VI
      Perforated rosette; perhaps a decorative attachment for a belt or harness. For parallel in iron from Pasargadae, see Stronach 1978:222–223, Fig. 96:12.
*310. 5612/60; 701; A; XI
      Disk with four small perforations on the rim
*311. 1852/60; 340; A; VIII
      Piece of a vessel handle?

293

311a. 5575/64; 842; A; VIII
Ornamental boss

*312. 2538/60; 411; A; VII
Pin fragment?

*313. 1735/60; 722; A; VII
Unidentified fragment

*314. 4158/60; 580; D; VI
Nail fragment?

*315. 2458/60; 405; A; VIII
Nail fragment?

*316. 1867/60; 340; A; VIII
Chain link

*317. 1857/60; 335; A; VIII (not illustrated)
Hook-shaped fragment

*318. 1762/61; 323; A; V
Chain link fragment

319. 1762/60; 323; A; V
Chain links

*320. 1754/60; 323; A; V
Chain links (cf. Carrière and Barrois
1927: Pl. LIV:107a)

*321. 6885/60; 1014; A; V
Fragment of helmet crest (?) (cf.
Lachish III: 387, Pl. 39:1)

*322. 1794/60; 323; A; V
Fragment of cosmetic stick?

*323. 107/60; 33; A; V
Pin fragment?

*324. 6213/60; 935; A; IIIa
Nail fragment

325. 8958/60; 1389; A; II
Nail fragment?

326. 4293/60; 727; D; VII
Bar

*327. 1/68; 1; Unstratified
Fragment of a buckle or of a horse
cheekpiece. For a possible parallel
from Post-Achaemenian Pasargadae,
see Stronach 1978:216–217, Fig.
93:5.

*328. 2407/60; 81; A; V
Small perforated disk

Iron

329. 11261/60; 1809; D; VI
Unidentified fragments

330. 2142/61; 50; A; I
Nail fragment?

Lead

*331. 1813/60; 324; A; VI
Sheet fragment

*332. 4266/60; 594; D; VII
Sheet fragment

333. 4229/60; 593; D; VII
Fragment of folded sheet

334. 6529/60A-C; 979; A; IX
Fragment of leaded-tin bronze hoop
with short piece of pipe attached and
two rivets

REFERENCES

Abel, M., and Barrois, A. 1928. Fouilles de l'Ecole Archéologique Francaise de Jérusalem effectuées à Neirab du 12 septembre au 6 novembre 1927. *Syria* 9:187–206, 303–319.

Amandry, P. 1958. Orfèvrerie achéménide. *Antike Kunst* 1:9–23.

Amiran, R. 1972. Achaemenian Bronze Objects from a Tomb at Kh. Ibsan in Lower Galilee. *Levant* 4:135–138.

Avila, R. A. J. 1983. *Bronzene Lanzen und Pfeilspitzen der griechischen Spätbronzezeit*. Munich.

Bass, G. F. 1967. *Cape Gelidonya: A Bronze Age Shipwreck*. Philadelphia.

Bliss, J. F., and Macalister, R. A. S. 1902. *Excavations in Palestine during the Years 1898–1900*. London.

Boardman, J. 1970. *Greek Gems and Finger Rings*. London.

Bouzek, J. 1978. Zu den Anfängen der Eisenzeit in Mitteleuropa. *Zeitschrift für Archäologie* 12:9–14.

Brovarski, E., Doll, S. K., and Freed, R. E. 1982. *Egypt's Golden Age: The Art of Living in the New Kingdom 1558–1085 B.C.* Boston.

Carrière, B., and Barrois, A. 1927. Fouilles de l'École Archéologique Francaise de Jérusalem effectuées à Neirab du 24 septembre au 5 novembre 1926. *Syria* 8:126–142; 201–212.

Chase, W. T. 1983. Bronze Casting in China: A Short Technical History. Pages 100–123 in: *The Great Bronze Age of China: A Symposium*. G. Kuwayama, ed. Los Angeles.

Chavane, M.-J. 1982. *Vases de bronze du Musée de Chypre (IXe-IVe s. av. J.-C.)*. Lyon.

Cleuziou, S. 1977. Les pointes de flèches "scythiques" au Proche et Moyen Orient. Pages 187–199 in: *Le Plateau Iranien et l'Asie Centrale des origines à la conquête islamique*. Paris.

Cooney, J. D. 1965. Persian Influence in Late Egyptian Art. *Journal of the American Research Center in Egypt* 4:39–48.

Craddock, P. T. 1978. The Composition of the Copper Alloys Used by the Greek, Etruscan and Roman Civilizations, 3. The Origins and Early Use of Brass. *JAS* 5:1–16.

Craddock, P. T. 1980. The First Brass: Some Early Claims Reconsidered. *MASCA Journal* I/5:131–133.

Craddock, P. T. 1986. Metallurgy and Composition of Etruscan Bronze. *Studi Etruschi* 52:211–271.

Craddock, P. T., Burnett, A. M., and Preston, K. 1980. Hellenistic Copper-base Coinage and the Origins of Brass. Pages 53–64 in: *Scientific Studies in Numismatics*. W. A. Oddy, ed. London.

Davis, D., Maddin, R., Muhly, J. D., and Stech, T. 1985. A Steel Pick from Mt. Adir in Palestine. *JNES* 44:41–51.

Gale, N., and Stos-Gale, Z. A. 1981. Ancient Egyptian Silver. *JEA* 67:103–115.

Gale, N. H., and Stos-Gale, Z. A. 1982. Bronze Age Copper Sources in the Mediterranean: A New Approach. *Science* 216:11–19.

Glueck, N. 1941. The Excavations of Solomon's Seaport: Ezion-geber. *Annual Report Smithsonian Institution*: 453–478.

Goldman, B. 1957. Achaemenian Chapes. *Ars Orientalis* 2:43–54.

Harding, G. L. 1950. An Iron Age Tomb at Meqabelein. *QDAP* 14:44–48.

Hughes, M. J., Curtis, J. E., and Hall, E. T. 1981. Analyses of Some Urartian Bronzes. *Anatolian Studies* 31:141–145.

Iakovidis, S. 1969–70. *Perati* (plates). Athens.

Johns, C. N. 1933. Excavations at 'Atlit (1930–31). The South-Eastern Cemetery. *QDAP* 2:41–104.

Jones, R. E. 1980. Analyses of Bronze and Other Base Metal Objects from the Cemeteries. Pages 447–459 in: *Lefkandi I: The Iron Age (Text)*. London.

Karageorghis, V. 1965. Sur quelques ornements de chevelure du bronze ancien de Chypre. *Syria* 42:141–154.

Karageorghis, V. 1986. L'archeologia a Cipro. *Archeo* 15:22–29.

Khalil, L. A. 1986. A Bronze Caryatid Censer from Amman. *Levant* 18:103–110.

Kraay, C. M., and Moorey, P. R. S. 1968. Two Fifth Century Hoards from the Near East. *Revue Numismatique* 10:181–235.

Kraay, C. M., and Moorey, P. R. S. 1981. A Black Sea Hoard of the Late Fifth Century B.C. *Numismatic Chronicle* 141:1–19.

Lefebvre, G. 1923. *Le tombeau de Petosiris*, vol. 3. Cairo.

Maxwell-Hyslop, K. R. 1971. *Western Asiatic Jewellery, c. 300–612 B.C.* London.

McKeon, J. F. X. 1973. Achaemenian Cloisonné-Inlay Jewellery, an Important New Example. Pages 109–117 in: *Orient and Occident: Festschrift Cyrus H. Gordon*. H. A. Hoffner, ed. Neukirchen-Vluyn.

Meshel, Z. 1977. Horvat Ritma – An Iron Age Fortress in the Negev Highlands. *Tel Aviv* 4:110–135.

Moorey, P. R. S. 1971. The Loftus Hoard of Old Babylonian Tools from Tell Sifr in Iraq. *Iraq* 33:61–86.

Moorey, P. R. S. 1975. Iranian Troops at Deve Hüyük in Syria in the Earlier Fifth Century B.C. *Levant* 7:108–117.

Moorey, P. R. S. 1980a. *Cemeteries of the First Millennium B.C. at Deve Hüyük, near Carchemish.* (British Archaeological Reports International Series 87.) Oxford.

Moorey, P. R. S. 1980b. Metal Wine Sets in the Ancient Near East. *Iranica Antiqua* 15:181–197.

Muhly, J. D. 1973. *Copper and Tin.* Hamden, Conn.

Muhly, J. D. 1982. How Iron Technology Changed the Ancient World –And Gave the Philistines a Military Edge. *BAR* 8/6:40–54.

Muscarella, O. W. 1982. An Aftercast of an Ancient Iranian Bronze. *Source: Notes in the History of Art* I/2:6–9.

Muscarella, O. W. 1985. Review of Curtis 1984. *JAOS* 105:729–730.

Oren, E. D. 1971. A Middle Bronze Age I Warrior Tomb at Beth-Shan. *ZDPV* 87:109–139.

Reade, J. 1986. A Hoard of Silver Currency from Achaemenid Babylon. *Iran* 24:79–89 (with appendices by M. J. Hughes and M. R. Cowell).

Richter, G. M. A. 1968. *Engraved Gems of the Greeks and the Etruscans.* London.

Rothenberg, B. 1975. Metals and Metallurgy. *Lachish V*: 72–83.

Shanks, H., and Eitan, A. 1986. BAR Interviews Avraham Eitan: Antiquities Director Confronts Problems and Controversies. *BAR* 12/4:30–38.

Shea, M., and Maxwell-Hyslop, K. R. 1979. A Gold Earring from the Great Shaft at Tell ed-Duweir. *Levant* 11:171–173.

Snodgrass, A. M. 1964. *Early Greek Armour and Weapons.* Edinburgh.

Snodgrass, A. M. 1981. Early Iron Swords in Cyprus. *RDAC*: 129–134.

Stech-Wheeler, T., Muhly, J. D., Maxwell-Hyslop, K. R., and Maddin, R. 1981. Iron at Taanach and Early Iron Metallurgy in the Eastern Mediterranean. *AJA* 85:245–268.

Stern, E. 1980. Achaemenian Tombs from Shechem. *Levant* 12:90–111.

Stern, E. 1982. *Material Culture of the Land of the Bible in the Persian Period, 538–332 B.C.E.* Warminster.

Stronach, D. 1978. *Pasargadae.* Oxford.

Stucky, R. A. 1976. Achämenidische Ortbänder. *Archäologischer Anzeiger* 1976:13–23.

Szilágyi, J. G. 1957. Some Problems of Greek Gold Diadems. *Acta Archaeologica Academiae Scientiarum Hungaricae* 5:45–93.

Tadmor, M. 1974. Fragments of an Achaemenid Throne from Samaria. *IEJ* 24:37–43.

von Bothmer, D. 1984. *A Greek and Roman Treasury.* New York.

Waldbaum, J. C. 1983. *Metalwork from Sardis: The Finds through 1974.* Cambridge, Mass.

Woolley, C. L. 1914–16. A North Syrian Cemetery of the Persian Period. *AAA* 7:115–129.

25b

Chemical Investigations of Metal Artifacts

by Alexandru Lupu

Metallic findings from the Tel Michal excavations total 528 objects, including fragments: 311 of copper and copper alloys, 14 of lead, 21 of silver or silver alloys (Tables 25.1–25.10), and 182 of iron. In addition, there were 16 samples of "slags" (Table 25.11). Iron objects make up 35 percent of the total. If we consider that iron corrodes more rapidly than the copper alloys, lead, or silver, we may presume that the total proportion of iron objects must originally have been much greater than 35 percent. Many iron objects undoubtedly corroded away, leaving nothing behind but (perhaps) a red stain in the soil. Consequently, the statistics presented here do not give the true picture of the relative use of ferrous and nonferrous metals in various chronological periods represented at the site.

Table 25.1. Nature of Nonferrous Metallic Artifacts

Metal	Number	Percentage
Copper	101	29.20
Arsenical bronze	19	5.50
Arsenical tin bronze	2	0.58
Tin arsenical bronze	21	6.07
Tin bronze	117	33.82
Leaded tin bronze	51	14.74
Lead	14	4.05
Silver	21	6.07
Total artifacts	346	100.03

Most of the nonferrous metal artifacts were analyzed in the metallurgical laboratories of the Institute of Archaeology of Tel Aviv University (Table 25.12).[1] The catalog numbers on this table refer to Chap. 25a (which also includes the iron objects).

Among nonferrous metals, copper and its alloys were most common until the time when iron use became widespread. Copper and copper alloys are defined as follows: *copper*: metallic copper with less than 0.3–0.4 percent arsenic; *arsenical bronze*: metallic copper with more than 0.3–0.4 percent arsenic and less than 0.3–0.4 percent tin; *arsenical tin bronze*: metallic copper with more arsenic than tin and both more than 0.3–0.4 percent; *tin arsenical bronze*: metallic copper with more tin than arsenic and both more than 0.3–0.4 percent; *tin bronze*: metallic copper with more than 0.3 percent tin and less than 0.3–0.4 percent arsenic; *leaded tin bronze*: metallic copper with more than 0.3–0.4 percent tin, 2.0 percent lead, and a relatively small percentage of arsenic.

Lead and silver objects comprise only 10.12 percent of the nonferrous metals. Copper objects (29.36 percent) are present in about the same proportions as tin bronzes (33.43 percent). Arsenical bronze (5.52 percent) is well represented in the later periods, despite the fact that the use of tin instead of arsenic had already been known for centuries. Arsenic as an alloying agent is more common in metal artifacts from countries with more prevalent arsenic ores than Israel or Sinai, since the local copper ores contain less than 0.1 percent arsenic (Bender 1968:140–146; Lupu and Rothenberg 1970).

Copper objects that contain nickel, cobalt, bismuth, antimony, or zinc may be of foreign origin, since local copper is very poor in these elements (less than 0.1 percent). In leaded tin bronzes, the lead was most likely added to obtain better casting properties or for economic reasons, since in ancient times lead was cheaper than tin. The presence of silver and gold in various copper alloys may indicate the presence of copper from foreign deposits containing those elements or the melting down of various small objects of gold or silver (or gold- or silver-plated copper alloys). The presence of zinc, generally rare before the Roman period, also points to a foreign origin. Copper-zinc ores may have come from Cyprus, where copper sulfide deposits containing zinc have been known since antiquity (Beer 1962:126).

The chemical composition of the metallic objects has been calculated in two ways (Table 25.12): chemical analy-

Table 25.2.   Distribution of Copper Artifacts

Artifact	Iron Age	Persian Period	Hellenistic Period	Roman Period	Arabic Period	Not Stratified	Total
Nails/tacks		33	11	2	2	4	52
Pins		8	4				12
Arrowheads	1	1				1	3
Bowl		1					1
Clamps/plaques		8					8
Disks		1	1				2
Earrings		1	1				2
Fibulae		1	1				2
Hook		1					1
Chain link		1					1
Needles/bodkins		2	2				4
Rings		3					3
Cosmetic sticks		1	1			2	4
Handle of vessel		1					1
Fragments		2	2			1	5
Total	1	65	23	2	2	8	101

sis of the artifact in its present condition and then the recalculation of these results by considering the total contents of the metallic elements (Cu, Sn, Zn, Fe, Pb, Ag, Au, As, Bi, Sb, Ni, Co) as 100 percent to obtain an approximate picture of the original metallic composition before corrosion. The recalculated percentages, wherever of sufficient interest, are enclosed in parentheses in the appropriate columns of Table 25.12. Oxygen, carbon dioxide, sulfur, silica, aluminum, calcium oxide, manganese oxide, and magnesium oxide are therefore eliminated in recalculation.

Recalculation is important because it is very difficult to compare the metallic composition of a very corroded metal object, having only 40 or 50 percent of its original metallic elements preserved, with other objects that have not been corroded at all or that contain (for example) 80–90 percent of their metallic elements. However, recalculation of the original composition by this method presents some prob-

lems, since the metallic elements have undergone various degrees of oxidation. For example, if direct analysis of a bronze object reveals only 50 percent copper and 10 percent tin, recalculation (considering the total metallic content of 60 percent as 100 percent) will give 83.33 percent copper and 16.66 percent tin. Here we have considered both of these elements as having the same degree of oxidation.

In reality, copper may be oxidized not only to cuprite (Cu_2O) or tenorite (CuO_2) but also to azurite ($2CuCO_3 \cdot Cu(OH)_2$) or malachite ($Cu(OH)_2CuCO_3$), where the copper content is only 55 or 57.65 percent, respectively, and the rest of the corrosion product (CO_3 and $(OH)_2$) equals 45 percent, representing an increased weight of about 100 percent of the original copper. The metallic tin (Sn) may be oxidized to cassiterite (SnO_2), with a tin content of 78.76 percent and an oxygen content of 21.24 percent. This means that the degree of oxidation — the increased weight — of the original metal will be only 27 percent compared with about 100 percent increased weight of the copper.

Considering the copper and tin as equally oxidized is not accurate; if we take this into account, however, and recalculate exactly the original content, instead of 83.33 percent copper and 16.66 percent tin, by direct calculation we will obtain 82.14 percent copper and 17.86 percent tin. The difference between the two results is not great, and the latter is nearer the original composition. The approximation is about 98.57 percent for copper and 107.20 percent for tin.

Another limitation of the recalculation method is caused by the weathering of corroded metallic elements, which may be dissolved by water in the soil to a greater or lesser extent. Nevertheless, since recalculation gives us a closer picture of the original metal composition, it is adopted here. Because of the complex nature of corrosion, it is doubtful whether greater precision would be possible even with a thorough and complicated quantitative mineralogical investigation.

Table 25.3.   Copper Artifacts of Foreign Origin (Remelted)

Artifact	Reg. No.	Impurities (%)
Pin fragment	107/60	0.31 Ag
Tack	410/60	0.12 Co
Fragment	1632/60	0.10 Ag
Pin	1680/60	0.15 Ni
Chain link	1762/61	0.13 Co
Pin	4090/60	0.44 Co
Nail	4166/60	0.22 Co
Nail	4198/60	0.14 Ag
Nail	4407/60	0.15 Co
Plaque with rivet	7709/60	0.17 Ni
Plaque with rivet	7710/60	1.50 Ni
Tack	8896/60	0.10 Ag

Table 25.4. Distribution of Arsenical Bronze Artifacts

Artifact	Late Bronze Age	Iron Age	Persian Period	Hellenistic Period	Roman Period	Not Stratified	Total
Nails/tacks			4	2			6
Arrowheads			1			1	2
Chisel			1				1
Bracelets			2				2
Lynch pin			1				1
Needles	1	1			1		3
Clamps/plaques			2				2
Cosmetic stick			1				1
Fragment					1		1
Total	1	1	12	2	2	1	19

Determination of the mineralogical composition of corrosion was done by microscopic analysis or differential thermal analysis.

25b.1 COPPER

Objects containing less than 0.3–0.4 percent tin and/or less than 0.3–0.4 percent arsenic represent about 30 percent of the total metallic artifacts (Table 25.2). These were distributed over all periods from the Middle Bronze Age to the Early Arab. Most came from the Persian period, however, which is represented by six strata on the high tell (Strata XI–VI) and by an extensive cemetery. Nails, tacks, and pins were the most common articles (52 nails/tacks and 12 pins). Their abundance may be explained by their use in wood or wood-metal joints; they were therefore not easy to recover. After the wood rots away, however, they are free.

Jewelry items (bracelets, earrings, fibulae, rings, cosmetic sticks, and the like) are the second most important group of copper objects. In reality their number may have been even greater, but since they are usually not thick they corrode faster and disappear in time.

Weapons and tools are poorly represented (only three arrowheads), since in comparison with bronze or iron, copper is much softer and therefore not suitable for such purposes.

The copper objects may have been produced locally from ores in the Arabah (Timna or Punon) or Sinai. Metallic copper from these locations is characterized by low content of other metallic elements: less than 0.1 percent Sn, As, Sb, Bi, Zn, Ni, Co, Ag, and Au and less than 0.2–0.4 percent lead (Bender 1968; Lupu 1970). Iron content cannot give information about the location of the deposit because it comes from the iron fluxes used in the smelting process and not from copper ores. In many cases, lead is added to the copper to achieve better casting properties. A lead alloy is cheaper and easier to produce since it has low melting and reduction points.

The chemical-metallurgical laboratory of the Institute of Archaeology of Tel Aviv University analyzed thousands of copper objects, ores, and slags from the Arabah and Sinai, as well as objects from Cypriote excavations, and we have

Table 25.5. Distribution of Tin Arsenical Bronze Artifacts

Artifact	Late Bronze Age	Persian Period	Hellenistic Period	Total
Nails		2	1	3
Pins	1	1	1	3
Arrowheads		2		2
Bracelets		4		4
Earrings		4		4
Cotter pin		1		1
Band		1		1
Ring		1		1
Cosmetic stick	1			1
Total	2	16	2	20

obtained a detailed picture of the composition of ancient copper objects. If the copper came from remelted scrap, elements may be present in higher percentages than are characteristic of local copper deposits. For example, contents of more than 0.1 percent silver or gold indicate remelting of silver or gold objects or copper objects that had been plated with silver or gold.

Most copper pieces found at Tel Michal seem to have been produced locally, except for 12 that contain elements not characteristic of local copper deposits (Table 25.3). Four items containing silver may be the result of a scrap process of remelting copper objects with silver or silver-plated pieces, whereas eight pieces with cobalt or nickel probably originated where copper deposits were rich in nickel and cobalt (Caley 1964:112).

25b.2 ARSENICAL BRONZE

The presence of more than 0.3–0.4 percent arsenic changes the properties of raw metallic copper. We prefer to call this alloy arsenical bronze instead of arsenical copper because copper-tin alloys with more than 0.3–0.4 percent tin are called bronzes (tin bronzes). Nineteen objects of arsenical

Table 25.6. Distribution of Tin Bronze Artifacts

Artifact	Iron Age	Persian Period	Hellenistic Period	Roman Period	Arab Period	Not Stratified	Total
Nails		4	3		1	5	13
Pins		6	2				8
Arrowheads		7					7
Sheet metal band		1					1
Bowls		2					2
Bracelets		11	1				12
Diadem						1	1
Disks-knobs		3					3
Earrings		10	1				11
Fibulae		11	3				14
Rosettes		1	1				2
Chain links		2					2
Needles		2					2
Rings		11					11
Cosmetic stick		5	1			8	14
Tweezer		1					1
Fragments	1	2	2		1	7	13
Total	1	79	14	0	2	21	117

Table 25.7. Distribution of Leaded Tin Bronze Artifacts

Artifact	Iron Age	Persian Period	Hellenistic Period	Roman Period	Arab Period	Not Stratified	Total
Nail		1					1
Pins		2					2
Arrowheads		10		1		2	13
Bead		1					1
Bracelets		10					10
Disk-knob		1					1
Fibulae	1	4	3				8
Fishing weight		1					1
Hoops		3					3
Ladle		1					1
Needle						1	1
Rings		1				1	2
Cosmetic sticks		3	1				4
Fragments		1				1	2
Unidentified			1				1
Total	1	39	5	1	0	5	51

Table 25.8. Distribution of Lead Artifacts

Artifact	Persian Period	Hellenistic Period	Not Stratified	Total
Weight	1			1
Clamps	1	1		2
Fishing weights	1	1		2
Rings	1		2	3
Fragments			3	3
Not classified			3	3
Total	4	2	8	14

Table 25.9. Distribution of Silver Artifacts

Artifact	Persian Period	Not Stratified	Total
Earrings	4	2	6
Rings	9	5	14
Pendant	1		1
Total	14	7	21

Table 25.10. Melting Points of Silver Artifacts

Reg. No.	Artifact	Cu (%)	Melting Point (°C)
1/64	Earring	5.45	920
1/65	Earring	7.48	907
25/60	Ring	36.96	805
3314/60	Signet ring	9.36	890
4210/60	Ring	3.4	935
4472/60	Earring	6.8	895
7680/60	Ring	0.85	970
7733/60	Earring	1.42	957
7733/62	Earring	1.03	960
9390/60	Earring	0.56	974
11612/60	Ring	1.28	965
11613/60	Ring	0.70	972
11633/60	Ring	3.3	935
11633/61	Ring	0.34	978
11645/60	Pendant	3.22	928
11720/60	Ring	13.9	855

bronze (Table 25.4) represent only 5.5 percent of all non-ferrous finds from Tel Michal.

The addition of arsenic to copper is an ancient technique, and most of these objects have a small arsenic content (0.3–0.6 percent As). This arsenic may come from melted scrap, from arsenical copper ores, or from the addition of small amounts of arsenic. There are only two items of typical arsenical bronze with a higher arsenic content: a cosmetic stick of the Persian period with 1.53 percent (recalculated as 1.60 percent) As (Reg. No. 3319/60) and a needle from the LB I stratum with 1.91 percent (recalculated as 2.25 percent) As (Reg. No. 10835/60). The needle may have been produced by a scrap melting process, judging by its iron and silver content of 1.63 percent (1.9 percent) Fe and 0.51 percent (0.58 percent) Ag, since the percentage in raw metallic copper is generally less than 0.2–0.5 percent iron and less than 0.1 percent silver. Therefore, whatever object(s) were melted here to give 1.91 percent (2.25 percent) As in the final alloy would have had a much higher content of arsenic.

Of the 19 arsenical bronze objects, 13 contain other metals such as silver or antimony, indicating a melted scrap origin. Objects containing antimony as an impurity (e.g., Reg. No. 4198) may indicate a northern origin for the copper, since northern copper-sulfidic ores contain a higher percentage of antimony than those from the Arabah or Sinai (0.01–0.04 percent Sb).

Like the pins and nails of pure copper, those of arsenical bronze are the most common objects, perhaps because they were affixed to wood that helped to protect them from direct contact with the soil. The only weapons in this group are arrowheads. One of these (Reg. No. 11202/60) must have come from melted scrap because it contains a relatively large amount of silver (0.24 percent Ag). Jewelry is represented by three items: a bracelet, a fibula, and a cosmetic stick.

25b.3 ARSENICAL TIN BRONZE

This alloy (defined as containing more than 0.3–0.4 percent arsenic and 0.3–0.4 percent tin) is represented by only two items. The first is a tack of the Hellenistic period, 15 mm long and 4 mm wide with a head 20 mm in diameter (Reg. No. 4103/60). For greater hardness, the piece contains 1.05 percent (recalculated as 1.09 percent) arsenic and 0.49 percent (0.51 percent) tin. The presence of other elements such as gold (0.14 percent), bismuth (0.19 percent), antimony (0.13 percent), and zinc (0.30 percent) indicates a scrap smelting process of metals from northern origins where sulfide copper deposits are found. The second item is a cosmetic stick of the Late Bronze Age, 8 cm long and 4 mm wide and weighing 10 g (Reg. No. 6542/60). It contains 0.43 percent Sn and 0.60 percent As.

25b.4 TIN ARSENICAL BRONZE

There are 20 items in this group, all containing more than 0.3–0.4 percent tin (Table 25.5). These pieces represent a transition from arsenical bronze to tin bronze, since arsenic, because of its noxiousness, was used less and less as time went by. The arsenic content is relatively low in all but three of these artifacts: 1.0–1.2 percent in Nos. 1108/60, 5270/60, and 10721/60. The zinc (1.05 percent), bismuth (0.15 percent), silver (0.3 percent), antimony (0.45 percent), and cobalt (0.11 percent) contents of Reg. No. 1108/60 (a Persian arrowhead) indicate a northern origin or scrap source.

The jewelry items (four earrings, four bracelets, and one finger ring) are relatively numerous, as this alloy may have been considered a luxury. Pins and nails are represented by only six pieces, since ordinary objects of this sort do not require expensive high-content tin alloys.

25b.5 TIN BRONZE

Bronzes of this alloy (consisting of more than 0.3–0.4 percent tin and less than 0.3–0.4 percent arsenic) are the most numerous, totaling 117 pieces or about 34 percent of all nonferrous artifacts (Table 25.6). Use is also more diversified, since tin bronze is suitable for more purposes than metallic copper because of superior casting qualities and mechanical properties. The latter include hardness (for arrowheads) and plasticity and elasticity (for jewelry such as fibulae, bracelets, and rings). The anticorrosive nature of tin bronze makes it a desirable alloy for all metal objects, but particularly for tableware and jewelry. There are 14 fibulae in this group (as compared with only 2 of copper), 12 earrings (versus 2 of copper), 11 finger rings (versus 3 of copper), and 12 bracelets (versus none of copper). Although copper continued to be used for such items, it was probably less affluent people who did so. Pins, nails, and tacks of tin bronze (like those of tin arsenical bronze) are less well represented (21 altogether) than the same items made of copper (64) for the same reason: tin was too expensive to be used for everyday items, and copper pins and

Table 25.11. Chemical Composition of Slags[a]

Reg. No.	Locus	SiO$_2$	CaO	MgO	FeO	Fe$_2$O$_3$[b]	Fe$_3$O$_4$[c]	MnO	Al$_2$O$_3$	Na$_2$O	K$_2$O	Cu	Ni	Sn	Zn	As	Magnetic
428/60	1070	30.59	11.68	2.05	···	43.00	···	0.07	2.83	n.d.[d]	n.d.	0.19	···	0.19	···	0.05	No
1504/60	219	12.35	4.67	2.14	···	62.30	···	2.14	1.53	n.d.	n.d.	0.18	···	0.18	···	0.04	No
1817/60	330	25.84	21.68	4.16	37.28	41.42	···	0.31	2.64	2.17	2.53	<0.1	0.008	0.01	0.008	···	No
1942/60	339	10.66	9.82	0.80	71.47	79.41	···	0.04	2.37	2.37	1.86	<0.1	0.009	0.02	0.004	···	No
2435/60	404	7.13	4.33	1.24	79.67	88.53	85.22	0.06	2.04	2.34	1.05	0.03	0.03	0.01	0.005	···	Yes
3613/60	500	6.2	6.93	0.95	70.24	78.04	75.14	0.05	1.18	2.10	1.1	0.02	0.04	0.04	0.005	···	Yes
3613/61	500	6.73	3.77	1.16	67.08	74.53	71.76	0.17	1.42	2.67	1.15	0.02	0.017	0.02	0.004	···	Yes
3629/60	160	7.78	5.22	2.97	77.95	71.66	···	0.17	1.5	2.16	1.24	<0.1	0.01	0.03	0.005	···	Yes
4002/60	551	4.14	1.34	0.35	79.11	87.90	84.63	0.15	1.24	2.7	1.08	<0.1	0.015	0.02	0.005	···	Yes
4026/60	551	9.56	4.56	1.38	64.5	71.66	69.0	0.07	1.41	2.14	1.34	<0.1	0.03	0.02	0.004	···	Yes
4074/60	560	15.26	10.71	0.95	53.06	59.00	56.76	0.24	1.78	2.25	1.58	<0.1	0.027	0.03	0.004	···	No
4094/60	568	9.7	8.9	2.66	62.72	70.00	67.1	0.12	1.80	2.77	1.34	0.07	0.015	0.02	0.005	···	Yes
4138/60	580	8.7	8.28	1.0	69.6	77.33	74.44	0.66	1.84	2.8	1.3	<0.1	0.03	0.05	0.003	···	Yes
4204/60	578	10.0	0.73	0.18	71.53	79.5	76.52	0.02	1.41	2.43	1.32	<0.1	0.05	0.03	0.004	···	Yes
5102/60	675	16.98	9.02	0.65	69.63	77.36	···	0.17	2.03	2.12	1.4	0.03	0.02	0.02	0.004	···	No
5205/60	690	7.33	0.61	0.19	78.22	86.92	83.66	0.01	1.4	2.42	1.08	<0.1	0.04	0.02	0.004	···	Yes

[a] Shown as percentages.
[b] FeO calculated as hematite.
[c] FeO calculated as magnetite.
[d] Not detected.

nails have enough mechanical strength for their purpose—to penetrate wood.

Four of the seven arrowheads are of the triangular Persian type. Their tin content is generally less than 1.0 percent, with the exception of Reg. No. 2433/60, which contains 6.88 percent tin. Compared with the leaded tin bronzes, the tin bronze arrowheads are less common (see below).

Some of the pieces, even those with a higher tin content (6–8 percent) are very corroded. Those with more than 9 percent tin are better preserved, with a surviving metal content of more than 87–90 percent.

Since the metallic copper found here may have been brought from the Arabah or Sinai, manufacture of bronze by alloying it with tin may have been done locally. Chemical analysis of the bronzes suggests that many of them may have been made using local copper together with tin imported from an international tin trade center, such as Mari (Malamat 1971; Muhly and Wertime 1974). The presence of characteristic elements such as Zn, As, Bi, Sb, Ni, and Co indicates a possible northern origin for 13 pieces. Three pieces with higher zinc content may have come from Cyprus or the Roman Empire.

The shallow tin bronze bowl (Reg. No. 1274/60) is typical of the Persian period. Its antimony content of 0.08 percent may indicate a foreign origin, since northern sulfidic-copper deposits contain this element as an impurity. One piece with an unusual composition is a Persian period pin weighing 1.48 g (Reg. No. 2060/60). It contains 11.75 percent zinc, 5.53 percent tin, 0.14 percent antimony, 0.11 percent bismuth, and 0.45 percent arsenic. The content of antimony, arsenic, and bismuth implies a northern copper-sulfidic deposit, but the high zinc content (more than the tin) makes this alloy closer to brass (zinc-copper alloy). In this period, the alloy may have been brought from the Roman Empire (Italy or some other European country) that possessed such sulfidic copper-zinc deposits. The Cyprus copper deposits, which also contain zinc, cannot be excluded as the origin of this alloy; at Kokkinopezoul and other places, ancient tools consisting of almost 60 percent metallic zinc have been found (Beer 1962:126).

25b.6 LEADED TIN BRONZE

Fifty-one pieces of tin-lead or lead-tin bronze containing more than 2 percent lead represent about 15 percent of the nonferrous metals (Table 25.7). Most of them are arrowheads (13), followed by bracelets (10) and fibulae (8). There are only one nail and two pins (one with 3.52 percent Pb and the second with 4.52 percent Pb) since this alloy has little mechanical strength. Lead was popular as an alloying component for certain objects because of its good casting properties (low melting temperature, fluidity, and better filling of the molds); good forging qualities for making small objects, such as jewelry; and good ballistic properties as a result of its relatively high specific gravity (11 g/cm^3 for lead as compared with 7.8 for copper). Another attraction may have been the fact that lead was "cheaper" than copper or tin, since rich lead-ore deposits are more widely diffused than copper ore deposits. The technique of extracting lead from ores was also more economical as a result of its low melting point (327°C) and low reduction temperature. It is therefore not surprising that this alloy was popular for arrowheads because of the ease of manufacture at low tem-

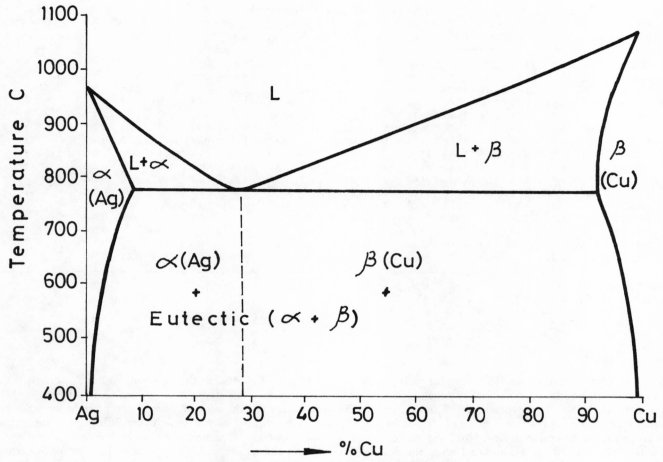

Figure 25.17. Melting points of silver-copper alloys.

peratures in ordinary stone or ceramic molds. Although the arrowheads are of various types, the Persian triangular type is most numerous. There are fewer of the rhomboid type (four pieces). In three of these, the tin content is very small (0.5–0.7 percent), whereas some have 5.0–16.0 percent tin. The lead in this group is between 4 and 60 percent, tending to higher proportions in the Persian type (more than 14 percent Pb, with the exception of Reg. No. 4530/60, which has only 4.24 percent Pb). Ten of the arrowheads, which contain arsenic, zinc, antimony, or silver, are apparently of foreign origin. Those containing only silver as an impurity (without the other metals) may have come from melted scrap, probably a major source for the production of arrowheads.

The second group of leaded tin bronzes consists of bracelets, most of them containing silver (0.1–0.15 percent), antimony (0.1–0.15 percent), and arsenic (0.4–0.72 percent) as impurities. The third group of leaded bronzes consists of eight fibulae, which contain 4–18 percent lead. The two rings, which contain nickel and antimony, are probably of foreign origin. The presence of silver in one of them indicates a scrap melting process.

25b.7 LEAD

Only pieces that have more than 90 percent lead are classified in this group of 14 (Table 25.8). Thirteen pieces are of this quality, according to chemical analysis; the one piece with a lower lead content (69.13 percent Pb) probably also contained more than 99 percent lead in its original state since no other metallic elements are present (except 0.1 percent Fe). The metallic lead was almost totally transformed into lead sulfate ($PbSO_4$).

The metallic impurities occur in very small proportions — less than 0.1–0.2 percent — with the exception of Reg. No. 348/60, which has 1.12 percent tin. This tin content may have come from lead ores, which often contain tin as an impurity. Most of the lead objects are from the Hellenistic and Persian periods. Lead was used mainly for weights of various types; two of our specimens are fishing weights.

25b.8 SILVER

There were 21 silver objects: 14 rings, 6 earrings, and 1 pendant (Table 25.9). The rings are made of silver copper alloys, some containing small quantities of copper (0.34–0.7 percent) and some with very high copper content (14.70–36.66 percent Cu). The copper content of the earrings is 0.56–7.38 percent; the impurities (Fe, Pb, Sn, Zn, Bi, Ni) vary from less than 0.1 to 1–2 percent.

Silver is used mainly as an alloy with copper. Figure 25.17 shows the characteristic melting points of silver-copper alloys. Adding copper decreases the melting point of silver (980°C) to 779°C when the silver contains 28.5 percent copper (the eutectic point). Among the silver objects only one, containing 36.96 percent copper, comes near this, with a melting point of 805°C. The rest of the objects have melting points as presented in Table 25.10.

Silver-copper alloys are very resistant to corrosion. Alloys with more than 7.5 percent copper are used for coins, and those with more than 90 percent silver are used for jewelry, since pure silver is too soft. Alloys at or around the eutectic composition (28.5 percent Cu) are used as solders since they are fluid and adhesive.

Gold is present only in very small quantities—from undetectable to 0.75 percent Au (0.64 percent in earring fragment Reg. No. 4472/60). The origin of the silver objects is very difficult to determine, as the jewelry undoubtedly was remelted and transformed over and over again. The presence of such impurities as arsenic, tin, zinc, and iron may indicate an origin from remelted objects. Nine of the 21 pieces contain such elements; for example, earring Reg. No. 1/64 has 0.39 percent zinc, 2.72 percent tin, 0.16 percent bismuth, 0.16 percent nickel, and 0.78 percent iron. All these impurities may have come from sulfidic deposits of copper and lead where silver and gold were also present. The presence of iron may be explained only by assuming a scrap melting process in which the melted objects contained small amounts of iron along with the silver.

25b.9 SLAGS

The large quantity of metallic artifacts, both ferrous and nonferrous, from the excavation is not associated with a corresponding amount of slag.

Only 16 pieces of so-called slag were found (Table 25.11), and only 2 of them are of nonferrous metals (copper or copper alloys). The rest are ferrous "slags," better defined as cinder material (Table 25.11). Their chemical composition indicates that they result from hot working rather than from melting in a crucible to extract iron from ores.

The iron ore deposits closest to Tel Michal are located near the Israel-Lebanon border (Menara). By smelting these ores together with fluxes, the Phoenicians obtained metallic iron and made ingots of various dimensions. These ingots were worked not by casting but by heat treatment and forging.

At Tel Michal, lumps of brown-black color commonly known as slags are similar to those obtained by casting or smelting, but they are not true slags. Microscopic examination reveals small particles of iron oxides joined together by heat but at a temperature below melting point (1,500°C). This cinder material is composed of iron scales that became detached in heating and beating the ingots. The iron content of these pieces is more than 70 percent (Fe_2O_3). Ten of the slags are magnetic, and magnetite (Fe_3O_4) is microscopically visible together with iron oxide (Fe_2O_3). No iron particles are present in these "slags," nor are there any silicates, which are the result of a casting or smelting process. Two of these lumps are not magnetic (Reg. Nos. 4074/60 and 1817/60), having 59 percent Fe_2O_3 and 41.42 percent Fe_2O_3, respectively. They are the result of forging, but the oxidation process was complete and no magnetite remained. The presence of 25.84 percent SiO_2, 21.68 percent CaO, and 4.16 percent MgO comes from the sandy soil of Tel Michal. The nickel content in the Lebanon deposits is very low (less than 0.1 percent). Copper, tin, and zinc contents (less than 0.1 percent each) are usual for iron ores.

Two of the lumps (Reg. Nos. 428/60 and 1504/60), which are not totally melted, may be skimming material that came from some scrap melting process in which various nonferrous (copper-based) metals and ferrous materials were melted together. The presence of 0.18–0.19 percent copper and 0.18–0.19 percent tin indicates a scrap source rich in tin, since the ratio of copper to tin is about 1:1.

NOTE

1. The editors wish to thank Netta Halperin, chemist at the Institute of Archaeology, Tel Aviv University, who not only performed many of the metallurgical analyses of the metal artifacts but also was very helpful in clarifying several technical points in the manuscript of the late Prof. Alexandru Lupu.

REFERENCES

Beer, L. M. 1962. *The Mineral Resources and Mining Industry of Cyprus 1.* Nicosia.

Bender, F. 1968. *Geologie von Jordanien.* Berlin-Stuttgart.

Caley, E. R. 1964. *Analysis of Ancient Metals.* London.

Lupu, A. 1970. Metallurgical Aspects of the Chalcolithic Copper Industry at Timna-Arava, Israel. *Bulletin of the Historical Metallurgy Group* 4(1):21–23. London.

Lupu, A., and Rothenberg, B. 1970. The Extractive Metallurgy of the Early Iron Age Copper Industry in the 'Arabah, Israel. *Archaeologia Austriaca* 47:91–130.

Malamat, A. 1971. Syro-Palestinian Destinations in a Mari Tin Inventory. *IEJ* 21:31–38.

Muhly, J. D. and Wertime, T. A. 1974. Evidence for the Source and Use of Tin during the Bronze Age of the Near East. *World Archaeology* 5:112–122.

Table 25.12. Chemical Composition of Metal Artifacts[a]

Reg. No.	Locus	Type of Object	Cat. No.	Cu	Sn	Zn	Fe	Pb	Ag	Au	As	Bi	Sb	Ni	Co	Weight[b] (g)
1/60	1	Copper handle	164	75.48 (98.50)	n.d.[c]	0.01	0.42	0.23	n.d.	0.08	0.28	0.04	0.04	n.d.	n.d.	
1/61	1	Tin bronze arrowhead	28	60.48 (98.12)	0.50	0.16	0.21	0.14	0.06	n.d.	n.d.	0.02	0.02	0.04	0.01	
1/62	1	Bronze arrowhead	17	68.18 (81.36)	3.48 (4.15)	0.04	0.12	11.52 (13.74)	0.05	n.d.	0.21	0.03	0.15	0.02	n.d.	
1/63	1	Leaded tin bronze arrowhead	16	68.64 (77.80)	3.32	0.23	0.14	16.46	0.06	n.d.	0.20	0.03	0.08	0.02	0.03	
1/64	1	Silver earring	198	5.45	2.72	0.39	0.78	0.45	90.91	0.42	n.d.	0.16	n.d.	0.16	n.d.	
1/65	1	Silver earring	199	7.48	2.25	0.27	0.67	0.33	89.82	0.3	n.d.	0.14	n.d.	0.13	n.d.	
1/66	1	Tin bronze pin	274	81.04 (96.56)	2.43 (2.89)	0.08	0.16	0.16	n.d.	n.d.	n.d.	0.02	0.04	n.d.	n.d.	
1/67	1	Copper needle	71	82.42 (99.04)	0.22	0.04	0.20	n.d.	n.d.	n.d. (0.37)	0.31	0.01	0.06	n.d.	n.d.	
1/67a	1	Copper hook	76	95.77	0.2	0.2	0.09	n.d.	n.d.	n.d.	0.20	0.02	0.02	n.d.	n.d.	
1/68	1	Leaded tin bronze buckle	327	75.38 (85.70)	4.27	0.06	0.12	7.79	0.02	n.d.	n.d.	0.05	0.25	0.02	n.d.	
1/69	1	Lead		0.06	n.d.	0.1	0.02	98.43 (99.8)	0.03	n.d.	0.25	0.04	0.06	n.d.	n.d.	
23/60	1	Tin bronze bracelet	230	89.3	9.53	0.009	0.13	0.70	0.08	n.d.	0.25	n.d.	n.d.	0.030	n.d.	
24a/60	2	Tin bronze fragment		78.12 (97.25)	1.22 (1.52)	0.034 (0.042)	0.75 (0.93)	0.034 (0.042)	n.d.	n.d.	<0.13	n.d.	n.d.	0.043	n.d.	
25/60	2	Silver ring	241	36.96				0.22	63.69							
103/60	43	Tin bronze earring	194	90.03	6.30	0.17	0.23	2.0	0.05	n.d.	0.27	n.d.	0.04	0.04	0.016	1.9523
107/60	33	Copper pin fragment	323	99.21	n.d.	0.02	0.001	0.27	0.31	n.d.	n.d.	n.d.	0.04	0.01	n.d.	4.1633
299/60	66	Copper nail	105	95.55	n.d.	0.035	0.17	0.076	0.02	n.d.	n.d.	n.d.	<0.04	0.026	0.043	
321/60	63	Copper nail	138	99.55	n.d.	0.007	0.036	0.25	0.07	n.d.	n.d.	n.d.	0.036	0.06	n.d.	7.4200
348/60	65	Lead clamp			1.12			98.80								47.5200
377/60	70	Copper hook	75	87.50	<0.25	0.03	0.075	n.d.	0.05	n.d.	<0.125	n.d.	n.d.	n.d.	n.d.	3.7714
410/60	63	Copper tack	130	98.13 (99.42)	n.d.	0.063	0.16	0.017	0.046	n.d.	<0.12	n.d.	n.d.	0.035	0.12	1.5677
535/60	87	Copper tack	120	94.88 (99.43)	0.03	0.019	0.18	n.d.	0.015	n.d.	n.d.	n.d.	n.d.	0.022	n.d.	1.8448
541/60	404	Tin bronze handle	163	64.00 (87.11)	8.96 (12.21)	0.034	0.25	0.04	0.02	n.d.	0.11	n.d.	n.d.	0.01	0.034	21.2942
918/60	129	Tin bronze fibula	260	93.41 (95.53)	5.37	0.06	0.18	0.66	0.11	n.d.	0.12	n.d.	0.046	0.032	n.d.	5.0741
1066/60	163	Copper nail		99.14	n.d.	0.03	0.26	0.05	0.04	n.d.	<0.40	n.d.	0.04	0.012	n.d.	27.0851
1108/60	165	Tin arsenic bronze arrowhead	14	87.85	6.50	1.05	0.65	1.23	0.31	0.21	1.17	0.15	0.45	0.15	0.11	2.5567
1256/60	176	Leaded tin bronze arrowhead	13	80.2	7.02	0.13	0.09	11.66	0.11	0.11	0.42	n.d.	0.21	0.03	0.02	2.0388
1256/61	176	Tin bronze arrowhead		85.0 (88.5)	10.5 (10.93)	0.03 (0.03)	0.25 (0.26)	0.10 (0.13)	0.015	n.d.	<0.42	n.d.	n.d.	0.02	0.012	3.4960
1266/60	176	Tin bronze bracelet	239	82.35	14.41	0.29	0.56	1.41	0.22	n.d.	n.d.	0.12	0.24	0.03	0.03	13.3723

Cat. no.	No.	Object	Sample													
1266/61	176	Tin bronze bracelet	228	80.05 (86.52)	9.85 (10.65)	0.27 (0.29)	0.20 (0.22)	1.35 (1.46)	0.1 (0.11)	0.03 (0.031)	0.34 (0.37)	0.081 (6.08)	0.20 (6.22)	0.03	0.02	8.2509
1271/60	1150	Tin bronze diadem	208	82.72	13.97	0.13	0.13	0.18	n.d.	n.d.	n.d.	0.04	n.d.	0.04	n.d.	18.4936
1273/60	46	Tin bronze bracelet	229	74.28 (85.0)	11.59 (13.32)	0.09 (0.1)	0.31 (0.36)	0.26 (2.30)	0.04 (0.05)	n.d.	0.29 (0.33)	0.06 (0.07)	0.04 (0.05)	0.02 (0.02)	n.d.	1.2600
1273/61	176	Tin arsenic bronze ring	170	63.5	9.26	0.06	0.69	0.20	0.04	0.06	0.63	0.13	0.21	0.04	0.05	0.6236
1274/60	183	Tin bronze bowl	161	86.80 (92.54)	5.55	0.03	0.76	0.22	0.02	0.01	0.29	0.08	0.08	0.02	0.02	175
1280/60	176	Tin bronze disk	283	93.32	5.97	0.25	0.21	0.17	0.075	n.d.	n.d.	n.d.	n.d.	0.008	n.d.	11.3247
1288/60	189	Tin bronze cosmetic stick		83.60 (87.70)	10.19 (10.70)	0.14 (0.15)	0.41 (0.43)	0.57 (0.60)	0.12 (0.13)	n.d. (n.d.)	0.13 (0.14)	0.03 (0.03)	0.1	0.03	n.d.	4.4469
1632/60	311	Copper fragment	311	99.3	n.d.	0.022	0.09	0.05	0.1	n.d.	0.25	n.d.	0.044	0.055	0.077	2.5220
1667/60	306	Copper nail	306	93.23 (99.64)	n.d.	0.013	0.04	0.034	0.09	0.014	0.1	n.d.	n.d.	0.01	0.025	
1680/60	38	Copper pin	272	99.30	n.d.	0.01	0.04	0.04	0.02	n.d.	0.34	0.06	0.03	0.15	n.d.	1.7055
1724/60	311	Copper cosmetic stick	296	99.43	<0.14	0.01	0.58	0.09	0.03	n.d.	n.d.	n.d.	0.06	0.06	0.05	8.4750
1734/60	310	Copper pin	310	98.4	n.d.	0.01	0.2	0.04	0.02	n.d.	0.3	n.d.	0.84	0.03	n.d.	2.0463
1735/60	722	Tin arsenic bronze nail	722	96.77	1.13	0.23	0.94	0.20	0.05	n.d.	0.55	0.13	0.13	0.12	n.d.	0.7088
1748/60	320	Tin bronze pin	313	91.30	7.88	0.02	0.10	0.13	0.04	n.d.	0.34	0.08	0.08	0.007	0.02	0.2488
1754/60	323	Copper link	320	87.84 (99.75)	n.d.	0.006	0.16	n.d.	0.03	n.d.	n.d.	n.d.	n.d.	0.007	0.02	3.2081
1761/60	323	Copper earring	323	82.24 (99.8)	n.d.	0.006	0.08	n.d.	0.03	n.d.	n.d.	n.d.	n.d.	0.008	0.04	0.2785
1762/60	323	Tin bronze links (5)	319	64.10 (90.26)	6.15 (8.66)	0.06	0.64	0.03	0.03	0.01	n.d.	n.d.	n.d.	n.d.	n.d.	1.9417
1762/61	323	Copper link fragments	318	95.42 (90.55)	<0.004	<0.004	0.12	0.02	0.02	n.d.	<0.08	n.d.	n.d.	0.02	0.13	1.5612
1794/60	323	Tin bronze fragment of cosmetic stick (?)	322	92.24	5.95	0.04	0.25	0.09	0.018	n.d.	0.18	n.d.	0.026	0.008	n.d.	0.8789
1802/60	323	Leaded tin bronze fibula	262	70.4 (88.14)	4.3 (5.4)	0.015	0.63	4.22	0.034	0.01	0.16	0.045	<0.045	0.013	n.d.	14.0445
1813/60	324	Lead fragment	331	n.d.	n.d.	n.d.	0.14	69.3	0.02	n.d.	n.d.	n.d.	0.05	n.d.	n.d.	13.7100
1852/60	340	Tin arsenical bronze fragment		89.85	3.77	0.02	<0.04	5.26	0.07	n.d.	0.48	n.d.	0.33	0.04	n.d.	10.3257
1853/60	323	Leaded tin bronze fibula	257	70.73 (82.60)	3.54	0.14	0.48	9.97	0.02	0.05	0.45	0.06	0.08	0.04	0.01	4.3447
1857/60	335	Copper hook	317	96.4 (99.13)	0.16	0.006	0.24	0.09	0.02	n.d.	0.29	n.d.	0.05	0.03	n.d.	5.4531
1864/60	342	Tin bronze pin	270	89.93 (95.63)	1.62	0.02	0.09	2.16	0.2	n.d.	0.014	n.d.	0.05	0.01	n.d.	2.5647
1867/60	340	Copper link	316	85.09 (99.07)	0.2	0.005	0.20	0.20	n.d.	n.d.	0.10	n.d.	0.04	0.01	0.04	0.8211
1886/60	343	Copper nail	343	67.20 (98.27)	n.d.	0.03	0.76 (1.11)	0.056	0.027	n.d.	0.35	n.d.	n.d.	0.01	n.d.	7.6200
1910/60	329	Tin arsenical bronze arrowhead	329	89.93 (91.51)	0.56	0.004	<0.02	6.46	0.13	n.d.	0.56	0.5	0.056	0.054	n.d.	4.0850
1911/60	344	Copper disk	344	99.1	0.15	0.03	0.2	0.03	0.04	n.d.	0.18	n.d.	0.03	0.02	n.d.	4.3569
1981/60	344	Leaded tin bronze fibula	244	70.90 (80.16)	11.69 (13.20)	0.05 (0.06)	0.44	4.60	0.17	0.02	0.38	0.08	0.06	0.03	0.02	28.0588
2041/60	352	Copper cosmetic stick	282	90.8 (99.82)	n.d.	0.009	0.076	<0.04	0.03	0.01	n.d.	n.d.	n.d.	n.d.	n.d.	2.6800

Table 25.12. Continued

Reg. No.	Locus	Type of Object	Cat. No.	Cu	Sn	Zn	Fe	Pb	Ag	Au	As	Bi	Sb	Ni	Co	Weight[b] (g)
2049/60	63	Leaded tin bronze weight	152	61.03	1.5	0.02	0.04	36.5	0.03	0.01	0.86	n.d.	0.06	0.06	0.03	1.4866
2060/60	63	Tin arsenical bronze cotter pin	151	78.08	5.53	11.75	1.76	2.82	0.05	n.d.	0.45	0.11	0.14	0.06	n.d.	2.1658
2077/60	352	Tin bronze fibula	252	70.4	4.97	0.016	0.47	0.12	0.05	0.009	0.18	n.d.	0.07	0.028	n.d.	3.4016
2095/60	357	Leaded tin bronze pin		92.31 (83.68)	6.52 (5.75)	0.29	1.31	3.35	0.06	0.01	0.29	0.02	0.10	0.13	0.02	0.6722
2127/60	357	Copper needle	73	84 (99.2)	0.2	0.004	0.20	0.04	n.d.	n.d.	0.16	n.d.	0.04	0.01	n.d.	0.5765
2221/60	367	Tin bronze ring		63.5 (82.31)	6.82 (9.6)	0.026	0.43	n.d.	0.05	n.d.	0.25	n.d.	n.d.	0.013	n.d.	1.4485
2250/60	60	Tin bronze nail		71.43 (88.62)	8.5 (10.55)	0.022	0.38	0.06	0.02	n.d.	0.14	n.d.	0.023	0.01	n.d.	0.3144
2407/60	81	Copper disk	328	94.87 (99.31)	0.22	0.01	0.22	n.d.	0.03	n.d.	0.16	n.d.	n.d.	0.018	n.d.	31.5936
2427/60	89	Copper nail	110	94.83	n.d.	0.02	0.10	0.22	0.02	n.d.	0.09	n.d.	0.03	0.01	n.d.	1.9169
2433/60	86	Tin bronze arrowhead	23	84.46 (92.06)	6.3 (6.88)	0.024	0.07	0.65	0.09	n.d.	0.11	n.d.	n.d.	0.03	n.d.	6.2300
2458/60	405	Copper nail fragment	315	95.93	<0.06	0.01	0.16	0.03	n.d.	n.d.	n.d.	n.d.	n.d.	n.d.	n.d.	1.2300
2489/60	415	Tin bronze nail		91.36	6.31	0.023	0.31	1.83	<0.02	n.d.	0.18	n.d.	n.d.	0.014	n.d.	6.5175
2538/60	411	Copper pin	312	93.07	n.d.	0.02	0.13	0.07	0.02	n.d.	0.15	n.d.	0.07	0.01	n.d.	30.8100
2551/60	423	Leaded tin bronze fibula	242	57.96 (74.02)	5.84 (7.46)	0.013	0.01	13.9 (17.75)	0.03	n.d.	0.39	n.d.	n.d.	0.015	n.d.	7.1247
2848/60	240	Tin bronze fragment	304	92.67	6.55	0.024	0.24	0.06	<0.02	n.d.	n.d.	n.d.	0.09	0.045	n.d.	0.4942
2853/62	255	Copper nail		96.34 (99.51)	n.d.	0.01	0.37	n.d.	n.d.	n.d.	n.d.	n.d.	n.d.	0.02	n.d.	3.4111
3314/60	466	Silver signet ring	174	9.36	0.27	0.17	0.32	1.21	87.43	0.55	0.34	0.16	n.d.	0.24	n.d.	6.6700
3319/60	466	Arsenical bronze chisel (?)	68	93.65 (97.54)	0.16	0.004	0.41	0.14	0.02	n.d.	1.53 (1.60)	n.d.	0.09	0.01	n.d.	2.4681
3321/60	466	Tin bronze rosette	309	82.35 (93.40)	4.71	0.04	0.34	0.16	0.02	0.03	0.27	0.08	0.08	0.07	0.02	14.9654
3328/60	469	Arsenical bronze lynch pin	148	98.18	n.d.	0.05	0.73	0.09	0.05	0.04	0.45	n.d.	0.07	0.03	0.02	5.4911
3653/60	508	Copper nail		99.40	n.d.	0.01	0.41	0.05	0.04	n.d.	n.d.	n.d.	n.d.	0.04	0.04	5.9424
3740/60	508	Lead fishing weight		0.09	<0.12	0.02	0.05	99.47	n.d.	n.d.	<0.24	n.d.	0.03	n.d.	n.d.	24.0361
3809/60	519	Copper nail	81	98.96	n.d.	0.004	0.09	n.d.	0.02	n.d.	0.076	n.d.	n.d.	0.008	n.d.	
3811/60	521	Tin arsenical bronze pin		82.30 (91.72)	4.12 (4.59)	0.26 (0.29)	0.27 (0.30)	2.06 (2.29)	0.08 (0.09)	0.06 (0.07)	0.41 (0.46)	0.04 (0.04)	0.08 (0.09)	0.05	n.d.	1.0616
3815/60	534	Lead weight	160	0.28	n.d.	0.01	0.05	98.84	0.02	n.d.	<0.19	n.d.	n.d.	n.d.	n.d.	30.2843
3819/60	534	Copper nail		97.74	n.d.	0.03	0.62	0.03	0.05	0.03	0.15	n.d.	0.05	0.02	n.d.	10.0036
4007/60	551	Copper fibula	551	97.83	n.d.	0.03	0.22	0.76	0.03	0.067	0.3	n.d.	0.04	0.03	0.055	2.5400
4008/62	556	Tin bronze nail		91.26	6.53	0.009	0.15	0.66	0.03	n.d.	0.3	n.d.	0.04	0.057	n.d.	1.9542
4046/60	551	Copper nail	104	90.52 (99.58)	n.d.	0.018	0.09	0.03	0.04	0.009	0.17	n.d.	n.d.	0.01	n.d.	1.3000
4054/60	560	Copper tack	121	99.5	n.d.	0.006	0.14	0.0571	0.03	n.d.	0.23	n.d.	0.038	0.02	n.d.	1.5469
4090/60	570	Copper pin		98.11	n.d.	0.02	0.58	0.036	0.02	n.d.	0.14	n.d.	0.03	0.04	0.44	0.8871
4103/60	570	Arsenical tin bronze tack	127	92.11 (95.95)	0.49	0.30	0.59	1.97	0.08	0.14	1.05	0.19	0.13	0.07	0.07	2.5760

Cat. no.	Sample	Object	No.													
4108/60	570	Tin bronze tack	128	97.22	0.46	0.30	0.29	1.17	0.06	0.05	0.37	0.14	0.14	0.10	0.04	2.2078
4108/61	570	Tin bronze cosmetic stick		94.27	3.51	0.02	0.47	2.92	0.06	n.d.	0.35	0.06	0.06	0.05	0.09	5.8507
4121/60	576	Leaded tin bronze nail	298	82.45	7.23	0.01	0.11	0.95	0.05	<0.01	0.31	n.d.	0.13	0.02	n.d.	
4128/60	576	Tin bronze pin		91.14	6.25	0.023	0.26	0.06	0.03	n.d.	0.35	n.d.	0.03	0.05	0.16	0.9948
4149/60	583	Copper nail		99.5	n.d.	0.015	0.17	0.12	0.04	n.d.	0.12	n.d.	0.03	0.02	0.012	0.3186
4158/60	580	Copper nail fragment	314	99.65	n.d.	0.01	0.07	0.04	<0.02	n.d.	0.14	n.d.	n.d.	n.d.	n.d.	4.2308
4162/60	579	Copper nail fragment	106	99.58	n.d.	0.01	0.08	0.08	0.03	n.d.	0.14	0.06	0.03	n.d.	0.01	0.5975
4166/60	588	Copper nail	82	93.38	n.d.	0.011	0.18	0.22	0.03	n.d.	0.16	n.d.	n.d.	0.04	0.22	4.7327
4198/60	585	Copper nail fragment		57.93 (98.48)	n.d.	0.05	0.09		0.14	n.d.	0.27	n.d.	0.11	<0.007	n.d.	4.9718
4210/60	580	Silver ring	171	3.4	n.d.	0.08	0.13	0.6	95.78	n.d.	n.d.	0.04	n.d.	0.01	n.d.	3.5070
4215/60	594	Tin bronze pin		92.06	7.42	0.02	0.19	0.02	0.01	n.d.	0.20	0.05	0.03	0.01	0.23	0.3813
4229/61	593	Tin bronze nail		73.99	7.63	0.08	0.19	0.18	0.05	n.d.	0.08	n.d.	0.03	0.01	n.d.	0.9086
4232/60	595	Tin bronze pin		83.8 (89.93)	8.1 (8.7)	0.14	0.4	0.52	0.017	n.d.	<0.07	n.d.	n.d.	0.12	<0.014	0.8665
4246/60	558	Copper nail	332	96.15	n.d.	0.019	0.096	0.05	0.038	n.d.	n.d.	n.d.	n.d.	n.d.	n.d.	0.9686
4266/60	594	Lead sheet fragment		0.08	n.d.	0.003	0.09	99.9	0.01	n.d.	n.d.	n.d.	n.d.	n.d.	n.d.	1.7900
4276/60	585	Tin bronze fibula	255	79.71 (86.02)	11.6 (12.52)	0.01	0.32	0.56	0.07	n.d.	0.23	n.d.	0.13	0.028	n.d.	6.2681
4282/60	572	Arsenical bronze pin		93.36 (99.02)	n.d.	0.013	0.08	0.04	0.07	n.d.	0.58	n.d.	0.1	0.033	n.d.	7.5846
4282/61	572	Copper pin		98.77	n.d.	0.03	0.62	0.03	0.05	0.03	0.15	n.d.	0.05	0.02	n.d.	1.3333
4288/60	588	Tin arsenical bronze bracelet fragment	226	84.91 (88.41)	10.06	0.05	0.19	0.08	0.03	n.d.	0.63	n.d.	0.06	0.03	n.d.	1.6615
4295/60	731	Copper nail	83	93.06 (99.63)	n.d.	0.006	0.12	<0.04	0.03	n.d.	0.1	n.d.	<0.04	n.d.	n.d.	1.2830
4298/80	593	Leaded copper bead		8.90	4.25	0.01	1.2	30.37	0.05	<0.96	0.23	n.d.	0.05	n.d.	n.d.	18.3676
4406/60	600	Tin bronze cosmetic stick		84.20 (89.43)	n.d.		0.4	5.2	0.03	0.013		n.d.		0.02	n.d.	4.1807
4407/60	600	Copper nail		99.43	n.d.	0.016	0.08	0.05	0.02	n.d.	0.19	n.d.	0.03	0.04	0.15	4.1400
4417/60	602	Tin bronze rivet	136	78.12 (91.05)	6.4 (7.5)	0.04	0.26	0.72	0.04	n.d.	0.18	n.d.	n.d.	0.016	n.d.	1.8154
4418/60	603	Leaded tin bronze ladle	166	84.75 (85.23)	9.61	0.02	0.11	4.52	0.07	n.d.	0.23	n.d.	0.08	0.05	0.05	31.6222
4422/60	601	Copper pin		99.34	n.d.	0.01	0.28	0.1	0.04	n.d.	0.23	n.d.	0.033	0.033	0.023	0.7607
4449/61	603	Tin bronze pin	267	93.18	6.21	0.035	0.14	0.2	0.03	n.d.	n.d.	n.d.	n.d.	n.d.	n.d.	1.4600
4451/60	602	Leaded tin bronze arrowhead	10	68.85 (75.96)	0.63 (0.70)	0.53	0.47	19.6 (21.62)	0.05	n.d.	0.3	n.d.	0.15	0.01	0.05	1.8400
4454/60	610	Tin bronze cotter pin	149	85.37 (91.67)	6.50	0.07	0.47	0.10	0.02	0.06	0.37	0.08	0.04	0.04	0.02	1.4324
4464/60	610	Tin bronze pin	268	93.26	5.76	0.08	0.32	0.07	0.11	n.d.	0.22	0.09	0.05	0.03	n.d.	0.5326
4472/60	610	Silver earring fragment	197	6.80 (7.99)	n.d.	0.60	0.52	0.37	76.0	0.64	0.02	n.d.	0.05	0.11	n.d.	
4495/60	612	Tin arsenical bronze nail		84.89	13.37	0.04	0.31	0.06	0.04	0.04	0.74	0.11	0.08	0.03	0.07	
4497/60	612	Tin bronze band	147	90.55 (98.0)	0.39 (0.42)	0.20	0.78	0.11	0.08	n.d.	0.20	0.03	0.03	0.03	110	6.5929
4503/60	614	Copper nail	84	97.5	n.d.	0.01	0.08	0.05	n.d.	n.d.	0.1	n.d.	0.05	n.d.	n.d.	25.5274
4522/60	618	Tin bronze cosmetic stick	285	56.54 (93.52)	1.64 (2.71)	0.04	0.51	1.54 (2.55)	0.04	n.d.	0.14	n.d.	n.d.	0.012	n.d.	5.9455

Table 25.12. Continued

Reg. No.	Locus	Type of Object	Cat. No.	Cu	Sn	Zn	Fe	Pb	Ag	Au	As	Bi	Sb	Ni	Co	Weight[b] (g)
4523/60	618	Tin bronze pin fragment	269	82.07	13.89	0.02	0.19	0.04	0.06	0.05	0.32	0.02	0.05	0.02	0.01	0.4400
4530/60	618	Leaded tin bronze arrowhead	1	89.3	5.36	<0.009	0.053	4.24	0.096	n.d.	0.12	<0.07	0.053	0.03	n.d.	3.2839
4541/60	618	Tin bronze fibula	248	81.63 (91.27)	5.7 (6.0)	0.016	0.22	1.98	0.03	n.d.	0.2	n.d.	0.05	0.05	0.04	2.2821
4550/60	22	Copper tack	132	99.79	n.d.	0.02	0.34	n.d.	0.02	n.d.	0.13	n.d.	n.d.	0.02	0.03	2.3116
4671/60	664	Copper nails (5)		84.76 (98.1)	<0.06	0.04	1.1	0.06	0.03	0.007	0.23	n.d.	0.03	0.015	0.03	47.4700
4821/60	653	Copper clamp	145	79.8 (99.25)	<0.12	0.034	0.19	0.047	0.033	n.d.	0.16	n.d.	n.d.	0.01	n.d.	4.9082
4822/60	653	Tin bronze tweezers	276	73.53 (96.62)	2.2 (2.9)	0.04	0.18	0.07	n.d.	n.d.	<0.07	n.d.	n.d.	0.007	n.d.	3.3125
4841/60	664	Copper nail	85	96.24	n.d.	0.01	0.14	0.10	0.04	n.d.	0.19	n.d.	0.05	n.d.	n.d.	38.5579
4845/60	666	Tin bronze pendant	204	81.97 (83.05)	9.84 (9.97)	0.05	0.16	6.65	0.02	0.08	n.d.	n.d.	0.02	0.02	n.d.	1.0377
4859/60	673	Tin bronze earring	194a	65.21 (88.18)	3.21 (5.15)	0.038	4.5 (6.08)	0.08	0.02	n.d.	0.28	n.d.	n.d.	0.03	n.d.	0.7200
4866/60	664	Long copper nail	86	91.1 (99.40)	<0.08	0.014	0.12	0.04	0.04	0.008	0.22	n.d.	0.01	0.02	n.d.	41.0682
4871/60	664	Copper nail	87	74.5 (99.07)	n.d.	0.03	0.46	<0.03	0.16	n.d.	0.13	n.d.	n.d.	0.03	n.d.	53.7438
4871/62	664	Copper nail	89	88.6 (99.49)	n.d.	0.03	0.24	0.03	0.03	n.d.	<0.08	n.d.	<0.03	0.02	0.026	35.0814
4871/63	664	Copper nail	90	82.03 (99.16)	n.d.	0.036	0.42	0.047	0.025	n.d.	0.12	n.d.	n.d.	0.012	0.03	40.0814
4871/64	664	Copper nail	91	91.91 (99.64)	n.d.	0.013	0.12	0.036	0.028	n.d.	0.1	n.d.	0.02	0.016	n.d.	55.3302
4874/60	825	Tin bronze bracelet	232	85.47 (89.9)	8.55 (9.0)	0.023	0.07	0.43	0.07	0.01	0.28	<0.04	0.08	0.038	0.01	8.3600
4879/60	664	Tin bronze ring	173	72.41 (92.51)	4.48 (5.72)	0.12	0.83	0.15	0.08	n.d.	0.17	n.d.	n.d.	0.03	n.d.	0.8812
4881/60	826	Leaded tin bronze bracelet	209	64.65 (84.95)	6.7 (8.8)	0.04	0.28	4.04 (5.31)	0.02	n.d.	0.34	n.d.	n.d.	0.017	n.d.	6.8113
4881/61	826	Leaded tin bronze bracelet	210	71.77 (82.72)	8.11 (9.41)	0.07	0.44	5.76	0.044	0.02	0.35	n.d.	0.044	0.02	0.03	11.5089
4881/62	826	Leaded tin bronze bracelet	211	48.8 (90.0)	3.14 (4.11)	0.03	0.23	3.93 (5.14)	0.027	n.d.	0.23	n.d.	0.04	0.01	n.d.	11.6905
4881/63	826	Leaded tin bronze bracelet	212	41.4 (58.8)	15.3 (21.73)	0.06	0.91	12.16 (17.27)	n.d.	n.d.	0.37	0.04	0.1	0.033	<0.02	2.8767
5112/60	678	Copper nail		99.78	n.d.	0.020	0.1	n.d.	0.02	0.02	n.d.	n.d.	n.d.	0.01	0.04	7.9630
5121/60	682	Arsenical bronze fragment	159	98.9	n.d.	0.05	0.14	0.046	0.06	0.02	0.57	n.d.	0.18	0.07	n.d.	5.8150
5146/60	686	Lead fishing weight		0.07	<0.24	0.01	0.03	99.66	n.d.	n.d.	n.d.	n.d.	n.d.	n.d.	n.d.	0.7825
5172/60	691	Copper pin fragment		95.11	n.d.	0.04	0.05	n.d.	0.04	n.d.	<0.09	0.10	n.d.	0.009	n.d.	1.3663
5196/60	689	Copper nail		97.77	n.d.	0.02	n.d.	2.12	0.06	n.d.	n.d.	n.d.	0.11	0.01	n.d.	2.6769
5202/60	684	Copper nail	105a	99.52	n.d.	0.02	0.05	0.16	0.04	n.d.	0.12	n.d.	0.08	n.d.	n.d.	2.9390
5240/60	687	Copper nail		96.7	0.2	0.066	0.07	0.05	0.03	n.d.	0.16	n.d.	0.03	0.01	n.d.	

Sample	No.	No.	Object													
5270/60	698		Tin arsenical bronze pin	85.45 (88.17)	8.30 (8.56)	0.05	0.44	0.88	0.04	0.14	1.17	0.09	0.15	0.12	0.03	2.2876
5453/60	320	205	Tin bronze pendant	71.20 (92.27)	4.9 (6.35)	0.022	0.74	0.06	0.025	n.d.	0.19	n.d.	n.d.	0.02	n.d.	1.4001
5456/60	713		Tin bronze arrowhead	87.21 (95.9)	3.5	0.05	0.28	0.044	0.014	n.d.	0.14	n.d.	n.d.	0.02	n.d.	2.3284
5457/60	311	125	Copper tack	99.43	n.d.	0.008	0.28	n.d.	<0.014	n.d.	n.d.	n.d.	n.d.	0.02	n.d.	1.9617
5469/60	344	213	Tin bronze bracelet	56.22 (85.6)	6.88 (10.5)	0.05	0.26	1.82	0.1	n.d.	0.26	n.d.	0.08	0.013	n.d.	4.1455
5486/60	701		Tin bronze pin	98.28	0.82	0.02	0.21	0.05	0.02	n.d.	0.32	0.15	0.08	0.04	n.d.	0.1134
5504/60	832	265a	Copper nail	99.26	0.18	0.019	0.095	n.d.	0.05	n.d.	0.27	n.d.	0.038	0.02	0.04	
5561/60	830	104a	Tin bronze fibula fragment	82.11 (86.96)	11.4 (12.07)	0.01	0.15	0.58	0.027	n.d.	0.13	n.d.	n.d.	0.015	n.d.	8.7161
5575/61	842		Copper nail	99.22	0.22	0.015	0.13	n.d.	0.026	n.d.	0.31	n.d.	n.d.	0.026	n.d.	4.9527
5609/60	845	98a	Tin bronze ring	73.17 (96.78)	0.73 (0.96)	0.012 (0.015)	0.22 (0.29)	1.37 (1.81)	0.012 (0.016)	n.d.	0.06 (0.08)	n.d.	n.d.	0.012	n.d.	0.6152
5612/60	701		Tin bronze disk fragment	60.70 (88.15)	7.52 (10.92)	0.019	0.24	0.17	0.06	n.d.	0.12 (0.17)	n.d.	n.d.	0.012	0.019 (0.027)	13.6895
5615/60	840	310	Tin bronze nail	90.43 (98.98)	0.65	0.02	0.16	0.08	0.02	n.d.	n.d.	n.d.	n.d.	0.01	n.d.	5.6148
5644/60	317	92	Copper nail	92.87 (99.74)	n.d.	0.004	0.04	<0.04	0.04	n.d.	0.11	n.d.	n.d.	0.01	n.d.	7.3544
5715/60	861	72	Copper hook	94.6 (99.44)	0.21	0.007	0.16	n.d.	0.016	n.d.	0.13	n.d.	n.d.	0.02	n.d.	0.3990
5716/60	704	93	Copper nail	97.54 (98.0)	0.12	0.03	0.12	0.02	0.03	<0.01	0.06	0.02	n.d.	0.04	0.07	30.4614
5751/60	334	247	Tin bronze fibula	82.96 (89.20)	7.30 (7.85)	0.01	0.55	1.9	0.04	n.d.	0.10	n.d.	0.044	0.026	n.d.	2.4607
5863/60	843		Copper "drawing" pin	96.15	n.d.	0.014	1.18	0.13	0.14	n.d.	0.23	n.d.	0.05	0.077	0.02	5.8220
5910/60	872		Copper arrowhead	99.67	0.11	0.007	0.04	0.028	0.013	n.d.	0.11	n.d.	n.d.	0.006	n.d.	5.0428
5932/60	837		Leaded tin bronze fragment	63.90 (87.02)	6.00 (8.17)	0.034	0.44	2.64 (3.60)	0.01	n.d.	0.24 (0.33)	n.d.	0.03	0.12		3.3018
6213/60	935		Copper nail	99.32	n.d.	0.007	0.36	0.05	0.02	n.d.	0.23	n.d.	0.02	0.033	n.d.	2.5515
6262/60	940	324	Tin bronze cosmetic stick	79.62 (76.7)	12.74	0.11	0.38	1.25	0.07	0.03	<0.13	0.05	0.11	0.21	n.d.	
6266/60	1309		Tin bronze fibula	90.04 (95.08)	4.02 (4.24)	0.007	0.18	0.19	0.013	n.d.	0.2	n.d.	0.04	0.02	n.d.	11.4337
6280/60	935	250	Tin bronze cosmetic stick	64.65 (98.0)	0.65 (0.97)	0.026	0.47 (0.70)	0.06	n.d.	0.05	n.d.	n.d.	0.017	0.017	n.d.	2.9564
6312/60	7	299	Leaded tin bronze arrowhead fragment	30.0 (41.24)	0.7 (0.96)	0.02	2.15 (2.94)	39.65 (54.20)	0.02 (0.03)	n.d.	0.22 (0.30)	n.d.	0.17 (0.23)	0.02 (0.03)	0.04	2.7439
6315/60	77		Copper bodkin	76.14 (99.36)	<0.12 (<0.016)	0.01	0.24	0.02	0.012	n.d.	0.07	n.d.	n.d.	0.017	n.d.	14.0824
6318/60	1308		Tin bronze fragment	45.62 (76.7)	13.5 (22.7)	0.016	0.2	<0.04 (<0.07)	0.02 (0.034)	n.d.	0.07 (0.12)	n.d.	n.d.	0.018 (0.03)	n.d.	4.6054
6336/60	948	305	Tin bronze chain links	64.9 (89.93)	7.02	0.01	0.1	0.038	n.d.	n.d.	0.096	n.d.	n.d.	0.01	n.d.	4.3200
6351/60	1312	288	Leaded tin bronze cosmetic stick	66.28 (70.0)	11.10 (11.72)	0.02	0.23	16.57 (17.50)	0.02	0.01	0.37 (0.54)	n.d.	0.06	0.02	0.02	5.6178
6368/60	1304		Tin bronze cosmetic stick	71.96 (99.02)	0.41 (0.56)	0.025 (0.034)	0.20 (0.27)	n.d.	0.025 (0.034)	n.d.	n.d.	n.d.	n.d.	0.053 (0.073)	n.d.	6.6474
6385/60	2	1317	Leaded tin bronze arrowhead	45.87 (62.5)	1.03 (1.4)	0.027	1.15	24.65 (33.74)	0.02	n.d.	0.17 (0.23)	0.09	n.d.	0.014	0.08	2.1504

Table 25.12. Continued

Reg. No.	Locus	Type of Object	Cat. No.	Cu	Sn	Zn	Fe	Pb	Ag	Au	As	Bi	Sb	Ni	Co	Weight[b] (g)
6434/60	99	Copper arrowhead	18	99.3	0.25	0.005	0.12	0.05	0.03	n.d.	0.25	n.d.	n.d.	n.d.	n.d.	6.6282
6529/60a	979	Leaded tin bronze hoop fragment with pipe attached and two rivets	334	73.41	5.56	0.02	0.08	21.43	0.06	0.06	n.d.	0.08	0.16	0.08	0.08	196
6529/60b				77.93 (89.90)	5.61 (6.47)	0.03	0.26	2.49	0.01	0.02	0.06	0.05	0.10	0.05	0.01	
6529/60c				94.06	0.50	0.02	0.10	2.23	0.02	n.d.	n.d.	0.05	0.09	0.03	0.02	
6555/60	984	Tin bronze fibula	243	89.0 (92.7)	5.76	0.028	0.31	0.4	0.05	n.d.	0.34	n.d.	0.07	0.034	0.034	4.4977
6542/60	956	Arsenical tin bronze cosmetic stick	279	95.75	0.43	0.02	0.40	0.08	<0.01	<0.01	0.60	0.02	n.d.	0.02	n.d.	10.1422
6624/60	985	Tin bronze cosmetic stick	294	71.43 (97.90)	0.71 (0.97)	0.033 (0.045)	0.52 (0.71)	0.047 (0.064)	0.028	n.d.	0.17 (0.23)	n.d.	n.d.	0.019 (0.026)	n.d.	4.2371
6626/60	985	Copper nail (long)		96.15 (99.48)	n.d.	0.019	0.072	<0.048	<0.053	n.d.	0.3	n.d.	n.d.	0.012	n.d.	35.5864
6825/60	685	Tin bronze fibula	263	83.06 (90.76)	6.68 (8.4)	0.018	0.06	0.38	0.035	n.d.	0.17	n.d.	0.04	0.033	n.d.	5.2020
6871/60	698	Copper needle	74	99.1	0.30	0.026	0.15	n.d.	0.036	n.d.	0.30	n.d.	n.d.	0.03	n.d.	0.4658
6884/60	1015	Tin bronze fibula	259	69.44 (94.31)	3.70 (5.00)	0.025	0.23	n.d.	0.04	n.d.	0.14	n.d.	n.d.	0.023	0.037	2.7353
6885/60	1014	Fragment of tin bronze helmet crest (?)	321	72.82 (89.40)	8.26 (10.13)	0.06	0.24	n.d.	n.d.	n.d.	0.08 (0.1)	n.d.	n.d.	0.023	0.019	31.7175
6893/61	1022	Copper cosmetic stick	289	93.18	0.26	0.01	0.09	0.05	0.03	0.01	<0.06	n.d.	0.02	0.02	0.01	4.8271
6902/60	693	Copper nail	107	92.4 (99.25)	n.d.	0.018	0.3	0.02	0.04	n.d.	0.21	n.d.	n.d.	0.026	0.06	17.1778
6910/60	693	Copper nail	108	99.3	0.21	0.007	0.17	0.04	0.03	n.d.	0.21	n.d.	n.d.	0.017	n.d.	2.9010
7105/60	1065	Tin bronze bracelet	240	85.91 (90.6)	6.87 (7.24)	0.008	<0.04	1.61 (1.7)	0.06	n.d.	0.21	n.d.	n.d.	0.02	n.d.	53.4462
7127/60	1072	Copper tack	126	98.37	n.d.	0.006	0.18	0.13	0.018	n.d.	0.23	n.d.	0.035	0.025	n.d.	2.2400
7242/60	1357	Lead ring	177	0.54	0.27	0.61	0.03	98.5	<0.03	n.d.	0.54	0.03	0.11	0.01	n.d.	0.7560
7244/60	1351	Leaded tin bronze ladle	165	68.97	10.12	0.09	0.12	18.75	0.03	n.d.	0.10	0.1	n.d.	0.03	n.d.	140
7348/60	1104	Tin bronze ring	169	77.41	6.12	0.04	0.33	1.57	0.028	n.d.	0.17	n.d.	0.07	0.042	0.024	1.1303
7369/60	1101	Tin bronze spatula (?)	308	78.6 (88.77)	9.9 (11.12)	0.07	0.4	0.12	0.03	n.d.	n.d.	n.d.	n.d.	0.016	n.d.	4.4872
7373/60	591	Tin bronze fibula	254	81.52 (88.87)	8.7 (9.48)	0.005	0.076	1.09	0.05	n.d.	0.13	n.d.	0.14	0.03	n.d.	11.4462
7378/60	1114	Copper nail		99.38	<0.22	0.01	0.045	n.d.	0.058	n.d.	0.22	n.d.	n.d.	0.01	n.d.	5.4561
7451/60	1128	Tin bronze fibula	247	70.5 (87.86)	8.46 (10.54)	0.026	0.63	0.28	0.056	n.d.	0.23	n.d.	n.d.	0.056	n.d.	29.0200
7468/60	1128	Copper nail	99	92.51 (99.62)	n.d.	0.01	0.07	0.04	n.d.	n.d.	0.2	n.d.	n.d.	0.01	n.d.	17.1968
7636/60	1162	Tin bronze earring fragment	182	48.48 (92.98)	3.33 (6.4)	0.064 (0.12)	0.24	n.d.	n.d.	n.d.	n.d.	n.d.	n.d.	0.03	n.d.	1.2045
7638/60	1163	Tin arsenical bronze bracelet	214	80.13 (89.28)	7.16 (7.98)	0.73	0.24	0.64	0.04	n.d.	0.38 (0.42)	n.d.	0.04	0.30	0.09	12.9869
7638/61	1163	Tin bronze bracelet	215	89.5	8.95	0.064	0.18	0.92	0.03	n.d.	0.31	n.d.	n.d.	0.018	0.037	10.6389

Cat. No.	No.	Object	Sample												
7644/60	1159	Tin bronze ring	167	83.8 (87.14)	11.06 (11.50)	<0.003	0.08	1.0	0.023	n.d.	0.13	0.03	0.04	n.d.	3.5421
7661/60	1178	Tin bronze nail	94	87.12 (97.2)	2.27 (2.53)	0.018	0.06	n.d.	0.05	n.d.	0.09	n.d.	0.02	n.d.	49.4613
7662/60	1178	Copper nail	95	93.36 (99.5)	<0.2	0.014	0.08	n.d.	0.03	n.d.	0.098	n.d.	0.02	0.03	34.6181
7663/60	1178	Tin arsenical bronze bowl	162	86.07	7.38	0.10	0.39	0.20	0.07	0.02	0.41	n.d.	0.06	0.02	280
7665/60	1174	Tin bronze earring	183	65.62 (95.60)	2.8 (4.18)	0.025	0.087	0.025	<0.012	n.d.	n.d.	n.d.	<0.006	n.d.	0.7941
7674/60	1178	Copper nail	96	98.80	0.17	0.01	0.22	0.07	0.02	n.d.	0.17	n.d.	0.05	0.04	49.2610
7675/60	1178	Copper nail	97	92.18 (99.47)	0.18 (0.19)	0.018	0.074	n.d.	0.018	n.d.	0.18	n.d.	0.022	n.d.	45.4153
7676/60	1180	Tin bronze bracelet	233	85.30	7.31	0.005	0.25	0.97	0.03	0.01	0.19	0.04	0.02	0.01	83.9882
7678/60	1184	Tin bronze bracelet	234	82.24	11.64	0.06	0.25	0.85	0.06	0.03	0.13	0.05	0.06	0.03	14.6000
7678/61	1184	Tin bronze bracelet	235	84.50	8.95	0.02	0.28	0.99	0.06	0.01	0.16	0.04	0.02	0.02	12.7430
7680/60	1178	Silver ring	176	0.85 (1.04)	n.d.	0.32	0.19	0.20	80.39 (97.93)	0.02	n.d.	0.04	0.01	n.d.	2.5767
7687/60	1186	Tin bronze bracelet	216	83.33	9.76	0.01	0.12	0.02	0.03	<0.01	0.06	0.10	0.08	0.02	38.8270
7690/60	1179	Tin bronze earring fragment	185	95.38	2.56	0.45	0.64	0.32	0.102	n.d.	0.32	n.d.	0.19	n.d.	1.8880
7690/61	1179	Tin bronze earring	186	95.26	3.81	0.076	0.42	0.076	0.06	n.d.	0.26	n.d.	0.031	n.d.	0.4745
7690/62	1179	Tin arsenical bronze earring	191	93.72	5.41	0.071	0.20	0.10	0.041	n.d.	0.41	n.d.	0.041	n.d.	0.6651
7690/63	1179	Tin arsenical bronze earring	187	96.14	2.74	0.114	0.33	<0.11	n.d.	n.d.	0.55	n.d.	0.026	n.d.	0.6384
7694/60	1159	Tin bronze earring	192	71.56 (91.61)	6.3 (8.06)	0.01	0.15 (0.19)	0.1	n.d.	n.d.	n.d.	n.d.	n.d.	n.d.	0.6933
7698/60	1159	Copper bracelet	217	87.81 (98.2)	<0.21	0.014	0.25	n.d.	0.02	n.d.	0.21	n.d.	0.02	n.d.	7.8000
7699/60	1191	Tin bronze earring	180	61.54 (90.73)	5.77 (8.51)	0.08	0.31	0.096	n.d.	n.d.	n.d.	n.d.	0.03	n.d.	0.3861
7703/60	1194	Arsenical bronze clamp	139	78.43 (99.03)	<0.20	0.008	0.12	<0.04	0.04	n.d.	0.31 (0.40)	0.04	0.01	n.d.	1.1900
7703/61	1194	Copper clamp	140	71.43 (90.03)	n.d.	0.07	0.24	0.07	0.05	n.d.	0.24	n.d.	0.03	n.d.	0.6171
7706/60	1194	Copper clamp	146	88.98 (94.82)	n.d.	0.19	0.75	n.d.	0.02	n.d.	n.d.	n.d.	0.04	n.d.	1.4304
7706/61	1194	Copper clamp	141	95.69 (99.48)	n.d.	0.02	0.15	n.d.	n.d.	0.05	0.24	n.d.	0.02	n.d.	0.6634
7706/62	1194	Copper clamp	142	94.34 (98.83)	n.d.	0.03	0.11	n.d.	n.d.	n.d.	n.d.	n.d.	0.02	n.d.	0.6671
7709/60	1194	Copper clamp	143	63.02 (98.6)	0.21 (0.33)	0.05	0.13	0.04	0.046	n.d.	0.19 (0.3)	0.042	0.17 (0.27)	n.d.	2.1733
7710/60	1194	Arsenical bronze clamp	144	74.40 (97.60)	<0.3	0.07	0.06	0.09	<0.03	n.d.	0.4 (0.52)	n.d.	1.5 (1.95)	n.d.	0.7900
7726/60	1183	Tin bronze bracelet		76.10 (87.87)	9.78 (11.3)	0.04	0.19	n.d.	0.12	n.d.	0.3	n.d.	0.07	n.d.	4.6386
7730/60	1193	Tin arsenical bronze earring	188	66.70 (85.24)	10.33 (13.20)	0.004 (0.007)	0.17 (0.22)	0.11 (0.14)	0.73 (0.93)	n.d.	0.78 (1.0)	0.07 (0.09)	0.008 (0.01)	n.d.	0.5377
7733/60	1193	Silver earring	196	1.42 (1.54)	n.d.	0.42 (0.46)	0.40	0.38	88.31 (95.84)	0.05	0.94 (1.02)	n.d.	0.03	n.d.	0.9336

Table 25.12.   Continued

Reg. No.	Locus	Type of Object	Cat. No.	Cu	Sn	Zn	Fe	Pb	Ag	Au	As	Bi	Sb	Ni	Co	Weight[b] (g)
7733/62	1193	Silver earring	195	1.03	n.d.	0.006	n.d.	0.14	98.66	n.d.	0.17	n.d.	n.d.	n.d.	n.d.	1.5937
8329/60	1029	Tin bronze fibula	251	80.36 (90.70)	6.07 (6.85)	0.005	0.2	1.43 (1.61)	0.025	n.d.	0.2	n.d.	0.3	0.32	n.d.	3.8495
8332/60	1033	Copper ring fragment		98.91	0.26	0.13	0.47	0.04	0.03	n.d.	0.18	n.d.	n.d.	0.02	0.08	0.4745
8736/60	1371	Arsenical bronze rod/pin		91.78	0.03	0.009	0.02	n.d.	0.11	0.008	0.43	0.03	n.d.	0.007	0.01	
8752/60	1371	Leaded tin bronze fibula	246	74.2	11.45	0.027	0.23	4.17	0.08	0.01	0.2	0.02	0.04	0.01	n.d.	27.2000
8896/60	1389	Copper tack	124	95.0	0.11	0.012	0.3	0.46	0.1	n.d.	0.23	0.02	n.d.	0.04	0.08	1.0674
8920/60	1391	Leaded tin bronze arrowhead		60.8	6.8	0.008	0.29	19.72	0.04	n.d.	0.35	0.02	0.02	0.01	0.06	
9225/60	942	Leaded tin bronze arrowhead	8	73.3	15.98	0.04	0.19	4.2	0.2	0.02	0.28	0.07	0.05	0.06	n.d.	3.9131
9328/60	948	Leaded tin bronze arrowhead	3	23.0	1.0	0.04	0.36	60.1	0.1	0.017	0.37	0.07	0.11	n.d.	n.d.	3.8900
9369/60	1308	Leaded tin bronze arrowhead	25	46.0	1.37	0.013	0.06	51.55	0.1	0.01	0.3	0.06	n.d.	n.d.	0.02	3.3379
9390/60	1308	Silver earring	198a	0.56	n.d.	0.03	0.1	0.03	99.2	n.d.	0.35	n.d.	0.02	0.004	n.d.	1.8271
9624/60	1500	Leaded tin bronze arrowhead	4	58.78	0.42	0.03	0.09	13.92	0.1	0.01	0.19	0.037	n.d.	0.05	n.d.	2.7981
9768/60	1558	Arsenical bronze needle	69	87.8	n.d.	0.017	0.87	0.13	0.08	0.01	0.6	n.d.	0.17	0.03	0.03	1.0710
10228/60	1012	Arsenical bronze needle		91.3	0.07	0.015	0.03	1.05	0.15	0.02	0.41	0.02	n.d.	0.07	n.d.	3.4836
10282/60	690	Leaded tin bronze ring with attached wire	150	92.82	0.90	0.02	0.27	5.75	0.1	0.016	0.4	0.04	n.d.	0.24	n.d.	4.4409
10283/60	690	Copper tack	123	95.92	0.05	n.d.	0.08	n.d.	0.07	0.01	0.19	0.02	n.d.	n.d.	n.d.	1.3688
10302/60	1631	Arsenical bronze pin/nail		97.7	0.12	0.02	0.04	0.06	0.1	n.d.	0.54	n.d.	n.d.	0.02	0.007	6.1738
10305/60	1640	Arsenical bronze nail	100	96.83	0.10	0.02	0.09	0.1	0.22	0.03	0.36	0.02	0.04	0.03	n.d.	7.8610
10314/60	1639	Leaded tin bronze arrowhead	5	41.93	2.33	0.07	0.78	54.9	0.07	n.d.	0.51	n.d.	0.04	0.01	0.05	4.6964
10351/60	1634	Tin bronze arrowhead	11	74.6	1.8	0.04	0.18	0.25	0.05	n.d.	0.13	n.d.	n.d.	0.04	n.d.	3.7292
10360/60	1641	Tin bronze spatula		80.27	0.64	0.014	0.28	0.35	0.06	0.01	0.26	0.03	0.02	n.d.	n.d.	2.5536
10380/60	1645	Leaded tin bronze arrowhead	12	72.6	4.57	0.1	0.81	13.94	0.06	n.d.	0.32	0.02	0.03	0.01	0.08	2.7206
10381/60	1646	Tin arsenical bronze arrowhead	20	94.63	1.8	0.007	0.14	0.02	0.05	0.02	0.34	0.03	n.d.	0.08	n.d.	6.9208
10424/60	1650	Arsenical bronze needle fragment		87.9	0.06	0.014	0.30	0.03	0.09	n.d.	0.36	0.02	0.03	0.01	n.d.	5.4500
10478/60	1659	Tin arsenical bronze arrowhead	303	67.95	5.0	0.013	0.05	0.02	0.05	n.d.	0.44	0.03	0.009	0.025	0.005	9.870
10711/60	1702	Tin arsenical bronze arrowhead		91.14	1.32	n.d.	0.14	0.27	0.10	0.02	0.44	0.02	n.d.	n.d.	n.d.	
10721/60	1364	Tin arsenical bronze cosmetic stick	295	85.6	1.45	0.03	0.73	0.25	0.15	n.d.	1.1	n.d.	0.14	0.07	0.01	1.0865
10733/60	1710	Arsenical bronze tack	131	94.9	0.1	0.01	0.05	0.12	0.91	0.02	0.4	0.05	0.04	0.025	n.d.	1.8705
10835/60	1730	Arsenical bronze needle	70	81.73	0.09	0.02	1.63	0.04	0.51	0.006	1.91	0.015	0.03	0.07	0.007	4.2002

Cat. no.	No.	Artifact	Sample	Cu	Sn	—	—	Pb	Ag	—	—	—	—	—	—	Total
11032/60	1739	Leaded tin bronze cosmetic stick	297	82.62	8.0	0.04	0.44	4.48	0.12	n.d.	0.15	n.d.	0.08	0.014	0.008	2.0545
11050/60	1776	Arsenical bronze needle	80	90.9	0.05	0.01	0.8	0.34	0.07	n.d.	0.54	n.d.	n.d.	0.02	n.d.	0.4140
11062/60	1772	Arsenical bronze nail		83.53	0.067	0.01	0.13	0.03	0.11	0.008	0.47	0.015	0.007	0.03	0.04	2.4341
11202/60	1804	Arsenical bronze arrowhead		95.07	0.11	0.02	0.03	0.06	0.24	0.05	0.61	0.02	n.d.	n.d.	n.d.	3.7400
11230/60	500	Copper nail	109	92.2	n.d.	0.01	0.05	n.d.	0.06	n.d.	0.14	n.d.	n.d.	n.d.	n.d.	3.2563
11286/60	1814	Leaded tin bronze arrowhead	6	50.91	3.35	0.02	0.74	36.6	0.06	n.d.	0.5	0.04	0.05	0.018	0.08	3.9531
11603/60	1851	Leaded tin bronze bracelet	236	84.03	10.86	0.016	0.38	4.12	0.11	0.02	0.40	0.06	0.07	0.04	0.017	13.8888
11603/61	1851	Arsenical bronze bracelet	237	89.0	0.12	0.012	0.14	0.02	0.08	0.014	0.36	0.03	n.d.	0.02	0.023	13.5733
11606/60	1853	Tin bronze earring	179	84.23	2.87	0.03	0.17	0.03	0.52	n.d.	0.15	n.d.	n.d.	0.02	0.01	1.7968
11612/60	1161	Silver ring	200	1.28	0.96	0.05	0.07	0.18	97.56	0.18	0.35	n.d.	0.02	0.006	n.d.	3.9708
11613/60	1851	Silver ring	201	0.7	n.d.	0.03	0.04	0.28	99.9	0.06	0.25	n.d.	n.d.	0.004	n.d.	4.1591
11626/60	1857	Leaded tin bronze bracelet	238	81.31	8.0	0.03	0.37	10.52	0.096	0.04	0.45	0.03	0.07	0.03	0.01	16.4758
11633/60	1858	Silver ring	202	3.3	n.d.	0.04	0.08	0.6	90.71	0.27	0.45	0.05	0.03	0.01	n.d.	1.4970
11633/61	1858	Silver ring	203	0.34	n.d.	0.03	0.06	0.04	92.36	n.d.	0.26	n.d.	n.d.	0.007	n.d.	1.1648
11645/60	1159	Silver pendant	207	3.22	0.12	n.d.	0.25	0.13	73.98	0.097	0.57	n.d.	n.d.	0.016	n.d.	0.8647
11669/60	1866	Arsenical bronze bracelet	220	99.36	0.07	0.01	0.16	0.026	0.15	0.002	0.45	0.03	0.03	0.02	n.d.	4.7692
11669/61	1866	Leaded tin bronze bracelet	221	78.43	9.34	0.02	0.35	3.14	0.13	0.02	0.42	0.06	0.06	0.04	0.009	4.68
11671/60	1870	Tin arsenical bronze earring		81.64	1.3	0.05	0.26	0.3	0.11	0.04	0.4	0.05	n.d.	0.02	n.d.	0.5636
11672/60	1870	Tin bronze earring	189	54.9	2.6	0.03	0.23	0.04	0.07	n.d.	0.28	0.03	n.d.	n.d.	n.d.	0.6600
11678/60	1871	Tin bronze cosmetic stick	287	85.33	6.34	0.015	0.17	0.14	0.07	n.d.	0.17	0.03	n.d.	n.d.	n.d.	5.7200
11684/60	1869	Leaded tin bronze bracelet	222	79.74	8.48	0.06	0.18	4.83	0.1	0.012	0.44	0.04	0.03	0.03	0.015	11.0153
11684/61	1869	Leaded tin bronze bracelet	223	75.7	8.76	0.04	0.13	5.51	0.11	0.013	0.66	0.06	0.016	0.03	0.016	9.9421
11690/60	1869	Tin bronze earring fragments	190	80.0	4.87	0.018	0.42	n.d.	0.08	n.d.	0.08	n.d.	n.d.	n.d.	n.d.	2.2100
11697/60	1875	Leaded tin bronze bracelet	224	83.6	5.8	0.46	0.5	2.3	0.096	n.d.	0.43	n.d.	0.23	n.d.	0.05	12.5300
11697/61	1875	Leaded tin bronze bracelet	225	72.2	6.33	0.13	0.46	3.45	0.11	n.d.	0.63	n.d.	0.27	0.02	0.05	12.9560
11706/60	1872	Tin bronze ring	168	78.12	3.23	0.07	0.42	0.03	0.22	n.d.	0.3	n.d.	n.d.	0.03	0.01	0.8765
11711/60	1872	Tin bronze cosmetic stick	290	77.7	5.34	0.02	0.27	0.05	0.05	n.d.	0.3	0.02	n.d.	n.d.	n.d.	6.9222
11720/60	1880	Silver ring	175	13.9	0.05	0.3	1.38	0.4	78.3	0.08	0.17	0.08	n.d.	0.01	n.d.	1.9117
11721/60	1159	Copper nail	103	87.2	0.09	0.02	0.30	0.02	0.15	0.03	0.5	0.025	n.d.	0.014	0.02	18.9842

a Shown as percentages.

b Some artifacts, mainly surface finds briefly lent to us by collectors, were not weighed; several others were too fragmentary to be worth weighing.

c Not detected.

26

Flint Implements

by Mordechai Lamdan

Because of Tel Michal's location on the seacoast, the only stone in the vicinity is the *kurkar* (sandstone) of which the coastal ridge is composed (see Chaps. 16 and 18). Consequently, every flake or core of flint found on the site must have been brought there by humans. Most of the 343 flint artifacts recorded in the excavations can be ascribed to historical periods when the site was occupied, whereas 33 of them are prehistoric. The latter were probably collected by the inhabitants from various prehistoric sites in the neighborhood.

26.1. FLINT ITEMS FROM HISTORICAL PERIODS

Sickle Blades (Fig. 26.1:1–9)

Sickle blades are the most abundant item in the lithic assemblage. They are all finely serrated and characterized by heavy sickle gloss, the result of their contact with stalks of the Gramineae family. Most of them are made of coarse brown flint. The butt is usually plain, but a few are dihedral. These blades are of several types:

Tip blades: 11 items (Fig. 26.1:1–2). These are elongated triangles, usually backed, for use in the tip of the sickle (Mozel 1978:152, Fig. 1:2; 1983: Fig. 1:1; Rosen 1982: 142).

Square blades: 21 items (Fig. 26.1:6–7). This category includes both square and short rectangular blades, usually made on brown or dark gray flint.

Elongated rectangular blades: 10 items (Fig. 26.1:5). These are made of the same kind of flint. Some of them are truncated on both the proximal and distal ends.

Rhomboids: 11 items (Fig. 26.1:3–4). Of brown or dark gray flint, these are roughly rhomboid in shape.

Canaanean blades: 14 items (Fig. 26.1:8–9). Whereas the other blades were produced on blank flakes or flake blades, these were apparently knapped as sickle blades from the beginning. Several of them are broken. The flint is usually gray or light gray in color.

Reaping knife. A long, wide reaping knife with sharp, smooth cutting edge and sickle gloss (Mozel 1978:152, Fig. 1:3) should be added to the above types.

Most sickle blades are quadrilaterals of one kind or another: square, rectangular, rhomboid, or trapezoidal. When mounted in the haft, these make up the long cutting edge of the sickle, whereas the elongated-triangular blades are mounted at the tip of the sickle (Rosen 1982:142; Mozel 1983).

On the basis of size, the sickle blades from Tel Michal can be classified as either long (tip blades, elongated blades, and Canaanite blades) or short (square blades and parallelograms). These two categories were noted also at Tel Nagila (Gilead 1973) and Tel Beer-sheba (Lamdan 1984:123).

Blank Flakes for Sickle Blades

Among the unretouched flakes are 14 large ones of coarse brown flint with plain butts of the same size as the retouched blades. Undoubtedly, these were blanks imported to the site for retouching as sickle blades.

Heavy Denticulated Implements

This group consists of 27 blades or long flakes with very rough denticulation on the ventral face and deep concavities between the denticulations. The dorsal face is retouched (Fig. 26.1:10–14). Two of these are reworked sickle blades in secondary use (Fig. 26.1:10–11). On three of them, the retouch is coarse enough to make them bifacials (Fig. 26.1:13–14), similar to crude chisels.

Other Tools

In addition to the two groups of sickle blades and the large denticulated implements, there are a small number of other items:

Denticulated pieces: two items. One of these (broken) is a very thick flake of breccoidal flint with white patina. The second, with a light patina and retouched edges, resembles a denticulated transversal scraper.

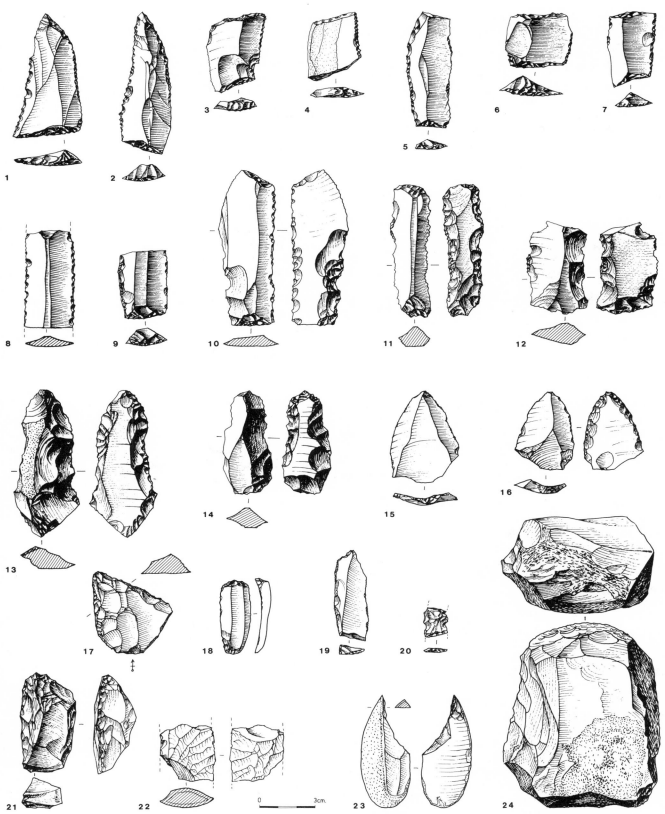

Figure 26.1. Historic and prehistoric flint tools.

No.	Item	Reg. No.	Locus	Stratum
1	Sickle blade (tip)	9495/50	1522	XIV
2	Sickle blade (tip)	9672/50	1535	XV
3	Sickle blade (rhomboid)	8803/50	1381	XVI
4	Sickle blade (rhomboid)	10443/50	1649	VII
5	Sickle blade (elongated)	9593/50	1512	XV
6	Sickle blade (square)	6429a/50	956	XV
7	Sickle blade (square)	5901/51	882	XVI
8	Sickle blade (Canaanite)	2549/50	409	IX
9	Sickle blade (Canaanite)	9539/50	1522	XIV
10	Heavy denticulated blade	9723/50	1554	XV
11	Heavy denticulated blade	10469/50	1659	XV
12	Heavy denticulated blade	10375/50	1660	XV
13	Heavy denticulated blade	9592/50	1512	XV
14	Heavy denticulated blade	8506/50	1366	Unstratified
15	Levallois point	10446/50	1649	VII
16	Levallois point	7492/50	1113	VIII
17	Acheulian side-scraper	137/50	33	V
18	Neolithic end-scraper	5562/50	842	VIII
19	Neolithic backed knife	3708/50	160	VI
20	Neolithic sickle blade	2144/50	367	IX
21	Neolithic adze	9758/50	1559	XVI
22	Bifacial (Neolithic?)	5970/50	857	X
23	Perforator	9659/50	1530	XV
24	Anvil	10441/50	1660	XV

Backed knife. This has irregular nibbling serration on the ventral face.

Perforator (Fig. 26.1:23). This piece, still with its natural cortex back, is retouched and reworked roughly at one end to form a sharp point.

Retouched pieces: four items. There is one broken flake of transparent flint with utilization retouch on its ventral face; one broken flake of breccoidal flint, retouched on both edges of its ventral face; one blade, broken at both proximal and distal ends, retouched on both edges; and one small broken flake partially retouched on its left edge.

Truncated pieces: two items. One of these has whitish patination; the other, truncated on the ventral face, is without patina.

The above tools, which were apparently fashioned on the spot for everyday domestic tasks as the need arose (Lamdan 1984), probably had no permanent function. We might call them "ad hoc" tools.

Rejuvenated blade. There is one blade with triangular section and cortical striking platform, apparently a rejuvenation of a prismatic core.

Miscellaneous Implements

Hammerstone. This fragment of a hammerstone on a flint pebble was apparently broken after being cracked in a fire. Such stones are commonly called *hammerstones* because they bear pounding marks, and it is of course possible that they were used as hammering instruments. However, the stone may have been nicked intentionally to give it a rough surface suitable for filing.

Anvil (Fig. 26.1:24). This is a large block of flint more than 10 cm high. One end is fairly wide and stable when set on a flat surface, whereas the other is pointed slightly and covered with hammering nicks. The anvil could have stood on the floor, its narrow face pointing upward and serving as a work surface. Such anvils were used by knappers for work that required hammering, such as retouching sickle blades (Bordaz 1969; Ronen 1984).

Debris

This category consists of flint items that are not tools. The flint is of various types but mostly brownish in color. There is nothing to indicate to which historical or prehistoric period they belong, since similar flakes are found in every period; however, it is very likely that those with a white or very light patina are prehistoric pieces that had been lying exposed on the surface over the millennia. There are 17 blanks in this group—8 unretouched flakes and 9 unretouched blades—that are potential tools. Of nine blades (all broken), five are ordinary and four are Canaanean.

Waste

In this group are 62 amorphous flakes or blade fragments that are of no potential use, 39 flint chips and flakes of less than 2 cm, and 33 chunks that seem to be core fragments.

Cores

There are 15 small cores from which bladelets and small flakes were struck and four large, formless cores. Six small cores are of brownish gray flint, most of them without patina, whereas nine have white or lightish patina, the latter with Epipaleolithic features. The others are from historical periods.

26.2 PREHISTORIC ITEMS

On the basis of typology, technique, and color, there are 33 prehistoric implements from Tel Michal (not including debris and waste items mentioned above). Their patina is whitish or light gray, differing from the brownish flints of historical times, which usually lack patina. Some of these were found on the surface of the site, but a large number was dispersed throughout the strata of historical periods. There were 15 items of the Lower Paleolithic (Acheulian culture) and 18 of the Neolithic period.

Acheulian Culture

Levallois points: six items (Fig. 26.1:15–16). Two of these are complete and four are broken. All have a convex butt. One point (No. 16) is retouched on the ventral face, but the rest are not retouched. One of the broken points has a reddish patina, whereas that of the others is light gray or white.

Levallois flake: has a convex base and is without patina.

Levallois blade: has gray patination.

Side-scrapers: three items. There is one straight/convex canted scraper with steep La Quina retouch and white patina (Fig. 26.1:17), one fragment of a double convex scraper, and one convex scraper with delicately retouched edges.

Point: This is a thick triangular flake with convergent, delicately retouched edges and broken butt.

Levallois cores and waste: There are two Levallois cores: one with white patina, broken and somewhat abraded; the second on a flake and without patina. There is also one very thin hand-axe waste flake.

Although the assemblage is without hand axes and has Mousterian affinities, the flint items are defined as Acheulian. The Mousterian culture is similar to the Acheulian but without hand axes (Lamdan 1982). Moreover, the Mousterian culture is practically absent in the Sharon coastal plain, whereas there are numerous Acheulian sites (Ronen and Lamdan, in press).

Neolithic Period

Adze (Fig. 26.1:21). One Neolithic adze was found at Tel Michal. It is short and almost square in section, and slightly polished on its ventral face.

Backed knives (Fig. 26.1:19). There were two, one complete and one broken. Both are truncated and backed with steep retouch. Similar tools were found in the neighborhood of the site (Gophna 1978:138, Fig. 2:2; Mozel 1978: Fig. 3:1).

Sickle blade (Fig. 26.1:20). The fragment is double-edged denticulated with reddish patina and bifacial retouch. Similar blades of the same period are known from north of the site (Mozel 1978: Fig. 3:4).

End-scrapers. There are three small, simple end-scrapers, one with abrupt retouch (Fig. 26.1:18).

Retouched items. One of these is purplish flint with alternate retouch. The other is a retouched blade fragment with light patina.

Waste. This category includes three flakes with light patina and four bladelets, two with light patina, a third, sand-

abraded specimen of brown flint, and a fourth bladelet of pinkish flint. There is also a white-patinated blade fragment partially abraded by wave action.

Bifacial (Fig. 26.1:22). This broken, brown flint bifacial with lens-shaped section has twisted pressure retouch. A similar tool was found near Naḥal Poleg (Mozel 1978: Fig. 3:8), although its pressure retouching was not twisted. This bifacial appears to be Neolithic, although it might be a fragment of an Egyptian implement.

The Neolithic assemblage from Tel Michal is too limited to permit any determination of the subperiod, and it is possible that the flints were collected from several different sites in the neighborhood.

26.3. DISTRIBUTION ACCORDING TO CHRONOLOGICAL PERIODS

As may be seen in Table 26.1, flint artifacts were most abundant in the Late Bronze Age and Persian period strata at Tel Michal. In comparing the assemblages of these two periods, however, we see significant differences in the quantities of different types. For example, if sickle blades are classified according to length (Table 26.2), long blades of both types—elongated rectangles and elongated, triangular tip blades—are more common in LB strata. However, in the Persian period loci there are more short blades, mainly rhomboids; in fact, there are practically no rhomboids from the Late Bronze Age, contrary to earlier information (Rosen 1982:142).

The raw material used for sickle blades in all the historical periods—a somewhat coarse brown flint—apparently came from the same source. In the Persian period, there are slightly more blanks of sickle blades than in the Late Bronze Age (Table 26.1).

During the Persian period it might seem that there was more production and use of flint than in other periods. Not only are there more finished products but also more by-products (debris and waste), indicating tool production on

Table 26.1. Flint Artifacts According to Periods at Tel Michal

| Period | Sickle Blades, Complete | Sickle Blades, Broken | Blank Flakes | Heavy Denticulates | Other Items | Miscellaneous Tools | Debris | | Waste | | | Cores | Total |
							Flakes	Blades	Flake Waste	Flint Chips	Flint Chunks		
Middle Bronze Age IIB	4	1							3	1		1	10
Late Bronze Age	21	13	3	13	3	2	1	1	21	9	7	7	101
Iron Age	6		2	1			1	1	7	2	4		24
Persian	22	6	7	10	2		5	6	24	15	16	8	121
Hellenistic/Hasmonean	4							1	3	8	4	1	21
Roman				1				1		1	1		4
Early Arab	1	1			2				3	1	1	1	10
Surface/unstratified	9		2	2	4		1		1	2		1	22
Total	67	21	14	27	11	2	8	10	62	39	33	19	313

FLINT IMPLEMENTS

Table 26.2. Sickle Blades According to Types and Periods

Period	Tip Blades	Elongated Rectangles	Rhomboids	Square Blades	Canaanean Blades	Broken Blades	Total
Middle Bronze Age IIB	2				2	1	5
Late Bronze Age	6	6	1	8	4	13	38
Iron Age			2	2	2		6
Persian	1	2	8	7	4	6	28
Hellenistic/Hasmonean	1	1		1	1		4
Early Arab					1	1	2
Surface/unstratified	1	1		2	1		5
Total	11	10	11	21	14	21	88

the spot. However, it should be remembered that the Persian period was the one most extensively represented at the site, both in size of excavated area and in number of strata. Persian period strata also yielded a greater number of Acheulian and Neolithic items that were probably collected by the inhabitants from prehistoric sites in the vicinity.

26.4. DISCUSSION

The use of flint, particularly for sickle blades, continued well into historical periods, since it is a cheap and easily workable material (Felix 1963:207; Avitsur 1966:23; 1976:23; Roth 1967; Gilead 1973). The Late Bronze Age strata may have large numbers of items because iron tools were not yet common. In the Persian period, on the other hand, the abundance of flint artifacts undoubtedly reflects the period's prosperity, since the site flourished at this time and was extensively populated. There is practically no significance for the isolated items found in later periods, since — unlike pottery that breaks and metal that rusts — flint tools usually remain intact and can be used secondhand and even thirdhand. Moreover, they have a tendency to "climb" from stratum to stratum.

As noted above, most of the sickle blades and blank flakes were made of the same kind of raw material. This, together with the presence of an anvil and the scarcity of cores of the size required to strike large blades, indicates that blank flakes were prepared in some other production center. There was most likely a village of flint-knappers located near the source of the raw material, probably in the foothills some 20 km east of Tel Michal. The large blank flakes were then sold to agricultural towns and villages in the plains, where they were retouched into sickle blades.

A similar pattern for the manufacture of blanks in regional production centers in the Early Bronze Age has been drawn by Rosen (1981; 1983:28) and has also been observed in Turkey (Bordaz 1969; Whallon 1978), where peasants today still use flint blades in their threshing sledges. At Tel Michal the unretouched blank flakes would have been given to an on-the-spot craftsman to retouch and fit into the sickle haft. Retouching was done on an anvil (Fig. 26.1.24), as it is done today by Turkish peasants and Australian aborigines. A similar anvil of the Neolithic peri-

od was found in the Sefunim cave (Bordaz 1969; Ronen 1984).

Most of the sickle blades, as noted above, are finely serrated, whereas the single reaping knife found at the site has a sharp, straight edge. According to our experience, and by analogy with modern harvesting machinery — in which serrated blades are replaced by smooth blades according to need — it seems that serrated sickle blades were used to reap dry cereal spikes and smooth blades were used to cut green stems, perhaps even reeds (Ronen 1983; 1984; J. Merenzon, personal communication).

In addition to sickle blades and heavily denticulated tools (whose function is not yet clear), other artifacts were improvised for impromptu domestic tasks. For this purpose the inhabitants apparently collected tools and scraps of flint wherever they came across them — for example, in nearby prehistoric sites. The Neolithic tools were probably found not too far from the tell (Prausnitz et al. 1970; Gophna 1978; Ronen and Lamdan, in press), or even possibly at a small Neolithic site under the historical strata of the tell itself. Acheulian sites are not present in the vicinity of the tell, the Acheulian culture in the coastal plain being confined to the third and easternmost kurkar range (Lamdan 1982). Consequently, Acheulian tools must have been brought from a distance at least 3 km east of the site. From this we surmise that the inhabitants of Tel Michal were accustomed to walk a distance of 3 km from their homes or that their fields stretched that far to the east — and perhaps even farther.

There are not many items of the type we have called ad hoc tools, probably because the tell is remote from any source of raw flint or pebbles and raw materials had to be brought from afar or gathered bit by bit in the fields.

In conclusion, it seems to us that the flint implements found in historical contexts are not merely a curiosity but a faithful reflection of the material culture and daily life of ordinary inhabitants, and they are worthy of study not only at Tel Michal but at other sites and periods.

REFERENCES

Avitsur, S. 1966. *Implements for Harvesting and Similar Purposes Used in the Traditional Agriculture of Eretz-Israel.* (Hebrew) Tel Aviv.

Avitsur, S. 1976. *Man and His Work: Historical Atlas of Tools and Workshops in the Holy Land.* (Hebrew) Jerusalem.

Bordaz, J. 1969. Flint Flaking in Turkey. *Natural History* 78:136–147.

Felix, J. 1963. *Agriculture in Palestine in the Period of the Mishna and Talmud.* (Hebrew) Tel Aviv.

Gilead, D. 1973. Flint Industry of the Bronze Age from Har Yeruham and Tel Nagila. Pages 133–141 in: *Excavations and Studies.* Y. Aharoni, ed. Tel Aviv.

Gophna, R. 1978. Archaeological Survey of the Central Coastal Plain, 1977. Preliminary Report. *Tel Aviv* 5:136–147.

Lamdan, M. 1982. The Upper Acheulian on the Israeli Coastal Plain. Pages 113–116 in: *The Transition from Lower to Middle Palaeolithic and the Origin of Modern Man.* A. Ronen, ed. Oxford.

Lamdan, M. 1984. Flint Artifacts from Tel Beer-sheba. *Beer-sheba II*: 122–124.

Mozel, I. 1978. A Note on the Flint Implements from Tel Michal and Naḥal Poleg. *Tel Aviv* 5:152–158.

Mozel, I. 1983. A Reconstructed Sickle from Tel Lachish. *Tel Aviv* 10:182–183.

Prausnitz, M., et al. 1970. Excavations at the Neolithic Site of Herzliyah, 1969. (Hebrew; English summary) *Mitekufat Haeven* 10:11–16.

Ronen, A. 1983. Les étapes principales de la domestication en Mediterranée Orientale. Pages 7–16 in: *L'histoire à Nice, actes du colloque internationale 1980,* vol. 1. Nice.

Ronen, A. 1984. *Sefunim Prehistoric Sites: Mount Carmel, Israel.* BAR International Series 230. Oxford.

Ronen, A., and Lamdan, M. In press. The Prehistory of the "Sharon." In *The Sharon (Coastal Plain).* (Hebrew) Tel Aviv.

Rosen, S. A. 1981. Historic Lithic Assemblages in Israel. Paper Presented at the Meeting of the Society for American Archaeology, May 1981, San Diego, Calif.

Rosen, S. A. 1982. Flint Sickle Blades of the Late Prehistoric and Early Historic Periods in Israel. *Tel Aviv* 9:135–145.

Rosen, S. A. 1983. The Canaanite Blade and the Early Bronze Age. *IEJ* 33:15–29.

Roth, Y. 1967. *History of the Sickle in Eretz-Israel.* (Hebrew) Tel Aviv.

Whallon, R.-J. 1978. Threshing-Sledge Flints: A Distinctive Pattern of Wear. *Paleorient* 4:319–324.

27

Numismatic Report

by Arie Kindler

Four seasons of excavation at Tel Michal yielded 182 coins (Table 27.1).

27.1. SIDONIAN

Twelve coins (Nos. 1–12) are Sidonian, from the end of the 5th century B.C.E. until shortly before the conquest by Alexander the Great, i.e., from the late Persian period. Most of them were struck by Straton I (370–358 B.C.E.) before the revolt of Tennes in about 350 B.C.E., and even the earliest coin of this series (No. 1) could still have been circulated under Straton I. At that time the king of Persia bestowed the coastal area from Dor to Jaffa upon the Sidonian king Eshmunezer. These coins clearly attest to the fact that Tel Michal was included in the above-mentioned enclave dominated by the Sidonians. One other coin of this period was struck at Tyre (13); another Tyrian coin, which could be dated to 359 B.C.E., was discovered in the cemetery on the northern hill during previous excavations (Avigad 1977:770).

27.2. GRECO-PERSIAN

Five coins of Greco-Persian type (14–18) that were obviously issued in Gaza in the late Persian period found their way northward to Tel Michal. This group consists mainly of local imitations of Athenian coins. One drachm (14) bears a ringlet on the cheek of Pallas Athena that no doubt stands for the עֿ of עֿזֿה (Gaza).

27.3. COINS OF ALEXANDER

The coins of Alexander the Great are of the usual types. They are represented here by a hoard of five tetradrachms (20–24), a single tetradrachm (25), a drachm (26), a hemidrachm (34), and seven bronzes (27–33). Two of the tetradrachms are from Aradus and so is the hemidrachm struck posthumously; one tetradrachm comes from Acco, one from Pella (Macedonia), and three from Babylon.

These latter three tetradrachms and the obol of Babylon, struck under Alexandrine rule (19), may have come to Tel Michal via the trade route from the east that terminated at the port of Gaza and from there may have traveled northward like the Greco-Phoenician coins.

27.4. PTOLEMAIC

The richest numismatic period at Tel Michal, however, is the 3d century B.C.E. when Palestine was under Ptolemaic rule. In single finds, Ptolemy I is represented by 4 bronze coins (82–85) and Ptolemy II by 13 coins (86–91, 94–101). A hoard of 47 tetradrachms (35–81; Kindler 1978) contained coins from Ptolemy I-III, including two rare portrait coins of Ptolemy III. Many of them were issued at the royal Ptolemaic mints, such as Sidon, Tyre, Ptolemais, Joppa, and Gaza on the Palestinian-Phoenician coast. Another small cache of five tetradrachms of Ptolemy II and Ptolemy III (91–93 and 102–103, respectively) was also discovered. These coins were minted at Sidon, Joppa, and Gaza.

27.5. MACEDONIAN

A small hoard of five Macedonian coins of Philip V (112–116) found in Locus 63 and a deposit of four bronze coins of Antiochus IV (123, 129, 131, and 135) struck at the mint of Ptolemais-Ake (Acco) complete the coin hoards.

Macedonian coins of Philip V (similar to our 112–116), as well as coins from Sidé (Pamphylia) of the particular type found at Tel Michal (110–111), are rather common finds in Israel, although the appearance of coins from mints so remote from Israel has not yet been satisfactorily explained.

27.6. SELEUCID

The Seleucid period is represented by bronze coins only. There are 6 specimens of Antiochus III (117–122), all of the same type; 13 of Antiochus IV (123–135), 4 of which came from the above-mentioned hoard; 1 of Demetrius I (136);

and 3 of Demetrius II's second period of sovereignty (137–139), all of the same type. Surprisingly, there are no coins of Antiochus VII (139–129 B.C.E.), whose commander-in-chief Kendebaeus wrought havoc to the region on his southward march against Simon Maccabeus (1 Macc. 15:38–41). Nor are there coins of Alexander Zabinas (128–123 B.C.E.), although these rulers were almost contemporaneous with Demetrius II, and their coins are generally well represented at other sites in Israel.

27.7. HASMONEAN, ROMAN, AND MAMELUKE

Seven coins of Alexander Jannaeus (140–146) and one of Agrippa I (156), all common types, rather poorly represent the Hasmonean and Herodian periods. The first half of the 1st century C.E. is, however, represented by nine coins of the following Roman procurators: Annius Rufus, Valerius Gratus, and Pontius Pilate (147–155). A coin from Alexandria (157), one from Gaba (158), and one from Antiochia ad Orontem (159) also belong to the first half of the 1st century C.E.

The Bar Kokhba coin (160) is pierced, suggesting that it was lost on the site after the war by an occasional visitor, either a Jew or a Roman legionary, who had worn it as a souvenir pendant.

The coin repertoire of the four excavation seasons ends with one surface find of an unidentifiable Late Roman coin, 4th century C.E. (161); 3 Mameluke coppers (162–164) of the 12th-14th centuries C.E.; and a group of 18 unidentifiable bronze coins (not included in the catalog), 4 or 5 of which might be Hellenistic and one probably Late Roman.

We may conclude that numismatic evidence is present at Tel Michal from circa 400 B.C.E. to 50 C.E. The three Mameluke coins may point to a post-Crusader occupation of the site, especially if we take into consideration that one of them was discovered in a tomb on the high tell.

REFERENCES

Avigad, N. 1977. Makhmish. *Enc. Arch. Exc. III*: 768–770.

Kindler, A. 1978. A Ptolemaic Coin Hoard from Tel Michal. *Tel Aviv* 5:159–169.

Newell, E. T. 1916. *The Dated Alexander Coinage of Sidon and Ake*: *Yale Oriental Series, Researches*, vol. 2. New Haven, Conn.

Rosenberger, M. 1975. *City-Coins of Palestine*, vol. 2. Jerusalem.

Svoronos, J. N. 1904–1908. *Nomismata tou kratous ton Ptolemaian*. Athens.

Table 27.1. Coins of Tel Michal

No.	Reg. No.	Locus	Metal[a]	Size (mm)	Weight (g)	Axis	Denomination	Ruler, Period of Reign, Date of Issue	Obverse	Reverse	Reference	Plate No.
1	2/61	1	AR	6.5–7.5	0.35	↑	32 of sheqel	Uncertain king. End 5th c. B.C.E.; Sidon	Persian king running-kneeling to r., holding spear transversely in r. hand and bow in l. hand; square incuse	War galley with oars to l.; sea indicated by two wavy lines; border of dots	BMC Phoenicia: 142, Nos. 14–15	72:2
2	1078/60	504	AR	7	0.25	↑	32 of sheqel	Straton I 'Abd-'ashtart; 370–358 B.C.E.; Sidon	Persian king running-kneeling to r., holding bow in r. hand and spear transversely in l. hand; square incuse	War galley to r.; border of dots; above: ᐁ	BMC Phoenicia: 146, No. 36	72:3
3	10/60	1	AR	7.5–8.5	0.63	↑	16th of sheqel	As No. 2	Persian king on l. fighting lion monster on r.; square incuse; between figures below: o	War galley to l.; below: two wavy lines indicating sea; above: ᐁ		
4	5743/60	347	AR	15–15.5	4.95	↑		As No. 2	Persian king in cart to l. drawn by two horses, driven by charioteer holding reins in both hands; incuse circle	War galley with oars; below: double line of waves; border of dots; above: date (obliterated)	BMC Phoenicia: 147–148, Nos. 46–52	
5	7475/60	1125	AE	14	4.30	↑		As No. 2	As No. 4	As No. 4	As No. 4	
6	6882/60	1024	AE	14.5–15	3.25	↖		As No. 2	As No. 4	As No. 4	As No. 4	
7	2070/60	352	AE	11–11.5	5.85			As No. 2	As No. 4	As No. 4	As No. 4	
8	26/60	3	AE	12.5–13.5	2.95	↑		As No. 2	Persian king running-kneeling to r., holding bow in r. hand, spear transversely in l. hand; border of dots	War galley with oars to l.; on board round shields; below: two wavy lines indicating sea; border of dots	BMC Phoenicia: 148, No. 53	72:9
9	17/60	1	AE	13–15	2.75	↑		As No. 2	As No. 8	As No. 8	As No. 8	
10	24a/60	2	AE	12–13	2.30	↑		As No. 2	As No. 8	As No. 8	As No. 8	
11	8347/60	1015	AE	12.5	1.80			As No. 2	Head of king to r., bearded; wearing low kidaris bound with diadem	War galley with oars; row of shields along bulwarks; without waves	BMC Phoenicia: 149, Nos. 60–62; Pl. XIX, Nos. 19–20	
12	19/65	1	AE	9.5–10		↑	16th of sheqel	Euagoras II of Cyprus (345–342 B.C.E.); Sidon	Persian king on l., fighting lion monster on r.; square incuse; between king and lion: o o	War galley to l.; below: two wavy lines indicating sea	BMC Phoenicia: 151, No. 2	72:12

No.	Inv. No.	No.	Metal	Diam.	Weight	Axis	Denomination	Date; Mint	Obverse	Reverse	Reference	Plate
13	4821/61	653	AR	6–7	0.20			4th c. B.C.E.; Tyre	Dolphin to r.	Hippocamp		72:13
14	7380/60	728	AR	15.5–16	3.50	↑	Drachm	Greco-Persian (4th c. B.C.E.); Gaza	Head of Pallas Athena to r., wearing crested helmet; on cheek: circle, which may stand for: ע = עזה	Owl standing to front; on l. above: olive spray; incuse square on r. downward: A Θ E		72:14
15	27/64	3	AR	7–9	0.10	→	Fraction of obol	As No. 14	Head to r.	Owl standing to r.; square incuse		
16	3608/60	160	AR	8	0.50	↑		As No. 14	Male head to r.; in upper r.: traces of legend: IΛ	Ram(?) standing to r., head turned backward; on l. above: branch (?); on r. below: bow(?)		
17	5161/60	687	AE	11–11.5	1.50			4th–3d c. B.C.E.	Head to r. with oriental hair style; border of dots	Obscure		
18	3799/60	531	AE	9.5–10	0.95			4th–3d c. B.C.E.	Head of Pallas Athena to r., wearing crested helmet	Owl standing to r.		
19	27/61	3	AR	8.5	0.28	↙	Fraction of obol	Alexandrine empire; Babylon	Lion walking to l.	Zeus seated to l. on throne	BMC Arabia: 183, Nos. 14–16; Pl. XXI, Nos. 8–9	72:19
20	3249/62	453	AR	24.5	16.80	→	Tetradrachm	Alexander the Great (336–323 B.C.E.); Babylon	Head of Heracles to r. wearing lion's skin	Zeus seated to l. on backless throne, holding eagle in r. hand and resting l. hand on scepter. On r., downward: ΑΛΕΞΑΝΔΡΟΥ; in exergue: ΒΑΣΙΛΕΩΣ; in field l.: monogram surrounded by wreath: [monogram]; between legs of chair: H.	SNG Oxford, Macedonia III: Nos. 3094–3104	
21	3249/63	453	AR	25–25.5	16.75	↑	Tetradrachm	Alexander the Great; Aradus	As No. 20	Type as No. 20, but between legs of throne: [monogram A/P]	Similar to: SNG Oxford, Macedonia III: Nos. 3094–3104	
22	3249/61	453	AR	25.5–26.5	16.60	→	Tetradrachm	As No. 21	As No. 20	Type as No. 20, but between legs of throne: [monogram A/P]	As No. 21	72:22

Table 27.1.   Continued

No.	Reg. No.	Locus	Metal[a]	Size (mm)	Weight (g)	Axis	Denomination	Ruler, Period of Reign, Date of Issue	Obverse	Reverse	Reference	Plate No.
23	3249/60	453	AR	25–26.5	16.50	↑	Tetradrachm	Alexander the Great; Acco	As No. 20	Type as No. 20, but on r. downward: ΑΛΕΞΑΝΔΡΟΥ: in field, 1.: III · ΛΛϽΟ = 33 ϽϞ	Newell 1916: 49, No. 36	
24	3249/64	453	AR	26.5–28	16.40	→	Tetradrachm	Alexander the Great; Babylon	As No. 20	Type as No. 20, but on r. downward: ΑΛΕΞΑΝΔΡΟΥ; between legs of throne, monograms:	SNG Oxford, Macedonia III: No. 3501	
25	4516/60	610	AR	25	16.5	↗	Tetradrachm	Alexander the Great; Pella, Macedonia	As No. 20	Type as No. 20, but on r., in quarter circle downward: ΑΛΕΞΑΝΔΡΟΥ	SNG Oxford, Macedonia III: No. 2529	
26	438/64	63	AE	16.5–19.5	4.15	→	Drachm	Alexander the Great	As No. 20	As No. 20, but legend effaced		72:26
27	1980/60	311	AE	15.5–16.5	5.50	↑		As No. 26	As No. 20	Club, bow, and quiver; between club and quiver: ΑΛΕΞΑΝΔΡΟΥ		
28	5584/60	322	AE	17–19.5	5.10	↑		As No. 26	As No. 20	As No. 27, but legend effaced		
29	2454/60	408	AE	16–17	4.70	→		As No. 26	As No. 20	As No. 27, but on r.: caduceus; on l. star: ΑΛΕΞΑΝΔΡΟΥ		72:29
30	7719/60	1173	AE	16–17	4.10	↗		As No. 26	As No. 20	As No. 27, but legend effaced		
31	4524/60	610	AE	16–19.5	4.00			As No. 26	As No. 20	As No. 27		
32	1956/60	750	AE	12	2.20			As No. 26	Obliterated	As No. 27, but legend effaced		
33	12/60	1	AE	13–13.5	1.85			As No. 26	As No. 20	As No. 27, but legend: ΑΛΕ[ΞΑΝΔΡΟΥ]		
34	2/60	1	AR	12–12.5	1.95	↑	Hemidrachm	Alexander the Great (posthumous); Aradus	As No. 20	As No. 20, but in field l. below: Σ; between legs of chair, monogram:	SNG Copenhagen, Macedonia II, No. 800; Macedonia III	

No.	Reg. No.	No.	Metal	Diam.	Weight	Axis	Denom.	Date / Mint	Obverse	Reverse	Reference	Plate
35–81b	852/1–47	125										
82	400/60	63	AE	18	4.25	↑		Ptolemy I (305–285 B.C.E.)	Head of Alexander the Great, diademed	Eagle with spread wings standing to l. on thunderbolt; in field l. below: Corinthian helmet to l.; around from l. below: ΠΤΟΛΕΜΑΙΟΥ ΒΑΣΙΛΕΩΣ	Svoronos 1904–1908: 30, No. 172; Pl. VI:16–17	72:82
83	26/61	3	AE	17–18	7.00	↑	Chalkous	As No. 82	Head of Alexander the Great in elephant's skin	Type as No. 82, but legend effaced; in field l. below: Ж = ΧΑΛΚΟΥΣ = chalkous	Svoronos 1904–1908: 38, No. 235; Pl. VIII:10	72:83
84	7357/60	1104	AE	13–14	2.20	↑		As No. 82	Head of Alexander the Great	As No. 82, but legend effaced	Svoronos 1904–1908: 39, No. 239; Pl. VIII:16	
85c	6832/60	1024	AE	26–26.5	14.10	↑		As No. 82	Head of Zeus to r., diademed; border of dots	Type as No. 82, but border of dots; in field l. below: Π	Similar to Svoronos 1904–1908: 48, No. 296; Pl. X:21	
86	7016/60	1065	AE	14–16	3.35	↑		Ptolemy II (285–247 B.C.E.); Tyre: 280 B.C.E.	Head of Alexander the Great to r., diademed; border of dots	Type as No. 82, but in field l.: club (= Tyre); above club: I = 6th year of Ptolemy II = 280 B.C.E.; border of dots	Svoronos 1904–1908: 95, No. 635; Pl. XIX:7	
87	5200/60	694	AE	19–20	7.45	↑		Ptolemy II: 285–266 B.C.E.	Head of Alexander the Great in elephant's skin	Type as No. 82, but in field, l. oblong shield; border of dots; legend from r., above: [ΒΑ]ΣΙΛΕΩΣ [ΠΤΟΛΕΜΑΙΟΥ] above shield: Σ	Svoronos 1904–1908: Pl. XIV:12–13	
88	5136/60	686	AE	13.5–14	3.50	↑		Ptolemy II; Tyre: 285–262 B.C.E.	Head of Alexander the Great to r., diademed	Type as No. 82, but legend effaced; in field, l. club	Svoronos 1904–1908: Pl. XIX:4–5	
89	1655/60	306	AE	12–12.5	2.60	↑		As No. 88	Type as No. 88	Effaced	As No. 88	
90	7367/60	1111	AE	16–17	4.35	↑		Ptolemy II; Tyre (?)	Type as No. 88	Type as No. 82, but in field l.: aphlaston (?); legend around from l. below: ΠΤΟΛΕΜΑΙΟΥ [ΒΑΣΙΛΕΩΣ]	Similar to Svoronos 1904–1908: 95, No. 635; Pl. XIX:4, 5, 7	

Table 27.1. Continued

No.	Reg. No.	Locus	Metal[a]	Size (mm)	Weight (g)	Axis	Denomination	Ruler, Period of Reign, Date of Issue	Obverse	Reverse	Reference	Plate No.
91	6856/63	1014	AR	24.5–26	13.65	↑	Tetra-drachm	Ptolemy II; Sidon: 256 B.C.E.	Head of Ptolemy I to r., diademed, wearing aegis; border of dots	Eagle standing to l. on thunderbolt; around from l. below: ΠΤΟΛΕΜΑΙΟΥ ΣΩΤΗΡΟΣ in field, r. above: ΚΘ = 29th yr. of Ptolemy II = 256 B.C.E.; l. above, mintmark: ΣΙ; l. below mintmaster: ΔΙ	Svoronos 1904–1908: 108, No. 730; Pl. XXI:12	
92	6856/62	1014	AR	25.5–27	13.10	↑	Tetra-drachm	Ptolemy II; Joppa: 249 B.C.E.	As No. 91	Type as No. 91, but in field: r. above: ΛϹ = 36th year of Ptolemy II = 249 B.C.E.; r. below, head mintmaster: ⊙ l. above, mintmark: ⟨symbol⟩	Svoronos 1904–1908: 121, No. 811; Pl. XXIII:14	
93	6856/60	1014	AR	25	13.50	↑	Tetra-drachm	Ptolemy II; Gaza: 248 B.C.E.	As No. 91, but graffiti: on r.: ⟨symbol⟩; on left: ⟨symbol⟩	Type as No. 91, but in field: r. above: ΛΙ = 37th year of Ptolemy II = 248 B.C.E.; r. below, mintmark: I; l. above, mintmark: ΙϜ l. below, mintmaster: ⟨symbol⟩	Svoronos 1904–1908: 124, No. 833; Pl. XXIV:12	
94	4281/60	591	AE	19.5–20.5	7.10	↑		Ptolemy II	As No. 87	Type as No. 82		
95	4148/60	579	AE	20.5–21	5.15	↑		Ptolemy II	As No. 87	Type as No. 82, but legend from r. above: [ΒΑ]ΣΙΛΕ[ΩΣ ΠΤΟΛΕ ΜΑΙΟΥ]		
96	11281/60	1813	AE	17.5–18.5	5.60	↑		Ptolemy II	As No. 87	Type as No. 82		
97	4534/60	619	AE	16	3.20	↑		Ptolemy II	As No. 87	Type as No. 82		
98	8931/60	1392	AE	16.5	7.30	↗		Ptolemy II	As No. 87	Type as No. 82		
99	7185/60	1067	AE	23	11.00	↑		Ptolemy II; Tyre	As No. 85	Type as No. 82, but legend from r. above: ΒΑΣΙΛΕΩΣ ΠΤΟΛΕ ΜΑΙΟΥ in field l.: club	Svoronos 1904–1908: 104, No. 708; Pl. XX:18	

No.	ID	Ref.No.	Metal	Diameter	Weight	Axis	Denomination	Date/Ruler	Obverse	Reverse	Reference
100	851/60	125	AE	22–23.5	12.05	↑		Ptolemy II	As No. 85	Type as No. 82, but legend around from r. above: [B]ΑΣΙΛΕ[ΩΣ] ΠΤΟΛΕΜΑΙΟΥ; in field: l., double cornucopia; border of dots	Svoronos 1904–1908: 112, No. 761; Pl. XXII:15
101	3236/60	453	AE	25.5–26.5		↑		Ptolemy II	As No. 85	Type as No. 82, but legend effaced	
102	6856/64	1014	AR	24.5–25.5	13.55	↑	Tetradrachm	Ptolemy III (247–221 B.C.E); Sidon: 242 B.C.E.	Head of Ptolemy I to r., diademed, wearing aegis	Eagle standing to l. on thunderbolt; border of dots; around from l. below: ΠΤΟΛΕΜΑΙΟΥ ΣΩΤΗΡΟΣ; in field: r. above; Δ = 4th year of Ptolemy III = 242 B.C.E.; r. below, mintmaster: M; l. above, mintmark: ΣΙ; l. below, mintmaster: I H	Svoronos 1904–1908: 162, No. 10291; Pl. XXXII:5
103	6856/61	1014	AR	24–25	13.50	↑	Tetradrachm	Ptolemy III; Joppa: 241 B.C.E.	Head of Ptolemy I to r., diademed; border of dots	Type as No. 102, but in field: r. above: E = 5th year of Ptolemy III = 241 B.C.E.; r. below, mintmaster: HP; l. above, mintmark:ΙΟΠ; l. below, head mintmaster: ⊙	Svoronos 1904–1908: 164, No. 1043; Pl. XXXII:24
104	11235/60	1804	AE	18–18.5	3.20	→		Ptolemaic: 3d c. B.C.E.	Head to r.	Eagle standing to l.; punchmark (incuse): trident	
105	4014/60	551	AE	17–17.5	5.55			As No. 104	Bearded head of Zeus to r.	Eagle standing to l.	
106	4144/60	579	AE	17.5	3.70			As No. 104	Obscure	Obscure	
107	19/66	1	AE	14	2.55			As No. 104	Obscure	As No. 82, but legend effaced	
108	11/60	1	AE	14.5	2.25			As No. 104	Head of Zeus to r.	PΘ = 109	
109	2019/60	352	AR	20–21.5	6.20	↑	Didrachm	Ptolemy IV and V (204–194 B.C.E.)	Head of Ptolemy to r., diademed; border of dots	Eagle standing to l. on thunderbolt; around from r. above: ΒΑ[ΣΙΛΕΩΣ] ΠΤΟΛΕΜΑΙΟΥ; in field: r.: Θ; l.: P = PΘ = 109	Svoronos 1904–1908: 199, No. 1216; Pl. XXXVIII:16

Table 27.1. Continued

No.	Reg. No.	Locus	Metal[a]	Size (mm)	Weight (g)	Axis	Denomination	Ruler, Period of Reign, Date of Issue	Obverse	Reverse	Reference	Plate No.
110	4102/61	570	AE	10.5–11	4.15	→		3d. c. B.C.E. Side, Pamphylia	Head of Athena to r., wearing Corinthian helmet	Pomegranate	BMC Lycia, Pamphylia: 150. Nos. 59–61; Pl. XXVIII:4	72:110
111	138/60	35	AE	12–13	1.65	↑		3d c. B.C.E.	As No. 110	As No. 110	As No. 110	
112	437/60	63	AE	15	3.05			Philip V of Macedon (220–179 B.C.E.)	Round ornamented Macedonian shield	Helmet seen from in front with cheekpieces	SNG Copenhagen, Macedonia III: No. 1253	72:112
113	438/62	63	AE	12–13	2.90			As No. 112	As No. 112	As No. 112	As No. 112	
114	438/60	63	AE	12–13	2.65			As No. 112	As No. 112	As No. 112	As No. 112	
115	438/63	63	AE	14	2.55			As No. 112	As No. 112	As No. 112	As No. 112	
116	438/61	63	AE	11–12	2.35			As No. 112	As No. 112	As No. 112	As No. 112	
117	7041/60	1059	AE	11–12	2.30	↗		Antiochus III (223–187 B.C.E.); Antiochia ad Orontem	Laureate head of Apollo to r.	Apollo standing to l., holding arrow in r. hand; l. hand resting on bow	SNG Copenhagen, Seleucid Kings: Nos. 154–156	
118	4159/60	554	AE	9	1.50			As No. 117	As No. 117	As No. 117	As No. 117	
119	27/62	3	AE	9–10	1.25			As No. 117	As No. 117	As No. 117	As No. 117	
120	27/65	3	AE	8–9	1.05			As No. 117	As No. 117	As No. 117	As No. 117	
121	80/60	35	AE	9–10	0.75			As No. 117	As No. 117	As No. 117	As No. 117	
122	27/60	3	AE	7.5–8.5	0.55			As No. 117	As No. 117	As No. 117	As No. 117	
123	19/64	1	AE	14–15	3.85			Antiochus IV (175–164 B.C.E.); Seleucia ad Tigrim	Head of Antiochus IV to r., radiate	Tyche seated to l. on throne, holding Nike in extended r. hand; bird at her feet to l.	SNG Copenhagen, Seleucid Kings: No. 180	
124[d]	28/63	3	AE	12.5–13	3.00	↑		Antiochus IV; Ptolemais-Ake	Head of Antiochus IV to r., radiate; border of dots; behind head: B	Veiled goddess (Atargatis) standing to front, holding long scepter in r. hand; border of dots; on r. downward: [BA]ΣΙΛΕ[ΩΣ]; on l. downward, reading outward: [A]NTIOXOY	SNG Copenhagen, Seleucid Kings: No. 198	
125	28/62	3	AE	14–14.5	2.45	↑			As No. 124, but no monogram	As No. 124, but legend effaced	As No. 124	
126	4108/62	570	AE	14	2.80	↑		As No. 124	As No. 124	As No. 124	As No. 124	
127	10988/60	1756	AE	13.5–14	2.60	↑		As No. 124	As No. 124	As No. 124	As No. 124	
128	29/60	3	AE	12.5–13	2.25	↑		As No. 124	As No. 124	As No. 124	As No. 124	
129	19/63	1	AE	13.5	2.20	↑		As No. 124	As No. 124	As No. 124, but on r.: BAΣΙΛΕΩΣ; on l.: ANTIOXOY	As No. 124	

No.	Accession	Qty.	Metal	Diam. (mm)	Wt. (g)	Axis	Denom.	Attribution	Obverse	Reverse	Reference	Plate
130	28/64	3	AE	13–13.5	2.05	↑			As No. 124	As No. 124, but ANTIOXOY on l.	As No. 124	
131	19/62	1	AE	12.5–14	2.00				As No. 124	As No. 124	As No. 124	
132	19/61	1	AE	12–13	1.95	↑			As No. 124	As No. 124, but on r.: ΒΑΣΙΛΕΩΣ; on l.: ANTIOXOY	As No. 124	
133	4429/60	600	AE	13–14.5	1.90	↑			As No. 124	As No. 124	As No. 124	
134	7128/60	1075	AE	12–13	1.50	↑			As No. 124	As No. 124, but on r.: ΒΑΣΙΛΕΩΣ; on l.: ANTIOXOY	As No. 124	
135	28/65	3	AE	11.5	1.50	↑			As No. 124	As No. 124	As No. 124	72:135
136	19/60	1	AE	12–12.5	2.60	↑		Demetrius I (162–150 B.C.E.); Antiochia ad Orontem	Bust of Artemis to r.; quiver at shoulder	Apollo, nude, standing to l.; legend effaced	SNG Copenhagen, Seleucid Kings: No. 243	
137	55/60	25	AE	17	5.30	↑	Chalkous	Demetrius II (129–125 B.C.E.; 2d reign); Antiochia ad Orontem	Laureate head of Zeus to r.; border of dots	Nike standing to l., holding palm branch over l. shoulder and wreath in extended r. hand. In four lines on r. and l.: [ΒΑ]ΣΙΛ[ΕΩΣ] ΔΗΜΗΤΡΙΟΥ ΘΕΟΥ ΝΙΚΑ ΤΟΡΟ[Υ]; in field, l. below: Ξ	SNG Copenhagen, Seleucid Kings: No. 349	72:137
138	5625/60	832	AE	16.5–17	5.00	↑	Chalkous		As No. 137	Type as No. 37, but in 4 lines on r. and l.: [ΒΑ]ΣΙ[ΛΕΩΣ] [ΔΗ]ΜΗΤΡ[ΙΟΥ] [ΘΕ]ΟΥ [ΝΙ]ΚΑΤΟΡ[ΟΣ]	As No. 137	
139	5135/60	686	AE	17	5.00	↑	Chalkous		As No. 137	Type as No. 137, but in 4 lines on r. and l.: [ΒΑ]ΣΙΛΑ[ΕΩΣ] Δ[ΗΜΗΤΡ]ΙΟΥ ΘΕΟΥ ΝΙΚΑΤΟΡΟ[Σ]	As No. 137	72:139
140	2339/60	363	AE	10–11	0.60		Hemilepton	Alexander Jannaeus (103–76 B.C.E.); after 96 B.C.E.	Star of 7 rays	Anchor within circle; traces of legend, reading outward: ΛΛ	BMC Palestine: 210–211, Nos. 1–18	72:140
141	5187/60	685	AE	9.5–10.5	0.50		Hemilepton	As No. 140	Star of 6 rays surrounded by circle of dots	Anchor within circle	As No. 140	72:141

Table 27.1. Continued

No.	Reg. No.	Locus	Metal[a]	Size (mm)	Weight (g)	Axis	Denomination	Ruler, Period of Reign, Date of Issue	Obverse	Reverse	Reference	Plate No.
142	5185/60	692	AE	9–9.5	0.50		Hemilepton	As No. 140	Star of 5 rays; traces of legend: ⋎∴∧	Anchor within circle; traces of legend: ⋎∴∧	As No. 140	
143	11018/60	1739	AE	9.5	0.45		Hemilepton	As No. 140	Star of 6 rays	Effaced	As No. 140	
144	11063/60	1772	AE	9.5–10	0.65		Hemilepton	As No. 140	Star surrounded by circle; traces of legend: ⊓Γ	Anchor within circle	As No. 140	
145	2853/61	255	AE	8.5–11	0.40		Hemilepton	As No. 140	Star of ? rays	Anchor within circle. Traces of legend: ΥΣ	As No. 140	
146	2853/60	255	AE	11.5–12	1.10		Lepton	As No. 140	Star of 8 rays, surrounded by dotted circle	Blank (uniface!)		
147	2018/60	60	AE	13–16	1.70		Dilepton	Annius Rufus: (12–15 C.E.) 12 C.E.	Ear of barley; legend from l. below: KAICA[PO]C	Palm tree with 8 branches and 2 bunches of dates; border of dots; across field, date of issue: LΛΘ = yr. 39 of Augustus = 12 C.E.	BMC Palestine: 248–249, Nos. 9–14	
148	6120/60	923	AE	14.5–16	2.10	↑	Dilepton	Annius Rufus: 14 C.E.	As No. 147, but legend: KAICAPOC	As No. 147, but date of issue: L MA = yr. 41 of Augustus = 14 C.E.	BMC Palestine: 249–250, Nos. 21–27	
149	5137/60	1002	AE	14.5–15	2.00	↙	Dilepton	Valerius Gratus: (15–26 C.E.) 18/19 C.E.	Wreath tied on bottom; border of dots; in 3 lines therein: TIB/KAI/CAP	Upright palm branch; across field: above IOYΛIA; below, date of issue: L E = yr. 5 of Tiberius = 18/19 C.E.	BMC Palestine: 255–256, Nos. 38–45	72:149
150	6759/60	1002	AE	14–15	1.30	↙	Dilepton	Valerius Gratus: 18/19 C.E.	Type and legend as No. 149	Type and legend as No. 149	As No. 149	
151	6771/60	1008	AE	15.5–16.5	2.15	↑	Dilepton	Valerius Gratus: 25 C.E.	Type and legend as No. 149	Type and legend as No. 149, but date of issue: L IA = yr. 11 of Tiberius = 25 C.E.	BMC Palestine: 256–257, Nos. 46–53	
152	10989/60	1756	AE	14.5	2.00		Dilepton	Valerius Gratus	Type as No. 149, but legend effaced	Type as No. 149 but traces of legend above only: [IO]YΛI[A]	BMC Palestine: 254–257, Nos. 31–53	

No.	Reg. no.		Metal	Diameter	Weight	Axis	Denomination	Attribution / Date	Obverse	Reverse	Reference	Plate
153	11034/60	1008	AE	9	0.60		Dilepton	Valerius Gratus	Type as No. 149, but legend effaced	Type as No. 149; traces of legend above: [I]OY[ΛIA]; below: date of issue: L (?)	As No. 152	
154	6167/60	918	AE	15–15.5	2.15	↓	Dilepton	Pontius Pilate (26–36 C.E.): 30 C.E.	Simpulum; border of dots; legend from l. below: TIBEP[IOC KAICAPOC] LIS = yr. 16 of Tiberius = 30 C.E.	3 ears of barley bound together; border of dots; in semicircle above from l.: IOYΛ[IA KAI]CAPOC	*BMC Palestine*: 257–258, Nos. 54–68	72:154
155	7215/60	1094	AE	11–14	1.80		Dilepton	Roman procurator, probably 1st half 1st c. C.E.	Effaced	Effaced		
156	5865/60	843	AE	15.5	2.10	↑	Dilepton	Agrippa I (37–44 C.E.): 42/43 C.E.	Canopy (umbrella) up-right; legend from r. above: [BACIΛEWC A] PIΠA	3 ears of barley; border of dots; across field, date of issue: [L]S = yr. 6 of Agrippa I = 42/43 C.E.	*BMC Palestine*: 236–237, Nos. 1–19	
157	310/60	58	AE	23	8.10	↑		Livia (died 29 C.E.); Alexandria	Bust of Livia to r.; hair in knot behind	Bust of Euthenia to r. bound with corns and carrying ears of corn in r. hand; legend effaced: [EYΘENIA]	*BMC Alexandria*: 4, No. 28; Pl. XXII, No. 28	72:157
158	11076/60	1776	AE	20.5–21	7.00	↑		Claudius (41–54 C.E.); Gaba	Bust of Claudius to r. laureate, drapery over shoulder	Female figure seated on throne to r., resting r. hand on spear or scepter and branch in l. hand; legend from r. KΛAY[ΔIEΩN ΦIΛIΠIΠH] NΩN	Rosenberger 1975, Vol. 2, Gaba: 43, No. 1	
159	324/60	61	AE	21	3.13	↗		1st half 1st c. C.E.; Antiochia ad Orontem	Bust of emperor to r.	Wreath; large S C therein		
160ᵉ	45/60	1	AE	26–28	9.35	→	Dupondius	Bar Kokhba War (132–135 C.E.): 133–134 C.E.	Palm tree with 7 branches; border of dots; across field: שמעון = Simon	Vine leaf; border of dots; legend from l. above: ש ב להר...ות ישראל (= Year 2 for the freedom of Israel)	*BMC Palestine*: 308–309, Nos. 47–59	72:160
161	24/60	2	AE	12.5	1.10			Late Roman (?) 4th c. C.E. (?)	Head of emperor to r.	Figure standing		
162	9680/60	1906	AE	18.5–19.5				Mameluke: 12th–14th c. C.E.	Traces of Arabic writing	Traces of Arabic writing		72:162
163ᵉ	6149/60	906	AE	14–16	0.90			Mameluke: 12th–14th c. C.E.	Effaced	Effaced		

Table 27.1. Continued

No.	Reg. No.	Locus	Metal[a]	Size (mm)	Weight (g)	Axis	Denomi-nation	Ruler, Period of Reign, Date of Issue	Obverse	Reverse	Reference	Plate No.
164	52/60	25	AE	15.5–17	1.15			Mameluke: 13th-c. C.E.	Outline of geometric design; border of dots	Effaced		

[a] AR = AR(gentum) = silver; AE = AE(s Cuprum) = copper/bronze.

[b] Nos. 35–81 are a hoard of 47 tetradrachms dating to the reigns of Ptolemy I–III (Kindler 1978).

[c] Edge of No. 85 is partly serrated.

[d] Nos. 124–136 have serrated edges.

[e] Nos. 160 and 163 are pierced.

28a

Seals and Seal Impressions

by Mira Barak and Shua Amorai-Stark

Although relatively few seals and bullae were retrieved from the excavations at Tel Michal, they represent an interesting diversification of periods, styles, and materials: steatite, jasper, white quartz, blue glass, and silver (Fig. 28.1). They date from the 10th to 4th centuries B.C.E.

28a.1. SEALS

1. *Stag (or ibex) with male figure* (Fig. 28.1:1; Pl. 73:1). Perforated conoid seal; base uneven circle. Steatite. Diameter 12 mm.

The exact nature of the motifs incised on the base is difficult to determine, but most probably one of them is a four-legged animal with a long curved tail and large horns. The two slightly curved horns protrude from the animal's head and turn backward. Two pointed lines extend forward from the animal's face—perhaps an exaggeration of an open mouth. All four legs are represented, curving slightly and ending abruptly in a sharp, thin curve without hooves. This is probably a highly schematic representation of an ibex or stag. Above the animal's head is a small globular motif, crossed by a thin line, probably a crack. It may be a sun disk or possibly a sacred shield. Another motif is incised diagonally in midair above the animal. It seems to be a schematic representation of a male figure or an insect. If a man, his arms protrude in small sharp lines from the lower part of his globular head and his legs continue from the sides of his body in two sharp, pointed strokes.

These motifs are engraved in a very stylized way. No details are added to the basic spiderlike incisions. The long body of the animal is incised with a comparatively wide drill and the legs, tail, and horns with very thin, curvilinear incisions, probably executed with a thin, sharp drill turned on its edge or by a scriber tool.

Representations of a man holding onto the horns of a bull (or hovering above a bull or stag) appear on Cretan seals (Kenna 1960: Nos. 13, 247, 249, 341) from the Early to Late Minoan periods. The motif of a man or an insect (usually a scorpion) hovering above a horned animal or

standing behind it appears also on post-Hittite conoid seals from Syria (Hogarth 1920: 85–86, Nos. 280–281, 295). Number 280 is especially close to the Tel Michal seal both in style and subject.

However, the nearest parallels to the Tel Michal seal in shape (perforated conoid with small uneven circular base), incision technique, and motif are seals from the 10th century B.C.E. onward. Examples are found in the following sites: Lachish: scaraboid with stag (*Lachish III*: Pls. 43A-44: Nos. 90–92); conoid seal with stag, identical leg treatment (*Lachish III*: Pl. 44A-45: No. 149); Megiddo: perforated conoid with stag and scorpion, identical style (*Megiddo I*: Pl. 69:15); perforated conoid with nursing stag or ibex and scorpion disk, identical style (*Megiddo I*: Pl. 69:22); perforated conoid with stag and scorpion, ostrich(?), similar style (*Megiddo I*: Pl. 69:40); see also Pl. 69:39, scaraboid with horned stag, hovering human above, another man in front; Samaria: scaraboid, human above a stag, identical leg style (*Samaria-Sebaste III*: Pl. XV:23); scaraboid with stag, standing man above (*Samaria 1924*: Pl. 56:e7); Beth-shemesh: elongated perforated conoid with nursing stag, large object above, similar style, mainly of legs and body (*Ain Shems III*: Fig. 3:16); Hazor Stratum XA: perforated conoid with stag and human above, similar leg and body style (*Hazor III-IV*: Pls. CCCLX: 6–7, CLXXIV: 19); Shechem: two-horned quadruped, scorpion above, other motif below (Wright 1962: Fig. 4).

In light of these numerous analogies, there is no doubt that our seal No. 1 belongs to the same milieu and glyptic tradition.

2. *Winged "sphinx"* (Fig. 28.1:2; Pl. 73:2). Perforated conical seal; base almost perfect circle, slightly convex. Quartz. Diameter 14 mm.

One large mythical animal is engraved on the base of the seal, facing right in profile. Two overlapping wings extend in a sharp angle from the point of juncture of the animal's head and body. The winged animal is depicted schematically. Its body, legs, tail, and neck are composed of wide, straight grooves engraved by wide and round drills, inter-

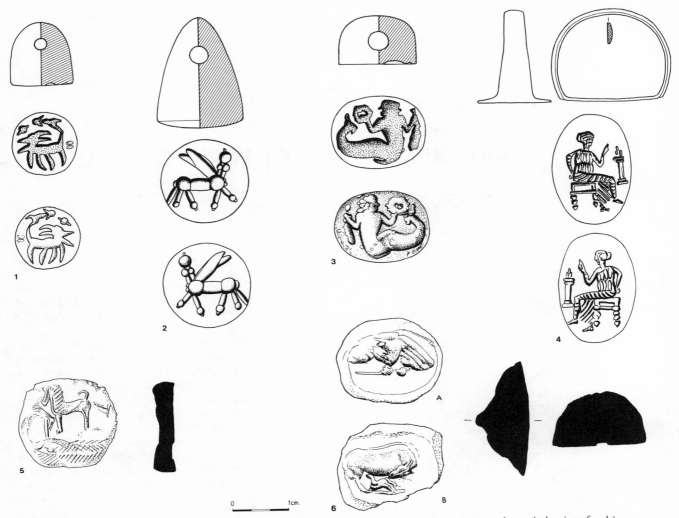

Figure 28.1. Seals, seal impressions, and bullae. (Seal impressions produced by us are shown underneath drawing of seal.)

Legend for Fig. 28.1

No.	Type	Reg. No.	Locus	Stratum	Material	Pl.
1	Seal	9578/60	1531	X	Steatite	73:1
2	Seal	1513/50	221	VIII/VI	White quartz	73:2
3	Seal	11710/50	1872	XI/VI	Blue glass	73:3
4	Signet ring	3314/60	466	VI	Silver	74:1
5	Bulla	9456/1	1501	X	Clay	74:2
6	Bulla	10323/1	1029	VII	Clay	74:3

spersed with round globules of various sizes (head, end of legs, and body) engraved with ball drills. The head is composed of two globules placed side by side (eyes?). A larger globule (crown?) appears above them. There is no suggestion of horns or mane. All four legs are depicted in diagonal angles to the body. Each leg ends with a round globule. The tail parallels the hind leg and looks more like a fifth leg than a proper tail; however, it does not end in a globule.

In spite of the elementary style of execution, a three-dimensional representation is achieved. Conical seals of this type are typical of Mesopotamian art, beginning with the Assyrian and Neo-Babylonian periods (von der Osten 1934:9, Pl. XXVII: 481–505). In such summary work, the figure lacks specific features and details.

This is undoubtedly a mythical winged creature, neither human nor avian, but it is impossible to determine whether it was intended to represent a winged lion, bull, or horse. Nevertheless, it may be called a "sphinx" in the broadest sense of this term. Winged bulls or lions are commonplace in Assyrian and Neo-Babylonian art. However, the so-called sphinx motif is less frequent on the conoid seals of these periods than other designs (including animals) that are associated with religious expression, although it too is known. A similar animal is depicted on the elliptical base of a seal from Ur (Woolley 1962: Pl. 30:489u), with a line-drilled technique and similar overall effect. However, its style is not identical to that of the Tel Michal seal: the animal's legs are vertical to the body, they do not end with round drillings, only one wing is visible, and the position of the tail is different. The Ur seal was found in the palace of E-nun-Mah, in a hoard of gold objects and jewelry from Nebuchadnezzer's period.

The use of seals of this type continues into the Persian period. A Babylonian seal discovered at En-gedi in the Persian stratum represents the common Mesopotamian seal subject of a priest praying before the emblems of Marduk (Mazar 1976). This seal was engraved in the same globular and linear style as our Seal No. 2. However, it is a much more refined work. The Tel Michal seal may therefore be either a later example of that style or, more likely, simply a more provincial product of the same period (6th-5th centuries B.C.E.).

3. *Triton* (Fig. 28.1:3; Pl. 73:3). Perforated scaraboid. Blue glass. Measures 12 mm × 18 mm.

This glass scaraboid has a plain convex back and flat oval base. As is typical of glass gems, the surface of the base is full of tiny air bubbles.

The figure of a Triton (half man, half fish), engraved on the horizontal axis, fills the area of the base. His human torso is depicted frontally, his human head turned sideways and backward toward his tail. His facial features and hair style are not clear. It is, however, possible to make out his beard, which appears above his shoulder. The Triton's arms are spread outward, bent at the elbows and raised symmetrically. In one hand he holds a large wreath of flowers and/or leaves, at which he seems to be looking. In the other hand, he holds an elongated object that widens at the bottom and may be either a wineskin or a dolphin held by its tail. Fins are discernible on both sides of the Triton's human waist. His large tail curves upward and is split at the end.

The engraver of this glass seal has adapted the Triton's body and attributes admirably to the oval shape of the scaraboid and has succeeded in representing all the typical characteristics of his subject with hardly any distortions. Possibly, even finer details were originally incised on the Triton.

This stylistic skill is typical of late Archaic or Classical Greek (or Greco-Phoenician) gems. Stylistically, the Tel Michal Triton is a work of the late 5th or early 4th century B.C.E. A sphinx engraved on the same material (blue glass) appears on a 5th-century conoid from Syria. It exhibits a similar combination of Syro-Phoenician elements (shape and material) with Greek stylistic devices (Boardman and Vollenweider 1978:41, No. 172). A later Triton, whose body also fills the base area of the gem, appears on a carnelian seal at the Musee d'Art d'Histoire in Geneva (Vollenweider 1966:118, Pl. 77:7). Technically, the Tel Michal seal was engraved with wide cylindrical drills that were probably rotated onto their sides in order to incise the thinner (but still rounded) parts of the design.

Glass scaraboids were very common in the ancient Near East. Blue or green glass scaraboids of the Phoenician type were commonly made in Syria-Phoenicia, especially from the 7th century onward (Boardman 1970a:377–378). Large glass scaraboids became popular in the Classical period. The use of glass as a gem material increased in the Hellenistic period, mainly for ring stones but occasionally also for scaraboids; the tiny air bubbles of glass gems are most typical of this period (Boardman and Vollenweider 1978:72).

Both the design and motif are clearly Grecian. A similarly stylized Triton appears on a Phoenician coin from Aradus dated to the mid-5th century B.C.E. (Moscati 1968:69, Fig. 28) and on a jasper seal from Tharros in Sardinia dated to the end of the 5th or the beginning of the 4th century (Harden 1962: Pl. 108h). The details of the Tritons on these two objects are clearer and therefore helpful in reading our Seal No. 3. The lack of detail on our seal should not be attributed to a different glyptic phase but rather to the material, since most glass seals tend to wear out and the details are often distorted or partially obliterated. The Triton on the Aradus coin holds a band in one hand (as does the Triton from Tel Michal) and a dagger in the other. His head is turned sideways exactly like that of the Tel Michal Triton. The headgear of the Triton on the Phoenician coin looks like a large skullcap, and his hair is gathered at the neck. The cap and hair style of the Triton on our seal were probably similar.

A similar glass seal was found in a tomb at Lachish (*Lachish III*: Pl. 44: 123). The excavators called the figure a Nereid or mermaid, but considering the parallels cited above it seems more likely that it is a Triton. The Tel Michal Triton is a product of the Greco-Phoenician school; both the material (glass) and form (scaraboid) are typically Syro-Phoenician, whereas the motif and style are Grecian. It is hardly surprising that this maritime motif was copied by the seafaring Phoenicians. The seal should be dated to the late 5th or early 4th century B.C.E.

4. *Unidentified seal*. Reg. No. 7342/80; Locus 1103 (Pl. 73:4). Scaraboid. Steatite. Measures 6 mm × 13 mm.

The design on this seal is not clear. It may possibly depict a winged scorpion. No parallels are known to us.

5. *Woman seated in front of altar* (Fig. 28.1:4; Pl. 74:1). Signet ring. Upright oval bezel. Silver. Measures 13 mm × 18 mm.

A seated female, facing right, is the main motif. In front of her but on a higher (more distant?) level is an altar (or incense burner) with flames that appears to be suspended in midair. There is no ground line, and the whole lower part of the composition slants slightly upward. The altar seems to lean to the left. The seated woman fills most of the seal area. Her proportions are much larger than those of the altar, although both are elongated and rather flat. The difference in size and location between the woman and the altar is striking but not uncommon. By depicting the altar at a higher level, the artist brought the woman's hand almost directly above the flames, thus emphasizing her cultic action.

The woman is seated on a carved stool with slightly curved legs. Her head and legs are shown in right profile, her body frontally. Her hair is tied behind her head in a chignon, possibly with a band. A small attribute (diadem or small modius) protrudes above her forehead. She wears a small round earring and is dressed in a long garment with tight sleeves, tied at the waist. On each shoulder is a large round pin molding a mantle(?) or long garment. Her right arm is bent at the elbow in a sharp angle behind her back and her right hand touches her hips. Her left arm, also bent at the elbow, is raised toward the altar. Possibly she is holding a small object or flower in her left hand, or she may be fueling the altar or incense burner. The altar is symmetrical, with two round base lines and two round rim lines; three small flames are burning on top.

The silver ring is typically Achaemenid in form (Boardman 1970a: 322). The silver seal is an upright oval. Ring and sealing area were cast in one piece, and then the incisions were added. The result, although schematic, is very attractive. The incision is linear drill work with shallow cutting, typical of the Achaemenid technique (Boardman 1970b). There is no development of volume and no real body modeling. The dress and hair were rendered by short linear drill strokes, the folds of the garment and the leg protruding from the "skirt" by different parallel linear angles, and the arms, seat, and altar by longer, thinner drill strokes. The decoration on the legs of the stool was executed with shorter and deeper strokes. The effect is flat and decorative.

Similar seals and signet rings of Greek origin and style were found throughout the Persian empire (Boardman 1970a). Most of the seals from Persepolis are in this style (*Persepolis II*: 46). Particularly common on Greek signet rings is a seated woman facing a cult object. A gold ring with a round bezel of the 4th century B.C.E. (Boardman 1970a: Pl. 753) presents exactly this subject. The sitting position in front of a flaming altar, the body stance and arm position, the type of chair, garment, and headdress – all are identical. The similar design of the garment is also noteworthy. In both rings, two groups of lines comprise the upper part of the garment, another group covers the leg protruding from under the garment, and a fourth group represents the descending folds of the garment. The difference between these two ring bezels is in the level of artistic execution. The one from Tel Michal is crudely engraved, whereas the other is in the best Greek tradition – one is an original art object, the other a provincial imitation.

Other rings with scenes that resemble ours include a silver ring bezel depicting a woman dressed in a long linear garment and seated on a decorated stool in front of a flamed altar (Boardman 1970a: No. 990) and a gold ring from the Oxus treasure in Bactria with a similar seated woman but without the altar (Dalton 1964: Pl. 16:103).

In conclusion, it is clear that our signet ring belongs to the large group of so-called Greco-Persian productions (Boardman 1970a:304), or more specifically to the mixed style (Boardman 1970a:312). These rings, which are the result of the cultural encounter between Greece and Persia, date to the 5th-4th centuries B.C.E.

28a.2. BULLAE

6. *Two horses (?)* (Fig. 28.1:5; Pl. 74:2). Clay bulla. Measures 17 mm × 17 mm.

The bulla has one impression on the face. There are papyrus impressions around the sides, partly crosshatched and partly diagonal parallel lines. Tiny pieces of clay are broken off, and the bulla, which was fired, is cracked in at least one place.

Apparently this is only a partial impression of the original seal. Most likely the original shape was basically an oblong or pyramidal stamp seal. Only the right half of the original seal was impressed on the bulla, with traces of the left half.

The motif, undoubtedly a standing horse, fills most of the area, as if it was intended to be the only motif of the impression. The horse's head and body are in strict profile to the left, the body incised with a wide, shallow drill. The upper part of the horse's head is obliterated. The two engraved legs are straight and stiff. His long tail curls upward above his back and a large mane is incised on his neck and shoulders in parallel diagonal lines, the outcome of sharp, thin drill work. Except for the tail (similar to a lion's tail), which is portrayed decoratively in an arrested movement, the horse is represented without any motion. The overall result is wooden, flat, and immobile. Another small linear motif that appears behind the horse may be a device typical of Achaemenid-Lydian pyramidal stamp seals (Boardman 1970b: Fig. 3:21), or perhaps a stylized plant.

Facing the horse are the remnants of another motif, which may be an animal, a human figure, an inanimate object, or an architectural device. If an animal, only the two front legs and perhaps the lower line of the body remain. One of the legs is straight; the other crosses it. The latter is bent in the typical posture of a walking horse, with the knee and upper muscles emphasized. We could therefore assume that on the original seal another horse was incised facing the first. However, if so, the second "horse" must have been larger than the first and their stances were different. Furthermore, if a large horse was actually portrayed on the left side of the original seal, the seal must either have been wider on the left, and hence unevenly shaped, or the larger "horse" was not standing upright.

Standing horses occasionally appear on their own on Achaemenid pyramidal seals of the Court style (Boardman 1970b: No. 169) or led by a Persian guard (Boardman 1970b: No. 71). However, they are invariably portrayed with all four legs. The lack of developed volume and linear incisions occurs at times on Achaemenid seals, but the still posture of the standing horse on the Tel Michal seal is very provincial. We have not found any direct analogy to it. It is therefore best to attribute this impression to a workshop of the Achaemenid period but not to any specific region and to acknowledge the uncertain identification of the second device.

7. *Bulla with two impressions* (Pl. 74:3): (A) *Eagle holding a snake(?)* (Fig. 28.1:6a); (B) *Nursing mare or cow* (Fig. 28.1:6b).

This is a two-sided "gabled" clay bulla with a flat base (17 mm × 22 mm). A different impression appears on each side. Imprints of a papyrus sheet and the tying strand are also visible, as well as the fingerprints of the person who stamped the impression. The bulla is chipped on the lower part of side A and worn out on the lower part of side B. The bulla was fired at some stage, which helped to preserve it.

It is impossible to determine whether the two impressions were made from two different seals (probably scarabs or scaraboids) or from two sides of a single multifaced seal incised with two or more independent motifs (Zwierlein-Diehl 1969: Nos. 125, 126, "Cypriote").

Both seal impressions are of animals: an eagle (A) and a nursing mare or cow (B). The shape of the two impressions is similar but not identical. Impression B has a "cable" band surrounding the design. The style of the animal engravings shows a familial similarity, but they were probably executed by two different hands. The execution of the nursing animal is superior to that of the eagle. These considerations favor the assumption that the impressions were made by two different seals. A doubly stamped bulla was found at Wadi ed-Daliyeh near Samaria (latest date 331 B.C.E.). One impression appears to be a representation of a Persian hero, the other a female figure (Nike) dressed in Greek garments (Cross 1974:28, No. 22A, B).

Side A: Eagle Holding a Snake(?)

The impression of the eagle on the bulla is partly worn out and probably incomplete. The upper left side is missing. The eagle is on the upper half of the impression, apparently in the sky; the lower part is empty. It is possible to make out the basic shape of the original seal, which was probably a horizontal oval. The deep impression in clay on the upper right side of this face of the bulla is also probably the original edge of the seal area. The eagle is depicted frontally, its wings spread symmetrically on both sides of its body and the tail in profile under the right wing. Very little is left of the head but it was probably turned to the left. In front of the bird's body, both talons hold (or catch) a snake(?) shaped like a long, thin rope. There is no ornamental band visible around the edge. The original seal engraving was done with thin and thick drills.

The basic shape of the bird was probably engraved with a wide cylindrical drill, the details with a thin wheel drill. The bird is portrayed with some volume and the overall design has a simple, balanced effect. However, the details of the bird's body (and talons) are schematic and symmetrical.

An eagle devouring a snake appears on some Greco-Phoenician gems from the second half of the 6th century B.C.E. and probably slightly later (Zwierlein-Diehl 1969:66, No. 138, with parallels). Two birds tearing an antelope are seen on Achaemenid pyramidal seals of the Orientalizing type (Boardman 1970b: Figs. 60–65). We have not found an exact parallel to the eagle from Tel Michal. However, as the above examples indicate, the subject was known in the 6th-5th centuries both in mainland Greece and western Anatolia (before and during the

Achaemenid Empire). The Tel Michal impression may be a crude provincial work from the same period.

Side B: Nursing Mare or Cow

The impression of the nursing mare or cow is clear, although the hindquarters of the larger animal are blurred. The bottom part of the impression is chipped off. The lower part of the original seal (scarab?) was probably not a clearly defined geometric shape, but more likely a squarish horizontal oval with rounded edges. Such irregularly shaped seals are typical of 6th-century "Greco-Phoenician" scarabs (usually of green jasper) (Zwierlein-Diehl 1969: Nos. 132, 135–136, 143–144; Boardman 1970a: Nos. 415–416). The base of these scarabs is always surrounded by an ornamental band. Traces of a continuous ornamental border, either crosshatched or the typical "cable," can be seen around the inner rim of our seal impression. Single human beings or animals surrounded by an ornamental band of this type are the most common motifs depicted on Orientalizing (7th century) and Archaic (including Greco-Phoenician) gems of the 6th-5th centuries and of the Classical period (Zwierlein-Diehl 1969: No. 168; Maaskant-Kleibrink 1978).

The nursing mare or cow and her young are portrayed standing in profile on a ground line, facing different directions. It is not entirely clear whether the animals are a cow nursing her calf or a mare nursing her foal. The calf/foal is schematically represented, the thin body in profile to the left, the head raised, and the calf/foal suckling. It seems to have a long bushy tail more typical of a horse than a cow. The figure of the nursing mother is excellent, and her realistic stance is both loving and tender.

The body of the nursing mother is portrayed in almost one continuous volume with slight variations of depth. The neck was engraved in a similar way with details incised on it. These basic large, round shapes were probably made with a wide cylindrical or disk-shaped drill with rounded edges. Details like the mane, the mother's legs, and the foal/calf were incised with thinner drills. The sure sense of volume indicates that this seal is not earlier than the 6th century. The minimal nondecorative and realistic details place it more probably in the early 5th century.

An animal nursing its young was a widespread motif in the art of the ancient world (Keel 1980). During the second half of the 1st millennium, it became even more common in glyptic art. Cows were the dominant subject until the middle of the 1st millennium and continued to be popular in later glyptic art, although a wider variety occurs: female deer and wolves, female sheep and goats, lionesses and mares (Zwierlein-Diehl 1969: No. 141, second half of 6th century; Nos. 167–168, 5th century, with many parallels).

Although nursing mares are not very common, the figure of the nursing mother on the Tel Michal bulla is probably a mare. The quite realistic depiction emphasizes the muscles and is true to the figure of a real horse down to the anatomic details: the elongated face (even including the teeth), the emphasized muzzle, and the large nostril that can be closed to keep out dust. The long flexible neck,

337

capable of stretching in various directions, is also clear (Groves 1974: 25–26). The mare is stretching her head backward in a typical manner so that the lower jaw is turned upward. Delicate lines representing the mane may be discerned on the neck, although they may possibly be interpreted as cow's horns. However, in most cow depictions the horns are much emphasized (Keel 1980:141), whereas here it seems that they are not horns at all since they are too small and straight to be cow's horns, which are usually depicted in two large curves. Although similar straight and back-pointed horns are at times portrayed on goats, the shape of our animal is obviously not that of a goat. The nursing animal's impression on the Tel Michal bulla was made by a Greco-Phoenician stone (most probably a blue or green jasper scarab) of the late 6th or early 5th century B.C.E.

As the above discussion has shown, the two impressions on this bulla date from the same period. However, stylistically they belong to two different subgroups: impression A (eagle) is most likely a provincial product of a Greco-Achaemenid workshop; impression B (nursing animal) is a Greco-Phoenician product. Therefore, the two impressions on the bulla most probably come from two independent seals, possibly impressed by two different persons. Hence the bulla might have been attached to a commercial document, sealed by each of the two interested parties.

REFERENCES

Boardman, J. 1970a. *Greek Gems and Finger Rings*. London.

Boardman, J. 1970b. Pyramidal Stamp Seals in the Persian Empire. *Iran* 8:19–45.

Boardman, J., and Vollenweider, M.-L. 1978. *Catalogue of the Engraved Gems and Finger Rings I: Greek and Etruscan*. Oxford.

Cross, F. M. 1974. The Papyri and Their Historical Implications. Pages 17–29 in: *Discoveries in the Wadi ed-Daliyeh*. P. W. Lapp and N. L. Lapp, eds. *AASOR* 41. Cambridge, Mass.

Dalton, O. M. 1964. *The Treasure of Oxus*. London.

Groves, C. P. 1974. *Horses, Asses and Zebras in the Wild*. London.

Harden, D. B. 1962. *The Phoenicians*. London.

Hogarth, D. G. 1920. *Hittite Seals*. Oxford.

Keel, O. 1980. *Das Böcklein in der Milch seiner Mutter und Verwandtes*. Freiburg.

Kenna, V. E. G. 1960. *Cretan Seals*. Oxford.

Maaskant-Kleibrink, M. 1978. *Catalogue of the Engraved Gems in the Royal Coin Cabinet, the Hague: The Greek, Etruscan and Roman Collections*. The Hague.

Mazar, B. 1976. En-Gedi. *Enc. Arch. Exc.* II: 370–378.

Moscati, S. 1968. *The World of the Phoenicians*. London.

Vollenweider, M.-L. 1966. *Die Steinschneidekunst und ihre Künstler in spätrepublikanischer und augusteischer Zeit*. Baden-Baden.

von der Osten, H. H. 1934. *Ancient Oriental Seals in the Collection of Mr. E. T. Newell*. Chicago.

Woolley, L. 1962. *Ur Excavations IX: The Neo-Babylonian and Persian Periods*. London.

Wright, G. E. 1962. Selected Seals from the Excavations at Balatah (Shechem). *BASOR* 167:5–13.

Zwierlein-Diehl, E. 1969. *Antike Gemmen in Deutschen Sammlungen II*. Munich.

28b

Notes on a Stamped Amphora Handle

by Diethelm Conrad

The upper part of an amphora with a stamp impression on the handle, discovered in the Persian period cemetery, was published in a preliminary report of the excavations at Tel Michal (Herzog et al. 1978:118 and n. 21; Fig. 12:120). By attributing the amphora to Cypriote Plain White ware VI, the excavators were able to date it to 475–400 B.C.E. The impression on the handle was referred to as a "schematic figure" but was not discussed—mainly because such an impression was hardly known at the time.

The impression (Fig. 28.2; Pl. 74:4), which was made by a stamp 22 mm high and 13 mm wide, has the shape of a slightly rounded rectangle. Three superimposed Greek capital letters are incised, almost filling the complete height of the rectangle. These letters are ligatured to each other, forming a monogram. It seems that they should be read as ΥΦΔ from top to bottom or ΔΦΥ from bottom to top. The stamp is impressed so that the upsilon points to the neck of the amphora.

At the time this stamped handle was found, the only similar impression known in the literature came from the 1973–74 excavations at the Kerameikos in Athens (Knigge 1975:456, Fig. 4). According to the archaeological context, this stamp impression can be dated before 440–436 B.C.E., corresponding very well with the date of the Tel Michal impression. The monogram of the Kerameikos impression has the same reading: upsilon-phi-delta or delta-phi-upsilon. However, the stamp is impressed in the opposite direction, with the delta pointing to the neck. Moreover, the stamp is more rounded at its base and straighter at the top. Additionally, either a small decorated band is incised at the top, or the stamp is not neatly pressed into the clay here. So even though the two impressions are very similar in shape and depict the same monogram, it is obvious that they were made by two different stamps.

The third example of a similar monogram impression, published in 1980, was found at Khirbet Kinniyeh near Tell Keisan (*Tell Keisan*: 253, No. 105, Pl. 87:90a, KK38).[1] Although most of the finds at Khirbet Kinniyeh date from the 4th century B.C.E., the stamp impression should be dated to the 5th century, since it is the same type

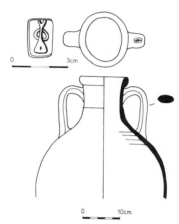

Figure 28.2. Amphora with stamped handle.

and very similar to both impressions mentioned above. However, as the drawing of the impression shows (*Tell Keisan*: 253, No. 105, Pl. 87:90a), the third lowest letter of the Khirbet Kinniyeh monogram is without any doubt an alpha, and not a delta. A check of the stamped handle confirmed this reading.

During the excavations conducted at Tel Akko since 1973, five more stamped handles were found, all of them bearing the monogram upsilon-phi-alpha or alpha-phi-upsilon (Pl. 74:5–8).[2] This supports the reading of the alpha on the Khirbet Kinniyeh impression and seems to indicate that this is actually the correct reading. We may therefore assume that the deltas of the examples from Tel Michal and the Kerameikos are badly incised alphas. It should be noted that the five impressions from Tel Akko were also made by different stamps.

So far, the meaning of the monogram is still unknown. The same applies to the place of origin of the Tel Michal amphora. The petrographic analysis (Chap. 24c: Sample 3) suggested an origin in "the Greek islands, Greece itself, or

Cyprus." As noted above, the excavators attributed this amphora to Cypriote Plain White ware VI (475–400 B.C.E.). On the one hand, this 5th-century date is corroborated by the context in which the Tel Michal amphora was found (i.e., the Persian period cemetery) and also by stratified finds of similar amphorae along the coast of Israel (e.g., at Tell Abu Hawam Stratum II, Atlit Tomb L35b; for additional examples, see *Tell Keisan*: 128, n. 35). On the other hand, no Cypriote example as drawn by Gjerstad (*SCE IV, 2*) fits our amphora completely; possible similarities in details range from Plain White V to VII wares.[3] Moreover, the attribution of the amphora to Cypriote Plain White ware does not necessarily mean that the Tel Michal amphora originated in Cyprus. Gjerstad has pointed out that the Plain White V amphorae are a purely Greek type and that those of Types VI-VII are also similar to the contemporary Greek amphorae of the 5th and 4th centuries (*SCE IV, 2*: 307). And, indeed, Grace (1971:75 f., Fig. 3) describes amphorae very similar to ours, also of the 5th century B.C.E., as possible "Samian amphoras," although this provenance is not at all certain.

The seven stamp impressions found in Israel were submitted to neutron activation analysis to determine whether the vessels bearing these impressions were made of the same clay—i.e., produced in the same place. The results will soon be published elsewhere. However, even without these results, there are strong arguments that all the amphorae bearing this particular monogram originated in the same locale. There are reasons to suppose that this could be somewhere in the eastern Aegean or the nearby mainland of western Anatolia. So far, however, all attempts have failed to connect these amphorae with a specific town from which they were exported (with wine?) to various parts of the Mediterranean.

To summarize, the Tel Michal amphora and all the others bearing the monogram impression upsilon-phi-alpha or alpha-phi-upsilon, whose meaning is unknown, can be dated with certainty to the middle of the 5th century B.C.E., but their place of origin is still unknown.[4]

NOTES

1. According to Grace (1971: n. 105), there are additional unpublished examples of monogram stamps of this type that were found in Egypt and in the region of the Black Sea.

2. I am indebted to Dr. Avner Raban, University of Haifa, for his advice and for permission to publish here photographs of the five impressions from Tel Akko.

3. For the best example of the rim, see *SCE IV, 2*: Pl. LVIII:24 (Plain White V); of the collar, *SCE IV, 2*: Pl. LXIII:11 (Plain White VI); and of the neck with collar, *SCE IV, 2*: Pl. LXIX:5 (Plain White VII).

4. For a discussion on the amphora, see Chap. 9.5 and Pl. 64:8.

REFERENCES

Grace, V. R. 1971. Samian Amphoras. *Hesperia* 40:52–95.

Herzog, Z., Negbi, O., and Moshkovitz, S. 1978. Excavations at Tel Michal, 1977. *Tel Aviv* 5:99–130.

Knigge, U. 1975. Kerameikos. Tataigkeitsbericht 1973/74. Archäologischer Anzeiger. *Beiblatt zum Jahrbuch des Deutschen Archäologischen Instituts* 90:456–468.

29

Egyptian Artifacts

by Raphael Giveon

The Egyptian finds from Tel Michal include a bulla with a seal impression of the Twelfth Dynasty; a relatively large group of Hyksos scarabs (none of which was found in a Middle Bronze Age II context); some New Kingdom objects, including a rare statuette of Mut; and a few Horus eyes.

29.1. HEAD OF MUT STATUETTE
(Fig. 29.1:1; Pl. 75:1)

What remains of this statuette is the upper part of the figurine, consisting of the head of a young woman with heavy locks descending to her neck, leaving her ears uncovered. She wears the double crown of Upper and Lower Egypt. On the back is a hieroglyphic inscription that reads: *dd mdw in Mwt*, "Words spoken by Mut."

An anepigraphic Mut statuette was found at Beth-shan (Rowe 1936:271, No. A21), and what may be an aegis of Mut turned up in the excavations at Gezer (Rowe 1936:272, No. A22). Amun, Mut, and Chons form the triad of Thebes. Mut was considered the wife of Amun, and at times she has been called the mother of Pharaoh. This, together with the play on words (*mwt* also means "mother"), may explain the use of Mut amulets by women in the hope of ensuring an easy delivery. (Regarding Mut, see also Bonnet 1952:491–494 and te Velde 1980:246–248).

29.2. HYKSOS SCARABS

This group includes one representational and four nonrepresentational types. Three of the latter are of the well-known *nbw* type, bearing the hieroglyph *nbw* ("gold") as the central design. In Egypt such scarabs are known from the Hyksos period as well as somewhat earlier.

Scarab, Representational Type
(Fig. 29.1:2; Pl. 75:2)

This scarab is slightly damaged on the left upper side of its base. Within a frame consisting of a single line there is a figure sitting on a low-backed chair, with legs shaped like an animal's (lion?) paws. The figure is wearing a long garment with shoulder straps, patterned with parallel lines; a headcloth falls to the shoulders. The left arm is lifted as if in prayer, while the right hand holds a flower. A similar seated figure (but without the flower) and an identical chair appear on a scarab found at Gezer (*Gezer III*: Pl. 202a:7).

The flower on our scarab is extraordinary in that it is bent downward. Dussaud (1949:90) has suggested that the motif of a person holding a wilted flower symbolizes the dead. Our representation may therefore be an early instance of this artistic convention. The parallel lines connecting the upright part of the stalk with the bent part are common in the Hyksos artistic tradition (Newberry 1907: Pl. 12, No. 37205). The chair stands on an *nb* ("lord") sign, and below the flower appears the sign *'nḫ* ("life").

The back of the scarab lacks a division between the prothorax and elythra, and instead there are two small triangular notches. The back is decorated with two beautifully executed crossed branches.

Scarab, nbw Type (Fig. 29.1:3; Pl. 75:3)

On each side of the *nbw* sign appears the sign *nfr* ("beautiful, good"), and above it is the sequence of hieroglyphs

r-n-'-ḫ', which make no sense. This is a variation of the 'Anra type of Hyksos scarabs, 'Anra being a fictitious royal

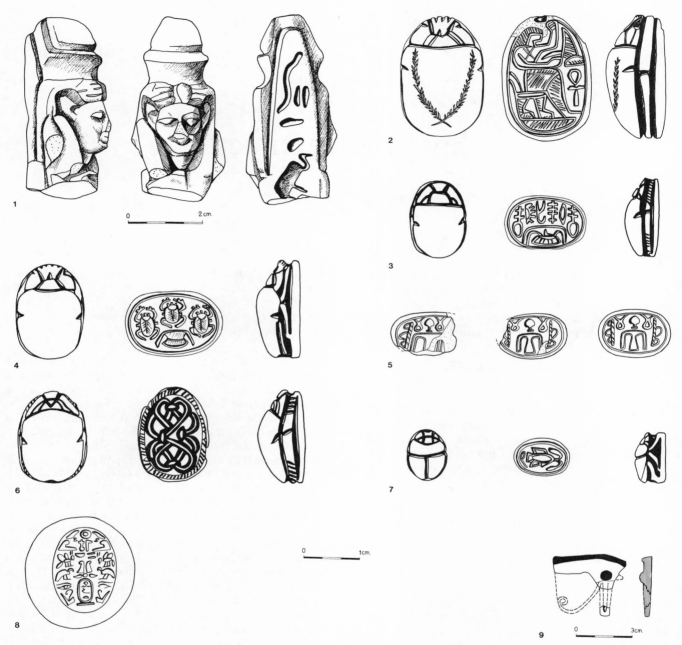

Figure 29.1. Egyptian artifacts.

Legend for Fig. 29.1

No.	Type	Reg. No.	Locus	Stratum	Material	Pl.
1	Head of Mut	25/80	2	Unstratified	Faience	75:1
2	Scarab	9809/80	965	XVI/XV	Steatite	75:2
3	Scarab	9801/80	983	XVI/XV	Steatite	75:3
4	Scarab	5787/80	882	XVI	Steatite	75:4
5	Seal impression	12/1	1	Unstratified	Clay	75:5
6	Scarab	10722/80	1702	XV	Steatite	75:6
7	Scarab	10449/80	1653	XV	Steatite	75:7
8	Bulla	15/1	1	Unstratified	Clay	75:8
9	Horus eye	11630/80	1858	XI/VI	Faience	75:9

name. Many such scarabs have been found in Egypt (van Seters 1966:64) and in Israel (Rowe 1936: Pl. 6, No. 222); the latter type is very similar but has *ʿnḫ* signs instead of *nfr* signs flanking the *nbw*.

Scarab, nbw Type (Fig. 29.1:4; Pl. 75:4)

This scarab is of the same type, with a similar back. The design, more simply drawn, consists of an *nbw* sign with three scarabs, one above and one at each side. No parallels are known to us.

Scarab Seal Impression, nbw Type (Fig. 29.1:5; Pl. 75:5)

This impression, also of the *nbw* type scarab, appears twice on the same fragment of pottery. Both impressions have lacunae, but the original design can be restored from a combination of the two. The center of the design is filled by a very tall *nbw* sign, flanked by the red crowns of Lower Egypt. The other three hieroglyphs on this impression are upside down; in the center there is a handleless pot, which undoubtedly represents the similar sign for *ib* ("heart"). The whole group should perhaps be interpreted as "Heart (wish, will) of his majesty."

Scarab, Rope Frame Type (Fig. 29.1:6; Pl. 75:6)

The carving of the back and base of this scarab is typical of the Hyksos period. Within a frame of rope design, there is an elaborate cord pattern. For parallels, see Rowe 1936: Pl. 3, Nos. 82, 88; Petrie 1925: Pl. 8, Nos. 145, 146.

29.3. NEW KINGDOM SCARAB
(Fig. 29.1:7; Pl. 75:7)

This shows a fish (tilapia) holding a plant in its mouth; behind its tail is a lotus bud. The tilapia symbolized regeneration to the Egyptians, who erroneously believed (since this fish is a mouth breeder) that its young were born in the mouth "ready-made," as a self-generation and continuation of life. The lotus also has the symbolic value of regeneration, and its appearance here reinforces the image and magic efficacy of the scarab as an amulet. The lotus bud, which has the phonetic value *nhm* ("to save"), is not infrequent in scarab designs.

For the symbolic value of tilapia, see Hornung et al. 1976:110–111; for parallels, see Hornung et al. 1976:375, No. B17, and Rowe 1936: Pl. XV:597.

29.4. BULLA OF AMENEMHAT III
(Fig. 29.1:8; Pl. 75:8)

The bulla bears the name of Amenemhat III, preceded by epithets and with *nfr* signs at both sides:

over the cartouche:

the cartouche:

both sides:

The sign at the top is the sun disk *re'*; below follows *ntr nfr* ("good god") as a royal epithet, and below this *nb t3.wy* ("lord of the two lands") but with an inversion showing the *nb* ("lord") sign after the signs for the two lands. Then comes the cartouche crowned by two Maat feathers. The cartouche has the fourth name of Amen-em-hat, *n-m3't-r'*.

At the side the following appears: above, flanking the sun disk, there are two falcons, representing Horus, the sky god, then *h3t* ("foremost"), then the bee as the symbol of Lower Egypt; the vulture that follows signifies in this context not Mut but the goddess Nekhbet, protectress of the king. Then follows the *wd3t* eye and the red crown of Lower Egypt. Although this grouping of signs does not yield any sense if read in sequence, all the signs have some relevance in context with the king represented in the center. This grouping of signs is typical of the Hyksos period, but there are some royal scarabs of the Twelfth Dynasty that show the same features. One example is a scarab of Amenemhat III (Hall 1913:14, No. 141), which has the Horus bird, *wd3t*, *h3t*, the red crown, and *nb t3.wy* as epithets over the cartouche. Another object of the same kind from the Ashmolean Museum (Newberry 1905: Pl. 9:26) has similar signs with the vulture depicted upside down. This seal impression from Tel Michal should therefore be added to the royal documents of the Twelfth Dynasty found in Israel (Giveon 1978:79).[1]

29.5. HORUS EYE (Fig. 29.1.9; Pl. 75:9)

This faience object (which has been partially restored) was found in a tomb of the Persian period. What remains is the eyebrow, in the form of an elegantly curved brown line. The white of the eye is represented by greenish material and the eyeball by a relatively small brownish circle. The eye representation, which was the most common type of amulet in Egypt, is often found in Israel. It symbolizes the eye of Horus, the sky god, in his form as a falcon. Horus's eye was damaged in a fight with Seth and completely replaced by Thot. The falcon eye as an amulet is therefore called *wd3t*, ("the whole one"), its magic propensities being obvious from its name.

Two additional Horus eye amulets, both mother-of-pearl (one complete and one broken), were found in the Persian period cemetery of Tel Michal and are published together with the beads (See Chap. 34.2: Nos. 129, 232).

NOTE

1. This bulla has been published previously with a different interpretation (Schulman 1978:148–151).

REFERENCES

Bonnet, H. 1952. *Reallexikon der ägyptischen Religionsgeschichte*. Berlin.

Dussaud, R. 1949. *L'art phénicien du IIᵉ millénaire*. Paris.

Giveon, R. 1978. *The Impact of Egypt on Canaan*. Freiburg.

Hall, H. R. 1913. *A Catalogue of Egyptian Scarabs, etc., in the British Museum*. Vol. I: *Royal Scarabs*. London.

Hornung, E., et al. 1976. *Skarabäen und andere Siegelamulette aus Basler Sammlungen*. Basel.

Newberry, P. E. 1905. *Scarabs*. London.

Newberry, P. E. 1907. *Scarab-shaped Seals*. Catalogue général du musée du Caire. London.

Petrie, W. M. F. 1925. *Buttons and Design Scarabs*. London.

Rowe, A. 1936. *A Catalogue of Egyptian Scarabs, Scaraboids, Seals and Amulets in the Palestine Archaeological Museum*. Cairo.

Schulman, A. 1978. Two Scarab Impressions from Tel Michal. *Tel Aviv* 5:148–151.

te Velde, H. 1980. Mut. Pages 246–248 in: *Lexikon der Ägyptologie IV*. Wiesbaden.

van Seters, J. 1966. *The Hyksos*. New Haven, Conn.

30

Calcite-Alabaster Vessels

by Christa Clamer

The calcite-alabaster vessels from Tel Michal originated in three periods: the Middle Bronze Age II-Late Bronze Age I, the Persian period, and the Hellenistic period. The earliest specimens are three fragmented small jars; all belong to common stone-vase types found in MB II-LB I contexts and were imported from Egypt, where they served as containers for ointments and aromatic oils.

A number of shallow bowls and fragments of alabastra date from the Persian period. These also are known as cosmetic articles and considered Egyptian in origin. However, the material, characterized by heavy banding and ranging from white/cream/pale yellow to tan/reddish brown, is often quite different from Bronze Age calcite-alabaster, which is crenulated and banded with lighter colors that vary from whitish to cream. The Persian period material apparently comes from a different quarry. The Hellenistic period is represented by two bowl fragments only.

Several fragments of alabastra were collected in fills of later strata and are dated here on a typological basis.

30.1. MIDDLE BRONZE AGE II- LATE BRONZE AGE I

1. Small, Squat, Bag-Shaped Jar (Fig. 30.1:1)

Preserved height 40 mm, maximum diameter 86 mm. Tapering sides, curving toward wide, flat base; contracted neck; chipped rim, part of base missing. The chipped rim seems to have been partially reworked in antiquity.

Small, squat, bag-shaped jars are known from Twelfth Dynasty Egypt (Petrie 1937: Pl. XXIX:605–607). They belong to the commonest class of baggy-shaped vases, introduced from Egypt during the Middle Bronze Age II (*TBM I*: 28–29, Pl. 42:1; *Jericho II*: Fig. 100:19; Oren 1973:91, Fig. 33:1–8). The squat forms in particular are comparable to the squat Cretan alabastra, and Cretan influence on Twelfth Dynasty Egyptian jars cannot be excluded (Warren 1969:4). A few crudely executed gypsum-alabaster specimens found in an MB II context indicate that they were copied by local craftsmen (*Jericho I*: Fig. 187:1; *Jericho II*: Figs. 171:9, 179:25); on this subject, see Ben-Dor 1945:101–102. Bag-shaped jars continued into the Late Bronze Age I.

2. Small Slender Jar (Fig. 30.1:2)

Height 83 mm, neck 28 mm, maximum diameter 42 mm, base 20 mm. Rounded shoulder, straight sides tapering downward to small flat base. Rim and neck missing. Interior drilled out tubularly with drill marks clearly visible. Mediocre workmanship.

A small projection at the shoulder suggests a truncated handle. The handle and upper part may have broken off in antiquity and the place of fracture smoothed. This small jar was found in a fill of Stratum IX containing mixed Late Bronze Age, Iron Age, and Persian period pottery.

Handleless jars with pronounced shoulder and straight, downward tapering sides can be traced to a long tradition in the Egyptian stone-vase repertoire. The smaller forms are well known from Middle Kingdom contexts. Calcite-alabaster specimens are also encountered in MB II-LB I Canaan (*Jericho II*: Fig. 100:18, Fig. 154:5–6, 11; Fig. 171:10) and locally produced in gypsum-alabaster copies (Ben-Dor 1945:102–103).

3. Small Slender Jar (Fig. 30.1:3)

Preserved height 64 mm, maximum diameter 40 mm. Rounded shoulder, sides tapering downward; rim/neck and base missing. Fine workmanship.

It is possible that the rim and neck, now missing, were worked separately and inserted into the body. This fragment was found in the fill of the Late Bronze Age I ramparts.

30.2. PERSIAN PERIOD

Following what Petrie (1937:14) referred to as a "remarka-

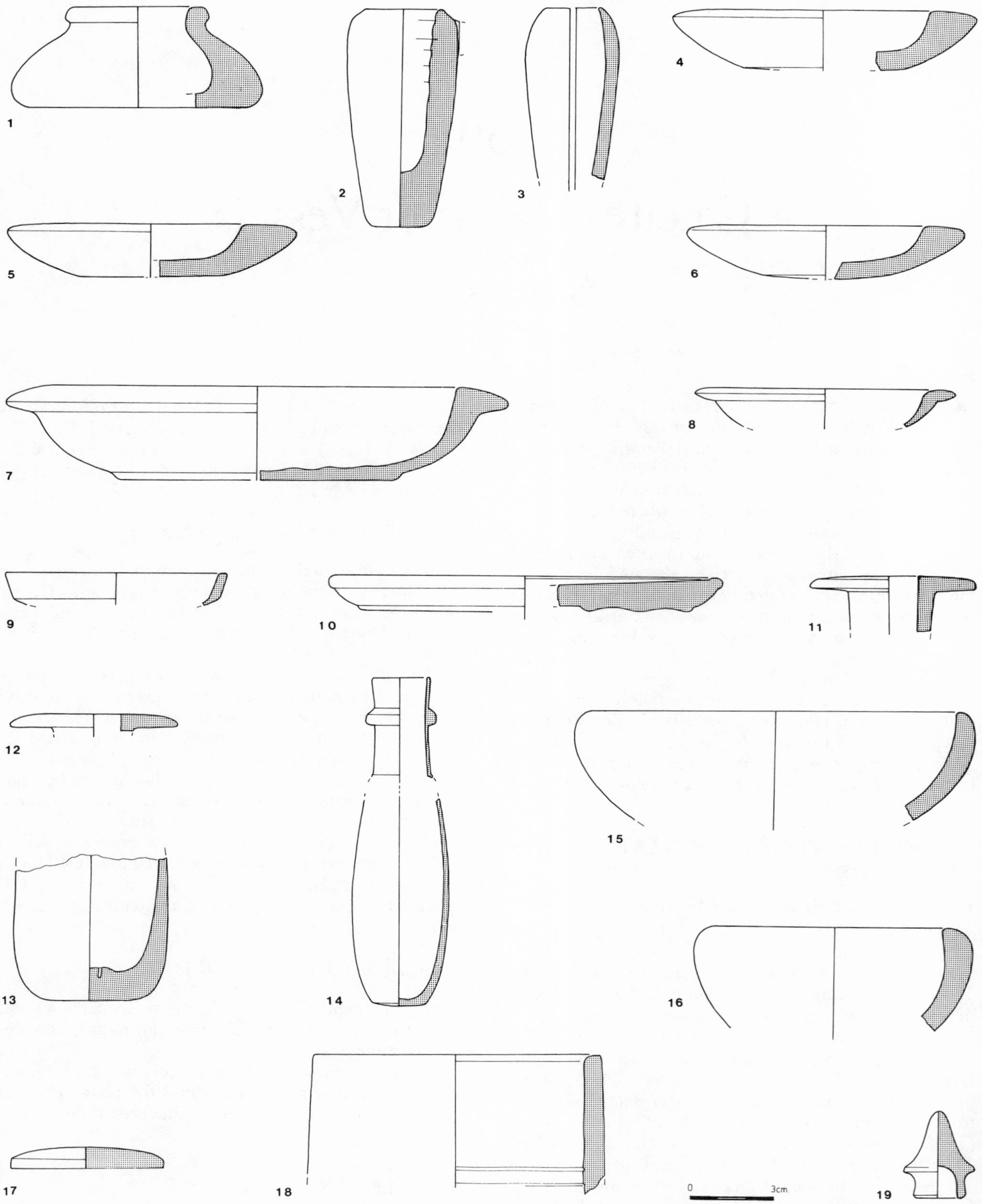

Figure 30.1. Calcite-alabaster vessels.

Legend for Fig. 30.1

No.	Type	Reg. No.	Locus	Stratum	Description
1	Jar	1755/50	317	VI	Crenulated, translucent, cream/white; polished (partly encrusted).
2	Jar	6435a/50	421	IX	Banded, crenulated, cream/brownish (surface weathered).
3	Jar	9795/50	1562	XVI	Crenulated, translucent, white; polished.
4	Bowl	11091/50	1776	VI	Heavily banded, glossy cream/white/tan, brownish inclusions; polished (slightly encrusted).
5	Bowl	5471/50	722	VII	Heavily banded, crenulated, translucent, cream/white/tan; slightly polished.
		6038/50	907	II	
6	Bowl	6240/50	935	IIIa	Heavily banded, translucent, pale cream/whitish/tan/reddish brown; polished (slightly encrusted).
7	Bowl	2449/50	405	VIII	Banded, crenulated, cream/tan; polished.
8	Bowl	6020/50	904	I	Mottled, banded, translucent, pale yellow/tan/reddish brown; polished.
9	Bowl	9815/50	988	IX	Heavily banded, translucent, glossy white/cream/tan; polished.
10	Plate	4060/50	551	V–IV	Heavily banded, white/pale cream; polished.
11	Alabastron	10214/50	1631	IX	Banded, translucent, white/pale cream; polished.
12	Alabastron	511/50	89	VIII	Banded, translucent, white/pale cream.
13	Alabastron	1745/50	317	VI	Banded, translucent, whitish/gray; polished.
14	Alabastron	1739/50	1881	XI/VI	Banded, crenulated (with inclusions), translucent, cream/pale yellow; polished.
15	Bowl	554/50	405	VIII	Banded, crenulated, translucent, glossy, white/cream; polished.
16	Bowl	4164/50	585	V	Banded, crystalline, translucent, white/cream; polished.
17	Lid	1715/50	317	VI	Banded, crenulated, cream/tan; slightly encrusted, chipped.
18	Neck fragment	424/50	66	II	Crenulated, translucent, cream/white.
19	Yoke terminal	10390/51	1631	IX	Calcite-alabaster (?), creamy, dense; polished.

ble absence of stone vases after the Ramesside times," Egyptian production and export revived after the Persian conquest. However, the repertoire remained limited. There were two main articles of calcite-alabaster that enjoyed great popularity throughout the Near East: the small bowl and the elongated alabastron. At Tel Michal, the bowl appears in three versions: (A) with a broad flat rim, (B) with a ledge or flanged rim, and (C) with carinated walls. Alabastra are represented by two types: (A) with a wide ledge or flanged rim and (B) with a plain rim and a bulging ridge on the neck. Except for Nos. 6, 8, and 10, these vessels all came from Persian period strata. Fragment No. 5 is composed of two pieces that join together, one from a Persian period stratum and the other from a Roman period stratum.

4. Shallow Bowl, Type A (Fig. 30.1:4)

Height 22 mm, maximum diameter 108 mm. Broad flat rim, sides tapering downward, flattened base; part of base missing. Fine workmanship.

5. Shallow Bowl, Type A (Fig. 30.1:5)

Height 22 mm, maximum diameter 108 mm. Broad flat rim, rounded sides, flattened base. Profile preserved.

6. Shallow Bowl, Type A (Fig. 30.1:6)

Height 21 mm, maximum diameter 101 mm. Broad flat rim, sides tapering down, flattened base; part of base missing.

Although the fragment is typologically of the Persian period, it was found in a Stratum IIIa (Late Hasmonean) robbers' trench.

In addition to this specimen, there are two unpublished bowls of the same type that came from the 1961 excavations at Tel Michal, now on permanent exhibition in the Israel Museum in Jerusalem. Similar to each other in size and shape, the bowls (Type A) have many parallels – e.g., from the Residency at Tel Lachish (Lachish III: Pls. 57:49, 64:2–3), from Samaria (Samaria 1924: 334, Fig. 206, Type 7d), Meqabelein (Stern 1982: Fig. 252), and Deve Hüyük (Moorey 1980: Fig. 8:145). All examples date to the 6th-5th centuries B.C.E.

7. Shallow Bowl, Type B (Fig. 30.1:7)

Height 35 mm, maximum diameter 172 mm, base 95 mm. Flat-topped flanged rim, rounded sides, disk base; part of base missing. Lathe-cut grooves on interior bottom of bowl. Fine workmanship.

Wheel grooving is also found on the footed plate (No. 10 below) and on pottery bowls (e.g., Samaria 1924: 174:52).

8. Shallow Bowl, Type B (Fig. 30.1:8)

Preserved height 15 mm, maximum diameter 94 mm. Flat-topped flanged rim, rounded sides, base missing. Fine workmanship.

Although retrieved from a Stratum I fill, this bowl must have originated in a Persian period stratum. It is comparable to the royal tableware from Persepolis (Persepolis II: Pl. 61:5-7) and to calcite-alabaster bowls from Samaria (Samaria 1924: 334, Fig. 206, Type 7c) and from Neirab in

Syria (Carrière and Barrois 1927: Pl. 53A:S141). It was also found in a burial cave in the Hinnom Valley in Jerusalem, excavated by G. Barkay (personal communication) and dated to the 6th-5th centuries B.C.E.

9. Carinated Bowl, Type C (Fig. 30.1:9)

Preserved height 12 mm, maximum diameter 80 mm. Narrow flat-topped rim; short, straight sides; carinated at bottom. Base missing. Fine workmanship.

10. Shallow (Footed?) Plate
(Fig. 30.1:10)

Preserved height 13 mm, maximum diameter 145 mm. Very shallow; bead rim; low, tapering sides; interior slopes slightly toward center of plate; three concentric wheel-cut

This very shallow plate is a rare shape in the stone vessel repertoire. Although found on the treading floor of the Hellenistic winepress, it seems to belong to a class of footed stone plates found among the Achaemenian tableware in the Treasury at Persepolis. Here, the foot is either splayed, high or low, or a pedestal with a ring base (*Persepolis II*: Pls. 57–58). The concentric grooves on the underside of the plate are also unusual. Two Achaemenian stone trays at Persepolis also have this feature (*Persepolis II*: Pl. 64:4, 6).

11. Alabastron, Type A (Fig. 30.1:11)

Preserved height 5 mm, rim 61 mm, neck 30 mm, mouth 20 mm. Wide flat-topped ledge rim, narrow tubular neck; body and base missing. Fine workmanship.

This rim-and-neck fragment seems to belong to a large alabastron similar to No. 12 below (cf. *Samaria 1924*: 333, Fig. 204:3a).

12. Alabastron, Type A (Fig. 30.1:12)

Preserved height 5 mm, rim 60 mm, mouth 20 mm (rim fragment only). This broad, flanged rim, slightly convex on top, is a typical alabastron shape; cf. Deve Hüyük (Moorey 1980: Fig. 8:124).

13. Alabastron, Type A (Fig. 30.1:13)

Preserved height 53 mm, maximum diameter 55 mm (lower body and base fragment only). Straight sides, tapering slightly upward, curving downward into a flattened base. Inside, center: groove from drilling the cylindrical core. Fine workmanship.

Similar alabastra with an almost cylindrical body and a flattened base come from Samaria (*Samaria 1924*: 33, Fig. 204:1a), from the Persian period tombs at Gezer (*Gezer I*: Figs. 152:2, 157:22), and from 'Ain 'Arrub (Stern 1982:79, Fig. 95). They date to the 5th century B.C.E. (Stern 1982:75, 79). Type A alabastra are fairly common in the Near East from the 6th to 4th centuries B.C.E. (For their distribution, see Stern 1982:149, n. 20; for fundamental

studies on alabastra, see von Bissing 1939:131–178; Moorey 1980:47–49.)

Shape and size vary considerably, the earlier specimens being more baggy shaped with rounded base, whereas the later ones are ovoid to elongated-narrow with convex to flattened base. They usually have two small knob handles at the upper part of the body. The necks of the earlier specimens are flaring, the later ones tubular, both types with wide, flanged rim (Petrie 1937: Pl. XXXVII:948–971). Alabastra were containers for spices or perfumed oils, which were apparently measured in fixed quantities; alabastra from Persepolis bore incised inscriptions indicating measured quantities (*Persepolis II*: 149). They were also copied in glass, as, for example, at Hazor (Stern 1982:149) and in pottery, as, for example, at Meqabelein (Stern 1982:125, Fig. 196).

14. Alabastron, Type B (Fig. 30.1:14)

Preserved height of body/base fragment 78 mm, of rim/neck fragment 37 mm, rim 21 mm, neck 19 mm, maximum diameter 35 mm, base diameter 18 mm. Plain rim; tubular, slightly concave neck with projecting ridge; elongated, slightly ovoid body; flattened base. Connecting link between neck and body missing. Fine workmanship.

This ridged-neck alabastron comes from a Persian period tomb. The ridge may have been intended to support a tubular lid (*Persepolis II*: Pl. 65:6) or to tie down a lid, plug, or cloth over the opening. A similar alabastron with flanged neck was found in the Hinnom Valley burial cave in Jerusalem of the 6th-5th centuries B.C.E. (G. Barkay, personal communication). Petrie (1937:15, Pl. XXVIII:993–995) dated this type of alabastron to the 1st century C.E. by analogy with a specimen from Mazghuneh in Egypt. Usually it seems to be handleless, but there are two specimens from Persepolis with a projecting ridge on a short, flaring neck and two vertical knob handles in the shape of degenerated duck-head handles. The two bottles were perhaps part of a composite vessel, inscribed with the name of Amasis of the 26th Dynasty (*Persepolis II*: 83, 90, Pls. 47:7a-b, 48:8b). They may therefore be an earlier version of our Type B.

Type B alabastra are encountered less frequently than those of Type A. The ridged neck, however, is found on clay copies of alabastra, as well as on Bes pitchers (Woolley 1914–16: Pls. XXVII:6–7).

30.3. HELLENISTIC PERIOD

15. Rounded Bowl (Fig. 30.1:15)

Preserved height 43 mm, maximum diameter 148 mm. Plain, slightly inverted rim; curved sides; base missing. The fragment was found in the fill above a Stratum VIII floor.

16. Rounded Bowl (Fig. 30.1:16)

Preserved height 30 mm, maximum diameter 100 mm. Plain, inverted rim; curving sides. Base missing.

For comparisons in stone, see Petrie 1937: Pl. XXXVIII:990, 991; *Samaria 1924*: 336, Fig. 209:5a (limestone). The shape is very common in the pottery of the Hellenistic period.

30.4. MISCELLANEOUS FRAGMENTS

17. Lid (Fig. 30.1:17)

Height 7 mm, maximum diameter 56 mm. Slightly convex top, lower side flat.

18. Neck Fragment (Fig. 30.1:18)

Preserved height 52 mm, maximum diameter 104 mm. Plain rim, straight side; two incised lines at bottom of segment.

This neck fragment may be a segment of a composite jar inserted into the shoulder (see *Kush V*: 30, Fig. 21: W609a).

19. Yoke Terminal (Fig. 30.1:19)

Yoke terminals belong to the chariot fittings of the Late Bronze Age. The Tel Michal specimen is Type B2 of James's classification (1978:103–115, Fig. 1:3). Yoke terminals are often referred to as stoppers (*Lachish IV*: 86, Pl. 26:44); perhaps they fulfilled this function in secondary use. Interestingly enough, Item 19 fits perfectly into the neck of Jar 2 above.

REFERENCES

Ben-Dor, I. 1945. Palestinian Alabaster Vases. *QDAP* 11:93–112.

Carrière, B., and Barrois, A. 1927. Fouilles de l'Ecole Archéologique Francaise de Jérusalem éffectuées à Neirab du 24 septembre au 5 novembre 1926. *Syria* 8:126–142; 201–212.

James, F. 1978. Chariot Fittings from Late Bronze Age Beth Shan. Pages 102–115 in: *Archaeology in the Levant*. P. Moorey and P. Parr, eds. Warminster.

Moorey, P. R. S. 1980. *Cemeteries of the First Millennium B.C. at Deve Hüyük, near Carchemish*. British Archaeological Reports International Series 87. Oxford.

Oren, E. D. 1973. *The Northern Cemetery of Beth Shan*. Leiden.

Petrie, W. 1937. *The Funeral Furniture of Egypt and Stone and Metal Vases*.

Stern, E. 1982. *Material Culture of the Land of the Bible in the Persian Period, 538–332 B.C.E.* Warminster.

von Bissing, F. W. 1939. Studien zur ältesten Kultur Italiens IV. Alabastra. *Studi Etruschi* 13:131–178.

Warren, P. 1969. *Minoan Stone Vases*. Cambridge.

Woolley, C. L. 1914–16. A North Syrian Cemetery of the Persian Period. *AAA* 7:115–129.

31

Stone and Clay Objects

by Lily Singer-Avitz

31.1. MORTARS

The mortar-and-pestle, already known in the Natufian period, is apparently the earliest implement for pounding or grinding cereals (Amiran 1956:47). At Tel Michal there were two types of mortars, one limestone, the other basalt.

Limestone Mortars (Fig. 31.1:1–7; Pl. 76:1–2)

This type is either V-shaped in section with a flat base or has curved walls and a rounded bottom. It appears at Tel Michal in Iron Age and Persian period strata. Mortars of similar shape but made of basalt were found in Area A, Stratum XB, at Hazor (*Hazor III-IV*: Pl. CLXXIII:11–12) and at Megiddo Stratum II (*Megiddo I*: Pl. 112:8).

Basalt Mortars (Fig. 31.2:1–7; Pl. 76:3)

These are shallow bowls with three legs carved in one piece with the body (Avitsur 1976:71). Amiran calls them tripod mortars (*Hazor I*: 43, Pl. LXXIII:11; 1958:117). At Tel Michal they were found in Iron Age, Persian, and Roman period contexts. A leg from one of these bowls (Fig. 31.2:6) has an incised base resembling an animal's paw, perhaps a lion's. Legs carved as animal paws or hooves were a common Assyrian decoration that appears on a wide variety of furniture and stands (Amiran 1958:117).

The small basalt mortar with two lug handles and very thick walls (Fig. 31.2:8; Pl. 77:1) has an unusual shape. Similar mortars of various sizes have been found in Egypt made of alabaster (von Bissing 1904: Pl. IV:18248, 7.5 cm high) or from what the author calls "black diorite" (von Bissing 1904: Pl. IV:18736, 45 cm high). Both are attributed to the *Spätzeit*, and are apparently from the Persian period.

31.2. MILLSTONES

Millstones were also used for grinding cereals, but they uti-lize the crushing principle better and were probably used to prepare larger quantities. Two types were found at Tel Michal: quernstones and frame millstones.

Quernstones

These come in pairs, usually elongated ovals (Pl. 76:7). The lower quern is flat on top (sometimes slightly concave); the upper quern, somewhat smaller, flat on the bottom and rounded on top, is used to crush the grain against the larger stone. These grinding stones first appeared in Pre-Pottery Neolithic cultures (e.g., Jericho, Jarmo) and continued throughout the ages with no technological improvements (Amiran 1956:46–49).

At Tel Michal, 47 quern fragments were found. The materials used were *kurkar*, basalt, limestone, and beach-rock, randomly distributed throughout all the strata of the site; it is probably only by chance that there were no basalt querns in the MB IIB or Iron Age strata and that beachrock did not appear before the Persian period.

Frame Millstones (Fig. 31.2:9–10; Pl. 76:4–5)

A different type of millstone appears from Iron Age II on-ward. Called a "frame millstone" by Amiran (1956:47), it operated according to the same rubbing principle as the first type but was more efficient. The upper stone has a projecting rectangular frame surrounding a long aperture in the center through which the grain could be poured during the grinding process. There is also a groove through the short end of the frame into which a rod could be inserted to move the upper stone.

According to analogies at Tell Zakariyeh, Tell Judeidah, Samaria, and Tell Halaf, Amiran (1956:49) concludes that this type of millstone first appeared in Iron Age II. Additional specimens have been discovered at Tel Mevorakh Stratum IIIA, at Shiloh (in an unclear context), in the Hellenistic temple at Oumm el-'Amed near Tyre (*Tel Mevorakh I*: 24), and in Area A at Ashdod Stratum 3b

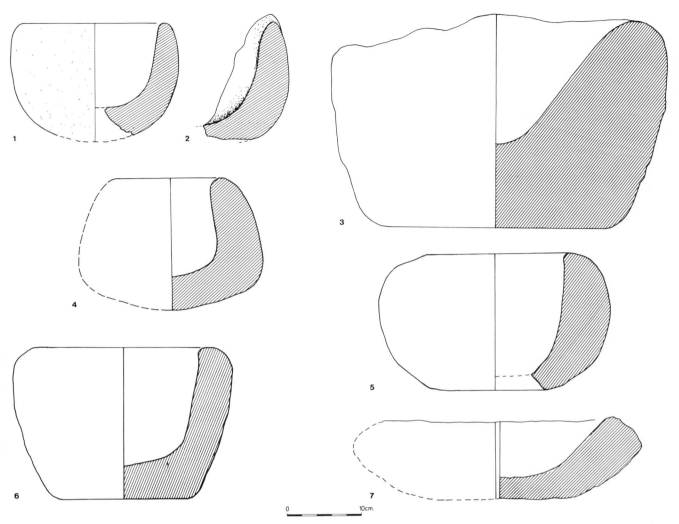

Figure 31.1. Limestone mortars.

Legend for Fig. 31.1

No.	Reg. No.	Locus	Stratum	Material	Pl.
1	9727/50	1261	XIV	Limestone	
2	2560/50	423	XIII	Limestone	
3	9407/50	1474	VII	Limestone	
4	6/50	1	Unstratified	Limestone	76:1
5	4/50	1	Unstratified	Limestone	76:2
6	5/50	1	Unstratified	Limestone	
7	10417/50	1649	VII	*Kurkar*	

(*Ashdod I*: Fig. 4:15). Others dating to the 6th century B.C.E. are known from the Greek islands and mainland, Italy, and Sicily (*Tel Mevorakh I*: 24, nn. 17–18).

At Tel Michal there were four frame millstones, all basalt. One of them was found in the lower city of the Persian period (Fig. 31.2:9; Pl. 76:4), lying next to the decorated leg of a tripod basalt mortar (Fig. 31.2:6). Another (Fig.

31.2:10; Pl. 76:5) came from a beaten-earth floor of the Roman fortress, where there was also an oven. Since the latter was found in situ, this room presumably was used for food preparation. The other two frame millstones were surface finds.

31.3. BOWLS

Basalt Bowls (Fig. 31.3)

Since these bowls are all smooth on the interior, it may be assumed that they—like the tripod basalt mortars—were also used as pounding/grinding vessels, but for crushing small quantities of materials - spices rather than cereal grains. Some of them are as small as 9 cm in diameter and very thick walled; the maximum diameter is 34 cm. The rims are sometimes cut sharply (Fig. 31.3:1–3) but are usually rounded (Fig. 31.3:4–14). Most of the bases are rounded or flattish, but one is concave (Fig. 31.3:14), and one is a ring base (Fig. 31.3:15).

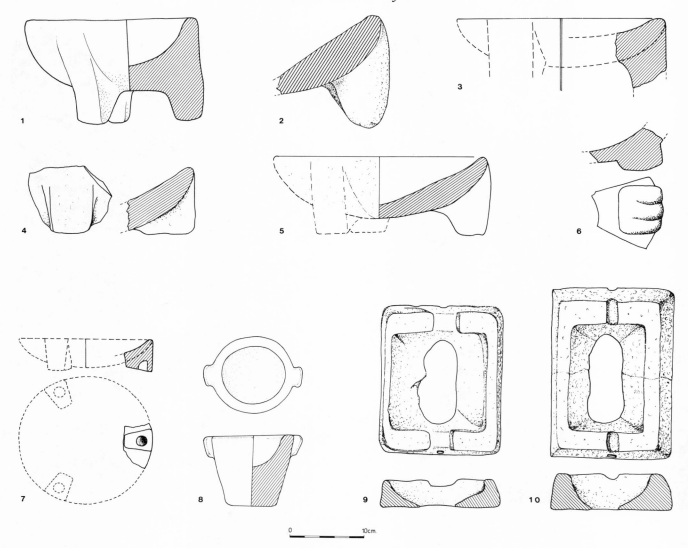

Figure 31.2. Basalt mortars and millstones.

Legend for Fig. 31.2

No.	Type	Reg. No.	Locus	Stratum	Pl.
1	Mortar	6190/50	906	Unstratified	76:3
2	Mortar	3/51	1	Unstratified	
3	Mortar	8447/50	1264	XIV	
4	Mortar	1883/50	344	IX	
5	Mortar	1172/50	165	VI	
6	Mortar	6809/50	803	II	
7	Mortar	8768/1	830	VIII	
8	Mortar	6047/50	915	IIIa	77:1
9	Millstone	1151/50	165	VI	76:4
10	Millstone	6059/50	913	II	76:5

The bowl with concave base (Fig. 31.3:14) has parallels in Stratum VI at Hazor (*Hazor II*: Pl. LXXVIII:1) and in Stratum XII (*Hazor III-IV*: Pl. CCXXXI:22). The ring-based bowl with traces of a handle or knob (Fig. 31.3:15) has parallels in Stratum VIII at Hazor (*Hazor II*: Pl. LXXVII:9).

Limestone Bowls

These are generally rounded with straight-cut rims (Fig. 31.4:1–6) or small and shallow with ledge rims (Fig. 31.4:9–12). The first type is the most common at Tel Michal, where it exists from the final phase of the Persian period into the Hellenistic and Early Hasmonean periods. Complete specimens usually have a flat or rounded base, like those from Area A, Stratum 2 (Hellenistic) at Ashdod (*Ashdod I*: Fig. 12:7). The concave disk base (Fig. 31.4:8) apparently belongs to a fairly large bowl of this type.

The ledged-rim limestone bowls, which came mainly

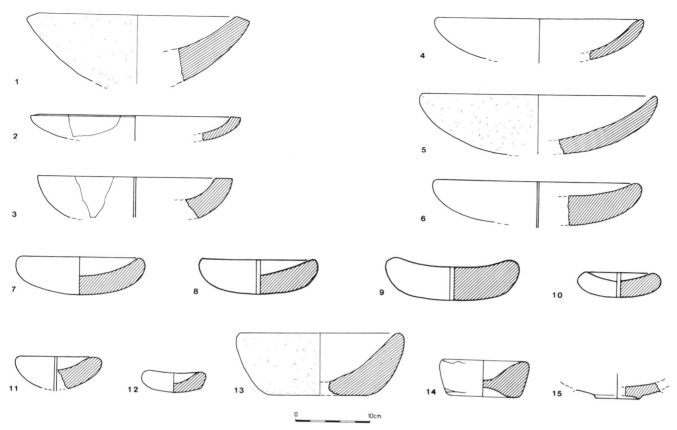

Figure 31.3. Basalt bowls.

Legend for Fig. 31.3

No.	Reg. No.	Locus	Stratum
1	10375/50	1660	XV
2	9480/50	1495	XI
3	5218/50	690	VI
4	6485/50	965	XVI/XV
5	2435/50	404	IX
6	6828/50	1012	IV
7	6797/50	800	IV
8	421/50	27	IV
9	54/50	61	II
10	1102/50	279	V
11	5510/50	832	V/IV
12	2011/50	352	VIII
13	4105/50	551	V-IV
14	4072/50	551	V-IV
15	8745/50	1373	XI

from Hellenistic contexts, seem to be imitations of alabaster cosmetic bowls (see Chap. 30, No. 8). Similar vessels were found at Lachish in the Residency of Stratum I (*Lachish III*: Pl. 64:5) and at Tell Keisan Stratum 2 (*Tell Keisan*: Pl. 16:2).

Another type of limestone bowl has a disk base, rounded walls, and two apparent ledge handles (Fig. 31.4:13). In the Iron Age, such bowls appear with knob handles, as at Lachish Stratum III (*Lachish III*: Pl. 65:9); in the Hellenistic period at Tell Keisan, there are similar vessels of basalt (*Tell Keisan*: Pl. 16:5).

Diorite Bowls

The diorite bowl fragment with everted rim and rounded ridge beneath it (Fig. 31.4:14) came from Stratum VII. Since the fragment is so small, the course of the ridge is unknown; in similar complete specimens, however, the ridge has two gaps in it on opposite sides of the bowl. This type of ridge may be the outcome of a long evolution of the bar handle, well known on pottery bowls. Similar stone bowls were found at Megiddo Stratum I (*Megiddo I*: Pl. 113:8) with rounded rim and at Stratum III (*Megiddo I*: Pl. 113:5, 9), made of basalt; at Hazor Stratum V (*Hazor I*: Pl. LIX:6–7), also of basalt; at Ashdod, Area A, surface (*Ashdod I*: Fig. 15:12); at Lachish Stratum II (*Lachish II*: Pl. 65:8), of basalt; and at Tell el-Qitaf (Amiran 1958: Pl. XIX:3). The high ring base (Fig. 31.4:15) is made of diorite, but it is not clear to what type of bowl it belonged.

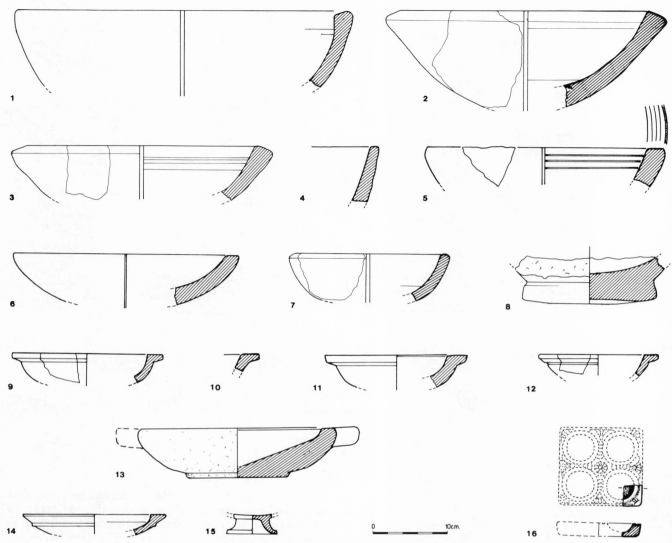

Figure 31.4. Limestone and diorite bowls.

Legend for Fig. 31.4

No.	Type	Reg. No.	Locus	Stratum	Material
1	Bowl	10883/50	1739	V	Limestone
2	Bowl	7369/50	1101	VI	Limestone
3	Bowl	5152/50	687	IIIb	Limestone
4	Bowl	6205/50	934	V	Limestone
5	Bowl	3789/51	160	VI	Limestone
6	Bowl	7400/50	1118	VII	Limestone
7	Bowl	2068/50	350	IIIb	Limestone
8	Bowl	10846/50	1743	VIII	Limestone
9	Bowl	11255/50	1804	Unstratified	Limestone
10	Bowl	11267/50	1809	VI	Limestone
11	Bowl	5634/50	311	V	Limestone
12	Bowl	84/50	36	V	Limestone
13	Bowl	3789/50	160	VI	Limestone
14	Bowl	8308/50	1013	VII	Diorite
15	Bowl	6686/50	997	IX	Diorite
16	Cosmetic palette	10309/50	1639	VIII	Marble

31.4. COSMETIC CONTAINERS

Cosmetic Palette

The marble cosmetic palette (Fig. 31.4:16) has been reconstructed in the drawing by analogy to the square marble palette with four round cups and a lotus design running between them that was found in the cemetery of Deve Hüyük in Syria (Moorey 1980: Fig. 8:146). In the corner of our fragment, traces of a lotus design can also be discerned. Another example of such a palette came from the Solar Shrine at Lachish (*Lachish III*: Pl. 64:10).

Multiple-Tubed Kohl Container

This is a tall rectangular clay vessel (3.2 cm × 3.2 cm and 9.2 cm in height) with four deep tubes and one shallow tube (Fig. 9.12:5; Pl. 77:3). Two small perforations run di-

Figure 31.5. Anchors, rollers, scrapers, and potter's wheel.

Legend for Fig. 31.5

No.	Type	Reg. No.	Locus	Stratum	Material	Pl.
1	Anchor	3/50	1	Unstratified	Limestone	76:8
2	Anchor	9630/50	1541	XV	Limestone	76:9
3	Anchor	8527/50	1371A	VIII	Limestone	76:10
4	Roller	5732/50	856	X	Limestone	
5	Roller	9568/50	1514	XIV	Limestone	
6	Potter's wheel	10856/50	1738	XV	Basalt	76:6
7	Scraper	2519/50	418	XIII	Scoria	77:2
8	Scraper	2548/50	423	XIII	Scoria	

agonally from the top of the vessel to its sides. The vessel has a grooved exterior. It was found in Locus 610 in the lower city of the Persian period, together with a number of rather unusual vessels (see Chap. 9.4.2).

By analogy with similar vessels from Egypt, this multiple-tubed container was apparently used for kohl. The four deep tubes contained the kohl, the shallow one held the cosmetic stick, and the two diagonal perforations could have been used for a lid attachment or for hanging up the vessel. In Egypt, such cosmetic containers are well known, with the number of tubes ranging from one to five;

they are made of stone (von Bissing 1904: Pl. IX:118611, 118541) or wood (Bénédite 1911: Pl. XVI:44.549, 44.552). See also Petrie 1927: Pl. XXXII:15–18. A bronze kohl box of four tubes arranged around a central pillar came from the cemetery at Atlit (Johns 1933: Fig. 64, Pl. XXVII:711).

31.5. ANCHORS

Three anchors, all of limestone and fairly flat, were discovered during the excavations (Fig. 31.5:1–3; Pl. 76:8–10). The earliest (Fig. 31.5:2; Pl. 76:9), found in secondary use in a Late Bronze Age wall, is rounded with a large hole in its center. The second, squarish with a relatively small hole near one corner (Fig. 31.5:3; Pl. 76:10), was built into a Persian period wall of Stratum VIII; it is broken on the left side. The third (Fig. 31.5:1; Pl. 76:8), which was retrieved from the beach below the tell, is square with a round hole in its upper part and is broken at the bottom.

According to McCaslin (1980:18–20), three main types of stone anchors were used in the eastern Mediterranean in the Late Bronze and early Iron Ages: (1) The composite anchor (which served as both a weight and sand anchor) with three holes (McCaslin 1980: Figs. 5, 7a). (2) The weight an-

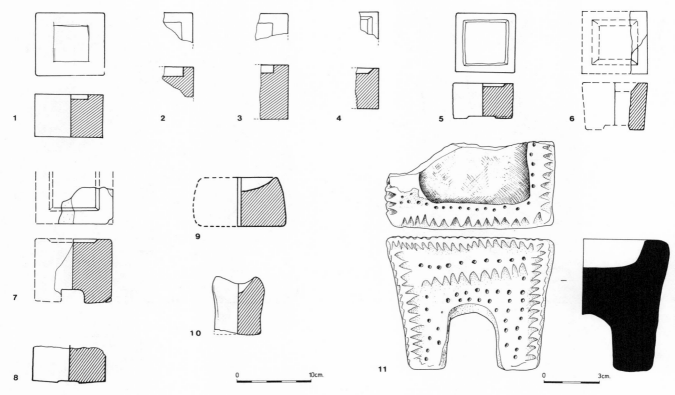

Figure 31.6. Incense altars.

Legend for Fig. 31.6

No.	Reg. No.	Locus	Stratum	Material	Pl.
1	4512/50	610	VI	Basalt	77:5
2	8965/50	1371	VIII	Basalt	
3	7164/50	1065	IV	Basalt	
4	8318/50	1634	IX	Limestone	
5	1045/50	1771	IX	Limestone	
6	1766/50	322	VI	Limestone	
7	850/50	129	VI	Limestone	
8	857/50	129	VI	Limestone	
9	709/50	121	VII-VI	Limestone	
10	5245/50	697	IV	Limestone	77:7
11	6833/1	1012	IV	Clay	77:6

chor, with a single hole for the hawser, which moored the ship securely by virtue of its sheer mass. Its weight should be at least 50 kg, according to McCaslin. (3) The sand anchor, which was usually smaller and had two or more holes. These anchors were added to the anchor line to increase the drag (McCaslin 1980: Fig. 7b).

The three anchors from Tel Michal are all single holed and should therefore be classified as weight anchors. The single complete example (Fig. 31.5:2; Pl. 76:9) is estimated to weigh about 55–60 kg. Weight anchors of various sizes and shapes have been found along the Syro-Phoenician coast at Atlit, Dor, Tel Megadim, Byblos, and Ugarit.

Many of the one-holed weight anchors from Atlit (Linder 1967; McCaslin 1980: Fig. 25, Group II) resemble ours but do not have any of the distinguishing features typical of a particular home port, such as the conical shape of one-holed Egyptian anchors with their rope-hole grooves (McCaslin 1980: Figs. 23, 25:19), the pyramidal shape of the Byblos weight anchors (McCaslin 1980: Fig. 27), or the squat, rectangular Ugaritic type that is very regular in section (McCaslin 1980: Fig. 28:1, 6–7). Among the numerous stone anchors found at Cape Andreas and nearby anchorages in Cyprus, there are also several that are similar to ours (McCaslin 1980: Fig. 15), but none of these have features that point to a specific port of origin.

31.6. ROLLERS

The two limestone rollers, one from an Iron Age context and the other from the Persian period (Fig. 31.5:4–5), are cylindrical in shape with sockets at both ends into which wooden handles could be inserted. These stone cylinders were used to smooth plaster on flat roofs. Mud roofs (probably supported by wooden beams and branches) would have required replastering annually to block the cracks made in the old plaster by the blistering summer sun and to prevent leakage in the winter. Similar stone cylinders are used up to this day in some Arab villages (Yeivin 1954:199, Pl. 22). Parallels are found in Strata VI and IA at Hazor (*Hazor III-IV*: Pls. CLXXXVIII:10, CCLXXXV:6).

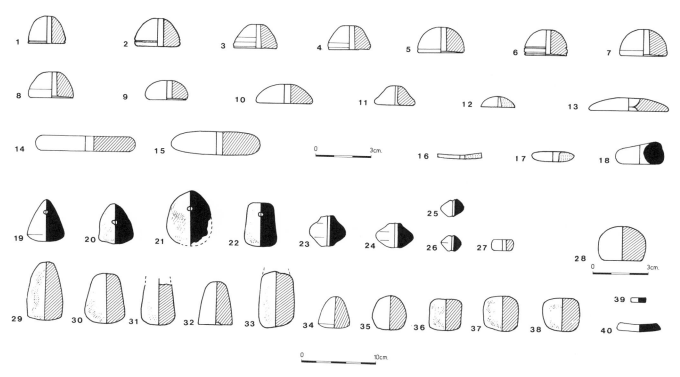

Figure 31.7. Spindle whorls, loom weights, pestles, and varia.

31.7. POTTER'S WHEEL

According to Amiran (1956:48), the potter's wheel has been known since the Early Bronze Age. The pivot stone of the wheel from Tel Michal (Fig. 31.5:6; Pl. 76:6) came from a Late Bronze Age stratum. It is rounded on the bottom like the one from Area C, Stratum 1B, at Hazor (*Hazor II*: Pl. CXXVII:22). Other pivot wheels have a flat surface (*Hazor I*: Pl. LXXXVII:24; *Hazor II*: 23; *Lachish II*: Pl. 49:12).

Amiran and Shenhav (1984:107–108) conducted experiments in an attempt to learn how the potter's wheel operated, and they discovered that if the potter applied any pressure at all to the upper stone in the course of his work, the rotary motion of the wheel would stop. They therefore conclude that a wooden disk (optimum diameter about 60 cm) was placed on the upper stone and that the potter worked on this surface instead of on the stone itself.

31.8. SCRAPERS

Two scoria scrapers came from Stratum XIII (Fig. 31.5:7–8; Pl. 77:2). Similar scrapers have been found in many excavations, including Hazor Strata VA, XB, and VI (*Hazor II*: Pl. CV:13, 16–17; *Hazor III-IV*: Pls. CLXXIII:4, CLXXXVIII:8–9) and Megiddo Strata VA and IV (*Megiddo II*: Pl. 264:5–10).

The first of our scrapers has a perforation through its relatively small handle that apparently enabled a (metal?) handle to be attached. The stone handle of the second scraper is much larger and easier to grasp, eliminating the need for a handle of another material.

31.9. INCENSE ALTARS

Nine rectangular incense altars (Fig. 31.6:1–9; Pl. 77:5), one decorated clay altar (Fig. 31.6:11; Pl. 77:6) and one horned altar (Fig. 31.6:10; Pl. 77:7) were found. Ranging from 5 to 8 cm in height, three of the rectangular altars are made of vasicular basalt and six of limestone.

Basalt Altars (Fig. 31.6:1–3; Pl. 77:5)

These flat-based rectangular altars all came from Persian and Hellenistic contexts. Basalt incense altars are rare in this country, and only one of this material has been found so far, at Megiddo (Stern 1982:186).

Limestone Altars (Fig. 31.6:4–9)

Some of these have flat bases, but usually they stand on four small, square legs. None is decorated. All belong to the Persian period.

In his study of cuboid incense burners in the Middle East, Shea (1983:93, 95) tried to put them into a chronological scheme according to body shape. In his opinion, the square altars should be dated to the early part of the Persian period, whereas their shape becomes more squat toward the end of the period. At Tel Michal, however, the flattest example is from Stratum IX (Fig. 31.6:5) and the tallest from Stratum VI (Fig. 31.6:7).

357

Legend for Fig. 31.7

No.	Type	Reg. No.	Locus	Stratum	Material	Weight	Pl.
1	Spindle whorl	1/50	1	Unstratified	Diorite	Not weighed[a]	
2	Spindle whorl	1/51	1	Unstratified	Diorite	Not weighed	
3	Spindle whorl	6334/50	1308	IX	Diorite	10.0035	
4	Spindle whorl	5440/50	339	IX	Diorite	10.1045	
5	Spindle whorl	9343/50	948	VIII	Diorite	13.1025	
6	Spindle whorl	7496/50	1113	VIII	Diorite	11.5434	77:4
7	Spindle whorl	6989/50	1027	VII	Diorite	14.3530	
8	Spindle whorl	11287/50	1814	VI	Diorite	13.0030	
9	Spindle whorl	6728/50	694	V	Diorite	9.2970	
10	Spindle whorl	10982/50	1739	V	Diorite	15.9789	
11	Spindle whorl	10264/51	1637	VI	Diorite	6.0863	
12	Spindle whorl	9355/40	1488	IX	Bone	1.6386	
13	Spindle whorl	5820/50	893	X	Alabaster	Not weighed	
14	Spindle whorl	11033/50	1759	II	Limestone	Not weighed	
15	Spindle whorl	7022/50	1054	II	Limestone	47.2380	
16	Spindle whorl	2136/40	364	IX	Bone	1.2107	
17	Spindle whorl	6494/40	973	VII	Ivory	2.4950	
18	Spindle whorl	1900/1	343	VII	Clay	12.686	
19	Loom weight	141/1	322	VI	Clay	130	
20	Loom weight	1750/1c	323	V	Clay	120	
21	Loom weight	1750/1b	323	V	Clay	210	
22	Loom weight	1750/1a	323	V	Clay	130	
23	Loom weight	148/1	322	VI	Clay	24.1	
24	Loom weight	1504/1	219	VIII/VI	Clay	17.2	
25	Loom weight	1124/1	279	V	Clay	82.9	
26	Loom weight	1125/1	279	V	Clay	71.45	
27	Loom weight	10304/50	1640	VII	Stone	23.5	
28	Weight	2564/50	418	XIII	Limestone	19.665	
29	Pestle	9767/50	1559	XVI	Basalt	. . .	
30	Pestle	2575/50	99	XIII	Basalt	. . .	
31	Pestle	10390/50	1631	IX	Basalt	. . .	
32	Pestle	7259/50	1069	VIII	Basalt	. . .	
33	Pestle	347/50	63	IV	Basalt	. . .	
34	Pestle	21/52	2	Unstratified	Basalt	. . .	
35	Pestle	6630/50	985	IX	Basalt	. . .	
36	Pestle	11082/50	1779	IX	Basalt	. . .	
37	Pestle	5945/50	886	XVI	Basalt	. . .	
38	Pestle	494/50	92	VIII	Limestone	. . .	
39	Disk	5918/1	885	XVI	Clay	. . .	
40	Disk	10433/1	1655	XV	Clay	. . .	

[a] Numbers 1 and 2 were not weighed because they came from private collections and were returned to them before this chapter was written; Nos. 13 and 14 are broken.

In Stern's opinion (1982:192), it is impossible to trace any significant morphological changes in the undecorated limestone altars. The specimens from Shiqmona, Gezer, Shomron, Tell en-Nasbeh, Tel Malḥata, and Beer-sheba range in date from the 8th century B.C.E. (Beer-sheba) through the 6th century (Tel Malḥata, Tell en-Nasbeh), the 5th century (Gezer), and up to the 4th century (Shiqmona). Thus, this type of altar is common from the end of the Iron Age and continues throughout the Persian period into Hellenistic times.

Horned Incense Altar (Fig. 31.6:10; Pl. 77:7)

This small limestone incense altar with four horns came from Stratum IV of the Hellenistic period. It is very rare, since most of the known altars of the period are the rectangular limestone type.

Clay Incense Altar (Fig. 31.6:11; Pl. 77:6)

The single altar of clay has four rather long legs, and its sides are decorated with a wedge-and-reed impressed pattern. Clay altars are very rare in Israel but are well known from Mesopotamia. There, too, they are rectangular, have four long legs, and are decorated with impressions and incisions. Dating from the Neo-Babylonian and Persian periods, they are found at Nippur (Legrain 1930: Pls. LXVI:360–364, LXVII:365–367), Uruk and Babylon (Ziegler 1942:224–240), and Ur (Woolley 1962: Pl. 36). From Asshur, only a few specimens are known (Ziegler 1942:231,

233). Since our clay altar is unique at Tel Michal, it may have been a Mesopotamian import.

Judging by the locations where these incense burners were found throughout the Middle East, Shea (1983:92) concludes that they were used domestically. Ziegler (1942:234) arrived at the same conclusion on the basis of her Mesopotamian research. To a certain extent, the evidence from Tel Michal tends to support this assumption. Most of the incense burners did not come from a cultic context. However, two of the limestone altars were found in Locus 129 (not far from the cache of seven closed lamps) in the area of the Iron Age temple on the eastern hillock that probably continued to be used as an open cult area in the Persian and Hellenistic periods.

31.10. SPINDLE WHORLS

The spindle whorls at Tel Michal are mostly made of stone, but there are a few of bone or clay and even one of glass (see Chap. 33.4). Morphologically, they are of two basic types: hemispheric or flat.

Hemispheric Spindle Whorls

The stone spindle whorls, all made of diorite, are hemispheric in section (Fig. 31.7:1–10; Pl. 77:4), except for one that is triangular (Fig. 31.7:11). The six whorls of the Persian period (Fig. 31.7:3–8), as well as the two surface finds (Fig. 31.7:1–2), all have one or two grooves near their bases, whereas those from the Hellenistic period do not have such grooves (Fig. 31.7:9–10).

Although none of the spindle whorls at Tel Michal can be dated before the Persian period, they are found in much earlier contexts elsewhere. At Megiddo they appear in the Late Bronze and Iron Ages (*Megiddo Tombs*: Fig. 175:7, 22, 25) and at Tel Mevorakh in Stratum VII of the 10th century (*Tel Mevorakh I*: Pl. 16:19–21). At Tell Keisan a large number (some grooved, some not) were found, but many were unstratified (*Tell Keisan*: Pl. 96:1–26).

The weights of the diorite spindle whorls at Tel Michal vary from 6 to 15 g. According to Nodet (1980:315), various sizes and weights were used according to the nature and thickness of the thread and the size of the spool. Higher spinning speeds can be reached with a whorl of larger diameter and flatter top (see Fig. 31.7:10).

One hemispheric whorl of bone was found in Stratum IX (Fig. 31.7:12). Bone whorls are not uncommon, as seen at Tell Keisan Stratum 2b (*Tell Keisan*: Pl. 96:21); Hazor Stratum II (*Hazor I*: Pl. LXXXII:9); Megiddo, Late Bronze Age (*Megiddo Tombs*: Pl. 153:4; *Megiddo I*: Pl. 95:38); and Samaria, Period IV (*Samaria-Sebaste III*: Fig. 92a:22).

Flat Spindle Whorls (Fig. 31.7:13–18)

Made of stone, bone, ivory or clay, these are usually elongated-oval in section, but some are convex at the top and some are quite thin and flat.

Of the stone whorls of this class, one is alabaster (Fig. 31.7:13) and two are limestone (Fig. 31.7:14–15). The latter is much heavier than any of the others. There is one bone whorl, very flat and thin (Fig. 31.7:16), and another that is apparently ivory (Fig. 31.7:17), both from the Persian period and quite light, weighing only 1–2 g each. The clay spindle whorl is made from a pottery sherd that was roughly rounded and pierced through its center (Fig. 31.7:18). Clay spindle whorls are known from various sites (e.g., *Tell Keisan*: Pl. 96:39–44; Lapp 1978: Pl. 25:9).

31.11. LOOM WEIGHTS

Loom weights, usually of clay, are used to keep the warp threads of the loom taut (Sheffer 1981). They come in various sizes and shapes, rounded in the earlier periods and conical or biconical in the Persian and Hellenistic periods. Dozens of such weights were found at Tel Michal, only a few of which are illustrated. There is a large group of heavier, larger weights and a small group of lighter, smaller weights.

Large Loom Weights (Fig. 31.7:19–22)

These vary from 100 to 130 g, although a few are even heavier. They come in three different shapes: conical with slightly convex sides and a pointed top (Fig. 31.7:19–20), conical with rounded sides and rounded top (Fig. 31.7:21), and conoid with flattish top (Fig. 31.7:22). The horizontal perforation is usually through the upper third of the weight, although in a few cases it is slightly lower.

Small Loom Weights (Fig. 31.7:23–26)

Most of these are biconical. Their weights seem to fall into three categories: 15–25 g, 45–65 g, and 70–85 g.

In some excavation reports, these weights are referred to as spindle whorls, but Nodet (1980:318) defines them as loom weights, pointing out not only that they are too crude and heavy to function as spindle whorls but that the perforation is too narrow for a spindle to pass through and they are not symmetrical. At Tell Keisan, such loom weights were found in Strata 3 and 2 (*Tell Keisan*: Pl. 97:1–6).

At Tel Michal, few loom weights were found singly, and in two cases they were lying in large concentrations: in Locus 322 of Stratum VI, 7 large ones (of the type shown in Fig. 31.7:19) were lying on a floor; in Pit 323 of Stratum V, there were 32 (of the types shown in Fig. 31.7:20–22), together with remains of carbonized wood (*Pistacia palaestina*), which might have come from a wooden loom.

It is interesting that small loom weights were found close to both of these concentrations, one in Locus 322 and two in Pit 323. At Tell Keisan, large loom weights appear in some instances in proximity to small ones: in one case 36 large ones and three small ones, and in another 20 large ones and one small loom weight. Nodet (1980:319) suggests that the smaller, lighter weights were used to stretch small groups of different colored threads, or threads of different widths. Therefore, each loom had a large group of heavier weights and a few small ones.

In addition to the clay loom weights, one small rectangular specimen of limestone was found (Fig. 31.7:27).

31.12. WEIGHT, PESTLES, AND CERAMIC DISKS

One small limestone weight of typical hemispheric shape, weighing 19.665 g, was found in Stratum XIII (Fig. 31.7:28).

The pestles (Fig. 31.7:29–38) are all made of basalt except for one of limestone (Fig. 31.7:38).

Fifteen ceramic disks, made of pottery sherds whose edges had been rounded off, were found in the various strata (Fig. 31.7:39–40); their diameters range from 2 to 5 cm. Such disks, which appear in almost every excavation (e.g., *Megiddo I*: Pl. 103), are called "stoppers" in most publications. Eleven such disks were found in the Iron Age II levels at Beth-zur (*Beth-zur 1968*: 83; Pl. 42b). The excavator is of the opinion that these disks are not suitable for jar lids because they are too flat and would have fallen off. By analogy with the practices of the American Indians, he suggests that they were gaming pieces. Dagani (as cited by the excavator) thinks that they may have been measuring weights and tries to find regularity in their weights. Of all the possibilities, the most likely seems to be that they were used either as lids for various types of small-mouthed vessels, or perhaps to plug the bungholes of wine jars, their removal enabling the fermentation gases to escape. In this case, to prevent the stopper from falling out it may have been wrapped in a piece of cloth or secured in place by some other material.

REFERENCES

Amiran, R. 1956. Millstones and the Potter's Wheel. (Hebrew) *EI* 4:46–49.

Amiran, R. 1958. A Stone Bowl of the Late Assyrian Period from Tell el-Qitaf in the Beth-shan Valley. (Hebrew) *'Atiqot* 2:116–118.

Amiran, R., and Shenhav, D. 1984. Experiments with an Ancient Potter's Wheel. Pages 107–212 in: *Pots and Potters*. P. M. Rice, ed. Los Angeles.

Avitsur, S. 1976. *Man and His Work: Historical Atlas of Tools and Workshops in the Holy Land*. (Hebrew) Jerusalem.

Bénédite, G. A. 1911. *Objets de toilette. Pt. 1*. Catalogue général des antiquités égyptiennes du Musée du Caire. Cairo.

Johns, C. N. 1933. Excavations at 'Atlit (1930–31). The South-Eastern Cemetery. *QDAP* 2:41–104.

Lapp, N. L. 1978. The Third Campaign at Tell el-Fûl: The Excavations of 1964. *AASOR* 45.

Legrain, L. 1930. *Terracottas from Nippur*. Philadelphia.

Linder, E. 1967. La ville phénicienne d'Athlit A-t-elle eu l'un des plus anciens ports artificiels de Méditerranée? *Archeologia* 17:25–29.

McCaslin, D. W. 1980. *Stone Anchors in Antiquity: Coastal Settlement and Maritime Trade Routes in the Eastern Mediterranean ca. 1600–1050 B.C. SIMA* 61.

Moorey, P. R. S. 1980. *Cemeteries of the First Millennium B.C. at Deve Hüyük, near Carchemish*. British Archaeological Reports International Series 87. Oxford.

Nodet, É. 1980. Fusaïoles et Pesons. *Tell Keisan*: 315–320.

Petrie, W. M. F. 1927. *Objects of Daily Use*. London.

Shea, M. O. 1983. The Small Cuboid Incense Burner of the Ancient Near East. *Levant* 15:76–109.

Sheffer, A. 1981. The Use of Perforated Clay Balls on the Warp-Weighted Loom. *Tel Aviv* 8:81–83.

Stern, E. 1982. *Material Culture of the Land of the Bible in the Persian Period, 538–332 B.C.E.* Warminster.

von Bissing, F. W. 1904. *Steingefässe*. Catalogue général des antiquités égyptiennes du Musée du Caire. Vienna.

Woolley, L. 1962. *Ur Excavations IX: The Neo-Babylonian and Persian Periods*. London.

Yeivin, S. 1954. Construction. (Hebrew) *Enc. Miqr.* II: 179–263.

Ziegler, L. 1942. Ton Kästchen aus Uruk, Babylon und Assur. *ZA (NF)* 13 (77): 224–240.

32

Terracottas and Worked Bone Artifacts

by Trude Kertesz

32.1. CLAY FIGURINES AND RELIEFS

1. Human Head (Fig. 32.1:1; Pl. 78:1)

This figurine is the head of a bearded warrior with high, round headgear covering his hair, which is depicted by a coil of diagonally incised lines. The eyes and other facial features are plastically molded. It seems to represent a Persian soldier, most likely a cavalryman like those shown on the Persepolis wall panels of the Achaemenian period (Ghirshman 1964: Pls. 184–185; see also the central panel of the frieze from the stairway of Artaxerxes III Ochus, Palace of Darius, in Persepolis, *BMP 1932*: Pls. 7–8). A bearded Parthian soldier wears the same headdress (Legrain 1930: Pl. XLVII:245–246), as well as a Scythian horseman from Memphis (*Memphis I*: Pl. XL:43, 46; see also Blinkenberg 1931: Pl. 89:1994–1999, 203; Haspels 1951: Pl. 37a) from the Greek Archaic period (6th-4th centuries B.C.E.). The hair style was worked with the same technique for a sitting figure with the same cap on a pitcher of the Cypriote Classical period, 475–400 B.C.E. (Spiteris 1970: Pl. 185). Apparently this technique of depicting the headdress was used throughout the eastern Mediterranean and much of the Near East during the Persian period.

2. Garment Fragment (Fig. 32.1:2; Pl. 78:2)

This fragment is the fold of a garment of a mold-produced figure, probably a peplos worn by a Nike or Aphrodite in a pacing movement. Although found in a Persian period locus, its style suggests the Hellenistic period. This technique was used in the workshops at Corinth. Similar material was found in the sanctuary of Demeter and Kore on Acrocorinth and the Heraeum at Perachora (Higgins 1967: Pl. 47C, Tanagra style; Pl. 47F, girl carrying an offering). I thank Dr. Moshe Fischer for calling this parallel to my attention.

3. Head of Pillar Figurine (Fig. 32.1:3; Pl. 78:3)

This is the head and neck of a pillar figurine made in a two-part mold. The eyes include traces of lashes, the nose is slightly damaged, the cheeks are high, and the lips are not separated. The wig is depicted by two rows of curls that cover the ears and forehead. The head flows into the neck, which was attached to the body by a clay "peg."

According to Holland (1977:124–125), there are two types of pillar figurines: Type A with solid, hand-modeled body, and Type B with hollow body, usually made on the wheel. The first type was most common during the Israelite period, from the middle of the Iron Age to about the 6th century B.C.E. The hollow-bodied type is less widespread and was apparently influenced by a peripheral culture. The clay peg at the end of the neck was usually attached to a hollow body, and therefore our example represents the second type.

The body very likely was a nude female figurine, which most authors believe represents some form of the "Mother Goddess" (Holland 1977:134). One of the earliest native examples of a mother goddess figurine carved in the round was found in Stratum III (Iron Age I) at Beth-shemesh (*Ain Shems IV*: 155–156, Pl. LI:28; Pritchard 1943:56–57). Other early examples came from Strata VII-VI at Megiddo (e.g., *Megiddo II*: Pl. 243:18, 22–23). According to Tufnell, however, the standing pillar-based figurine first began to appear only in the 8th century B.C.E. (*Lachish III*: 374, Pls. 27:4, 8; 28:10–11, 13; 31:1–14; 32:3). These pillar figurines have been found at numerous sites, including Beth-shemesh, Stratum II (*Ain Shems IV*: Pl. LI:21–24, 29–31); Tell Beit Mirsim, Stratum A (*TBM III*: Pls. 54:1–8; 56:1–4); Tell en-Nasbeh (*TN I*: Pl. 85); Beer-sheba, Stratum II (*Beer-sheba I*: Pl. 27:4–9); and Samaria (*Samaria-Sebaste III*: Pl. XI:2, 4, 8).

4. Human Mask (Fig. 32.1:4; Pl. 78:4)

This mask is of a molded head, about 4.5 cm high, which may have belonged to a panel. It has a pointed cap that

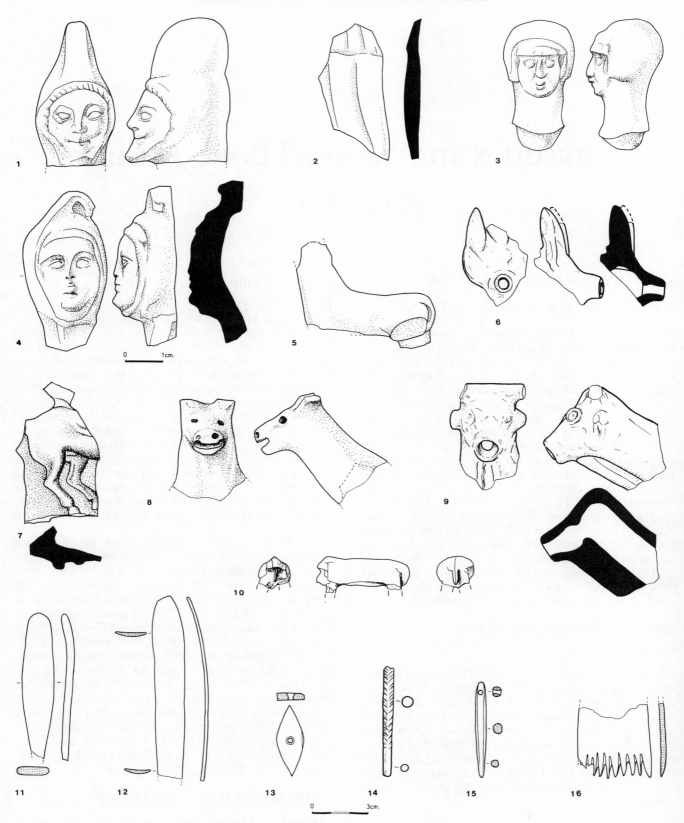

Figure 32.1. Terracottas and worked bone artifacts.

Legend for Fig. 32.1

No.	Object	Reg. No.	Locus	Stratum	Description of Material	Pl.
1	Human head	7458/1	1113	VIII	Brownish clay, gray core.	78:1
2	Garment fragment	8757/1	1371	VIII	Brown clay, gray core.	78:2
3	Head of pillar figurine	6414/1	955	VI	Brownish clay, brownish gray core; white wash.	78:3
4	Human mask	4285/1	579	Unstratified	Reddish clay, orange-gray core.	78:4
5	Zoomorphic figurine	8766/1	1381	XVI	Brownish clay, red core.	78:5
6	Spout of zoomorphic vessel	18/1	1	Unstratified	Reddish clay, light-orange core, white wash.	78:6
7	Hindquarters of horse	10862/1	1709	VII	Brown clay, white wash.	78:7
8	Head of cow (?)	2325/1	50	I	Brown clay, gray core, white grits; white wash.	78:8
9	Spout of zoomorphic vessel	22/1	2	Unstratified	Light brown clay, grayish core.	78:9
10	Body of quadruped	14/1	1	Unstratified	Brownish clay, gray core.	78:10
11	Spatula	6543/40	983	XVI/XV	Bone.	78:11
12	Spatula	6508/40	973	VII	Bone.	78:12
13	Gavel head (?)	9701/40	983	XVI/XV	Bone.	78:13
14	Pin	1117/40	174	XVII	Bone.	78:14
15	Pendant	9509/40	1513	XIII	Bone.	78:15
16	Comb	10447/40	1649	VII	Bone.	78:16

covers the chin. Its style suggests the Hellenistic period. The features are modeled naturalistically, the lips slightly parted, the eyelids accentuated.

Soldiers wearing this kind of headdress are seen on the Alexander sarcophagus (Havelock 1971: Figs. 150–151); see also Breitenstein 1948: Pls. 2:10–11; 3:16, of the same period. But this cap also appears in the Persian period, e.g., at Meqabelein (Harding 1950: Pl. XIII:1), at Shiqmona (*Shiqmona I*: Pl. XLIII:690), and at Lindos in Cyprus (Blinkenberg 1931: Pl. 90:2012).

5. Zoomorphic Figurine (Fig. 32.1:5; Pl. 78:5)

This body fragment of a handmade quadruped, perhaps part of a horse, came from Stratum XIV. Such animal figurines may have had some role in the cultic practices of the period (Holland 1977:153). A similar fragment was found in an Iron Age context in the Citadel of Jerusalem (Amiran and Eitan 1973: Pl. 42:2). See also *Lachish III*: Pl. 32:5 (part of a horse); *TBM III*: Pl. 58:11–16, Stratum A; and *Samaria-Sebaste III*: Pl. XII:2.

6. Spout of Zoomorphic Vessel (Fig. 32.1:6; Pl. 78:6)

This fragment, a surface find, is apparently part of a calf's head. The hollow projecting muzzle, one eye, and one ear are preserved. A rhyton with this kind of spout came from the Persian period at Tel Mevorakh (*Tel Mevorakh I*: Pl. 43:1). Similar vessels are also known from the Early Arab period (Baramki 1944: Fig. 16:18–19).

7. Hindquarters of Horse (Fig. 32.1:7; Pl. 78:7)

This is a fragment of a mold-produced relief. It may have been a decoration on a vessel since it is slightly curved on the underside. Horses, usually with riders, are common on the terracottas of the Hellenistic period throughout the Mediterranean area (Breitenstein 1948: Pl. 81:664, 665, Hellenistic; *Corinth XII*: Pl. 27:308–311, late 4th-early 3rd centuries B.C.E.; Higgins 1967: Pl. 47:E, Hellenistic). It may therefore be assumed that this fragment belongs to the Hellenistic period, although it was found in the debris above a Persian period floor.

8. Head of Cow? (Fig. 32.1:8; Pl. 78:8)

The eyes and nostrils of this handmade head were indented with a pointed stick and the muzzle was divided by inserting a flat stick. It resembles the animal heads from the Early Arab period at Khirbet el-Mefjer (Baramki 1944: Figs. 9:33; 16:18–19; Pl. XVII:2) and Ramla (Rosen-Ayalon and Eitan 1969: Pl. 2:1).

9. Spout of Zoomorphic Vessel (Fig. 32.1:9; Pl. 78:9)

This bovine head has a rounded, hollow muzzle, eyes accentuated by surrounding circles, and broken ears. The spout may have come from an Iron Age kernos. Kernoi decorated with this style of spout and eyes were found at Ashdod (*Ashdod I*: Fig. 44; *Ashdod II-III*: Fig. 66, Pls. LX, LXI, LXII:1–3). It is also possible that it comes from the Early Arab period, as No. 8 above.

10. Body of Quadruped (Fig. 32.1:10; Pl. 78:10)

The body, head, tail, and stumps of the four legs are preserved on this fragment. The tail is short and thick and the muzzle pinched. It may represent a sheep. Although a surface find, it might have come from one of the earlier periods at Tel Michal. A similar animal was found in Megiddo, Stratum XIV (*Megiddo II*: Pl. 245:15).

32.2. WORKED BONE ARTIFACTS

11. Spatulas (Fig. 32.1:11–12; Pl. 78:11–12)

These flat bone implements were used for mixing and spreading small quantities of cosmetics or ointments, in which case they had one or more rounded ends, connected by a shaft. Another type, used for medical purposes such as opening and cleaning wounds or piercing abscesses, had pointed ends. Four of the round-ended type were found at Tel Michal, ranging in width from 20 mm to 40 mm and in length from 6 cm to 10 cm, but none are completely preserved.

The first (Fig. 32.1:11) was found in Strata XVI-XV, together with a large quantity of Late Bronze Age pottery; it is rounded on one end but broken at the other; the second (Fig. 32.1:12), which came from a Persian period locus, may be slightly chipped on the rounded end but is definitely broken at the other end; the other two (Reg. No. 4510/40, Locus 610, Stratum VI; Reg. No. 5138/40, Locus 697, Stratum IV) both had rounded extremities but disintegrated into too many fragments to be drawn or photographed.

Most of the published parallels are the type with pointed extremities, e.g., *Megiddo I*: Pl. 95:39–62, Iron Age; *Samaria-Sebaste III*: Fig. 115:4–6. Numerous examples of the rounded type were found in the Pre-Pottery Neolithic period at Jericho (*Jericho IV*: Fig. 234:1–4, 7–10, 20–29); among the many pointed ones, there is also a round-ended type at Lachish (*Lachish III*: Pl. 63:22).

12. Gavel Head? (Fig. 32.1:13; Pl. 78:13)

This is a flat, trapezoidal implement of bone or ivory, pointed at both extremities and pierced through the center. A bone object of similar appearance (perhaps less flat; it is illustrated only by a frontal photograph) was found at Lachish (*Lachish III*: Pl. 37:6), where it is included among the classes of bone objects so far "found exclusively in Palestine" whose use "has never been satisfactorily explained," although some think they may have been divination rods (*Lachish III*: 381–382). There is also a bone object of similar shape at Lachish listed as a spindle whorl (*Lachish III*: Pl. 55:11); however, the objects generally considered to be spindle whorls are usually circular (see Chap. 31.10).

13. Pin (Fig. 32.1:14; Pl. 78:14)

This pin (broken at one end), with incised herringbone pattern, was found in an MB II context. Pins of this sort were used for attaching garments together at the shoulder,

primarily before the appearance of the fibula. A similarly incised bone pin was found at Gezer (*Gezer II*: Fig. 277). Incised herringbones are seen on a bone pin from Boğozköy (Boehmer 1972: Pl. LXXIII:2046) and on an LB II bone spindle from Megiddo (*Megiddo Tombs*: Pl. 95:49).

14. Pendant (Fig. 32.1:15; Pl. 78:15)

This needlelike bone pendant (5.2 cm in length) from a Persian period locus may have been an amulet, but its narrow shape suggests that it had a practical function, such as sewing together strips of loosely woven material. Similar pendants or needles, most of them decorated with incised lines, were found, for example, from Strata IV-III at Megiddo (*Megiddo I*: Pl. 97:33) and in an Iron Age context at Lachish (*Lachish III*: Pl. 55:17).

15. Comb (Fig. 32.1:16; Pl. 78:16)

This comb of whitish bone came from a Persian period stratum. It is broken at the top and has very short teeth. Wooden combs of this type are also known. Parallels in bone come from Strata XIV-XIII at Megiddo (*Megiddo II*: Pl. 201:7–8), from the Bronze Age at Lachish (*Lachish IV*: Pl. 28:16), and from the Iron Age at Gezer (*Gezer II*: Fig. 295).

REFERENCES

Amiran, R., and Eitan, A. 1973. Excavations in the Citadel, Jerusalem, 1968–1969 (Preliminary Report). *EI* 11:213–218. (Hebrew).

Baramki, D. C. 1944. The Pottery from Khirbet el Mefjar. *QDAP* 10:65–103.

Blinkenberg, C. 1931. *Lindos: Fouilles de l'Acropole 1902–1914, I: Les petits objets*. Berlin.

Boehmer, R. M. 1972. *Die Kleinfunde von Boğozköy*. Berlin.

Breitenstein, N. 1948. *Catalogue of Terracottas. Danish National Museum*. Copenhagen.

Ghirshman, R. 1964. *The Arts of Ancient Iran*. New York.

Harding, G. L. 1950. An Iron-Age Tomb at Meqabelein. *QDAP* 14:44–48.

Haspels, C. H. E. 1951. *La cité de Midas, céramique et trouvailles diverses. Phrygie 3*. Paris.

Havelock, C. M. 1971. *Hellenistische Kunst*. Vienna.

Higgins, R. A. 1967. *Greek Terracottas*. London.

Holland, T. A. 1977. A Study of Palestinian Iron Age Baked Clay Figurines with Special Reference to Jerusalem: Cave 1. *Levant* 9:121–156.

Legrain, L. 1930. *Terracottas from Nippur*. Philadelphia.

Pritchard, J. B. 1943. *Palestinian Figurines in Relation to Certain Goddesses Known through Literature*. New Haven, Conn.

Rosen-Ayalon, M., and Eitan, A. 1969. *Ramla Excavations: Finds from the VIII Century C.E.* Israel Museum Catalogue 66. Jerusalem.

Spiteris, T. 1970. *The Art of Cyprus*. New York.

33

Glass Artifacts

by Trude Kertesz

More than 100 pieces of glass that could be identified as parts of various vessels were found at Tel Michal, as well as another 50 unidentifiable fragments. All of them came from residential and industrial areas, none from the Persian period cemetery. It may therefore be assumed that they were used domestically, the earlier items (from the Persian period strata) as pots for ointments and salves, containers for cosmetic oils, and perfume bottles. Later on, in the Hellenistic and Roman periods, glass vessels also served as tableware.[1]

The most typical production techniques and decorations from each period are represented in the Tel Michal finds, and since they were found in stratified contexts, sometimes together with coins, it is easy to assume their dates. The finds are grouped below according to the techniques of manufacture.

33.1. CORE-FORMED GLASS VESSELS

From the Late Bronze Age to the end of the Hellenistic period, the basic method for making glass containers was the core technique. After a core of a sandy clay mixture was modeled to the desired shape on a copper rod, the glassmaker wound threads of semimolten glass around it. This was reheated until the threads coalesced, and then the surface was smoothed with a flat tool or rolled on a flat bench (marver). Patterns were made by coiling glass threads of various colors around the surface and moving them up or down with a pointed tool to create a wavy, zigzag, or other desired decorative effect. The vessel was then rolled again to embed the added glass flush into the surface. When the vessel was ready, the core was removed.

At Tel Michal, nine pieces of glass produced by the technique described above were found, five in Persian period strata (XI-VI) and the rest in Hellenistic strata (V-IV).

1. Shoulder Piece of Amphoriskos with Handle

Reg. No. 8882/70, Locus 1386, Stratum XI. The shoulder has a zigzag pattern of white and black threads; the handle is white. Parallels include Fossing 1940: Figs. 44, 50; Hayes 1975: Pls. 1:12, 2:19 (5th century B.C.E.). According to Fossing (1940:44), zigzag or festoon patterns are most common in the 6th-4th centuries B.C.E. See also von Saldern et al. 1974: Fig. 146, amphoriskos (6th-5th centuries B.C.E.); Freyer-Schauenburg 1973: Pls. XIII:e, XVI (6th-5th century); Johns 1933: Pl. XVIII:416 (5th century).

2. Festooned Body Fragment

Reg. No. 8889/70, Locus 1386, Stratum XI, white background with green festoon thread decoration. This could be a piece of a kohl tube or an alabastron. Parallels include Barag 1975: Fig. 5 (5th or early 4th century B.C.E.); Barag 1970:155, Fig. 42; Fossing 1940: Figs. 31–32 (6th-5th centuries B.C.E.).

3. Zigzag Threaded Body Fragment

Reg. No. 5454/70, Locus 339, Stratum IX. Fragment of black vessel (possibly an aryballos) with yellow and white inlaid zigzag pattern above two inlaid threads. Parallel: Goldstein 1979: No. 262.

4. Zigzag Threaded Body Fragment

Reg. No. 10321/70, Locus 1639, Stratum VIII. Yellow with green and white five-threaded zigzag pattern and green bordering thread. Parallel: *Corinth XII*: Pl. 54:582 (Greek period).

5. Horizontally Threaded Body Fragment

Reg. No. 3690/70, Locus 508, Stratum VI. Black with two horizontal yellow threads.

6. Handle Fragment

Reg. No. 11031/70, Locus 1739, Stratum V. Blue with three yellow threads.

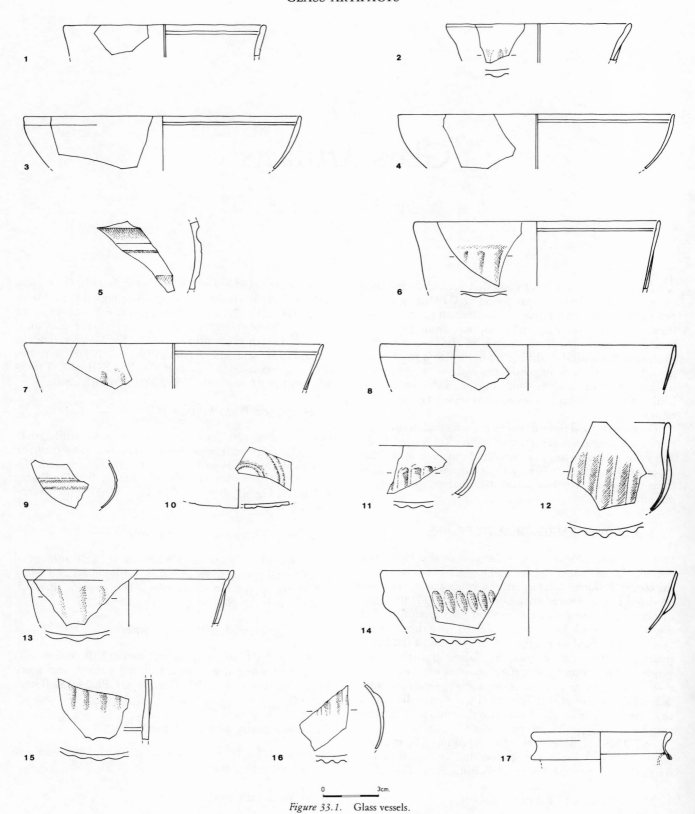

Figure 33.1. Glass vessels.

Legend for Fig. 33.1

No.	Type	Reg. No.	Locus	Stratum	Description
1	Bowl	6180/70	1489	VI	Mold-cast, wheel-grooved, brown.
2	Bowl	8301/70	1003	IV	Mold-cast, wheel-grooved, ribbed, light blue.
3	Bowl	6078/70	930	IV	Mold-cast, wheel-grooved, light blue.
4	Bowl	10238/70	689	I	Mold-cast, wheel-grooved, greenish.
5	Bowl	5285/70	1003	IV	Mold-cast, wheel-grooved, greenish, iridescent.
6	Bowl	6025/70	901	Unstratified	Mold-cast, wheel-grooved, ribbed, light blue.
7	Bowl	7075/70	1050	Unstratified	Mold-cast, wheel-grooved, ribbed, light blue.
8	Bowl	5152/70	687	IIIb	Mold-cast, wheel-grooved, light blue.
9	Bowl	6827/70	685	IIIb	Mold-cast, wheel-grooved, light blue.
10	Bowl (base)	5468/70	722	VII	Mold-cast, wheel-grooved, whitish.
11	Bowl	5282/70	806	V	Mold-cast, ribbed, light blue.
12	Bowl	5180/70	697	IV	Mold-cast, ribbed, light blue.
13	Bowl	5170/70	685	IIIb	Mold-cast, wheel-grooved, ribbed, light blue.
14	Bowl	300/70	58	II	Mold-cast, ribbed, greenish black.
15	Bowl	420/70	66	II	Mold-cast, ribbed, blue.
16	Bowl	6073/70	918	II	Mold-cast, ribbed, light blue.
17	Bottle (neck)	7112/70	1050	Unstratified	Blown glass, green.

7. Feather-Patterned Body Fragments

Reg. Nos. 4060/70, 4109/70, Loci 551, 551B, Stratum V-IV. Blue with white inlaid feather pattern. The first fragment was found together with a Ptolemaic coin (Chap. 27: No. 105) on the treading floor of the Hellenistic winepress.

8. Rim and Neck of Perfume Bottle

Reg. No. 4108/70, Locus 570, Stratum V-IV. Black with three yellow inlaid threads on neck; ledge rim. The piece was found together with a coin from Sidé, Pamphylia, 3d century B.C.E. (Chap. 27: No. 195). Parallels (all 2d-1st centuries B.C.E.): Hayes 1975: Pl. 2:28–29, 31–32; Goldstein 1979: No. 267, Late Hellenistic alabastron; Harden 1969: Fig. 3.

33.2. MOLD-CAST VESSELS

Bowls with Wheel-Cut Body Grooves (Fig. 33.1:1–9)

These are either conical with vertical rims (Fig. 33.1:1–2, 6–7) or hemispheric with rounded bases (Fig. 33.1:3–4, 8–9) and thick walls, commonly about 3 mm although some may be as thick as 5 mm (Fig. 33.1:5). They are usually decorated with a single horizontal groove cut on the lapidary's wheel just below the rim around the inner circumference; occasionally there are two grooves (Fig. 33.1:9) or even three (Fig. 33.1:6). Some of those at Tel Michal are also ribbed (Fig. 33.1:2, 6–7). Most are light blue or greenish, although the color often appears to be gray or white, perhaps as a result of the earthy weathering that characterizes most of these bowls. Many also are iridescent, with a silvery crust.

The vessels were cast in two-part molds, then polished on both surfaces, the interior wheel polished and the exterior fire polished. Such cast bowls were the first glass vessels to be used in antiquity as tableware. Most of the fragments found at Tel Michal came from the Hellenistic/Hasmonean strata, although a few were found in Persian period loci (where they were probably intrusive) and a few in later contexts or on the surface. One fragment (Fig. 33.1:5) was found together with a coin of Demetrius II (Chap. 27: No. 138), and one green body fragment (Reg. No. 4108/71, Locus 570, Stratum V-IV, unillustrated) with a coin of Antiochus IV (Chap. 27: No. 126).

Bowls of this type are known from the Hellenistic/Hasmonean period at Tel Anafa (Weinberg 1970: Figs. 1–2, 7–10) and Kibbutz Hagoshrim in the Upper Galilee (Weinberg 1973: Fig. 3:1–6). At Tel Anafa they are classified as bowl Type A and dated from the second half of the 2d century B.C.E. to the end of the Hellenistic occupation (Grose 1979: Figs. 3–4). The earliest specimens came from the Athenian Agora, where they are dated to the 2d century B.C.E. (Weinberg 1961: Pl. 91:1; Grose 1979:57–58). They are also known at Samaria in the last quarter of the 1st century B.C.E. (*Samaria-Sebaste III*: 403–404, Fig. 93:2, 4), in the Jewish Quarter of Jerusalem from 50 to 40 B.C.E. (Avigad 1972: Fig. 4, Pl. 45:B; 1980: Fig. 219), at Ashdod from the mid-2d century B.C.E. (Barag 1967: Fig. 105:1, Pl. XCVIII:1; 1971: Bowls 2–6). In the west they lasted until somewhat later (Hayes 1975: Fig. 1:41–42, 44, 1st century B.C.E.-1st century C.E.; van Lith 1977: Fig. 12, Pl. 3:10, 1st century C.E.). They were found in Morgantina, Sicily, from the 1st century B.C.E. to the 1st century C.E. (Grose 1982: Figs. 2, 7) and in Crete until the 1st century C.E. (Grose 1979:58).

Base with Wheel-Cut Circles (Fig. 33.1:10)

This base, with two concentric circles cut into it, belongs either to a vessel with wheel-cut grooves of the type described above or to a ribbed bowl. Parallels: Grose 1979: Fig. 1 (1st century B.C.E.); van Lith 1978–79: Pl. 13:221–228 (1st century C.E.); Berger 1960: Pl. 9:140 (1st century C.E.).

Ribbed Bowls (Fig. 33.1:11–16)

These bowls, also cast in two-part molds, are generally hemispheric, deep or shallow, with flat or rounded bottoms and vertical or slightly flared fire-polished rims. Their colors are light green, light blue, or transparent, although many of them are discolored by earthy weathering or covered with a silver crust. A few of the ribbed pieces are also grooved (Fig. 33.1:2, 7, 13), but ribbing, which appeared only occasionally on the Strata V-IV vessels, became more common in Strata III-II, and grooving, although still found in Stratum IIIb (Fig. 33.1:13) tended to disappear. Fourteen pieces of different bowls of this type were found, six in the Hellenistic/Hasmonean strata and eight in the Early Roman stratum.

The earliest bowls of this type were found in the east at Tel Anafa (Weinberg 1970:17–27, Figs. 11A, 12), where they are classified as bowl Type C (Grose 1979: Figs. 5–7), and at Kibbutz Hagoshrim in the Upper Galilee (Weinberg 1973:35–51, Fig. 3:20–21, 43, 47–48), all with densely spaced ribs and dating from 150 to 75 B.C.E. Elsewhere in the east, they date from the 1st century B.C.E. into the 1st century C.E.: at Samaria (*Samaria-Sebaste III*: 403, 406, Fig. 93:1, with widely spaced ribs), Ashdod (Barag 1967: Fig. 16:10), and Jerusalem (Johns 1950:139, Fig. 10a; Avigad 1980: Fig. 220). In the west, these bowls appear somewhat later (Isings 1957: Form 3, 1st century C.E.). At Morgantina in Sicily they are dated from the 1st century B.C.E. to the 1st century C.E. (Grose 1982: Fig. 8), at Velsen in the Netherlands to the second half of the 1st century C.E. (van Lith 1977: Pls. 1–2), and at Valkenburg (Netherlands) they lasted into Period 6 (178–260 C.E.) but were probably produced earlier as well (van Lith 1978–79:23–36, Fig. 1:4, 6, Pls. 5–6). At this site most of the bowls had widely spaced ribs, but in all periods some had densely spaced ribs (van Lith 1978–79:23–36, Nos. 37, 47, 49, 74, 78, 85, 88, 99, 101); therefore, densely spaced ribs like those at Tel Michal cannot be ascribed to any particular period. At Köln (Fremersdorf 1958: Pls. 23–27), such bowls were found with widely spaced ribs in a 1st-century C.E. context; at Vindonissa they date to the same period, until 100 C.E. (Berger 1960: Pls. 2:24–27, 18:29–38, Forms 28–29).

At Tel Michal, one piece (Fig. 33.1:14) was found together with a coin of Livia (Chap. 27: No. 157) and another (Fig. 33.1:16) with a coin of Pontius Pilate (Chap. 27: No. 154).

The type with short ribs around the shoulder (Fig. 33.1:14) has good parallels at Vindonissa (Berger 1960: Pls. 2:23, 9:139, 18:31), in Cyprus (*SCE IV, 3*: Fig. 41:5, 8), and at Ashdod (Barag 1967: Fig. 16:7, 9), all 1st century C.E., and at Samaria (*Samaria-Sebaste III*: Fig. 93:1), 1st century B.C.E.

33.3. BLOWN GLASS

The pieces made by this method include: (1) A flared bottle neck with collar ridge at junction of body (Fig. 33.1:17); the collar is made of a hollow strip of blown glass. This piece may be part of a Roman bottle (see Isings 1957: Form 70, 2d century C.E.). (2) Two green lamp bases with wick holders. One of these was found in the watchtower of Stratum I (Reg. No. 2194/70, Locus 50) and the other at the surface (Reg. No. 3624/70, Locus 531). This type of lamp first appears in the 4th century C.E. and continues into the Early Arab period (Isings 1957: Form 134, 4th-5th centuries C.E.; Philippe 1970: Fig. 39; Lehrer 1972:68, Nos. 10–11). (3) Five vertical or slightly flared rims and 15 light green body fragments from the Early Arab stratum.

33.4. OTHER GLASS ARTIFACTS

In addition to numerous glass beads found at the site (Chap. 34), there were three glass objects that are not parts of vessels.

1. Glass Rod

Reg. No. 7275/70, Locus 1086, Stratum V, greenish color, 35 mm long, 3 mm in diameter; a similar rod from Samaria was described as a pin or kohl stick (*Samaria-Sebaste III*: 420; Avigad 1980: Fig. 222).

2. Spindle Whorl

Reg. No. 6758/70, Locus 1002, Stratum II, gray glass, 3 mm in diameter, flat bottom, convex upper side. No parallels of spindle whorls made from glass are known to me. (For spindle whorls of stone and bone found at Tel Michal, see Chap. 31.10 and Fig. 31.7.)

3. Child's Bracelet

Reg. No. 513/70, Locus 94, Stratum I, 13.7 cm in diameter, made of a white thread, D-shaped in section, 3.5 mm. This was found in an infant burial of the Early Arab period. Parallels: *Gerar*: Pl. 67:4–8.

33.5. SUMMARY

Glass vessels were used at Tel Michal from the Persian period; the earliest piece comes from Stratum XI. In these early times, the vessels were manufactured by the core technique and were used mainly as containers for cosmetic materials and perfumes. In the Hellenistic and Hasmonean periods, glass vessels cast in two-part molds and decorated with horizontal wheel-cut grooves or vertical ribbing were common. Bowls of this type were abundant at the site. From the Roman period on, glass-blown vessels were produced, but only a few of these (namely, the lamps with wick holders known up to the Early Arab period) were found at Tel Michal in a state permitting identification.

NOTE

1. I am indebted to Gusta Lehrer-Jakobson, curator of the Glass Pavilion of the Haaretz Museum, for her advice and for the use of the museum library.

REFERENCES

Avigad, N. 1972. Excavations in the Jewish Quarter of the Old City in Jerusalem. *IEJ* 22:193–200.

Avigad, N. 1980. *The Upper City of Jerusalem*. (Hebrew) Jerusalem.

Barag, D. 1967. The Glass Vessels. *Ashdod I*: 36–37.

Barag, D. 1970. Mesopotamian Core-Formed Glass Vessels (1500–50 B.C.) Pages 131–174 in: *Glass and Glass-Making in Ancient Mesopotamia*. A. L. Oppenheim et al., eds. New York.

Barag, D. 1971. The Glass Vessels. *Ashdod II-III*: 202–206.

Barag, D. 1975. Rod-formed Kohl Tubes in the Mid-First Millennium B.C. *Journal of Glass Studies* 17:23–36.

Berger, L. 1960. *Römische Gläser aus Vindonissa*. Basel.

Fossing, A. 1940. *Glass Vessels before Glass-Blowing*. Copenhagen.

Fremersdorf, F. 1958. *Römisches Buntglas aus Köln*. Cologne.

Freyer-Schauenburg, B. 1973. Die Glasfunde aus Pitane (Çandarli). *Anadolu* 17:141–175.

Goldstein, S. M. 1979. *Pre-Roman and Early Roman Glass in the Corning Museum of Glass*. New York.

Grose, D. F. 1979. The Syro-Palestinian Glass Industry in the Late Hellenistic Period. *MUSE* 13:54–65.

Grose, D. F. 1982. The Hellenistic and Early Roman Glass from Morgantina (Serra Orlando) Sicily. *Journal of Glass Studies* 24:20–29.

Harden, D. B. 1969. Ancient Glass I: Pre-Roman. *Archaeological Journal* 125:46–72.

Hayes, J. W. 1975. *Roman and Pre-Roman Glass in the Royal Ontario Museum: Catalogue*. Toronto.

Isings, C. 1957. *Roman Glass from Dated Finds*. Groningen.

Johns, C. N. 1933. Excavations at 'Atlit (1930–31). The South-Eastern Cemetery. *QDAP* 2:41–104.

Johns, C. N. 1950. The Citadel, Jerusalem. *QDAP* 14:121–190.

Lehrer, G. 1972. Three Fragments of Rare Vessels from the Museum Collection. *Museum Haaretz Bulletin* 14:127–137.

Philippe, J. 1970. *Le monde byzantin dans l'histoire de la verrerie*. Bologna.

van Lith, S. M. E. 1977. Römisches Glas aus Velsen, Z.H. *Oudheindkundige Medelingen uit het Ryksmuseum van Oudhedente* 48: 1–62.

van Lith, S. M. E. 1978–79. *Römisches Glas aus Valkenburg, Z.H.* Leiden.

von Saldern, A., et al. 1974. *Gläser der Antike Sammlung Oppenländer*. Cologne.

Weinberg, G. R. (Davidson). 1961. Hellenistic Glass Vessels from the Athenian Agora. *Hesperia* 30:380–393.

Weinberg, G. R. (Davidson). 1970. Hellenistic Glass from Tel Anafa in Upper Galilee. *Journal of Glass Studies* 12:17–27.

Weinberg, G. R. (Davidson). 1973. Notes on Glass from Upper Galilee. *Journal of Glass Studies* 15:35–51.

34

Beads and Pendants

by Trude Kertesz

Of the 275 or so beads found at Tel Michal (including a few pendants and amulets), more than 240 came from the Persian period cemetery and another 13 of the same period were found scattered individually in the various excavation areas.[1] There were few beads from the earlier Iron Age and later Hellenistic to Early Arab periods and none from the Middle or Late Bronze Age strata, probably because these settlements were represented by fewer strata and no cemetery. The nomenclature for bead shapes and types used in the following descriptions comes from Beck (1928).

34.1. IRON AGE

The earliest bead found at the site came from Iron Age Stratum XIV/XIII (Reg. No. 6970/80, Locus 117; Pl. 79:1). This is a long cylinder frit bead (5 mm in diameter and 15 mm long). Frit (often called "paste" or "composition"), although composed of the same or similar materials as glass (mainly powdered quartz sand), is baked at a low temperature until the grains are partially fused but not vitrified. As described by Kuschke (1970), "the sand grains adhere so loosely that one can scrape them away with the fingernail." Such is the case with this Iron Age example, whose surface is cracked and partially crumbled away. Its color is bright blue (for the composition of what is known as "Egyptian blue frit," see Lucas 1962:340–344).

Frit beads have been known in Egypt since the Old Kingdom (Brunton 1928: Pl. C:75:2). Long cylindrical beads of frit, which became popular in Egypt in the Ramesside period, have been found in numerous excavations in Israel (e.g., *Lachish II*: Pl. 34:39, 41, Pl. 36:103; *Lachish III*: Pl. 66:37; *CPP*: Nos. D50, 64, 105, 134).

The other Iron Age beads were found together in a jug of Stratum XIII (Reg. No. 553/80, Locus 99; Pl. 79:2). This hoard – which may have been collected by the inhabitants from earlier strata – included six cowrie shells from the Red Sea, two faience beads, one frit bead, one spacer made of clay, and two gaming pieces.

The shells (*Cypraea carneola*) varied from 10 to 15 mm in length and 5 to 8 mm in diameter. The dorsal sides were broken away, perhaps to permit stringing. Petrie has suggested that this type of shell was used by the Egyptians, who also imitated it in gold (de Morgan 1895: Pl. XVII) as an amulet for protection against the evil eye (Petrie 1914:27, Pl. XIVa-e). Such shells were found in Iron Age contexts both at Megiddo and Lachish (*Megiddo II*: Pl. 217:129, Stratum VA; *Lachish III*: Pl. 67:116).

The two long, cylindrical faience beads (5 mm in diameter and 12 mm in length) were made by coating a thread with a frit paste, rolling it on a board while still moist, and then cutting the long cylinder to the required lengths with a knife. The thread was burnt out during the firing process, leaving a hole for stringing. This frit core was then dipped into a silica glaze, producing a glassy surface of various colors according to the oxides present in the components of the glaze (Lucas 1962:44–45; Kuschke 1970: 157–163).

The frit bead from this hoard is white standard circular (12 mm × 12 mm). Frit beads of this shape were very common from the Middle Kingdom on (Engelbach 1923:80, J312, glazed; *Megiddo II*: Pl. 213:62; *Megiddo Tombs*: Pl. 161:10–11). An Iron Age example is seen in *Lachish III*: Pl. 38:2.

Among the objects in the hoard was a spacer (19 mm wide and 4.5 cm in length) of gray clay with three perforations. Spacers, usually elongated and flattened, with two or more perforations, were used to separate multiple strands of beads. Our rectangular specimen belongs to Group XVII of Beck's classification (Beck 1928:13). Rectangular spacers made of various materials such as gold, carnelian, or faience are common since Old Kingdom times in Egypt; for Iron Age examples, see *Lachish III*: Pl. 54:8; *Gezer II*: Fig. 290.

The other two items in the hoard were not beads but gaming pieces. They are about 19 mm high and have a conical base topped by an unperforated convex button. Gaming pieces of this and other types are known from Egyptian wall paintings of the Ramesside period (Michalowski 1968: Fig. 564). For local examples, see *Lachish IV*: Pl. 54:6, Late Bronze Age; *Gezer II*; Fig. 281; *Megiddo II*: Pl. 191:12–15, Strata VI-IV; *Megiddo I*: Pl. 101:14, Stratum III.

 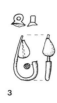  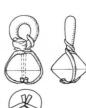 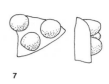

1   2   3   4   5   6   7

0 ⊢————————⊣ 1cm.

Figure 34.1. Persian period beads, according to catalog numbers: (1) granulated disk bead (No. 7); (2) eye bead (Nos. 26–27); (3) bronze earring with bead of turquoise faience (No. 96); (4) eye bead (Nos. 122–126); (5) carnelian bead mounted in silver frame for suspension (No. 192); (6) eye bead (No. 233); (7) plate with frit bead insets (No. 246).

34.2. PERSIAN PERIOD

About 240 beads were found in the Persian period cemetery (Nos. 1–241 in catalog), most of them in groups, from which we assume that they had been strung together as bracelets, armlets, necklaces, anklets, or some other kind of personal adornment. There were eight burials with large bead groups, one of them (Burial 666) with as many as 40 items. In Burial 1869 there were two separate clusters of beads, presumably from two different strings of jewelry. Some of the graves contained only two or three beads (and many none at all), but it must be remembered that a large number of these burials lay close to the surface and were robbed or badly damaged by erosion. Many of the beads made of softer materials such as frit must have disintegrated in the ground. Some of the beads (Nos. 240–241) were retrieved from the sand around the graves, where they had probably been washed from the burials.

It is not known whether these beads were simply the personal possessions of the deceased, who had worn them when still alive, or whether they were burial offerings or had some other cultic significance (see *Kamid el-Lōz 2*: 40–41). Those burials rich in other grave goods often had a large number of beads (see Chap. 11 tables).

It is not known how or in what order the beads were strung together; in the photographs of the groups (Pls. 79:3–7; 80:1–2), we have simply tried to show some of the representative bead types from the larger groups.

Thirteen beads were found in various loci of the inhabited area, mostly in Strata VIII–VI on the high tell and a few in Area C (Nos. 242–254 in catalog). They were exactly the same types as were found in the cemetery.

34.2.1. Catalog of Persian Period Beads

Measurements are given according to diameter × length unless otherwise specified. Parallels have been limited to a few examples only, from the Persian period whenever possible.

Burial 1869: Reg. No. 11679/80: Pl. 79:3

1. Standard, carnelian, 9 × 9 mm, red. Parallels: Hachmann 1970: Pl. 3:11; *Kamid el-Lōz 2*: Pl. 9, 9:13–14, etc.
2. Long barrel, zoned, marble, 11 × 17 mm, gray with white stripe around circumference. Parallels: *Megiddo I*:

Pl. 90:54, 66 (Iron Age); *Kamid el-Lōz 2*: Pl. 9, 9:18, Pl. 12, 15:23, Pl. 21, 74:9.
3. Standard, limestone, 8 × 7 mm, gray.
4. Scaraboid, plain back, sides and base, serpentine, 10 × 14 mm, dark green. Probably Egyptian import. Parallels: *Gerar*: Pl. XXV:123–24 (New Kingdom); *Kamid el-Lōz 2*: Pl. 17, 47:11 (limestone).
5–6. Long barrel, zoned, marble, 6 × 9 mm, 11 × 13 mm, gray (see No. 2).
7. Granulated disk, frit, 8 mm diam., 2 mm thick, gray. The granules are placed around the axis in the shape of a flower (Fig. 34.1:1). Parallels: Hachmann 1970: Pl. 3:17; *Kamid el-Lōz 2*: Pl. 4, 2:5, 6, Pl. 9, 9:3, Pl. 12, 15:10–11; Beck 1928: Fig. 23A; *CPP*: Pl. 98, 105 (silver).
8–9. Long barrel, frit, 7 × 8 mm, green. Parallels: Hachmann 1970: Pl. 3:32; *Kamid el-Lōz 2*: Pl. 16, 63:14.
10–11. Long cylinder, plaster, 5 × 6 mm, 9 × 10 mm, white. Parallels: Hachmann 1970: Pl. 13:16; *Kamid el-Lōz 2*: Pl. 4, 1:24 (frit).

Burial 1869; Reg. No. 11688/80: Pl. 79:4

12–13. Flattened, lenticular, bone, 8 × 3 mm, whitish.
14–15. Flattened, lenticular, stone, 7 × 4 mm, 5 × 2 mm, whitish.
16–25. Disk cylinder, plaster, 5 × 2 mm, white. Parallels: *Kamid el-Lōz 2*: 3, 1:6–8.
26–28. Standard eye beads, glass, 5 × 5 mm, one broken. Green matrix; each bead with four blue protruding eyes surrounded by white circle (Fig. 34.1:2). Parallels: *Kamid el-Lōz 2*: Pl. 11, 13:5, 7; *Corinth XII*: Pl. 122:2469.
29–31. Standard grain beads, frit, 4 × 4 mm. Brown matrix, green and red grains. Parallels: Hachmann 1970: Pl. 3, 3:20, 22; *CPP*: Pl. 36 (26th Dynasty).

Burial 1163: Reg. No. 7638/80: Pl. 79:5

32–33. Cowrie shells, *Cypraea carneola* (see Section 34.1). Parallels from Persian period: *Kamid el-Lōz 2*: Pl. 11, 13:20.
34–36. Short barrel, carnelian, 9 × 4 mm, red. Parallels: *Kamid el-Lōz 2*: Pl. 16, 38:5.
37. Long barrel, zoned, stone, 7 × 16 mm, grayish with white stripe (see No. 2).
38–49. Standard grain beads, frit, 4.5 × 4.5 mm, brown with blue and green grains (see Nos. 29–31).

371

50–54. Drop-shaped pendants, frit, 5 × 12 mm, yellow and turquoise. Parallels: Hachmann 1970: Pl. 4:12.

55–58. Flattened cylinder, glass, 5 × 6 mm, greenish. Unperforated. Parallels: *Corinth XII*: Pl. 122: No. 2469 (Roman period).

Burial 666: Reg. No. 4845/80: Pl. 79:6

59. Long barrel, carnelian, 6 × 11 mm, red with whitish stripes. Parallels: Hachmann 1970: Pl. 3:32; *Kamid el-Lōz 2*: Pl. 11, 13:19, etc.

60–65. Two standard barrel, carnelian, 6 × 7 mm, red; two limestone, 6 × 7 mm, yellow; two onyx, 6 × 7 mm, black. For carnelian parallels, see No. 1; for limestone and onyx, see *Kamid el-Lōz 2*: Pl. 19, 63:28.

66–67. Shells (*Ceritium erithraconense*), 6 × 14 mm, 6 × 16 mm.

68–79. Standard cylinder, plaster, 6 × 6 mm, white. Parallels: *Kamid el-Lōz 2*: Pl. 4, 2:22, etc.

80–84. Standard disk, frit, 2 × 3 mm to 1 × 3 mm, dark blue. Parallels: *Kamid el-Lōz 2*: Pl. 15, 28:11.

85–86. Long cylinder, gadrooned, frit, 1 × 7 mm, 2 × 7 mm, green. Parallel: Beck 1928: Fig. 12 (500 B.C.E., made of gold); *Kamid el-Lōz 2*: Pl. 4, 2:34.

87–88. Long granulated, frit, 2 × 6 mm, green with brown (similar to No. 7 but longer).

89–91. Short standard eye beads, glass, 5 × 3 mm. Green matrix, dark blue eyes surrounded by two white circles; eyes not protruding. Parallels: *Kamid el-Lōz 2*: Pl. 11, 13:6, Pl. 25, 28:7; *Persepolis II*: Pl. 43:11.

92–93. Drop-shaped pendants, glass, 6 × 13 mm, blue. Parallels: resemble serpentine amulet from Hachmann 1970: Pl. 3:19.

94–95. One flattened, one biconical standard, glass, 5 × 3 mm, 5 × 4 mm, blue. Parallels: *Corinth XII*: 255, 282; Pl. 148c. Probably imported from Egypt.

96. Bronze earring decorated with drop-shaped bead of greenish turquoise faience; bead is affixed to upper part of half-round bronze thread of earring; upper extremity of ring is broken (Fig. 34.1:3). Parallels: *Kamid el-Lōz 2*: 55, Pl. 3, 1:12–17, Pl. 4, 2:9–10, Pl. 6, 5:3, etc.

Burial 1184: Reg. No. 7683/80: Pl. 79:7

97–98. Cowrie shells, 11 × 15 mm, white (see Nos. 32–33).

99–109. Long cylinder, plaster, 5 × 8 mm, white (see Nos. 10–11).

110. Granulated disk, frit, 5 × 2 mm, black (see No. 7).

111–121. Short disk, frit, 1.5 × 2 mm, brown. Parallels: *Kamid el-Lōz 2*: Pl. 4, 2:28.

122–126. Short standard eye beads, glass, 5 × 3 mm (Fig. 34.1:4). Green matrix, blue eyes; one blue and one white circle around each (see Nos. 89–91).

Burial 1875: Reg. No. 11698/80: Pl. 80:1

127–128. Cowrie shells, 11 × 15–17 mm (see Nos. 32–33).

129. Amulet, 7 × 7 mm, mother-of-pearl. "Eye of Horus," white. Parallels: *Kamid el-Lōz 2*: Pl. 11, 13:1–4 (faience).

130–133. Standard grain beads, frit, 5 × 5 mm, brown matrix with green and white grains (see Nos. 29–31).

Burial 1871: Reg. No. 11707: Pl. 80:2

134. Short bicone, carnelian 12 × 7 mm, red. Parallels: *Kamid el-Lōz 2*: Pl. 9, 9:12, Pl. 14, 22:2.

135–142. Standard cylinder, plaster, 4 × 3 mm, white (see Nos. 68–79).

143–155. Short barrel, carnelian, 2 × 1 mm, red (see Nos. 34–36).

156. Long bicone, frit, 8 × 12 mm, white. This type is usually made of carnelian, e.g., *Kamid el-Lōz 2*: Pl. 23, 76:48 (see also Nos. 8–9).

157–171. Short standard, carnelian, 8 × 5 mm, red (not all stringable). Parallel: *Kamid el-Lōz 2*: Pl. 16, 40:9.

172. Granulated disk, frit, 2 × 1 mm, black (see No. 7).

Burial 663: Reg. No. 4842

173–174. Short bicone, frit, 5 × 4 mm, green. Parallels: *Kamid el-Lōz 2*: Pl. 4, 2:27.

Burial 664: Reg. No. 4877: Pl. 80:3

175–182. Long cylinders, probably of bone, 10 × 12 mm, brown. Each has three holes, one at each end, but not perforated, and one on its circumference. These may possibly be hinges of a small box (suggested by G. Barkay).

Burial 826: Reg. No. 4881/80: Pl. 80:4 (Nos. 183–191); Pl. 80:5 (No. 192)

183–191. Long cylinder, frit, 5 × 10–12 mm, brown. Parallels: *Kamid el-Lōz 2*: Pl. 4, 2:26 etc. (faience).

192. Bead as amulet. Standard bicone, carnelian, 5 × 5 mm, red. Mounted in silver frame for suspension (Fig. 34.1:5). Parallels: *Gezer I*: Fig. 157: 10–12.

193. Long cylinder, irregularly shaped, frit, 5 × 10 mm, brownish.

Burial 1160: Reg. No. 7627

194. Long barrel, stone, 10 × 16 mm, gray. Parallels: *Kamid el-Lōz 2*: Pl. 23, 76:49 etc. (malachite).

Burial 1179: Reg. Nos. 7689/7690

195. Standard cylinder, frit, 7 × 6 mm, white. Parallels: *Kamid el-Lōz 2*: Pl. 19, 63:7–8.

196–205. Flattened lenticular grain beads, frit, 5–7 mm, 4–10 mm, brown matrix with yellow, white, and green grains (cf. Nos. 29–31, standard).

206. Drop shaped, limestone, 4 × 4 mm, brown (cf. Nos. 50–54, frit).

Burial 1183: Reg. No. 7725/80: Pl. 80:6 (Nos. 207–210); Reg. No. 7728 (Nos. 211–214)

207–210. Short circular, limestone, 6 × 5 mm, light brown.

211. Long barrel, gadrooned, marble, 5 × 7 mm, gray (cf. Nos. 85–86, frit). Parallel: Beck 1928: Fig. 21:A2d (2000 B.C.E.).

212–213. Standard barrel, limestone, 7 × 7 mm, light brown (cf. Nos. 60–65, carnelian).

214. Pendant, broken, mother-of-pearl, white, representing part of wings.

Burial 1193: Reg. Nos. 7732/80 (No. 215);
7733/80 (Nos. 216–219)

215. Short bicone, frit, 9 × 4 mm, green. Parallel: *Kamid el-Lōz 2*: Pl. 13, 18:11–12, etc. (faience).

216–218. Short convex bicone, glass, 5 × 4 mm, green. Parallels: *Kamid el-Lōz 2*: Pl. 4, 2:31–32.

219. Short bicone, frit, yellow (see No. 215).

Burial 1851: Reg. No. 11611/80

220–226. Broken eye bead, glass, white matrix, green circles; broken glass bead, green; long barrel, frit, 8 × 10 mm, green (see Nos. 8–9); cowrie shell (see Nos. 32–33); three unidentifiable shell parts.

Burial 1858: Reg. No. 11629/80: Pl. 80:7

227. Long square serpentinite, 15 × 22 mm, gray with black. Parallels: *Lachish III*: Pl. 66 (resin); Beck 1928: Group IX; *CPP*: No. E10, from 18th–19th Dynasties (carnelian).

Burial 1859: Reg. No. 11649/80

228. Long cylinder, plaster, 3 × 9 mm, white (see Nos. 10–11).

229–230. Long cylinder, frit, 4 × 10 mm, white (see Nos. 183–191).

Burial 1861: Reg. No. 11644/80: Pl. 80:8

231. Standard bicone, carnelian, red. Parallels: *Kamid el-Lōz 2*: Pl. 9, 9:12, etc.

232. Amulet, broken, mother-of-pearl (?). May be part of a Horus eye like that shown in Figure 29.1:9. Parallels: *Kamid el-Lōz 2*: Pl. 11, 13:1, etc. (faience).

233. Short barrel glass eye bead, 4 × 3 mm (Fig. 34.1:6); black matrix, dark blue eyes surrounded by white circles (see Nos. 89–91).

Burial 1866: Reg. No. 11667/80

234. Standard bicone, glass, 4 × 4 mm, green. Parallels: *Kamid el-Lōz 2*: Pl. 4, 2:31–32, etc.

235. Disk barrel, frit, 2 × 1 mm, brown. Parallels: *Kamid el-Lōz 2*: Pl. 15, 28:1, 15–16.

Burial 1867: Reg. No. 11660/80

236–237. Irregularly shaped, frit, 5 × 5 mm, blue.

Burial 1872: Reg. No. 11712/80 (No. 238):
Pl. 80:9; Reg. No. 11710/80 (No. 239)

238. Standard bicone, frit, 13 × 12 mm, greenish gray. Parallels: *Kamid el-Lōz 2*: Pl. 4, 2:27, etc.

239. Long cylinder, frit, 8 × 15 mm, white (see Nos. 183–191).

Burial(?) 1159 (sand next to graves): Reg.
No. 11675/80 (No. 240): Pl. 80:10; Reg.
No. 11646/80 (No. 241)

240. Long barrel, zoned, alabaster, 13 × 17 mm, gray with white stripe around circumference (see No. 2).

241. Long barrel, zoned, limestone, 9 × 14 mm, gray with white stripe around circumference (see No. 2).

Locus 1639: Reg. No. 10326/80

242. Long cylinder, frit, 8 × 10 mm, white.

243. Standard, carnelian, 3 × 5 mm, red (see No. 1).

Locus 842: Reg. No. 5575/80

244. Long barrel, faience, 4 × 11 mm, black with golden glaze (see No. 8).

Locus 357: Reg. No. 2079/80: Pl. 80:11

245. Pendant, triangular, tortoise shell, 7–10 × 16 mm (broken), white. Parallels: *Lachish III*: Pl. 67:137 (marble).

Locus 1122: Reg. No. 7414/80

246. Pendant (?). Piece of triangular frit plate inlaid with three tiny standard circular blue frit beads (Fig. 34.1:7).

Locus 608: Reg. No. 4448/80

247. Standard circular, faience, 6 × 6 mm, greenish.

Locus 593: Reg. No. 4298/80: Pl. 80:12

248. Standard circular, stone, 10 × 10 mm, greenish, with crumbs of natural copper embedded in stone.

Locus 233: Reg. No. 2813/80

249. Disk, glass, broken, dark blue.

Locus 315: Reg. No. 1693/70

250. Standard concave, unidentifiable black material (resin or wood?), 16 × 16 mm, rod inserted through perforation.

Locus 322: Reg. No. 5584/80

251. Standard bicone, glass, broken, green (see No. 234).

Locus 602: Reg. No. 4414/50

252. Pendant (?), triangular, stone, 20 × 17 × 17 mm (broken), brown with yellow stripe, polished.

Locus 690: Reg. No. 5205/80

253. Short bicone, glass, 9 × 8 mm, green (see No. 234).

Locus 1640: Reg. No. 6976/70

254. Scaraboid, glass, 6 × 11.5 mm, broken, unperforated, black. Parallels: Beck 1928, Group XXXVI of pendants (see No. 4).

34.2.2. Summary of Persian Period Beads

Because of the great number of beads found in the Persian period cemetery, where there is practically no chance that they are intrusive, we are able to determine the most popular types at Tel Michal during this period. Of the 250 or so beads from the Persian period cemetery or settlement, some 85 were frit; there were probably many more, even in the graves that were not robbed or eroded, but because of the extreme friability of the material (see description of frit in Section 34.1), they may simply have disintegrated. Long cylindrical, long barrel or long bicone frit beads were the most common (Nos. 8–9, 156, 183–91, 193, 229–30). Grain frit beads were also abundant (Nos. 29–31, 38–49, 131–33, 196–205). The core of a grain frit bead is made of rough quartz grains of different colors cemented by fusion with an alkali or lime; the different colors of the grains are then visible in the core as well as on the outside of the bead. Another type of frit bead (Fig. 34.1:1) had small spherical granules placed around the central perforation to produce what looks like daisy petals (Nos. 7, 87–88, 110, 172). This type imitates silver and gold beads from Persia (Ghirshman 1964:560–563).

The second most popular type of material was natural stone; 38 beads of carnelian and 26 of marble, alabaster, or limestone were found. These may have been produced on the spot, since the manufacturing technique was simple (see Lucas 1962:43).

Other natural materials used for beads were bone (Nos. 12–13, as well as the presumed box hinges, Nos. 175–182) and shell. The cowrie shells (Nos. 32–33, 97–98, 127–128, 223), which are naturally open on the ventral side, all had broken dorsals that made them stringable. These shells probably came from the Red Sea. There were also two amulets of mother-of-pearl in the form of a Horus eye, one complete and one broken (Nos. 129, 232). Such amulets are Egyptian in origin (Engelbach 1923: Pl. L:38; Beck 1928: Fig. 28A) and were probably imported from there. (A third Horus eye, of faience, was found in Burial 1858; see Chap. 29.5.)

There were 34 plaster beads (Nos. 10–11, 16, 25, 68–79, 99–109, 135–142), most long, cylindrical, and white, like those from the tombs of Kamid el Lōz. These beads were probably imported.

Thirty glass beads were found, 17 of plain glass in various shapes, and mostly blue or green. Four of them were unperforated (Nos. 55–58), a phenomenon for which we can offer no explanation. There were 13 "eye beads" (Nos. 26–28, 89–91, 122–126, 220, 233). Such beads were made by placing a drop of colored glass onto the matrix and rolling it in while still soft; then another drop of a different color was placed in the center so that the first drop left a ring around the second. In the Persian period this technique achieved a very high standard. The eye beads from Burial 666 (Nos. 89–91) are very similar to those found at Persepolis, whence they and similar ones from Kamid el-Lōz were probably imported.

34.3. HELLENISTIC, ROMAN, AND EARLY ARAB PERIODS

There were four beads from Hellenistic Strata V-IV and one from Late Hasmonean Stratum IIIb: one of blue glass (long bicone), one of black frit (short barrel), one of gray marbled stone (long barrel), and one short standard circular eye bead with blue matrix and black eye surrounded by white circle.

The Late Hasmonean, Roman, and Early Arab periods yielded one glass bead each: Stratum IIIb: short circular barrel, dark blue; Stratum II: standard circular, black; Stratum I: standard circular, blue matrix with brown and yellow bands around the circumference.

NOTE

1. Also included in this chapter are a few small items found together with the bead groups, such as the gaming pieces from the Iron Age hoard and what may be stone hinges from the Persian period cemetery.

REFERENCES

Beck, H. C. 1928. Classification and Nomenclature of Beads and Pendants. *Archaeologia* 77:1–76.
Brunton, G. 1928. *Qau Badari II: Amulet and Bead Corpus*. London.
de Morgan, J. 1895. *Fouilles à Dahchour I*. Vienna.
Engelbach, R. 1923. *Harageh II: Corpus of Beads*. London.
Ghirshman, R. 1964. *The Arts of Ancient Iran*. New York.
Hachmann, R. 1970. *Bericht über die Ergebnisse der Ausgrabungen in Kāmid el-Lōz (Libanon) in den Jahren 1966 und 1967*. Bonn.
Kuschke, A. 1970. Fayence und Fritte. Pages 157–163 in: *Archäologie und Altes Testament, Festschrift für Kurt Galling*. A. Kuschke and E. Kutsch, eds. Tübingen.
Lucas, A. 1962. *Ancient Egyptian Materials and Industries*, 4th ed. London.
Michalowski, K. 1968. *Art of Ancient Egypt*. New York.
Petrie, W. M. F. 1914. *Amulets*. Warminster.

35

Iron Age and Persian Period Pottery from Tel Poleg

by Lily Singer-Avitz

Tel Poleg, which lies about 14 km north of Tel Michal near the estuary of Naḥal Poleg, was excavated in 1959 and 1964 by Dr. R. Gophna, a member of the Tel Michal expedition. Although the site was apparently occupied, sporadically at least, during several stages of the 2d and 1st millennia, only the Middle Bronze Age II finds were published (Gophna 1973; Kochavi et al. 1979), since the later periods were not represented by substantial architecture.[1]

The proximity of Tel Poleg to Tel Michal suggested that we might be able to establish the date of its Iron Age and Persian period levels by comparing their pottery assemblages with those of the relevant levels at Tel Michal and other sites, particularly those lying in the coastal zone of the Sharon plain.

35.1. IRON AGE POTTERY

The Iron Age pottery at Tel Poleg was found mainly in Area C (Gophna 1973: Figs. 1, 3). According to Gophna (personal communication), the remains of this period lay directly above the MB IIA settlement and included fragmentary walls of brick and stone, although no architectural units were distinguished. The settlement, apparently unfortified, was built in the concavity inside the walls of the MB fort, which were still partially standing at the time. There were no ash layers nor signs of destruction by fire, and the settlement was probably abandoned.

During the excavations an attempt was made to separate the baskets of the lower Iron Age phase (IIc) from those of the two phases above it (IIb-IIa). However, no typological differences in the pottery were revealed from one phase to the next. For this reason and because of the paucity of the material, the whole assemblage is treated here as a single unit. It consists entirely of common domestic wares: bowls, cooking pots, and a few storage jars.

Bowls

As in Iron Age Strata XIV-XIII at Tel Michal, most of the bowls are covered inside and out with hand-burnished red slip. The burnish is usually horizontal on the upper part of the bowl and vertical from the carination to the base. The carinated red-slipped and hand-burnished bowl (Fig. 35.1:1) is relatively thick walled and has a ring base. Similar bowls were found at Megiddo Strata VA-IVB (*Megiddo I*: Pl. 28:98) and Taanach, Period IIB (*Taanach I*: Fig. 45:2, 8). The bowl with rounded walls and internally thickened rim (Fig. 35.1:2) is smeared with reddish brown paint and hand burnished; parallels are known at Hazor Stratum XB (*Hazor III-IV*: Pl. CLXXI:6) and at Tel Mevorakh Stratum VII (*Tel Mevorakh I*: Fig. 12:24). The red-slipped and hand-burnished bowl with simple rim (Fig. 35.1:3) is an extremely common type that usually has a ring base. Similar bowls are found in Area A, Strata X-IX, at Hazor (*Hazor I*: Pl. XLV:5), Megiddo Strata VA-IVB (*Megiddo I*: Pl. 30:123), and Tell Qasile Stratum IX (Mazar 1977: Pl. 56:1). Mazar (1977:269–272) notes that these rounded bowls with simple rim are the largest and most varied group of bowls at Tell Qasile, appearing in Strata XII-IX without morphological change, although the surface treatment (slip, burnish, and decoration) varies. The rounded bowl with inward-sloping rim, grooved on the outer edge (Fig. 35.1:4), is red slipped and hand burnished. These bowls, very common in the 10th century B.C.E., are found at Tel Michal in Stratum XIV (Fig. 7.1:3; for parallels, see Chap. 7, Section 7.1.1). The ring bases of Figure 35.1:5–6, with red slip and chordal burnishing on the inner surface, belong to the range of bowls described above.

Kraters

The relatively small carinated krater (Fig. 35.1:7) with rounded, thickened rim is red slipped and hand burnished

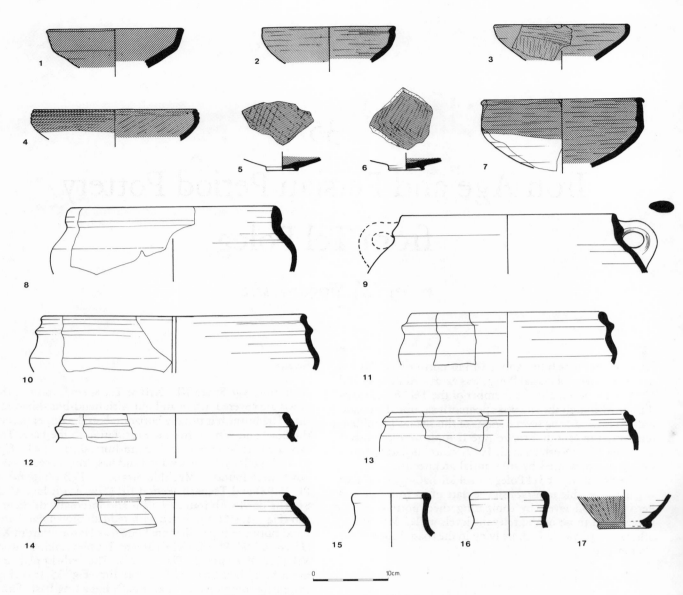

Figure 35.1. Iron age pottery from Tel Poleg.

Legend for Fig. 35.1

No.	Type	Reg. No.	Phase	Description
1	Bowl	15/64	IIa	Brown (gray), small white and gray grits; red slip, hand burnished.
2	Bowl	15a/64	IIa	Gray (gray), small white and large gray grits; red-brown slip, hand burnished.
3	Bowl	19/64	IIb	Brown-gray (gray-black), small white grits; red slip, hand burnished.
4	Bowl	21/64	IIc	Brown (gray), white small grits; red slip, hand burnished.
5	Bowl	9/64	IIb	Brown-gray (gray), small white grits; red slip, hand burnished.
6	Bowl	10/64	IIc	Brown-gray (gray), small white and gray grits; red slip, hand burnished.
7	Small krater	8/64	IIa	Brown-orange (gray), white and gray grits; red slip, hand burnished.
8	Krater	20/64	IIc	Brown (gray), small and large white grits.
9	Cooking pot	6a/64	IIa	Brown (gray), small white and gray grits.
10	Cooking pot	6/64	IIa	Brown (gray), small white grits.
11	Cooking pot	17/64	IIb	Brown (gray), white and gray grits.
12	Cooking pot	18/64	IIb	Brown (black), small and large white grits.
13	Cooking pot	10a/64	IIc	Brown-gray (black), small white grits.
14	Cooking pot	21a/64	IIc	Brown-gray (gray-brown), small white grits.
15	Storage jar	9a/64	IIa	Brown-orange (brown-orange), small white grits.
16	Storage jar	6/64	IIa	Brown-orange (gray), small and large white grits.
17	Jug	15b/64	IIa	Brown-gray (gray), small white grits; red slip, hand burnished.

inside and out. Comparisons of this bowl with complete specimens, such as those found at Tel Michal (e.g., Stratum XIV, Fig. 7.1:4, and parallels in Section 7.1.1), indicate that it should have a ring base and a pair of loop handles extending from the rim down to the carination. Such kraters come in different sizes, and their thickened rims appear at many 10th-century sites.

The closed krater (Fig. 35.1:8) has a rounded body, folded rim, and ring base. Such kraters are known at Taanach, Periods IIB-IA (*Taanach I*: Figs. 7:1-5, 16:1-5, 24:4, 28:2-3, 42:1-4, 43), Megiddo Strata VIII-VIA (*Megiddo II*: Pls. 61:23, 78:14, 84:20-22), Beth-shan Stratum VI (*Beth-shan 1966*: Fig. 54:2), Afula Strata IIIA-IIIB (Dothan 1955: Figs. 12:15-18, 17:12-19), Tel 'Amal Stratum IV (Levy and Edelstein 1972: Fig. 15:20), Tell Keisan Stratum 9a (*Tell Keisan*: Pl. 64:8), in Burial VII on Mount Carmel (Guy 1924: Pl. 3:28), Tel Mevorakh Strata VIII-VII (*Tel Mevorakh I*: Figs. 13:1-5, 20:4-5), and Tell Qasile Strata X-IX (Mazar 1977: Figs. 31:10, 48:29, 49:21). From the analogies, it appears that kraters of this type originated in the north of the country and may be dated to the 11th-10th centuries B.C.E.

Cooking Pots

The cooking pots, which are all wide and shallow with carinated bodies, have two different types of rims: an externally concave triangular rim (Fig. 35.1:9-12) and a short, triangular rim (Fig. 35.1:13-14), the latter characteristic of Strata X-IX (extending into Stratum VIII) at Hazor. According to R. Amiran, they belong to the transitional Iron Age I-II period; for parallels, see *Hazor I*: Pl. XLV:19-20; *Hazor II*: Pl. LI:11; *Hazor III-IV*: Pl. CLXXI:21-27; *Tell Keisan*: Pl. 55:8, 8a; and Gezer (Gitin 1979: Vol. II: Pl. 9:21, 24).

Storage Jars and Jugs

The storage jar rims (Fig. 35.1:15-16) belong to elongated, egg-shaped jars with rounded shoulders, two loop handles, long straight neck, and thickened, slightly inverted rim. Such jars are found at Megiddo in Stratum V (e.g., *Megiddo I*: Pl. 20:120, 122).

The ring base of the red-slipped and vertically burnished jug (Fig. 35.1:17), which is most characteristic of Iron Age II, could belong to various jug types, such as those at Megiddo Stratum VA (*Megiddo II*: Pl. 88:3, 4) and Tel 'Amal Stratum IV (Levy and Edelstein 1972: Fig. 11).

Summary

The assemblages from the three Iron Age phases at Tel Poleg are very similar, so they must also be very close in time. The comparisons, particularly with the pottery from the coastal sites and those in the northern part of Israel, show that the Iron Age material should be dated to the second half of the 10th century B.C.E. The chronological range corresponds with Strata XIV-XIII at Tel Michal, Megiddo VA-IVB, Tel 'Amal IV-III, Tell Abu Hawam III, Taanach IIB, Hazor X-IX, Tel Mevorakh VII, Tell Qasile IX-VIII,

Tell Keisan 8, and Gezer VIIA. Certain vessels, such as the closed kraters with thickened rims and possibly also the egg-shaped jars, have northern affinities. But the assemblage on the whole is local in character, and the absence of imported wares is notable.

35.2. PERSIAN PERIOD POTTERY

The Persian period pottery at Tel Poleg came from Areas A, B, and C. Architectural elements were found in all three areas, but the excavations were discontinued before any complete units were exposed. The assemblage is poor, consisting mainly of bowl rims, storage jars, and a few jugs.

Bowls

The bowls with rippled outer surface, externally thickened rim, and high ring base, commonly known as "mortaria" (Fig. 35.2:1-2, 14), are abundantly present in the Persian strata of Tel Michal (Figs. 9.1:1-2, 16-18; 9.2:1-2; 9.7:1-2; 9.8:2). The bowl of Figure 35.2:3 also belongs to this group, although it has an everted curved rim. This type usually has a flat or concave disk base. There is a similar bowl in Hazor Stratum II (*Hazor I*: Pl. LXXIX:18). The rounded bowl with sharply inverted rim is known at Tel Mevorakh Stratum V (*Tel Mevorakh I*: Fig. 4:9), Megiddo Stratum I (*Megiddo I*: Pl. 25:62), and at Ramat Raḥel (*Ramat Raḥel II*: Fig. 12:11, 13).

Kraters

Kraters were rare in the Persian period and have been found at only a few sites. The krater with rounded rim and rounded body (Fig. 35.2:4) may have had a pair of loop handles; such kraters were found at Samaria (*Samaria 1924*: Fig. 168:11A) and Lachish (*Lachish III*: 282, Pl. 91:403). The krater of Figure 35.2:15, with a folded rim hollow at the center, is paralleled at Megiddo Stratum I (*Megiddo I*: Pl. 13:66). The externally burnished krater fragment with everted rim is impressed with a wedge decoration (Fig. 35.2:16); similarly decorated kraters were found at En-gedi (Stern 1982; Photo 220) and Tell en-Nasbeh (*TN II*: Pl. 66:496). This decoration, common throughout the country, is characteristic only of the early part of the Persian period (from the end of the 6th to the end of the 5th centuries B.C.E.). The burnishing on some of the vessels with this decoration also points to an early date in the Persian period, since burnishing ceased sometime during the 5th century and is completely absent in the 4th century (Stern 1982:136).

Storage Jars

Storage jars, relatively plentiful in the assemblage, may be classified into four groups:

Elongated Type (Fig. 35.2:5)

These jars, with rounded rim, convex pointed base, and

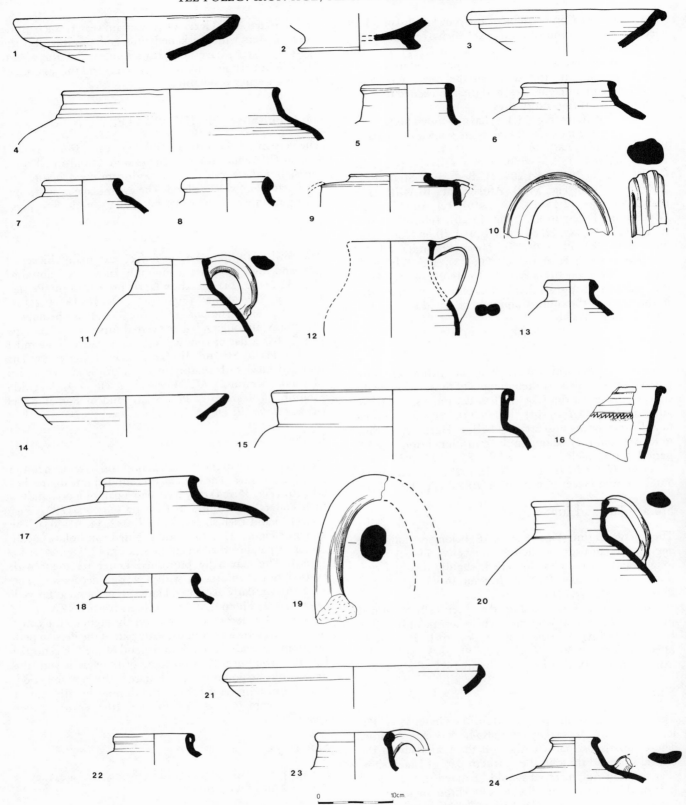

Figure 35.2. Persian period pottery from Tel Poleg (Area A: 1–13; Area B: 14–20; Area C: 21–24).

Legend for Fig. 35.2

No.	Type	Reg. No.	Description
1	Bowl	1009/1	Buff (orange), small white and gray grits.
2	Bowl	1017/10	Orange (orange), small white and gray grits.
3	Bowl	1017/1	Buff (gray), small red and white grits, large white grits.
4	Krater	1020/1	Light orange (gray), large and small white grits.
5	Storage jar	1020/5	Light gray (gray), small and large white grits.
6	Storage jar	1020/2	Brown (gray), small white grits, large gray grits.
7	Storage jar	1021/4	Light brown (gray), small gray and white grits.
8	Storage jar	1022/2	Buff (gray), small gray and white grits.
9	Storage jar	1017/5	Light orange (gray).
10	Storage jar	1017/9	Buff (brown-pink), small gray and white grits.
11	Jug	1016/15	Orange (orange), small white grits.
12	Jug	1017/8	Buff-gray (gray), small white grits.
13	Jug	1009/6	Light brown (gray), small brown and white grits, large white grits.
14	Bowl	3001/4	Brown-orange (brown), small gray and white grits.
15	Krater	3001/2	Brown-orange (gray), small gray and white grits, large white grits.
16	Krater	3001/1	Orange (gray), small gray and white grits.
17	Storage jar	3004/5	Brown-pink (gray), small white grits.
18	Storage jar	3005/3	Light brown (gray), small brown and white grits.
19	Storage jar	3004/7	Buff (brown), small gray and white grits.
20	Jug	3001/3	Light brown (gray), small gray and white grits.
21	Bowl	7/64	Pink (pink), small white grits.
22	Storage jar	7a/64	Light orange (light orange), small gray grits.
23	Jug	7b/64	White (gray), small white grits.
24	Decanter	3-4/64	Light orange (gray), small white grits.

pair of loop handles extending from shoulder to body, are very common at Tel Michal, especially in Strata IX-VIII, where they differ mainly in their body dimensions (see Chap. 9, Section 9.5, Jar Type 1).

Bag-Shaped Type (Fig. 35.2:6–8, 17–18, 22)

The jars of this group have a very short neck, a ridge at the junction of neck and shoulder, and two shoulder handles. They are present at Tel Michal only in Strata X-IX, and they are particularly abundant in the latter stratum (see Section 9.2.3, Jar Type 2).

Flat-Shouldered Type (Fig. 35.2:9)

From comparisons with complete vessels, we assume that the specimen from Tel Poleg had a pair of distorted loop handles extending from its right-angled shoulders to its swollen body, which slopes down to a pointed base. These jars first appear in the 8th-7th centuries and continue to exist throughout the Persian period. Their geographic distribution is also widespread; apart from Israel, they are common along the Phoenician coast, Cyprus, Rhodes, and in Punic sites in the Mediterranean (see Section 9.2.3, Jar Type 3).

Basket-Handled Type (Fig. 35.2:10, 19)

The handles shown here belong to a round-shouldered jar with elongated body ending in a pointed base and with two basket handles rising above the rim. At Tel Michal these jars were found mainly in Strata XI-IX, with a few sherds in Strata VIII-VI. Such jars, which began to appear at the end of the Iron Age, were very common all along the eastern Mediterranean coast throughout the Persian period and were apparently used extensively in maritime trade. It is generally assumed that they are of eastern Greek origin, but some may have been local imitations (see Section 9.2.1, Jar Type 5, and the results of the petrographic analysis in Chap. 24c (Samples 5–7).

Jugs

The most characteristic jug at Tel Poleg has a wide cylindrical neck, thickened rim, and swollen body (Fig. 35.2:11–12, 20, 23). Such jugs are particularly abundant in coastal sites. Very common at Tel Mevorakh (Tel Mevorakh I: 36, Fig. 9:2–3), they are also found at Atlit (Johns 1933:92, Fig. 71), Tel Megadim (Stern 1982: Photo 172), and Taanach Period VIA (Taanach I: Fig. 83:4, 5).

The narrow-necked decanter (Fig. 35.2:24) has a ridge at the base of the neck (unlike the usual decanter with mid-neck ridge), ring rim, and bag-shaped body. A loop handle extends from ridge to shoulder. A similar decanter was found at En-gedi (Stern 1969: Pl. 25:5). The decanter is typical of the end of the Iron Age, continuing into the 6th and beginning 5th centuries in a degenerated form, particularly in the south (Stern 1982:116).

Summary

Persian period pottery from the three excavated areas is homogeneous, the different types of vessels ("mortaria," ridged storage jars, and wide-necked jugs) appearing in all three. Despite the limited assemblage, there are sufficient data to date it to the early part of the Persian period. Vessels such as the krater with wedge-impressed decoration, the storage jars with ridge at the base of the neck, and the decanter are not known in the 4th century at all, whereas they are characteristic of the end of the 6th and 5th centuries B.C.E. At this coastal site, one might have expected to find some sherds of glazed black Attic ware, common at the end of the 5th and during the 4th centuries. The total absence of this ware at Tel Poleg is an additional indication of the early date of the assemblage. From the parallels, it appears that the Persian period settlement at Tel Poleg was contemporaneous with Strata X-IX at Tel Michal.

NOTE

1. I wish to thank Dr. R. Gophna for making available the material in this study and for providing the ceramic drawings.

REFERENCES

Dothan, M. 1955. Excavations at 'Afula. *'Atiqot* 1:19–70. English series.

Gitin, S. 1979. *A Ceramic Typology of the Late Iron II, Persian and Hellenistic Periods at Tell Gezer*, I–III. Ph.D. dissertation. Hebrew Union College, Cincinnati, Ohio.

Gophna, R. 1973. The Middle Bronze Age II Fortifications at Tel Poleg. *EI* 11:111–119 (Hebrew); 26 (English summary).

Guy, P. L. O. 1924. Mt. Carmel, an Early Iron Age Cemetery near Haifa Excavated September 1922. *Bulletin, British School of Archaeology in Jerusalem* 5.

Johns, C. N. 1933. Excavations at 'Atlit (1930–31). The South-Eastern Cemetery. *QDAP* 2:41–104.

Kochavi, M., Beck, P., and Gophna, R. 1979. Aphek-Antipatris, Tel Poleg, Tel Zeror and Tel Burga: Four Fortified Sites of the Middle Bronze Age IIA in the Sharon Plain. *ZDPV* 95:121–165.

Levy, S., and Edelstein, G. 1972. Cinq années de fouilles à Tell 'Amal (Nir David). *RB* 79:325–367.

Mazar, A. 1977. *The Temples of Tell Qasile*. (Hebrew) Ph.D. dissertation, Hebrew University, Jerusalem.

Stern, E. 1969. *The Material Culture of Palestine in the Persian Period (538–332 B.C.)*. (Hebrew) Ph.D. dissertation. Hebrew University, Jerusalem.

Stern, E. 1982. *Material Culture of the Land of the Bible in the Persian Period, 538–332 B.C.E.* Warminster.

36

The "Lord of Heaven" at Tel Michal

by Anson F. Rainey

Pottery sherds bearing traces of incised writing were found in 1987 on the northeastern hillock of Tel Michal, originally excavated under the name Makmish by N. Avigad (Avigad 1959; 1977). The sherds were discovered by Yehuda Friedman, an amateur archaeologist who brought them to us. The present writer found that the pieces could be fitted together and that a Phoenician inscription was partially preserved on it. Subsequently the fragments were cleaned and glued together in the laboratory of the Institute of Archaeology.

The joined pieces came from the upper part of a Persian period krater with thickened, everted rim and sloping neck, where the inscription appeared (Fig. 36.1; Pl. 84). Although kraters are quite rare in the Persian period (Stern 1982:99), a similar rim and neck fragment was found at Sheikh Ibrahim (Stern 1982:99, Fig. 125). The only other kraters at Tel Michal (Stratum IX, Fig. 9.2:3; Stratum VII, Fig. 9.8:1) have a vertical rather than sloping neck.

After photographing the fragment, we made a hand tracing of the inscription on transparent paper; the tracing was photocopied with the photograph as background (Fig. 36.2). The text of the inscription is as follows:

[מ]מ̇ש̇ על בר[בל]

[מ]מ̇ש̇ /̇ʿ /̇ḃ /̇ [/]

[Belonging to] Baal-sham[êm].

The nature of the inscription is commonplace. It indicates that the jar or its contents were devoted to the deity known as Baal-shamêm, "Lord of the Heavens." In accordance with the usual custom, such inscriptions are generally introduced by the *lamed* preposition, signifying the votive nature of the vessel or its contents. Therefore, we have not hesitated to supply a *lamed* at the beginning of the inscription. Given the known onomasticon of eastern Mediterranean deities, the only reasonable possibility is to interpret the tail of the letter after *shin* as a *mem* and to supply a second *mem* in brackets. The spelling בעלשמם =

b'lšmm is well attested in Phoenician inscriptions from Byblos, Cyprus, Cilicia, Sardinia, and Carthage (Röllig 1965:273), and the spelling בעלשמין = *b'lšmyn* is attested in Aramaic from Hamath. In the treaty between Esarhaddon and Baal of Tyre it is spelled ᵈ*Ba-al-sa-me-me* (Borger 1959: §69 IV 10). Philo of Byblos renders it Βεελσάμην (Jacoby 1969:807, 24; Baumgarten 1981:13); in the Punic portion of Plautus's Poenulus (1027) it is written *balsamem*; and Augustine spells it *Baalsamen*. It is also documented in Aramaic contexts and even has a counterpart in North Arabia (Höfner 1965:429–430). Temples to this deity are known especially from Sî' in the Ḥaurân and from Palmyra.

It is possible that most of the cult figurines (those of the bearded deity) found by Avigad (1959; 1977) are representations of Baal-shamêm, "Lord of the Heavens."

From the standpoint of paleography, the *lamed* is of the earlier type, with its angular shape; it does not have the tick added to the foot as in the Cypriote, Byblian, or Sidonian-Tyrian traditions and in the "General Series" during later periods. On the contrary, it may be compared with the Isis statue and the Sardinia stele (Peckham 1968:109, Nos. 3, 5) of the 6th century B.C.E.; in the cursive script of this series, however, there are even earlier parallels (Peckham 1968:110, Nos. 1–3). The *shin* is of the three-pronged type but with the middle stroke slightly left of center; the form is known from the Isis statue and the Sardinia stele (Peckham 1968:109, Nos. 3, 5), but the best parallel is suggested

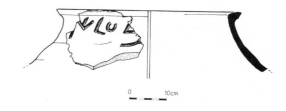

Figure 36.1. Inscribed krater fragment (Reg. No. 47/1; Locus 22; dark brown clay; brown core; few white grits).

0   3cm.

Figure 36.2   Drawing of inscription "[To] Baal-shamê[m]." The *lamed* supplied at beginning and particular shapes of *mem*'s are conjectural.

by the Saqqarah papyrus where the *shin* with off-center middle stroke appears alongside the more trident-shaped form (Peckham 1968:110, No. 3). The *bet* is not complete, but the surviving tail—pulled far to the left in what appears to be a sweeping curve—is not typical of Phoenician inscriptions in general. Nevertheless, it seems closest to the "General Series" toward the end of the 6th or beginning of the 5th century B.C.E. (Peckham 1968:107, Nos. 8–9; 109, Nos. 1, 3), especially with the obviously triangular, as opposed to rounded, head. Only the tail of the *mem* is visible, but at the top it appears to come curving down from the left; that is, it may have resembled the type found on the Sardinia stele (Peckham 1968:108, No. 4) or on the Elephantine ostraca of the 5th century (Peckham 1968:110, Nos. 4–6). Our restoration in the hand drawing is strictly conjectural, of course.

Alongside these seemingly early forms, it is surprising to find the *'ayin* open at the top. Such forms appear in the "General Series" by the 5th century (Peckham 1968:164). In the Sidonian and Tyrian sequence, the *'ayin* is never opened until the late 3d century (Peckham 1968:98), whereas at Byblos it does appear in the early 5th century (Peckham 1968:61). In Cyprus the *'ayin* may open in the late 4th century (Peckham 1968:36). On our present text, one may observe that inside the U-shaped *'ayin* there is the beginning of another stroke near the left arm; perhaps the writer sought to close the *'ayin* but his stroke was blocked by the protruding rim of the vessel.

Given these details—several letters typical of the 6th century with an *'ayin* more typical of the 5th—one is tempted to fall back on a vague commitment to dating such as "late 6th-early 5th century B.C.E." This would point to a time contemporary with the first or second forts established on the high tell (i.e., Stratum XI or X). Beyond that, one must hesitate to establish a date.

REFERENCES

Avigad, N. 1959. Excavations at Makmish, 1958. Preliminary Report. *IEJ* 10:90–96.

Avigad, N. 1977. Makmish. *Enc. Arch. Exc. III*: 768–770.

Baumgarten, A. I. 1981. *The Phoenician History of Philo of Byblos. A Commentary*. Leiden.

Borger, R. 1956. *Die Inschriften Asarhaddons Königs von Assyrien*. Archiv für Orientforschung Beiheft 9. Osnabrück.

Höfner, M. 1965. Die Stammesgruppen Nord- und Zentralarabiens in vorislamischer Zeit. Pages 407–481 in: *Götter und Mythen im vorderen Orient*. H. W. Haussig, ed. Stuttgart.

Jacoby, F. 1969. *Die Fragmente der Griechischen Historiker*. Dritter Teil: Geschichte von Städten und Volkern (Horographie und Ethnographie). C. Autoren über einzelne Länder, Nr. 608a-856 (Zweiter Band: Illyrien-Thrakien Nr. 709–856). Leiden.

Peckham, J. B. 1968. *The Development of the Late Phoenician Scripts*. Harvard Semitic Series 20. Cambridge, Mass.

Röllig, W. 1965. Baal-Šamēm. Page 273 in: *Götter und Mythen im vorderen Orient*. H. W. Haussig, ed. Stuttgart.

Stern, E. 1982. *Material Culture of the Land of the Bible in the Persian Period, 538–332 B.C.E.* Warminster.

Appendixes

Appendix I
Loci

Locus	Stratum[a]	Area	Square(s)	Description	Figure(s)
1	Unstratified	. . .		Surface (private collection)	
2	Unstratified	. . .		Surface (private collection)	
3	Unstratified	. . .		Surface	
22	Unstratified	. . .		Surface	
23	Unstratified	. . .		Surface	
25	Unstratified	A	R/S/T14	Surface	
27	IV	A	S/T14	Floor east of Room 32	12.8
28	Unstratified	A	U14	Surface	
30	VI	A	U14	Fill north of Fort 324	8.19
32	IV	A	T15	Room in Structure 35	12.8
33	V	A	T15	Courtyard between Structures 333 and 35	12.3
35	V	A	S15	Room in Structure 35	12.3
36	V	A	T14–15	Part of Courtyard 33	12.3
37	VI	A	S15	Fill under Floor 324	8.19
38	V	A	S15	Room in Structure 35	12.3
39	Unstratified	A	T15	Surface	
43	VI	A	S15	Fill under Floor 324	8.19
50	I	A	L/M15	Watchtower	15.1
54	I	A	M14–15	Plastered installation north of Wall M151	15.1
56	Unstratified	A	M14	Surface	
58	II	A	M13	Room in Roman fortress	14.2
60	I	A	M14–15	Robbers' trench of Wall M150	15.1
61	II	A	M15	Lime pavement in Courtyard 812	14.2
62	II	A	L/M13–14	Foundation trench of Wall M131 of Roman fortress	14.2
63	IV	A	M15	Disturbed floor in Courtyard 63 of Fort 691	12.7
65	IV	A	M13	Fill under Courtyard 63	12.7
66	II	A	M/N14	Fill under northern part of Courtyard 907	14.2
70	VI	A	M13	Fill southeast of Structure 1024	8.20
74	IV	A	M11–12	Room in Fortress 691	12.7
80	I	A	G15	Mameluke grave	
81	V	A	G15	Room in Fortress 806	12.2
85	VII	A	G15	Ash pit west of Structure 86	4.5; 8.17
86	VII	A	G14–15	Room in Structure 86	4.5; 8.15; 8.17
87	VII	A	G15	Floor west of Structure 86	8.17
88	XIV–XIII	A	E15	Debris dumped on southern slope	6.2; 6.4
89	VIII	A	G15	Courtyard in Structure 89	8.10; 8.12
92	VIII	A	F/G15	Storeroom in Structure 89	8.12
93	VIII	A	F/G15	Stone-lined silo in Room 92	8.12
94	I	A	G15	Mameluke grave	
98	IX	A	F/G15	Fill under Room 412	8.9
99	XIV–XIII	A	F/G15	Room in Structure 423	6.2; 6.4
100	Unstratified	B	G16–17	Fill south of Structure 108	8.23
101	Unstratified	B	G17	Avigad's excavations (1958–60)	8.23
103	VII–VI	B	G16	Courtyard south of Structure 108	8.23
104	VII–VI	B	G16–17	Fill under courtyard south of Structure 112	8.23

Locus	Stratum[a]	Area	Square(s)	Description	Figure(s)
106	Unstratified	B	H16	Avigad's excavations (1958–60)	8.23
108	VII–VI	B	H17	Room in Structure 108	8.23
109	XIV/XIII	B	H18	Fill north of Structure 117	6.7
110	VII–VI	B	H16	Brick platform east of Structure 108	8.23
111	VII–VI	B	H16	Pavement in Structure 108	8.23
112	VIII–VI	B	G18	Room in Structure 112	8.23
116	XIV/XIII	B	G16–17	Courtyard south of Structure 117	6.7
117	XIV/XIII	B	G/H16	Structure 117	6.6; 6.7
118	VII–VI	B	H18	Fill north of Structure 112	8.23
121	VII–VI	B	E18	Fill	8.23
124	XIV–XIII	B	H18	Structure 124	6.7; 6.8
125	V	C	O4	Sand fill	8.22
126	Unstratified	C	N4	Surface	
128	XIV/XIII	C	O4–5	Pit north of Structure 300	6.5
129	VII/VI	C	N4	Paved area east of Structure 143	8.22
130	VII/VI	C	M4	Fill south of Structure 143	8.22
131	I	C	N4	Plastered installation	
134	XIV/XIII	C	O5	Pit north of Structure 300	6.5
135	V	C	N4	Silo	8.22
137	VII–VI	C	N5	Drainage channels	8.22
138	Unstratified	C	O3	Surface	
139	XIV/XIII	C	O3	Pit northeast of Structure 300	
140	XIV/XIII	C	O5	Pit north of Structure 300	6.5
143	VII–VI	C	N4–5	Room in Structure 143	8.22
144	XIV	C	O4	Fill north of Structure 300	6.5
145	XII	C	M4	Fill	6.5
147	XIV	C	N5	Ash pit	6.5
160	VI	D	G15	Sloping stone surface	8.21
163	VI	D	G15	Brick debris	8.21
165	VI	D	G16	Fill	8.21
174	XVII	D	G16	Fill	8.21
176	XI/VI	E	B2	Burial (?)	11.1
178	XI/VI	E	C2	Cist burial	11.1
179	XI/VI	E	B2	Cist burial	11.1
180	XI/VI	E	B1	Pit burial	11.1
181	XI/VI	E	B1	Pit burial	11.1
182	XI/VI	E	B1	Cist burial	11.1
183	XI/VI	E	B2	Cist burial	11.1
185	XI/VI	E	C2	Pit burial	11.1
186	XI/VI	E	C1	Cist burial	11.1
188	XI/VI	E	C3	Disturbed burial	11.1
189	XI/VI	E	E1	Pit burial	11.1
190	XI/VI	E	F3–4	Jar burial	11.1
191	XI/VI	E	D1	Cist burial	11.1
193	XI/VI	E	E3–4	Cist burial	11.1
200	Unstratified	F	E/F10–11	Surface	
203	VIII/VI	F	E10	Red sand	8.13
204	VIII/VI	F	E11	Refuse dump	8.13
205	Unstratified	F	E/F12	Surface	
207	VIII/VI	F	E12	Pottery kiln	8.13
210	VIII/VI	F	F11	Red sand	
211	VIII/VI	F	F11	Occupational surface	
212	VIII/VI	F	E11	Refuse dump	8.13
215	VIII/VI	F	D/E10–11	Pottery kiln	8.13
219	VIII/VI	F	G/H2	Debris on slope	
220	VIII/VI	F	H2–3	Ash dump	
221	VIII/VI	F	H2	Red sandy debris	
225	VII/VI	B	C17	Fill north of Structure 237	8.23
227	VII/VI	B	E19	Stone debris	8.23
230	XIV/XIII	B	C17	Robbers' trench of wall in Structure 246	6.8
233	VII/VI	B	C16	Lime-burning pit	8.23

Locus	Stratum[a]	Area	Square(s)	Description	Figure(s)
237	VII/VI	B	B/C17	Room in Structure 237	8.23
238	XIV/XIII	B	B16	Room in Structure 249	6.8
240	XIV/XIII	B	B17	Robbers' trench of Wall B174 in Structure 246	6.8
241	VII/VI	B	B17	Ashy fill under Room 237	8.23
242	VII/VI	B	B16	Pit east of Structure 237	8.23
246	XIV/XIII	B	B17	Room in Structure 246	6.6; 6.8
249	XIV/XIII	B	B16	Room in Structure 249	6.8; 6.9
255	IIIb	H		Hasmonean winepress	12.11
278	VI	D	G/H14	Fill	8.21
279	V	D	G16	Ash pit	8.21
281	VI	D	G16	Fill	8.21
292	VII	A	G15	Silo	8.17
293	XVI/XV	A	E15	Mixed LB I–II deposit on southern slope	4.6
300	XIII	C	N4	Structure	6.5
302	XIII	C	N4	Fill east of Structure 300	6.5
303	XIII	C	N4	Stone platform in Structure 300	6.5
304	VII–VI	C	N5	Room in Structure 143	8.22
305	V	A	R/S15	Fill east of Structure 35	12.3
306	IV	A	R14	Room in Structure 306	12.8
307	IV	A	R14	Ash pit	12.8
310	V	A	R14	Fill east of Structure 35	12.3
311	V	A	R13–14	Fill east of Structure 35	12.3
314	V	A	R14	Pit east of Structure 35	12.3
315	VI	A	R15	Fill under Floor 324	8.19
317	VI	A	R15	Part of Courtyard 324	8.19
320	V	A	S13	Fill	12.3
322	VI	A	S14	Entryway to Fort 324	8.19
323	V	A	S/T14	Pit in Courtyard 33	12.3
324	VI	A	S15	Courtyard in Fort 324	8.18; 8.19
325	V	A	R14–15	Pit east of Structure 35	12.3
329	VII	A	R15	Courtyard in Fort 329	8.15; 8.16
330	VI	A	R14	Room in Structure 330	8.18; 8.19
332	VI	A	R14	Part of Room 330	8.19
333	V	A	T14	Room in Structure 333	12.3
334	V	A	T14	Room in Structure 333	12.3
335	VIII	A	S15	Part of Courtyard 340	8.11
338	IX	A	T14	Floor west of Structure 344	8.8
339	IX	A	R14	Floor between Structures 349 and 898	8.8
340	VIII	A	S14	Courtyard in Fort 340	8.10; 8.11
341	VII	A	R14	Room in Structure 341	8.16
342	VIII	A	S15	Room in Fort 340	8.11
343	VII	A	S14	Room north of Structure 341	8.16
344	IX	A	S14	Courtyard in Structure 344	8.7; 8.8
345	IX	A	S15	Fill south of Structure 344	8.8
347	VII	A	R14	Part of Room 341	8.16
350	IIIb	A	M15	Room in Fort 696A	12.10
352	VIII	A	M16	Floor west of Structure 1304	4.3; 8.12
353	VI	A	M16	Fill	4.3; 8.20
354	V	A	M15	Room in Fort 806	12.2
355	VII	A	M16	Ash pit west of Structure 1061	4.3; 8.17
356	IIIb	A	M15	Room in Fort 696A	12.10
357	VIII	A	M16	Wash near surface	8.12
361	IX	A	L/M16	Floor west of Structure 1308	8.9
362	VIII	A	M16	Installation basin west of Structure 1304	8.12
363	IIIb	A	M15	Robbers' trench of Wall M155	8.20; 12.10
364	IX	A	M16	Fill west of Structure 1308	4.3; 8.9
367	IX	A	M16	Fill west of Structure 1308	4.3; 8.9
368	IIIa	A	L/M15	Room in Fort 684	12.10
369	VI	A	M15	Room south of Structure 1024	8.20
370	I	A	L15	Robbers' trench	15.1
372	I	A	L15	Plastered floor south of Structure 50	15.1

Locus	Stratum[a]	Area	Square(s)	Description	Figure(s)
373	I	A	L15	Robbers' trench	15.1
374	XIII	A	M16	Room (?)	6.4
378	XIV	A	M17	Fill in pit (?)	4.3; 6.2
382	IIIb	A	L15	Room in Fort 696A	12.10
388	VII	A	M15	Room (?) in Structure 388	8.17
393	X	A	M16	Ash pit	
397	IX	A	M16	Ash fill west of Structure 1308	4.3; 8.9
401	Unstratified	A	F14	Surface	
403	VI	A	G14–15	Fill	8.20
404	IX	A	G15–16	Floor west of Structure 412	4.5; 8.9
405	VIII	A	G14–15	Lane	4.5; 8.12
407	IX	A	G15–16	Stone installation	8.9
408	VI	A	G14	Silo	8.20
409	IX	A	G16	Fill west of Structure 412	8.9
410	IX	A	G16	Stone-lined silo west of Structure 412	8.9
411	VII	A	G14	Fill under Room 86	8.17
412	IX	A	G14–15	Room	4.5; 8.7; 8.9
413	VIII	A	G14–15	Drainage channel	8.12
415	XI	A	G15	Pit	4.5; 8.3
416	IX	A	F16	Fill southwest of Structure 412	8.9
418	XIV–XIII	A	F15–16	Room in Structure 423	6.2; 6.4
420	XI	A	F15	Pit	8.3
421	IX	A	G15–16	Fill northwest of Structure 412	4.5; 8.9
423	XIV–XIII	A	G/H14–15	Courtyard in Structure 423	4.5; 6.1; 6.2; 6.4
450	Unstratified	C	M5	Surface	
452	Unstratified	C	N3	Surface	
453	VI	C	N3	Red sandy soil and debris east of Structure 143	
454	XII	C	M5	Red sandy soil and debris	6.5
458	XIV–XIII	C	M5	Red sandy soil	6.5
461	XIV	C	N3	Stone pavement east of Structure 300	6.5
462	XIV	C	O/N4	Fill east of Structure 300	6.5
463	XIV	C	N4	Fill north of Structure 300	6.5
464	XII	C	N4	Pit near Platform 303	6.5
466	VI	C	P2	Brick debris	
467	XIV	C	N5	Part of Structure 300	6.5
468	Unstratified	C	P3	Surface	
469	VI	C	P3	Brick debris	
470	VI	C	P3	Gray fill	
471	XIV/XIII	C	P3	Red fill	
473	XIV/XIII	C	N3	Red sandy soil	
500	Unstratified	D	I14	Surface	
504	VI	D	H16	Room	8.21
505	VI	D	H16	Fill	8.21
506	VI	D	H16	Fill	8.21
508	VI	D	H16	Room	8.21
510	VIII	D	I13	Small winepress	8.21
512	Unstratified	D	I14	Surface	
515	VIII	D	I14	Collecting vat of Winepress 510	8.21
516	Unstratified	D	I14	Robbers' trench of Winepress 510	
519	VI	D	G15	Fill	8.21
521	VI	D	G15	Pavement east of Wall G152	8.21
524	VI	D	G14	Ash pit	8.21
525	VIII	D	I13	Drainage channel	8.21
528	VIII	D	I14	Floor	8.21
530	VI	D	I14	Fill west of Wall G151	8.21
531	Unstratified	D	G17	Surface	
532	VIII	D	I14	Fill	8.21
533	VI	D	G17	Room	8.21
534	VI	D	G17	Room	8.21
551	V–IV	D	I20	Floor in Winepress 556	12.4
551A	V–IV	D	I20	Vat in Winepress 556	12.4

LOCI

Locus	Stratum[a]	Area	Square(s)	Description	Figure(s)
551B	V–IV	D	I/K19–20	Vat in Winepress 556	12.4
552	V–IV	D	I20	Pavement around Winepress 556	12.4
553	V–IV	D	K20	Pavement around Winepress 556	12.4
554	V–IV	D	H/I20	Pavement around Winepress 556	12.4
556	V–IV	D	I19	Treading floor of Winepress 556	12.4
558	VI	D	K20	Fill	8.21
560	VI	D	K19	Floor	8.21
562	VI	D	K20	Fill east of Winepress 556	8.21
563	VI	D	K19	Floor	8.21
565	Unstratified	D	K19	Pit cutting into Winepress 556	12.4
567	IV	D	I/K19	Small compartment north of Treading Floor 556	12.4
568	IV	D	K19	Part of Treading Floor 556	12.4
569	VI	D	H19	Room	8.21
570	V–IV	D	I18	Pavement around Winepress 556	12.4
571	V	D	I/K19	Small compartment north of Treading Floor 556	12.4
572	VII	D	K19	Floor	8.21
575	IV	D	I18	Small compartment north of Treading Floor 556	12.4
576	VI	D	I18	Floor	8.21
577	VI	D	I18	Fill east of Winepress 556	8.21
578	VI	D	H20	Fill	8.21
579	Unstratified	D	G19	Surface	
580	VI	D	H19	Fill	8.21
584	V	D	H20	Drainage channel in Winepress 556	12.4
585	V	D	F19	Fill	
586	III (?)	D	I19	Robbers' trench of Wall I192	12.4
588	VI	D	G19	Fill	8.21
591	V	D	K/L19	Pit north of Winepress 556	12.4
592	VI	D	H19	Fill	8.21
593	VII	D	G19	Fill	8.21
594	VII	D	E19	Fill	
596	VI	D	G19	Fill	8.21
600	V/IV	D	D/E6	Eroded floor	
601	VI	D	A7	Brick debris	
602	VI	D	A7	Occupational surface	
603	VII	D	B7	Brick debris	
605	VII	D	B7	Ash fill	
606	VI	D	B7	Brick debris	
607	VII	D	B7	Oven	
608	VII	D	A7	Ashy fill	
610	VI	D	C7	Occupational surface	
611	VII	D	A7	Brick debris	
612	VI	D	C7	Occupational surface	
614	VII	D	A7	Fill	
615	VII	D	D6	Fill	
618	VII	D	C7	Fill	
619	VII	D	A7	Fill	
651	XI/VI	E	E2	Jar burial	11.1
652	XI/VI	E	F2	Jar burial	11.1
653	XI/VI	E	E2–3	Cist burial	11.1
654	XI/VI	E	F2–3	Jar in cist burial	11.1
658	XI/VI	E	B3	Cist burial	11.1
659	XI/VI	E	B3	Cist burial	11.1
662	XI/VI	E	B3	Jar burial	11.1
663	XI/VI	E	B3	Jar burial	11.1
664	XI/VI	E	B4	Cist burial	11.1
665	XI/VI	E	B3	Jar burial	11.1
666	XI/VI	E	B4	Cist burial	11.1
667	XI/VI	E	D1–2	Sand in cemetery	11.1
671	XI/VI	E	A/B–3	Cist burial	11.1
672	XI/VI	E	A3	Cist burial	11.1
673	XI/VI	E	A3	Jar burial	11.1

Locus	Stratum[a]	Area	Square(s)	Description	Figure(s)
674	XI/VI	E	D1–2	Cist burial	11.1
675	Unstratified	A	N/O/P14–15	Surface	
677	I	A	O14	Courtyard north of Structure 50	15.1
678	I	A	N15	Courtyard north of Structure 50	15.1
680	I	A	O15	Courtyard north of Structure 50	15.1
682	II	A	N14–15	Ash pit north of Tower 1002	14.2
683	I	A	N/O15	Plastered basin north of Structure 50	15.1
684	IIIa	A	N/O14	Paved courtyard in Fort 684	12.9; 12.10
685	IIIb	A	O14	Room in Fort 696A	12.10
686	IIIa	A	O14	Stone paving in Fort 684	12.10
687	IIIb	A	O15	Room in Fort 696A	12.10
689	I	A	N15	Robbers' trench in Stratum II wall	
690	VI	A	N16	Fill southwest of Structure 1017	8.20
691	IV	A	O14	Room in Fortress 691	12.7
692	IIIa	A	O/N15	Room in Fort 684	12.10
693	Unstratified	A	O16	Surface	
694	V	A	O14	Room in Fortress 806	12.2
696	II	A	N14	Ash pit east of Tower 1002	14.2
696A	IIIb	A	O13	Courtyard of Fort 696A	12.9; 12.10
697	IV	A	O15	Room in Fortress 691	12.7
698	V	A	O15	Fill west of Fortress 806	12.2
701	XI	A	S14	Fill in Wall S144	8.2
702	XI–	A	S14	Fill under Floor 872	8.2
704	VII–VI	A	R/S14–15	Drainage channel	8.16; 8.19
705	X	A	R15	Fill	8.5
706	XVI	A	R15	Fill	4.7
709	X	A	S13	Room east of Courtyard 856	8.5
710	VIII	A	S14	Oven in Courtyard 340	8.11
711	XVI	A	S15	Drainage channel in Structure 873	4.7
712	XVI	A	S15	Gray fill	4.7
713	X	A	S13	Room east of Courtyard 856	8.5
714	VIII	A	S13	Part of Courtyard 340	8.11
716	XVII	A	S15	*Hamra* layer and glacis	4.7
717	X	A	T15	Floor in part of Courtyard 856	8.5
718	VIII	A	R14	Part of Courtyard 340	8.11
719	XVII	A	S15	Sand fill under Glacis 716	4.7
721	IX	A	S15	Pit west of Structures 344 and 898	8.8
722	VII	A	R13	Room in Structure 341	8.16
722A	VIII	A	R13–14	Part of Courtyard 340	8.11
723	XVII	A	R15	Continuation of Platform 782	4.7
724	IV	A	T14	Ash pit	12.8
727	VII	D	H19	Fill	8.21
728	VI	D	K/L19	Fill	8.21
731	VII	D	K/L19	Fill	8.21
750	VI	A	S13	Part of Entryway 322	8.19
776	XVI/XV	A	M17	Robbers' trench	4.6
777	XIV	A	M16	Floor west of Structure 1522	6.1; 6.2
780	VIII	A	M15	Part of Courtyard 1304	8.12
782	XVII	A	M17	Brick layer of Platform 782	4.1; 4.3
800	IV	A	O15	Room in Fortress 691	12.7
803	II	A	P14	Entry hall of Roman fortress	14.2
804	II	A	P14	Drainage channel in Roman fortress	14.2
805	IIIb	A	O14	Room in Fort 696A	12.10
806	V	A	O13	Fill under courtyard in Fortress 806	12.1; 12.2
807	IIIb	A	O13	Room in Fort 696A	12.10
808	II	A	N13	Room in Roman fortress	14.2
809	IIIa	A	N/O13	Room in Fort 684	12.10
811	II	A	P14	Continuation of Channel 804	14.2
812	II	A	N/O13–14	Central courtyard in Roman fortress	14.1; 14.2
813	IIIa	A	O14	Room in Fort 684	12.10
825	XI/VI	E	D3	Jar burial	11.1

Locus	Stratum[a]	Area	Square(s)	Description	Figure(s)
826	XI/VI	E	A2	Jar burial	11.1
827	XI/VI	E	A2	Cist burial	11.1
828	XI/VI	E	F2	Jar burial	11.1
830	VIII	A	U14	Room in Fort 340	8.11
831	Unstratified	A	S12	Surface	
832	V/IV	A	R12	Eroded floor	12.3
833	VIII	A	R13	Part of Courtyard 340	8.11
834	V	A	R12	Pit	12.3
835	Unstratified	A	R12	Circular installation	
836	VII/VI	A	R12	Drainage channel (?)	
837	XI	A	U14	Fill north of Structure 872	8.2
838	X	A	U14	Gray floor north of Courtyard 856	8.5
839	IX	A	R13–14	Open space between Structures 349 and 898	8.8
840	IX	A	R12	Storage pit in Structure 344	8.8
841	IX	A	R13	Fill south of Structure 344	8.8
842	VIII	A	T13	Floor north of Courtyard 340	8.11
843	Unstratified	A	U13	Eroded slope	
844	VII/VI	A	R13	Drainage channel (part of Channel 704)	8.16; 8.19
845	X	A	T13	Part of Courtyard 856	8.5
847	V	A	R12	Paved floor	12.3
850	X	A	U13	Fill	8.5
856	X	A	S/T13–14	Courtyard	8.4; 8.5
857	X	A	R13	Floor south of Wall R132	8.5
858	XIII	A	T14	Floor	6.3
859	VIII	A	T12–13	Stairway leading to Fort 340	8.11
861	X	A	T14	Floor of Courtyard 856	8.5
864	X	A	S13–14	Pit in Courtyard 856	8.5
866	XI	A	T13	Room in Structure 872	8.2
870	XI	A	T13	Storage bin in Room 866	8.2
872	XI	A	T14	Courtyard in Structure 872	8.1; 8.2
873	XVI	A	S14	Courtyard in Structure 873	4.7; 4.8
874	XI	A	U14	Room in Structure 872	8.2
876	XI	A	U14	Fill under Room 874	8.2
877	XVI	A	R14	Room in Structure 873	4.7
879	X	A	T13	Fill north of Wall T132	8.5
881	X	A	R/S13	Pit in Room 713	8.5
882	XVI	A	T14	Fill under Courtyard 813	4.7
885	XVI	A	R14	Gray fill	4.7
886	XVI	A	S14	Gray fill under Courtyard 873	4.7
887	XI	A	U13	Fill north of Structure 872	8.2
892	XIII	A	R13–14	Drainage channel	6.4
893	X	A	T13	Fill east of Courtyard 856	8.5
895	X	A	U14	Foundation trench of Wall U148	8.5
897	XI	A	S13	Gray surface east of Structure 872	8.2
898	IX	A	R14–15	Room in Structure 898	8.8
901	Unstratified	A	M14	Surface	
904	I	A	L14	Fill south of Structure 50	15.1
906	Unstratified	A	M17	Surface	
907	II	A	L14–15	Enclosed area in Courtyard 812 of Roman fortress	14.2
911	XVII	A	M17	Mixed *hamra* and debris layer of Platform 782	4.3
912	II	A	L/M13	Room in Roman fortress	14.2
913	II	A	L13	Room in Roman fortress	14.2
914	IIIa	A	L14	Room in Fort 684	12.10
915	IIIa	A	L14	Room in Fort 684	12.10
916	XVII	A	M17	Sand fill of Platform 782	4.3
917	IIIb	A	L/M14–15	Room in Fort 696A	12.10
918	II	A	L13	Fill under Room 913	14.2
919	II	A	L13	Fill under Room 912	14.2
921	IIIb	A	L14	Room in Fort 696A	12.10
922	XVII	A	M17	Sand layer in Fill 927	4.3
923	II	A	L13	Drainage channel in Roman fortress	14.2

Locus	Stratum[a]	Area	Square(s)	Description	Figure(s)
927	XVII	A	M17	Ash layer of Platform 782	4.3
929	XVII	A	M17	Consolidated sand (bedrock)	4.3
930	IV	A	L14–15	Floor in Fortress 691	12.7
931	VI	A	L13	Room in Structure 931	8.20
934	V	A	L14–15	Ash fill	12.2
935	IIIa	A	L14–15	Robbers' trench of Strata IV wall	12.7
937	VI	A	L15	Ash pit south of Room 369	8.20
938	II	A	L15	Fill under Courtyard 907	14.2
940	VII	A	L15	Patch of lime floor	8.17
942	VII	A	L15	Brick debris	8.17
943	V	A	L14	Plastered floor	12.2
944	II	A	L14	Fill under Courtyard 907	14.2
945	VII	A	L14	Floor west of Structure 1061	8.17
947	VII	A	L/M13–14	Ash fill west of Room 1061	8.17
948	VIII	A	L14–15	Room in Structure 1304	8.12
951	VIII	A	F/G13–15	Fill in retaining Wall F151	8.12
952	VII	A	F15	Pit south of Structure 86	8.17
954	VII	A	F/G14	Pit east of Structure 86	8.17
955	VI	A	F15	Silo	8.20
956	XV	A	F/G15–16	*Hamra* layer	4.5; 4.6
958	XV	A	G14–15	Ashy soil (occupational surface?)	4.5; 4.6
961	XV	A	G14	*Hamra* glacis of Rampart 971	4.5; 4.6
962	XV	A	F15	Brick debris	4.6
963	XV	A	G15	*Hamra* glacis of Rampart 971	4.5; 4.6
964	XV	A	F16	Sand layer in Rampart 971	4.5; 4.6
965	XVI/XV	A	F16	Mixed LB I–II deposit on southern slope	4.6
966	VII	A	F14	Pit south of Structure 86	8.17
970	XVI/XV	A	G16	Brick material	4.6
971	XV	A	G15	Sand layer in Rampart 971	4.5; 4.6; 4.8
973	VII	A	F16	Fill	8.17
974	XV	A	G16	Ashy soil (occupational surface?)	4.5; 4.6; 4.8
979	IX	A	F14–15	Fill south of Structure 412	8.9
983	XVI/XV	A	E16	Mixed LB I–II deposit on southern slope	4.6
984	IX	A	G13	Fill west of Structure 412	4.6; 8.9
985	IX	A	F14–15	Pit east of Structure 412	8.9
986	IX	A	G14	Fill north of Structure 412	4.5; 8.9
988	IX	A	G14	Pit east of Structure 412	8.9
991	XIV–XIII	A	F/G14–15	Room in Structure 423	6.2; 6.4
995	XV	A	G14	Ashy soil (occupational surface?)	4.5; 4.6
996	XVI/XV	A	F15	Mixed LB I–II deposit on southern slope	4.6
997	IX	A	G14	Stone-lined silo east of Structure 412	8.9
999	IX	A	G14	Fill east of Structure 412	8.9
1000	Unstratified	A	P3	Surface	
1001	I	A	N14	Courtyard north of Structure 50	15.1
1002	II	A	N15–16	Tower in Courtyard 812 of Roman fortress	14.2
1003	IV	A	P14	Fill north of Fortress 691	12.7
1007	IIIb	A	O13	Room in Fort 696A	12.10
1008	II	A	N/O13	Room in Roman fortress	14.2
1012	IV	A	N14	Room in Fortress 691	12.7
1013	VII	A	O13–14	Courtyard in Structure 1013	8.15; 8.17
1014	V	A	O15	Room in Fortress 806	12.2
1015	Unstratified	A	Q13–14	Surface	
1016	VI	A	N/O15	Room west of Courtyard 1024	8.20
1017	VI	A	O14	Oven in Courtyard 1024	8.20
1018	Unstratified	A	P15–16	Surface	
1019	II	A	P15–16	Room in Roman fortress	14.2
1021	II	A	O/P15–16	Fill under Courtyard 812	14.2
1022	VII	A	N/O14–15	Room in Structure 1013	8.17
1024	VI	A	N/O13–14	Courtyard in Structure 1024	8.18; 8.20
1025	V	A	O15	Room in Fortress 806	12.2
1027	VII	A	O15	Room in Structure 1013	8.17

Locus	Stratum[a]	Area	Square(s)	Description	Figure(s)
1028	VIII	A	O14	Room in Structure 1032	8.12
1029	VII	A	N13–14	Silo in Structure 1013	8.17
1032	VIII	A	O15	Room in Structure 1032	8.12
1033	VIII	A	N/O14	Room in Structure 1032	8.12
1050	Unstratified	A	K/L/M10	Surface	
1054	II	A	K/L/M12	Fill east of Roman fortress	14.2
1059	V–IV	A	L12	Room in Fortresses 806 and 691	12.2; 12.7
1060	VI	A	M12	Floor	8.20
1061	VII	A	L/M12–13	Room in Structure 1061	8.15; 8.17
1062	V	A	M12	Room in Fortress 806	12.2
1065	IV	A	K12	Room in Fortress 691	12.7
1067	V	A	L11–12	Fill east of Fortress 806	12.2
1068	V	A	M12	Fill under room of Fortress 806	12.2
1069	VIII	A	K/L11–12	Fill under Structure 1069	8.12
1070	II	A	L/M/N12	Room in Roman fortress	14.2
1071	VII	A	K12	Floor south of Structure 1061	8.17
1072	V	A	M11	Fill east of Fortress 806	12.2
1073	VII	A	L11	Fill east of Structure 1061	8.17
1076	VIII	A	K11	Fill under Structure 1069	8.12
1078	IIIb	A	N12	Room in Fort 696A	12.10
1079	IIIb	A	N11–12	Room in Fort 696A	12.10
1080	IIIb	A	M11–12	Room in Fort 696A	12.10
1084	VIII	A	M11	Room in Structure 1084	8.10; 8.12
1086	V	A	N11	Fill east of Fortress 806	12.2
1087	II	A	N/O12	Room in Roman fortress	14.2
1091	VIII	A	N10–11	Fill under Structure 1084	8.12
1100	VI	D	M19	Floor	8.21
1101	VI	D	M18	Floor	8.21
1103	VI	D	L19	Floor	8.21
1104	VI	D	M17	Floor	8.21
1107	VI	D	H17	Fill under room	8.21
1109	VI	D	H17	Courtyard (?)	8.21
1110	VI	D	H19	Courtyard (?)	8.21
1111	V	D	H18	Pavement around Winepress 556	12.4
1113	VIII	D	K/L19	Pit	8.21
1114	VII	D	M17	Floor	8.21
1118	VII	D	M18	Floor	8.21
1119	VII	D	M19	Floor	8.21
1120	VII	D	M19	Ash fill	8.21
1121	VII	D	M18	Ash fill	8.21
1122	VII	D	L19	Floor	8.21
1125	Unstratified	D	L18	Surface	
1128	VIII	D	L19	Fill	8.21
1150	Unstratified	E	D1	Surface	11.1
1151	XI/VI	E	A2	Robbed burial	11.1
1152	XI/VI	E	A2	Robbed burial	11.1
1154	XI/VI	E	A4	Sand in cemetery	11.1
1155	XI/VI	E	A2	Cist burial	11.1
1156	XI/VI	E	A2	Jar burial	11.1
1157	XI/VI	E	G2	Pit burial	11.2
1158	XI/VI	E	G2	Cist burial	11.2
1159	XI/VI	E	C/D3	Burial (?)	11.1
1160	XI/VI	E	H2	Jar burial	11.2
1161	XI/VI	E	H2	Burial	11.2
1162	XI/VI	E	H2	Cist burial	11.2
1163	XI/VI	E	J2	Jar burial	11.2
1164	XI/VI	E	J2	Cist burial	11.2
1165	XI/VI	E	C3	Pit (?) burial	11.1
1166	XI/VI	E	C3	Robbed cist burial	11.1
1167	XI/VI	E	B/C2–3	Pit burial	11.1
1168	XI/VI	E	C2–3	Pit burial	11.1

Locus	Stratum[a]	Area	Square(s)	Description	Figure(s)
1169	XI/VI	E	C2–3	Pit burial	11.1
1170	XI/VI	E	K2	Cist burial	11.2
1171	XI/VI	E	K2	Cist burial	11.2
1172	XI/VI	E	K2	Jar burial	11.2
1173	XI/VI	E	L2	Cist burial	11.2
1174	XI/VI	E	L2	Cist burial	11.2
1175	XI/VI	E	L2–3	Cist burial	11.2
1176	XI/VI	E	M2	Jar burial	11.2
1177	XI/VI	E	L2	Cist burial	11.2
1178	XI/VI	E	L2	Cist burial	11.2
1179	XI/VI	E	C3	Cist burial	11.1
1180	XI/VI	E	C3	Cist burial	11.1
1181	XI/VI	E	C3	Pit burial	11.1
1182	XI/VI	E	C3	Cist burial	11.1
1183	XI/VI	E	L2	Cist burial	11.2
1184	XI/VI	E	C3	Cist burial	11.1
1185	XI/VI	E	L2	Pit burial	11.2
1186	XI/VI	E	L2	Cist burial	11.2
1187	XI/VI	E	D3	Jar burial	11.1
1188	XI/VI	E	D3	Jar burial	11.1
1189	XI/VI	E	D3	Cist burial	11.1
1190	XI/VI	E	D3	Pit burial	11.1
1191	XI/VI	E	D3	Pit burial	11.1
1192	XI/VI	E	D3–4	Cist burial	11.1
1193	XI/VI	E	L1	Cist burial	11.2
1194	XI/VI	E	D2–3	Cist burial	11.1
1195	XI/VI	E	M2–3	Cist burial	11.2
1251	IX	A	G13	Stone-lined silo east of Structure 412	8.9
1252	IX	A	G13	Fill east of Structure 412	8.9
1253	IX	A	G13	Fill east of Structure 412	8.9
1254	IX	A	F13–14	Ash fill east of Structure 412	8.9
1259	XVI/XV	A	E16	Mixed LB I–II deposit on southern slope	4.6
1260	XVI/XV	A	E15–16	Mixed LB I–II deposit on southern slope	4.6
1261	XIV	A	G13	Ash fill	6.2
1262	XV	A	G14	Ḥamra glacis of Rampart 971	4.5; 4.6
1264	XIV	A	F/G14	Ash fill	6.2
1265	XIV	A	G13	Ash fill	6.2
1300	VIII	A	L/M14–15	Part of Courtyard 1304	8.12
1303	VII	A	L14	Ash fill	8.17
1304	VIII	A	L15	Courtyard in Structure 1304	8.10; 8.12
1308	IX	A	L14/15	Courtyard in Structure 1308	8.7; 8.9
1309	VII	A	L/M14	Robbers' trench	8.17
1311	IX	A	M15–16	Ash fill west of Structure 1308	8.9
1312	VIII	A	L14	Brick debris in Room 948	8.12
1317	VIII	A	L15	Fill under Room 1304	8.12
1322	IX	A	L/M15	Room in Structure 1308	8.9
1323	X	A	L14	Fill under Courtyard 1454	8.6
1351	X	A	L10	Room east of Courtyard 1454	8.4; 8.6
1354	V/IV	A	M10	Pit	
1357	X	A	L10	Fill east of Room 1351	8.6
1358	X	A	M10	Fill north of Room 1351	8.6
1360	X	A	L10	Fill under Room 1351	8.6
1364	X	A	N10	Fill north of Room 1351	8.6
1366	Unstratified	A	M10	Mixed debris on surface	4.1; 4.4
1369	V	A	K10	Kiln	12.1
1371	VIII	A	A1	Debris on slope	8.11
1371A	VIII	A	N11	Anchor reused in Wall N111	8.12
1372	XI	A	U14	Fill under Room 874	8.2
1373	XI	A	A14	Fill north of Structure 872	8.2
1378	XIV	A	A14	Ash and sand layer under Structure 1401	6.2; 6.3
1381	XVI	A	U14	Fill in Rampart 1381	4.7; 4.8

Locus	Stratum[a]	Area	Square(s)	Description	Figure(s)
1382	XVI	A	T15	*Ḥamra* and ash fill in Courtyard 873	4.7
1383	XVI	A	A14	*Ḥamra* glacis of Rampart 1381	4.7
1385	X	A	S14	Pit in Courtyard 856	8.5
1386	XI	A	U13	Fill north of Structure 872	8.2
1387	VII	A	U13	Pit	8.12
1388	XIV	A	U13	Fill	6.3
1389	II	A	Q14	Fill under Ramp 1760	14.2
1390	II	A	Q14	Room in Roman fortress (staircase?)	14.2
1391	II	A	Q14	Fill north of Roman fortress	14.2
1392	II	A	Q15	Room in Roman fortress	14.2
1399	XVI/XV	A	R14	Robbers' trench of Walls R1414 and S139	4.7
1400	XII	A	U13	Debris on slope	6.3
1401	XIV	A	A14	Room in Structure 1401	6.1; 6.3
1451	I	A	M14	Fill	15.1
1453	IX	A	L15	Part of Courtyard 1308	8.9
1454	X	A	L/M15	Courtyard	8.4; 8.6
1458	VII	A	M14	Brick debris on top of Wall M141	8.17
1459	IIIb	A	M13	Ash fill under Courtyard 696A	12.10
1461	VII	A	M14–15	Robbers' trench of Wall M141	8.17
1467	VII	A	L/M14	Pit west of Structure 1061	8.17
1474	VII	A	M/N14	Floor south of Structure 1013	8.17
1475	VI	A	M14	Silo south of Structure 1024	8.20
1483	IX	A	M13	Room	8.7; 8.9
1485	V	A	L13	Fill under Fortress 806	12.2
1486	II	A	L/M13	Foundation trench of Wall M131	14.2
1488	IX	A	M13	Robbers' trench of Wall M134	8.9
1489	VI	A	L13	Robbers' trench of Wall L139	8.20
1490	VIII	A	L13–14	Room east of Structure 1304	8.12
1491	X	A	M13	Floor northeast of Courtyard 1454	8.6
1495	XI	A	M13	Ash fill	8.3
1498	X	A	M14	Room north of Courtyard 1454	8.6
1499	VIII	A	L13	Room east of Structure 1304	8.12
1500	XI	A	L14–15	Fill	8.3
1501	XII; X	A	L13	Pavement with reused Iron Age vessels	8.6
1503	XI	A	L15	Silo cutting into Pit 1519	8.3
1504	XI	A	M15	Oven	8.3
1505	XI	A	M15	Oven	8.3
1506	X	A	M14	Room north of Courtyard 1454	8.6
1507	XI	A	L14	Oven	8.3
1508	XI	A	L15	Oven	8.3
1509	X	A	L13	Paved area east of Courtyard 1454	8.6
1510	XIII	A	L14–15	Stone-paved floor in Structure 1513	6.4
1512	XV	A	M13	Brick and ash layer of Rampart 1701	4.1; 4.6
1513	XIII	A	L14	Room with oven in Structure 1513	6.4
1514	XIV	A	L13–14	Floor and oven in Structure 1522	6.2
1515	XI	A	L/M14	Ash pit	8.3
1516	XI	A	L14	Ash pit	8.3
1518	XIV	A	L13	Floor near Structure 1522	6.2
1519	IX	A	L14–15	Pit cut by Silo 1503	8.3
1520	XIV	A	L13–14	Robbers' trench of Wall L1320 in Structure 1522	6.2
1521	X	A	L13	Pit	11.3
1522	XIV	A	L14	Room in Structure 1522	6.1; 6.2
1523	XIV	A	L14–15	Paved room in Structure 1522	6.2
1526	XIV	A	M13–14	Robbers' trench of Wall L1317 in Structure 1522	6.2
1529	XIV	A	L13–14	Silo in Room 1522	6.2
1530	XV	A	M14–15	Gray fill under Structure 1534	4.6
1531	X	A	M13	Fill northeast of Courtyard 1454	8.6
1534	XV	A	L15	Paved room in Structure 1534	4.6; 4.8
1535	XV	A	L13	Brick and stone debris east of Structure 1534	4.6
1537	XV	A	L13	Pavement in Structure 1534	4.6
1538	XV	A	N13	Sand fill in Rampart 1701	4.9

Locus	Stratum[a]	Area	Square(s)	Description	Figure(s)
1539	XIV	A	L/M14	Silo in Room 1523	6.2
1540	XV	A	K/L13	Ash fill east of Structure 1534	4.6
1541	XV	A	L14	Pavement east of Structure 1534	4.6
1542	XI	A	L15	Pit	8.3
1554	XV	A	F/G15–16	Scattered bricks in Rampart 971 sand layer	4.5; 4.6
1555	XVI	A	G16	*Hamra* glacis of Rampart 1562	4.5; 4.6
1556	XVI	A	F/G14–15	Debris layer in Rampart 1562	4.5; 4.6
1557	XIV	A	G16	Washed fill under Room 418	6.2
1558	XVI	A	G15	Bricks in Rampart 1562	4.5; 4.6
1559	XVI	A	F/G14–15	Debris layer in Rampart 1562	4.5; 4.6
1560	XVI	A	F/G14–15	Sand fill in Rampart 1562	4.5; 4.6
1562	XVI	A	G14–15	Sand and *hamra* fill in Rampart 1562	4.5; 4.6; 4.8
1631	IX	A	O13–14	Stone pavement	8.9
1633	VIII	A	N/O15	Room in Structure 1032	4.9; 8.12
1634	IX	A	O15	Fill under room	8.9
1635	V	A	N14	Robbers' trench of Wall O132	12.2
1637	VI	A	M/N14	Robbers' trench of Wall N135	8.20
1639	VIII	A	O15	Fill under Structure 1032	8.12
1640	VII	A	O14–15	Room in Structure 1013	8.17
1641	X	A	N14	Fill	8.6
1642	VIII	A	M/N14	Fill north of Structure 1304	8.12
1644	IX	A	O14	Floor	8.9
1645	IX	A	N/O15	Floor	4.9; 8.9
1646	X	A	O13	Fill	8.6
1647	XV	A	N14	Brick and ash layer in Rampart 1701	4.1; 4.6
1649	VII	A	L/M14	Ash fill under Floor 1474	8.17
1650	IX	A	O14	Pit	8.9
1653	XV	A	O15	Brick and ash layer in Rampart 1701	4.6; 4.9
1655	XV	A	N/O15	Fire pit	4.9
1656	X	A	O14	Pavement	8.6
1657	XVII	A	N14	Sand layer in Rampart 1903	4.9
1658	XIV	A	M14	Ash pit	6.2
1659	XV	A	M14	Brick and ash layer in Rampart 1701	4.6; 4.9
1660	XV	A	O14	Pavement	4.6
1661	XIV	A	O15	Brick debris	4.9
1662	XVI	A	M/N14	Ash pit	4.6
1663	XVII	A	M14	Sand layer in Rampart 1903	4.9
1664	XVII	A	O15	*Hamra* layer in Platform 782	4.1; 4.9
1665	XVII	A	O13	*Hamra* glacis of Rampart 1903	4.6
1666	XI	A	O15	Ash pit	
1700	XVI/XV	A	M10	Western part of Glacis 1902	
1701	XV	A	M10	Sand fill in Rampart 1701	4.1; 4.4; 4.8
1702	XV	A	M10	*Hamra* glacis of Rampart 1701	4.4
1709	VII	A	K12	Floor south of Structure 1061	8.17
1710	VIII	A	N10	Fill under Structure 1084	8.12
1712	II	A	H13	Room in Roman fortress	14.2
1715	IIIb	A	K13–14	Room in Fort 696A	12.10
1716	II	A	K13	Room in Roman fortress	14.2
1717	VII	A	H12	Fill	8.17
1718	XVI	A	M10	*Hamra* glacis of Rampart 1722	4.4
1720	V	A	H/K12	Fill east of Fortress 806	12.2
1722	XVI	A	M10	Sand layer in Rampart 1722	4.1; 4.4; 4.8
1725	IIIb	A	H/K12–13	Room in Fort 696A	12.10
1726	VII	A	K12	Ash pit south of Structure 1061	8.17
1727	XVI	A	M10	Ash layer in Rampart 1722	4.4
1728	II	A	H13	Room in Roman fortress	14.2
1730	XVI	A	M10	Brick and ash debris in Rampart 1722	4.4
1731	XVI	A	M10	Sand layer in Rampart 1722	4.4
1732	VIII	A	H11	Fill	8.12
1734	IV	A	H13	Fill under Room 1065	12.7
1735	V	A	H13	Fill	12.2

Locus	Stratum[a]	Area	Square(s)	Description	Figure(s)
1736	XV	A	M8	Sand layer in Rampart 1701	4.4
1737	XV	A	M8	*Ḥamra* glacis of Rampart 1701	4.4
1738	XV	A	M9	Foundation trench of Wall M91	4.4
1739	V	A	O/P12	Fill north of Fortress 806	12.2
1743	VIII	A	M8	Stone and brick debris	4.4
1744	IIIb–IIIa	A	N/O13	Drainage channel in Forts 696A and 684	12.10
1745	VII	A	K12	Fill south of Structure 1061	8.17
1746	XVI	A	M9	Brick and ash debris in Rampart 1722	4.4
1747	II	A	H13–14	Room in Roman fortress	14.2
1750	XVI	A	M8	Brick and ash debris in Rampart 1722	4.4
1753	IIIb	A	K13	Room in Fort 696A	12.10
1756	IV	A	O12	Fill north of Fortress 691	12.7
1757	VI	A	O12	Fill east of Structure 1024	8.20
1758	VIII	A	K11	Fill under Structure 1069	8.12
1759	II	A	K13–14	Room in Roman fortress	14.2
1760	II	A	P/Q12	Approach ramp to Roman fortress	14.2
1761	XVI	A	M8	Sand layer in Rampart 1722	4.4
1763	II	A	O/P12–13	Room in Fortress 812	14.2
1764	XVI	A	M8	Ash layer in Rampart 1722	4.4
1766	V/IV	A	L11	Pit	
1767	XVII	A	M8	Pit (sand fill in *ḥamra* quarry)	4.1; 4.4
1768	IX	A	K/L11	Fill south of Room 1771	8.9
1769	VI	A	O11	Fill east of Structure 1024	8.20
1771	IX	A	L/M11	Room in Structure 1771	8.7; 8.9
1772	V	A	N12	Room in Fortress 806	12.2
1773	V	A	N/O12	Fill under Courtyard 806	12.2
1774	V–IV	A	N11–12	Room in Fortress 806 and 691	12.2; 12.7
1775	V–IV	A	N12	Fill under Courtyard 806	12.2; 12.7
1776	VI	A	O/P11	Fill east of Structure 1024	8.20
1777	X	A	O11	Fill	8.6
1779	IX	A	L11	Fill under Room 1771	8.9
1803	IX/VIII	D	C20	Pottery kiln	8.13; 8.14
1804	Unstratified	D	C20	Surface	
1805	Unstratified	D	L13	Surface	
1806	VI	D	L13	Fill	8.21
1807	VI	D	K14	Fill	8.21
1808	Unstratified	D	R19	Surface	
1809	VI	D	P/Q19	Paved courtyard	
1812	IX/VIII	D	C20	Opening of firing chamber in Kiln 1803	8.13
1813	Unstratified	D	G7	Surface	
1814	VI	D	G7	Fill	
1850	XI/VI	E	L3	Pit burial	11.2
1851	XI/VI	E	L/M3	Cist burial	11.2
1852	XI/VI	E	L1	Jar burial	11.2
1853	XI/VI	E	L1	Pit burial	11.2
1854	XI/VI	E	M3	Pit burial	11.2
1855	XI/VI	E	L3–4	Cist burial	11.2
1856	XI/VI	E	L4	Cist burial	11.2
1857	XI/VI	E	L4	Cist burial	11.2
1858	XI/VI	E	L3	Jar burial	11.2
1859	XI/VI	E	L3	Jar burial	11.2
1860	XI/VI	E	K3	Pit burial	11.2
1861	XI/VI	E	K3	Cist burial	11.2
1862	XI/VI	E	A/B12	Pit (?) burial	
1863	XI/VI	E	E3	Pit burial	11.1
1864	XI/VI	E	E3	Jar burial	11.1
1865	XI/VI	E	E3	Cist burial	11.1
1866	XI/VI	E	D3	Cist burial	11.1
1867	XI/VI	E	D/E3	Cist burial	11.1
1868	XI/VI	E	L1	Jar burial	11.2
1869	XI/VI	E	L1	Cist burial	11.2

Locus	Stratum[a]	Area	Square(s)	Description	Figure(s)
1870	XI/VI	E	L1	Jar burial	11.2
1871	XI/VI	E	D/E4	Cist burial	11.1
1872	XI/VI	E	E4	Cist burial	11.1
1873	XI/VI	E	L1	Cist burial	11.2
1874	XI/VI	E	D4	Jar burial	11.1
1875	XI/VI	E	D4–5	Jar burial	11.1
1876	XI/VI	E	C/D4	Cist burial	11.1
1877	XI/VI	E	D4	Pit burial	11.1
1878	XI/VI	E	L1	Pit burial	11.2
1879	XI/VI	E	B4	Jar burial	11.1
1880	XI/VI	E	C4	Pit burial	11.1
1881	XI/VI	E	C/D3–4	Cist burial	11.1
1882	XI/VI	E	C4	Pit burial	11.1
1883	XI/VI	E	K/L1	Cist burial	11.2
1884	XI/VI	E	D3–4	Cist burial	11.1
1885	XI/VI	E	C4	Pit burial	11.1
1886	XI/VI	E	E4	Pit burial	11.1
1900	XVI	A	M/N13	*Ḥamra* layer in Rampart 1722	4.9
1901	XVII	A	L14	*Ḥamra* glacis of Rampart 1903	4.9
1903	XVII	A	L/M13	Sand layer in Rampart 1903	4.1; 4.9
1906	I	A	H14	Mameluke grave	
1908	XVI	A	M13	Sand fill in Rampart 1722	4.9
1909	IX	A	R/S13	Room in Structure 344	8.8
2900	XIV/XIII	I	E1–2	Treading floor in Winepress 2900	6.9
2901	XIV/XIII	I	E1	Large vat in Winepress 2900	6.9
2902	XIV/XIII	I	E1	Small vat in Winepress 2900	6.9
2903	XIV/XIII	I	D1–2	Treading floor in Winepress 2900	6.9
2904	XIV/XIII	I	D1	Large vat in Winepress 2900	6.9
2905	XIV/XIII	I	D1	Small vat in Winepress 2900	6.9
2906	XIV/XIII	I	A2–3	Treading floor in Winepress 2910	6.9
2907	XIV/XIII	I	A2	Large vat in Winepress 2910	6.9
2908	XIV/XIII	I	A2	Small vat in Winepress 2910	6.9
2910	XIV/XIII	I	B2–3	Treading floor in Winepress 2910	6.9
2911	XIV/XIII	I	A/B2–3	Rectangular basin in Winepress 2910	6.9
2912	XIV/XIII	I	D/E1–2	Rectangular basin in Winepress 2900	6.9
2913	XIV/XIII	I	B2	Large vat in Winepress 2910	6.9
2916	XIV/XIII	I	B2	Small vat in Winepress 2910	6.9

[a] See Table 1.1 for chronological correlation of strata.

[b] Loci with strata separated by a hyphen were in use in both strata; a slash between stratum numbers gives the possible stratigraphic span of the locus.

Appendix II
Participants

1977

Ambers, Steven
Cleveland OH

Aron, Tricia
Pauma Valley CA

Bernstein, Claudia
Brooklyn NY

Blatt, Karl-Rheinhard
Göttingen, Germany

Bosek, Rebecca
Alexandria MN

Boshard, Jonathan
Denver CO

Brandes, Friederike

Brandl, Kathy
Minneapolis MN

Brennan, Verna
Hermosa Beach CA

Brody, Lisa
Philadelphia PA

Burbank, Alison
Provo UT

Busis, Judy
Philadelphia PA

Cerny, Katarina
Minneapolis MN

Cerny, Nina
Minneapolis MN

Christenson, Bethany
Stillwater MN

Combe, Ulrike
Wiesenfild, Germany

Cook, Jaclyn
Minneapolis MN

Creighton, Millie
Richfield MN

Davis, Clifford
Salt Lake City UT

Davis, Marcia
Salt Lake City UT

Dawidowicz, Nicole
Holon, Israel

Dorbecker, Reinhard
Schwalnstadtz, Germany

Duerden, Richard
Provo UT

Eames, Bruce
Green Bay WI

Eiger, Kenneth
Minneapolis MN

Emfield, Scott
St. Paul MN

Engler, Uwe
Heidelberg, Germany

Foster, Thomas
Morgan MN

Furman, Linda
Grassy Lake, Canada

Furman, Mary Jean
Oakland CA

Grenell, Suzanne
Minneapolis MN

Gunther, Lloyd
Brigham City UT

Gunther, Metta
Brigham City UT

Hansen, Richard
Rupert ID

Harris, Debra
Idaho Falls ID

Haugerud, Ann
St. Paul MN

Hebrew, Esther
Lehi UT

Heuer, Susanne
Giessen, Germany

Higgins, Mike
Wilmington NC

Houanes, Joyce
Minneapolis MN

Imholte, Sara
Morris MN

Ingersoll, Julie
Salt Lake City UT

Jackson, William
Fair Oaks CA

Jephson, Jolene
Idaho Falls ID

Jermasele Johnson, Lori
Minneapolis MN

Kaufmann, Petra
Berlin, Germany

Kirstadter, Freimut
Heidelberg, Germany

Korman, Charles
Merion PA

Krasny, Janis
Cresskill NJ

Laveman, David
Houston TX

Levine, Joyce
Hopkins MN

Lieberson, Robert
Huntington Valley PA

Lieblein, Edward
Great Neck NY

Meira Penna, Cecilia
Oslo, Norway

Melcher, Brigitte
Hanover, Germany

Minsberg, Michael
St. Paul MN

Mueller, Jill Alice
St. Paul MN

Muhly, Alexis
Philadelphia PA

Muhly, Elizabeth
Philadelphia PA

Muhly, Nicholas
Philadelphia PA

Nelson, Stephen
Salt Lake City UT

Nicholls, Dana
Orem UT

Nissen, Elaine
Minneapolis MN

Otto, Jonathan
Philadelphia PA

Owen, Melanie
Flintridge CA

Parker, Kathryn
Portland OR

Patterson, Cynthia
Cortez CO

Peitz, Rudiger
Herford, Germany

Perry, David
Boston MA

Porat, Seffy
Holon, Israel

Prusse, Joan
Denver CO

Quebbeman, Susan
LaGrande OR

Rohloff, Sabine
Berlin, Germany

Salz, Tammy
Philadelphia PA

Schafer, Pamela
Minneapolis MN

Schneider, Hiltrud
Sandhausen, Germany

Siemers, Heinke
Marburg, Germany

Spangler, Eugenie
Sauk Centre MN

Stefanucciala, Maria E.
Rome, Italy

Stone, Leslie
Valhalle NY

Summerson, Phil
Columbus OH

Vogel, Susan
Elkins Park PA

Waring, Dawn
Pasadena CA

Warzecha, Cynthia
Melrose MN

1978

Angerhofer, Norman
Provo UT

Ballard, David
Salt Lake City UT

Balza, Robert
Bear DE

Barnes, Lee
Blaine MN

Barnwell, Elizabeth
Marquette MI

Bell, Jennifer
Crystal MN

Bernskov, Helle Birgit
Ballerup, Denmark

Blewett, Dan
Anoka MN

Boardman, Ian
Narberth PA

Brant, Elaine
St. Paul MN

Brug, John
West Newton PA

Bushman, Douglas
Provo UT

Busis, Richard
Pittsburgh PA

Carr-Henry, Melvin
Ridgewood NY

Christensen, James
Orem UT

Cohen, Nancy
West Williamsville NY

Davidi, Orit
Holon, Israel

Davies, Nathan
Orem UT

Donaldson, Susan
Batel UT

Dukoff, Patricia
Woodmere NY

Engebretson, Mikael
New Brighton MN

Eshel, Yehuda
Petach Tikvah, Israel

Eshet, Reuven
Tel Aviv, Israel

Fennell, Steven
Wilmington NC

Frochlich, Richard
Denmauk WI

Furman, Mary Jean
Oakland CA

Gast, Kenneth
Tomah WI

Gast, Roberta
Tomah WI

Gavish, Judith
Ramat Gan, Israel

Gawrisch, Wilbert R.
Mequon WI

Giesen, Audrey
New Prague MN

Goeglein, Mark
Wauwatosa WI

Gross, Steven
River Edge NJ

Gullixson, Theodore
Minot ND

Gurgel, Karl
Lake Mills WI

Gwiliam, Donna
Newport Beach CA

Haberkorn, Keith
Manitowik WI

Hadley, Judith
Perrysburg OH

Hanson, Virjean
Belleville WI

Happee, Nienlee
Heiden, Holland

Harper, Jody
Placenkia CA

Harstad, Adolph
Alma MI

Higgins, Miles
Raleigh NC

Hill, Christopher
Duluth MN

Hochmuth, Donald
Mason City IA

Hokkanen, Karin
Maitland FL

Huffman, Roger
Mankato MN

Jacobs, Henry
Jerusalem, Israel

Jahnke, Gene
Detroit MI

Jeske, Eleonore
Mequon WI

Jeske, John
Mequon WI

Johnson, Wendelin
Detroit Lakes MN

Karl, Ruth
St. Paul MN

Kehaya, Elizabeth
Wilmington NC

Kelm, Paul
Madison WI

Kert, Robert
Toronto, Canada

Kock, Eugene
Minocqua WI

Krueger, Silas
Tucson AZ

Kujawski, Nancy
Boyne City MI

Larson, Grace
Minneapolis MN

Laterman, Anna
Ramat Gan, Israel

Lenz, Greg
Ann Arbor MI

Liestman, Terri Lynn
Mound MN

Lindberg, Evonne C.
Minneapolis MN

Long, Lydia
Wilmington NC

Marble, Haws
Provo UT

Marble, Rodney
Davis CA

Marin, Deborah
Lexington MA

May, Lawrence Allen, Jr.
Bradenton FL

McHose, Mary
Southport NC

Mead, Pamela
Minneapolis MN

Mills, Barry
Willard NC

Moss, Carol
Duluth MN

Nachtsheim, Stephen
St. Paul MN

Nass, Thomas
Jefferson WI

Nelson, Dean
Shoreview MN

Nevyas, Anita
Narberth PA

Nissen, Elaine
Minneapolis MN

Nitz, Carol
Mequon WI

Nitz, Paul
Mequon WI

Nugent, Cynthia
Minneapolis MN

Palmer, Marla
Kirtland NM

Panning, Armin
Mequon WI

Papenfuss, Jo
Lincoln NE

Parish, John
Grants Pass OR

Perkins, Evan K.
Sacramento CA

Peters, Kevin
Roscommon MI

Raindorf, Julie
Fair Lawn NJ

Rapp, Karen
Duluth MN

Rapp, Kathy
Duluth MN

Ray, Keith
St. Saline MI

Riley, Archibald
Philadelphia PA

Robertson, Deborah
Los Angeles CA

Robinson, Adele
Bethesda MD

Ross, Charles
Lake Elmo MN

Schlussel, Meryl
Teaneck NJ

Schmitzer, Alois
Frankenmoth MI

Schroeder, George
Provo UT

Schwab, Rodney
Kawrawlin MI

Seifert, John
Midland MI

Serling, Jane
New Haven CT

Sill, James
Las Vegas NV

Soukup, John
Circle Pines MN

PARTICIPANTS

Spevacek, Kirby
Maribel WI

Sprain, Roger
Medellin, Colombia

Stanger, Tobie L.
Summit NJ

Stein, Jeffrey
Duluth MN

Strack, Kenneth
Tecumseh MI

Trapp, Carol
Stambaugh MI

Trapp, Thomas
Stambaugh MI

Van Pelt, Warren
Provo UT

Voeltz, Brenda
Lake Elmo MN

Vogt, John
Jacksonville FL

Vogt, Sandra
Jacksonville FL

Voss, Verne
Jordan MN

Walstrom, Wendie
Anoka MN

Weber, Richard
Lake Geneva WI

Weiss, Danny
Ranana, Israel

Wilde, John
Vero Beach FL

Yarbrough, Jennifer
Ogden UT

Zarling, John
Sedona AZ

Zarling, Mark
Benton Harbor MI

Zarling, Waldemar
Benton Harbor MI

1979

Aboulafia, David
Farmington Hills MI

Aharoni, Dan
Rehovot, Israel

Aharoni, Gad
Rehovot, Israel

Ashton, Terry
Burwood, Australia

Atkins, Laurie
Scottsdale AZ

Bailey, Margaret
Turramurra, Australia

Bennion, Owen
Provo UT

Bernstein, Paul
Minneapolis MN

Bischoff, Anya
Costa Mesa CA

Block, Leslie
Palos Verdes CA

Bondfield, Verity
Sydney, Australia

Borow, Hilary
Martinsville NJ

Brett, Florence
St. Paul MN

Brown, Merilyn
Phoenix AZ

Buckingham, Janis
Arcadia CA

Butler, Thayer A.
Duluth MN

Catler, James
West Hartford CT

Clarke, Trevor
Nerang, Australia

Cluff, Annette
Provo UT

DeRugter, Thomas
Renville MN

Dibbs, Stewart
Pymble, Australia

Donaldson, Martha
Bountiful UT

Donaldson, Susan
Batel UT

Dybiec, Paul
St. Paul MN

Esser, Heather
Grand Rapids MN

Fehr, Lee
Bloomer WI

Flegenheimer, Eve
Roslyn NY

Foxworthy, Bazzell
Kansas City MO

Foxworthy, Roberta
Kansas City MO

Friedman, Amy
Brooklyn NY

Furman, Michael
Scranton PA

Garnder, Charee
Kenn WA

Gilboa, Dani
Tel Aviv, Israel

Ginzburg, Ady
Petach Tikvah, Israel

Girod, Pamela
St. Paul MN

Gitelman, Leslie
Pittsburgh PA

Glass, Michele
Berrien Springs MI

Glass, Phillip
Berrien Springs MI

Goldberg, Janet
Scarsdale NY

Goldstein, Debbie
Montreal, Canada

Goossens, Filip
Louvain, Belgium

Gornall, Sarah
St. Ives, Australia

Greenberg, Karen
Ottawa, Canada

Gross, Andrea
Philadelphia PA

Grunberg, Rebecca
Bayside NY

Harris, Leota
Independence MO

Harris, Merrill
Independence MO

Haskins, JoAnne
Midvale UT

Herzog, Chen
Ramat-Hasharon, Israel

Hewitt, Heather
St. Ives, Australia

Hobson, Jim
Minneapolis MN

Hochstadt, Shari
Brooklyn NY

Hoyt, Sharon
Scottsdale AZ

Johnson, Susan
Grand Rapids MN

Jones, Jana
Pymble, Australia

Kaiman, Andrea
Matawan NJ

Kaplan, Marc
St. Newton MA

Kaplan, Shmuel
Jerusalem, Israel

Katz, Debra Faith
Minneapolis MN

Kenison, Dave
Payson UT

Lambert, Lynn
Two Harbors MN

Lambert, Timothy
Two Harbors MN

Laughlan, Joseph
Mankato MN

Leppington, Richard
Northwood, England

Leslie, Donna
London, England

Mandel, Glenn
Fox Lake IL

Martineau, Rebecca
Salt Lake City UT

Mazer, Margaret
Harnson NY

McCue, Elizabeth
Minneapolis MN

McCue, Margaret
Eugene OR

McKnight, Richard
Stillwater MN

McLauchlan, Peggy
Duluth MN

McMullin, Tom
Minneapolis MN

Mills, Lois
Racine WI

Mosher, Raquel
Dallas TX

Nachtsheim, Stephen
St. Paul MN

Nalick, Marilyn
St. Louis MO

Nemy, Garth
Winnipeg, Canada

Newberger, Nancy
Meadowbrook PA

Orlins, Michelle
Ft. Myers FL

Pertzik, Marvin
St. Paul MN

Petersen, Camille
Duluth MN

Pirmantgen, Toni
Austin MN

Platzman, Ellen
Short Hills NJ

Plitzuweit, Jerald
Watertown WI

Radeck, Herman J.
San Francisco CA

Remole, Mary
Minneapolis MN

Rich, Lisa
New Hope MN

Rigor, Madelyn
Salt Lake City UT

Roseman, Ruth
Westmont NJ

Rosenfeld, Jerry
Toronto, Canada

Roth, Nancy
Jericho NY

Russell, Connie
La Canada CA

Schneeberg, Judy
Cheix PA

Schöne, Angelika
Heidelberg, Germany

Schow, Cheryl
Twin Falls ID

Schwartz, Jill
Irvington NY

Scott-Virtue, Eileen Lianne
West Ryde, Australia

Shoval, Dalia
Givataim, Israel

Shukur, Margaret
Milwaukee WI

Shvarzchild, Meir
Haifa, Israel

Siegel, Owen
Lausdale PA

Stallings, Meralee
Idaho Falls ID

Stead, Roberta
Melbourne, Australia

Stevens, Christine
Sydney, Australia

Talbot-Windeyer, Veronica
North Ryde, Australia

Tavor, Nimrod
Ramat-Hasharon, Israel

Thompson, Annette
Salt Lake City UT

Thompson, Keith, Jr.
Salt Lake City UT

Thomson, Margaret
West Chester PA

Tishler, Boaz
Ramat-Aviv, Israel

Tory, Joanne
Don Mills, Canada

Tsouroulla, Katena
Anmandale, Australia

Volkov, Shaul
Minneapolis MN

Watkins, Rebecca
Lombard IL

Watts, Kenneth
Loveland CO

Weinberg, Michelle
Brooklyn NY

Weiss, Bradley
Brooklyn NY

Weiss, Ricky
Flushing NY

Werdin, Kristi
Roseville MN

Willette, Katherine
Delavan MN

Wingerath, Halina
Heidelberg, Germany

Wittkopf, Eric
Hastings MN

Wolff, Cheryl
Merrick NY

1980

Adar, Yael
Ramat Gan, Israel

Alexander, Mary
Boston MA

Alony, Efrat
Netanya, Israel

Balge, Daniel
Mequon WI

Balge, Richard
Mequon WI

Barnstorf, Lori
Duluth MN

Baumler, Gary
Watertown WI

Beck, Joan
Epping, Australia

Bekker, Isfriede
North Rocks, Australia

Bekker, Tihamer
North Rocks, Australia

Brenchley, Elizabeth
McMahons Pt., Australia

Brooks, Alec
Rosebush MI

Busch, Richard
Edina MN

Busch, Robert
Edina MN

Bushman, Nephi
Salt Lake City UT

Cady, Richard
Albany MN

Coverdale, Cherry
St. Paul MN

Crawley, Hal
Mt. Pleasant MI

Crawley, Nancy
Mt. Pleasant MI

Davies, James
Bend OR

Davies, Martha
Bend OR

Dibbs, Stewart
Pymble, Australia

Douglass, Carolinda
Warrenville IL

Eldridge, Victor
Eastwood, Australia

Epstein, Lise
Merion PA

Ericson, Lester
Vienna, Austria

Euchman, Josefine
Jerusalem, Israel

Ewings, Jerry
Jim Falls WI

Fitzpatrick, Judith
Everett MA

Foy, Joan
London, England

Gassner, Shirley
Petach Tikvah, Israel

Gerlach, Joel
Mequon WI

Gerlach, Lillian
Mequon WI

Goldberg, Ron
Plymouth MN

Graff, Francine
Salt Lake City UT

Graff, Leslie
Salt Lake City UT

Greenberg, Isidore
Brooklyn NY

Guetta, Judith
Holon, Israel

Guetta, Tali
Holon, Israel

Hadas, Nurit
Ramat Gan, Israel

Hamel, Marcie
Minneapolis MN

Hamel, Tom
Minneapolis MN

Harman, Susan
Orem UT

Hensley, Arlene
Madison WI

Herzog, Anat
Tel Aviv, Israel

Herzog, Mirit
Tel Aviv, Israel

Himm, Dennis
Milwaukee WI

Himm, Kay
Milwaukee WI

Huebner, John
Sarasota FL

Jeffs, Martha
Mountain View CA

Jeffs, Ralph
Mountain View CA

Jenkins, H. James
Portland OR

Jeske, Eleonore
Mequon WI

Jeske, John
Mequon WI

Jeske, Mary
Mequon WI

Johengen, Edward
Mt. Pleasant MI

Johnston, Robert
Stevensville MI

Katz, Bert
New York NY

Katz, Craig
Cherry Hill NJ

Kelley, Audrey
Oroville CA

Kelley, Gray
Oroville CA

Kennedy, Trevor
Victoria, Australia

Kestenbaum, Connie
Washington DC

Kezar, Edward
Eden NC

Kezar, Kirsten
Eden NC

Lacoba, Fatima
Sydney, Australia

Lemke, Laura L.
Monroe MI

Lesher, Scott
King of Prussia PA

Leslie, Donna
London, England

Levit, Dov
Nof Yam, Israel

PARTICIPANTS

Likins, William
St. Paul MN

Lipschultz, Dorothy
St. Paul MN

Lipten, Lori
Huntington Woods MI

Londgren, Jeff
Marshall MN

Mandelkom, Ariana
Neve-Shalem, Israel

Marble, Haws
Provo UT

Marggraf, Paul
Watertown WI

Martineau, Rebecca
Salt Lake City UT

Michels, Mary
Strum WI

Nitz, Paul
Mequon WI

Olson, Lawrence
Cedarburg WI

Olson, Mary
Cedarburg WI

Otto, Robert
Somers WI

Paltiel, Ellen
Westmount, Canada

Pankhurst, Alula Andrew
London, England

Panning, Armin
Mequon WI

Radeck, Herman
San Francisco CA

Rieke, Mark
Tomah WI

Robb, Kelly
Orem UT

Rutheiser, Charles
Rockville Centre NY

Rykel, Martin
Roseville MN

Schenk, Joel
New Ulm MN

Schmidt, James
Morgan MN

Schmitt, Christina
St. Paul MN

Schultz, David
Mesa AZ

Shalen, Elsia
Trumball CT

Shavit, Eran
Tel Aviv, Israel

Shillestad, Christine
West Hartford CT

Soderquist, Catherine
Minneapolis MN

Stevens, Franklin B.
Duluth MN

Stevens, Portia
Duluth MN

Stokes, Leon Wayne
Dothan AL

Sweet, David
East Lansing MI

Thompson, Annette
Jerusalem, Israel

Thompson, Evelyn
London, Canada

Thompson, Glen
Lusaka, Zambia

Thompson, Keith, Jr.
Jerusalem, Israel

Thomson, Margaret
West Chester PA

Unke, Timothy A.
Manitowoc WI

Velenchik, Tess
Fairfield CT

Vernier, Kendra
Newark DE

Wallace, Dorothy
Duluth MN

Wallace, Martin
Duluth MN

Werdin, Kristi
Roseville MN

Westlin, Bonnie
Crystal MN

Wilson, Barbara
Duluth MN

Wolfson, Wendy
Des Moines IA

Wright, Steve
Bismarck ND

Yuknavage, Kathy
Gobles MI

Plates

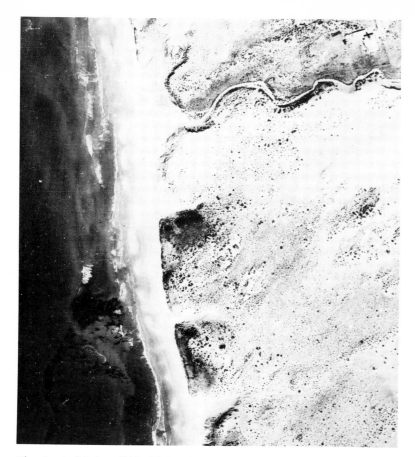

Plate 1. Aerial view of Tel Michal and vicinity (photographed in 1949), showing original course of Naḥal Gelilot.

Plate 2. Aerial view of Tel Michal and vicinity (photographed in 1977, after first excavation season). Note vestigial *kurkar* ridge.

Plate 3. High tell before excavation, looking west.

Plate 4. High tell after removal of overlying sand dunes from eastern slope (photographed in 1979).

Plate 5. Stepped trench on western side of high tell, from west (Fig. 4.3).

Plate 6. Excavation of eastern slope of high tell.

Plate 7. Retaining Wall S156 of Middle Bronze Age IIB Platform 782 with sand Fill 716 in front.

Plate 8. Section on southern slope showing layer of scattered bricks (Locus 1554) incorporated into Rampart 971 (Stratum XV).

Plate 9. Section through eastern slope of Ramparts 1722 (Stratum XVI) and 1701 (Stratum XV) with Wall M91 in center.

Plate 10. Rampart 1562 (Stratum XVI; Fig. 4.5).

Plate 11. Earthworks at center of high tell: (1) sand Fill 1903 (Stratum XVII); (2) hard-packed *hamra* Fill 1901 (Stratum XVII); (3) sand Fill 1538 (Stratum XV).

Plate 12. Rampart layers in center of high tell (Strata XVI–XV; compare Fig. 4.9).

Plate 13. Building 1534 at center of high tell (Stratum XV; Fig. 4.6). Note anchor in secondary use at lower right.

Plate 14. Room 1513 at center of high tell (Stratum XIII; Fig. 6.4).

Plate 15. Building 423 (Strata XIV–XIII). Retaining Wall F151 of Stratum VIII at left.

411

Plate 16. Cultic building (Structure 300) on eastern hillock (Stratum XIII; Fig. 6.5).

Plate 17. Structure 117 on southeastern hillock (Strata XIV/XIII; Fig. 6.7).

412

Plate 18. Iron Age Winepress Complex 2910, south of Tel Michal.

Plate 19. Vat 2907 of Winepress Complex 2910. At right: foothold ledges in vat and depression for holding jar.

Plate 20. Limestone block found next to Iron Age winepress complexes.

413

Plate 21. Persian period pits at center of high tell (Stratum XI; Fig. 8.3) cutting through earlier strata.

Plate 22. Persian period ovens (Stratum XI; Fig. 8:3) with pits of same stratum beginning to appear.

Plate 23. Pottery cylinders and stone roller in Courtyard 856 (Stratum X; Fig. 8.5).

414

Plate 24. Persian period Storeroom 92 at southern end of high tell (Stratum VIII; Fig. 8:12).

Plate 25. Silo 93 with intact storage jars in Storeroom 92 (Stratum VIII; Fig. 8:12).

Plate 26. Brick Wall S141 and Drain 704 of Persian period Fort 329 (Stratum VII).

Plate 27. Persian period silo in Building 1013 at center of high tell.

Plate 28. Foundation course and scattered pottery on floor of Room 504 on northern hill (Stratum VI; Fig. 8:21).

Plate 29. Persian period Building 143 (Stratum VI) and Hellenistic period Silo 135 (Stratum V) on eastern hillock (Fig. 8.22).

Plate 30.   Persian period pottery kiln (1803) on northern hill showing opening of fire chamber (Stratum VIII; Figs. 8.13; 8.14).

Plate 31.   Interior of Kiln 1803.

Plate 32.   Broken storage vessels in Kiln 1803.

Plate 33. Persian period Winepress 510 on northern hill (Stratum VIII; Fig. 8.21).

Plate 34. Persian period pottery kiln (215) on southwestern side of northern hill (Stratum VIII; Fig. 8.13).

Plate 35. Stones from dismantled Persian period structures (Stratum VI) laid as protective mantle around Hellenistic winepress (Stratum V) on northern hill.

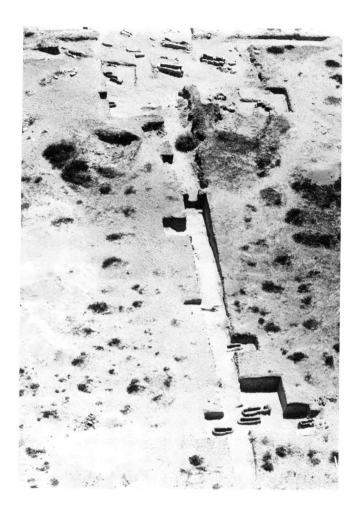

Plate 36. Aerial view of Persian period cemetery on northern hill (Area E; Figs. 11.1; 11.2).

Plate 37. Stone-walled cist burials.

419

Plate 38. Preservation of badly deteriorated skeleton in Persian period cemetery.

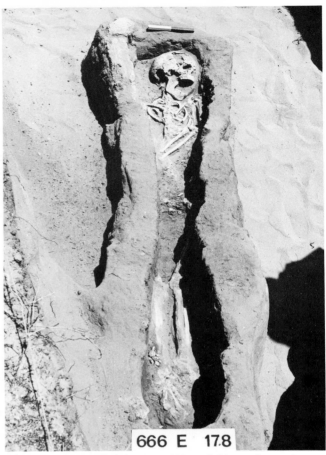

Plate 39. Ḥamra-walled cist grave (666), probably wood covered.

Plate 40. Jar Burial 190 with capping of unbaked clay.

Plate 41. Foundation of western wall (O159) of Hellenistic Fortress 806 (Stratum V; Fig. 12.2) with ashlar incorporated into superstructure. Above lies Basin 683 of Early Arab period (Stratum I).

Plate 43. Hellenistic Structure 306 (Stratum IV; Fig. 12.8).

Plate 42. Room 1014 of Hellenistic Fortress 806 (Stratum V; Fig. 12.2). At right, foundations of Roman period Tower 1002 and Early Arab basin.

Plate 44. Hellenistic Winepress 556 on northern hill (Strata V–IV; Fig. 12.4).

Plate 45. Winepress 556 in process of preservation (Figs. 12.4; 12:5).

422

Plate 46. Vat 551A of Hellenistic Winepress 556 (Strata V–IV).

Plate 47. Hasmonean Winepress 255 (Stratum III; Fig. 12.11).

475 N 18

Plate 48. Room 685/813 of Hasmonean fort (Strata IIIb–IIIa; Fig. 12.10). Buttresses inside room belong to Stratum IIIa.

Plate 49. Drainage Channel 1744 of Hasmonean Fort 696/684 (Strata IIIb–IIIa; Fig. 12.10) cut by walls of Roman fortress (Stratum II).

Plate 50. Ashlar threshold leading from Courtyard 907 into Room 913 of Roman fortress (Stratum II; Fig. 14:2).

Plate 51. Drainage Channel 804 draining central Courtyard 812 of Roman fortress.

425

Plate 52. Concrete foundations (L150) of buttressed corner of Tower 50 of Early Arab period (Stratum I; Fig. 15:1).

Plate 53. Basin 683 used in preparing lime plaster for Stratum I constructions.

Plate 54. Expedition camp at Nof Yam.

Plate 55. Afternoon pottery study session in expedition camp.

Plate 56. The late Shmuel Moshkovitz, surveyor and stratigraphic consultant of the Tel Michal expedition.

Plate 57. Local Bronze Age pottery: 1. bowl (Fig. 5.2:23); 2. bowl (Fig. 5.5:8); 3. krater (Fig. 5.5:13); 4. krater (Fig. 5.5:14); 5. krater (Fig. 5.8:11); 6. cooking pot (Fig. 5.6:8); 7. cooking pot (Fig. 5.6:7); 8. cooking pot (Fig. 5.6:2); 9. cooking pot (Fig. 5.6:1); 10. juglet (Fig. 5.7:8); 11. storage jar (Fig. 5.9:1); 12. storage jar (Fig. 5.7:14).

428

Plate 58. Imported Bronze Age pottery: 1. bowl (Fig. 5.10:16); 2. bowl (Fig. 5.10:4); 3–4. bowls (Fig. 5.10:1–2); 5. bowl (Fig. 5.10:5); 6. bowl (Fig. 5.10:8); 7. Minoan sherd (6533/1, Locus 956); 8. Bichrome sherd (Fig. 5.9:13).

Plate 59. Iron Age pottery: 1. small krater (Fig. 7.1:4); 2. bowl (Fig. 7.5:2); 3. bowl (Fig. 7.5:1); 4–5. chalices (Fig. 7.5:6–7); 6. cooking pot (Fig. 7.5:9); 7–9. jugs (Fig. 7.3:3–5); 10. juglet (Fig. 7.5:14); 11–12. juglets (Fig. 7.3:7–8); 13. storage jar (Fig. 7.2:11); 14. storage jar (Fig. 7.3:15); 15. holemouth jar (Fig. 7.3:16); 16. storage jar (Fig. 7.5:18).

Plate 60. Local Persian period pottery (high tell): 1. bottle (Fig. 9.2:14); 2. bottle (Fig. 9.2:12); 3. decanter (Fig. 9.2:6); 4–5. amphoriskoi (Fig. 9.8:8–9); 6. bowl (Fig. 9.10:8); 7. jug (Fig. 9.10:1); 8. lamp (Fig. 9.9:6); 9. amphora (Fig. 9.3:11); 10. storage jar (Fig. 9.3:2).

431

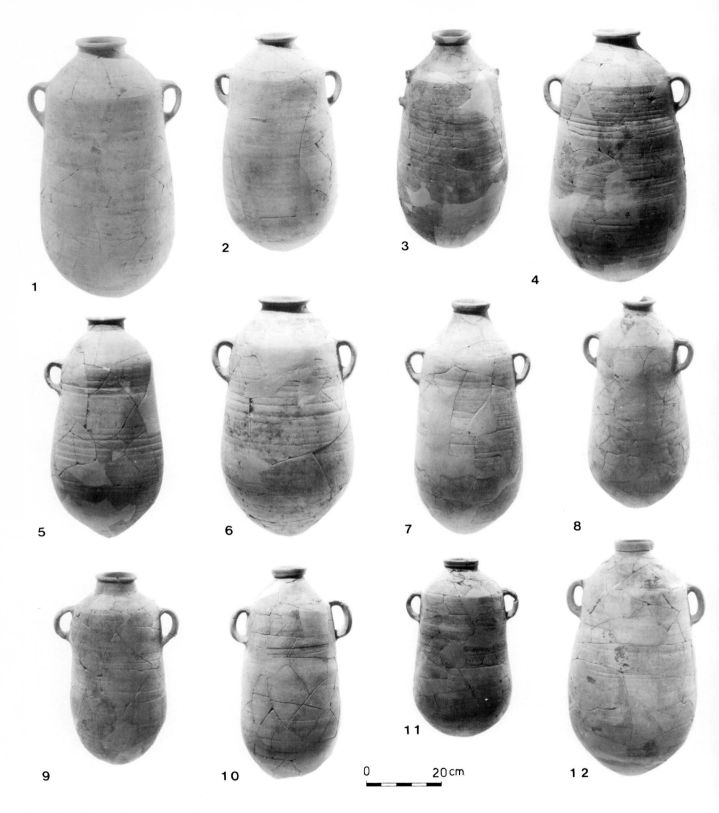

1   **2**   **3**   **4**

5   **6**   **7**   **8**

9   **10**   **11**   **12**

0   20 cm

Plate 61.   Persian period storage jars (Locus 92): 1 (Fig. 9.4:1); 2–3 (Fig. 9.4:3–4); 4 (Fig. 9.4:6); 5 (Fig. 9.4:9); 6 (Fig. 9.4:8); 7 (Fig. 9.4:5); 8–9 (Fig. 9.4:11–12); 10–12 (Fig. 9.5: 2–4).

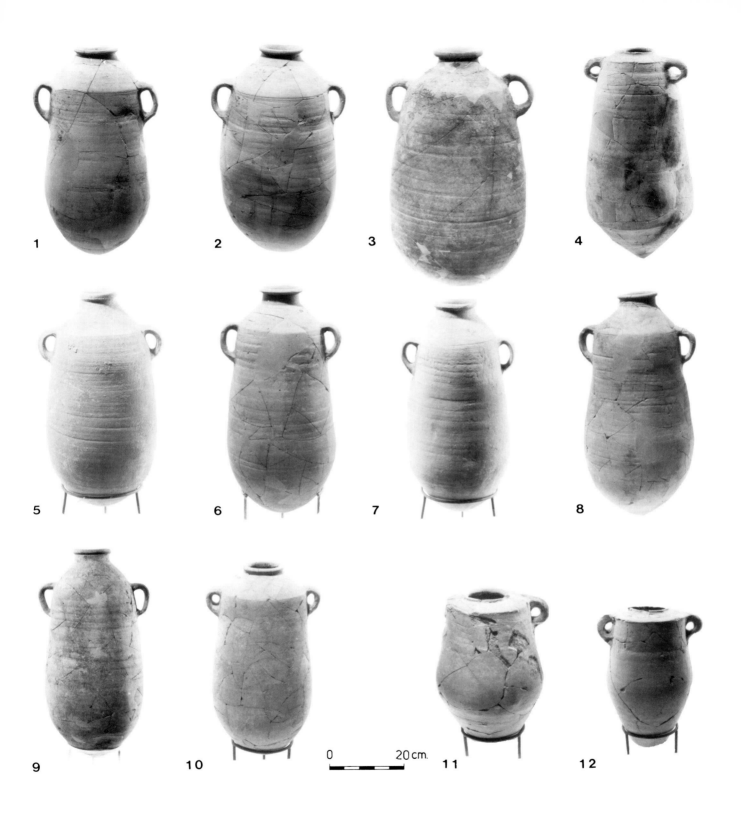

Plate 62. Persian period storage jars (Loci 92, 93, 1031, 955): 1–2 (Fig. 9.5:5–6); 3–4 (Fig. 9.5:8–9); 5–8 (Fig. 9.6:2, 4–6); 9 (Fig. 9.7:10); 10 (Fig. 9.10:3); 11–12 (Fig. 9.10:5–6).

433

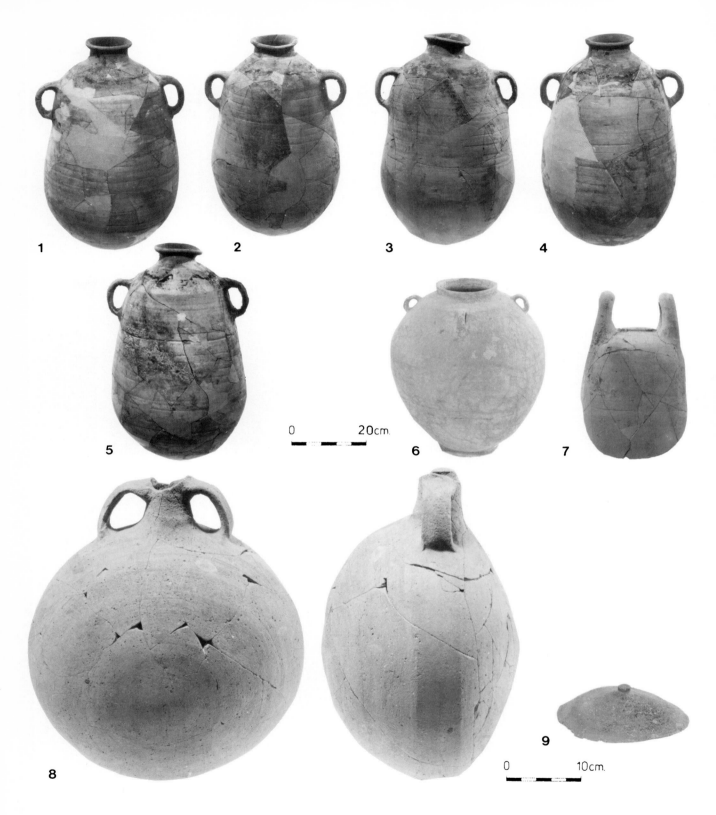

Plate 63. Local Persian period pottery (northern hill): 1–5. storage jars from kiln (Fig. 9.12:6–10); 6. storage jar (Fig. 9.12:3); 7. storage jar (Fig. 9.13:19); 8. flask (Fig. 9.13:16); 9. lid (Fig. 9.13:15).

Plate 64.   Persian period pottery (cemetery and eastern hillock): 1–2. storage jars (Fig. 9.14:1–2); 3. storage jar (Fig. 9.14:5); 4. storage jar (Fig. 9.14:9); 5. storage jar (Fig. 9.14:8); 6. storage jar (Fig. 9.14:7); 7. storage jar (Fig. 9.14:10); 8. amphora (Fig. 9.15:7); 9. bowl (Fig. 9.15:8); 10. lamps (Fig. 9.11:3–8).

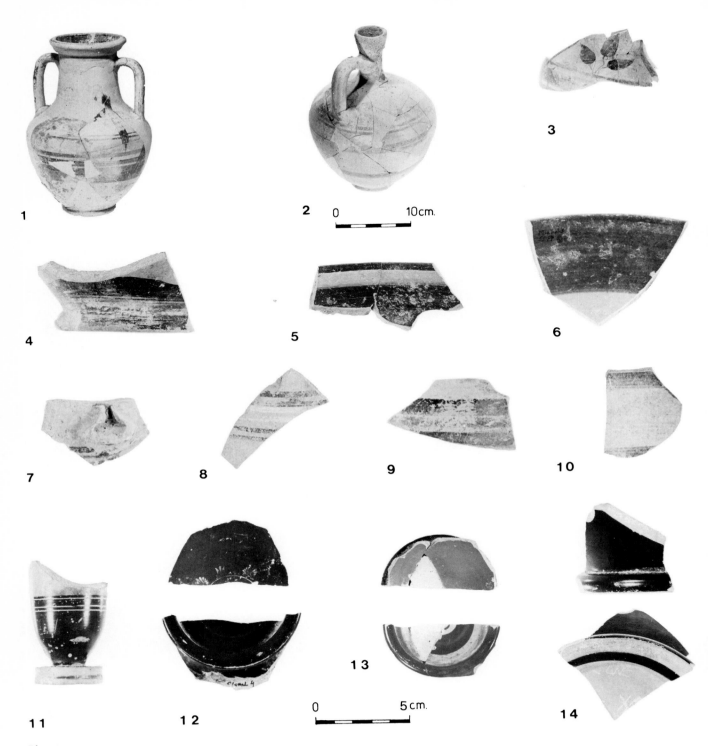

Plate 65. Imported Persian period pottery: 1. amphora (Fig. 10.1:1); 2–3. jugs (Fig. 10.1:2, 4); 4. amphora (Fig. 10.1:5); 5–6. bowls (Fig. 10.1:6–7); 7. askos (Fig. 10.1:8); 8–10. jugs (Fig. 10.1:9–11); 11. lekythos (Fig. 10.2:16); 12. bolsal (Fig. 10.2:11); 13. bolsal (Fig. 10.2:12); 14. skyphos (Fig. 10.2:8).

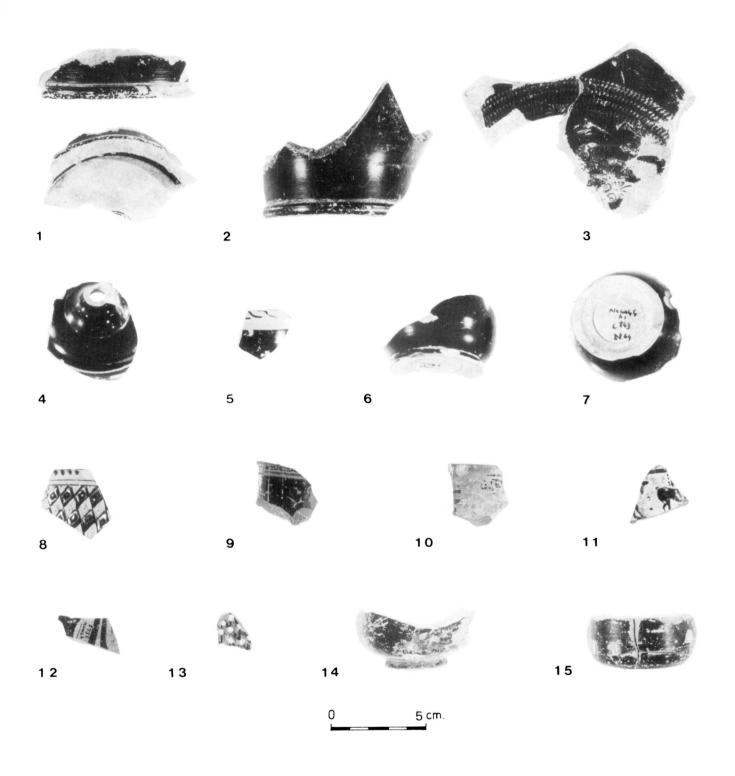

1

2

3

4

5

6

7

8

9

10

11

1 2

1 3

14

15

0   5 cm.

Plate 66.   Imported Persian period pottery: 1. skyphos (Fig. 10.2:15); 2. skyphos (Fig. 10.2:10); 3. bowl (Fig. 10.2:13), 4–7. lekythoi (Fig. 10.2:18–21); 8–9. skyphoi (Fig. 10.2:25–26); 10–13. lekythoi (Fig. 10.2:27–30); 14–15. lamps (Fig. 10.2:32–33).

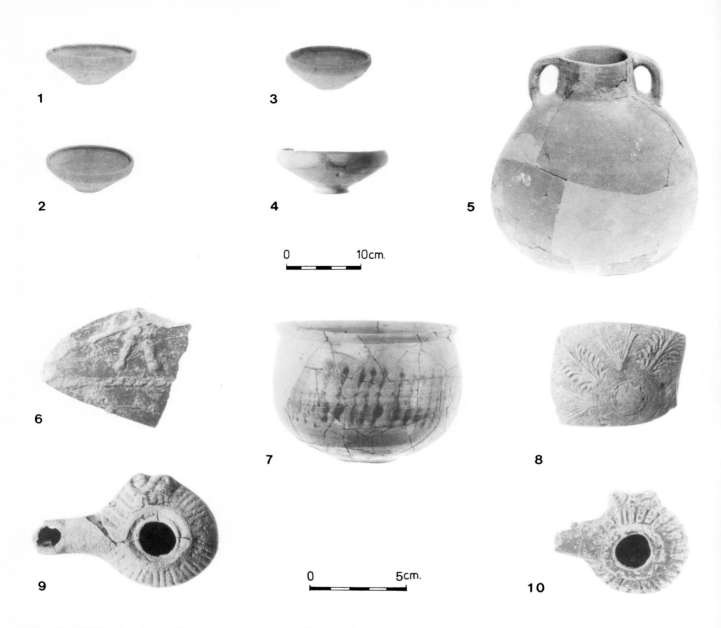

Plate 67.   Hellenistic pottery: 1. bowl (Fig. 13.2:3); 2. bowl (Fig. 13.2:2); 3. bowl (Fig. 13.2:4); 4. bowl (Fig. 13.2:8); 5. cooking pot (Fig. 13.1:10); 6. bowl (Fig. 13.2:22); 7. bowl (5217/1, Locus 689); 8. Megarian bowl (339/1, Locus 65); 9. lamp (Fig. 13.1:14); 10. lamp (Fig. 13.2.24).

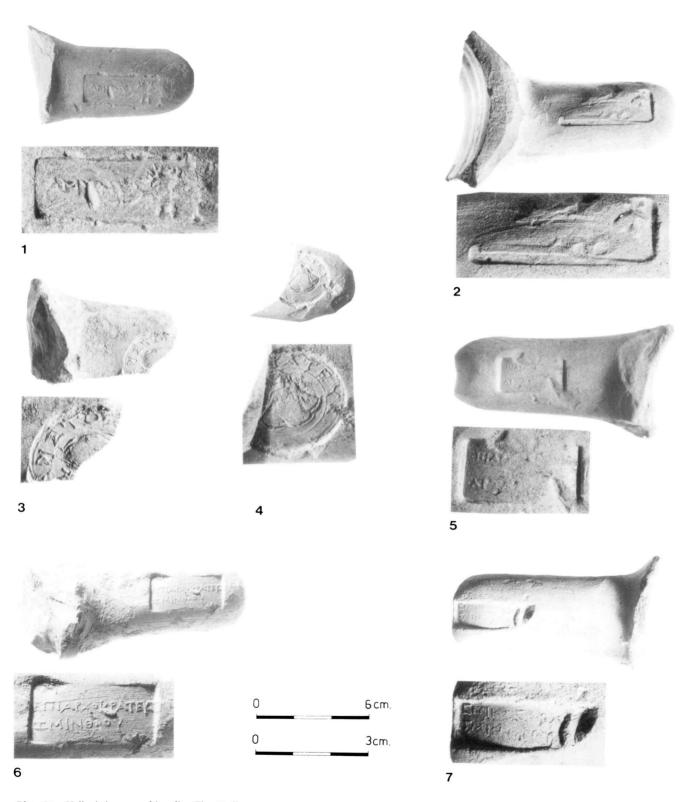

0 ⸻ 6 cm.

0 ⸻ 3 cm.

Plate 68. Hellenistic stamped handles (Fig. 13.4).

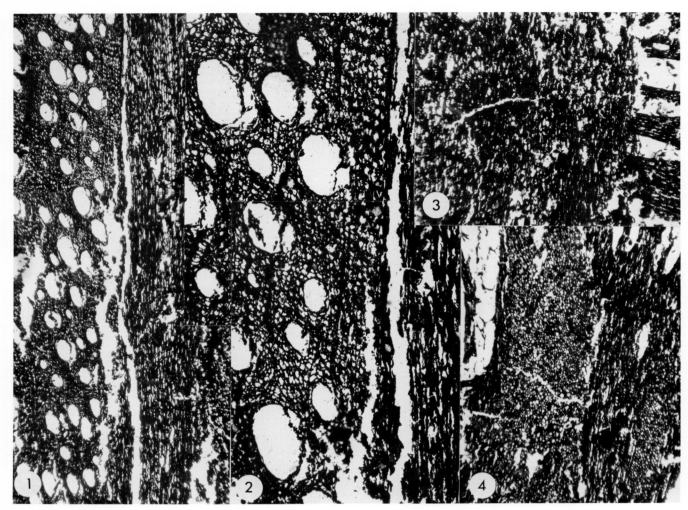

Plate 69. Sections of *Quercus ithaburensis* wood: 1. cross section (× 50); 2. cross section (× 135); 3. tangential longitudinal section (× 50); 4. radial longitudinal section (× 50).

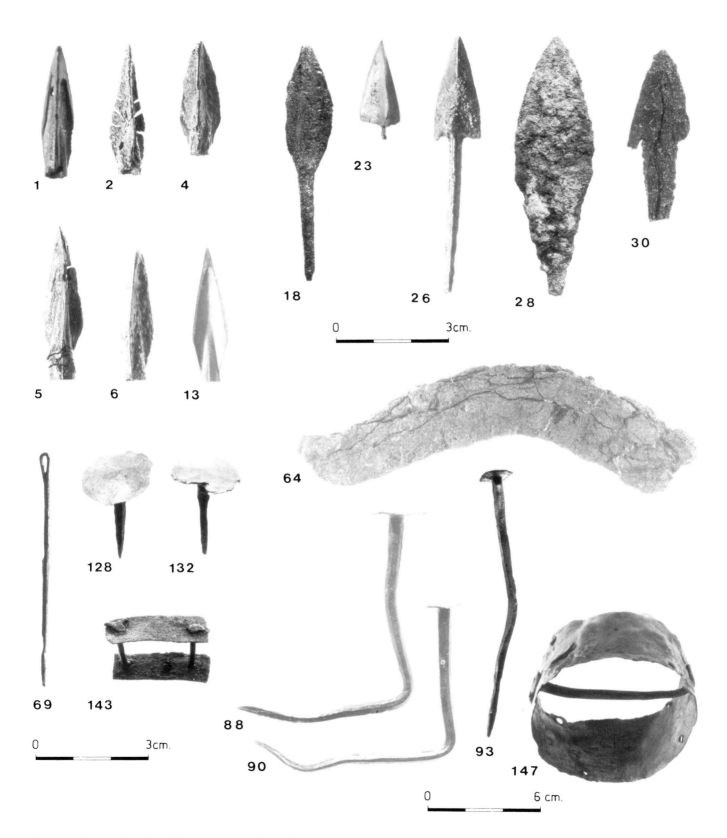

Plate 70. Metal artifacts (according to catalog numbers, Chap. 25a).

441

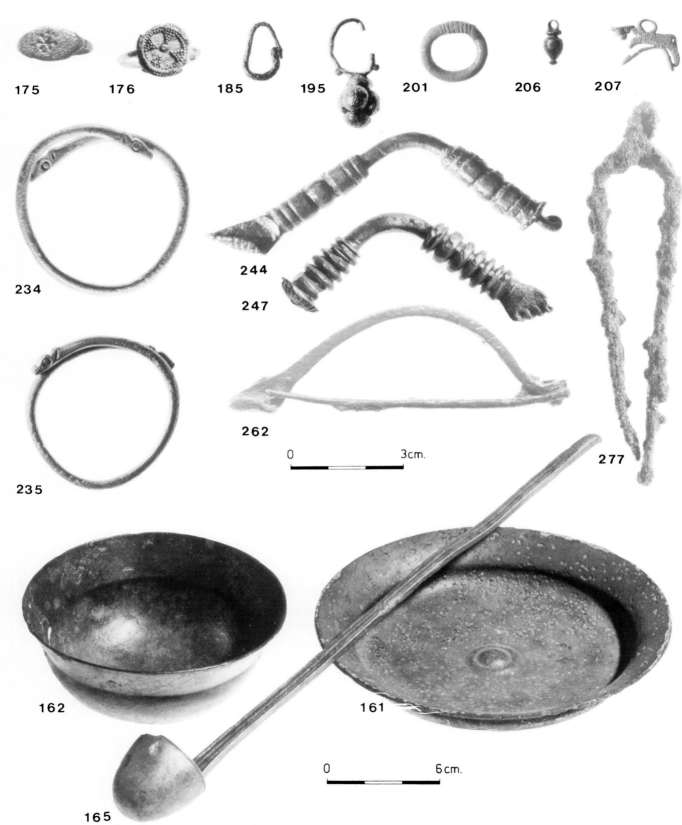

175   176   185   195   201   206   207

234   244   247   277

235   262

0   3cm.

162   161   165

0   6cm.

Plate 71. Metal artifacts (according to catalog numbers, Chap. 25a).

442

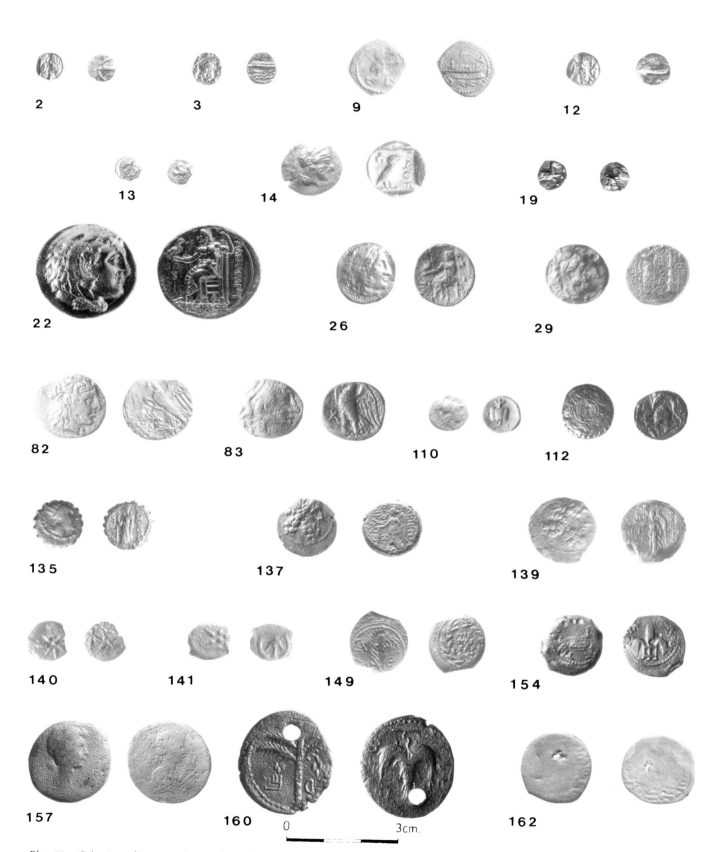

Plate 72. Coins (according to catalog numbers, Chap. 27).

443

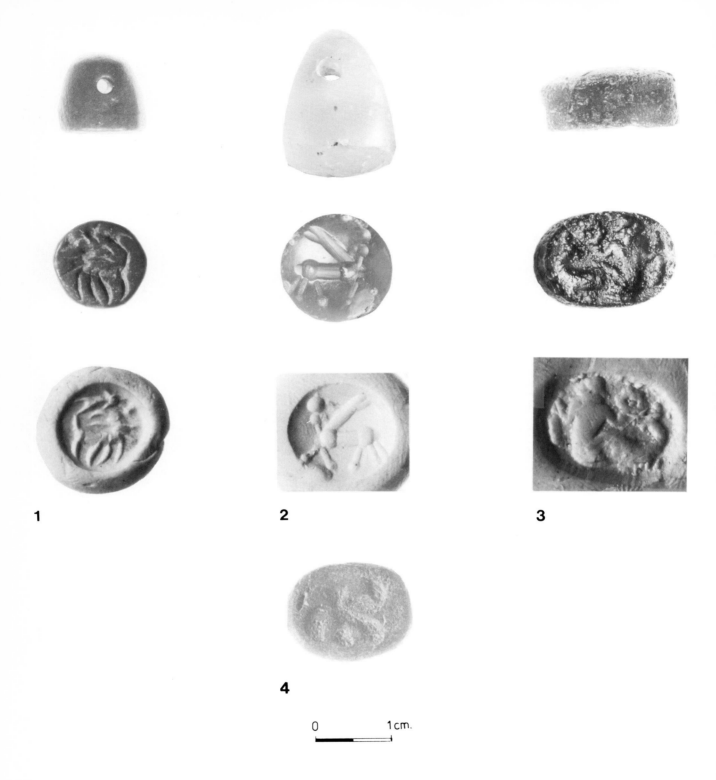

Plate 73.   Stamp seals: 1–3 (Fig. 28.1:1–3); 4 (7342/80, Locus 1103).

444

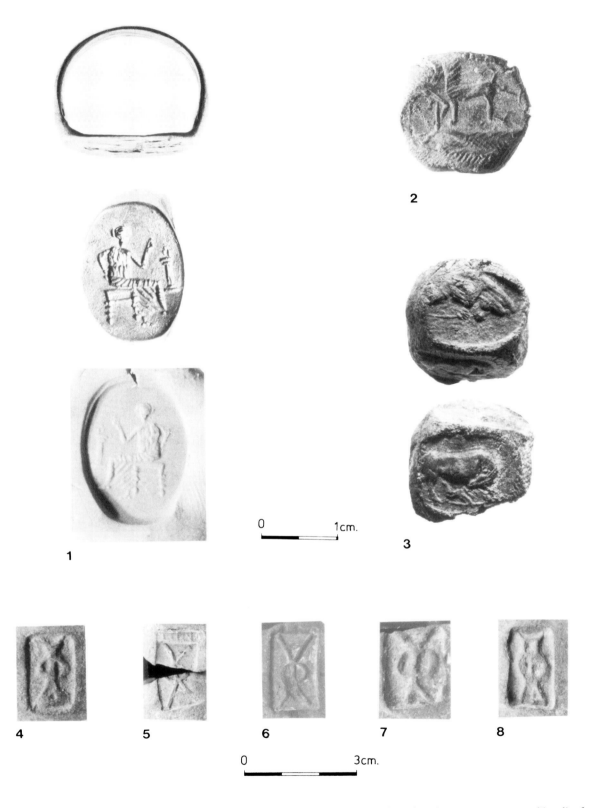

Plate 74. Seals: 1. signet ring (Fig. 28.1:4); 2–3. stamp impression (Fig. 28.1:5–6); 4. stamped handle (Fig. 28.2); 5–8. stamped handles from Akko.

445

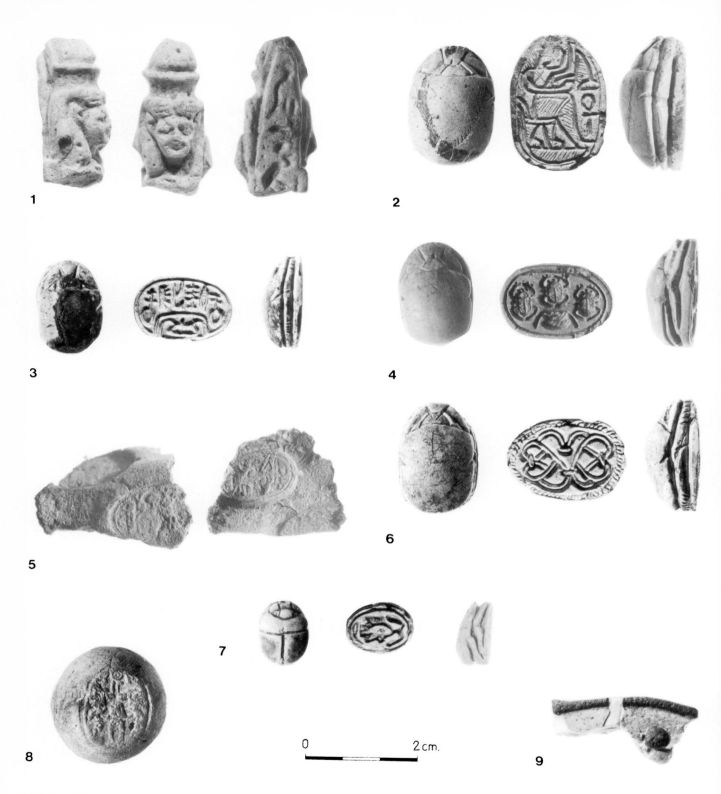

1

2

3

4

5

6

7

8

0   2 cm.

9

Plate 75.   Egyptian artifacts (Fig. 29.1).

446

Plate 76. Stone implements: 1–2. mortars (Fig. 31.1:4–5); 3. mortar (Fig. 31.2:1); 4–5. millstones (Fig. 31.2:9–10); 6. potter's wheel (Fig. 31.5:6); 7. grinding stone (6575/50, Locus 423); 8–10. anchors (Fig. 31.5:1–3).

447

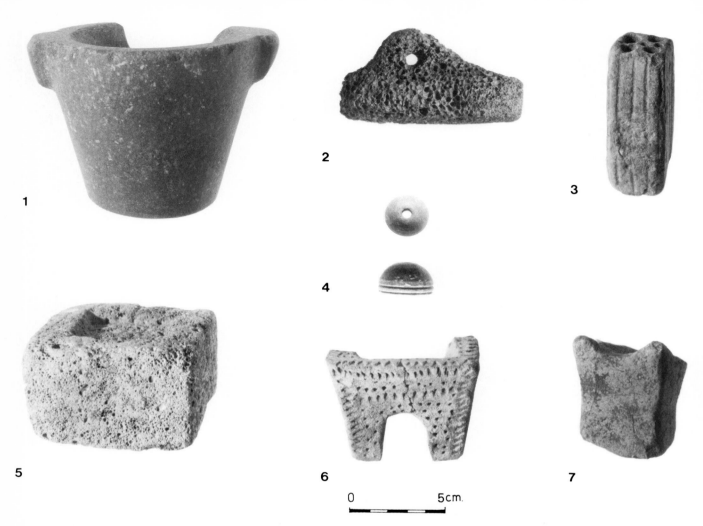

Plate 77.   Stone and clay implements: 1. mortar (Fig. 31.2:8); 2. scraper (Fig. 31.5:7); 3. kohl container (Fig. 9.12:5); 4. spindle whorl (Fig. 31.7:6); 5–7. altars (Fig. 31.6:1, 10, 11).

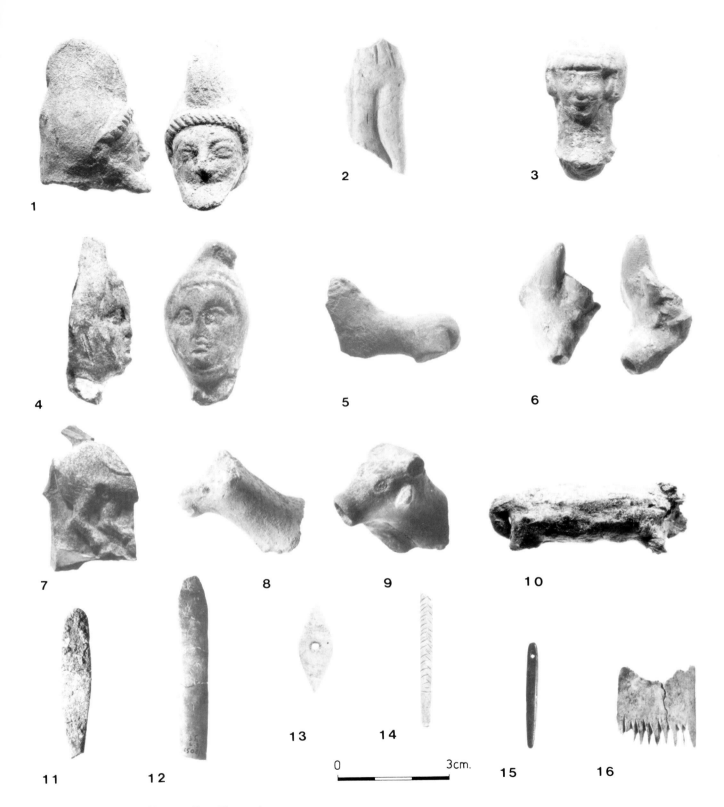

1   2   3

4   5   6

7   8   9   10

11   12   13   14   0   3cm.   15   16

Plate 78.   Terracottas and bone artifacts (Fig. 32.1).

449

Plate 79. Beads (Chap. 34): 1. Iron Age frit bead; 2. hoard from Iron Age jug; 3. Burial 1869: Nos. 1–11; 4. Burial 1869: Nos. 12–31; 5. Burial 1163: Nos. 32–58; 6. Burial 666: Nos. 59–96; 7. Burial 1184: Nos. 97–126.

450

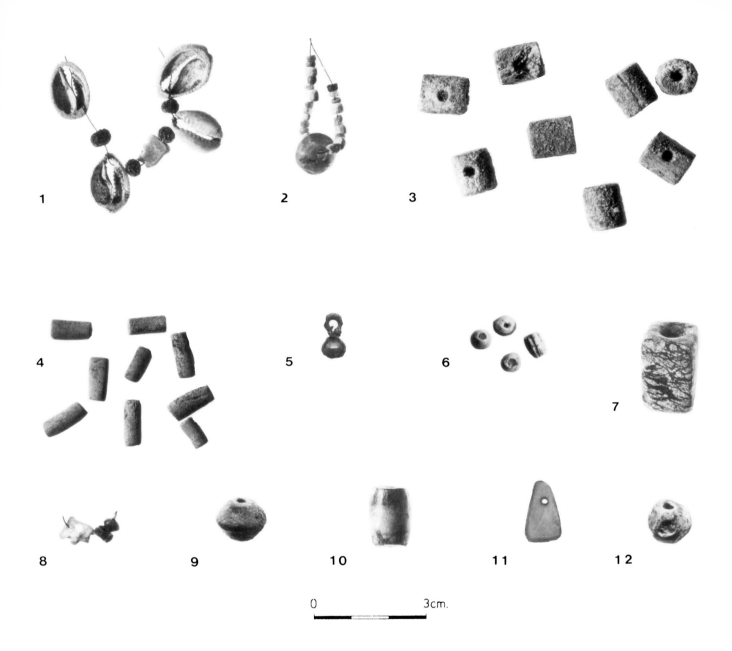

Plate 80. Beads (Chap. 34): 1. Burial 1875: Nos. 127–133; 2. Burial 1871: Nos. 134–172; 3. Burial 664: Nos. 175–182; 4. Burial 826: Nos. 183–191; 5. Burial 826: No. 192; 6. Burial 1183: Nos. 207–210; 7. Burial 1858: No. 227; 8. Burial 1861: Nos. 231–233; 9. Burial 1872: No. 238; 10. Burial (?) 1159: No. 240; 11. Locus 354: No. 245; 12. Locus 593: No. 248.

Plate 81. Microslumping exposed in south balk of stratigraphic trench A2 (west slope of high tell). Sediment of Locus 929 is Tel Aviv *kurkar* fill (unconsolidated), overlain by Netanya *ḥamra* fill.

Plate 82. Section along south side of Naḥal Gelilot, about 100 m inland from shore, showing nature of contact between Netanya *ḥamra* (paludal facies) and overlying friable Tel Aviv *kurkar* (calcarenite). The contact is transitional, with oxidized *ḥamra* sediment intermixed with calcarenite grains, as well as cobble-size clasts of semiconsolidated calcarenite lodged in *ḥamra* just below pure calcarenite.

Plate 83. Persian period cemetery (Area E), west balk of Square W14, showing section of mudbrick cist tomb. Tomb floor is cut into Tel Aviv *kurkar*; it is covered with corbeled Netanya *ḥamra* mudbricks and reburied by Ḥadera dune sand that comprises uppermost sedimentary unit of area.

Plate 84. Fragment of large krater bearing inscription "[To] Baal-shamê[m]."

453

Index

Note to Index

Most sites, settlements, streams, and so forth mentioned in this volume obviously have more than one name or form: historical (biblical and/or classical), Arabic, modern Hebrew. The individual authors have used the form most appropriate to their respective subjects.

The system of diacritical marks used follows the generally accepted practice in transliterating Semitic languages: Hebrew ḥet is represented by ḥ and Hebrew ṣade by ṣ, except in Chap. 2, where the author uses ḫ and ẕ in modern Hebrew place names (Naẖal instead of Naḥal) in conformance with official government maps. Full diacritical marks appear only in Chaps. 2 and 29. Hebrew/Arabic *'ayin/'ayn* is represented by a single left quotation mark. *Alef* is not indicated except in Chap. 2 and the bibliographic references, where it is represented by a single right quotation mark. Names of several well-known places in Israel have been anglicized.

General Index

INDEX

Geographic Index

Ze'ev Herzog is senior lecturer in the Department of Archaeology and Ancient Near Eastern Studies at Tel Aviv University. He studied at the Hebrew University of Jerusalem and at the Free University of Berlin, received his Ph.D. from Tel Aviv University in 1977, and has been a visiting scholar at the University of Pennsylvania and Harvard University. Herzog served as archaeological field director at the Tel Michal excavations; his field experience also includes excavations at Tel Beer-sheba and Tel Gerisa for Tel Aviv University and at Arad, Megiddo, and Hazor for the Hebrew University of Jerusalem. Widely published, he is author of *Beer-sheba II, the Early Iron Age Settlement* (Tel Aviv University, 1984) and *Das Stadttor in Israel und in den Nachbarländern* (Philipp von Zabern, Mainz, 1986).

George Rapp, Jr., is dean of the College of Science and Engineering at the University of Minnesota, Duluth, professor of geology and archaeology, and director of the Archaeometry Laboratory. He also serves as professor in the Center for Ancient Studies at the University of Minnesota, Minneapolis. Rapp was the first recipient of the Archaeological Geology award from the Geological Society of America and is a member of numerous professional societies. He is a manuscript reviewer for many journals and proposal reviewer for the National Science Foundation, the National Geographic Society, and other organizations. His publications include *Archaeological Geology*, co-edited with John A. Gifford (1985), *Excavations at Nichoria in Southwestern Greece, Volume I: Site, Environs, and Techniques* (University of Minnesota Press), co-edited with S. E. Aschenbrenner and *The Minnesota Messenia Expedition: Reconstructing a Bronze Age Regional Environment* (University of Minnesota Press), co-edited with W. A. McDonald.

Ora Negbi is associate professor in the Department of Archaeology and Ancient Near Eastern Studies at Tel Aviv University. She received her Ph.D. in 1964 from the Hebrew University, Jerusalem. She was a visiting scholar at the University of London, the School of Divinity at Harvard University, Wolfson College at Oxford University, and the University of the Sorbonne. She has participated in expeditions at Toumba tou Skourou (Harvard University) and Kalavasos Ayios Dhimitrios (Brandeis University), both in Cyprus, and at Tel Michal and Tel 'Ira (Tel Aviv University). Negbi has contributed articles to *Expedition, Qadmoniot,* the *American Journal of Archaeology*, and the *Report of the Department of Antiquities of Cyprus*. She is the author of two monographs entitled *A Deposit of Terracottas and Statuettes from Tel Ṣippor* ('Atiqot VI, 1966) and *The Hoards of Goldwork from Tell el-'Ajjul* (Studies in Mediterranaean Archaeology 25, 1974). She has also written a book: *Canaanite Gods in Metal* (Tel Aviv University, 1976).

DATE DUE

HIGHSMITH   #LO-45220